THE SCARECROW AUTHOR BIBLIOGRAPHIES

1. John Steinbeck—1929-71 (Tetsumaro Hayashi). 1973.
   See also no. 64.
2. Joseph Conrad (Theodore G. Ehrsam). 1969.
3. Arthur Miller (Tetsumaro Hayashi). 2nd ed., 1976.
4. Katherine Anne Porter (Waldrip & Bauer). 1969.
5. Philip Freneau (Philip M. Marsh). 1970.
6. Robert Greene (Tetsumaro Hayashi). 1971.
7. Benjamin Disraeli (R.W. Stewart). 1972.
8. John Berryman (Richard W. Kelly). 1972.
9. William Dean Howells (Vito J. Brenni). 1973.
10. Jean Anouilh (Kathleen W. Kelly). 1973.
11. E.M. Forster (Alfred Borrello). 1973.
12. The Marquis de Sade (E. Pierre Chanover). 1973.
13. Alain Robbe-Grillet (Dale W. Frazier). 1973.
14. Northrop Frye (Robert D. Denham). 1974.
15. Federico García Lorca (Laurenti & Siracusa). 1974.
16. Ben Jonson (Brock & Welsh). 1974.
17. Four French Dramatists: Eugène Brieux, Francois de Curel,
    Emile Fabre, Paul Hervieu (Edmund F. Santa Vicca). 1974.
18. Ralph Waldo Ellison (Jacqueline Covo). 1974.
19. Philip Roth (Bernard F. Rodgers, Jr.). 2nd ed., 1984.
20. Norman Mailer (Laura Adams). 1974.
21. Sir John Betjeman (Margaret Stapleton). 1974.
22. Elie Wiesel (Molly Abramowitz). 1974.
23. Paul Laurence Dunbar (Eugene W. Metcalf, Jr.). 1975.
24. Henry James (Beatrice Ricks). 1975.
25. Robert Frost (Lentricchia & Lentricchia). 1976.
26. Sherwood Anderson (Douglas G. Rogers). 1976.
27. Iris Murdoch and Muriel Spark
    (Tominaga & Schneidermeyer). 1976
28. John Ruskin (Kirk H. Beetz). 1976.
29. Georges Simenon (Trudee Young). 1976.
30. George Gordon, Lord Byron (Oscar José Santucho). 1977.
31. John Barth (Richard Vine). 1977.
32. John Hawkes (Carol A. Hryciw). 1977.
33. William Everson (Bartlett & Campo). 1977.
34. May Sarton (Lenora Blouin). 1978.
35. Wilkie Collins (Kirk H. Beetz). 1978.
36. Sylvia Plath (Lane & Stevens). 1978.
37. E.B. White (A.J. Anderson). 1978.
38. Henry Miller (Lawrence J. Shifreen). 1979.
39. Ralph Waldo Emerson (Jeanetta Boswell). 1979.
40. James Dickey (Jim Elledge). 1979.
41. Henry Fielding (H. George Hahn). 1979.
42. Paul Goodman (Tom Nicely). 1979.
43. Christopher Marlowe (Kenneth Friedenreich). 1979.
44. Leo Tolstoy (Egan & Egan). 1979.
45. T.S. Eliot (Beatrice Ricks). 1980.
46. Allen Ginsberg (Michelle P. Kraus). 1980.

Tennessee Williams:

A Bibliography

second edition

by
DREWEY WAYNE GUNN

Scarecrow Author Bibliographies, No. 89

The Scarecrow Press, Inc.
Metuchen, N.J., & London
1991

British Library Cataloguing-in-Publication data available

Library of Congress Cataloging-in-Publication Data

Gunn, Drewey Wayne, 1939-
    Tennessee Williams, a bibliography / by Drewey Wayne Gunn.
-- 2nd ed.
        p.   cm. -- (Scarecrow author bibliographies ; no. 89)
    Includes indexes.
    ISBN 0-8108-2495-7 (alk. paper)
    1. Williams, Tennessee, 1911-1983--Bibliography. I. Title.
II. Series.
Z8976.424.G85 1991
[PS3545.I5365]
016.812'54--dc20   91-34939

CONTENTS

iii

224432

PRELIMINARY NOTES

This new edition of a work which first appeared in 1980 has been completely recast to create what I hope is a handier reference. Materials have been systematically grouped with cross-references between sections, the principles of organization for each section being explained in the headnote to that section. The work remains an enumerative bibliography. It lists those materials by and about Williams as I knew of them through summer 1990, though publication delays allowed me to add items through summer 1991. To keep it up to date, scholars should turn to *Modern Drama* (in which Charles A. Carpenter has done a masterful job of bringing out the year's bibliography), starting with the 1992 annual listing; to the *Modern Language Association International Bibliography*, starting with the 1990 volume; and to the *Tennessee Williams Literary Journal*. There are likewise annual bibliographies in the *Journal of Modern Literature* and in the *Mississippi Quarterly*.

The major research library remains the Humanities Research Center at the University of Texas, Austin. The original collection of materials catalogued by Andreas Brown is a trove for the scholar. Recently Kenneth Craven has brought more information to light by creating a horizontal file of the many clippings and programs accumulated there. George Freedley assembled a file for the New York Public Library Theater Collection, mainly of newspaper clippings, programs, and other secondary sources arranged by year. Other significant collections are at Columbia University and the University of Delaware. The Harvard Theater Collection holdings, to become available in 1992, will be extremely important. The Chicago Public Library, the University of Iowa, the New Orleans Public Library, and Washington University in St. Louis have small collections of materials. The University of Missouri has several important items scattered among three archives, each with its own catalogue. A large collection of theses and dissertations exists at the University of Mississippi.

I began assembling a Williams bibliography in 1962 while working on my master's thesis and continued gathering notes for the next three decades. I worked in the libraries at Duke University, University of Houston, University of Mississippi, University of Missouri, University of North Carolina at Chapel Hill, University of North Carolina at

Greensboro, Rice University, University of Texas, Texas A&I
University, Trinity University, and Washington University,
as well as the Chicago and New Orleans Public Libraries, the
Bibliothèque Nationale, the British Embassy reading room in
Paris, various municipal libraries in South Texas, and many
a bookstore. My friend Carole France explored the New York
Public Library for me.

Of the bibliographies listed in Section I the most
helpful for me were those by Thomas P. Adler et al., Andreas
Brown, Charles A. Carpenter, Carpenter and Elizabeth Cook,
Alan M. Cohn, Nandine Dony, John S. McCann, and Delma E.
Presley. McCann performed an invaluable service in bringing
to light unreprinted articles in New York newspapers, especially *Variety*, *Village Voice*, and the *New York Morning
Telegraph*. Floyd Eugene Eddleman's and, above all, George
Miller's reviews of the first edition of this bibliography
were instructional. The seven issues of *The Tennessee Williams Newsletter* (renamed *The Tennessee Williams Review*),
1979-83, and the three issues to date of *The Tennessee Williams Literary Journal*, beginning 1989, contain much
information.

The following were also useful: *Play Index*, ed.
Estelle A. Fidell, Dorothy Margaret Peake, Dorothy Herbert
West, and/or Juliette Yaakow (New York: Wilson, 1953-83);
Ottemiller's Index to Plays in Collections, ed. Billie M.
Connor and Helene G. Mochedlover (Scarecrow, 1988); *Index to
Plays in Periodicals*, ed. Dean H. Keller (Scarecrow, 1979);
Drama Criticism, ed. Arthur Coleman and Gary R. Tyler (Den-
ver: Swallow, 1966); *Modern Drama: A Checklist of Critical
Literature on 20th Century Plays*, ed. Irving Adelman and
Rita Dworkin (Scarecrow, 1967); *A Guide to Critical Reviews*,
ed. James M. Salem (Scarecrow, 1973-84); *American Drama
Criticism*, ed. Floyd E. Eddleman (Hamden, CT: Shoe String,
1976); *Index to Critical Film Reviews...*, ed. Stephen E.
Bowles (New York: Franklin, 1974); *Index to Motion Pictures
Reviewed by Variety 1907-1980*, ed. Max Joseph Alvarez
(Scarecrow, 1982).

It is a delight to remember the kind people who helped
me in so many ways. Above all I appreciate the many articles that my friends Pam Hill and Earl Herrick brought to my
attention. (And I remember with pleasure the similar role
the late Donna Vogt played in the first edition.) Other
friends who have mailed me numerous items through the years
are Kent Asmussen and Gretchen Vik. Without their diligence
many a mystery would not have been solved. Many other
friends, colleagues, and students at Texas A&I University
and at the Université de Metz added bits and pieces: Ward
Albro, Kathie Birat, Nicole Boireau, Taylor Cage, May Camp-

bell, Doris Clatanoff, Melissa Dawson, David Deacon, Norma
Beth Drake, Don Howell, Jack Lampe, Glenda Langley, Lou
Martin, Antonio Martinez, Gunther Mende, Ronnie Ormond,
Dorothy Pace, Allen B. Page, David Sabrio, Joel and Loyd
Self, Robert Scott, Julia Smith, Al Tellinghuisen, and Jacki
and Peter Thomas.

The staff of the Texas A&I Library were most helpful.
I especially thank George Boatright, Milton Clausen, Paul
Goode, the late Margaret Hancock, David Laughlin, Jesuita
Ayala-Schueneman, and Bruce Schueneman. At other libraries
the following were most kind: Lauren Bufferd, Chicago Public; Ken Craven, Ellen Dunlap, and Goldia Hester, University
of Texas; George Gause, Pan American University; Holly Hall
and Carole Prietto, Washington University. Other librarians
who supplied important pieces of information via telephone
and post were Larry Berk, Key West Community College; Craig
Campbell, Academy of Motion Pictures Arts and Sciences;
Shelly J. Croteau, University of Missouri; Earl M. Rogers,
University of Iowa; and Emily C. Walhout, Harvard University.

Some key information was uncovered by Vincent Curcio,
general manager of the White Barn Theatre; George McCue,
graduate of the University of Missouri; Brian Peterson, a
student at the University of Vancouver; and Carol Waycaster,
a Houston collector. Also helpful were Pearl A. McHaney,
bibliographer for *The Tennessee Williams Literary Journal*;
Stephen S. Stanton, editor of *The Tennessee Williams Newsletter*; and Hersh Zeifman of *Modern Drama*. Though they
added no entries, I appreciate the kindness of the following
in answering inquiries: George Crandall of Auburn University, Peggy L. Fox of New Directions, William S. Gray of
Randolph-Macon College, lawyer Robert Lantz, Joan M. Ling of
the English Theatre Guild, and Donovan Rhynsburger, Fred L.
Lee, and Madge Fisher Harrah of the University of Missouri.

For their contributions at various stages I equally
thank Ed Hammonds, who planted the seed for this bibliography by bringing me his program for the New York production of *Period of Adjustment*; George M. Harper, who directed
my master's thesis; my mother, Josephine S. Gunn; Josephine
Harper, who made several helpful suggestions about organization; and Jacques Murat, who took many notes for me and
listened many an hour. I am indebted to Gerald Liner and
the Texas A&I University Computer Users Committee for grant-
ing me the computer on which the work was completed; to the
Department of Language and Literature, with Doris Clatanoff
as chair, for buying the program I used; to John Bonno for
loading it for me; to my current chair, Emil Mucchetti, for
obtaining me one-fourth release time to work on the project

during the spring 1990; and to my dean, Armando Arias, for
helping me work through program problems by lending me his
able assistants Joyce Ley and Mark Fassold. James Stanley
proofread copy; Jacques Murat verified the French; Monika
Hardy, the German; Ricardo Szmetan, the Spanish; and Zach
Christodoulides, the Greek.

    Other important people are acknowledged in the intro-
ductions to Sections G and H.

Drewey Wayne Gunn
Texas A&I University
9 August 1991

WILLIAMS'S LITERARY CAREER: AN OVERVIEW

Thomas Lanier Williams - native of Mississippi, resident in St. Louis - began his literary career auspiciously. At age 16 he placed in a national essay contest and saw his entry published in *Smart Set*. The next year he had a story accepted by *Weird Tales*. Upon entering the University of Missouri he placed in a college-wide writing contest with a short play and saw it produced in 1930. Other successes followed. But then came setbacks. Suffering from the Depression, his father removed him from school to work, much like Tom in *The Glass Menagerie*, in a shoe company. Williams continued to write feverishly until the frustrations of the menial job and the time spent late at his writing desk resulted in a nervous breakdown. Recuperating in Memphis, he saw a play of his produced by a little theatre there. This was followed by four other productions in or near St. Louis, works generally of social criticism such as were popular during the 1930s. During the same period he had over thirty poems and an occasional short story accepted by a little magazine or school journal. But by the time he finally received his B.A. from the University of Iowa at the age of 27, he appeared after all to have advanced little on his elusive career.

Dramatists seem to take longer to mature than poets or even novelists. But apparently feeling the need to start afresh, in 1939 Williams changed his name: Tennessee Williams came into existence. The sobriquet appeared to function as a talisman. *Story* accepted a work, he obtained an agent in New York, and he won both a Group Theatre prize for a series of short plays and a Rockefeller grant. (Tennessee Williams also shed three years: the Group Theatre contest was for playwrights 25 or younger. Consequently, some biographies continue to report his birthdate as 1914.) Then in 1940, just short of his thirtieth year, a play was optioned by the New York Theatre Guild. But the fates again withheld fame. *Battle of Angels* closed in Boston. He did publish seven short plays and a collection of twenty-seven poems during the lean years 1940-44, but that was about all. He had to support himself by odd jobs around the country, including a stint as scriptwriter in Hollywood.

Then the day after Christmas 1944 the name Tennessee Williams entered the annals of theatre history forever. *The Glass Menagerie* marched triumphantly from Chicago to New

York to capture the Drama Critics' Circle Award on the first
ballot. The play ran for 561 performances. Finally finan-
cially free, Williams plunged into a multitude of projects.
For nineteen years he alternated between a greater and a
lesser success. *You Touched Me!* had only 109 performances,
but *A Streetcar Named Desire* ran for 855 and swept the theatre awards including the Pulitzer Prize. *Summer and Smoke*
barely made it to 100 on Broadway (though its later Circle-
in-the-Square production launched the off-Broadway move-
ment); *The Rose Tattoo* had 306. *Camino Real* hurt the most
with only 60; but it was followed by *Cat on a Hot Tin Roof*
with 694 and a second Pulitzer. The rewrite of *Battle of
Angels*, *Orpheus Descending*, was another disappointment with
only 68 performances (its off-Broadway production was likewise more successful); however, it was followed by *Suddenly
Last Summer*, off Broadway, for an extensive run and *Sweet
Bird of Youth*, on Broadway, for 383. *Period of Adjustment*
opened for only 132; but *The Night of the Iguana* had 316.
The Milk Train Doesn't Stop Here Anymore opened in New York
in the midst of a newspaper strike and still had a healthy
run of 65 performances. At the same time there were important publications: a collection of short plays, *27 Wagons
Full of Cotton*; two collections of short stories, *One Arm*
and *Hard Candy*; a novel, *The Roman Spring of Mrs. Stone*,
which was briefly on the *New York Times* best sellers list;
and a collection of poems, *In the Winter of Cities*. Ten
films, including an original, *Baby Doll*, added to his fame.

But Williams was rarely accorded the position that was
rightfully his during those great years; like Joyce, Lawrence, and O'Neill he was often lionized by completely
irrelevant appraisals and battered by equally irrelevant
assaults. His very popularity on stage and screen was sus-
pect to many. Others gingerly recoiled from his scarcely
veiled sexuality. Though all realized that his was a presence, few critics seemed able to look at him calmly, stead-
ily, and in perspective. It is easy to forget today that
Williams was one of the most important warriors in gaining
freedom for the stage and screen to treat formerly forbidden
matters. Reviewers often reacted (or felt they had to re-
act) with shock to works now routinely taught in colleges
and shown at any hour by the local television station. Some
London critics still tend to twitter.

Thus some people seemed almost pleased when Williams's
record started sliding precipitously. Suffering from the
death of his companion, Frank Merlo, and from addiction
problems, Williams rewrote *Milk Train* in a darker vein and
opened it in New York on the first day of 1964. The un-
thinkable happened: a Williams play closed after four performances. As he entered the world he had helped form, Wil-

liams, probably because of substance abuse, seemed more and more lost. From then until his death nineteen years later, his New York production record remained bleak. In his last years his natural bent was increasingly for the experimental short play as he explored new forms and modes of expression. But in quest of money and acclaim he incessantly returned to Broadway and the full-length play after equally incessant announcements that he would never write for that market again. His next presentation there, *Slapstick Tragedy*, closed after 7 performances; *The Seven Descents of Myrtle* after 29; *In the Bar of a Tokyo Hotel* after 25. Not until *Small Craft Warnings* did he have another successful run in the city: 200 performances. Then followed *Out Cry*, 12; *The Red Devil Battery Sign*, which closed in its Boston tryout; *The Eccentricities of a Nightingale*, 24; *Vieux Carré*, 5; *A Lovely Sunday for Creve Coeur*, 36; and the final humiliation of *Clothes for a Summer Hotel*, 15. Two more collections of short stories, *The Knightly Quest* and *Eight Mortal Ladies Possessed*; a collection of short plays, *Dragon Country*; a collection of poems, *Androgyne, Mon Amour*; a novel, *Moise and the World of Reason*; and a collection of essays, *Where I Live*, were greeted lukewarmly. Only Williams's *Memoirs* was a relative success.

To many critics and teachers Williams began to seem a period piece. For a decade his reputation suffered the most curious ups and downs. In 1968-69 Whit Burnett, for a new edition of his anthology *This Is My Best*, polled authors, teachers, bookstore managers, readers of literary magazines, and diverse other groups interested in literature to find out who they considered America's most distinguished living authors to be. Williams received the greatest number of mentions, outstripping Steinbeck and MacLeish and being far ahead of such critical favorites as Bellow and Lowell. The academic and critical worlds reacted with shock. In 1969 Williams was awarded the Gold Medal for Drama by the American Academy and the National Institute of Arts and Letters. But on June 10 *Life* magazine (as that magazine tried to ward off its own impending demise) unabashedly announced the death of his talent in a full-page advertisment in the *New York Times*. Meanwhile, revivals from the earlier period did do well in New York: a 1965 production of *Glass* ran for 175 performances; the 1974-75 revised *Cat* had 160. All the early great plays were perennial favorites in summer stock and regional and college theatres. Throughout the 1970s various articles noted that only Shakespeare was more popular on American stages. College and high-school introduction to drama textbooks routinely included *Glass*. But college American literature anthologies rarely looked at him.

Perhaps the picture was confused because there had always been several Williamses. The offspring of both Chekhov and Strindberg, such diverse playwrights as Brecht, García Lorca, O'Neill, Pirandello, Shaw, and Wilder also left their mark. One Williams was sensitive, lyrical, and pensive. Another was boisterous, vulgar, and somewhat pretentious. The best work occurred when these two fused. The deeply introspective plays won him critical acclaim; the violently sexual ones brought him notoriety. In these two areas he staked out the terrain that came to be recognized as his. But Williams became restive within these confines. Yet another Williams, especially in his last period, wanted to explore the terrors of communication by using the elliptical patterns cultivated by Beckett and Pinter. And still another Williams sought, even as early as *Camino Real* and increasingly in the 1970s, an intense fusion of all the elements of theatre, including dance, song, and mime. When audiences refused to follow him in these new directions, he returned to more familiar territory. But only in the late autobiographical plays did he seem relatively brilliant. It will take us years to sort out the impressions he left.

Only in the last few years of his life was Williams regarded correctly as one of our most important writers. The *New York Times* (14 Jan. 1979, sec. 2: 1, 10) polled eighteen playwrights (plus Williams) to name the "most nearly perfect examples of the dramatist's art" they knew. One-third cited Williams's work. Now that his career is in place the critical climate has shifted. *The Glass Menagerie* and *A Streetcar Named Desire* are recognized for what they are: masterpieces of American literature. Revivals of lesser plays generate excitement even on Broadway. And critical attention has embraced the entire canon, including the earlier one-acts and the later failures. An appreciable body of solid criticism has begun to take shape. Few textbooks, whether introductions to drama or anthologies of American literature, now ignore him - although all too often he is still represented only by *Glass*. His name routinely mentioned in the same sentence as O'Neill's, Williams's position in American letters finally seems relatively secure.

1907 Marriage (2 June) of Edwina Dakin (1884-1980) and Cor-
      nelius Coffin Williams (1879-1957).

1909 Birth of daughter, Rose (17 Nov.).

1911 Birth of Thomas Lanier Williams in Columbus, Missis-
      sippi (26 March: fourth Sunday of Lent). Childhood
      spent in various towns in Mississippi and Tennessee,
      often with grandparents Rev. and Mrs. Walter E. Dakin.

1918 Family moved to St. Louis, Missouri.

1919 Birth of brother, Dakin (21 Feb.).

1927 Pub. essay "Can a Good Wife Be a Good Sport?"

1928 First trip to Europe. Pub. story "The Vengeance of
      Nitocris."

1929 Graduated University City High School. Enrolled Uni-
      versity of Missouri; joined Alpha Tau Omega frater-
      nity.

1930 Prod. "Beauty Is the Word" (honorable mention, campus
      play contest).

1931 Won honorable mention for story "Something by Tol-
      stoi." Summer, began work for St. Louis shoe company.

1932 Won honorable mentions for play "Hot Milk at Three in
      the Morning" and story "Big Black." Left university.

1933 Won prize for poem "Under the April Rain."

1935 Won first prize St. Louis Writers Guild contest for
      story "Stella for Star."   Nervous breakdown; joined
      grandparents in Memphis; discovered Chekhov. Prod.
      "Cairo Shanghai, Bombay!" Audited courses Washington
      University, St. Louis.

1936 Won St. Louis Wednesday Club Literary Contest with
      "Sonnets for the Spring." Prod. "The Magic Tower,"
      Webster Groves; "Headlines," St. Louis.   Enrolled

Washington University. Friendship with Clark Mills
McBurney and William Jay Smith; discovered Hart Crane.

1937   Prod. *Candles to the Sun, Fugitive Kind*, St. Louis;
        refused honorable mention in play contest for "Me,
        Vashya." Enrolled University of Iowa; wrote unpro-
        duced play *Spring Storm*. Rose underwent prefrontal
        lobotomy.

1938   Wrote unproduced play *Not about Nightingales*. Re-
        ceived bachelor's degree (5 Aug). Moved to Chicago,
        then New Orleans.

1939   Headed West with Jim Parrott. Won Group Theatre award
        for short plays; Audrey Wood became agent; moved to
        New York. Pub. story "The Field of Blue Children,"
        first work to appear under name Tennessee Williams.

1940   Enrolled in New School for Social Research; received
        Rockefeller Grant. Prod. "The Long Goodbye," New
        York; *Battle of Angels*, Boston. From now through 1944
        itinerant writer and worker at odd jobs in Acapulco,
        Key West, Los Angeles area, Macon (GA), Mexico City,
        New Orleans, New York, Provincetown, St. Louis, Taos.
        Friendships with Tallulah Bankhead, Leonard Bernstein,
        Paul Bigelow, Paul and Jane Bowles, Oliver Evans, Hans
        Hoffmann, William Inge, Christopher Isherwood, Margo
        Jones, Kip Kiernan, Lincoln Kirstein, Jordan Massee,
        Gilbert Maxwell, Harold Norse, Jackson Pollock, Tony
        Smith, Marion Black Vaccaro, Donald Windham.

1943   Prod. *You Touched Me*, Cleveland, Pasadena.

1944   Death of maternal grandmother (6 Jan.). Pub. *Five
        Young American Poets*; prod. *The Glass Menagerie*, Chi-
        cago.

1945   Prod. *The Glass Menagerie*, New York (Drama Critics'
        Circle, Sidney Howard, Donaldson Awards); *Stairs to
        the Roof*, Pasadena; *You Touched Me*, New York. Sojourn
        in Mexico.

1946   Friendship with Francisco Rodriguez, Carson McCullers.

1947   Prod. *Stairs to the Roof*, Pasadena; *Summer and Smoke*,
        Dallas; *A Streetcar Named Desire*, New York, beginning
        collaboration with Elia Kazan (Pulitzer Prize, Drama
        Critics' Circle, Donaldson Awards, 1948). Met Frank
        Phillip Merlo (born c. 1921).

1948   Pub. stories *One Arm*; prod. "Portrait of a Madonna,"
        TV; *Summer and Smoke*, New York. Second trip to Eu-
        rope. Thereafter always spent part of each year
        abroad; in the States alternated between homes in Key
        West, New Orleans, New York. Friendships with Maria
        Britneva, Truman Capote, Anna Magnani, Alberto Mora-
        via, Gore Vidal, Luchino Visconti.

1950   Pub. novel *The Roman Spring of Mrs. Stone*; prod. film
        The Glass Menagerie; *The Rose Tattoo*, Chicago.

1951   Prod. *The Rose Tattoo*, New York (Tony Award); film *A
        Streetcar Named Desire* (New York Film Critics' Circle
        Award; screenplay nominated for Academy Award, 1952).

1952   Recorded works; worked on Visconti's *Senso*; became
        acquainted with José Quintero; elected to National
        Institute of Arts and Letters. Ballet *A Streetcar
        Named Desire* (choreography by Bettis), Montreal.

1953   Prod. *Camino Real*, New York; "Lord Byron's Love Let-
        ter," TV; directed Windham's *The Starless Air*, Hous-
        ton.

1954   Pub. stories *Hard Candy*.

1955   Prod. opera "Lord Byron's Love Letter," New Orleans;
        Cat on a Hot Tin Roof, New York (Pulitzer Prize, Drama
        Critics' Circle, Donaldson Awards); "Three Players of
        a Summer Game," Westport, CT; *A Streetcar Named Desire*
        (excerpts), TV; film *The Rose Tattoo*. Deaths of
        maternal grandfather (14 Feb.), Jones; friendship with
        Lilla van Saher.

1956   Pub. poems *In the Winter of Cities*; prod. *Sweet Bird
        of Youth*, Miami; *Baby Doll* (screenplay nominated for
        Academy Award, 1957), controversy caused by Cardinal
        Spellman.

1957   Prod. *Orpheus Descending*, New York. Death of father
        (27 Mar.). Began psychoanalysis with Frank S. Kubie.
        Ballets "This Property Is Condemned," New York, and
        "The Purification," Westport, CT.

1958   Prod. *Garden District*, New York; "The Last of My Solid
        Gold Watches," "Moony's Kid Don't Cry," "This Property
        Is Condemned," TV; *Period of Adjustment*, Miami. Film
        Cat on a Hot Tin Roof (screenplay by others). Ended
        visits with Kubie.

1959   Prod. *Sweet Bird of Youth*, New York (last collabora-
        tion with Kazan); "The Night of the Iguana," Spoleto,
        Italy. First trip to Far East. Film *Suddenly Last
        Summer* (screenplay by Vidal).

1960   Prod. *The Night of the Iguana*, Miami; *Period of
        Adjustment*, New York; film *The Fugitive Kind*. Cover
        story, *Time* magazine. Death of Diana Barrymore.

1961   Prod. "Hello from Bertha," "I Rise in Flame...," "The
        Lady of Larkspur Lotion," "The Purification," TV; *The
        Night of the Iguana*, New York (Drama Critics' Circle
        Award, 1962). Films *The Roman Spring of Mrs. Stone*
        (screenplay by Lambert), *Summer and Smoke* (screenplay
        by others).

1962   Prod. *The Milk Train Doesn't Stop Here Anymore*, Spo-
        leto, Italy. Films *Period of Adjustment* (screenplay
        by Lennart), *Sweet Bird of Youth* (screenplay by
        Brooks).

1963   Prod. *The Milk Train Doesn't Stop Here Anymore*, New
        York, Abingdon, VA. Donated papers to University of
        Texas. Death of Merlo (21 Sept.).

1964   Prod. *The Milk Train Doesn't Stop Here Anymore*, New
        York; *The Eccentricities of a Nightingale*, summer
        stock; recording *The Glass Menagerie*. Started seeing
        Dr. Max Jacobson. Film *The Night of the Iguana*
        (screenplay by others).

1965   Recorded Hart Crane poems. *The Night of the Iguana*
        won London Critics' Poll. Received Brandeis Univer-
        sity Creative Arts Award. Friendship with William
        Glavin.

1966   Pub. stories *The Knightly Quest*; prod. *Slapstick Trag-
        edy*, New York; "Ten Blocks on the Camino Real," *The
        Glass Menagerie*, TV. Film *This Property Is Condemned*
        (screenplay by others).

1967   Prod. *The Two-Character Play*, London; recording *The
        Rose Tattoo*. Death of McCullers.

1968   Prod. *The Seven Descents of Myrtle*, New York; film
        Boom!. Deaths of Bankhead, Van Saher.

1969   Prod. *In the Bar of a Tokyo Hotel*, New York. Awarded
        honorary degree, University of Missouri; Gold Medal
        for Drama, American Academy of Arts and Letters. Con-
        verted briefly to Roman Catholicism; committed to St.

Louis mental ward for three months. Film *Last of the Mobile Hot-Shots* (screenplay by Vidal).

1970   Prod. "I Can't Imagine Tomorrow," "Talk to Me like the Rain...," TV. Met Dodson Rader. Deaths of Yukio Mishima, Vaccaro.

1971   Prod. opera *Summer and Smoke* (libretto by Wilson), St. Paul; "Confessional," Bar Harbor, ME; *Out Cry*, Chicago. Break with Wood; Bill Barnes became agent.

1972   Prod. *Small Craft Warnings*, New York (Williams's first professional appearance on stage). Received National Theatre Conference Annual Award; honorary degrees, University of Hartford, Purdue University. Juror, Venice Film Festival. Met Robert Carroll.

1973   Prod. *Out Cry*, New York; *Tennessee Williams's South*, Canadian TV (script by Rasky); revised *Cat on a Hot Tin Roof*, West Springfield; *The Glass Menagerie*, TV; recording *A Streetcar Named Desire*. Received medal, Cathedral Church of St. John the Divine. Deaths of Magnani, Jane Bowles, Inge.

1974   Pub. stories *Eight Mortal Ladies Possessed*; prod. *The Migrants*, TV (script by Wilson); *The Latter Days of a Celebrated Soubrette*, New York. Received Entertainment Hall of Fame Award.

1975   Pub. *Memoirs*; novel *Moise and the World of Reason*; prod. *The Red Devil Battery Sign*, Boston; *The Two-Character Play*, New York. Received Medal of Honor for Literature, National Arts Club; elected three-year term, Governing Council of Dramatists Guild.

1976   Prod. *This Is (An Entertainment)*, San Francisco; *The Eccentricities of a Nightingale*, TV, New York; *Cat on a Hot Tin Roof*, TV. President, Cannes Film Festival Jury.

1977   Pub. poems *Androgyne, Mon Amour*; prod. *Vieux Carré*, New York; *The Red Devil Battery Sign*, London. Elected member American Academy of Arts and Letters. Rift with Capote, Windham.

1978   Prod. *Tiger Tail*, Atlanta; *Vieux Carré*, London; *Creve Coeur*, Charleston, SC. German film *Bourbon Street Blues*. Mitch Douglas became agent.

1979   Prod. A *Lovely Sunday for Creve Coeur, Kirche, Kutchen, und Kinder*, "Lifeboat Drill," New York. Reported mugged in Key West. Honored by Washington Kennedy Center; subject special session, Modern Language Association Conference; first issue *Tennessee Williams Newsletter*, Stephen S. Stanton, editor.

1980   Prod. *Will Mr. Merriwether Return from Memphis?*, dedication of Tennessee Williams Fine Arts Center, Florida Keys Community College; *Clothes for a Summer Hotel*, Washington, Chicago, New York; opera "I Rise in Flame ...," New York; "Some Problems for the Moose Lodge," Chicago. Awarded Presidental Medal of Freedom. Death of mother (1 June).

1981   Prod. *A House Not Meant to Stand*, Chicago; *Something Cloudy, Something Clear*, New York; *The Notebook of Trigorin*, Vancouver. Received Common Wealth prize (with Harold Pinter). Luis Sanjurjo became representative. Deaths of Evans, Henry Faulkner. Journal became *Tennessee Williams Review*, co-editor, S. Alan Chesler.

1982   Prod. *A House Not Meant to Stand*, Chicago; opera *Summer and Smoke*, TV. Received honorary degree, Harvard University. Jerrold A. Phillips, editor, *Tennessee Williams Review*.

1983   Evening of 24-25 Feb., death in New York hotel; burial in St. Louis (5 Mar.); will left manuscripts to Harvard. Last issue *Tennessee Williams Review*.

1984   *A Streetcar Named Desire*, *Cat on a Hot Tin Roof*, TV. Ballet, *In the Winter of Cities*. Death of Capote.

1985   *Collected Stories*. Death of Wood.

1986   Tennessee Williams in Key West Literary Seminar and Festival. French film *Noir et Blanc*.

1987   Film *The Glass Menagerie*. First annual Tennessee Williams/New Orleans Literary Festival.

1988   "Secret Places of the Heart," British radio. Papers actually go to Harvard.

1989   *Sweet Bird of Youth*, TV. First issue *Tennessee Williams Literary Journal*, W. Kenneth Holditch, editor. Death of Vassilis Voglis.

1990   "27 Wagons Full of Cotton," *Orpheus Descending*, TV; paintings shown, Key West.

CHRONOLOGICAL LIST OF PUBLICATIONS

The following is a short-title list of Williams's publications in roughly chronological order. His primary American publishers have been New Directions (ND), Dramatists Play Service (DPS), and New American Library (NAL). His primary British publishers have been Secker and Warburg (S&W) and Penguin. Canadian publications (not listed below) have been tied in to ND editions since 1964. Program notes (D 1), individual letters (D 3), paintings (E 2), student editions, and reprints of truly secondary importance, which are listed at appropriate places in the main bibliography, are not entered here. An asterisk (*) marks the first publication of all or part of a work. The reference at the end of each entry codes the reader to the relevant section of the main bibliography, where alphabetical order is followed.

1. *"Can a Good Wife Be a Good Sport?" *Smart Set* May 1927. D 1.

2. *"The Vengeance of Nitocris." *Weird Tales* Aug. 1928. B 1.

3. *"A Lady's Beaded Bag." *Columns* May 1930. B 1.

4. *"Not without Knowledge." *Savitar of 1932.* C 1.
5. *"October Song." *Neophyte* 1932-33. C 1.

6. *"Under the April Rain." *Inspiration* Spring 1933. C 1.
7. *"Modus Vivendi." *Counterpoint* July 1933. C 1.
8. *"Ave Atque Vale." *Alouette* Oct. 1933. C 1.

9. *"After a Visit"; "Cacti." *Voices* Aug.-Sept. 1934. C 1.
10. "After a Visit." *Literary Digest* 1 Sept. 1934. C 1.

11. *"Sonnets for the Spring (A Sequence)." *St. Louis Star-Times* 26 Mar. 1936. C 1.
12. *"Twenty-Seven Wagons Full of Cotton." *Manuscript* Aug. 1936. B 1.
13. *"Changling"; "Sonnet for Pygmalion." *Eliot* Nov. 1936. C 1.
14. *"Two Metaphysical Sonnets"; "No Shaken Seas." *Eliot* Dec. 1936. C 1.

15. *"Lyric"; "Clover"; "Lament." *College Verse* Jan. 1937.
    C 1.
16. *"Recollection." *Eliot* Feb. 1937. C 1.
17. *"Swimmer and Fish Group." *College Verse* Mar. 1937.
    C 1.
18. *"Mummer's Rhyme." *Eliot* Mar. 1937. C 1.
19. *"The New Poet." *American Prefaces* Apr. 1937. C 1.
20. *"Inheritors." *College Verse* Apr. 1937. C 1.
21. *"Sacre de Printemps." *College Verse* May 1937. C 1.
22. *"Diver"; "Letter to an Old Love." *Eliot* May 1937.
    C 1.
23. *"Ole 'Sephus..."; "Valediction"; "What College Has Not
    Done for Me"; "Penates"; "Sanctuary"; "The Shallow
    Pool." *Eliot* June 1937. C 1; D 1.
24. *"The Shuttle." *Poetry* June 1937. C 1.
25. *"Lyric"; "Odyssey"; "This Cryptic Bone." *Eliot* Nov.
    1937. C 1.
26. *"Reveille"; "With Military Honors." *Eliot* Dec. 1937.
    C 1.

27. *"The Field of Blue Children." *Story* Sept.-Oct. 1939.
    B 1.

28. *"Moony's Kid Don't Cry." *The Best One-Act Plays of
    1940*. Dodd, Mead, 1941. A 1.
29. *"Landscape with Figures." *American Scenes*. John Day,
    1941. A 1.
30. *"In Memoriam to Jane Taussig." *Eliot* May 1941. C 1.

31. *"The Lady of Larkspur Lotion." *The Best One-Act Plays
    of 1941*. Dodd, Mead, 1942. A 1.
32. *"Problem." *Eliot* Jan. 1942. C 1.
33. *"The Last of My Solid Gold Watches." *The Best One-Act
    Plays of 1942*. Dodd, Mead, 1942. A 1.

34. *"The Kitchen Door Blues." *Maryland Quarterly* 1944.
    C 1.
35. *"Dos Ranchos, or The Purification." *New Directions
    1944*. ND, 1944. A 1.
36. **Five Young American Poets*. ND, 1944. C 1.

37. *"27 Wagons Full of Cotton." *The Best One-Act Plays of
    1944*. Dodd, Mead, 1945. A 1.
38. **Battle of Angels*; "The History of a Play (with Paren-
    theses)." *Pharos* Spring 1945. A 1; D 1.
39. *"The Author Tells Why It Is Called 'The Glass Menag-
    erie.'" *New York Herald Tribune* 15 Apr. 1945.
    D 1.
40. *"The Malediction." *Town and Country* June 1945. B 1.
41. *"Everyman." *Contemporary Poetry* Summer 1945. C 1.
42. **The Glass Menagerie*. Random House, 1945. A 1.

43. *"The Important Thing." *Story* Nov.-Dec. 1945. B 1.
44. *27 Wagons Full of Cotton.... ND, 1945. A 2.
45. *"The Unsatisfactory Supper." *The Best One-Act Plays of 1945.* Dodd, Mead, 1945. A 1.

46. *"Something about Him." *Mademoiselle* June 1946. B 1.
47. *"A Liturgy of Roses." *Chicago Review* Summer 1946. C 1.
48. *Blue Mountain Ballads: Cabin.* Schirmer, 1946. C 1.
49. *Blue Mountain Ballads: Heavenly Grass.* Schirmer, 1946. C 1.
50. *Blue Mountain Ballads: Lonesome Man.* Schirmer, 1946. C 1.
51. *Blue Mountain Ballads: Sugar in the Cane.* Schirmer, 1946. C 1.
52. *"Three Poems." *New Directions in Prose and Poetry.* ND, 1946. C 1.
53. *"Which Is My Little Boy?" *Experiment* Fall 1946. C 1.
54. *"An Appreciation." *New York Times* 15 Dec. 1946. D 1.

55. *You Touched Me!* (with Donald Windham). Samuel French, 1947. A 1.
56. *Three.* Hargail Music, 1947. C 1.
57. *"The Yellow Bird." *Town and Country* June 1947. B 1.
58. *["Facts about Me."] *Boston Herald* 2 Nov. 1947. D 1.
59. *"On a Streetcar Named Success." *New York Times* 30 Nov. 1947. D 1.
60. *A Streetcar Named Desire.* ND, 1947. A 1.

61. "The Catastrophe of Success." *Story* Spring 1948. D 1.
62. *Brief comment: "My Current Reading." *Saturday Review of Literature* 6 Mar. 1948. D 1.
63. *"Desire and the Black Masseur." *New Directions in Prose and Poetry.* ND, 1948. B 1.
64. *"A Movie Named 'La Terra Trema.'" *'48* June 1948. D 1.
65. *"Testa dell' Efebo." *Harper's Bazaar* Aug. 1948. C 1.
66. *One Arm and Other Stories.* ND, 1948. B 2.
67. *American Blues....* DPS, 1948. A 2.
68. *The Glass Menagerie.* DPS, 1948. A 1.
69. *The Glass Menagerie.* John Lehmann, 1948. A 1.
70. *"Questions without Answers." *New York Times* 3 Oct. 1948. D 1.
71. *"On the Art of Being a True Non-Conformist." *New York Star* 7 Nov. 1948. D 1.
72. *Summer and Smoke.* ND, 1948. A 1.
73. *"Rubio y Morena." *Partisan Review* Dec. 1948. B 1.

74. *"An Appreciation." *Derrière le Miroir* Jan. 1949. D 1.

75. *"Tuesday's Child." *Partisan Review* Apr. 1949. C 1.
76. *"The Harp of Wales." *Prairie Schooner* 1949. C 1.
77. *"Rubio y Morena"; "Three Poems." *New Directions in Prose and Poetry*. ND, 1949. B 1; C 1.
78. *"The Christus of Guadalajara"; "The Stonecutter's Angels." *Botteghe Obscura* 1949. C 1.
79. *27 Wagons Full of Cotton*.... John Lehmann, 1949. A 2.
80. *A Streetcar Named Desire*. John Lehmann, 1949. A 1.
81. *The Glass Menagerie*. ND, 1949. A 1.
82. *"An Allegory of Man and His Sahara." *New York Times Book Review* 4 Dec. 1949. D 1.

83. *"The Resemblance between a Violin Case and a Coffin." *Flair* Feb. 1950. B 1.
84. "The Resemblance between a Violin Case and a Coffin." *Penguin New Writing*. Penguin, 1950. B 1.
85. *Brief comment: "What I look for in a Film." *Films in Review* Mar. 1950. D 1.
86. *Summer and Smoke*. DPS, 1950. A 1.
87. *A Streetcar Named Desire*. ND, n.d. A 1.
88. *"Foreword." *Young Man with a Screwdriver* by Oliver Evans. Univ. Nebraska Pr., 1950. D 1.
89. *"Foreword." *Constructing a Play* by Marian Gallaway. Prentice-Hall, 1950. D 1.
90. *"Introduction: This Book." *Reflections in a Golden Eye* by Carson McCullers. ND, 1950.
91. "Which Is My Little Boy?" *Mademoiselle* July 1950. C 1.
92. *"A Writer's Quest for a Parnassus." *New York Times Magazine* 13 Aug. 1950. D 1.
93. *The Roman Spring of Mrs. Stone*. ND, 1950. B 1.
94. *The Roman Spring of Mrs. Stone*. John Lehmann, 1950. B 1.
95. *"Eight Poems." *New Directions in Prose and Poetry*. ND, 1950. C 1.
96. *"The Human Psyche - Alone." *Saturday Review of Literature* 23 Dec. 1950. D 1.

97. *"Concerning the Timeless World of a Play." *New York Times* 14 Jan. 1951. D 1.
98. *["The Meaning of *The Rose Tattoo*."] *Vogue* 15 Mar. 1951. D 1.
99. *The Rose Tattoo*. ND, 1951. A 1.
100. *I Rise in Flame, Cried the Phoenix*.... James Laughlin, 1951. A 1.
101. *A Streetcar Named Desire*. NAL, 1951. A 1.
102. *"The Interior of the Pocket." *New Directions in Prose and Poetry*. ND, 1951. C 1.

134. *Four Plays.* S&W, 1956. A 2.
135. *Cat on a Hot Tin Roof.* S&W, 1956. A 1.
136. *"On Meeting a Young Writer." *Harper's Bazaar* Aug.
         1956. D 1.
137. *Baby Doll....* ND, 1956. A 1.
138. *The Script for the Film Baby Doll.* NAL, 1956. A 1.

139. *Baby Doll....* S&W, 1957. A 1.
140. *Baby Doll....* Penguin, 1957. A 1.
141. *Cat on a Hot Tin Roof.* Penguin, 1957. A 1.
142. *The Roman Spring of Mrs. Stone.* S&W, 1957. B 1.
143. *A Streetcar Named Desire.* S&W, 1957. A 1.
144. *Summer and Smoke.* S&W, 1957. A 1.
145. *"A Talk with Tennessee Williams." *New York Post Maga-
         zine* 17 Mar. 1957. D 1.
146. *"Tennessee Williams on the Past, the Present and the
         Perhaps." *New York Times* 17 Mar. 1957. D 1.
147. "The World I Live In." *London Observer* 7 Apr. 1957.
         D 1.
148. *"Author and Director: A Delicate Situation." *Play-
         bill* 30 Sept. 1957. D 1.
149. *Orpheus Descending* [excerpts]. *The Best Plays of
         1956-1957....* Dodd, Mead, 1957. A 1.

150. *"The Writing Is Honest." *New York Times* 16 Mar. 1958.
         D 1.
151. "Introduction." *The Dark at the Top of the Stairs* by
         William Inge. Random House, 1958. D 1.
152. *Orpheus Descending, with Battle of Angel.* ND, 1958.
         A 1.
153. *Suddenly Last Summer.* ND, 1958. A 1.
154. *Camino Real.* S&W, 1958. A 1.
155. *Orpheus Descending.* S&W, 1958. A 1.
156. *Cat on a Hot Tin Roof.* NAL, 1958. A 1.
157. *"A Perfect Analysis Given by a Parrot." *Esquire* Oct.
         1958. A 1.
158. *Cat on a Hot Tin Roof.* DPS, 1958. A 1.
159. *Suddenly Last Summer.* DPS, 1958. A 1.
160. *Suddenly Last Summer.* ND, n.d. A 1.
161. *The Rose Tattoo; Camino Real.* Penguin, 1958. A 2.

162. *A Streetcar Named Desire; The Glass Menagerie.* Pen-
         guin, 1959. A 2.
163. *"The Enemy: Time." *Theatre* Mar. 1959. A 1.
164. *"Williams' Wells of Violence." *New York Times* 8 Mar.
         1959. D 1.
165. *Sweet Bird of Youth.* *Esquire* Apr. 1959. A 1.
166. *Garden District: Two Plays....* S&W, 1959. A 2.
167. *Orpheus Descending.* DPS, 1959. A 1.
168. *"Man Bring This Up Road." *Mademoiselle* July 1959.
         B 1.

169. *Hard Candy....* ND, 1959.
170. **Sweet Bird of Youth.* ND, 1959. A 1.

171. *Brief comment: "'As if a rose might somehow be a
     throat'...." *Words and Music.* RCA Victor, n.d.
     D 1.
172. *The Glass Menagerie.* DPS, n.d. A 1.
173. *A Perfect Analysis Given by a Parrot....* DPS, n.d.
     A 1.

174. *Suddenly Last Summer.* NAL, 1960. A 1.
175. *The Fugitive Kind....* NAL, 1960. A 1.
176. *Three Players of a Summer Game....* S&W, 1960. B 2.
177. *"Reflections on a Revival of a Controversal Fantasy."
     New York Times 15 May 1960. D 1.
178. *"Tennessee Williams Presents His POV." *New York Times
     Magazine* 12 June 1960. D 1.
179. *"Prelude to a Comedy." *New York Times* 6 Nov. 1960.
     D 1.
180. **Period of Adjustment....* Esquire* Dec. 1960. A 1.
181. **Period of Adjustment....* ND, 1960. A 1.

182. *"Five Fiery Ladies." *Life* 3 Feb. 1961. D 1.
183. *Sweet Bird of Youth.* S&W, 1961. A 1.
184. *Period of Adjustment.* S&W, 1961. A 1.
185. **Period of Adjustment.* DPS, 1961. A 1.
186. *Orpheus Descending; Something Unspoken; Suddenly Last
     Summer.* Penguin, 1961. A 2.
187. *"The Author." *Saturday Review* 23 Sept. 1961. D 1.
188. *The Roman Spring of Mrs. Stone.* NAL, 1961. B 1.
189. *Summer and Smoke.* NAL, 1961. A 1.
190. *"A Summer of Discovery." *New York Herald Tribune* 24
     Dec. 1961. D 1.

191. **The Night of the Iguana.* Esquire* Feb. 1962. A 1.
192. **The Night of the Iguana.* ND, 1962. A 1.
193. *Sweet Bird of Youth.* NAL, 1962. A 1.
194. *Sweet Bird of Youth; A Streetcar Named Desire; The
     Glass Menagerie.* Penguin, 1962. A 2.
195. *Five Plays....* S&W, 1962. A 2.
196. *Period of Adjustment.....* NAL, 1962. A 1.
197. *Sweet Bird of Youth.* DPS, 1962. A 1.
198. *"The Agent as Catalyst." *Esquire* Dec. 1962. D 1.

199. **The Milk Train Doesn't Stop Here Anymore* [excerpts].
     The Best Plays of 1962-1963.... Dodd, Mead, 1963.
     A 1.
200. *Period of Adjustment; Summer and Smoke.* New English
     Library, 1963. A 2.
201. *The Night of the Iguana.* S&W, 1963. A 1.
202. **The Night of the Iguana.* DPS, 1963. A 1.

203. *"T. Williams's View of T. Bankhead." *New York Times*
     29 Dec. 1963. D 1.

204. *The Milk Train Doesn't Stop Here Anymore.* ND, 1964.
     A 1.
205. *The Milk Train Doesn't Stop Here Anymore.* DPS, 1964.
     A 1.
206. *The Milk Train Doesn't Stop Here Anymore.* S&W, 1964.
     A 1.
207. *Grand.* House of Books, 1964. D 1.
208. *Three Plays....* ND, 1964. A 2.
209. *The Eccentricities of a Nigtingale and Summer and
     Smoke.* ND, 1964. A 1.
210. *In the Winter of Cities: Poems.* ND, 1964. C 2.
211. *The Night of the Iguana.* NAL, 1964. A 1.
212. *The Night of the Iguana.* Penguin, 1964. A 1.

213. *"Mama's Old Stucco House." *Esquire* Jan. 1965. B 1.
214. "Man Bring This Up Road." *International* (London)
     Spring 1965. B 1.
215. "Mama's Old Stucco House." *London Weekend Telegraph* 7
     May 1965. B 1.
216. *Camino Real.* DPS, n.d. A 1.
217. *The Rose Tattoo.* DPS, n.d. A 1.
218. *Slapstick Tragedy....* *Esquire* Aug. 1965. A 1.
219. *Three Players of a Summer Game....* Penguin, 1965.
     B 2.
220. *Note on Hart Crane. *Tennessee Williams Reads Hart
     Crane.* Caedmon Records, 1965. E 1.

221. *"The Wolf and I." *New York Times* 20 Feb. 1966. D 1.
222. *"I Can't Imagine Tomorrow." *Esquire* Mar. 1966. A 1.
223. *The Glass Menagerie.* American Printing House for
     Blind, 1966. A 1.
224. *A Streetcar Named Desire.* American Printing House for
     Blind, 1966. A 1.
225. *The Night of the Iguana.* American Printing House for
     Blind, 1966. A 1.
226. *Brief comment: "Gore Vidal." *Double Exposure.* Dela-
     courte, 1966. D 1.
227. "'Grand.'" *Esquire* Nov. 1966. D 1.
228. *The Knightly Quest....* ND, 1966. B 2.
229. *The Glass Menagerie.* ND, 1966. A 1.
230. *27 Wagons Full of Cotton....* ND, 1966. A 2.

231. *"Kingdom of Earth." *Esquire* Feb. 1967. A 1.
232. *The Gnädiges Fräulein....* DPS, 1967. A 1.
233. *The Mutilated....* DPS, 1967. A 1.
234. *One Arm....* ND, 1967. B 2.
235. *Hard Candy....* ND, 1967. B 2.

264. *The Theatre of Tennessee Williams.* Vol. I. ND, 1971.
        A 2.
265. *The Theatre of Tennessee Williams.* Vol. II. ND,
        1971. A 2.
266. *The Theatre of Tennessee Williams.* Vol. III. ND,
        1971. A 2.

267. *The Theatre of Tennessee Williams.* Vol. IV. ND,
        1972. A 2.
268. *"We Are Dissenters Now." *Harper's Bazaar* Jan. 1972.
        D 1.
269. *Small Craft Warnings.* ND, 1972. A 1.
270. *Summer and Smoke: Opera* by Lanford Wilson. Belwin-
        Mills, 1972. A 1.
271. *"Survival Notes: A Journal." *Esquire* Sept. 1972.
        D 1.
272. "Happy August the 10th." *Esquire* Dec. 1972. B 1.

273. *"Homage to Key West." *Harper's Bazaar* Jan. 1973.
        D 1.
274. "Survival Notes: A Journal." *London Times Saturday
        Review* 20 Jan. 1973. D 1.
275. *"The Inventory at Fontana Bella." *Playboy* Mar. 1973.
        B 1.
276. *"Let Me Hang It All Out." *New York Times* 4 Mar. 1973.
        D 1.
277. *"Where My Head Is Now and Other Questions." *Perform-
        ing Arts* Apr. 1973. D 1.
278. *"To William Inge: An Homage." *New York Times* 1 July
        1973. D 1.
279. *Small Craft Warnings.* S&W, 1973. A 1.
280. *Out Cry.* ND, 1973. A 1.
281. *"Sabbatha and Solitude." *Playgirl* Sept. 1973. B 1.
282. *"Miss Puma, Miss Who?" *Antaeus* Autumn 1973. C 1.
283. *Brief comment. *Working with Kazan.* Wesleyan Univ.
        Pr., 1973. D 1.
284. *"Miss Coynte of Greene." *Playboy* Dec. 1973. B 1.

285. *Brief comment. *Dramatists Guild Quarterly* Winter
        1974. D 1.
286. *"Red Part of a Flag, or Oriflamme." *Vogue* Mar. 1974.
        B 1.
287. *Eight Mortal Ladies Possessed....* ND, 1974. B 2.
288. *Eight Mortal Ladies Possessed....* S&W, 1974. B 2.

289. *Battle of Angels.* DPS, 1975. A 1.
290. *Cat on a Hot Tin Roof.* ND, 1975. A 1.
291. *Sweet Bird of Youth.* ND, 1975. A 1.
292. *Moise and the World of Reason.* Simon, 1975. B 1.
293. *Memoirs.* Doubleday, 1975. D 1.

294. *"Some Words Before." *The Lonely Hunter* by Virginia
     Spencer Carr. Doubleday, 1975. D 1.
295. *"W. H. Auden: A Few Reminiscences." *Harvard Advocate*
     1975. D 1.

296. *The Theatre of Tennessee Williams*. Vol. V. ND, 1976.
     A 2.
297. *Moise and the World of Reason*. W. H. Allen, 1976.
     B 1.
298. *Memoirs*. W. H. Allen, 1976. D 1.
299. *Cat on a Hot Tin Roof; The Milk Train Doesn't Stop
     Here Anymore; The Night of the Iguana*. Penguin,
     1976. A 2.
300. *The Rose Tattoo; Camino Real; Orpheus Descending*.
     Penguin, 1976. A 2.
301. *Tennessee Williams' Letters to Donald Windham 1940-65*.
     Sandy M. Campbell, 1976. D 3.
302. *Four Plays....* NAL, 1976. A 2.
304. *Three by Tennessee....* NAL, 1976. A 2.
305. *Memoirs*. Bantam, 1976. D 1.
306. *Moise and the World of Reason*. Bantam, 1976. B 1.
307. *The Roman Spring of Mrs. Stone*. Bantam, 1976. B 1.
308. *"Foreword." *Feminine Wiles* by Jane Bowles. Black
     Sparrow, 1976. D 1.
309. *Brief comment: "The Arts in America." *New York Times*
     29 Aug. 1976. D 1.
310. *"The Blessings and Mixed Blessings of Workshop Produc-
     tions." *Dramatists Guild Quarterly* Autumn 1976.
     D 1.
312. *"'I Have Rewritten a Play for Artistic Purity.'" *New
     York Times* 21 Nov. 1976. D 1.

313. *"Mother Yaws." *Esquire* May 1977. B 1.
314. *"Candida: A College Essay." *Shaw Review* May 1977.
     D 1.
315. *"'I Am Widely Regarded as the Ghost of a Writer.'"
     New York Times 8 May 1977. D 1.
316. *"Androgyne, Mon Amour." *Ambit* 1977. C 1.
317. *Androgyne, Mon Amour....* ND, 1977. C 2.
318. *The Eccentricities of a Nightingale*. DPS, 1977. A 1.
319. *Tennessee Williams' Letters to Donald Windham 1940-
     1965*. Holt, 1977. D 3.
320. *Selected Plays*. Franklin Library, 1977. A 2.
321. *Memoirs*. W. H. Allen, 1977. D 1.
322. *The Roman Spring of Mrs. Stone*. Panther, 1977. B 1.

323. *"The Killer Chicken and the Closet Queen." *Christo-
     pher Street* July 1978. B 1.
324. *Where I Live: Selected Essays*. ND, 1978. D 2.
325. *The World of Tennessee Williams*. Putnam's, 1978.
     F 1.

326. *Brief comment. *A Portrait of the Theatre*. Crown,
       1979. D 1.
327. *Brief comment. "A Playwrights' Choice of 'Perfect
       Plays.'" *New York Times* 14 Jan. 1979. D 1.
328. *"Note." *Tennessee Williams in Tangier*. Cadmus, 1979.
       D 1.
329. *Vieux Carré*. ND, 1979. A 1.
330. *The Two-Character Play*. ND, 1979. A 1.
331. *Kingdom of Earth*.... DPS, n.d. A 1.
332. *Eight Plays*. Doubleday, 1979. A 2.

333. *"Tent Worms." *Esquire* May 1980. B 1.
334. *Steps Must Be Gentle*.... William Targ, 1980. A 1.
335. *Selected Plays*. Franklin Library, 1980. A 2.
336. *"Foreword." *The Bar Bizarre* by Dakin Williams. Sun-
       rise, 1980. D 1.
337. *Tennessee Williams' Letters to Donald Windham*....
       Penguin, 1980. D 3.
338. *A Streetcar Named Desire*. ND, 1980. A 1.

339. *"Das Wasser ist kalt." *Antaeus* Winter-Spring 1981.
       B 1.
340. *Note on Eve Adamson. *Other Stages* 30 July 1981. D 1.
341. *It Happened the Day the Sun Rose*. Sylvester, 1981.
       B 1.
342. *The Theatre of Tennessee Williams*. Vol. VI. ND,
       1981. A 2.
343. *The Theatre of Tennessee Williams*. Vol. VII. ND,
       1981. A 2.
344. *Clothes for a Summer Hotel*. DPS, 1981. A 1.
345. *Brief comment. *Conjunctions* Fall 1981. D 1.
346. *"The Travelling Companion." *Christopher Street* Dec.
       1981. A 1.

347. *"The Blond Mediterraneans: A Litany." *Christopher
       Street* 1982. C 1.
348. *"The Man in the Overstuffed Chair." *Antaeus* Spring-
       Summer 1982. D 1.
349. *The Donsinger Woman and Their Handy Man Jack*. Devil-
       lier-Donegan, 1982. E 1.
350. *Period of Adjustment; Summer and Smoke; Small Craft
       Warnings*. Penguin, 1982. A 2.
351. *A Streetcar Named Desire*. Limited Editions Club,
       1982. A 1.
352. *"Notes for *The Two-Character Play*"; Note on Eve Adam-
       son. *Tennessee Williams Review* 1982. D 1.

353. *Last Will and Testament. *Tennessee Williams Review*
       1983. D 4.
354. *Clothes for a Summer Hotel*. ND, 1983. A 1.

355. *"Beauty Is the Word"; "Hot Milk at Three in the Morn-
     ing." *Missouri Review* 1984. A 1.
356. **The Remarkable Rooming-House of Mme. Le Monde.*
     Albondocani, 1984. A 1.
357. **Stopped Rocking and Other Screenplays.* ND, 1984.
     A 2.
358. *Tennessee Williams.* Gale Research, 1984. F 1.
359. *Three Players of a Summer Game....* Everyman, 1984.
     B 2.

360. **Collected Stories.* ND, 1985. B 2.
361. *The Roman Spring of Mrs. Stone.* Ballantine, 1985.
     B 1.

362. *Collected Stories.* Ballantine, 1986. B 2.
363. *Collected Stories.* S&W, 1986. B 2.
364. **Conversations with Tennessee Williams.* Univ. Pr. of
     Mississippi, 1986. F 1.
365. *The Roman Spring of Mrs. Stone.* Listen for Pleasure,
     1986. B 1.

366. *The Glass Menagerie.* Penguin, 1987. A 1.
367. *The Glass Menagerie.* NAL, 1987. A 1.

368. **The Red Devil Battery Sign.* ND, 1988. A 1.

369. **Five O'Clock Angel: Letters....* Knopf, 1990. D 3.

370. *"We Have Not Long to Love." *Poetry* Feb. 1991. C 1.
371. **Baby Doll & Tiger Tail.* ND, 1991. A 1.
372. *"The Chalky White Substance." *Antaeus* Spring 1991. A
     1.
373. *Five O'Clock Angel: Letters....* Deutsch, 1991. D 3.
374. *Five O'Clock Angel: Letters....* Penguin, 1991.

A. PLAYS AND SCREENPLAYS

A 1 is the most complex section of the bibliography.
It lists Williams's published and/or produced plays and
screenplays in alphabetical order. For each title I have
tried to sort out the often complicated publishing history
(of which more is said below). Next comes the play's inclusion (if any) in textbooks, arranged alphabetically by edi-
or. Then appears, in alphabetical order by author, any
criticism of the work. (One should also turn to A 3).
Last, there is a record in chronological order of significant productions.

For the full-length plays the première of each new version has always been included, followed by important revivals (importance being defined generally by the amount of attention the production received; sometimes by the power of
the cast). The *Best Play/Burns Mantle Yearbook* series and
Theatre World have been very useful for tracking down American productions. For the short plays I am less certain of
the production record. Unless I note a première one should
not assume that the first listing is necessarily such.

Reviews are entered at the appropriate places: first
alphabetically by journal for anonymous reviews or those for
which I did not find the reviewers' names; then alphabetically by reviewer. I have omitted titles as largely mean-
ingless, though I regret not being able to demonstrate how
many copy editors have felt "A *Crass* Menagerie," among other
wordplays, is fresh and witty.

A 2 lists, in alphabetical order, collections of plays.
A 3 contains critical books and articles that analyze more
than one work, listed alphabetically by author. (F 1 offers
further information about a play's background and production). A 4 lists reports on conferences. Finally A 5 contains parodies and various kinds of attacks that seem to
fall outside the realm of literary criticism. In two ways I
have departed from conventions for the sake of clarity.
Newspapers and some magazines use quotation marks for titles
within titles; I have italicized them instead. Similarly I
have italicized titles within the titles of books and video-
cassettes.

Many of the plays exist in several versions; Williams,
instead of being satisfied with a work once it was in

print, often revised. Small revisions sometimes appeared
with no warning between one printing and another. Some
early British editions differed significantly from American
editions. And often he would rewrite a work, publishing a
new version any time from 3 to 35 years after it had first
appeared. Thus the textual editor of any definitive collection of his works will have enormous problems. Also,
twelve of the short stories listed in B 1 relate to published plays. Critical attention to revisions has not been
extensive; most critics simply accept the New Directions
texts as definitive.

     There follow 75 main entries. There have been 37 one-
act plays published, four of them in more than one version
(nine if one counts expansions into longer works). Six
others were produced but remain unpublished (though one became a longer published play). There have been 22 long
plays published, 14 to 17 (depending on how one considers
one acts and a screenplay) in anything from two to five different versions. Eleven others were produced but remain
unpublished. Finally six screenplays, three of which were
totally original, have been published, and two filmed; four
other screen adaptations were filmed but remain unpublished.
(All the other 12 unpublished screenplays, including a German version of a one-act play and two English and one French
versions of fiction, were written by others.)

              1. INDIVIDUAL TITLES, WITH PRODUCTIONS

ALL GAUL IS DIVIDED: see A *Lovely Sunday for Creve Coeur*

"AT LIBERTY": Drama about a trapped, frustrated Mississippi
   actress dying of consumption.

   *Landscape with Figures: Two Mississippi Plays. American
      Scenes.* Ed. William Kozlinko. New York: John Day,
      1941. Contents: Autobiographical Note; "At Liberty,"
      175-82; "This Property Is Condemned," 183-93.

   25 Non-Royalty One-Act Plays for All-Girl Casts. Ed.
      Betty Smith. New York: Greenberg, 1942. 60-67.

                         Criticism

   Weales, Gerald C. "Tennessee Williams' 'Lost' Play."
      American Literature 37 (Nov. 1965): 321-23.

Production

3 Small Plays by Big Playwrights.   New York: Quaigh Theatre, 7 Mar. 1978.   Ted Mornel, dir.

"AUTO-DA-FÉ: A TRAGEDY IN ONE ACT":   Drama about a sexually
repressed New Orleans postal worker.   Ms., Texas (G).

27 Wagons Full of Cotton, 1945, 1953: 105-20 (A 2).

27 Wagons Full of Cotton, 1949: 101-14 (A 2).

Theatre, Vol. 6, 1981: 129-51 (A 2).

Trans. (H):   Czech, Italian.

Production

Ten by Tennessee.   Acting Company.   New York: Lucille
Lortel Theatre, 11 May-29 June 1986 (53).   Michael Kahn,
dir.   Derek McLane, Ann Hould-Ward, Dennis Parichy, de-
sign.   Lee Hoiby, music.   With Richard Howard (Eloi),
Lisa Banes (Mme. Duvenet).   Reviews, Prod. Notes:
  New York Times 25 June 1986, sec. 3: 23.
  Freedman, Samuel G.   *New York Times* 18 May 1986, sec.
    2: 1, 6.   [Interview with Kahn]
  Gussow, Mel.   *New York Times* 20 May 1986, sec. 3: 17.
  Oliver, Edith.   *New Yorker* 2 June 1986: 74-75.
  Simon, John.   *New York* 16 June 1986: 76.

BABY DOLL/TIGER TAIL: Screenplay, *Baby Doll*, based on the
  plays "27 Wagons Full of Cotton" and "The Unsatisfactory
  Supper" (A 1 below) about the awakening of a Mississippi
  woman to her sexual potential; play, *Tiger Tail*, based on
  screenplay.   Mss., Columbia, Congress, Delaware, Princeton, Texas (G).
    Williams began work with Elia Kazan in 1952 on the
  script which would result in *Baby Doll*.   Finished early
  1956, there are many differences, including the ending,
  between the published screenplay and the film.   Cardinal
  Spellman created a controversy by banning the film for
  Catholics.   The screenplay, nevertheless, was nominated
  for an Academy Award.   In the 1970's Williams rewrote it
  for the stage as *Tiger Tail*.

Screenplay

*Baby Doll: The Script for the Film...Incorporating the
  Two One-Act Plays Which Suggested It: 27 Wagons Full of*

*Cotton; The Long Stay Cut Short, or The Unsatisfactory
Supper.* New York: New Directions, 1956. 208 pp. *Baby
Doll: The Script for the Film.* London: Secker & War-
burg, 1957. 140 pp. Ils. Contents: Publisher's
Note, 3; *Baby Doll*, 5-140; [New Directions only: "27
Wagons Full of Cotton" (A 1): 143-90; "... The Unsatis-
factory Supper" (A 1): 191-208]. Reviews:
  Reporter 20 Sept. 1956: 48.
  Davis, Helen. *Mainstream* 9 (Nov. 1956): 50-51.
  Freedley, George. *New York Morning Telegraph* 1 Oct.
    1956: 2.
  Phelps, Robert. *National Review* 15 Sept. 1956: 20.

The Script for the Film Baby Doll. Signet Book. New
  York: New American Library, 1956. 128 pp. Ils.

Baby Doll: The Script for the Film. Harmondsworth: Penguin Books, 1957. 123 pp. Ils.

Baby Doll, etc., 1958: 7-89 (A 2).

Baby Doll & Tiger Tail, 1991: 1-116 (below).

Trans. (H): Arabic, French, Italian.

Play

Baby Doll & Tiger Tail: A Screenplay and Play. New York:
  New Directions, 1991; Markham, Ont.: Penguin Books
  Canada, 1991. Also New Directions Paperbook. Con-
  tents: *Baby Doll*, 1-116; *Tiger Tail*, 117-220.

Criticism

Dusenbury, Winifred. "*Baby Doll* and *The Ponder Heart*."
  Modern Drama 3 (Feb. 1961): 393-95.

Hilfer, Anthony C., and R. Vance Ramsey. "*Baby Doll*: A
  Study in Comedy and Critical Awareness." *Ohio University Review* 11 (1969): 75-88.

Johnson, Carla Jean. "A Tiger by the Tail: The Five Finished Versions of Tennessee Williams' 'Twenty-Seven
  Wagons Full of Cotton.'" Diss., Univ. of Notre Dame,
  1988. *Dissertation Abstracts International* 49 (1989):
  1802 A.

Kahn, Sy. "*Baby Doll*: A Comic Fable." Tharpe (A 3):
  292-309.

Wooten, Carl. "The Country Wife and Contemporary Comedy:
A World Apart." *Drama Survey* 2 (Winter 1963): 333-43.

Productions

Baby Doll. Newtown Production. Warner Brothers, 18 Dec.
1956 (première). Elia Kazan, dir. Boris Kaufman, camera. Richard Sylbert, design. Kenyon Hopkins, music.
With Carroll Baker (Baby Doll), Eli Wallach (Silva), Karl
Malden (Archie), Mildred Dunnock (Aunt Rose). Music
soundtrack: Columbia Records, 1956. Reviews, Prod.
Notes, Report on Controversy:
    America 96 (15 Dec. 1956): 320.
    America 96 (29 Dec. 1956): 367.
    America 96 (5 Jan. 1957): 386.
    Commonweal 65 (11 Jan. 1957): 371-72.
    Cosmopolitan Jan. 1957: 23.
    Life 11 June 1956: 111-12. [Filming]
    Life 7 Jan. 1957: 60-65.
    Look 25 Dec. 1956: 95.
    Look 12 Mar. 1957: 124.
    National Parent-Teacher Jan. 1957: 36.
    New York Post 13 Dec. 1956: 31. [Editorial against
      Spellman]
    New York Times 28 Nov. 1956: 28.
    New York Times 17 Dec. 1956: 28. Rpt. Van Antwerp (F
      1): 164-66. [Spellman's denouncement]
    New York Times 18 Dec. 1956: 39.
    New York Times 20 Dec. 1956: 36. [Indianapolis]
    New York Times 21 Dec. 1956: 18.
    New York Times 23 Dec. 1956, sec. 1: 17.
    New York Times 24 Dec. 1956: 14. [Response by Bishop
      Pike]
    New York Times 27 Dec. 1956: 21. [Ban by chain]
    New York Times 28 Dec. 1956: 17. [Bookings]
    New York Times 30 Dec. 1956, sec. 1: 2.
    New York Times 1 Jan. 1957: 19. [Syracuse, Troy, NY]
    New York Times 3 Jan. 1957: 28.
    New York Times 4 Jan. 1957: 19.
    New York Times 5 Jan. 1957: 11. [Providence, RI]
    New York Times 6 Jan. 1957, sec. 1: 86. [Providence]
    New York Times 7 Jan. 1957: 20. [France]
    New York Times 8 Jan. 1957: 26.
    New York Times 20 Jan. 1957, sec. 1: 76; sec. 2: 5.
    New York Times 24 Jan. 1957: 34. [Gary, IN]
    New York Times 30 Jan. 1957: 30. [[Aurora, IL]
    New York Times 4 Feb. 1957: 22.
    New York Times 10 Mar. 1957, sec. 1: 76. [Philadel-
      phia]
    New York Times 25 May 1957: 25.
    New York Times Magazine 22 Apr. 1956: 47. [Filming]

Newsweek 17 Dec. 1956: 106.

Newsweek 31 Dec. 1956: 59.

Spectator 138 (4 Jan. 1957): 22.

Theatre Arts Nov. 1956: 30-32, 89. [Interview with
   Kazan]

Time 24 Dec. 1956: 61.

Time 14 Jan. 1957: 100.

Variety 5 Dec. 1956: 6.

Anderson, Lindsay. *New Statesman* 53 (5 Jan. 1957): 14.

Baker, Carroll. *Baby Doll: An Autobiography.* New
   York: Arbor House, 1983. 142-61.

Berger, Meyer. *New York Times* 22 Oct. 1956: 23.

Bingham, Robert. *Reporter* 24 Jan. 1957: 36.

Bolton, Whitney. *New York Morning Telegraph* 18 Feb.
   1957: 2.

Butcher, Maryvonne. *Commonweal* 67 (22 Nov. 1957): 202-
   04.

Cameron, Kate. *New York Sunday News* 2 Dec. 1956, sec.
   2: 3.

Carr, William H. A., and Malcolm Logen. *New York Post*
   17 Dec. 1956: 5, 42. [Kazan's, Williams's responses
   to Spellman]

Ciment, Michel, ed. *Kazan on Kazan.* London: Secker,
   1973. 73-81. Rpt. Van Antwerp (F 1): 171-75.

Cogley, John. *Commonweal* 65 (11 Jan. 1957): 381.

---. *Commonweal* 65 (1 Feb. 1957): 465.

Cook, Alton. *New York World-Telegram* 19 Dec. 1956: 18.

Corliss, Richard. *Film Comment* 4 (Summer 1968): 44-47.

Crowther, Bosley. *New York Times* 9 Dec. 1956, sec. 2:
   5.

---. *New York Times* 19 Dec. 1956: 40. Rpt. *New York
   Times Film Reviews.*

---. *New York Times* 6 Jan. 1957, sec. 2: 1.

Dent, Alan. *Illustrated London News* 12 Jan. 1957: 80.

Downing, Robert. *Films in Review* 7 (Dec. 1956): 534-
   35.

Dyer, Peter John. *Films and Filming* Feb. 1957: 21-22.

Esterow, Milton. *New York Times* 26 Feb. 1956, sec. 2:
   5.

Finley, James Fenlon. *Catholic World* 184 (Jan. 1957):
   302.

---. *Catholic World* 184 (Apr. 1957): 62-63.

Hart, Henry. *Films in Review* 8 (Jan. 1957): 32-33.

Hartung, Philip. *Commonweal* 65 (28 Dec. 1956): 335.

Hatch, Robert. *Nation* 183 (29 Dec. 1956): 567. Rpt.
   Van Antwerp (F 1): 166-67.

Hewes, Henry. *Saturday Review* 29 Dec. 1956: 23-24.
   Rpt. George Oppenheimer, ed., *The Passionate Playgoer...* (New York: Viking, 1971): 250-54.

Hume, Rod. *Films and Filming* Dec. 1956: 9.

ﾟﾟﾟ

Kael, Pauline. *Kiss Kiss Bang Bang*. Boston: Little,
   Brown, 1968. 232.
Kaufman, Boris. "Filming *Baby Doll*." *American
   Cinematographer* Feb. 1957: 92-93, 106-07.
Kazan, Elia. *A Life* (F 1): 561-64.
Kites, Jim. "Elia Kazan: A Structural Analysis."
   Cinema 7 (Winter 1972): 25-36.
Knight, Arthur. *Saturday Review* 29 Dec. 1956: 22-23.
Kurnitz, Harry. *Holiday* Feb. 1957: 93, 103.
Marcorelles, Louis. *Sight and Sound* 26 (Winter 1956-
   57): 150-51.
Mardore, Michel. *Nouvel Observateur* 17-23 Nov. 1980:
   98-99.
Marowitz, Charles. *Village Voice* 12 Sept. 1956: 9-10.
---. *Village Voice* 23 Jan. 1957: 6.
McCarten, John. *New Yorker* 29 Dec. 1956: 59-60.
Pryor, Thomas. *New York Times* 23 Dec. 1956, sec. 4: 8.
---. *New York Times* 25 May 1957: 25. [Profit]
Quigly, Isabel. *Spectator* 4 Jan. 1957: 22.
Quint, Bert. *New York Herald Tribune* 17 Dec. 1956: 1,
   15. [Spellman]
Sarris, Andrew. *Film Culture* 3 (1957): 19-20.
Scott, Nathan A. Jr. *Christian Century* 74 (23 Jan.
   1957): 110-12.
Seldin, Joel. *New York Herald Tribune* 27 Nov. 1956,
   sec. 4: 1, 19.
Speicher, Charlotte Bilkey. *Library Journal* 81 (1 Dec.
   1956): 2838.
Tailleur, Roger. *Elia Kazan* (F 1).
Winn, Janet. *New Republic* 136 (21 Jan. 1957): 21.
Zinsser, Sam. *New York Herald Tribune* 19 Dec. 1956:
   17.

Tiger Tail. Atlanta: Alliance Theatre, 19 Jan.-4 Feb.
1978 (première). Harry Rasky, dir. John Wulp, design.
With Elizabeth Kemp (Baby Doll), Nick Mancuso (Silva),
Thomas Toner (Archie Lee), Mary Nell Santacroce (Aunt
Rose). Reviews, Prod. Notes:
  Bain, Carl E. *Tennessee Williams Newsletter* 1.1
     (Spring 1979): 21-23.
  Rasky, Harry. *Tennessee Williams* (F 1): 115-21.
  Smith, Helen C. *Atlanta Constitution* 20 Jan. 1978,
     sec. B: 2. Rpt. Van Antwerp (F 1): 342-44.
  Thomas, Barbara. *Atlanta Journal* 20 Jan. 1978, sec. B:
     8.
  Warren, Steve. *Advocate* 22 Mar. 1978: 30.
  Wilson, Earl. *New York Post* 27 Jan. 1978: 52.

Tiger Tail. Gainesville, FL: Hippodrome Theater Workshop, 2 Nov.-1 Dec. 1979. Marshall New, dir. Carlos F.
Asse, Kerry McKenney, Lisa Martin, design. With Jennifer

Pritchett (Baby Doll), Jon Schwartz (Silva), Michael
Doyle (Archie Lee), Dana Moser (Aunt Rose). Review:
  Gale, Steven H. *Theatre Journal* 32 (Oct. 1980): 397–
  98.

BATTLE OF ANGELS: see *Orpheus Descending*

"BEAUTY IS THE WORD": Melodrama set on a South Pacific
island, on which the gospel of beauty overpowers religious intolerance. Ms., Missouri, Texas (G).
   The script won honorable mention in the 1929-30 University of Missouri play contest and was Williams first
play to be produced.

Missouri Review 7 (1984): 187–95.

                         Production

Two Plays in the Round. Columbus: Missouri Workshop
(Univ. of Missouri), Apr. 1930 (première). Nelson Baker,
dir. Review:
  Daily Missourian 12 Apr. 1930: 2.

BLOOD KIN: see *Kingdom of Earth*

BOOM!: see *The Milk Train Doesn't Stop Here Anymore*

"CAIRO, SHANGHAI, BOMBAY!": Unpublished comedy, written
1935 in collaboration with Bernice Dorothy Shapiro, about
two sailors and their love problems. Ms., Texas (G).
   This was Williams's first off-campus production.

Cairo, Shanghai, Bombay! Garden Players. Memphis: Rose
Arbor Playhouse, 12 July 1935 (première). Arthur B.
Scharff, dir. Program: Leavitt (F 1): 25; Van Antwerp
(F 1): 22.

CAMINO REAL: Fantasy, quasi-allegorical in nature, about
various historical, literary, and invented characters
trapped in a fallen world and seeking a way out. Mss.,
Columbia, Delaware, New York Public, Texas (G).
   A shorter version, "Ten Blocks on the Camino Real," was
written 1946. Elia Kazan urged Williams to expand it for
a 1953 Broadway production, *Sixteen Blocks on the Camino
Real* (shortened to *Camino Real*). The play ran for only a

short period. Disappointed, Williams revised it extensively. Something of his intentions appears in the two
essays included with the play and his "Reflections on a
Revival of a Controversial Fantasy" (D 1).

When Whit Burnett in 1969 asked Williams to choose his
best piece of writing for inclusion in an anthology, he
picked a scene from this play.

Publication: Shorter Version

"Ten Blocks on the Camino Real." *American Blues*, 1948:
   43-77 (A 2).

Publication: Expanded Version

Camino Real. Norfolk, CT: New Directions, 1953. xvi,
   161 pp. Il. New York: New Directions, 1970; Toronto:
   McClelland & Stewart, 1970. New Directions Paperbook.
   xiv, 161 pp. Contents: "Foreword" (D 1), viii-xi;
   "Afterword," xii-xiii; Editor's Note, xiv; play, 1-161.
   Review:
      Hawkins, William. *Theatre Arts* Oct. 1953: 26-27,
         96.

Theatre Arts 38 (Aug. 1954): 34-64. Ils.

Four Plays, 1956: 229-320 (A 2).

Camino Real. London: Secker & Warburg, 1958. 96 pp.

Rose Tattoo, etc., 1958, 1976: 119-233 (A 2).

Six American Plays for Today. Ed. Bennett Cerf. New
   York: Modern Library, 1961. 1-114.

Famous American Plays of the 1950's. Ed. Lee Strasberg.
   New York: Dell, 1962. 127-227.

Three Plays, 1964: 157-329 (A 2).

Camino Real: A Play. New York: Dramatists Play Service,
   [1965]. 96 pp.

"The Departure of Lord Byron." *America's 85 Greatest
   Living Authors Present: This Is My Best in the Third
   Quarter of the Century*. Ed. Whit Burnett. Garden
   City: Doubleday, 1970. Contents: Letter, 649; *Camino
   Real*, Block 8, 650-55.

Theatre, Vol. 2, 1971: 417-591 (A 2).

Selected Plays, 1977: 279-387; *Selected Plays*, 1980: 181-282 (A 2).

Famous American Plays of the 1940s and 1950s. Ed. Henry Hewes and Lee Strasberg. Garden City: Fireside Theatre, 1988.

Trans. (H): Czech, German, Greek, Norwegian, Romanian, Spanish.

Inclusion in Textbooks (Expanded Version)

Jacobus, Lee, ed. *The Longman Anthology of American Drama*. White Plains, NY: Longman, 1982.

Miller, Jordan Y., ed. *American Dramatic Literature: Ten Modern Plays in Historical Perspective*. New York: McGraw-Hill, 1961. 139-91.

Sanders, Thomas E., ed. *The Discovery of Drama*. Glenview, IL: Scott, Foresman, 1968. 526-602.

Ulanov, Barry, ed. *Makers of the Modern Theatre*. New York: McGraw-Hill, 1961.

Criticism

Broussard, Louis. *American Drama: Contemporary Allegory from Eugene O'Neill to Tennessee Williams*. Norman: Univ. of Oklahoma Pr., 1962. 111-16.

Buchloh, Paul G. "Verweisende Zeichen in Tennessee Williams: *Camino Real*." *Anglia* 77 (1959): 173-203. Rpt. *Amerika...*, ed. Franz H. Link (Frankfurt: Atheneum, 1968): 434-54.

Campbell, Michael L. "The Theme of Persecution in Tennessee Williams' *Camino Real*." *Notes on Mississippi Writers* 6 (1973): 35-40.

Cless, Downing. "Alienation and Contradiction in *Camino Real*: A Convergence of Williams and Brecht." *Theatre Journal* 35.1 (1983): 41-50.

Coakley, James. "Time and Tide on the *Camino Real*." Tharpe (A 3): 232-36. Rpt. Bloom (A 3): 95-98.

Ferlita, Ernest. *The Theatre of Pilgrimage*. New York: Sheed, 1971. 95-110.

Henenberg, Rosemary Elaine.   "The Psychomachian Dilemma
   in the Middle Ages and in the Twentieth-Century in
   Camino Real by Tennessee Williams and in Paintings by
   Max Beckmann."   Diss., Ohio Univ., 1973.   *Dissertation
   Abstracts International* 34 (1974): 5834 A.

Hill, F. A.   "The Disaster of Ideals in *Camino Real* by
   Tennessee Williams."   *Notes on Mississippi Writers* 1
   (Winter 1969): 100-09.

Miller, Jordan Y.   "*Camino Real*."   *The Fifties: Fiction,
   Poetry, Drama*.   Ed. Warren French.   DeLand, FL:
   Everett/Edwards, 1970.   241-48.

---.   "The Three Halves of Tennessee Williams's World."
   Studies in the Literary Imagination 21 (Fall 1988): 83-
   95.

Olley, Francis R.   "Last Block on the *Camino Real*."
   Drama Critique 7 (Fall 1965): 103-07.

Renaux, Sigrid.   "The Real and the Royal in Tennessee
   Williams' *Camino Real*."   *Ilha do Desterro* 7 (1982): 43-
   66.

Turner, Diane E.   "The Mythic Vision in Tennessee Williams' *Camino Real*."   Tharpe (A 3): 237-51.

Whiting, John. "*Camino Real*: An Appreciation."   *The Rose
   Tattoo*, etc. (A 2): 117-18.

Wolf, Morris Philip.   "Casanova's Portmanteau: *Camino
   Real* and Recurring Communication Patterns of Tennessee
   Williams."   Tharpe (A 3): 252-76.

---.   "Casanova's Portmanteau: A Study of *Camino Real* in
   Relation to the Other Plays of Tennessee Williams,
   1945-1955."   Diss., Univ. of Georgia, 1959.   *Dissertation Abstracts* 20 (1960): 2817.

Productions

Camino Real. Previews: New Haven, Philadelphia. New
York: Martin Beck Theatre, 19 Mar.-9 May 1953 (première:
60). Elia Kazan, Anna Sokolow, dirs. Lemuel Ayers,
design. Bernardo Segall, music. With Eli Wallach (Kilroy), Jo Van Fleet (Marguerite), Joseph Anthony (Casanova), Barbara Baxley (Esmeralda), Frank Silvera (Gutman), Hurd Hatfield (Byron). Program: Leavitt (F 1):
99. Reviews, Prod. Notes:
Newsweek 30 Mar. 1953: 63.

Time 30 Mar. 1953: 46
Times (London) 15 May 1953: 10.
Variety 25 Mar. 1953: 72.
Atkinson, Brooks. *New York Times* 20 Mar. 1953: 26.
    Rpt. *New York Times Theatre Reviews; New York
    Theatre Critics' Reviews* 14: 331.
---. *New York Times* 29 Mar. 1953, sec. 2: 1. Rpt. *New
    York Times Theatre Reviews.* Response: *New York
    Times* 5 Apr. 1953, sec. 2: 3 (inc. Shirley Booth,
    Edith Sitwell), rpt. Leavitt (F 1): 102; *New York
    Times* 3 May 1953, sec. 2: 3.
Bentley, Eric. *New Republic* 30 Mar. 1953: 30-31. Rpt.
    The Dramatic Event... (New York: Horizon, 1954;
    Boston: Beacon, 1956): 107-110; *What Is Theatre?...*
    (New York: Atheneum, 1968): 74-78.
Bolton, Whitney. *New York Morning Telegraph* 21 Mar.
    1953: 3.
Brown, John Mason. *Saturday Review* 18 Apr. 1953: 28-
    30.
Calta, Louis. *New York Times* 19 Mar. 1953: 34. [Open-
    ing]
Chapman, John. *New York Daily News* 20 Mar. 1953: 63.
    Rpt. *New York Theatre Critics' Reviews* 14: 331.
---. *New York Sunday News* 29 Mar. 1953, sec. 2: 3.
Clurman, Harold. *Nation* 176 (4 Apr. 1953): 293-94.
    Rpt. *Lies like Truth...* (New York: Macmillan, 1958):
    83-86; *The Divine Pastime...* (New York: Macmillan,
    1974): 21-23.
Coleman, Robert. *New York Daily Mirror* 20 Mar. 1953:
    50-51. Rpt. *New York Theatre Critics' Reviews* 14:
    330.
Freedley, George. *New York Morning Telegraph* 25 Mar.
    1953: 3.
Gibbs, Wolcott. *New Yorker* 28 Mar. 1953: 69-70.
Hawkins, William. *New York World-Telegram* 20 Mar.
    1953: 28. Rpt. *New York Theatre Critics' Reviews*
    14: 332.
---. *New York World-Telegram & Sun Saturday Magazine*
    28 Mar. 1953. Rpt. Van Antwerp (F 1): 141-42.
Hayes, Richard. *Commonweal* 17 Apr. 1953: 51-52.
Hewes, Henry. *Saturday Review* 10 Oct. 1953: 32.
Kazan, Elia. *A Life* (F 1): 494-98.
---. "Playwright's 'Letter to the World.'" *New York
    Herald Tribune* 15 Mar. 1953, sec. 4: 1-2.
Kerr, Walter F. *New York Herald Tribune* 20 Mar. 1953:
    12. Rpt. *New York Theatre Critics' Reviews* 14: 331-
    32; Van Antwerp (F 1) 137-39.
---. *New York Herald Tribune* 29 Mar. 1953, sec. 4: 1.
Lewis, Theophilus. *America* 89 (4 Apr. 1953): 25.
---. *America* 89 (11 Apr. 1953): 59-60.

McClain, John. *New York Journal-American* 20 Mar. 1953:
20. Rpt. *New York Theatre Critics' Reviews* 14: 332.
Nathan, George Jean. *New York Journal-American* 5 Apr.
1953, sec. L: 18.
---. *Theatre Arts* June 1953: 14, 88. Rpt. *The Theatre
in the Fifties* (New York: Knopf, 1953): 109-12.
Sheaffer, Louis. *Brooklyn Eagle* 20 Mar. 1953: 8.
Watts, Richard Jr. *New York Post* 20 Mar. 1953. Re-
sponse: John Steinbeck, *New York Post* 10 Apr. 1953;
rpt. *John Steinbeck: A Life in Letters*, ed. Elaine
Steinbeck and Robert Wallsten (New York: Viking,
1975): 441-42.
---. *New York Post* 29 Mar. 1953, amusement sec.: 12.
---. *New York Post* 12 Apr. 1953, amusement sec.: 14.
White, Stephen. *Look* 5 May 1953: 17.
Wyatt, Euphemia Van Rensselaer. *Catholic World* 197
(May 1953): 148.

Camino Real. International Playwrights' Theatre Company.
London: Phoenix Theatre, 8 Apr.-1 June 1957 (63). Peter
Hall, dir. With Denholm Elliott (Kilroy), Diana Wynyard
(Marguerite), Harry Andrews (Casanova), Elisabeth Seal
(Esmeralda), Harold Kasket (Gutman), Robert Hardy (By-
ron). Reviews, Prod. Notes:
English 11 (Summer 1957): 186.
New York Times 9 Apr. 1957: 41. Rpt. *New York Times
Theatre Reviews*.
Times (London) 17 May 1957: 3.
Trewin, J. C. *Illustrated London News* 230 (27 Apr.
1957): 702.
Tynan, Kenneth. *Curtains...* New York: Atheneum, 1961.
175-76.
Watt, David. *Spectator* 198 (12 Apr. 1957): 488.
Worsley, T. C. *New Statesman* 53 (13 Apr. 1957): 473-
74.

Camino Real. Chicago: Goodman Theatre, 21 Mar.-5 Apr.
1958. Charles McGaw, dir. Jim Marorek, Sylvia Wintle,
G. E. Naselius, design. With Frank Roach (Kilroy), Bev-
erly Younger (Marguerite), Charles Grunwell (Casanova),
Martin Streicher (Gutman), Thom Koutsoukas (Byron).
Reviews:
Cassidy, Claudia. *Chicago Daily Tribune* 24 Mar. 1958.
Dettmer, Roger. *Chicago American* 22 Mar. 1958.
Harris, Sydney J. *Chicago Daily News* 22 Mar. 1958.
Syse, Glenna. *Chicago Sun-Times* 22 Mar. 1958.

Camino Real. Circle-in-the-Square. New York: St. Mark's
Playhouse, 16 May-31 July 1960 (89). José Quintero, dir.
Keith Cuerden, Patricia Zipprodt, Patricia Collins, de-
sign. With Clinton Kimbrough (Kilroy), Nan Martin (Mar-

guerite), Addison Powell (Casanova), David Doyle (Gut-
man), Lester Rowlins (Byron). Reviews, Prod. Notes:
  New York Times 5 Apr. 1960: 43.
  Variety 1 June 1960: 72.
  Atkinson, Brooks. *New York Times* 17 May 1960: 42.
    Rpt. *New York Times Theatre Reviews*.
  ---. *New York Times* 29 May 1960, sec. 2: 1. Rpt. *New
    York Times Theatre Reviews*.
  Bogdanovich, Peter. *Village Voice* 21 July 1960: 7-8.
  Bolton, Whitney. *New York Telegraph* 18 May 1960: 2.
  Crist, Judith. *New York Herald Tribune* 17 May 1960:
    22.
  Freedley, George. *New York Morning Telegraph* 23 May
    1960) 2, 10.
  Gassner, John. *Educational Theatre Journal* 12 (Oct.
    1960): 227. Rpt. *Dramatic Soundings...*, ed. Glenn
    Loncy (New York: Crown, 1968): 585.
  Herridge, Frances. *New York Post* 17 May 1960: 66.
  Lewis, Theophilus. *America* 103 (2 July 1960): 422-24.
  Malcolm, Donald. *New Yorker* 28 May 1960: 92-94.
  McClain, John. *New York Journal-American* 17 May 1960:
    15.

Ten Blocks on the Camino Real. National Educational
Tevision Playhouse. PBS-TV, 7 Oct. 1966. Jack Lendan,
dir. With Mark Sheehan (Kilroy), Lotte Lenya, Albert
Dekker, Carrie Nye, Hurd Hatfield, Janet Margolin (Esme-
ralda). Reviews:
  Gardella, Kay. *New York Daily News* 8 Oct. 1966: 14.
  Gould, Jack. *New York Times* 8 Oct. 1966: 63.

Camino Real. New York: Vivian Beaumont Theatre, 8 Jan.-
21 Feb. 1970 (52). Milton Katselas, dir. Peter Hexler,
John Gleason, design. Bernardo Segall, music. With Al
Pacino (Kilroy), Jessica Tandy (Marguerite), Jean-Pierre
Aumont (Casanova), Susan Tyrrell (Esmeralda), Victor
Buono (Gutman), Clifford Davis (Byron). Reviews:
  Time 19 Jan. 1970: 61.
  Variety 14 Jan. 1970: 84.
  Barnes, Clive. *New York Times* 9 Jan. 1970: 42. Rpt.
    *New York Times Theatre Reviews; New York Theatre
    Critics' Reviews* 31: 395-96.
  Clurman, Harold. *Nation* 26 Jan. 1970: 93-94.
  Gill, Brendan. *New Yorker* 17 Jan. 1970: 50-52.
  Gottfried, Martin. *Women's Wear Daily* 9 Jan. 1970.
    Rpt. *New York Theatre Critics' Reviews* 31: 398-99.
  Harris, Leonard. CBS-TV, 8 Jan. 1970. Rpt. *New York
    Theatre Critics' Reviews* 31: 399.
  Hewes, Henry. *Saturday Review* 24 Jan. 1970: 24.
  Isaac, Dan. *New Leader* 53 (19 Jan. 1970): 32-33.

Kerr, Walter. *New York Times* 18 Jan. 1970, sec. 2: 1.
   Rpt. *New York Times Theatre Reviews; New York*
   Theatre Critics' Reviews 31: 396-97; *God on the Gym-*
   nasium Floor... (New York: Simon, 1969): 172-76.
Kroll, Jack. *Newsweek* 19 Jan. 1970: 82.
Lewis, Theophilus. *America* 122 (7 Feb. 1970): 140-42.
Newman, Edwin. NBC, 8 Jan. 1970. Rpt. *New York*
   Theatre Critics' Reviews 31: 399.
O'Connor, John J. *Wall Street Journal* 12 Jan. 1970.
   Rpt. *New York Theatre Critics' Reviews* 31: 397-98.
Richardson, Jack. *Commentary* Mar. 1970: 20-24.
Silver, Lee. *New York Daily News* 9 Jan. 1970: 60.
   Rpt. *New York Theatre Critics' Reviews* 31: 395.
Simon, John. *New York* 26 Jan. 1970: 64.
Tucker, John Bartholomew. ABC-TV, 8 Jan. 1970. Rpt.
   New York Theatre Critics' Reviews 31: 399.
Washburn, Martin. *Village Voice* 22 Jan. 1970: 45.
Watts, Richard Jr. *New York Post* 9 Jan. 1970: 61.
   Rpt. *New York Theatre Critics' Reviews* 31: 398.

Camino Real. Williamstown Theatre Festival. Williams-
town, MA: Adams Memorial Theatre, 28 June 1979.   Nikos
Psacharopoulos, dir.   John Conklin, Jess Goldstein, Jen-
nifer Tipton, design.   Arthur Rubinstein, music.   With
Williams Burns (Kilroy), Carrie Nye (Marguerite), Richard
Kneeland (Casanova), Richard Woods (Gutman).   Videotaped.
Review:
   Stanton, Stephen S. *Tennessee Williams Newsletter* 1.2
   (Fall 1979): 37-38.

Other Productions:
   Coakley, James. *Drama Critique* 11 (Winter 1968): 52-
   56. [Ann Arbor]
   Crowther, John. *New York Morning Telegraph* 10 Jan.
   1970: 3. [London]
   Shrimpton, Nick. *Plays and Players* May 1978: 39.
   [London]

CANDLES TO THE SUN: Unpublished melodrama, written 1936,
about Alabama coal miners and the injustices they suffer.
Mss., California-Los Angeles, Texas (G).
   The newspaper accounts which Williams used as a basis
for the play are on file at the University of Texas.   A
1938 Dramatist Guild reader's report on the script is reproduced in Van Antwerp (F 1): 36.

Candles to the Sun. Mummers.   St. Louis: Wednesday Club
Auditorium, 18 and 20 Mar. 1937 (première).   Willard H.
Holland, dir.   Program: Leavitt (F 1): 26.   Review, Prod.
Notes:

Eliot (Washington Univ.) Mar. 1937: 6.
Eliot (Washington Univ.) Apr. 1937: 7.
Unidentified clipping. Rpt. Van Antwerp (F 1): 33.

"THE CASE OF THE CRUSHED PETUNIAS: A LYRICAL FANTASY": Symbolic drama, dated 1941, about a prim and proper New Eng-
lander's conversion to life.

American Blues, 1948: 22-32 (A 2).

Ten Short Plays. Ed. Morton Jerome Weiss. New York:
Dell, 1963. 31-53.

The Small Town in American Literature. Ed. David M. Cook
and Craig G. Wanger. New York: Dodd, Mead, 1969.

Trans. (H): German, Hungarian, Italian.

Productions

"The Case of the Crushed Petunias." Cincinnati: Shel-
terhouse Theatre, 31 May 1973. Pirie MacDonald, dir.

The Wonderful Ones! Abingdon, VA: Barter Theatre, 18 May
1979. Rex Partington, dir.

CAT ON A HOT TIN ROOF: Drama set on a Mississippi planta-
tion: a woman trying to hold onto her marriage and an
alcoholic husband worrying about "mendacity." Mss.,
Columbia, Delaware, Texas (G).
  The materials which evolved into the play began rather
distantly with a short story "Three Players of a Summer
Game" (B 1). (Williams also prepared a staged version of
the story; see title below.) *Cat* was ready by 1954, but
as Williams explained in his note to the play, Elia Kazan
disliked the original third act, causing the playwright
to rewrite it for the 1955 production. Unhappy with his
decision, Williams published both third acts. The
original ending was used in the 1958 London production.
In addition to Williams's essay published with the play,
see "Critic Says 'Evasion'" (D 1). By 1973 Williams had
prepared a final version of the play, returning to the
original third act but maintaining the best moments from
the Kazan version.
  The unpublished 1958 screenplay (which was nominated for
an Academy Award) was the work of James Poe and Richard
Brooks. According to an article in *Newsweek* (17 Nov.
1980: 70), originally Bobby Ewing in the television se-

ries *Dallas* "was modeled after the ne'er-do-well playboy
son in *Cat on a Hot Tin Roof*" but later changed.

Publication: First Version

Cat on a Hot Tin Roof. New York: New Directions, 1955.
  London: Secker & Warburg, 1956. xiv, 197 pp. Il.
  Contents: "Person-to-Person" (D 1), vi–x; play, 1–150;
  Note of Explanation, 151–52; Act Three as Played in New
  York Production, 153–97. Reviews:
    New York Herald Tribune 7 July 1955: 19.
    Times Literary Supplement 10 Feb. 1956.
    Variety 13 July 1955: 56.
    Freedley, George. *New York Morning Telegraph* 8
      Sept. 1955: 3.
    Kinnaird, Clark. *New York Journal-American* 9 Oct.
      1955, sec. L: 52.
    McClain, John. *New York Journal-American* 13 May
      1955: 25.
    Rosselli, John. *Spectator* 196 (2 Mar. 1956): 284.

The Best Plays of 1954-1955.... Ed. Louis Kronenberger.
  New York: Dodd, Mead, 1955. 288–312. Excerpts.

Theatre '55. Ed. John Chapman. New York: Random House,
  1955. 69–93. Excerpts.

*Critics' Choice: New York Drama Critics' Circle Prize
  Plays 1935-1955.* Ed. Jack Gaver. New York: Hawthorn,
  1955. 643–57.

Theatre Arts 41 (June 1957): 33–71. Ils.

Cat on a Hot Tin Roof. Harmondsworth: Penguin Books,
  1957. 132 pp. Includes E. Martin Browne, Editorial
  Note, 15.

Cat on a Hot Tin Roof. Signet Book. New York: New American Library, 1958. 158 pp. Ils. New ils., 1985.

Best American Plays, Fourth Series, *1951-1957.* Ed. John
  Gassner. New York: Crown, 1958. 91–132.

Five Plays, 1962: vii–123 (A 2).

Milk Train Doesn't Stop Here Anymore, etc., 1969 (A 2).

Theatre, Vol. 3, 1971: 1–215 (A 2).

Cat on a Hot Tin Roof, etc., 1976: 5–132 (A 2).

Eight Plays, 1979: 399-536 (A 2).

Publication: "Acting" Version

Cat on a Hot Tin Roof...: A Play in Three Acts. New
York: Dramatists Play Service, 1958. 85 pp. Il.
Contents: play, 5-81.

Publication: Final Version

Cat on a Hot Tin Roof. New York: New Directions, 1975;
Toronto: McClelland & Stewart, 1975. 173 pp. Also New
Directions Paperbook. Contents: Notes for the De-
signer, 15-16; play, 17-173.

Another edition: 168 pp. [book club?].

Selected Plays, 1977: 383-474; *Selected Plays*, 1980: 285-
374 (A 2).

Trans. (H): Arabic, Chinese, Czech, Danish, French,
German, Greek, Hungarian, Italian, Japanese, Korean,
Norwegian, Persian, Spanish (version uncertain).

Publication: Student Edition

Cat on a Hot Tin Roof. Ed. Berthold Sturm. Frankfurt:
Hirschgraben, 1989. 120 pp.

Inclusion in Textbooks (Final Version)

Goodman, Randolph, ed. *Drama on Stage....* 2nd ed. New
York: Holt, 1978.

Howe, Irving, et al., eds. *Literature as Experience: An
Anthology*. New York: Harcourt, 1979. 1009-92.

Klaus, Carl, et al., eds. *Stages of Drama: Classical to
Contemporary Theatre*. New York: Wiley, 1981. 877-
920.

Scholes, Robert, ed. *Elements of Literature: Essay, Fiction, Poetry, Drama, Film*. New York: Oxford, 1978.
1147-1229.

Criticism

Allen, Dennis W. "Homosexuality and Artifice in *Cat on a
Hot Tin Roof*." *Coup de Théâtre* 5 (Dec. 1985): 71-78.

Barrick, Mac E. "Maggie the Cat: Tennessee Williams'
    Yerma." *American Notes and Queries:* Supplement I:
    Studies in English and American Literature. Troy, NY:
    Whitston, 1979. 312-15.

Blackwelder, James R. "The Human Extremities of Emotion
    in *Cat on a Hot Tin Roof.*" *Research Studies* (Washing-
    ton State Univ.) 38 (1970): 13-21.

Dukore, Bernard F. "The Cat Has Nine Lives." *Tulane
    Drama Review* 8 (Fall 1963): 95-100.

Funatsu, Tatsumi. "A Study of *Cat on a Hot Tin Roof.*"
    Kyushu American Literature 2 (May 1959): 33-39.

Gerbaud, C. "Famille et Homosexualité dans *Cat on a Hot
    Tin Roof.*" *Coup de Théâtre* 5 (Dec. 1985): 55-70.

Gobnecht, Eleanor Alberta. "A Descriptive Study of the
    Value Commitments of the Principal Characters in Four
    Recent American Plays...." Diss., Univ. of Southern
    California, 1963. *Dissertation Abstracts* 24 (1963):
    433-34.

Hagopian, John V. "*Cat on a Hot Tin Roof.*" *Insight:
    Analyses of Modern British and American Drama.* Ed.
    Hermann J. Weiand. Frankfurt: Hirschgraben, 1975. 4:
    269-75.

Hale, Allean. "How a Tiger Became the Cat." *Tennessee
    Williams Literary Journal* 2.1 (Winter 1990-91): 33-36.

Hethmon, Robert. "The Foul Rag-and-Bone Shop of the
    Heart." *Drama Critique* 7 (Fall 1965): 94-102.

Higgs, Robert J. *Laurel & Thorn: The Athlete in American
    Literature.* Lexington: Kentucky Univ. Pr., 1981. 141-
    44.

Huzzard, Jere. "Williams' *Cat on a Hot Tin Roof.*" *Ex-
    plicator* 43.2 (1985): 46-47.

Isaac, Dan. "Big Daddy's Dramatic Word Strings." *Amer-
    ican Speech* 40 (Dec. 1965): 272-78.

Kalson, Albert E. "A Source for *Cat on a Hot Tin Roof.*"
    Tennessee Williams Newsletter 2.2 (Fall 1980): 21-22.
    [J. B. Priestly, *Dangerous Corner*]

Kataria, Gulshan R.   "A Hetaira of Tennessee Williams:
    Maggie." *Indian Journal of American Studies* 12.1
    (1982): 45-55.

Kerjan, Liliane.   *"La chatte sur un toit brûlant*: L'en-
    droit du decor."   *Coup de Théâtre* 5 (Dec. 1985): 29-43.

Kolin, Philip C.   "Obstacles to Communication in *Cat on a
    Hot Tin Roof.*"   *Western Speech Communication* 39 (1975):
    74-80.

Lolli, Giorgio.   "Alcoholism and Homosexuality in Tennes-
    see Williams' *Cat on a Hot Tin Roof.*"   *Quarterly Jour-
    nal of Studies on Alcohol* 17 (1956): 543-53.

Long, Deborah Marie.   "The Existential Quest: Family and
    Form in Selected American Plays."   Diss., Univ. of Ore-
    gon, 1986.   *Dissertation Abstracts International* 47
    (1986): 1119 A.

Mansur, R. M.   "The Two 'Cats' on the Tin Roof: A Study
    of Tennessee Williams's *Cat on a Hot Tin Roof.*"   *Jour-
    nal of the Karnatak University: Humanities* 14 (1970):
    150-58.

Martin, J.   "Du geste à la parole dans *Cat on a Hot Tin
    Roof.*" *Bulletin de la Societé de Stylistique Anglaise*
    7 (1985): 149-60.

May, Charles E.   "Brick Pollitt as Homo Ludens: 'Three
    Players of a Summer Game' and *Cat on a Hot Tin Roof.*"
    Tharpe (A 3): 277-91; short ed.: 49-63.

Mayberry, Susan Neal.   "A Study of Illusion and the Gro-
    tesque in Tennessee Williams' *Cat on a Hot Tin Roof.*"
    Southern Studies 22 (1983): 359-65.

Millhauser, Milton.   "Science, Literature, and the Image
    of Man." *Humanist* 23 (May-June 1963): 85-88.

Morgan, Edward.   "That Uncertain Feeling." *Encore* May
    1958.   Rpt. *The Encore Reader,* ed. Charles Marowitz et
    al. (London: Methuen, 1965): 52-56.

Nathan, George Jean.   "Tennessee Williams and Sex." *New
    York Journal-American* 2 Apr. 1955: 16.

Peterson, William.   "Williams, Kazan, and the Two *Cats.*"
    New Theatre Magazine (Bristol) 7 (Summer 1967): 14-20.

Pitavy, François L.   "*Cat on a Hot Tin Roof*: Le jeu du mot et de la chose."   *Coup de Théâtre* 5 (Dec. 1985): 79-88.

Pitavy-Souques, Danièle.   "Au soir de la fête: Notes sur l'espace dans *Cat on a Hot Tin Roof*."   *Coup de Théâtre* 5 (Dec. 1985): 45-54.

Powers, Harvey M. Jr.   "Theatrical Convention: The Conditions of Acceptability."   *Bucknell Review* 7 (May 1957): 20-26.

Proehl, Geoffrey Scott.   "Coming Home Again: American Family Drama and the Figure of the Prodigal."   Diss., Stanford Univ., 1988.   *Dissertation Abstracts International* 49 (1989): 2455 A.

Sacksteder, William.   "The Three *Cats*: A Study in Dramatic Structure."   *Drama Survey* 5 (Winter 1966-67): 252-66.

Taubman, Howard.   "Not What It Seems."   *New York Times* 5 Nov. 1961, sec. 2: 1.

Productions

Cat on a Hot Tin Roof.   Playwrights' Company.   New York: Morosco Theatre, 24 Mar. 1955-17 Nov. 1956 (première: 694).   Elia Kazan, dir.   Jo Mielziner, Lucinda Ballard, design.   With Ben Gazzara (Brick), Barbara Bel Geddes (Maggie), Burl Ives (Big Daddy), Mildred Dunnock (Big Mama), Madeleine Sherwood (Mae).   Program: Leavitt (F 1): 107.   Winner Pulitzer Prize for Drama, New York Drama Critics' Circle Award, Donaldson Award.   Reviews, Prod. Notes:
  Life 18 Apr. 1955: 137-42.
  New York Herald Tribune 20 Mar. 1955, sec. 4: 1.
    [Interview with Bel Geddes]
  New York Times 7 Apr. 1955: 23.   [Censorship]
  New York Times 13 Apr. 1955.   [Drama Critics' Circle Award]
  New York Times 3 May 1955: 30.   [Pulitzer Prize]
  Newsweek 4 Apr. 1955: 54.
  Theatre Arts June 1955: 18-19.
  Theatre Arts July 1955: 74-79, 96.
  Time 4 Apr. 1955: 98.
  Time 23 May 1955: 54.   [Prizes]
  Times (London) 22 Apr. 1955: 16.
  Variety 30 Mar. 1955: 63, 66.
  Atkinson, Brooks.   *New York Times* 25 Mar. 1955: 18.
    Rpt. *New York Times Theatre Reviews; New York The-*

atre Critics' Reviews 16: 344; Van Antwerp (F 1):
144-46 (see also Van Antwerp: 147).

---. New York Times 3 Apr. 1955, sec. 2: 1. Rpt. New
York Times Theatre Reviews.

Beaufort, John. Christian Science Monitor 2 Apr. 1955:
36.

Becker, William. Hudson Review 8 (Summer 1955): 268-
72. Response: Hudson Review 8 (Winter 1956): 633-
35.

Bentley, Eric. New Republic 4 Apr. 1955: 22.

---. New Republic 11 Apr. 1955: 28. Rpt. What Is The-
atre?... (New York: Atheneum, 1968): 224-31; Van
Antwerp (F 1): 146-52. Responses: New Republic 18
Apr. 1955: 22-23; New Republic 25 Apr. 1955: 23.

Blotner, Joseph. Faulkner.... New York: Random House,
1974. Vol. 2: 1529-30.

Bolton, Whitney. New York Morning Telegraph 26 Mar.
1955: 2.

Calta, Louis. New York Times 24 Mar. 1955: 39. [Open-
ing]

---. New York Times 5 July 1955: 36. [Donaldson
Award]

Chapman, John. New York Daily News 25 Mar. 1955: 65.
Rpt. New York Theatre Critics' Reviews 16: 343.

Coleman, Robert. New York Daily Mirror 25 Mar. 1955.
Rpt. New York Theatre Critics' Reviews 16: 343.

Downing, Robert. "From the Cat-Bird Seat: The Production Stage Manager's Notes on Cat on a Hot Tin
Roof." Theatre Annual 14 (1956): 46-50.

Fehl, Fred. On Broadway: Performance Photographs. Ed.
William Stott and Jane Stott. Austin: Univ. of
Texas Pr., 1978. 258-59. Il.

Freedley, George. New York Morning Telegraph 11 Apr.
1955: 2-3.

Gibbs, Wolcott. New Yorker 2 Apr. 1955: 68.

Grutzner, Charles. New York Times 3 May 1955: 1, 28.
[Pulitzer Prize]

Hatch, Robert. Nation 180 (9 Apr. 1955): 314-15.

Hawkins, William. New York World-Telegram 25 Mar.
1955: 28. Rpt. New York Theatre Critics' Reviews
16: 342.

Hayes, Richard. Commonweal 62 (3 June 1955): 230-31.

Herridge, Frances. New York Post 11 Apr. 1955: 38.
[Censorship]

Hewes, Henry. Saturday Review 9 Apr. 1955: 32-33.

---. Saturday Review 30 Apr. 1955: 26. [Drama
Critics' Circle Award]

Kazan, Elia. A Life (F 1): 540-44.

Hivnor, Mary. Kenyon Review 18 (Winter 1956): 125-26.

Kerr, Walter F. New York Herald Tribune 25 Mar. 1955:
12. Rpt. New York Theatre Critics' Reviews 16: 342.

---. *New York Herald Tribune* 3 Apr. 1955, sec. 4: 1.
Mannes, Marya. *Reporter* 15 May 1955: 41-43. Rpt. *The*
   Reporter Reader, ed. Max Ascoli (Freeport, NY: Books
   for Libraries, 1969): 145-50; Van Antwerp (F 1):
   152-55. Response: *Reporter* 30 June 1955: 4.
McClain, John. *New York Journal-American* 25 Mar. 1955:
   20. Rpt. *New York Theatre Critics' Reviews* 16: 344.
---. *New York Journal-American* 11 Apr. 1955: 17.
Mitgang, Herbert. *New York Times* 17 Apr. 1955, sec. 2:
   3. [Interview with Ives]
Nathan, George Jean. *Esquire* Apr. 1956: 48.
O'Hara, John *Collier's* 2 Mar. 1956: 2.
Rosselli, John. *Spectator* 196 (2 Mar. 1956): 284.
Watts, Richard Jr. *New York Post* 25 Mar. 1955: 57.
   Rpt. *New York Theatre Critics' Reviews* 16: 343-44.
---. *New York Post* 3 Apr. 1955: 20.
---. *New York Post* 10 Apr. 1955: 16.
---. *New York Post* 17 Apr. 1955: 24. [On Kazan]
---. *New York Post* 17 May 1955: 40. [Censorship]
Wyatt, Euphemia Van Rensselaer. *Catholic Word* 181 (May
   1955): 147-48.
Young, Vernon. *Southwest Review* 41 (Spring 1956): 194-
   97.
Zolotow, Maurice. *New York Times* 8 Apr. 1955: 18.
   [Elephant joke]
---. *Theatre Arts* June 1955: 22-23, 93.

Cat on a Hot Tin Roof. London: Comedy Theatre, 30 Jan.
1958 (première). Peter Hall, dir. With Paul Massie
(Brick), Kim Stanley (Maggie), Leo McKern (Big Daddy).
Reviews:
   New York Times 31 Jan. 1958: 24. Rpt. *New York Times*
      Theatre Reviews.
   Times (London) 31 Jan. 1958: 3.
   Times (London) 6 June 1958: 6.
   Inglis, Brian. *Spectator* 200 (7 Feb. 1958): 174.
   Tynan, Kenneth. *Curtains*.... New York: Atheneum,
      1961. 202-04.
   Worsley, T. C. *New Statesman* 55 (8 Feb. 1958): 166.

Cat on a Hot Tin Roof. Screenplay by James Poe and Rich-
ard Brooks. Avon Productions. MGM, 6 Aug. 1958 (pre-
mière). Richard Brooks, dir. William Daniels, camera.
William A. Horning, Urie McCleary, design. With Paul
Newman (Brick), Elizabeth Taylor (Maggie), Burl Ives (Big
Daddy), Judith Anderson (Big Mama), Madeleine Sherwood
(Mae). Reviews, Prod. Notes:
   Cosmopolitan Sept. 1958: 18.
   Filmfacts 1 (1958): 161.
   Newsweek 1 Sept. 1958: 56.
   New York Times 10 July 1955, sec. 1: 52. [Film rights]

New York Times Magazine 30 Aug. 1958: 34.
Spectator 201 (17 Oct. 1958): 516.
Time 15 Sept. 1958: 92.
Variety 13 Aug. 1958: 6.
Alpert, Hollis. *Saturday Review* 13 Sept. 1958: 58.
Baker, Peter. *Films and Filming* Nov. 1958: 21.
Beckley, Paul. *New York Herald Tribune* 19 Sept. 1958:
    17.
Crowther, Bosley. *New York Times* 19 Sept. 1958: 24.
    Rpt. *New York Times Film Reviews.*
---. *New York Times* 21 Sept. 1958, sec. 2: 1.
Dent, Alan. *Illustrated London News* 233 (18 Oct.
    1958): 660.
Downing, Robert. *Films in Review* 9 (Oct. 1958): 454-
    55.
Hartung, Philip T. *Commonweal* 68 (26 Sept. 1958): 637.
Hatch, Robert. *Nation* 187 (11 Oct. 1958): 220.
Houston, Penelope. *London Observer* 12 Oct. 1958: 19.
Huskins, D. Gail. *Magill's Survey of Cinema: English
    Language Films.* 1st ser. Ed. Frank N. Magill.
    Englewood Cliffs, NJ: Salem, 1980. 308-11.
Johnson, Albert. *Film Quarterly* 12 (Winter 1958): 54-
    55. Rpt. Van Antwerp (F 1): 190-91.
Kauffmann, Stanley. *New Republic* 29 Sept. 1958: 21-23.
    Rpt. *A World on Film...* (New York: Harper, 1966):
    79-81.
McCarten, John. *New Yorker* 27 Sept. 1958: 141.
McManigal, Rod. *Sight and Sound* 28 (Winter 1958): 36.
Oumano, Elena. *Paul Newman.* New York: St. Martin's,
    1989. 70-73.
Speicher, Charlotte Bilkey. *Library Journal* 83 (1 Oct.
    1958): 2667.
Walsh, Moira. *America* 99 (27 Sept. 1958): 679.
---. *Catholic World* 188 (Nov. 1958): 153-54.

Cat on a Hot Tin Roof. West Springfield, MA: Stage West
Theatre, 9 Nov. 1973 (première). John Ulmer, dir.
Charles G. Stockton, Susan Glenn, Harvout, design. With
Armand Assante (Brick), Linda Selman (Maggie), Maury
Cooper (Big Daddy), Charlotte Jones (Big Mama). Review:
    Gussow, Mel. *New York Times* 12 Nov. 1973: 50.

Cat on a Hot Tin Roof. Stratford, CT: American Shakespeare Theatre, 10 July 1974 (26); New York: ANTA Theatre, 24 Sept. 1974-8 Feb. 1975 (160). Michael Kahn,
dir. John Conklin, Marc B. Weiss, Jane Greenwood, design. With Keir Dullea (Brick), Elizabeth Ashley (Maggie), Fred Gwynne (Big Daddy), Kate Reid (Big Mama).
Videotaped. Playbill: Leavitt (F 1). Reviews, Prod.
Notes:
    Variety 2 Oct. 1974: 68.

Barnes, Clive. *New York Times* 25 Sept. 1974: 26.   Rpt.
   New York Theatre Critics' Reviews 35: 242; *Stages of
   Drama*..., ed. Carl Klaus et al. (New York: Wiley,
   1981): 921.
Barthel, Joan. *New York Times* 22 Sept. 1974, sec. 2:
   1, 3. [Interview with Ashley]
Clurman, Harold. *Nation* 219 (12 Oct. 1974): 349-50.
Collins, Pat. CBS-TV, 24 Sept. 1974. Rpt. *New York
   Theatre Critics' Reviews* 35: 246.
Feingold, Michael. *Village Voice* 3 Oct. 1974: 77-78.
Gill, Brendan. *New Yorker* 7 Oct. 1974: 73.
Gottfried, Martin. *New York Post* 25 Sept. 1974: 46.
   Rpt. *New York Theatre Critics' Reviews* 35: 243.
Gussow, Mel. *New York Times* 22 July 1974: 40.
Hughes, Catherine. *America* 131 (12 Oct. 1974): 194.
---. *Plays and Players* 22 (Oct. 1974): 45.
Kalem, T. E. *Time* 7 Oct. 1974: 107.
Kauffmann, Stanley. *New Republic* 19 Oct. 1974: 16, 33-
   34. Rpt. *Persons of the Drama*... (New York: Harper,
   1976): 152-55.
Kerr, Walter. *New York Times* 6 Oct. 1974, sec. 2: 1,
   3.
Kroll, Jack. *Newsweek* 7 Oct. 1974: 73.
Novick, Julius. *New York Times* 28 July 1974, sec. 2:
   3.
Probst, Leonard. NBC-Radio, 25 Sept. 1974. Rpt. *New
   York Theatre Critics' Reviews* 35: 246.
Sharp, Christopher. *Women's Wear Daily* 25 Sept. 1974.
   Rpt. *New York Theatre Critics' Reviews* 35: 244.
Simon, John. *New York* 12 Aug. 1974: 48-49.
Snyder, Louis. *Christian Science Monitor* 27 Sept.
   1974. Rpt. *New York Theatre Critics' Reviews* 35:
   244-45.
Watt, Douglas. *New York Daily News* 25 Sept. 1974: 74.
   Rpt. *New York Theatre Critics' Reviews* 35: 242-43.
---. *New York Daily News* 6 Oct. 1974, sec. 3: 3.
Watts, Richard Jr. *New York Post* 28 Sept. 1974: 16.
Wilson, Edwin. *Wall Street Journal* 27 Sept. 1974.
   Rpt. *New York Theatre Critics' Reviews* 35: 243-44.

Cat on a Hot Tin Roof. NBC-TV, 6 Dec. 1976. With Robert
Wagner (Brick), Natalie Wood (Maggie), Laurence Olivier
(Big Daddy), Maureen Stapleton (Big Mama). Reviews:
   Kalem, T. E. *Time* 6 Dec. 1976: 97-98.
   O'Connor, John J. *New York Times* 5 Dec. 1976, sec. 2:
      29-30.

Cat on a Hot Tin Roof. Showtime-TV, 19 Aug. 1984. American Playhouse. PBS-TV, 24 June 1985. Jack Hofsiss,
dir. David Jenkins, design. Tom Scott, music. With
Tommy Lee Jones (Brick), Jessica Lange (Maggie), Rip Torn

(Big Daddy), Kim Stanley (Big Mama), David Dukes
(Grooper). Reviews, Prod. Notes:
  New York Times 21 July 1982, sec. 3: 15. [TV rights]
  People Weekly 27 Aug. 1984: 9.
  James, Noah. *New York Times* 19 Aug. 1984, sec. 2: 20.
  Kaplan, Peter W. *New York Times* 11 Aug. 1984, sec. 1:
    48.
  Leahy, Michael. *TV Guide* 18 Aug. 1984: 8-9, 12-13.
    [Interview with Lange]
  O'Toole, Lawrence. *Maclean's* 24 June 1985: 62.
  Plutzik, Roberta. *USA Today* 17 Aug. 1984, sec. D: 7.
    [Interview with Jones]
  Zoglin, Richard. *Time* 27 Aug. 1984: 51.

Cat on a Hot Tin Roof. London: Lyttleton Theatre, 3
Feb.-17 Sept. 1988. Howard Davies, dir. William Dudley,
Mark Henderson, design. Ilona Sekacs, music. With Ian
Charleson (Brick), Lindsay Duncan (Maggie), Eric Porter
(Big Daddy), Barbara Leigh Hunt (Big Mama). Reviews:
  Sunday Times (London) 7 Feb. 1988, sec. C: 6.
  Times (London) 4 Feb. 1988: 16.
  Billington, Michael. *Guardian* 4 Feb. 1988. Rpt.
    London Theatre Record 8: 135.
  Conway, Lydia. *What's On* 10 Feb. 1988. Rpt. *London
    Theatre Record* 8: 141.
  Coveney, Michael. *London Financial Times* 4 Feb. 1988.
    Rpt. *London Theatre Record* 8: 135.
  Edwards, Christopher. *Spectator* 20 Feb. 1988. Rpt.
    London Theatre Record 8: 136.
  Fender, Stephen. *Times Literary Supplement* 12 Feb.
    1988: 164.
  Gordon, Giles. *Drama* 168 (1988): 32.
  Hirschhorn, Clive. *London Sunday Express* 7 Feb. 1988.
    Rpt. *London Theatre Record* 8: 137.
  Hurren, Kenneth. *London Mail on Sunday* 7 Feb. 1988.
    Rpt. *London Theatre Record* 8: 134.
  Jameson, Sue. London Broadcasting, 4 Feb. 1988. Rpt.
    London Theatre Record 8: 139.
  King, Francis. *London Sunday Telegraph* 7 Feb. 1988.
    Rpt. *London Theatre Record* 8: 138.
  Morley, Sheridan. *Punch* 19 Feb. 1988. Rpt. *London
    Theatre Record* 8: 136.
  Nathan, David. *Jewish Chronicle* 12 Feb. 1988. Rpt.
    London Theatre Record 8: 135-36.
  Paton, Maureen. *London Daily Express* 4 Feb. 1988.
    Rpt. *London Theatre Record* 8: 139.
  Radin, Victoria. *New Statesman* 115 (19 Feb. 1988): 40.
    Rpt. *London Theatre Record* 8: 137.
  Ratcliffe, Michael. *London Observer* 7 Feb. 1988. Rpt.
    London Theatre Record 8: 139-40.
  Rich, Frank. *New York Times* 16 Feb. 1988, sec. C: 15.

St. George, Eric. *London Daily Telegraph* 5 Feb. 1988.
  Rpt. *London Theatre Record* 8: 138.
Shorter, Eric. *London Daily Telegraph* 5 Feb. 1988.
  Rpt. *London Theatre Record* 8: 140.
Shulman, Milton. *London Evening Standard* 4 Feb. 1988.
  Rpt. *London Theatre Record* 8: 140-41.
Tinker, Jack. *London Daily Mail* 4 Feb. 1988. Rpt.
  London Theatre Record 8: 136-37.

Cat on a Hot Tin Roof. Boston: Shubert Theatre, Mar.
1990; New York: Eugene O'Neill Theatre, 21 Mar. 1990.
Howard Davies, dir. William Dudley, Mark Henderson, de-
sign. Ilona Sekacz, music. With Daniel Hugh Kelly
(Brick), Kathleen Turner (Maggie), Charles Durning (Big
Daddy), Polly Holliday (Big Mama). Reviews, Prod. Notes:
  Tennessee Williams Literary Journal 2.1 (Winter 1990-
    91): 73-74.
  Barnes, Clive. *New York Post* 22 Mar. 1990. Rpt. *New
    York Theatre Critics' Reviews* 51: 353-54.
  Beaufort, John. *Christian Science Monitor* 18 Apr.
    1990. Rpt. *New York Theatre Critics' Reviews* 51:
    359.
  Brady, James. *Parade* 22 July 1990: 15. [Interview
    with Durning]
  Capuzzo, Mike. Knight-Ridder release. *Corpus Christi
    Caller* 7 Mar. 1990, sec. E: 8.
  Crisp, Quentin. *Christopher Street* 144 (1990): 10-11.
  Disch, Thomas M. *Nation* 250 (7 May 1990): 644.
  Henry, William A. III. *Time* 2 Apr. 1990: 71-72. Rpt.
    New York Theatre Critics' Reviews 51: 357.
  Hluchy, Patricia, and Brian D. Johnson. *Maclean's* 28
    May 1990: 63.
  Kahn, Toby. *People Weekly* 4 June 1990: 117-18. [In-
    terview with Durning]
  Kaplan, James. *Vanity Fair* Mar. 1990: 158-62, 216-22.
    [Interview with Turner]
  King, Larry. *USA Today* 2 Apr. 1990: 2. [Interview with
    Durning]
  Kramer, Mimi. *New Yorker* 2 Apr. 1990: 88.
  Kroll, Jack. *Newsweek* 2 Apr. 1990: 54. Rpt. *New York
    Theatre Critics' Reviews* 51: 355.
  O'Malley, T. P. *America* 162 (21 Apr. 1990): 410.
  Rich, Frank. *New York Times* 22 Mar. 1990: 81. Rpt.
    New York Theatre Critics' Reviews 51: 356-57.
  Rothstein, Mervyn. *New York Times* 2 Apr. 1990, sec. B:
    1. [Interview with Durning]
  Siegel, Joel. WABC-TV, 21 Mar. 1990. Rpt. *New York
    Theatre Critics' Reviews* 51: 359.
  Simon, John. *New York* 2 Apr. 1990: 93.
  Snead, Elizabeth. *USA Today* 28 Mar. 1990, sec. D: 4.
    [On Turner's lingerie]

Stearns, David Patrick. *USA Today* 22 Mar. 1990, sec.
  D: 1. Rpt. *New York Theatre Critics' Reviews* 51:
  359.
Watt, Douglas. *New York Daily News* 30 Mar. 1990.   Rpt.
  New York Theatre Critics' Reviews 51: 355.
Weber, Bruce, and Kathleen Beckett. *New York Times* 18
  Mar. 1990, sec. 2: 5.   [Interview with Turner]
Wilson, Edwin. *Wall Street Journal* 26 Mar. 1990.   Rpt.
  New York Theatre Critics' Reviews 51: 357.
Winer, Linda. *New York Newsday* 22 Mar. 1990.   Rpt. *New
  York Theatre Critics' Reviews* 51: 358.

Other Productions:
  Tennessee Williams Literary Journal 1.2 (Winter 1989-
    90): 65.   [Stratford, Ont.]
  Times (London) 2 June 1958: 7.   [Unlicensed Liverpool
    prod., May 1958, Sam Wanamaker, dir.]
  Times (London) 5 June 1958: 16.   [Banned Irish prod.].
  Times (London) 6 June 1958: 6.   [Liverpool]
  Dubois, Rochelle H. *Tennessee Newsletter* 2.2 (Fall
    1980): 44-46 [Cranford, NJ]
  Sidnell, M. J. *Journal of Canadian Studies* 29 (Winter
    1989-90): 157.   [Stratford, Ont.]
  Tynan, Kenneth. *Curtains....* New York: Atheneum,
    1961.   204-05.

"THE CHALKY WHITE SUBSTANCE": Scene of betrayal in a place
of desolation.

Antaeus 66 (Spring 1991): 467-73.

CLOTHES FOR A SUMMER HOTEL: Fantasy based on the life of F.
Scott and Zelda Fitzgerald.
    His last play produced on Broadway, Williams hoped that
it would mark his critical comeback.   After its failure,
he revised the script.   The New Directions text is a
slight revision of the Dramatists Play Service script.

  Clothes for a Summer Hotel: A Ghost Play.   New York:
    Dramatists Play Service, 1981.   55 pp.   Contents: The
    Set, 5; play, 7-52.

  Clothes for a Summer Hotel: A Ghost Play.   New York: New
    Directions, 1983; Toronto: George J. McLeod, 1983.
    xii, 77 pp.   Also New Directions Paperbook.   Contents:
    Author's Note, xi; The Set, xii; play, 1-77.   Reviews:
      Booklist 80 (1 Oct. 1983): 219.
      Choice 21 (Nov. 1983): 428.

Grecco, Stephen. *World Literature Today* 58 (Spring 1984): 269.

Criticism

Adler, Thomas P.   "When Ghosts Supplant Memories: Tennessee Williams' *Clothes for a Summer Hotel*." *Southern Literary Journal* 19 (Spring 1987): 5-19.

Anderson, Hilton.   "Tennessee Williams' *Clothes for a Summer Hotel*: Feminine Sensibilities and the Artist." *Publications of the Mississippi Philological Association* 1988: 1-8.

Dana, Robert.   "*Clothes for a Summer Hotel*: A Ghost Play." *Playbill* (Univ. of Iowa) 63 (June 1984): 22-24.

Production

Clothes for a Summer Hotel.   Washington: Kennedy Center, 29 Jan. 1980 (première: 39); Chicago: Blackstone Theatre, 26 Feb. 1980; New York: Cort Theatre, 26 Mar.-6 Apr. 1980 (15).   José Quintero, dir.   Oliver Smith, Theoni V. Aldredge, Marilyn Rennagel, design.   Michael Valenti, music.   With Geraldine Page (Zelda), Kenneth Haigh (Scott), Robert Black (Hemingway).   Reviews, Prod. Notes:
 Barnes, Clive.   *New York Post* 27 Mar. 1980: 50-51.
  Rpt. *New York Theatre Critics' Reviews* 41: 311-12.
 ---.   *New York Post* 10 Apr. 1980: 41, 46.
 Beaufort, John.   *Christian Science Monitor* 27 Mar.
  1980: 14.   Rpt. *New York Theatre Critics' Reviews*
  41: 313.
 Brustein, Robert.   *New Republic* 3 May 1980: 27.
 Clurman, Harold.   *Nation* 230 (19 Apr. 1980): 427.   Rpt.
  Van Antwerp (F 1): 359-61.
 Gill, Brendan.   *New Yorker* 7 Apr. 1980: 116-18.
 Healy, Paul.   *New York Daily News* 12 Mar. 1980: 43.
  [Interview with Page]
 Helbing, Terry.   *Advocate* 29 May 1980: 47.
 Herridge, Frances.   *New York Post* 21 Mar. 1980: 42.
  [Interview with Quintero]
 Kakutani, Michiko.   *New York Times* 18 Jan. 1980, sec.
  C: 9.
 ---.   *New York Times* 23 Mar. 1980, sec. 2: 1, 26.
 ---.   *New York Times* 22 June 1980, sec. 2: 1, 7.
  Response: *New York Times* 13 July 1980, sec. 2: 3, 10
  (Harold Clurman).   [See Williams's letter (D 3)]
 Kerr, Walter.   *New York Times* 27 Mar. 1980, sec. C: 15.
  Rpt. *New York Theatre Critics' Reviews* 41: 312-13.
 Kissel, Howard.   *Women's Wear Daily* 27 Mar. 1980.   Rpt.
  New York Times Theatre Critics' Reviews 41: 310-11.

Kroll, Jack. *Newsweek* 7 Apr. 1980: 95. Rpt. *New York Theatre Critics' Reviews* 41: 314.

Novick, Julius. *Village Voice* 7 Apr. 1980: 74-75.

Raidy, William A. *Plays and Players* June 1980: 33-34.

Ray, Melanie. *ScriptWriter* Apr. 1980: 22-23.

Reed, Rex. *New York Daily News* 28 Mar. 1980, Friday sec: 3.

Siegel, Joel. ABC-TV, 26 Mar. 1980. Rpt. *New York Theatre Critics' Reviews* 41: 314.

Simon, John. *New York* 7 Apr. 1980: 82-84.

Stanton, Stephen S. *Tennessee Williams Newsletter* 2.1 (Spring 1980): 40-42. [Summary of reviews]

Watt, Douglas. *New York Daily News* 27 Mar. 1980. Rpt. *New York Theatre Critics' Reviews* 41: 310.

Weales, Gerald. *Georgia Review* 34 (Fall 1980): 497-508.

Weatherby, W. J. *Sunday Times* (London) 30 Mar. 1980: 38.

Wilson, Edwin. *Wall Street Journal* 1 Apr. 1980. Rpt. *New York Theatre Critics' Reviews* 41: 313.

"CONFESSIONAL": see *Small Craft Warnings*

CREVE COEUR: see *A Lovely Sunday for Creve Coeur*

"THE DARK ROOM": Drama about an Italian tenement family with an unmarried pregnant daughter.
    The short story of the same title (B 1) is closely related.

American Blues, 1948: 15-21 (A 2).

Trans. (H): German, Italian.

"THE DEMOLITION DOWNTOWN": Absurd drama about human breakdown and attempts to cope in a post-revolutionary America of the future. Ms., California-Los Angeles (G).

Esquire 75 (June 1971): 124-27, 152.

Theatre, Vol. 6, 1981: 329-58 (A 2).

Production

"The Demolition Downtown." London: Carnaby Street Thetre, Jan. 1976. Review:
    Wardle, Irving. *Times* (London) 13 Jan. 1976.

"DOS RANCHOS": see "The Purification"

THE ECCENTRICITIES OF A NIGHTINGALE: Conflict between the body and the soul, set in Mississippi near the beginning of the century. Ms., Delaware (G).

Related to the short story "The Yellow Bird" (B 1), the play is a 1951 rewrite of *Summer and Smoke* (A 1 below) - although Donald Windham (F 1) has argued that the work predates that play. This text was later extensively revised. Williams's essay for the New York opening was "I Have Rewritten a Play for Artistic Purity" (D 1).

Publication: First Version

The Eccentricities of a Nightingale and Summer and Smoke: Two Plays. New York: New Directions, 1964; Toronto: McClelland & Stewart, 1964. ii, 248 pp. Contents: Author's Note, 4; *The Eccentricities of a Nightingale*, 5-107; *Summer and Smoke* (A 1 below), 109-248. Review:
   Freedley, George. *New York Morning Telegraph* 17
      Feb. 1965: 2.

Theatre, Vol. 2, 1971: 1-111 (A 2).

Trans. (H): German, Japanese.

Publication: Second Version

The Eccentricities of a Nightingale. New York: Dramatists Play Service, 1977. 57 pp. Author's Note, 5; play, 7-55.

Productions

The Eccentricities of a Nightingale. Nyack, NY: Tappan Zee Playhouse, 25 June 1964 (première). Also other summer stock productions, summer 1964.

The Eccentricities of a Nightingale. Chicago: Goodman Theatre 13 Jan.-5 Feb. 1967. Bella Itkin, dir. Marc Cohen, Marna King, design. With Dolores Sutton (Alma), Lee Richardson (John), Beverly Younger (Mrs. Buchanan).

The Eccentricities of a Nightingale. Guildford, Eng.: Yvonne Arnaud Theatre, Oct. 1967. With Sian Phillips (Alma). Review:
   Curtiss, Thomas Quinn. *International Herald Tribune* 14
      Oct. 1967.

The Eccentricities of a Nightingale. Theatre in America.
PBS-TV, 16 June 1976. With Blythe Danner (Alma), Frank
Langella (John). Review:
    Leonard, John. *New York Times* 16 June 1976: 79.

The Eccentricities of a Nightingale. Buffalo: Studio
Arena Theatre, 8 Oct.-6 Nov. 1976 (39); New York: Morosco
Theatre, 23 Nov.-12 Dec. 1976 (24). Edwin Sherwin, dir.
William Ritman, Theoni V. Aldredge, Marc Weiss, design.
Charles Cross, music. With Betsy Palmer (Alma), David
Selby (John). Program: Van Antwerp (F 1): 318; play-
bills: Leavitt (F 1). Reviews:
    Barnes, Clive *New York Times* 24 Nov. 1976: 23. Rpt.
       New York Theatre Critics' Reviews 37: 107; Van
       Antwerp (F 1): 318-19.
    Beaufort, John. *Christian Science Monitor* 26 Nov.
       1976. Rpt. *New York Theatre Critics' Reviews* 37:
       109.
    Gill, Brendan. *New Yorker* 6 Dec. 1976: 134-35.
    Gottfried, Martin. *New York Post* 24 Nov. 1976. Rpt.
       New York Theatre Critics' Reviews 37: 108.
    Kalem, T. E. *Time* 6 Dec. 1976: 98. Rpt. *New York*
       Theatre Critics' Reviews 37: 107.
    Kerr, Walter. *New York Times* 5 Dec. 1976, sec. 2: 3,
       26.
    Kissel, Howard. *Women's Wear Daily* 24 Nov. 1976. Rpt.
       New York Theatre Critics' Reviews 37: 108.
    Probst, Leonard. NBC, 23 Nov. 1976. Rpt. *New York*
       Theatre Critics' Reviews 37: 110.
    Watt, Douglas. *New York Daily News* 24 Nov. 1976. Rpt.
       New York Theatre Critics' Reviews 37: 109.
    Wilson, Edwin. *Wall Street Journal* 13 Oct. 1976. Rpt.
       New York Theatre Critics' Reviews 37: 110.

  Other Productions:
    Catinelli, Joseph. *New York Times* 14 Oct. 1979, sec.
      11: 16-17. [Teaneck, NJ]
    Faber, Charles. *Advocate* 5 Apr. 1979. [Long Beach,
      CA, with Sandy Dennis, Perry King, Nan Martin]
    Frankel, Haskel. *New York Times* 28 Oct. 1979, sec. 22:
      14. [Westchester, NY]

"THE ENEMY: TIME": see *Sweet Bird of Youth*

"THE FROSTED GLASS COFFIN": Tragicomedy about Florida re-
   tirees. Mss., Congress, Texas (G).

Dragon Country, 1969: 197-214 (A 2).

Theatre, Vol. 7, 1981: 197-214 (A 2).

Trans. (H): Spanish.

Productions

"The Frosted Glass Coffin." Key West Players. Key West:
Waterfront Playhouse, 1 May 1970 (première). Tennessee
Williams, dir.

"The Frosted Glass Coffin." Atlanta: Alliance Theatre,
11 Feb. 1980. Gary Tucker, dir. Nick Mancuso, design.
With Jim Loring (One), Leonard Shinew (Two), Thomas Campbell (Three).

Tennessee Laughs: Three 1-Act Plays. Chicago: Goodman
Theatre, 8-23 Nov. 1980. Gary Tucker, dir. Joseph
Nieminski, Ellen Ryba, Robert Christen, design. With
Nathan Davis (One), Les Podewell (Two), Scott Jaeck
(Three). Review:
  Kalson, Albert E. *Tennessee Williams Review* 3.1
    (1981): 25-27.

FUGITIVE KIND: Unpublished drama, written 1936-38, about
derelicts in a flophouse. Mss., Delaware, Texas (G).

Fugitive Kind. Mummers. St. Louis: Wednesday Club Audi-
torium, 30 Nov. and 4 Dec. 1937 (première). Willard H.
Holland, dir. Program: Van Antwerp (F 1): 35. Review:
  Hynds, Reed. *St. Louis Star-Times* 1 Dec. 1937: 17.
    Rpt. Van Antwerp (F 1): 34-35.

THE FUGITIVE KIND: see *Orpheus Descending*

GARDEN DISTRICT: see "Something Unspoken" and *Suddenly Last
Summer*

THE GLASS MENAGERIE: Semi-autobiographical drama about a
St. Louis writer's attempts to forget his mother and
sister, both misfits in a new world. Mss., Columbia,
Delaware, Princeton, Texas, Virginia (G).
  Williams's first book, the work was begun 1943. "Por-
trait of a Girl in Glass" (B 1) is a related short story.
The pre-Broadway essay, Williams's first written for the
occasion, was "The Author Tells Why It Is Called *The
Glass Menagerie*" (D 1). Since 1970 all the New Direc-

tions texts have had slightly revised stage directions and
typographical changes from the 1945 text.

For the 1948 acting edition Williams omitted a screen
device, added dialogue, and somewhat changed Jim's character. This script was revised, according to Lester Beaurline (below), in the 1950s. The first British edition seems
to be essentially the same script. In 1950 Williams and
Peter Bernis prepared the unpublished screenplay. All subsequent films returned to stage versions. In 1952 Williams
recorded a portion of the play (E 1).

Publication: First ("Reading") Version

The Glass Menagerie: A Play. New York: Random House,
   1945. xii, 124 pp. Ils. Contents: The Characters,
   vii; Production Notes, ix-xii; play, 3-124. Rpt. same
   text, plus "The Castatrophe of Success" (D 1), xiii-
   xix: New York: New Directions, 1949. New Classics.
   Ils. New York: New Directions, 1966; Toronto: McClelland & Stewart, 1966. New Classic/New Directions
   Paperbook. Reviews:
      MacBride, James. *New York Times Book Review* 2 Sept.
         1945: 8.
      Nichols, Lewis. *New York Times* 9 Sept. 1945, sec.
         2: 1.

The Best Plays of 1944-45.... Ed. Burns Mantle. New
   York: Dodd, Mead, 1945. 140-75. Excerpts.

Best Plays of the Modern American Theatre, Second Series.
   Ed. John Gassner. New York: Crown, 1947. 1-38.

New York Post Magazine 1 Oct. 1950: 7-13.

Six Modern American Plays. New York: Modern Library,
   1950. 271-340.

*Critics' Choice: New York Drama Critics' Circle Prize
   Plays 1935-1955*. Ed. Jack Gaver. New York: Hawthorn,
   1955. 290-326.

Six Great Modern Plays. New York: Dell, 1956. 435-512.

Four Plays, 1956: vii-63 (A 2).

Streetcar Named Desire, etc., 1959; 121-207 (A 2).

Sweet Bird of Youth, etc., 1962: 227-313 (A 2).

The Glass Menagerie: A Play. Louisville, KY: American
   Printing House for the Blind, 1966.

50 Best Plays of the American Theatre.   Ed. Clive Barnes.
New York: Crown, 1969. 3: 137-74.

Revised Version

The Glass Menagerie.   New Classic/New Directions Paperbook.   New York: New Directions, 1970; Toronto: McClelland & Stewart, 1970.   115 pp.

Theatre, Vol. 1, 1971: 122-237.

Selected Plays, 1977: 1-78; *Selected Plays*, 1980: 1-76 (A
2).

Eight Plays, 1979: 1-90 (A 2).

A Modern Southern Reader....   Ed. Ben Forkner and Patrick
Samway. Atlanta: Peachtree, 1986.   407-55.

The Glass Menagerie.   Signet Classic. New York: New
American Library, 1987.   139 pp.   Ils.

The Glass Menagerie....   Harmondsworth: Penguin Books,
1987.   92 pp.

Publication: Second ("Acting") Versions

The Glass Menagerie...: Play in Two Acts.   New York: Dramatists Play Serice, 1948.   viii, 62 pp.   Another ed.,
viii, 64 pp.   Contents: Staging the Play: Practical
Suggestions by the Publisher, iv-v; Author's Production
Notes, vi-viii; play, 1-62.

The Glass Menagerie: A Play in Two Acts.   London: John
Lehmann, 1948.   95 pp.   Contents: Introduction...:
"The Catastrophe of Success" (D 1), v-x; Notes on the
Characters, xiii; Author's Production Notes, xv; The
Music, xvii, The Lighting, xix; play, 21-95.

The Glass Menagerie...: Play in Two Acts.   New York: Dramatists Play Service, n.d.   70 pp.   Contents: Staging
the Play..., 5-6; Author's Production Notes, 7-8; play,
9-68.

Trans. (H): Arabic, Catalan, Chinese, Czech, Danish,
Estonian, French, German, Greek, Hindi, Italian,
Japanese, Korean, Marathi, Norwegian, Portuguese,
Romanian, Russian, Slovak, Spanish, Swedish, Tamil,
Turkish, Welsh (version uncertain).

Publication: Student Editions

The Glass Menagerie.   Ed. Shoichi Saeki.   Tokyo: Eihosha,
    1953.   144 pp.

The Glass Menagerie.   Ed. Heinz Nyszkiewicz.   Frankfurt:
    Hirschgraben, 1963.   64 pp.

The Glass Menagerie.   Ed. Heinz Pahler.   Paderborn: Fer-
    dinand Schoningh, 1963.

The Glass Menagerie.   Ed. E. R. Wood.   Hereford Plays.
    London: Heinemann Educational, 1968.   xxiv, 76 pp.

Inclusion in Textbooks

Abcarian, Richard, and Marvin Klotz, eds.   *Literature:*
    The Human Experience.   2nd ed.   New York: St. Martin's,
    1978.   211-64.

Allison, Alexander W., et al., eds.   *Masterpieces of the*
    Drama.   4th ed.   New York: Macmillan, 1979.   823-58.

American Literature.   Scribner Literature Series, Signa-
    ture Ed.   Mission Hills, CA: Glencoe, 1989.   712-52.

Anderson, Robert, et al., eds.   *Elements of Literature.*
    Fifth Course: *Literature of the United States.*   Austin,
    TX: Holt, 1989.   786-829.   Inc. *Memoirs* (excerpt).

Auburn, Mark S., and Katherine H. Burkman, eds.   *Drama*
    through Performance.   Boston: Houghton Mifflin, 1977.

Bain, Carl E., et al., eds.   *The Norton Introduction to*
    Literature.   2nd ed.   New York: Norton, 1977.

Barnet, Sylvan, ed.   *An Introduction to Literature: Fic-*
    tion, Poetry, Drama.   4th ed.   Boston: Little, 1961.
    694-748.

---, et al., eds.   *Types of Drama.*   5th ed.   Boston: Lit-
    tle, 1989.

Barranger, Milly S., ed.   *Understanding Plays.*   Needham
    Heights, MA: Allyn, 1989.

Barrows, Marjorie Westcott, et al., eds.   *The American*
    Experience: Drama.   New York: Macmillan, 1968.

Bergman, David, and Daniel Mark Epstein, eds. *The Heath
    Guide to Literature*. 2nd ed. Lexington, MA: Heath,
    1987. 867-911.

Blair, Walter, et al., eds. *The United States in Litera-
    ture*. Glenview, IL: Scott, 1968. 720-59.

Block, Haskell, and Robert G. Shedd, eds. *Masters of Mo-
    dern Drama*. New York: Random House, 1962. 989-1017.

Bloomfield, Morton W., and Robert C. Elliot, eds. *Great
    Plays, Sophocles to Brecht*. New York: Holt, 1965.

Bonazza, Blaxe, and Emil Roy, eds. *Studies in Drama,
    Form A*. New York: Harper, 1963. 279-333.

Boynton, Robert Whitney, and Maynard Mack, eds. *Intro-
    duction to the Play: In the Theater of the Mind*. 2nd
    ed., rev. Rochelle Park, NJ: Hayden, 1976.

Bradley, Sculley, et al., eds. *The American Tradition in
    Literature*. Norton Anthology. 4th ed. New York:
    Grosset, 1974. 1090-1146.

Brown, Leonard Stanley, ed. *A Quarto of Modern Litera-
    ture*. 5th ed. New York: Scribner, 1964. 345-73.

Cassady, Marshall, and Pat Cassady, eds. *An Introduction
    to Theatre and Drama*. Lincolnwood, IL: NTC, 1989.

Clark, Barnett H., and William H. Davenport, eds. *Nine
    Modern American Plays*. New York: Appleton, 1951. 341-
    79.

Cohn, Ruby, and Bernard F. Dukore, eds. *Twentieth Cen-
    tury Drama*.... New York: Random House, 1966. 331-402.

Cooper, Charles W., ed. *Preface to Drama*. New York:
    Ronald, 1955.

Corbin, Richard K., and Miriam Balf, eds. *Twelve Amer-
    ican Plays 1920-1960*. New York: Scribner, 1969.

Corrigan, Robert W., ed. *The Modern Theatre*. New York:
    Macmillan, 1964. 1219-47

Cubeta, Paul M., ed. *Modern Drama for Analysis*. New
    York: Sloan, 1950.

Dean, Leonard F., ed. *Twelve Great Plays*. New York:
    Harcourt, 1970. 681-737.

Dietrich, Richard Farr, et al., eds. *The Art of Drama.*
New York: Holt, 1969.

Downer, Alan S., ed. *American Drama.* New York: Crowell,
1960. [Acting ed.]

Elkins, William R., et al., eds. *Literary Reflections.*
New York: McGraw, 1967.

Elliott, Emory, et al., eds. *American Literature: A
Prentice-Hall Anthology.* Englewood Cliffs, NJ:
Prentice-Hall, 1991. 2: 1448-96.

Gassner, John, ed. *A Treasury of the Theatre....* New
York: Simon, 1950. 1039-59.

---, and Morris Sweetkind, eds. *Introducing the Drama.*
New York: Holt, 1963.

Hall, Donald, ed. *To Read Literature: Fiction, Poetry,
Drama.* 2nd ed. New York: Holt, 1987. 1167-1216.

Hardison, Osborne Bennett, and Jerry Mills, eds. *The
Forms of Imagination.* Englewood Cliffs, NJ: Prentice-
Hall, 1972.

Hatcher, Harlan, ed. *Modern American Drama.* New ed.
New York: Harcourt, 1949. 233-74.

Hatlen, Theodore W., ed. *Drama: Principles & Plays.* New
York: Appleton, 1967. 457-96.

Havighurst, Walter, et al., eds. *Selection: A Reader for
College Writing.* New York: Dryden, 1955. 607-38.

Jacobus, Lee A., ed. *The Bedford Introduction to Drama.*
New York: St. Martin's, 1989.

Kennedy, X. J., ed. *Literature: An Introduction to Fiction, Poetry, and Drama.* 2nd ed. Boston: Little,
1979. 1282-1328.

Kirszner, Laurie G., and Stephen R. Mandell, eds. *Literature: Reading, Reacting, Writing.* Fort Worth: Holt,
1990.

Knickerbocker, Kenneth L., and H. Willard Rininger, eds.
Interpreting Literature. New York: Holt, 1955.

Landy, Alice S., and Robert F. Sommer, eds. *Heath Literature for Composition.* Lexington, MA: Heath, 1990.

Laverty, Carroll D., et al., eds. *The Unity of English.*
New York: Harper, 1971.

Lawn, Beverly, ed. *Literature: 150 Masterpieces of Fiction, Poetry, and Drama.* New York: St. Martin's, 1991.

Lief, Leonard, and James F. Light, eds. *The Modern Age:
Literature.* 2nd ed. New York: Holt, 1972.

Litz, A. Walton, ed. *The Scribner Quarto of Modern Literature.* New York: Scribner, 1978.

McAvoy, William C., ed. *Dramatic Tragedy.* New York:
McGraw-Hill, 1971.

McFarland, Phillip, et al., eds. *Perceptions in Literature.* Boston: Houghton Mifflin, 1972.

McMichael, George, ed. *Anthology of American Literature.*
2nd ed. New York: Macmillan, 1980. 2: 1485-1530.

McNamee, Maurice B., et al., eds. *Literary Types and
Themes.* New York: Rinehart, 1960.

Meyer, Michael, ed. *The Bedford Introduction to Literature.* New York: St. Martin's, 1987. 1467-1513, 1696-
98.

Miller, James E., et al., eds. *United States in Literature.* Glenview, IL: Scott, 1979. 502-40. [Acting
ed.]

Miller, Jordan Y., ed. *The Heath Introduction to Drama*
.... Lexington, MA: Heath, 1976. 727-83.

Montague, Gene, and Marjorie Henshaw, eds. *The Experience of Literature.* Englewood Cliffs, NJ: Prentice-
Hall, 1966.

Perrine, Laurence, ed. *Dimensions of Drama.* New York:
Harcourt, 1973. 425-78.

---, ed. *Literature: Structure, Sound and Sense.* New
York: Harcourt, 1970. 1279-1332.

Pickering, Jerry V., ed. *A Treasury of Drama, Classical
through Modern.* St. Paul, MN: West, 1975. 417-85.

Reinert, Otto, ed. *Modern Drama: Nine Plays.* Boston:
Little, 1961. 387-449.

---, ed. *Six Plays: An Introductory Anthology*.   Boston:
Little, 1973. 324-85.

Roberts, Edgar V., and Henry E. Jacobs, eds. *Literature:
An Introduction to Reading and Writing*. Englewood
Cliffs: Prentice-Hall, 1986. 1565-1617.

Roberts, Nedra Pesold, ed. *The Play's the Thing: An
Introduction to Drama*. Wesley Hills, MA: Independent
School Press, 1981.

Rohrberger, Mary, et al., eds. *An Introduction to Literature*. New York: Random House, 1968. 886-948.

Shaw, Patrick W., ed. *Literature: A College Anthology*.
Boston: Houghton Mifflin, 1977. 859-910. [Acting ed.]

Shroyer, Frederick B., and Louis G. Gardemal, eds. *Types
of Drama*. Glenview, IL: Scott, 1970. 511-99.

Simonson, Harold P., ed. *Quartet: A Book of Stories,
Plays, Poems, and Critical Essays*. New York: Harper,
1970. *Trio: A Book of Stories, Plays, and Poems*. 3rd
ed. New York: Harper, 1970.

Somer, John L., ed. *Dramatic Experience: The Public
Voice*. Glenview, IL: Scott, 1970.

---, and Joseph Cozzo, eds. *Literary Experiences: Public
and Private Voices*. Glenview, IL: Scott, 1971.

Soule, George, ed. *The Theatre of the Mind*. Englewood
Cliffs, NJ: Prentice-Hall, 1974.

Sper, Felix, ed. *Living American Plays*. New York:
Globe, 1954.

Stafford, William T., ed. *Twentieth Century American
Writing*. New York: Odyssey, 1965.

Steinberg, M. W., ed. *Aspects of Modern Drama*. New
York: Holt, 1960. 559-615.

Styan, J. L., ed. *The Challenge of the Theatre*. Encino,
CA: Dickensen, 1972.

Waite, Harlow O., and Benjamin B. Atkinson, eds. *Literature for Our Time*. New York: Holt, 1953.

Wall, Vincent, and James Patton McCormick, eds. *Seven
Plays of the Modern Theatre*. New York: American, 1950.

Warnock, Robert, ed. *Representative Modern Plays: American*. Chicago: Scott, 1952. 580-653.

---, ed. *Representative Modern Plays: Ibsen to Tennessee
Williams*. Glenview, IL: Scott, 1964. 584-650.

Watson, E. Bradlee, and Benfield Pressey, eds. *Contemporary Drama: Eleven Plays*.... New York: Scribner,
1956. 137-69.

Weiss, Samuel A., ed. *Drama in the Modern World: Plays
and Essays*. Lexington, MA: Heath, 1964.

---, ed. *Drama in the Western World: 15 Plays with Essays*. Lexington, MA: Heath, 1968. 685-739. *Drama in
the Western World: 9 Plays with Essays*. Lexington, MA:
Heath, 1968.

Criticism

Beaurline, Lester A. "The Director, the Script, and
Author's Revisions: A Critical Problem." *Papers in
Dramatic Theory and Criticism*. Ed. David M. Knauf.
Iowa City: Univ. of Iowa, 1969. 78-91 (esp. 87-89).

---. "*The Glass Menagerie*: From Story to Play." *Modern
Drama* 8 (Sept. 1965): 142-49. Rpt. Bloom (below): 21-
29; Parker (below): 44-52.

Berkowitz, Gerald M. "The 'Other World' of *The Glass
Menagerie*." *Players* 48 (Apr.-May 1973): 150-53.

Berutti, Elaine. "*The Glass Menagerie*: Escapism as a Way
Out of Fragmentation." *Etudos Anglo-Americanos* 12-13
(1988-89): 78-89.

Bloom, Harold, ed. *Tennessee Williams' The Glass Menagerie*. New York: Chelsea, 1988. vii, 152 pp.

Bluefarb, Sam. "*The Glass Menagerie*: Three Visions of
Time." *College English* 24 (Apr. 1963): 513-18.

Borny, Geoffrey. "The Two Glass Menageries: An Examina-
tion of the Effects on Meaning That Result from Directing the Reading Edition as Opposed to the Acting Edition of the Play." *Page to Stage*.... Ed. Ortrun
Zuber-Skerritt. Amsterdam: Rodopi, 1984. 117-36.
Rpt. Bloom (above): 101-17.

Bryer, Jackson R. *The Glass Menagerie (Tennessee Williams)*. Phonotape-Cassette. DeLand, FL: Everett/
Edwards, 1971.

Buchloh, Paul G. "Zum Problem kultureller und medialer
Umsetzung von Dramatik: Tennessee Williams' *The Glass
Menagerie*." *Die amerikanische Literatur in der Welt-
literatur*. Berlin: Schmidt, 1982. 339-62.

Casty, Alan. "Tennessee Williams and the Small Hands of
the Rain." *Mad River Review* 1 (Fall-Winter 1965): 27-
43.

Cate, Hollis C., and Delma E. Presley. "Beyond Stereo-
type: Ambiguity in Amanda Wingfield." *Notes on Mississippi Writers* 3 (Winter 1971): 91-100.

Choudhuri, A. D. *The Face of Illusion in American Drama*.
Atlantic Highlands, NJ: Humanities, 1979. 112-28.

Clay, J. H. "The Broken Unicorn - Or, Why Is the Theater
So Rentlessly Dull?" *Tennessee Williams Newsletter* 2.2
(Fall 1980): 47-52.

Click, Patricia C. "The Uncertain Universe of *The Glass
Menagerie*: The Influence of the New Physics on Tennessee Williams." *Journal of American Culture* 12 (Spring
1989): 41-45.

Dakoske, Mary Beth. "Archetypal Images of the Family in
Selected Modern Plays." Diss., Univ. of Notre Dame,
1980. *Dissertation Abstracts International* 41 (1980):
1598 A.

Davis, Joseph K. "Landscapes of the Dislocated Mind in
Williams' *The Glass Menagerie*." Tharpe (A 3): 192-206.

Debusscher, Gilbert. "Tennessee Williams's Unicorn Broken Again." *Revue Belge de Philologie et d'Histoire* 49
(1971): 875-85. Rpt. Bloom (above): 47-57.

---. *Tennessee Williams: The Glass Menagerie*. York
Notes. London: Longman, 1982.

De la Cruz, Edgardo. "Things Loved, Things Remembered:
Joaquín's *Portrait* and Williams's *Menagerie*." *Philip-
pine Studies* 14 (1961): 243-52.

Dudley, Bronson. *The Glass Menagerie: A Scene-by-Scene
Analysis with Critical Commentary*. New York: American,
1965. 70 pp.

Durham, Frank. "Tennessee Williams: Theatre Poet in
    Prose." *South Atlantic Bulletin* 36 (Mar. 1971): 3-16.
    Rpt. Bloom (above): 59-73; Parker (below): 121-24.

Ellis, Brobury Pearce. "'The True Originall Copies.'"
    Tulane Drama Review 5 (Sept. 1960): 113-16.

Fisher, Kerk. "The Front Porch in Modern American Drama:
    The Promise of Mobility in O'Neill, Williams, and
    Inge." Diss., Univ. of Georgia, 1989. *Dissertation
    Abstracts International* 51 (1990): 1048 A.

Greenfield, Thomas A. *Work and the Work Ethic in Ameri-
    can Drama 1920-1970.* Columbia: Missouri Univ. Pr.,
    1982. 119-25.

Grieff, Louis K. "Fathers, Daughters, and Spiritual Sis-
    ters: Marsha Norman's *'night, Mother* and Tennessee Wil-
    liams's *The Glass Menagerie.*" *Textual Peformance
    Quarterly* 9 (1989): 224-28.

Gunn, Drewey Wayne. "'More than Just a Little Chekhov-
    ian': *The Sea Gull* as a Source for the Characters in
    The Glass Menagerie." *Modern Drama* 33 (Sept. 1990):
    313-21. Resume:
        Coughlin, Ellen K. *Chronicle of Higher Education* 28
        Nov. 1990, sec. A: 5, 10.

Guthrie, Tyrone. "Poetry Is Where You Find It." *New
    York Times* 18 Apr. 1965, sec. 2: 1, 3.

Hays, Peter L. "Arthur Miller and Tennessee Williams."
    Essays in Literature 4 (Fall 1977): 239-49.

Howell, Elmo "The Function of Gentlemen Callers: A Note
    on Tennessee Williams' *The Glass Menagerie.*" *Notes on
    Mississippi Writers* 2 (Winter 1970): 83-90. Rpt. Bloom
    (above): 43-46.

Hurd, Myles Raymond. "Bullins' *The Gentleman Caller*:
    Source and Satire." *Notes on Contemporary Literature*
    14.3 (1984): 11-12.

Ishizuka, Koji. "Two Memory Plays: Williams and Miller."
    American Literature in the 1940's. Annual Report.
    Tokyo: American Literary Society, 1975. 208-12.

Jones, John H. "The Missing Link: The Father in *The
    Glass Menagerie.*" *Notes on Mississippi Writers* 20.1
    (1988): 29-38.

Joven, Nilda G.   "Illusion and Reality in Tennessee Wil-
    liams' *The Glass Menagerie.*" *Dillman Review* 14 (Jan.
    1966): 81-89.

King, Thomas L.   "Irony and Distance in *The Glass Menag-
    erie.*" *Educational Theatre Journal* 25 (May 1973): 207-
    14. Rpt. Bloom (A 3): 85-94; Parker (below): 75-86.

Lees, Daniel E.   "*The Glass Menagerie*: A Black *Cinder-
    ella.*" *Unisa English Studies* 11 (Mar. 1973): 30-34.

Luhr, Friedrich Wilhelm.   "*The Glass Menagerie.*" *Zeit-
    genossische amerikanische Dichtung.* Ed. Warner Hullen
    et al. 3rd ed. Frankfurt: Hirschgraben, 1969. 147-
    58. [In German]

Mansur, Rajshekhar.   "The Emissary in Tennessee Williams'
    The Glass Menagerie: A Study of the Role of Jim O'Con-
    nor.*" *Journal of the Karnatak University: Humanities*
    28 (1984): 25-36.

Merritt, Francine.   "Staging *The Glass Menagerie.*" *Dra-
    matics* 20 (Dec. 1948): 18.

Modern Drama: Williams - The Glass Menagerie. Audiocas-
    sette. Stamford, CT: Educational Dimensions, 1974.

Napieralski, Edmund A.   "Tennessee Williams' *The Glass
    Menagerie*: The Dramatic Metaphor.*" *Southern Quarterly*
    16 (Oct. 1977): 1-12.

Nolan, Paul T.   "Two Memory Plays: *The Glass Menagerie*
    and *After the Fall.*" *McNeese Review* 17 (1966): 27-38.
    Rpt. Parker (below): 144-53.

Nyszkiewicz, Heinz.   "Drama, Bild und Wort in Tennessee
    Williams' *Glassmenagerie.*" *Padagogische Provinz* 17
    (1963): 308-20.

Osada, Mitsunobu.   "'Life' and 'Shadow' - *The Glass
    Menagerie* as a Reflection of Disintegrated Modern Civi-
    lization.*" *Amerika Bungaku Kenkyu* (Tokyo) 16 (1979):
    93-116.

Parker, R. B(rian).   "The Composition of *The Glass Menag-
    rie*: An Argument for Complexity.*" *Modern Drama* 25
    (1982): 409-22. Rpt. D. Parker (A 3): 12-26; Parker
    (below): 53-61.

---, ed. *The Glass Menagerie: A Collection of Critical Essays*. Englewood Cliffs, NJ: Prentice-Hall, 1983. ix, 166 pp.

Pavlov, Grigor. "A Comparative Study of Tennessee Williams' *The Glass Menagerie* and 'Portrait of a Girl in Glass.'" *Annuaire de l'Universite de Sofie* (Faculte des Lettres) 62 (1968): 111-31.

Pebworthy, Ted-Larry, and Claude Jay Summers. *Williams' The Glass Menagerie*. New York: Barrister, 1966.

Potter, Alex. "*The Glass Menagerie* by Tennessee Williams." *CRUX* 14.2 (1980): 20-26.

Presley, Delma E. *The Glass Menagerie: An American Memory*. Boston: Twayne, 1990. xvi, 117 pp.

Rama Murthy, V. *American Expressionistic Drama, Containing Analyses of Three Outstanding American Plays....* Delhi: Doaba, 1970. 102 pp.

Rathbun, Gilbert L. *Tennessee Williams' The Glass Menagerie: A Critical Commentary*. New York: Monarch, 1967. 75 pp.

Roberts, James L. *The Glass Menagerie and A Streetcar Named Desire: Notes*. Lincoln, NE: Cliff's Notes, 1965. 77 pp.

Robey, Cora. "Chloroses - Pales Roses and Pleurosis - Blue Roses." *Romance Notes* 13 (Winter 1971): 250-51.

Rowland, James L. "Tennessee's Two Amandas." *Washington State University Research Studies* 35 (1967): 331-40. Rpt. Parker (above): 62-74.

Sakellaridon-Hadzipyrou, Elsie. "The Glass Spectrum in *The Glass Menagerie*." *Epistemonike Epeterida...* (1978): 347-55.

Sasahara, Hiraku. "Tennessee Williams to Emily Dickinson - *The Glass Menagerie* wo Chushin ni." *Eigo Seinen* 120 (1974): 270-72.

Scheidler, Katherine P. "*Romeo and Juliet* and *The Glass Menagerie* as Reading Programs." *English Journal* 70 (Jan. 1981): 34-36.

Scheye, Thomas E. "*The Glass Menagerie*: 'It's no tragedy, Freckles.'" Tharpe (A 3): 207-13.

Sharma, Jaidev, and V. P. Sharma. "America, the Salesman, and the Artist: A Study of *The Glass Menagerie*,
The Iceman Cometh, and *Death of a Salesman*." *Perspectives on Arthur Miller*. Ed. Atma Ram. Madras:
Emerald, 1988. 62-74.

Stein, Roger B. "*The Glass Menagerie* Revisited: Catastrophe without Violence." *Western Humanities Review* 18
(Spring 1964): 141-53. Rpt. Bloom (above): 7-20; Parker (above): 135-43; Stanton (A 3): 36-44 (abr.).

Strickland, Arney L. "Abrogation of the Laws of Nature."
Tennessee Williams Review 3.1 (1981): 42-43.

Taubman, Howard. "Diverse, Unique, Amanda." *New York
Times* 16 May 1965, sec. 2: 1.

Thierfelder, William R. "Williams's *The Glass
Menagerie*." *Explicator* 48 (1990): 284-85.

"Through a Glass Starkly." *English Journal* 57 (Feb.
1968): 209-12, 220. [Honors English class project]

Uogintaite, Undine. "Plastivio teatro principai Tennessee Williams pjeseje *Stiklinds zverynas* iv amerikeciu
nacionalive drama." *Literatura* (Vilnius) 16.3 (1984):
77-85.

Watson, Charles S. "The Revision of *The Glass Menagerie*:
The Passing of Good Manners." *Southern Literary Journal* 8 (Spring 1976): 74-78. Rpt. Bloom (above): 75-78.

Wells, Arvin R. "*The Glass Menagerie*." *Insight: Analysis of American Literature*. Ed. John V. Hagopian and
Martin Doch. Frankfurt: Hirschgraben, 1967. 1: 172-
80.

Productions

The Glass Menagerie. Chicago: Civic Theatre, 26 Dec.
1944 (première); New York: Playhouse Theatre, 31 Mar.
1945-3 Aug. 1946 (561). Eddie Dowling, Margo Jones,
dirs. Jo Mielziner, design. Paul Bowles, music. With
Eddie Dowling (Tom), Laurette Taylor (Amanda), Julie
Haydon (Laura), Anthony Ross (Jim). Winner New York Drama Critics' Circle Award, Sidney Howard Memorial Award,
Donaldson Award. Music: Dramatists Play Service. Reviews, Prod. Notes:
  Life 30 Apr. 1945: 81-83.
  Life 11 June 1945: 12-14.

New York Herald Tribune 11 Apr. 1945. Rpt. Van Antwerp
  (F 1): 67-68.
New York Times 11 Apr. 1945: 18.
New York Times 1 July 1945, sec. 1: 19. [Donaldson
  Award]
New York Times 27 Jan. 1946, sec. 2: 1. [Washington
  Command Performance]
New York Times 31 Mar. 1946, sec. 2: 1.
New York Times 11 Apr. 1945: 18. [Drama Critics' Cir-
  cle Award]
New York Times 11 Jan. 1946.
New York Times 2 June 1946, sec. 2: 2.
New York Times Magazine 4 Mar. 1945: 28-29.
New York Times Magazine 15 Apr. 1945: 28.
Newsweek 2 Apr. 1945: 86-87.
Theatre Arts 29 (May 1945): 263.
Theatre Arts 29 (Oct. 1945): 554.
Time 9 Apr. 1945: 86-88.
Time 23 Apr. 1945: 88. Rpt. Leavitt (F 1) 58. [Drama
  Critics' Circle Award]
Variety 22 Nov. 1944: 40.
Variety 4 Apr. 1945: 52.
Bentley, Eric. *Sewanee Review* 54 (Spring 1946): 314-
  15.
Brown, John Mason. *Saturday Review* 14 Apr. 1945: 34-
  36. Rpt. *Seeing Things* (New York: McGraw-Hill,
  1948): 266-72.
Cassidy, Claudia. *Chicago Tribune* 27 Dec. 1944: 11.
  Rpt. Van Antwerp (F 1): 59-61.
---. *Chicago Tribune* 7 Jan. 1945, Books: 3. Rpt. Van
  Antwerp (F 1): 61-64.
Chapman, John. *New York Daily News* 2 Apr. 1945: 25.
  Rpt. *New York Theatre Critics' Reviews* 6: 236.
Courtney, Marguerite. *Laurette*. New York: Rinehart,
  1955.
Freedley, George. *New York Morning Telegraph* 3 Apr.
  1945: 2.
---. *New York Morning Telegraph* 3 Apr. 146: 2.
Garland, Robert. *New York Journal-American* 2 Apr.
  1945: 6. Rpt. *New York Theatre Critics' Reviews* 6:
  235.
Gibbs, Wolcott. *New Yorker* 7 Apr. 1945: 40.
Gilder, Rosamond. *Theatre Arts* 29 (June 1945): 325-28.
  Rpt. *Theatre Arts Anthology* (New York: MacGregor,
  1950): 554.
Goldsmith, Theodore. *New York Times* 1 July 1945, sec.
  2: 1. [Interview with Ross]
Guernsey, Otis L. Jr. *New York Herald Tribune* 2 Apr.
  1945: 10. Rpt. *New York Theatre Critics' Reviews* 6:
  236.
Hewitt, Barnard. *Player's* Sept.-Oct. 1945: 5, 17.

Kronenberger, Louis. *New York Newspaper PM* 2 Apr.
    1945. Rpt. *New York Theatre Critics' Reviews* 6:
    235-36.
Krutch, Joseph Wood. *Nation* 160 (14 Apr. 1945): 424-
    25.
Lewis, Lloyd. *New York Times* 14 Jan. 1945, sec. 2: 2.
Mielziner, Jo. "Scene Designs for *The Glass Menager-
    ie*." *Theatre Arts* 29 (Apr. 1945): 211.
Morehouse, Ward. *New York Sun* 2 Apr. 1945. Rpt. *New
    York Theatre Critics' Reviews* 6: 234-35.
Murdock, Henry T. *Chicago Sun* 28 Dec. 1944: 11.
Nathan, George Jean. *New York Journal-American* 4 Apr.
    1945. Rpt. Van Antwerp (F 1): 64-65.
---. *Theatre Book of the Year 1944-1945*. New York:
    Knopf, 1946. 324-27.
Nichols, Lewis. *New York Times* 2 Apr. 1945: 15. Rpt.
    *New York Times Theatre Reviews; New York Theatre
    Critics' Reviews* 6: 235.
---. *New York Times* 8 Apr. 1945, sec. 2: 1. Rpt. *New
    York Times Theatre Reviews*.
---. *New York Times* 15 Apr. 1945, sec. 2: 1. [Drama
    Critics' Circle Award]
Phelan, Kappo. *Commonweal* 20 Apr. 1945: 16-17.
Pollock, Robert. *Chicago Times* 27 Dec. 1944: 24.
Rascoe, Burton. *New York World-Telegram* 2 Apr. 1945.
    Rpt. *New York Theatre Critics' Reviews* 6: 237.
Stevens, Ashton. *Chicago Herald American* 27 Dec. 1944:
    10.
Waldorf, Wilella. *New York Post* 2 Apr. 1945. Rpt. *New
    York Theatre Critics' Reviews* 6: 236-37.
Wyatt, Euphemia Van Rensselaer. *Catholic World* 161
    (May 1945): 166-67. Resume: *Catholic World* 161
    (June 1945): 263-64.
Young, Michael C. *Tennessee Williams Newsletter* 2.2
    (Fall 1980): 32-35. [Interview with Haydon]
Young Stark. *New Republic* 112 (16 Apr. 1945): 505.
    Rpt. *Immortal Shadows* (New York: Scribner, 1948):
    249-53; George Oppenheimer, ed., *The Passionate
    Playgoer...* (New York: Viking, 1958): 488-91; Parker
    (Criticism above): 15-19.
Zolotow, Sam. *New York Times* 6 June 1945: 17. [Sidney
    Howard Memorial Award]

The Glass Menagerie. London: Theatre Royal, Haymarket,
28 July 1948. John Gielgud, dir. Jo Mielziner, design.
Paul Bowles, music. With Phil Brown (Tom), Helen Hayes
(Amanda), Frances Heflin (Laura), Hugh McDermott (Jim).
Reviews:

New York Times 25 July 1948: 19.
New York Times 29 July 1948: 17. Rpt. *New York Times
    Theatre Reviews*.

Punch 11 Aug. 1948: 132-33. Rpt. Van Antwerp (F 1):
   113-14.
Times (London) 29 July 1948: 6.
Barrow, Kenneth. *Helen Hayes*.... Garden City: Double-
   day, 1985. 151-55.
Fleming, Peter. *Spectator* 181 (6 Aug. 1948): 173.
Hayes, Helen, with Katherine Hatch. *My Life in Three*
   Acts. San Diego: Harcourt, 1990. 164-69.
Hayman, Ronald. *John Gielgud*. New York: Random House,
   1971. 161.
Trewin, J. C. *Illustrated London News* 213 (28 Aug.
   1948): 250.
Worsley, T. C. *New Statesman* 36 (7 Aug. 1948): 113.

The Glass Menagerie. Warner Brothers, 7 Sept. 1950 (pre-
mière). Irving Rapper, dir. Robert Burke, camera.
Robert Haas, design. Max Steiner, music. With Kirk
Douglas (Tom), Gertrude Lawrence (Amanda), Jane Wyman
(Laura), Arthur Kennedy (Jim). Reviews, Prod. Notes:
Christian Century 67 (22 Nov. 1950): 1407.
Good Housekeeping Aug. 1950: 215.
New York Herald Tribune 7 Jan. 1949: 16. [Screenplay]
New York Times Magazine 4 June 1950: 58.
Newsweek 9 Oct. 1950: 90.
Scholastic 18 Oct. 1950: 28.
Screen Hits Annual 5 (1950): 46-50. [Synopsis]
Sequence 13 (New Year 1951): 16-17.
Time 2 Oct. 1950: 74.
Variety 20 Sept. 1950: 6.
Aldrich, Richard Stoddall. *Gertrude Lawrence as Mrs.*
   O: An Intimate Biography of the Great Star. New
   York: Greystone, 1954. Chap. 17.
Brady, Thomas F. *New York Times* 22 Jan. 1950, sec. 2:
   5. [Filming]
Cook, Alton. *New York World-Telegram* 29 Sept. 1950:
   26.
Crowther, Bosley. *New York Times* 29 Sept. 1950: 51.
   Rpt. *New York Times Film Reviews*.
---. *New York Times* 8 Oct. 1950, sec. 2: 1.
Friedlich, Ruth K. *Films in Review* Oct. 1950: 25-26.
Gilbert, Justin. *New York Daily Mirror* 29 Sept. 1950:
   46.
Griffith, Richard. *Saturday Review* 14 Oct. 1950: 32-
   33.
Hartung, Philip T. *Commonweal* 52 (6 Oct. 1950): 631-
   32.
Hatch, Robert. *New Republic* 23 Oct. 1950: 22.
Hayes, J. J. *Christian Science Monitor Magazine* 15
   Apr. 1950: 8.
Hine, Al. *Holiday* Aug. 1950: 14-16.
Lockhart, Jane. *Rotarian* Jan. 1951: 38.

MacMullan, Hugh. "Translating *The Glass Menagerie* to
    Film." *Hollywood Quarterly* 5 (Fall 1950): 14-32.
McCarten, John. *New Yorker* 30 Sept. 1950: 60.
Morley, Sheridan. *Gertrude Lawrence: A Biography.* New
    York: McGraw-Hill, 1981. 181-82.
Sayers, Frances Clark. *Library Journal* 75 (15 Oct.
    1950): 1843.

The Glass Menagerie. New York: City Center Theatre, 21
Nov. 1956. Alan Schneider, dir. Peggy Clark, design.
With James Daly (Tom), Helen Hayes (Amanda), Lois Smith
(Laura), Lenny Chapman (Jim). Reviews:
    Theatre Arts Feb. 1957: 24.
    Atkinson, Brooks. *New York Times* 22 Nov. 1956: 50.
        Rpt. *New York Times Theatre Review; New York Theatre
        Critics' Reviews* 17: 193; Parker (Criticism above):
        20-21.
    ---. 2 Dec. 1956, sec. 2: 1. Rpt. *New York Times The-
        atre Reviews.*
    Chapman, John. *New York Daily News* 22 Nov. 1956: 60.
        Rpt. *New York Theatre Critics' Reviews* 17: 191.
    Coleman, Robert. *New York Daily Mirror* 22 Nov. 1956:
        28. Rpt. *New York Theatre Critics' Reviews* 17: 192.
    Donnelly, Tom. *New York World-Telegram* 23 Nov. 1956:
        22. Rpt. *New York Theatre Critics' Reviews* 17: 191.
    Hewes, Henry. *Saturday Review* 8 Dec. 1956: 29.
    Kerr, Walter. *New York Herald-Tribune* 22 Nov. 1956:
        20. Rpt. *New York Theatre Critics' Reviews* 17: 190.
    McClain, John. *New York Journal-American* 23 Nov. 1956:
        22. Rpt. *New York Theatre Critics' Reviews* 17: 192.
    Watts, Richard Jr. *New York Post* 23 Nov. 1956: 66.
        Rpt. *New York Theatre Critics' Reviews* 17: 190.
    Wyatt, Euphemia Van Rensselaer. *Catholic World* 184
        (Jan. 1957): 307.

The Glass Menagerie. Theatre Guild American Repertory
Company. Washington: National Theatre, Mar. 1961; European and South American tour, spring-summer 1961. With
James Broderick (Tom), Helen Hayes (Amanda), Nancy Coleman (Laura), Leif Erikson (Jim). Reviews, Prod. Notes:
    New York Times 20 Mar. 1961: 32. [Brussels]
    New York Times 1 Apr. 1961: 11. Rpt. *New York Times
        Theatre Reviews.* [Athens]
    New York Times 11 Apr. 1961: 43. Rpt. *New York Times
        Theatre Reviews.* [Tel Aviv]
    New York Times 1 May 1961: 35. Rpt. *New York Times The-
        atre Reviews.* [West Berlin]
    New York Times 19 May 1961: 22. Rpt. *New York Times
        Theatre Reviews.* [Stockholm]
    New York Times 31 May 1961: 28. Rpt. *New York Times
        Theatre Reviews.* [Rome]

New York Times 16 June 1961: 27. Rpt. *New York Times*
   Theatre Reviews. [Paris]
New York Times 21 Aug. 1961: 20. Rpt. *New York Times*
   Theatre Reviews. [Bogota]
Funke, Lewis. *New York Times* 5 Mar. 1961, sec. 2: 1.
Handler, M. S. *New York Times* 21 Apr. 1961: 29. Rpt.
   New York Times Theatre Reviews. [Vienna]
Taubman, Howard. *New York Times* 6 Mar. 1961: 30. Rpt.
   New York Theatre Reviews.
Underwood, Paul. *New York Times* 28 Mar. 1961: 32 [Bel-
   grade]
Zolotow, Sam. *New York Times* 25 Aug. 1960: 24.

The Glass Menagerie. Chicago: Goodman Theatre, 10-29
Jan. 1964. Patrick Henry, dir. James Maronek, Uta
Olson, design. With Peggy Wood (Amanda). Reviews:
   New York Times 12 Nov. 1963: 46.
   Cassidy, Claudia. *Chicago Tribune* 11 Jan. 1963.
   Christiansen, Richard. *Chicago Daily News* 13 Jan.
      1963.
   Richards, Stanley. *Chicago Daily News Panorama* 4 Jan.
      1963.

The Glass Menagerie. Caedmon recording, 1964. Howard
Sackler, dir. With Montgomery Clift (Tom), Jessica Tandy
(Amanda), Julie Harris (Laura), David Wayne (Jim). Notes
by Williams and William Inge in container; note by John
Gassner on cover. Review:
   Publishers Weekly 5 Apr. 1991: 115.

The Glass Menagerie. Minnesota Theatre Company. Min-
neapolis: Tyrone Guthrie Theatre, summer 1964. Alan
Schneider, dir. Lois Brown, design. Herbert Pilhofer,
music. With Lee Richardson (Tom), Ruth Nelson (Amanda),
Ellen Gweer (Laura), Ed Flanders (Jim). Reviews:
   New York Times 7 June 1964, sec. 2: 3.
   Clurman, Harold. *Nation* 10 Aug. 1964: 60. Rpt. *The
      Naked Image*... (New York: Macmillan, 1966): 142-43.
   Taubman, Howard. *New York Times* 20 July 1964: 18.
      Rpt. *New York Times Theatre Reviews*.

The Glass Menagerie. Guildford: Yvonne Arnaud Theatre,
fall 1965; London: Haymarket, 4 Dec. 1965. Vivian Mata-
lon, dir. With Ian McShane (Tom), Gwen Ffrangeon-Davies
(Amanda), Anna Massey (Laura), George Baker (Jim).
Reviews:
   Benedictus, David. *London Observer* 5 Dec. 1965: 24.
   Brien, Alan. *London Sunday Telegraph* 5 Dec. 1965: 12.
   Hobson, Harold. *Christian Science Monitor* 9 Dec. 1965:
      20.
   Lambert, J. W. *Drama* 80 (Spring 1966): 22.

Spurling, Hilary. *Spectator* 215 (10 Dec. 1965): 778.

The Glass Menagerie. Milburn, NJ: Paper Mill Playhouse,
30 Mar. 1965; New York: Brooks Atkinson Theatre, 4 May-2
Oct. 1965 (175). George Keathley, dir. James A. Taylor,
Robert T. Williams, Patton Campbell, V. C. Fuqua, design.
Paul Bowles, music. With George Gizzard (Tom), Maureen
Stapleton (Amanda), Piper Laurie (Laura), Pat Hingle
(Jim). Reviews, Prod. Notes:
    New York Daily News 18 Aug. 1965: 81. [Cast changes]
    New York Times 2 May 1965, sec. 2: 1.
    Time 14 May 1965: 64.
    WPAT Gaslight Review July 1965: 31-36.
    Cassidy, Claudia. *Life* 28 May 1965: 16.
    Gilman, Richard. *Newsweek* 17 May 1965: 92. Rpt. *Com-
        mon and Uncommon Modes...* (New York: Random House,
        1971): 148-49.
    Kerr, Walter. *New York Herald Tribune* 5 May 1965: 19.
        Rpt. *New York Theatre Critics' Reviews* 26: 334.
    Lewis, Theophilus. *America* 112 (19 June 1965): 888-89.
    Little, Stuart W. *New York Herald Tribune* 17 Mar.
        1965: 16. [Milburn]
    McCarten, John. *New Yorker* 15 May 1965: 158.
    McClain, John. *New York Journal-American* 5 May 1965;
        sec. L: 32. Rpt. *New York Theatre Critics' Reviews*
        26: 332.
    Nadel, Norman. *New York World-Telegram* 5 May 1965: 39.
        Rpt. *New York Theatre Critics' Reviews* 26: 333.
    Sheed, Wilfred. *Commonweal* 82 (9 June 1965): 356-57.
    Stang, Joanne. *New York Times* 16 May 1965, sec. 2: 1,
        3. [Interview with Stapleton]
    Taubman, Howard. *New York Times* 5 May 1965: 53. Rpt.
        New York Times Theatre Reviews.
    ---. *New York Times* 16 May 1965, sec. 2: 1. Rpt. *New
        York Times Theatre Reviews*; Parker (Criticism,
        above): 22-25.
    Watt, Douglas. *New York Daily News* 5 May 1965: 92.
        Rpt. *New York Theatre Critics' Reviews* 26: 333.
    Watts, Richard Jr. *New York Post* 5 May 1965: 78. Rpt.
        New York Theatre Critics' Reviews 26: 332.
    Zolotow, Sam. *New York Times* 1 June 1965: 45.

The Glass Menagerie. Cut by Williams. CBS-TV, 8 Dec.
1966. Michael Elliott, dir. John Clements, design.
With Hal Holbrook (Tom), Shirley Booth (Amanda), Barbara
Loden (Laura), Pat Hingle (Jim). Reviews:
    New York Post 9 Dec. 1966: 94.
    New York Times 10 June 1966: 91.
    New York Times 4 Dec. 1966, sec. 2: 23.
    New York World-Journal Tribune Magazine 4 Dec. 1966:
        13.

Variety 14 Dec. 1966: 33.

Gardella, Kay. *New York Sunday News* 4 Dec. 1966, sec.
    S: 32.

Gould, Jack. *New York Times* 9 Dec. 1966: 95.

Gross, Ben. *New York Daily News* 9 Dec. 1966: 100.

Musel, Robert. *TV Guide* 3 Dec. 1966: 38-40. [Inter-
    view with Booth]

Salerno, Al. *New York World-Journal Tribune* 9 Dec.
    1966: 39.

The Glass Menagerie. ABC-TV, 16 Dec. 1973. Anthony Har-
vey, dir. With Sam Waterston (Tom), Katherine Hepburn
(Amanda), Joanna Miles (Laura), Michael Moriarty (Jim).
Reviews, Prod. Notes:

New York Times 20 June 1973: 82.

Variety 26 Dec. 1973: 21.

Variety 2 Jan. 1974: 30. [Repeat showing]

Adams, Val. *New York Daily News* 11 Apr. 1973: 48.

Edwards, Anne. *A Remarkable Woman....* New York: Mor-
    row, 1985. 379-82. [Hepburn]

Gardella, Kay. *New York Sunday News* 9 Dec. 1973, sec.
    3: 19.

---. *New York Daily News* 14 Dec. 1973: 114.

Higham, Charles. *New York Times* 9 Dec. 1973, sec. 2:
    3, 21. [Interview with Hepburn]

Kael, Pauline. *New Yorker* 31 Dec. 1973: 50-51. Rpt.
    Reeling (Boston: Little, Brown, 1976): 246-47.

Mead, Mimi. *Christian Science Monitor* 14 Dec. 1973:
    24.

O'Connor, John J. *New York Times* 14 Dec. 1973: 94.

Reed, Rex. *New York Daily News* 14 Dec. 1973: 106.

---. *New York Sunday News* 9 Dec. 1973, sec. 3: 5.

Waters, Harry F. *Newsweek* 17 Dec. 1973: 61.

Weisman, Steven R. *New York Times* 29 May 1974: 82.
    [Emmys]

Williams, Bob. *New York Post* 14 Dec. 1973: 81.

The Glass Menagerie. New York: Circle-in-the-Square
Theatre, 18 Dec. 1975-22 Feb. 1976 (78). Theodore Mann,
dir. Ming Cho Lee, Thomas Skelton, Sydney Brooks, de-
sign. Craig Wasson, music. With Rip Torn (Tom), Maureen
Stapleton (Amanda), Pamela Playton-Wright (Laura), Paul
Rudd (Jim). Reviews:

Barnes, Clive. *New York Times* 19 Dec. 1975: 52. Rpt.
    New York Theatre Critics' Reviews 36: 125.

Beaufort, John. *Christian Science Monitor* 26 Dec.
    1975. Rpt. *New York Theatre Critics' Reviews* 36:
    127.

Clurman, Harold. *Nation* 3 Jan. 1976: 28.

Gottfried, Martin. *New York Post* 19 Dec. 1975. Rpt.
    New York Theatre Critics' Reviews 36: 125-26.

Hughes, Catherine. *America* 134 (31 Jan. 1976): 75.
Kalem, T. E. *Time* 12 Jan. 1976: 61.
Kauffmann, Stanley. *New Republic* 17 Jan. 1976: 28.
Kerr, Walter. *New York Times* 28 Dec. 1975, sec. 2: 5.
Kissel, Howard. *Women's Wear Daily* 19 Dec. 1975. Rpt.
  New York Theatre Critics' Reviews 36: 127.
Probst, Leonard. NBC, 18 Dec. 1975. Rpt. *New York
  Theatre Critics' Reviews* 36: 128.
Watt, Douglas. *New York Daily News* 19 Dec. 1975. Rpt.
  New York Theatre Critics' Reviews 36: 128.
Wilson, Edwin. *Wall Street Journal* 23 Dec. 1975. Rpt.
  New York Theatre Critics' Reviews 36: 126-27.

The Glass Menagerie. New York: Eugene O'Neill Theatre, 1
Dec. 1983-19 Feb. 1984 (100). John Dexter, dir. Ming
Cho Lee, Patricia Zipprodt, Andy Phillips, design. Paul
Bowles, music. With Bruce Davidson (Tom), Jessica Tandy
(Amanda), Amanda Plummer (Laura), John Heard (Jim). Re-
views:
Barnes, Clive. *New York Post* 2 Dec. 1983. Rpt. *New
  York Theatre Critics' Reviews* 44: 104.
Beaufort, John. *Christian Science Monitor* 7 Dec. 1983.
  Rpt *New York Theatre Critics' Reviews* 44: 106-07.
Brustein, Robert. *New Republic* 9 Jan. 1984: 25-26.
Corliss, Richard. *Time* 12 Dec. 1983: 108. Rpt. *New
  York Theatre Critics Reviews* 1983: 107-08.
Cunningham, Dennis. WCBS-TV, 1 Dec. 1983. Rpt. *New
  York Theatre Critics' Reviews* 44: 108-09.
Denby, David. *Atlantic* Jan. 1985: 38-39.
Gill, Brendon. *New Yorker* 12 Dec. 1983: 157-58.
Hughes, Catherine. *American* 150 (21 Jan. 1984): 34.
Kissel, Howard. *Women's Wear Daily* 2 Dec. 1983. Rpt.
  New York Theatre Critics' Reviews 44: 105.
Kroll, Jack. *Newsweek* 12 Dec. 1983: 113. Rpt. *New
  York Theatre Critics' Reviews* 44: 108.
Rich, Frank. *New York Times* 2 Dec. 1983. Rpt. *New
  York Theatre Critics' Reviews* 44: 103.
Sauvage, L. *New Leader* 26 Dec. 1983: 17.
Siegel, Joel. WABC-TV, 1 Dec. 1983. Rpt. *New York
  Theatre Critics' Reviews* 44: 108.
Simon, John. *New York* 12 Dec. 1983: 93.
---, and Rhoda Koenig. *New York* 19 Sept. 1983: 52.
  [Interview with Tandy]
Watt, Douglas. *New York Daily News* 2 Dec. 1983. Rpt.
  New York Theatre Critics' Reviews 44: 102.
Weales, Gerald. *Commonweal* 111 (10 Feb. 1984): 88.
Wilson, Edwin. *Wall Street Journal* 7 Dec. 1983. Rpt.
  New York Theatre Critics' Reviews 44: 104-05.

The Glass Menagerie. London: Greenwich, 20 May-29 June
1985. Alan Strachan, dir. Bernard Culshaw, Ricardo

Yori, design. Ilona Sekacz, music. With Gerard Murphy
(Tom), Constance Cummings (Amanda), Ioria Fuller (Laura),
Michael J. Shannon (Jim). Reviews:
  Barber, John. *London Daily Telegraph* 22 May 1985.
    Rpt. *London Theatre Record* 5: 471.
  Billington, Michael. *Guardian* 22 May 1985. Rpt. *London Theatre Record* 5: 472.
  Hurren, Kenneth. *London Mail on Sunday* 26 May 1985.
    Rpt. *London Theatre Record* 5: 473.
  King, Francis. *London Sunday Telegraph* 26 May 1985.
    Rpt. *London Theatre Record* 5: 473.
  Morley, Sheridan. *Punch* 29 May 1985. Rpt. *London Theatre Record* 5: 471.
  Nightingale, Benedict. *New Statesman* 31 May 1985.
    Rpt. *London Theatre Record* 5: 473.
  Shulman, Milton. *London Standard* 21 May 1985. Rpt.
    London Theatre Record 5: 472.
  Tinker, Jack. *London Daily Mail* 29 May 1985. Rpt.
    London Theatre Record 5: 472-73.
  Wolf, Matt. *Plays and Players* July 1985: 29.

The Glass Menagerie. Williamstown Theatre Festival.
Williamstown, MA: 20-25 Aug. 1985. New Haven: Long Wharf
Theatre, Mar.-Apr. 1986. Nikos Psacharopoulos, dir.
With John Sayles [Williamstown], Treat Williams [New
Haven] (Tom); Joanne Woodward (Amanda); Karen Allen
(Laura); James Naughton (Jim). Reviews, Prod. Notes:
  Advocate 5 July 1986: 35.
  Henry, William A. III. *Time* 2 Sept. 1985: 72.
  Luzzi, Michael. *USA Today* 8 Apr. 1986, sec. D: 6.
    [Interview with Woodward]

The Glass Menagerie. Cineplex Odeon, 12 May 1987. Paul
Newman, dir. Michael Ballhaus, camera. Tony Walton, de-
sign. Henry Mancini, music. With John Malkovich (Tom),
Joanne Woodward (Amanda), Karen Allen (Laura), James
Naughton (Jim). Music soundtrack: MCA Records, 1987.
Reviews, Prod. Notes:
  People Weekly 9 Nov. 1987: 110-11.
  People Weekly 23 Nov. 1987: 14.
  USA Today 30 Apr. 1986.
  Variety 13 May 1987: 139.
  Bemrose, John. *Maclean's* 28 Sept. 1987: 42.
  Bernard, Jami. *New York Post* 23 Oct. 1987: 31.
  Boyum, Joy Gould. *Glamour* Dec. 1987: 159.
  Buckley, Michael. *Films in Review* Jan. 1988: 44.
  Denby, David. *New York* 2 Nov. 1987: 95.
  Edelstein, David. *Village Voice* 10 Nov. 1988: 66.
  Haller, S. *People Weekly* 23 Nov. 1987: 14.
  Ivory, James. *Sight & Sound* Spring 1988: 135.
  Kauffmann, Stanley. *New Republic* 23 Nov. 1987: 25.

McGrady, Mike. *Newsday* 23 Oct. 1987, sec. 3: 3.
Maslin, Janet. *New York Times* 23 Oct. 1987, sec. 3:
    14.
Scheuer, D. *Scholastic Update* 20 Nov. 1987: 12-13.
Stearns, David Patrick. *USA Today* 3 Dec. 1987. [In-
    terview with Malkovich]
Stern, Stewart. *No Tricks in My Pocket: Paul Newman
    Directs.* New York: Grove, 1989. viii, 231 pp.
Sterritt, David. *Christian Science Monitor* 28 Oct.
    1987: 21.
Sweet, Louise. *Monthly Film Bulletin* Jan. 1988: 15.
Williams, Jeannie. *USA Today* 13 Apr. 1987.

The Glass Menagerie. Washington, DC: Arena Stage Kreeger
Theater, fall 1989. Tazewell Thompson, dir. Loy
Arcenas, Nancy Schertler, design. With Jonathan Earl
Peck (Tom), Ruby Dee (Amanda), Tonia Rowe (Laura), Ken
LaRon (Jim). Reviews:
    Tennessee Williams Literary Journal 1.2 (Winter 1989-
        90): 67. [Also see below]
    Burns, Morris U. *Theatre Review* 42 (May 1990): 267-69.
    Winer, Laurie. *New York Times* 16 Oct. 1989: 25.

Other Productions:
    American Theater Mar. 1991: 17. [Princeton McCarter
        Theater with Shirley Knight as Amanda]
    New York Herald Tribune 3 Dec. 1965: 2. [Japanese TV
        with Helen Hayes]
    New York Times 21 Sept. 1962: 35. [Canceled rights to
        prods.]
    Tennessee Williams Literary Journal 1.1 (Spring 1989):
        79. [Cleveland with Ruby Dee as Amanda]
    USA Today 19 Aug. 1985, sec. D: 2. [Chautauqua, NY,
        with Tom Hulce, Melissa Gilbert]
    Variety 8 Mar. 1950: 60. [Dublin]
    Beaufort, John. *Christian Science Monitor* 18 Sept.
        1950: 4. [Theatre Guild on the Air with Helen
        Hayes]
    Brady, Owen E. *Tennessee Williams Newsletter* 2.2 (Fall
        1980): 36-39. [Guthrie Touring Company]
    Evans, Everett. *Houston Cronicle* 22 Feb. 1987: 34.
        [Houston]
    Gelb, Arthur. *New York Times* 15 Dec. 1957, sec. 2: 3.
        [Off-Broadway]
    Gussow, Mel. *New York Times* 6 Nov. 1980, sec. C: 16.
        [Off-Broadway with Julie Haydon as Amanda]
    ---. *New York Times* 21 Jan. 1991, sec. B: 1.
        [Princeton McCarter Theater with Shirley Knight]
    Hewes, Henry. *Saturday Review* 25 Nov. 1967: 71. [New
        Haven with Mildred Dunnock]

Klein, Reva. *Times Educational Supplement* 10 Mar.
    1989: 18. [Young Vic Touring Company]
Lahr, John. *Guardian* 2 Feb. 1988: 11. [Peter Hall
    prod.]
Lambert, J. W. *Sunday Times* (London) 23 Mar. 1958: 11.
    [Stratford-on-Avon]
Marowitz, Charles. *Plays and Players* Sept. 1977: 26-
    27. [London]
Martin, Jeffrey B. *Tennessee Williams Review* 3.1
    (1981): 12-13. [Durham, NH]
Rice, Vernon. *New York Post* 18 July 1949: 25. [With
    Helen Hayes]
Shaland, Irene. *Theatre Review* 42 (Mar. 1990): 121-23.
    [Cleveland Playhouse, Apr. 1989]
Taylor, John Russell. *Drama* Apr. 1980: 47. [London
    with Gloria Grahame]
Tromley, F. B. *Journal of Canadian Studies* 20.4 (Win-
    ter 1985-86): 145-56. [Stratford, Ont.]
Voelker, Paul D. *Tennessee Williams Newsletter* 2.1
    (Spring 1980): 36-39. [Minneapolis, 1979]
Wilkinson, J. Norman. *Tennessee Williams Newsletter*
    2.2 (Fall 1980): 40-43. [Durham, NH]
Winer, Laurie. *New York Times* 16 Oct. 1989: 25.
    [Washington with Ruby Dee]
Yeaton, Kelly. *Players* 26 (May 1950): 180-82. [Penn-
    sylvania State Univ. Arena]
Young, Michael C. *Tennessee Williams Newsletter* 2.2
    (Fall 1980): 29-31. [Scranton, PA]

**"THE GNÄDIGES FRÄULEIN"/*THE LATTER DAYS OF A CELEBRATED SOU-
BRETTE*:** Comedy of the absurd about an aging, wounded
artist trying to cope on Cocaloony Key. Mss., California-Los Angeles, Columbia, Delaware, Harvard, Texas (G).
    With "The Mutilated" the play was produced under the
collective title *Slapstick Tragedy*. The Broadway opening
essay was "The Wolf and I" (D 1). More interesting is
the Preface to the 1965 publication. There are textual
variations between the 1965 and 1967 texts. Williams
expanded "Fräulein" into an unpublished work, *The Latter
Days of a Celebrated Soubrette*, produced 1974.

Slapstick Tragedy: Two Plays. Esquire 64 (Aug. 1965):
    95-102, 130-34. Contents: Preface, 95; "The Muti-
    lated," 96-101; "The Gnädiges Fräulein," 102, 130-34.

The Gnädiges Fräulein...: A Play in One Act. New York:
    Dramatists Play Service, 1967. 37 pp. Il. Contents:
    Production Notes, 4; play, 5-35.

Dragon Country, 1969: 215-62 (A 2).

Theatre, Vol. 7, 1981: 215-62 (A 2).

Trans. (H): Spanish.

Criticism

Debusscher, Gilbert. *"The Gnädiges Fräulein*: Williams's
Self-Portrait among the Ruins." *New Essays in American
Drama*. Ed. Gilbert Debusscher and Henry I. Schvey.
Amsterdam: Rodopi, 1989. 63-74.

Ishida, Akira. [Tennessee Williams' *Slapstick Tragedy*.
Annual Report of Studies] (Kyoto, Japan) 20 (1969):
439-65.

Productions

Slapstick Tragedy. New York: Longacre Theatre, 22-26
Feb. 1966 (première: 7). Alan Schneider, dir. Ming Cho
Lee, Noel Taylor, Martin Aronstein, design. Lee Hoiby,
music. With Margaret Leighton (Fräulein), Zoe Caldwell
(Polly), Kate Reid (Molly). Reviews, Prod. Notes:
    Time 4 Mar. 1966: 88.
    Times (London) 7 Mar. 1966: 9.
    Variety 2 Mar. 1966: 56.
    Bolton, Whitney. *New York Morning Telegraph* 24 Feb.
        1966: 3.
    Brustein, Robert. *New Republic* 26 Mar. 1966: 34-35.
        Rpt. *The Third Theatre* (New York: Knopf, 1969): 98-
        100.
    Callaghan, Barry. *Tamarack Review* 39 (Spring 1966):
        52-58.
    Clurman, Harold. *Nation* 202 (14 Mar. 1966): 309. Rpt.
        Stanton (A 3): 71-73.
    Gilman, Richard. *Newsweek* 7 Mar. 1966: 90. Rpt. *Com-
        mon and Uncommon Modes* (New York: Random House,
        1971): 150-51.
    Hardwick, Elizabeth. *New York Review of Books* 28 Apr.
        1966: 8-9.
    Hewes, Henry. *Saturday Review* 12 Mar. 1966: 28. Rpt.
        Leavitt (F 1): 145.
    Kauffmann, Stanley. *New York Times* 23 Feb. 1966: 42.
        Rpt. *Persons of the Drama* (New York: Harper, 1976):
        165-68; *New York Theatre Critics' Reviews* 1966: 361-
        62; *New York Times Theatre Reviews*. Correction:
        New York Times 26 Feb. 1966: 15.
    ---. *New York Times* 6 Mar. 1966, sec. 2: 1. Rpt. *New
        York Times Theatre Reviews*.
    Kerr, Walter. *New York Herald Tribune* 23 Feb. 1966:
        18. Rpt. *New York Theatre Critics' Reviews* 1966:
        359.

McCarten, John. *New Yorker* 5 Mar. 1966: 83-84.
McClain, John. *New York Journal-American* 23 Feb. 1966:
    17. Rpt. *New York Theatre Critics' Reviews* 1966:
    360; Van Antwerp (F 1): 242-43.
Nadel, Norman. *New York World-Telegram* 23 Feb. 1966:
    30. Rpt. *New York Theatre Critics' Reviews* 1966:
    362.
Sheed, Wilfred. *Commonweal* 84 (8 Apr. 1966): 82.
Smith, Michael. *Village Voice* 3 Mar. 1966: 19.
Watt, Douglas. *New York Daily News* 23 Feb. 1966. Rpt.
    New York Theatre Critics' Reviews 1966: 361.
Watts, Richard Jr. *New York Post* 23 Feb. 1966. Rpt.
    New York Theatre Critics' Reviews 1966: 360.
Weales, Gerald *Reporter* 24 Mar. 1966: 49-50.
West, Anthony. *Vogue* 1 Apr. 1966: 109.
Zolotow, Sam. *New York Times* 27 Nov. 1963: 33.
    [Plans]
---. *New York Times* 6 Oct. 1964: 34. [Plans]
---. *New York Times* 17 Feb. 1966: 29.

The Latter Days of a Celebrated Soubrette. New York:
Central Arts Cabaret Theatre, 16 May 1974 (première).
Luis Lopez-Cepero, dir. With Anne Meacham (Fräulein),
Robert Frink (Molly), William Pritz (Polly). Reviews:
    Gussow, Mel. *New York Times* 29 May 1974: 48.
    Novick, Julius. *Village Voice* 30 May 1974: 73.

"HEADLINES": Unpublished plea for pacifism, prepared 1936
as a curtain raiser for Irwin Shaw's *Bury the Dead.*

"Headlines." Mummers. St. Louis: Wednesday Club Auditorium, 11, 13, 14 Nov. 1936 (première). Willard H. Holland, dir. Program: Van Antwerp (F 1): 32.

"HELLO FROM BERTHA": Drama about a washed-out prostitute in
East St. Louis. Ms., Texas (G).

27 Wagons Full of Cotton, 1945, 1953: 181-93 (A 2).

27 Wagons Full of Cotton, 1949: 169-80 (A 2).

The Disinherited: Plays. Ed. Abe C. Ravitz. Encino, CA:
    Dickensen, 1974.

Theatre, Vol. 6, 1981: 229-44 (A 2).

Trans. (H): Greek, Italian, Norwegian.

Productions

Four by Tennessee. Play of the Week. PBS-TV, 6 Feb.
1961. With Maureen Stapleton (Bertha), Eileen Heckart
(Goldie), Salome Jens (Lena). Review:
    Shanley, John P. *New York Times* 7 Feb. 1961: 67.

"Hello from Bertha." Boston Conservatory, 8 Nov. 1989.
Julia Howard, dir. With Terry Merrill, Jennifer Fisk,
Amy Langer. Videocassette.

Other Productions:
    Theatre Arts Nov. 1956: 66. [New York]
    Times (London) 14 Sept. 1961: 16. [Dublin]

"HOT MILK AT THREE IN THE MORNING": see "Moony's Kid Don't
Cry"

A HOUSE NOT MEANT TO STAND/**"SOME PROBLEMS FOR THE MOOSE
LODGE"**: Unpublished autobiographical drama about the
dissolution of a Mississippi family. Ms., Columbia, New
York Public (G).
    The play began as the one act "Some Problems for the
Moose Lodge," produced 1980. Gary Moser urged Williams
to expand it into a full-length work, *A House Not Meant
to Stand*, first produced 1981 and revised 1982. It was
Williams's last new text to be produced in his lifetime.

Tennessee Laughs: Three 1-Act Plays. Chicago: Goodman
Theatre, 8-23 Nov. 1980 (première). Gary Tucker, dir.
With Les Podewell (Cornelius), Marji Bank (Bella), Scott
Jaeck (Charlie), Rachel Stephens (Jessie). See "Frosted
Glass Coffin."

A House Not Meant to Stand. Chicago: Goodman Theatre, 1
Apr. 1981 (première). Gary Tucker, dir. Joseph Nie-
minski, Ellen Ryba, Robert Christen, design. With George
Womach (Cornelius), Marji Bank (Bella), Scott Jaeck
(Charlie), Rachel Stephens (Jessie). Reviews:
    Variety 18 Mar. 1981: 311.
    Variety 13 May 1981: 410.
    Christiansen, Richard. *Chicago Tribune* 3 Apr. 1981,
        sec. 2: 3
    Syse, Glenna. *Chicago Sun-Times* 2 Apr. 1981: 80.

A House Not Meant to Stand. Chicago: Goodman Theatre,
16 Apr.-23 May 1982 (41). Andre Ernotte, dir. Karen

Schulz, Christa Scholtz, Rachel Budin, design. With
Frank Hamilton (Cornelius), Peg Murray (Bella), Scott
Jaeck (Charlie), Scotty Bloch (Jessie). Reviews, Prod.
Notes:
>Christiansen, Richard. *Chicago Tribune* 28 Apr. 1982,
>   sec. 3: 12. Rpt. Van Antwerp (F 1): 381-82.
>---. *Chicago Tribune Arts & Books* 9 May 1982: 5-6.
>   Rpt. Van Antwerp (F 1): 382-86.
>Karlson, Albert E. *Theatre Journal* 34 (Dec. 1982):
>   539-41.
>Scott, Stephen B., and Timothy Stevenson, eds. *Tennes-*
>   *see Williams' A House Not Meant to Stand.* The Good-
>   man Theatre Guide. [Chicago: Goodman Theatre,
>   1982.]

Other Productions:
>Clarke, Gerald, and Marilyn Alva. *Time* 28 June 1982.
>   [Miami]

"I CAN'T IMAGINE TOMORROW": Drama about two people living
in Dragon Country, unable to connect with each other or
with the rest of the world.
  Textual variations exist between the 1966 and the 1969
texts, including the cutting of several speeches.

Esquire 65 (Mar. 1966): 76-79.

Dragon Country, 1969: 131-50 (A 2).

The Best Short Plays 1971. Margaret Mayorga Series. Ed.
    Stanley Richards. Philadelphia: Chilton, 1971. 75-95.

Theatre, Vol. 7, 1981: 131-50 (A 2).

Trans. (H): Spanish.

Criticism

Phillips, Jerrold A. "Imagining *I Can't Imagine Tomor-*
    row." *Tennessee Williams Review* 3.2 (1982): 27-29.

Productions

I Can't Imagine Tomorrow. PBS-TV, 3 Dec. 1970 (premiere). Glenn Jordan, dir. With Kim Stanley (One), William Redfield (Two). Review:
>Gould, Jack. *New York Times* 4 Dec. 1970: 95.

Ten by Tennessee. New York: Lucille Lortel Theatre, 11
May–29 June 1986. Michael Kahn, dir. With Mary Lou
Rosato (One), Randle Mell (Two). See "Auto-da-Fé."

"I RISE IN FLAME, CRIED THE PHOENIX: A PLAY ABOUT D. H.
LAWRENCE": Drama about Lawrence's final days in Vence,
France. Ms., Texas (G).
   The play was written 1941 after a visit with Frieda
Lawrence at Taos. Williams later inexplicably marred one
of his finest works by substituting a sentimental ending
for his original realistic view of human nature. He also
translated the German scattered through Frieda's
speeches. According to George Miller (I: Gunn) this
revision was published in 1952. Thomas J. Flanagan
created an opera, 1980.

Publication: Original Version

*I Rise in Flame, Cried the Phoenix: A Play about D. H.
   Lawrence*...with a Note by Frieda Lawrence. Norfolk,
   CT: James Laughlin, 1951. 42 pp. Contents: A Preface
   by the Author, 5–6; A Note by Frieda Lawrence, 7–8;
   play, 9–42. Limited edition.

New World Writing: First Mentor Selection. New York: New
   American Library, 1952. 46–67.

Ramparts Jan. 1968: 14–19.

Publication: Revised Version

I Rise in Flame, Cried the Phoenix: Acting Edition: A
   Play in One Act about D. H. Lawrence. New York: Dramatists Play Service, n.d. 19 pp. Contents: Note, 3;
   play, 5–18.

Dragon Country, 1969: 55–75 (A 2).

Theatre, Vol. 7, 1981: 55–75 (A 2).

Trans. (H): Czech, French, Italian, Slovene, Spanish
   (version uncertain).

Productions: Play

Two Short Plays. New York: Theatre de Lys, 14 Apr. 1959.
Tom Brennan, dir. With Alfred Ryder (Lawrence), Viveca
Lindfors (Frieda), Nan Martin (Brett). Reviews:
   Village Voice 22 Apr. 1959: 7.

Calta, Louis. *New York Times* 15 Apr. 1959: 30. Rpt.
New York Times Theatre Reviews.
Hewes, Henry. *Saturday Review* 25 Apr. 1959: 23.

Four by Tennessee. Play of the Week. PBS-TV, 6 Feb.
1961. With Alfred Ryder (Lawrence), Jo Van Fleet
(Frieda). See "Hello from Bertha."

Production: Opera

"I Rise in Flame, Cried the Phoenix." Opera by Thomas J.
Flanagan. Golden Fleece. New York: 7 Feb. 1980 (pre-
miere). John Klingberg, accomp. With John Jellison
(Lawrence), Lucille Sullam (Frieda), Sally Ann Sward
(Bertha). Review:
Hughes, Allen. *New York Times* 9 Feb. 1980: 45.

"THE IMPORTANT THING": see B 1

IN THE BAR OF A TOKYO HOTEL: Drama written 1960-69 about
the final, frenzied visions of a painter and the schemes
of his rapacious wife in Tokyo. Mss., Columbia, Congress, New York Public (G).
    The pre-opening essay was "Tennessee, Never Talk to an
Actress" (D 1). Williams wrote an interesting letter to
his cast, "Tennessee Williams Talks about His Play" (D
3).

In the Bar of a Tokyo Hotel. New York: Dramatists Play
    Service, 1969. 45 pp. Il. Contents: play, 5-40.

Dragon Country, 1969: 1-53 (A 2).

Theatre, Vol. 7, 1981: 1-53 (A 2).

Trans. (H): French, German, Spanish.

Productions

In the Bar of a Tokyo Hotel. New York: Eastside Play-
house, 11 May-1 June 1969 (première: 45, inc. previews).
Herbert Machiz, dir. Neil Peter Jampolis, Stanley Sim-
mons, Hayward Morris, design. With Anne Meacham (Mir-
iam), Donald Madden (Mark), Jon Lee (Barman), Lester Raw-
lins (Leonard). Reviews, Prod. Notes:
New York Times 28 May 1969: 34. [Closing]
Time 23 May 1969: 75.
Barnes, Clive. *New York Times* 12 May 1969: 54. Rpt.
New York Times Theatre Reviews.

Clurman, Harold. *Nation* 208 (2 June 1969): 709-10.
Hewes, Henry. *Saturday Review* 31 May 1969: 18.
Kanfer, Stefan. *Life* 13 June 1969: 10. Rpt. as ad:
  New York Times 10 June 1969: 96. Response: *New York
  Times* 22 June 1969, sec. 2: 11; *Variety* 23 July
  1969: 67 (Audrey Wood).
Kerr, Walter. *New York Times* 25 May 1969, sec. 2: 5.
  Rpt. *New York Times Theatre Reviews*.
Kroll, Jack. *Newsweek* 26 May 1969: 133.
Watts, Richard Jr. *New York Post* 31 May 1969: 17.
  Rpt. Van Antwerp (F 1): 255-56.

In the Bar of a Tokyo Hotel. New York: Jean Cocteau Rep-
ertory Theatre, 20 Apr.-10 June 1979. Eve Adamson, dir.
James S. Payne, Charles Elliott, Karla Barker, Andy Mac-
Cracken, design. With Amy K. Posner (Miriam), Harris
Berlinsky (Mark), Andy MacCracken (Barman), Craig Smith
(Leonard). Review:
  Stanton, Stephen S. *Tennessee Williams Newsletter* 2.2
  (Fall 1979): 24, 29, 31.

KINGDOM OF EARTH: Black comedy about two half-brothers in a
contest over a woman and Mississippi property. Mss.,
Columbia, Congress, Texas (G).
  The play grew out of a short story "The Kingdom of
Earth" (B 1). Its 1966 publication in a general collection of his stories must have stimulated Williams's imagination, for 1967 he published "Kingdom of Earth: A One
Act Play" that sketched in the plot of the full-length
work. The 1968 and 1969 texts are essentially the same,
with a few speeches reworked or shuffled. The play was
produced under the title of *The Seven Descents of Myrtle*
and quickly closed. The pre-opening essay was entitled
"Happiness Is Relevant" (D 1). In an attempt to win a
new production Williams drastically cut the script. This
version was printed, 1976; the editing has left a few in-
consistencies.
  Gore Vidal prepared the 1969 unpublished screenplay, a
very loose adaptation of the 1968-69 versions; the film
was released in the United States as *Last of the Mobile
Hot-Shots* and abroad as *Blood Kin*.

Publication: One-Act Version

"Kingdom of Earth." *Esquire* 67 (Feb. 1967): 98-100, 132-
  34.

Publication: First Expanded Versions

Kingdom of Earth (The Seven Descents of Myrtle).   New
York: New Directions, 1968.   vi, 111 pp.   Contents:
play, 1-111.   On spine: *The Kingdom of Earth*.   Reviews:
 Choice 6 (July 1969): 667.
 Willers, A. C.   *Library Journal* 94 (15 Feb. 1969):
 775.

Kingdom of Earth (The Seven Descents of Myrtle)...: A
Play in Seven Scenes.   New York: Dramatists Play Serv-
ice, 1969.   87 pp.   Il.   Contents: A Note on the Song
Excerpts Included in the Play, 3-4; play, 7-81.

Publication: Revised Version

Theatre, Vol. 5, 1976: 121-214 (A 2).

Kingdom of Earth (The Seven Descents of Myrtle).   New
York: Dramatists Play Service, n.d.   102 pp.   Contents:
play, 7-96.

Trans. (H): Czech, French, German, Russian, Slovak.

Criticism

Adler, Thomas P.   "Two Plays for Puritans."   *Tennessee
Williams Newsletter* 1.1 (Spring 1979): 5-7.   [*Desire
under the Elms*]

Clinton, Craig D.   "Tennessee Williams's *Kingdom of
Earth*: The Orpheus Myth Revisited."   *Theatre Annual* 33
(1977): 25-37.

Derounian, Kathryn Zabelle.   "'Kingdom of Earth' and
Kingdom of Earth (The Seven Descents of Myrtle): Ten-
nessee Williams' Parody."   *University of Mississippi
Studies in English* 4 (1983): 150-58.

Hirsch, Foster.   "Sexual Imagery in Tennessee Williams'
Kingdom of Earth."   *Notes on Contemporary Literature*
1.2 (1971): 10-13.

Kalson, Albert E.   "Tennessee Williams' *Kingdom of Earth*:
A Sterile Promontory."   *Drama and Theatre* (Purdue) 8
(Winter 1969-70): 90-93.

Phillips, Jerrold A.   "*Kingdom of Earth*: Some Approaches."   Tharpe (A 3): 349-53.

Productions

The Seven Descents of Myrtle. Preview: Philadelphia.
New York: Ethel Barrymore Theatre, 27 Mar.-20 April 1968
(première: 29). José Quintero, dir. Jo Mielziner, Jane
Greenwood, design. With Estelle Parsons (Myrtle), Harry
Guardino (Chicken), Brian Bedford (Lot). Playbill:
Leavitt (F 1): 139. Reviews, Prod. Notes:
   New York Times 21 Feb. 1968: 61. [Title change]
   Time 5 Apr. 1968: 72.
   Variety 13 Mar. 1968: 68.
   Variety 2 Apr. 1968: 72.
   Village Voice 4 Apr. 1968: 42.
   Barnes, Clive. *New York Times* 28 Mar. 1968: 54. Rpt.
      *New York Times Theatre Reviews; New York Theatre
      Critics' Reviews* 29: 313.
   Bruce, Alan N. *Christian Science Monitor* 9 Apr. 1968:
      6.
   Chapman, John. *New York Daily News* 28 Mar. 1968, sec.
      5: 3. Rpt. *New York Theatre Critics' Reviews* 29:
      313.
   Clurman, Harold. *Nation* 206 (15 Apr. 1968): 516-17.
   Cooke, Richard F. *Wall Street Journal* 29 Mar. 1968.
      Rpt. *New York Theatre Critics' Reviews* 29: 315.
   Gill, Brendan. *New Yorker* 6 Apr. 1968: 109-10.
   Hewes, Henry. *Saturday Review* 13 Apr. 1968: 30.
   Howell, Chauncey. *Women's Wear Daily* 28 Mar. 1968.
      Rpt. *New York Theatre Critics' Reviews* 29: 316.
   Kerr, Walter. *New York Times* 7 Apr. 1968, sec. 2: 1,
      3. Rpt. *New York Times Theatre Reviews; Thirty
      Plays Hath November...* (New York: Simon, 1968): 224-
      30.
   Kroll, Jack. *Newsweek* 8 Apr. 1968: 131.
   Sheed, Wilfred. *Life* 26 Apr. 1968: 18.
   Simon, John. *Commonweal* 88 (3 May 1968): 208-09.
   ---. *Hudson Review* 21 (July 1968): 322-24.
   Watts, Richard Jr. *New York Post* 28 Mar. 1968: 67.
      Rpt. *New York Theatre Critics' Reviews* 29: 316; Van
      Antwerp (F 1): 249-50.
   Zolotow, Sam. *New York Times* 11 July 1967: 29.
   ---. *New York Times* 25 Jan. 1968: 33.
   ---. *New York Times* 21 Feb. 1968: 61. [Quintero's
      walkout]
   ---. *New York Times* 29 Feb. 1968: 30. [Quintero's
      return]

Last of the Mobile Hot Shots. Screenplay by Gore Vidal.
Warner Brothers/Seven Arts, 17 Dec. 1969 (première).
Sidney Lumet, dir. James Wong Howe, camera. Quincy
Jones, music. With Lynn Redgrave (Myrtle), Robert Hooks
(Chicken), James Coburn (Jeb). Reviews, Prod. Notes:

New York Times 8 Dec. 1967. [Film rights]
Newsweek 2 June 1969: 61. [Casting]
Time 19 Jan. 1970: 67.
Variety 31 Dec. 1969: 6.
Canby, Vincent. *New York Times* 15 Jan. 1970: 38.
Oberbeck, S. K. *Newsweek* 26 Jan. 1970: 75.
Reed, Rex. *Holiday* Mar. 1970: 37.
---. *New York Times* 8 June 1969, sec. 2: 15, 17.
   [Filming]

Kingdom of Earth. McCarter Theatre Company. Princeton,
NJ: 6 Mar. 1975 (première). Garland Wright, dir. Paul
Zalon, David James, Marc B. Weiss, design. With Marilyn
Chris (Myrtle), David Pendleton (Chicken), Courtney Burr
(Lot). Review:
   Barnes, Clive. *New York Times* 12 Mar. 1975: 28.

Kingdom of Earth. Bristol Old Vic Company. London: New
Vic, 14 Feb. 1978. Mike Newell, dir. John Elvery, de-
sign. With Gillian Borge (Myrtle), Peter Postlethwaite
(Chicken), Jonathan Kent (Lot). Review:
   Anderson, Michael. *Plays and Players* Apr. 1978: 39.

Kingdom of Earth. London: Hampstead, 17 Apr.-26 May
1984. Kenneth MacMillan, dir. Laurie Dennett, John B.
Read, John A. Leonard, design. With Nichola McAuliffe
(Myrtle), Stephen Rea (Chicken), David Taylor (Lot).
Reviews:
   Billington, Michael. *Guardian* 28 May 1984. Rpt.
      London Theatre Record 4: 350.
   Gordon, Giles. *Spectator* 5 May 1984. Rpt. *London
      Theatre Record* 4: 356.
   Hirschhorn, Clive. *London Sunday Express* 6 May 1984.
      Rpt. *London Theatre Record* 4: 355.
   Hurren, Kenneth. *London Mail on Sunday* 6 May 1984.
      Rpt. *London Theatre Record* 4: 355.
   King, Francis. *London Sunday Telegraph* 6 May 1984.
      Rpt. *London Theatre Record* 4: 350, 355.
   Radin, Victoria. *London Observer* 6 May 1984. Rpt.
      London Theatre Record 4: 350.
   Shalman, Milton. *London Standard* 2 May 1984. Rpt.
      London Theatre Record 4: 355.
   Tinker, Jack. *London Daily Mail* 10 May 1984. Rpt.
      London Theatre Record 4: 350.
   Todd, Susan. *New Statesman* 4 May 1984: 32. Rpt. *Lon-
      don Theatre Record* 4: 350.
   Vosburgh, Dick. *Punch* 9 May 1984. Rpt. *London Theatre
      Record* 4: 356.

Other Productions:
   Galligan, David. *Advocate* 8 Jan. 1985: 36.   [Theatre
   West]

KIRCHE, KUTCHEN, UND KINDER: Unpublished black comedy about
a New York hustler and his family.   Ms., Delaware (G).
The spelling is Williams's.

   Kirche, Kutchen, und Kinder.   New York: Jean Cocteau Rep-
   ertory Theatre, Sept. 1979 (première).   Eve Adamson, dir.
   With Craig Smith (Man), Phyllis Deitschel (Hausfrau),
   Coral S. Potter (Lutheran Minister), Harris Berlinsky
   (Fraulein).   Reviews, Prod. Notes:
      New York Daily News 25 Dec. 1979: 13.
      New York Times 16 Sept. 1979, sec. D: 7.
      Hornak, Richard Wray. *Tennessee Williams Newsletter*
         2.1 (Spring 1980): 33-35.
      Patterson, John S. *Villager* 20 Sept. 1979: 13.

"THE LADY OF LARKSPUR LOTION":   Drama about two dreamers in
New Orleans.   Ms., Texas (G).
   The setting and the character of the landlady were used
again in *Vieux Carre* (A 1 below).

   The Best One-Act Plays of 1941.   Ed. Margaret Mayorga.
   New York: Dodd, Mead, 1942.   121-32.

   27 Wagons Full of Cotton, 1945, 1953: 63-72 (A 2).

   27 Wagons Full of Cotton, 1949: 65-72 (A 2).

   Theatre, Vol 6, 1981: 79-89 (A 2).

   Trans. (H):   German (inc. film *Bourbon Street Blues*),
   Greek, Italian, Norwegian.

Criticism

Gerigk, H.-J.   "Tennessee Williams und Anton Cechov."
   Zeitschrift fur Slavische Philogie 39 (1976): 157-65.

Productions

The Lady of Larkspur Lotion.   American Club Theatre.
Paris: Monceau Theatre, 8 July 1949.   George Voskovec,
dir.   Review:
   New York Times 9 July 1949: 9.   Rpt. *New York Times*
   Theatre Reviews.

Four by Tennessee. Play of the Week. PBS-TV, 6 Feb.
1961. With Jo Van Fleet (Mrs. Harwicke-Moore). See
"Hello from Bertha."

"The Lady of Larkspur Lotion." London: Carnaby Street
Theatre, Jan. 1976. See "Demolition Downtown."

Ten by Tennessee. New York: Lucille Lortel Theatre, 11
May-15 June 1986. Michael Kahn, dir. With Mary Lou
Rosato (Mrs. Hardwicke-Moore), Randle Mell (Writer), Lisa
Banes (Mrs. Wire). See "Auto-da-Fé."

Other Productions:
   Lipton, Victor. *Show Business* 25 Oct. 1973. [New
   York]

LANDSCAPE WITH FIGURES: see "At Liberty" and "This Property
Is Condemned"

"THE LAST OF MY SOLID GOLD WATCHES": Drama about a fading
Mississippi salesman. Ms., Columbia, Texas (G).

The Best One-Act Plays of 1942. Ed. Margaret Mayorga.
   New York: Dodd, Mead, 1942. 1-15.

27 Wagons Full of Cotton, 1945, 1953: 73-85 (A 2).

27 Wagons Full of Cotton, 1949: 73-84 (A 2).

Theatre, Vol. 6, 1981: 91-105 (A 2).

Trans. (H): German.

Inclusion in Textbooks

Burgess, Charles Ower, ed. *Drama: Literature on Stage.*
   Philadelphia: Lippincott, 1969.

Mansfield, Roger, ed. *The Playmakers: One.* Hudders-
   field: Schofield, 1976.

Productions

4 Short Plays. Actors' Lab. Los Angeles: Las Palmas
Theatre, 13 Jan. 1947. Joks Dassin, dir. With Vincent
Price (Charlie). Playbill: Van Antwerp (F 1): 78.
Review:
   Oliver, W. E. *Los Angeles Herald-Express* 16 Jan. 1947,
   sec. B: 6. Rpt. Van Antwerp (F 1): 77-79.

Trilogy of One Act Plays. Theatre '47. Dallas: Gulf Oil
Playhouse, Sept. 1947. Margo Jones, dir. With Vaughan
Gloser (Charlie), Tod Andrews (Bob). Reviews, Prod.
Notes:
    Jones, Margo. *Theatre-in-the-Round.* New York: McGraw-
        Hill, 1965. 149-50.
    Rosenfield, John. *Dallas Morning News* 23 Sept. 1947.

Three by Tennessee. Kraft Television Theatre. NBC-TV,
16 Apr. 1958. Sidney Lumet, dir. With Thomas Chambers
(Charlie), Gene Saks (Bob). Reviews:
    Coppola, Jo. *New York Post* 17 Apr. 1958: 30.
    Gould, Jack. *New York Times* 17 Apr. 1958: 63.

LAST OF THE MOBILE HOT-SHOTS: see *Kingdom of Earth*

THE LATTER DAYS OF A CELEBRATED SOUBRETTE: see "The
Gnadiges Fraulein"

"LIFEBOAT DRILL": Black comedy, set on a cruise ship, about
an old couple's problems with life.

Theatre, Vol. 7, 1981: 279-96 (A 2).

Production

The Invitational. New York: Ensemble Studio Theatre, 14
Nov.-30 Dec. 1979 (première). Curt Dempster, dir. Brian
Martin, Marie Louise Moreto, Madeline Cohen, Marcia L.
Whitney, design. With John Wardwell (Mr. Taske), B. Con-
stance Barry (Mrs. Taske). Review:
    Gill, Brendan. *New Yorker* 14 Dec. 1979: 72-73.

"THE LONG GOODBYE": Dream play set in a Midwestern city
about a man's memories of his fallen sister. Ms., Texas
(G).

27 Wagons Full of Cotton, 1945, 1953: 159-79 (A 2).

27 Wagons Full of Cotton, 1949: 149-67 (A 2).

Theatre, Vol. 6, 1981: 201-27 (A 2).

Trans. (H): Arabic, German, Greek, Italian, Norwegian.

Inclusion in Textbooks

Bain, Carl E., et al., eds. *The Norton Introduction to
    Literature.* 2nd ed. New York: Norton, 1977. 1235-47.

Hogins, James Burl, ed. *Literature.* 3rd ed. Chicago:
    SRA, 1984. 701-15.

Productions

"The Long Goodbye." New York: New School for Social Research, 9, 10, 14 Feb. 1940 (première). Note:
    Daily Worker 10 Feb. 1940: 7.

Two One-Act Plays. Nantucket, MA: Straight Wharf Theatre, 1-3 Sept. 1946. Albert Penalosa, dir. With Sam
Holmes (Joe), Albert Penalosa (Silva), Rita Gam (Myra).
Program: Leavitt (F 1): 69; playbill: Van Antwerp (F 1):
77.

Ten by Tennessee. New York: Lucille Lortel Theatre, 11
May-15 June 1986. Michael Kahn, dir. With Randle Mell
(Joe), Derek D. Smith (Silva), Lisa Banes (Myra). See
"Auto-da-Fé."

"THE LONG STAY CUT SHORT":   see "The Unsatisfactory Supper"

"LORD BYRON'S LOVE LETTER": Drama about one of Byron's
aging lovers, now living in New Orleans. Ms, Texas (G).
Raffaello de Banfield composed the 1955 opera to a libretto by Williams.

Publication: Play

27 Wagons Full of Cotton, 1945, 1953: 121-32 (A 2).

27 Wagons Full of Cotton, 1949: 115-26 (A 2).

English One-Act Plays of Today. Ed. Donald Fitzjohn.
New York/London: Oxford Univ. Pr., 1962.

The Best American One-Act Plays. Ed. Kazua Ogawa and
Tatsumi Funatsu. Tokyo: Kaibunsha, 1964. 1-16.

The Mentor Book of Short Plays. Ed. Richard H. Goldstone
and Abraham H. Lass. New York: New American Library,
1969.

Theatre, Vol. 6, 1981: 153-67.

Trans. (H):   Czech, Greek, Italian.

Production: Play

"Lord Byron's Love Letter." Omnibus, CBS-TV, 30 Mar.
1953. Andrew McCullough, dir. Henry May, design. With
Ethel Barrymore, Patricia Collinge, Nydia Westman, John
C. Becher.

Publication: Opera

Lord Byron's Love Letter: Opera in One Act by Raffaello
de Banfield; Libretto by Tennessee Williams. New York:
Ricordi, 1955. 16 pp. Contents: Foreword, 2; libretto, 3-16.

Trans. (H):   Italian.

Productions: Opera

"Lord Byron's Love Letter." New Orleans Opera Guild.
New Orleans: Dixon Hall (Tulane Univ.), 17 Jan. 1955
(première). Nicola Rescigno, cond. With Patricia Neway
(Grandmother), Gertrude Ribla (Spinster). Program:
Leavitt (F 1). Reviews, Prod. Notes:
   New Orleans Times-Picayune 8 Dec. 1954: 62. [Composi-
      tion]
   New Orleans Times-Picayune 16 Jan. 1955, sec. 2: 9.
   Newsweek 31 Jan. 1955: 81.
   Atkinson, Brooks, and Ewing Poteet. *New York Times* 19
      Jan. 1955: 23. Rpt. *New York Times Theatre Reviews*.
   Loeb, Harry B. *Musical America* 1 Feb. 1955: 33.

"Lord Byron's Love Letter." Chicago: Lyric Theatre, 21
Nov. 1955. Nicola Rescigno, cond. Gerald Ritholz, de-
sign. With Astrid Varney (Grandmother), Gertrude Ribla
(Spinster). Review:
   Talley, Howard. *Musical America* 15 Dec. 1955: 7.

Lord Byron's Love Letter. RCA Victor, 1958. Nicola Rescigno, cond. With Astrid Varney (Grandmother), Gertrude
Ribla (Spinster). [Recorded in Rome 1956]

"Lord Byron's Love Letter." Spoleto USA Festival. Charleston, SC: Dock Street Theatre, May 1986.

THE LOSS OF A TEARDROP DIAMOND: Drama of a wealthy pariah's
search for love and her encounter with a poor young man,
set in Memphis and nearby Mississippi in the 1920s. Ms.,
Delaware (G).

A. H. Weiler (*New York Times* 28 July 1957, sec. 2: 5) reveals that Williams was working on the script then. He forgot it until the 1970s. The *Tennessee Williams Newsletter* 2.2 (Fall 1980): 6, says it was then finished.

Stopped Rocking and Other Screenplays, 1984: 95-192 (A 2).

A *LOVELY SUNDAY FOR CREVE COEUR/ALL GAUL IS DIVIDED*: Drama about the frustrations of St. Louis women trying to cope with illusions and reality during the 1920s. Ms., Columbia (G).

According to Williams's note, the screenplay, *All Gaul Is Divided*, was written late 1950s, then laid aside and forgotten until after A *Lovely Sunday for Creve Coeur*, then known simply as *Creve Coeur*, was written mid-1970s.

Publication: Screenplay

All Gaul Is Divided. Stopped Rocking and Other Screenplays, 1984: 1-93 (A 2).

Publication: Play

A *Lovely Sunday for Creve Coeur*. New York: New Directions, 1980; Toronto: George J. McLeod, 1980. x, 82 pp. Il. Contents: play, 1-82. Also New Directions Paperbook. Reviews:
> *Choice* 18 (Oct. 1980): 251.
> Witham, Barry B. *Library Journal* 105 (15 Mar. 1980); 740.

Best American Plays, Eighth Series: *1974-1982*. Ed. Clive Barnes. New York: Crown, 1983. 106-32.

Trans. (H): Slovak.

Productions

Creve Coeur. Spoleto Festival U.S.A. Charleston, SC: Dock Street Theatre, 1 June 1978 (première). Keith Hack, dir. Steve Rubin, Craig Miller, design. With Shirley Knight (Dorothea), Jan Miner (Bodey), Charlotte Moore (Helena). Reviews:
> Barnes, Clive. *New York Post* 12 June 1978: 23.
> DeVitis, A. A. *Tennessee Williams Newsletter* 1.1 (Spring 1979): 24-25.
> Ferillo, Traynor. *Charleston Evening Post* 2 June 1978, sec. B: 4.

Furtwangler, William. *Charleston News and Courier* 2
    June 1978: 1, 4.
Gussow, Mel. *New York Times* 7 June 1978, sec. C: 19.
Hamilton, Ian. *New Statesman* 96 (25 Aug. 1978): 251–
    52.
Kalem, T. E. *Time* 12 June 1978: 84.
Kalson, Albert E. *Educational Theatre Journal* 30 (Dec.
    1978): 552–53.
Simon, John. *New York* 26 June 1978: 60–61. Rpt. Van
    Antwerp (F 1): 345–47.

A *Lovely Sunday for Creve Coeur*. New York: Hudson Guild
Theatre, 17 Jan.–18 Feb. 1979 (36). Keith Hack, dir.
John Conklin, Craig Miller, Linda Fisher, design. With
Shirley Knight (Dorothea), Peg Murray (Bodey), Charlotte
Moore (Helena). Reviews:

Barnes, Clive. *New York Post* 22 Jan. 1979: 35. Rpt.
    New York Theatre Critics' Reviews 40: 338.
Beaumont, John. *Christian Science Monitor* 26 June
    1979: 18. Rpt. *New York Theatre Critics' Reviews*
    40: 339–40.
Chesley, Robert. *Advocate* 22 Mar. 1979: 40.
Clurman, Harold. *Nation* 228 (10 Feb. 1979): 156–57.
Cunningham, Dennis. CBS-TV, 21 Jan. 1979. Rpt. *New
    York Theatre Critics' Reviews* 40: 340.
Eder, Richard. *New York Times* 22 Jan. 1979, sec. C:
    15. Rpt. *New York Theatre Critics' Reviews* 40: 337–
    38.
Fox, Terry Curtis. *Village Voice* 5 Feb. 1979: 76–77.
Hughes, Catherine. *America* 140 (24 Feb. 1979): 135.
Kerr, Walter. *New York Times* 4 Feb. 1979, sec. D: 26.
Klein, Alvin. *New York Theatre Review* 3 (Mar. 1979):
    19.
Kroll, Jack. *Newsweek* 5 Feb. 1979: 68. Rpt. *New York
    Theatre Critics' Reviews* 40: 340.
Oliver, Edith. *New Yorker* 5 Feb. 1979: 99–101.
Raidy, William A. *Plays and Players* Apr. 1979: 37.
Sharp, Christopher. *Women's Wear Daily* 24 Jan. 1979.
    Rpt. *New York Theatre Critics' Reviews* 40: 339.
Tallmer, Jerry. *New York Post* 19 Jan. 1979: 38, 47.
    [Interview with Knight]
Watt, Douglas. *New York Daily News* 22 Jan. 1979: 27.
    Rpt. *New York Theatre Critics' Reviews* 40: 339.
Weales, Gerald. *Commonweal* 106 (16 Mar. 1979): 146–47.
    Rpt. Van Antwerp (F 1): 348–50.

A *Lovely Sunday for Creve Coeur*. London: Old Red Lion,
Islington, 1–19 July 1986. Sydnee Blake, dir. Alice
Prier, Gill McBride, Jennifer Cook, design. With Eliza-
beth Richardson (Dorothea), Marlene Sidaway (Bodey),
Rowan Stuart (Helena). Reviews:

Billington, Michael. *Guardian* 3 July 1986. Rpt.
  London Theatre Record 6: 695-96.
Coveney, Michael. *London Financial Times* 2 July 1986.
  Rpt. *London Theatre Record* 6: 696.
Pascal, Julia. *Jewish Chronicle* 11 July 1986. Rpt.
  London Theatre Record 6: 695.
Wolf, Matt. *Plays and Players* Sept. 1986: 39.

"THE MAGIC TOWER":   Unpublished romance about a young
married couple.

"The Magic Tower." Webster Groves Theatre Guild. Webster Groves, MO: 13 Oct. 1936 (première). David Gibson,
dir. Program: Van Antwerp (F 1): 31. Review:
  Jennings, Anne H. *Webster Groves News-Times* 16 Oct.
  1936: 1, 2. Rpt. Van Antwerp (F 1): 31-33.

"ME, VASHYA":   Drama with a vague European setting, written
1937: a love triangle between a princess, a munition
maker, and a poet. Mss., Texas, Washington (G).
   According to Dakin Williams (F 1), the play was broadcast in St. Louis about 1938.

THE MIGRANTS: see E 3

THE MILK TRAIN DOESN'T STOP HERE ANYMORE/BOOM!:   Quasi-
allegorical drama of a dying actress's final days on the
Italian coast. Mss., California-Los Angeles, Columbia,
Congress, Delaware, Texas (G).
   The play grew out of a short story "Man Bring This Up
Road" (B 1). Under way by 1959 Williams labored hard
over the script, but it met repeated failures. In earlier versions Mrs. Goforth accepts Chris Flanders; in
later versions she dies. According to Howard Taubman
(below), the 1965 version created a more humane Mrs.
Goforth and a more mystical Chris. Williams's unpublished 1967-68 screenplay was superior to the resulting
film. By 1980 Williams had finished yet another version
of the play, *Goforth*. But only one version of the play
has been published in full. Note: A very brief passage
in Scene 5 of the British editions (p. 62, 1st ed.) does
not appear in the American texts.

Publication: Early Version

The Best Plays of 1962-63.... Ed. Henry Hewes. New
  York: Dodd, Mead, 1963. 151-69. Excerpts.

Publication: Standard Versions

The Milk Train Doesn't Stop Here Anymore. New York: New
   Directions, 1964. iv, 118 pp. Contents: Author's
   Notes, 1-2; play, 3-118. Review:
     Freedley, George. *New York Morning Telegraph* 13
        July 1964: 2.

The Milk Train Doesn't Stop Here Anymore. New York: Dramatists Play Service, 1964. 90 pp.

The Milk Train Doesn't Stop Here Anymore: A Play.   London: Secker & Warburg, 1964. 94 pp. Review:
     Times Literary Supplement 29 Oct. 1964: 985.

Milk Train Doesn't Stop Here Anymore, etc., 1969 (A 2).

Cat on a Hot Tin Roof, etc. 1976: 133-224 (A 2).

Theatre, Vol. 5, 1976: 1-120.

Trans. (H): French, German.

Criticism

Debusscher, Gilbert. "French Stowaways on an American
   Milk Train: Williams, Cocteau, and Peyrefitte." *Modern
   Drama* 25 (1982): 399-408.

Heuermann, Hartmut. "Die Psychomachie im Tennessee Williams' *The Milk Train Doesn't Stop Here Anymore.*"
   Amerikastudien 19 (1974): 266-79.

McBride, Mary. "Prisoners of Illusion: Surrealistic
   Escape in *The Milk Train Doesn't Stop Here Anymore.*"
   Tharpe (A 3): 341-48.

Productions

The Milk Train Doesn't Stop Here Anymore. Festival of
Two Worlds. Spoleto, Italy: Teatro Nuovo, 10-11, 13 July
1962 (première). Herbert Machiz, dir. Ben Sheeter,
Peter Hall, Nikola Cernovich, design. With Hermione Baddeley (Mrs. Goforth), Paul Roebling (Chris), Mildred Dunnock (Witch of Capri), Leora Dens (Blackie). Reviews:
     New York Times 12 July 1962: 19. Rpt. *New York Times
        Theatre Reviews.*
     Time 20 July 1962: 40.
     Times (London) 6 Feb. 1963: 13.
     Lo Bello, Nino. *Paris Herald Tribune* 12 July 1962.

The Milk Train Doesn't Stop Here Anymore. Preview: New
Haven, Boston, Philadelphia. New York: Morosco Theatre,
16 Jan.–16 Mar. 1963 (65). Herbert Marchiz, dir. Jo
Mielziner, Fred Voelpel, Peter Hall, design. Paul
Bowles, music. With Hermione Baddeley (Mrs. Goforth),
Paul Roebling (Chris), Mildred Dunnock (Witch of Capri),
Ann Williams (Blackie). Program: Leavitt (F 1): 141.
Reviews:
  Newsweek 28 Jan. 1963: 79.
  Theatre Arts Feb. 1963: 66.
  Time 25 Jan. 1963: 53.
  Times (London) 6 Feb. 1963: 13.
  Variety 5 Dec. 1962: 55. [Boston preview]
  Variety 23 Jan. 1963: 72.
  Baxandall, Lee. *Encore* May–June 1963: 8-13.
  Bolton, Whitney. *New York Morning Telegraph* 18 Jan.
    1963: 2.
  Brustein, Robert. *New Republic* 2 Feb. 1963: 27. Rpt.
    Seasons of Discontent... (New York: Simon, 1965):
    129.
  Chapman, John. *New York Theatre Critics' Reviews* 24:
    391.
  Clurman, Harold. *Nation* 196 (2 Feb. 1963): 106.
  Coleman, Robert. *New York Theatre Critics' Reviews* 24:
    392.
  Freedley, George. *New York Morning Telegraph* 25 Jan.
    1963: 2, 7.
  Funke, Lewis. *New York Times* 4 Nov. 1962, sec. 2: 1.
    [Casting]
  Gassner, John. *Educational Theatre Journal* 15 (May
    1963): 186-87. Rpt. *Dramatic Soundings...*, ed.
    Glenn Loncy (New York: Crown, 1968): 588-89.
  Gilman, Richard. *Commonweal* 77 (8 Feb. 1963): 515-17.
    Rpt. *Common and Uncommon Modes...* (New York: Random
    House, 1971): 144-47.
  Grande, Luke M. *Drama Critique* 6 (Spring 1963): 60-
    64.
  Hewes, Henry. *Saturday Review* 2 Feb. 1963: 20-21.
  Kerr, Walter. *New York Theatre Critics' Reviews* 24:
    392-93. Rpt. *Thirty Plays Hath November...* (New
    York: Simon, 1968): 222-23.
  Lewis, Theophilus. *America* 108 (30 Mar. 1963): 449.
  Little, Stuart W. *New York Herald Tribune* 14 Nov.
    1962: 21. [Rehearsals]
  Mannes, Marya. *Reporter* 25 Apr. 1963: 48-50.
  McCarten, John. *New Yorker* 26 Jan. 1963: 72.
  McClain, John. *New York Theatre Critics' Reviews* 24:
    393.
  Nadel, Norman. *New York Theatre Critics' Reviews* 24:
    393-94.

Prideaux, Tom. *Life* 1 Feb. 1963: 14-15.
Pryce-Jones, Alan. *Theatre Arts* Feb. 1963: 66.
Simon, John. *Hudson Review* 16 (Spring 1963): 87-89.
   Rpt. *Uneasy Stages...* (New York: Random House,
   1975): 6-8.
Smith, Michael. *Village Voice* 24 Jan. 1963: 20.
Taubman, Howard. *New York Theatre Critics' Reviews* 24:
   394. Rpt. *New York Times Theatre Reviews* (18 Jan.
   1963).
Von Dreele, W. H. *National Review* 14 (9 Apr. 1963):
   291-93.
West. Anthony. *Show* Apr. 1963: 40-41.

The Milk Train Doesn't Stop Here Anymore. Abingdon, VA:
Barter Theatre, 16 Sept. 1963 (première). Adrian Hall,
dir. Bobby Soule, design. With Claire Luce (Mrs. Go-
forth), Donald Madden (Chris), Mary Finnery (Witch of
Capri), Nancy Wilder (Blackie). Reviews, Prod. Notes:
   New York Times 18 Sept. 1963: 32. Rpt. *New York Times
      Theatre Reviews.*
   Times (London) 28 Sept. 1963: 12. [Rewrite]
   Zolotow, Sam. *New York Times* 10 Sept. 1963: 47.
      [Announcement]

The Milk Train Doesn't Stop Here Anymore. New York:
Brooks Atkinson Theatre, 1 Jan. 1964 (4). Tony Rich-
ardson, dir. Rouben Ter-Artunian, Martin Aronstein,
design. Ned Rorem, music. With Tallulah Bankhead (Mrs.
Goforth), Tab Hunter (Chris), Ruth Ford (Witch of Capri),
Marian Seldes (Blackie). Reviews:
   Newsweek 13 Jan. 1964: 70.
   Time 10 Jan. 1964: 52.
   Variety 8 Jan. 1964: 272.
   Bolton, Whitney. *New York Morning Telegraph* 3 Jan.
      1964: 2.
   Chapman, John. *New York Daily News* 2 Jan. 1964: 55.
      Rpt. *New York Theatre Critics' Reviews* 25: 399.
   Davis, James. *New York Daily News* 1 Jan. 1964: 35.
      [Opening]
   Gassner, John. *Educational Theatre Journal* 16 (Mar.
      1964): 76-77. Rpt. *Dramatic Soundings...*, ed. Glenn
      Loncy (New York: Crown, 1968): 590.
   Hewes, Henry. *Saturday Review* 18 Jan. 1964: 22.
   Kerr, Walter. *New York Herald Tribune* 2 Jan. 1964: 11.
      Rpt. *New York Theatre Critics' Reviews* 25: 400;
      Thirty Plays Hath November... (New York: Simon,
      1968): 223.
   McClain, John. *New York Journal-American* 2 Jan. 1964:
      17. Rpt. *New York Theatre Critics' Reviews* 25: 398.

Nadel, Norman. *New York World-Telegram* 2 Jan. 1964:
    18. Rpt. *New York Theatre Critics' Reviews* 25: 397-
    98.
Rorem, Ned. *The Later Diaries* (F 1): 71, 73-76.
Smith, Michael. *Village Voice* 9 Jan. 1964: 10.
Taubman, Howard. *New York Times* 2 Jan. 1964: 33.   Rpt.
    *New York Times Theatre Reviews; New York Theatre
    Critics' Reviews* 25: 399.
Watt, Douglas. *New York Daily News* 19 Nov. 1963: 50.
    [Plans]
Watts, Richard Jr. *New York Post* 2 Jan. 1964: 42.
    Rpt. *New York Theatre Critics' Reviews* 25: 397.
Zolotow, Sam. *New York Times* 3 Jan. 1964: 13.
    [Closing]

The Milk Train Doesn't Stop Here Anymore. Actors Workshop Guild. San Francisco: Encore Theatre, 23 July 1965
(première: 47). John Hancock, dir. Warren Travis, Ken
Margolis, J. Thompson Poynter, design. Morton Subotnik,
music. With Winifred Mann (Mrs. Goforth), Robert Benson
(Chris), Joyce Lancaster (Witch of Capri), Sally Kemp
(Blackie). Review:
    Taubman, Howard. *New York Times* 27 July 1965: 25.
    Rpt. *New York Times Theatre Reviews.*

Boom! Limites/World Film Services. Universal, May 1968
(première). Joseph Losey, dir. Douglas Slocombe, cam-
era. Richard MacDonald, design. John Barry, Nazirali
Jairazbhoy, Viram Jasani, music. With Elizabeth Taylor
(Mrs. Goforth), Richard Burton (Chris), Noel Coward
(Witch of Capri), Joanna Shimkus (Blackie), Michael Dunn
(Rudy). Reviews, Prod. Notes:
    Filmfacts 11 (1968): 216.
    New York Times 3 Oct. 1967: 55. [Casting]
    Time 31 May 1968: 56.
    Variety 29 May 1968: 20.
    Canby, Vincent. *New York Times* 27 May 1968: 56. Rpt.
        New York Times Film Reviews.
    Gow, Gordon. *Films and Filming* Mar. 1969: 43.
    Hartung, Philip T. *Commonweal* 88 (14 June 1968): 385.
    Johnson, William. *Film Quarterly* Winter 1968-69: 52-
        55.
    Kauffmann, Stanley. *New Republic* 8 June 1968: 26.
    Knight, Arthur. *Saturday Review* 1 June 1968: 19.
    Rothschild, Elaine. *Films in Review* 19 (Aug.-Sept.
        1968): 454.
    Schickel, Richard. *Life* 21 June 1968: 12.
    Shivas, Mark. *Movie* 16 (Winter 1968-69): 39.
    ---. *New York Times* 15 Oct. 1967, sec. 2: 15. [Film-
        ing]
    Walsh, Moira. *America* 118 (8 June 1968): 760-61.

Zimmerman, Paul D. *Newsweek* 3 June 1968: 104.

The Milk Train Doesn't Stop Here Anymore. London: Tower
Theatre, fall 1968. Edgar Davies, dir. Sue Plummer,
design. With Sara Randall (Mrs. Goforth). Review:
  Wardle, Irving. *Times* (London) 2 Dec. 1968: 16.

The Milk Train Doesn't Stop Here Anymore. New York: WPA
Theatre, 4 Nov. 1987. Kevin Conway, dir. With Elizabeth
Ashley (Mrs. Goforth), Luis Ramos (Chris), Ava Haddad
(Witch of Capri), Amanda Plummer (Blackie). Reviews:
  Disch, Thomas M. *Nation* 246 (23 Jan. 1988): 100.
  Gussow, Mel. *New York Times* 23 Nov. 1987, sec. 3: 18.
  Kramer, Mimi. *New Yorker* 7 Dec. 1987: 165-66.
  Simon, John. *New York* 11 Jan. 1988: 58.
  Winer, Laurie. *New York Times* 8 Nov. 1987, sec. 2: 5.

Other Productions:
  Faber, Charles. *Advocate* 9 July 1981. [San Fernando
    Valley]

"MOONY'S KID DON'T CRY"/"HOT MILK AT THREE IN THE MORNING":
Drama about a dreamer trapped by his family. Mss., Columbia, Missouri, Texas (G).
  The first version, "Hot Milk at Three in the Morning,"
won honorable mention in the 1931-32 University of Missouri play contest. Classmate George McCue feels certain
it was not produced. Rewritten as "Moony's Kid Don't
Cry," 1934, it was Williams's first play to be published.

Publication: Earlier Version

"Hot Milk at Three in the Morning." *Missouri Review* 7
  (1984): 196-200. Early note:
    Columbia Missourian 24 Apr. 1932 (?).

Publication: Later Version

"Moony's Kid Don't Cry." *The Best One-Act Plays of 1940.*
  Ed. Margaret Mayorga. New York: Dodd, Mead, 1941. 29-
  44.

American Blues, 1948: 5-14 (A 2).

Trans. (H): French, German, Greek, Italian, Japanese.

Productions

Two One-Act Plays. Nantucket: Straight Wharf Theatre, 1,
3 Sept. 1946. Albert Penalosa, dir. With Albert Pena-

losa (Moony), Rita Gam (Jane). Program: Leavitt (F 1):
69; playbill: Van Antwerp (F 1): 77.

4 Short Plays. Actors' Lab. Los Angeles: Las Palmas
Theatre, 13 Jan. 1947. Alfred Ryder, dir. With Frank
White (Moony), Mary Davenport (Jane). Playbill: Van
Antwerp (F 1): 78. See "Last of My Solid Gold Watches."

Three by Tennessee. Kraft Television Theatre. NBC-TV,
16 Apr. 1958. Sidney Lumet, dir. With Ben Gazzara
(Moony), Lee Grant (Jane). See "Last of My Solid Gold
Watches."

Other Productions:
    Schmidt, Sandra. *Village Voice* 1 Aug. 1963: 12. [New
    York]

"THE MUTILATED": Drama about two lonely women in New Or-
    leans. Mss., California-Los Angeles, Delaware, Harvard,
    Texas (G).
    The play was produced together with "The Gnadiges Frau-
    lein" under the title *Slapstick Tragedy*.

Publication: First Version

Slapstick Tragedy, 1965: 96-101 (see "Gnädiges Fräulein,"
    above).

Publication: Second Version

The Mutilated...: A Play in One Act. New York: Drama-
    tists Play Service, 1967. 48 pp. Il. Contents: Pro-
    duction Notes, 4; play, 5-42; Variations, 43-46.

Publication: Third Version

Dragon Country, 1969: 77-130 (A 2).

Theatre, Vol. 7, 1981: 77-130 (A 2).

Trans. (H): German, Spanish.

Production

Slapstick Tragedy. New York: Longacre Theatre, 22-26
Feb. 1966 (première: 7). Alan Schneider, dir. With Margaret Leighton (Trinket), Kate Reid (Celeste). See "Gnadiges Fraulein."

THE NIGHT OF THE IGUANA: Drama of trapped people who have
come to the end of their resources in Mexico but who
still continue to live with grace. Mss., California-Los
Angeles, Columbia, Congress, Delaware, Harvard, New York
Public, Texas (G).
Only the title, the central symbol, a storm, and a very
different prototype for Hannah come from the short story
"The Night of the Iguana" (B 1). The play began 1959 as
an unpublished one act and expanded into a full-length
work. There are a few minor differences between the
Esquire and the New Direction texts. The Dramatists Play
Service text is a severe cutting, especially of the third
act, which removes much of the poetry and some of the
overwritten passages. For a discussion of the play's
origins see Williams's essay "A Summer of Discovery" (D
1). The unpublished 1964 screenplay was the work of
Anthony Veiller and John Huston.

Publication: First Versions

Esquire 57 (Feb. 1962): 47-62, 115-30.

The Night of the Iguana. New York: New Directions, 1962.
   128 pp. Il. Contents: Note on setting, 5; play, 7-
   127; Nazi Marching Song, 128. Reviews:
      Booklist 58 (15 May 1962): 638.
      Bookmark 21 (June 1962): 258.
      Freedley, George. *New York Morning Telegraph* 22
         Mar. 1962: 2, 8.

The Best Plays of 1961-1962.... Ed. Henry Hewes. New
   York: Dodd, Mead, 1962. 170-87. Excerpts.

The Night of the Iguana: A Play. London: Secker & Warburg, 1963. 107 pp. Review:
      Times Literary Supplement 12 July 1963: 510.

Best American Plays, Fifth Series: *1957-1963*. Ed. John
   Gassner. New York: Crown, 1963. 55-104.

The Night of the Iguana. Signet Book. New York: New
   American Library, 1964. 127 pp. Ils.

The Night of the Iguana. Penguin Play. Harmondsworth:
   Penguin Books, 1964. 117 pp.

Plays and Players May 1965, June 1965.

The Night of the Iguana. Louisville, KY: American Printing House for the Blind, 1966.

Night of the Iguana, etc., 1968 (A 2).

Best Plays of the Sixties. Ed. Stanley Richards. Garden City: Doubleday, 1970. 119-240.

Theatre, Vol. 4, 1972: 247-376 (A 2).

Three by Tennessee, 1976 (A 2).

Cat on a Hot Tin Roof, etc., 1976: 225-329 (A 2).

Selected Plays, 1977: 561-665; *Selected Plays*, 1980: 463-565 (A 2).

Eight Plays, 1979: 737-843 (A 2).

Trans. (H): Arabic, Czech, French, German, Hungarian, Italian, Polish, Portuguese, Slovak, Spanish, Turkish.

Publication: Second (Acting) Version

The Night of the Iguana. New York: Dramatists Play Service, 1963. 93 pp. Il. Contents: Note on setting, 4; play, 5-78; Nazi Marching Song, 80.

Inclusion in Textbook (First Version)

Dukore, Bernard, ed. *17 Plays: Sophocles to Baraka*. New York: Crowell, 1976. 698-771.

Criticism

Adler, Jacob H. "*Night of the Iguana* A New Tennessee Williams?" *Ramparts* Nov. 1962: 59-68.

Carpenter, David A. *Masterplots II: Drama Series*. Ed. Frank N. Magill. Pasadena, CA: Salem, 1990. 1143-47.

Embrey, Glenn. "The Subterranean World of *The Night of the Iguana*." Tharpe (A 3): 325-40; short ed.: 65-80.

Hendrick, George. "Jesus and the Osiris-Isis Myth: Lawrence's *The Man Who Died* and Williams' *The Night of the Iguana*." *Anglia* 84 (4 Mar. 1966): 398-406.

Kahn, Sy. *The Night of the Iguana (Tennessee Williams)*. Audiocassette. DeLand, FL: Everett/Edwards, 197-.

Leon, Ferdinard. "Time, Fantasy, and Reality in *Night of the Iguana*." *Modern Drama* 11 (May 1968): 87-96.

Moorman, Charles. "*The Night of the Iguana*: A Long Introduction, a General Essay, and No Explication at
All." Tharpe (A 3): 318-24.

Moritz, Helen E. "Apparent Sophoclean Echoes in Tennessee Williams's *Night of the Iguana.*" *Classical and
Modern Literature* 47 (1985): 305-14.

Productions

"The Night of the Iguana." Festival of Two Worlds. Spo-
leto, Italy: Teatro Caio Melisso, 2 July 1959 (première).
Frank Corsaro, dir. Paul Sylbert, design. Werner Torka-
nowsky, music. With Patrick O'Neal (Shannon), Rosemary
Murphy (Hannah). Playbill: Leavitt (F 1). Review:
   Hewes, Henry. *Saturday Review* 1 Aug. 1959: 30.

The Night of the Iguana. Miami: Coconut Grove Playhouse,
summer 1960 (première). Frank Corsaro, dir. Prod. Note:
   Variety 31 Aug. 1960: 54.

The Night of the Iguana. Previews: Rochester, Detroit,
Cleveland, Chicago. New York: Royale Theatre, 28 Dec.
1961-29 Sept. 1962 (316). Frank Corsaro, dir. Oliver
Smith, Jean Rosenthal, Noel Taylor, Edward Beyer, design.
With Patrick O'Neal (Shannon), Bette Davis, later Shelley
Winters (Maxine), Margaret Leighton, later Patricia Roe
(Hannah), Alan Webb, later Leo Lucker (Nonno), James
Farentino (Pedro). Winner New York Drama Critics' Circle
Award. Reviews, Prod. Notes:
   Life 13 Apr. 1962: 67-70.
   Newsweek 8 Jan. 1962: 44.
   Time 5 Jan. 1962: 53.
   Times (London) 11 Jan. 1962: 14.
   Variety 8 Nov. 1961: 75. [Rochester preview]
   Variety 3 Jan. 1962: 56.
   Brustein, Robert. *New Republic* 22 Jan. 1962: 20-23.
      Rpt. *Seasons of Discontent...* (New York: Simon,
      1965): 126-29.
   Chapman, John. *New York Daily News* 29 Dec. 1961: 44.
      Rpt. *New York Theatre Critics' Reviews* 22: 131.
   ---. *New York Sunday News* 14 Jan. 1962, sec. 2: 1.
   Clurman, Harold. *Nation* 194 (27 Jan. 1962): 86. Rpt.
      The Naked Image... (New York: Macmillan, 1966): 126-
      29.
   Coleman, Robert. *New York Mirror* 29 Dec. 1961: 28.
      Rpt. *New York Theatre Critcs' Reviews* 22: 134.
   Davis, Bette. *The Lonely Life: An Autobiography.* New
      York: Putnam's, 1962. Final chap.
   Downer, Alan S. *Quarterly Journal of Speech* 48 (Oct.
      1962): 261-70.

Driver, Tom F. *Christian Century* 79 (7 Feb. 1962):
    169.
Forrey, Robert. *Mainstream* 15 (Aug. 1962): 62-64.
Freedley, George. *New York Morning Telegraph* 30 Dec.
    1961: 2.
Gassner, John. *Educational Theatre Journal* 14 (Mar.
    1962): 69. Rpt. *Dramatic Soundings...*, ed. Glenn
    Loncy (New York: Crown, 1968): 588.
Gilman, Richard. *Commonweal* 75 (26 Jan. 1962): 460-61.
    Rpt. *Common and Uncommon Modes...* (New York: Random
    House, 1971): 140-43.
Griffin, Hilary. *Catholic World* 194 (Mar. 1962): 380-
    81.
Hewes, Henry. *Saturday Review* 20 Jan. 1962: 36.
Hunningher, Benjamin. *Toneel* 83 (Jan.-Feb. 1962): 15-
    19.
Kerr, Walter. *New York Herald Tribune* 29 Dec. 1961: 8.
    Rpt. *New York Theatre Critics' Reviews* 22: 134.
---. *New York Herald Tribune* 7 Jan. 1962, sec. 4: 1,
    3.
Laurence, Paula. "How It Feels to Be a Standby."
    Playbill 7 Oct. 1963: 33-37.
Lewis, Theophilus. *America* 106 (3 Feb. 1962): 604.
Mannes, Marya. *Reporter* 1 Feb. 1962: 45.
McCarten, John. *New Yorker* 13 Jan. 1962: 61.
McClain, John. *New York Journal-American* 29 Dec. 1961:
    9. Rpt. *New York Theatre Critics' Reviews* 22: 132-
    33.
Miano, Louis S. *Show* Dec. 1961: 33.
Nadel, Norman. *New York World-Telegram* 29 Dec. 1961:
    10. Rpt. *New York Theatre Critics' Reviews* 22: 133.
Oliver, Edith. *New Yorker* 13 Jan. 1962: 61.
Peck, Seymour. *New York Times Magazine* 29 Oct. 1961:
    34-35. [Rehearsals]
Richards, Stanley. *Players* 38 (Apr. 1962): 218-19.
Simon, John. *Hudson Review* 14 (Spring 1962): 83-92.
---. *Theatre Arts* Mar. 1962: 57. Rpt. Van Antwerp (F
    1): 226-28.
Sorell, Walter. *Cresset* Mar. 1962: 21.
Tallmer, Jerry. *Village Voice* 4 Jan. 1962: 9.
Taubman, Howard. *New York Times* 29 Dec. 1961: 10.
    Rpt. *New York Times Theatre Reviews; New York
    Theatre Critics' Reviews* 22: 132; Van Antwerp (F 1):
    224-26.
---. *New York Times* 7 Jan. 1962, sec. 2: 1. Rpt. *New
    York Times Theatre Reviews.*
Watts, Richard Jr. *New York Post* 29 Dec. 1961: 20.
    Rpt. *New York Theatre Critics' Reviews* 22: 131.
---. *New York Post* 14 Jan. 1962, amuse. sec.: 21.
Zolotow, Sam. *New York Times* 27 Dec. 1960: 23.
    [Plans]

---. *New York Times* 11 Apr. 1962: 46. [New York
   Critics' Circle Award]

The Night of the Iguana. Screenplay by Anthony Veiler
and John Huston. John Huston/Ray Stark Production.
MGM/Seven Arts, 31 June 1964 (première). John Huston,
dir. Gabriel Figueroa, cameraman. Stephen Grimes, art
director. Benjamin Frankel, music. With Richard Burton
(Shannon), Ava Gardner (Maxine), Deborah Kerr (Hannah),
Cyril Delevanti (Nonno), Sue Lyon (Charlotte). Music
soundtrack: MGM Records, 1964. Reviews, Prod. Notes:
   Filmfacts 7 (1964): 146.
   New York Times 7 Aug. 1964: 14. [Public opening]
   Newsweek 13 July 1964: 85.
   Spectator 213 (11 Sept. 1964): 340.
   Time 8 Nov. 1963: 69. [Filming]
   Time 17 July 1964: 86-88.
   Variety 1 July 1969: 6.
   Cook, Alton. *New York World Telegram* 8 Aug. 1964: 15.
   Crist, Judith. *New York Herald Tribune Magazine* 1 July
      1964: 14-15.
   Crowther, Bosley. *New York Times* 1 July 1964: 42.
      Rpt. *New York Times Film Reviews.*
   Dent, Alan. *Illustrated London News* 245 (26 Sept.
      1964): 480.
   Didion, Joan. *Vogue* 1 Sept. 1964: 106.
   Eyles, Allen. *Films and Filming* Oct. 1964: 28.
   Haedens, Kleber. *Candide* 13-20 May 1964: 10 ff.
   Hale, Wanda. *New York Daily News* 1 July 1964: 77.
   Hartung, Philip T. *Commonweal* 80 (21 Aug. 1964): 580.
   Higham, Charles. *Ava: A Life Story.* New York:
      Delacourte, 1974. 175-82.
   Houston, Penelope. *New Statesman* 68 (11 Sept. 1964):
      370.
   Huston, John. *An Open Book.* New York: Knopf, 1980.
      306-12.
   Kaminsky, Stuart. *John Huston....* Boston: Houghton
      Mifflin, 1978. 155-60.
   Kennedy, Paul P. *New York Times* 1 Dec. 1963: 5.
      [Filming]
   Kerr, Deborah. "The Days and Nights of. the Iguana: A
      Journal." *Esquire* May 1964: 128-42. [Filming]
   Knight, Arthur. *Saturday Review* 18 July 1964: 22.
   Lawrenson, Helen. *Show* Jan. 1964: 46-49, 104-05.
   Madsen, Axel. *John Huston.* Garden City: Doubleday,
      1978. 200-08.
   Mishkin, Leo. *New York Morning Telegraph* 1 July 1964:
      2.
   Nolan, William F. *John Huston....* Los Angeles: Sher-
      bourne, 1965. 203-17.
   Oliver, Edith. *New Yorker* 15 Aug. 1964: 84-85.

Oulahan, Richard. *Life* 20 Dec. 1963: 69-74. [Filming]
---. *Life* 10 July 1964: 11.
Pratley, Gerald. *The Cinema of John Huston.* Cranbury,
    NJ: Barnes, 1977; London: Tantivy, 1977. 142-46.
Quigly, Isabel. *Spectator* 213 (11 Sept. 1964): 340.
Rothschild, Elaine. *Films in Review* 15 (Aug.-Sept.
    1964): 439-41.
Sarris, Andrew. *Village Voice* 13 Aug. 1964: 12.
Silke, James. *Cinema* Oct.-Nov. 1964: 48.
Sussex, Elizabeth. *Sight and Sound* 33 (Autumn 1964):
    198-99.
Taylor, Stephen. *Film Quarterly* Winter 1964: 50-52.
Thomas, Bob. *New York Post* 24 Oct. 1963: 21. [Film-
    ing]
Victor, Thelda, with Muriel Davidson. "The Drama the
    Cameras Missed." *Saturday Evening Post* 11 July
    1964: 27-32. [Filming]
Walsh, Moira. *America* 111 (15 Aug. 1964): 161.
Weales, Gerald. *Reporter* 8 Oct. 1964: 49-50.
Winston, Archer. *New York Post* 1 July 1964: 54.

The Night of the Iguana. Croydon: Ashcroft Theatre, Feb.
1965; London: Savoy Theatre, 24 Mar. 1965. Philip Wise-
man, dir. Peter Farmer, design. With Mark Eden (Shannon), Vanda Godsell (Maxine), Sian Phillips (Hannah),
Donald Eccles (Nonno). Playbill: Leavitt (F 1). Winner
London Critics' Poll for Best Foreign Play. Reviews:
    Times (London) 18 Feb. 1965: 16.
    Times (London) 25 Mar. 1965: 16.
    Bryden, Ronald. *New Statesman* 19 (2 Apr. 1965): 546.
    Gilliatt, Penelope. *London Observer* 28 Mar. 1965: 24.

The Night of the Iguana. New York: Circle-in-the-Square
Theatre, 16 Dec. 1976-20 Feb. 1977 (77). Joseph Hardy,
dir. H. R. Poindexter, Noel Taylor, design. With Richard Chamberlain (Shannon), Sylvia Miles (Maxine), Dorothy
McGuire (Hannah), William Roerick (Nonno). Reviews:
    Barnes, Clive. *New York Times* 17 Dec. 1976, sec. C: 2.
        Rpt. *New York Theatre Critics' Reviews* 37: 62-63.
    Beaufort, John. *Christian Science Monitor* 17 Dec.
        1976. Rpt. *New York Theatre Critics' Reviews* 37:
        64-65.
    Clurman, Harold. *Nation* 224 (1 Jan. 1977): 28-29.
    Crossette, Barbara. *New York Times* 26 Nov. 1976, sec.
        C: 3. [Interview with Chamberlain]
    Gill, Brendan. *New Yorker* 27 Dec. 1976: 52.
    Gottfried, Martin. *New York Post* 17 Dec. 1976. Rpt.
        New York Theatre Critics' Reviews 37: 63-64.
    Hughes, Catherine. *America* 136 (8 Jan. 1977): 20.
    Kalem, T. E. *Time* 27 Dec. 1976: 39. Rpt. *New York
        Theatre Critics' Reviews* 37: 65.

Kerr, Walter. *New York Times* 19 Dec. 1976, sec. 2: 3.
Kissel, Howard. *Women's Wear Daily* 17 Dec. 1976. Rpt.
  New York Theatre Critics' Reviews 37: 64.
Probst, Leonard. NBC, 16 Dec. 1976. Rpt. *New York
  Theatre Critics' Reviews* 37: 65.
Watt, Douglas. *New York Daily News* 17 Dec. 1976. Rpt.
  New York Theatre Critics' Reviews 37: 62.
Wilson, Edwin. *Wall Street Journal* 20 Dec. 1976. Rpt.
  New York Theatre Critics' Reviews 37: 65.

The Night of the Iguana. Baltimore: Mechanic Theatre, 15
Oct.-9 Nov. 1985. Arthur Sherman, dir. Oliver Smith,
Lucinda Ballard, Feder, design. With Michael Moriarty
(Shannon), Eileen Brenner (Maxine), Jeanne Moreau (Han-
nah), Roy Dotrice (Nonno). Prod. Note:
  Time 7 Oct. 1985.

The Night of the Iguana. New York: Circle-in-the-Square,
26 June-4 Sept. 1988 (81). Theodore Mann, dir. Zack
Brown, Richard Nelson, Jennifer von Mayrhauser, design.
With Nicholas Surovy (Shannon), Jane Alexander (Maxine),
Maria Tucci (Hannah), William Le Massena (Nonno).
Reviews:
  Barnes, Clive. *New York Post* 27 June 1988. Rpt. *New
    York Theatre Critics' Reviews* 49: 217-18.
  Gussow, Mel. *New York Times* 27 June 1988, sec. 3: 16.
    Rpt. *New York Theatre Critics' Reviews* 49: 216.
  Hochman, Sandra. *New York Times* 26 June 1988, sec. 2:
    24.
  Kissel, Howard. *New York Daily News* 27 June 1988.
    Rpt. *New York Theatre Critics' Reviews* 49: 218.
  Oliver, Edith. *New Yorker* 11 July 1988: 77.
  Simon, John. *New York* 18 July 1988: 48.
  Waleson, Heidi. *New York Times* 26 June 1988, sec. 2:
    5. [Casting]
  Watt, Douglas. *New York Daily News* 8 July 1988. Rpt.
    New York Theatre Critics' Reviews 49: 218.
  Wilson, Edwin. *Wall Street Journal* 8 July 1988. Rpt.
    New York Theatre Critics' Reviews 49: 218.
  Winer, Linda. *New York Newsday* 27 June 1988. Rpt. *New
    York Theatre Critics' Reviews* 49: 219.

Other Productions:
  Goodman, Walter. *New York Times* 7 Oct. 1986, sec. 3:
    14. [Stanford, CT]
  Klein, Alvin. *New York Times* 30 July 1989, sec. 22:
    17. [Dobbs Ferry, NY]
  Mitchner, Robert W. *Tennessee Williams Review* 3.1
    (1981): 19-21. [Key West]

"NOW THE CAT WITH JEWELLED CLAWS":   Absurd exchanges in a
restaurant between two women friends, between two hust-
lers (and lovers), and with an aging gay manager. Ms.,
Columbia (G).

Theatre, Vol. 7, 1981: 297-330 (A 2).

THE NOTEBOOK OF TRIGORIN: Unpublished adaptation of *The Sea
Gull* by Anton Chekhov.

The Notebook of Trigorin. Vancouver: Playhouse Theatre,
12 Sept.-10 Oct. 1981 (première). Roger Hodgman, dir.
Toni Onley, Marti Wright, Jeffrey Dallas, design. With
Jim Mezon (Trepliev), Patricia Hamilton (Arkadina),
Roland Hewgill (Trigorin), Martha Burns (Nina). Review:
   Edmonstone, Wayne. *Vancouver Sun* 14 Sept. 1981, sec.
   B: 6.

The Notebook of Trigorin. Colony Production. Silver
Lake (Los Angeles): Studio Theatre Playhouse, Sept. 1982.
Terrence Shank, dir. With Robert O'Reilly (Trepliev),
Nan Martin (Arkadina), Ronald Morhous (Trigorin), Suzanne
Celeste (Nina). Reviews:
   Faber, Charles. *Advocate* 14 Oct. 1982: 51.
   Lochte, Dick. *Los Angeles* 27 (Sept. 1982): 266-68.

ONE ARM: Screenplay probably dating from mid-1960s, an
adaptation of the short story of the same title (B 1).
Ms., California-Los Angeles.
   A news item in the *New York Sunday News* (14 Apr. 1968,
sec. 5: 13) announced that it would be filmed, but nothing came of the project. Lanford Wilson was somehow connected with it: see Shewey (F 1).

Stopped Rocking and Other Screenplays, 1984: 193-291 (A
   2).

ORPHEUS DESCENDING/BATTLE OF ANGELS/THE FUGITIVE KIND:
Drama of a wandering artist who stirs up the repressed
sexuality of the women, the hidden sins, and the latent
violence in a small Mississippi community. Mss., Columbia, Congress, Delaware, New York Public, Texas (G).
   Battle of Angels was Williams's first play scheduled for
Broadway, but it closed during its Boston tryout in 1940.
Williams revised the script, adding a prologue and an
epilogue, and published this new version in 1945.

He continued brooding over the story, making changes in characterization, development, and symbolism but following always the same basic plot. In 1957 a further revision, *Orpheus Descending*, was produced; it too closed quickly. See Williams's two essays "The History of a Play" and "The Past, the Present, and the Perhaps" (D 1 and below).

When Williams prepared the acting version, 1959, he skillfully reordered some of the material, but he marred his fire symbolism. With Meade Roberts, he prepared the unpublished 1959 screenplay, *The Fugitive Kind* (the title of an earlier but quite different play).

Williams returned to *Battle* 1975, creating an acting edition that retains the structure of the original (minus prologue and epilogue) but introduces some of the better scenes from *Orpheus*. The script's editing is blemished, however.

Raffaello de Banfield began creating an unfinished and unpublished opera from *Orpheus Descending*.

Publication: First Version

Battle of Angels. Pharos 1/2 (Spring 1945): 5-109. Also "The History of a Play (with Parentheses)," 110-21.

Orpheus Descending, 1958: 119-238 (below).

Theatre, Vol. 1, 1971: 1-122 (A 2).

Trans. (H): Spanish.

Publication: Second Version

The Best Plays of 1956-1957.... Ed. Louis Kronenberger. New York: Dodd, Mead, 1957. 248-68. Excerpts.

Orpheus Descending, with Battle of Angels: Two Plays. New York: New Directions, 1958. x, 238 pp. Contents: "The Past, the Present, and the Perhaps" (D 1), v-x; *Orpheus Descending*, 1-118; *Battle of Angels* (above), 119-238. Reviews:
  Booklist 54 (15 June 1958): 581.
  Davis, Helen. *Mainstream* Apr. 1958: 55-57.
  Freedley, George. *Library Journal* 83 (1 Apr. 1958): 1108.
  ---. *New York Morning Telegraph* 6 Aug. 1958: 2.
  Justice, Donald. *Poetry* 93 (Mar. 1959): 402-03.

Theatre Arts 42 (Sept. 1958): 26-55.

Orpheus Descending: A Play.   London: Secker & Warburg,
   1958.   96 pp.   Contents: "The Past, the Present, and
   the Perhaps" (D 1); play, 9-96.   Review:
   Times Literary Supplement 14 Nov. 1958: 652.

*The Fugitive Kind (Original Play Title: Orpheus Descend-
   ing).*   Signet Book.   New York: New American Library,
   1960.   144 pp.   Ils.

Orpheus Descending, etc., 1961 (A 2).

Five Plays, 1962: 283-374 (A 2).

Best American Plays, Fifth Series, *1957-1963.*   Ed. John
   Gassner.   New York: Crown, 1963.   509-51.

Night of the Iguana, etc., 1968 (A 2).

Theatre, Vol. 3, 1971: 219-342 (A 2).

Four Plays, 1976: 1-144 (A 2).

Rose Tattoo, etc., 1976: 235-347 (A 2).

Eight Plays, 1979: 537-641 (A 2).

Trans. (H):   Arabic, Bulgarian, Chinese, Czech, Danish,
   French, German, Greek, Hungarian, Italian, Japanese,
   Romanian, Russian, Spanish.

Publication: Third Version

Orpheus Descending...: A Play in Three Acts.   New York:
   Dramatists Play Service, 1959.   83 pp.   Contents: play,
   5-78.

Publication: Fourth Version

Battle of Angels.   New York: Dramatists Play Service,
   1975.   76 pp.   Il.   Contents: play, 5-73.

Inclusion in Textbook (Second Version)

Gordon, Walter K., ed.   *Literature in Critical Perspectives....*   New York: Appleton, 1968.   529-73.

Criticism

Attar, Samar.   *The Intruder in Modern Drama.*   Frankfurt:
   Lang, 1981.   41-52.

Belli, Angela. *Ancient Greek Myths and Modern Drama.*
New York: New York Univ. Pr., 1969. 38-49.

Buell, John. "The Evil Imagery of Tennessee Williams."
Thought 38 (Summer 1963): 167-89.

Bunsch, Iris. "Tennessee Williams: *Orpheus Descending.*"
*Theater und Drama in Amerika: Aspekte und Interpreta-
tionen.* Ed. Edgar Lohner and Rudolf Haas. Berlin:
Schmidt, 1978. 278-94.

Chesler, S. Alan. "*Orpheus Descending.*" *Players* Oct.
1977: 10-13.

Dickinson, Hugh. *Myth on the Modern Stage.* Urbana:
Univ. of Illinois Pr., 1969. 278-309.

Ditsky, John. *The Onstage Christ: Studies in the Per-
sistence of a Theme.* London: Vision, 1980. 123-35.

King, Kimball. "The Rebirth of *Orpheus Descending.*"
Tennessee Williams Literary Journal 1.2 (Winter 1989-
90): 18-33.

Lee, M. Owen. "Orpheus and Eurydice: Some Modern Versions." *Classical Journal* 56 (Apr. 1961): 307-13.

Matthew, David C. "'Toward Bethlehem': *Battle of Angels*
and *Orpheus Descending.*" Tharpe (A 3): 172-91.

Quirino, Leonard. "Tennessee Williams' Persistent *Battle
of Angels.*" *Modern Drama* 11 (May 1968): 27-39. Rpt.
Bloom (A 3): 43-54.

Traubitz, Nancy Baker. "Myth as a Basis of Dramatic
Structure in *Orpheus Descending.*" *Modern Drama* 19
(Mar. 1976): 57-66. Rpt. D. Parker (A 3): 3-11.

Wallace, Jack E. "The Image of Theater in Tennessee Williams's *Orpheus Descending.*" *Modern Drama* 27 (1984):
324-35.

Watts, Richard Jr. "Orpheus Ascending." *Theatre Arts*
Sept. 1958: 25-26.

Productions

Battle of Angels. Theatre Guild. Boston: Wilbur Theatre, 30 Dec. 1940-11 Jan. 1941 (première). Margaret
Webster, dir. Cleon Throckmorton, design. Colin McPhee,
music. With Wesley Addy (Val), Miriam Hopkins (Myra),

Doris Dudley (Cassandra), Katherine Raht (Vee). Reviews,
Prod. Notes:
  Boston Globe 31 Dec. 1940: 7.
  Boston Post 22 Dec. 1940: 9.
  Boston Post 31 Dec. 1940: 8. Rpt. Van Antwerp (F 1):
    42-43.
  Boston Post 7 Jan. 1941: 8. Rpt. Van Antwerp (F 1):
    43-44.
  Boston Transcript 28 Dec. 1940, sec. 3: 4-5.
  New York Herald Tribune 25 Jan. 1942, sec. 6: 2.
    [Rewrite]
  New York Times 31 Dec. 1940: 18. Rpt. *New York Times*
    Theatre Reviews.
  New York Times 5 Jan. 1941, sec. 2: 1. Rpt. *New York*
    Times Theatre Reviews.
  New York Times 9 Mar., sec. 9: 3. [Apology; see Van
    Antwerp (F 1): 45]
  St. Louis Daily Globe-Democrat 24 Nov. 1940. Rpt. Van
    Antwerp (F 1): 40-42.
  Variety 1 Jan. 1941: 45.
  Hastings, Morris. *Boston Evening Transcript* 31 Dec.
    1940: 14.
  Norton, Elliot. *Boston Post* 12 Jan. 1941: 25.
  Webster, Margaret. "A Note on *Battle of Angels*."
    Pharos 1-2 (Spring 1945): 122-23.
  Williams, Alexander. *Boston Herald* 31 Dec. 1940: 10.
    Rpt. Leavitt (F 1): 46.

Orpheus Descending. Producers Theatre. Previews: Wash-
ington, Philadelphia. New York: Martin Beck Theatre, 21
Mar.-18 May 1957 (première: 68). Harold Clurman, dir.
Boris Aronson, Lucinda Ballard, Feder, design. With
Cliff Robertson (Val) [Robert Loggia in previews], Mau-
reen Stapleton (Lady), Lois Smith (Carol), Joanna Roos
(Vee). Program: Leavitt (F 1): 116. Reviews:
  America 6 Apr. 1957: 4.
  Harper's May 1957: 76-77.
  Newsweek 1 Apr. 1957: 81.
  Theatre Arts May 1957: 20.
  Time 1 Apr. 1957: 61.
  Variety 27 Feb. 1957: 58. [Washington preview]
  Variety 27 Mar. 1957: 66.
  Atkinson, Brooks. *New York Times* 22 Mar. 1957: 28.
    Rpt. *New York Times Theatre Reviews*; *New York*
    Threatre Critics' Reviews 18: 310.
  ---. *New York Times* 31 Mar. 1957, sec. 2: 1. Rpt. *New*
    York Times Theatre Reviews.
  Bolton, Whitney. *New York Morning Telegraph* 23 Mar.
    1957: 2.
  Calta, Louis. *New York Times* 23 Aug. 1956: 24.
    [Booking]

Chapman, John. *New York Daily News* 22 Mar. 1957: 52.
    Rpt. *New York Theatre Critics' Reviews* 18: 310.
Clurman, Harold. *Nation* 186 (25 Jan. 1957): 86-87.
Coleman, Robert. *New York Daily Mirror* 22 Mar. 1957:
    32. Rpt. *New York Theatre Critics' Reviews* 18: 311.
Donnelly, Tom. *New York World-Telegram* 22 Mar. 1957:
    22. Rpt. *New York Theatre Critics' Reviews* 18: 311.
---. *New York World-Telegram* 1 Apr. 1957: 10.
Driver, Tom F. *Christian Century* 74 (10 Apr. 1957):
    455-56.
Freedley, George. *New York Morning Telegraph* 1 Apr.
    1957: 2.
Gassner, John. *Theatre at the Crossroads* (A 3): 223-
    26.
Gibbs, Wolcott. *New Yorker* 30 Mar. 1957: 84-86. Rpt.
    Van Antwerp (F 1): 179-82.
Hatch, Robert. *Nation* 184 (6 Apr. 1957): 301-02.
Hayes, Richard. *Commonweal* 66 (26 Apr. 1957): 94-97.
Hewes, Henry. *Saturday Review* 30 Mar. 1957: 26.
Kerr, Walter. *New York Herald Tribune* 22 Mar. 1957:
    12. Rpt. *New York Theatre Critics' Reviews* 18: 313.
---. *New York Herald Tribune* 31 Mar. 1957, sec. 4: 1-
    2.
Lewis, Theophilus. *America* 97 (27 Apr. 1957): 148-50.
Mannes, Marya. *Reporter* 18 Apr. 1957: 43.
Marshall, Margaret. *New Republic* 8 Apr. 1957: 21.
McClain, John. *New York Journal American* 22 Mar. 1957:
    18. Rpt. *New York Theatre Critics' Reviews* 18: 312.
McCord, Bert. *New York Herald Tribune* 29 Aug. 1956:
    12. [Production]
Watts, Richard Jr. *New York Post* 22 Mar. 1957: 60.
    Rpt. *New York Theatre Critics' Reviews* 18: 312.
Wyatt, Euphemia Van Rensselaer. *Catholic World* 185
    (June 1957): 226-27.

Orpheus Descending. London: Royal Court Theatre, 14 May
1959. Tony Richardson, dir. With Gary Cockrell (Val),
Isa Miranda (Lady). Reviews:
    New York Times 15 May 1959: 23. Rpt. *New York Times
        Theatre Reviews*.
    Times (London) 15 May 1959: 6.
    Alvarez, A. *New Statesman* 57 (23 May 1959): 721-22.
    Brien, Alan. *Spectator* 202 (22 May 1959): 725-26.
    Duprey, Richard A. *Catholic World* 189 (June 1959):
        192-93.
    Whitebait, William. *New Statesman* 60 (10 Sept. 1960):
        336.

Orpheus Descending. New York: Gramercy Arts Theatre, 5
Oct. 1959; Greenwich News Theatre, 10 Feb. 1960. Adrian
Hall, dir. Robert Soules, design. With John Rasmon-

detta, later Bruce Dern (Val), Ann Hamilton (Lady), Diane
Ladd (Carol). Reviews:
   Variety 21 Oct. 1959: 82.
   Aston, Frank. *New York World Telegram* 6 Oct. 1959: 20.
   Calta, Louis. *New York Times* 6 Oct. 1959: 45. Rpt.
      New York Times Theatre Reviews.
   Crist, Judith. *New York Herald Tribune* 6 Oct. 1959,
      sec. 2: 6.
   Herridge, Frances. *New York Post* 6 Oct. 1959: 66.
   McClain, John. *New York Journal-American* 6 Oct. 1959:
      15.
   Tallmer, Jerry. *Village Voice* 14 Oct. 1959: 9.

The Fugitive Kind. United Artists, 8 Apr. 1960 (pre-
miere). Sidney Lumet, dir. Boris Kaufman, camera.
Richard Sylbert, design. Kenyon Hopkins, music. With
Marlon Brando (Val), Anna Magnani (Lady), Joanne Woodward
(Carol), Maureen Stapleton (Vee). Music soundtrack:
United Artists, 1960. Reviews, Prod. Notes:
   Filmfacts 1 (1958): 161.
   Newsweek 25 Apr. 1960: 115.
   Time 18 Apr. 1960: 81.
   Variety 13 Apr. 1960: 6.
   Alpert, Hollis. *Saturday Review* 23 Apr. 1960: 28.
   Beckley, Paul V. *New York Herald Tribune* 15 Apr. 1960:
      9.
   ---. *New York Herald Tribune* 24 Apr. 1960, sec. 4: 1,
      6.
   Bogdanovich, Peter. *Film Quarterly* 13 (Winter 1960):
      18-23. [Interview with Lumet]
   Crowther, Bosley. *New York Times* 15 Apr. 1960: 13.
      Rpt. *New York Times Film Reviews.*
   ---. *New York Times* 14 Apr. 1960, sec. 2: 1. Rpt. *New
      York Times Film Reviews.*
   Dent, Alan. *Illustrated London News* 237 (17 Sept.
      1960): 498.
   Foster, Frederick. "Filming *The Fugitive Kind.*"
      American Cinematographer June 1960: 354-55, 379-82.
   Gelb, Arthur. *New York Times* 8 Dec. 1959: 58.
      [Williams booed at preview]
   Hartung, Philip T. *Commonweal* 72 (29 Apr. 1960): 127-
      28.
   Jordan, Rene. *Marlon Brando.* New York: Galahad, 1973.
      89-94.
   Kauffmann, Stanley. *New Republic* 2 May 1960: 21-22.
      Rpt. *A World on Film...* (New York: Harper, 1966):
      79-87.
   Kuhn, Helen Weldon. *Films in Review* 11 (May 1960):
      290-92.

Macdonald, Dwight. *Esquire* June 1960: 63–65. Rpt.
  Dwight Macdonald on Movies (Englewood Cliffs, NJ:
  Prentice-Hall, 1969): 146–48.
Marek, Richard. *McCalls* June 1960: 179–80.
McCarten, John. *New Yorker* 23 Apr. 1960: 147–48.
Mekas, Jonas. *Village Voice* 20 Apr. 1960: 6.
Nason, Richard *New York Times* 5 July 1959, sec. 2: 5.
  [Filming]
Powell, Dilys. *Sunday Times* (London) 4 Sept. 1960: 35.
Prouse, Derek. *Sight and Sound* 29 (Summer 1960): 144–
  45.
Pryor, Thomas M. *New York Times* 2 Apr. 1958: 36.
  [Casting]
———. *New York Times* 1 Dec. 1958: 35. [Casting]
Quigly, Isabel. *Spectator* 205 (9 Sept. 1960): 372–74.
Roberts, Meade. "Tennessee Rising" (F 1).
Thomas, Bob. *Marlon....* New York: Random House, 1973.
  152–56.
Thomas, Tony. *The Films of Marlon Brando*. Secaucus,
  NJ: Citadel, 1973. 122–27.
Tyler, Parker. *Film Quarterly* 13 (Summer 1960): 47–49.
Walsh, Moira. *America* 103 (30 Apr. 1960): 201.
Whitebait, William. *New Statesman* 60 (10 Sept. 1960):
  336.
Whitehall, Richard. *Films and Filming* Aug. 1960: 23–
  24.
Winsten, Archer. *New York Post* 15 Apr. 1960: 19.

Battle of Angels. Circle Repertory Company. New York:
Circle Theatre, 3 Nov. 1974 (première: 32). Marshall W.
Mason, dir. John Lee Beatty, Dennis Parichy, Jennifer
von Mayrhauser, design. Norman L. Berman, music. With
Max (Val), Tanya Berezin (Myra), Trish Hawkins (Cassan-
dra), Conchata Ferrell (Vee). Reviews:
  New York Times 8 Oct. 1974: 35. [Announcement]
  Gussow, Mel. *New York Times* 4 Nov. 1974: 51.
  Kerr, Walter. *New York Times* 17 Nov. 1974, sec. 2: 5.
  Watt, Douglas. *New York Sunday News* 17 Nov. 1974, sec.
    3: 3.

Orpheus Descending. Peter Hall Company. London: Theatre
Royal, Haymarket, 13 Dec. 1988–18 Feb. 1989. Peter Hall,
dir. With Jean-Marc Barr (Val), Vanessa Redgrave (Lady),
Julie Covington (Carol), Miriam Margoyles (Vee).
Reviews:
  Times (London) 15 Nov. 1988: 22.
  Times (London) 7 Dec. 1988: 19. [Interview with Hall]
  Billington, Michael. *Guardian* 15 Dec. 1988. Rpt.
    London Theatre Record 8: 1731–32.
  Conway, Lydia. *What's On* 9 Jan. 1989. Rpt. *London
    Theatre Record* 8: 1728.

Coveney, Michael. *London Financial Times* 14 Dec. 1988.
    Rpt. *London Theatre Record* 8: 1730-31.
Edwards, Christopher. *Spectator* 24 Dec. 1988: 87.
    Rpt. *London Theatre Record* 8: 1726-27.
Henry, William A. III. *Time* 2 Jan. 1989: 102.
Hirschhorn, Clive. *London Sunday Express* 18 Dec. 1988.
    Rpt. *London Theatre Record* 8: 1729.
Hurren, Kenneth. *London Mail on Sunday* 18 Dec. 1988.
    Rpt. *London Theatre Record* 8: 1730.
Jones, Dan. *London Sunday Telegraph* 18 Dec. 1988.
    Rpt. *London Theatre Record* 8: 1729.
Kellaway, Kate. *London Observer* 18 Dec. 1988. Rpt.
    London Theatre Record 8: 1728-29.
Kroll, Jack. *Newsweek* 9 Jan. 1989: 52.
Morley, Sheridan. *International Herald Tribune* 21 Dec.
    1988: 7.
---. *Punch* 6 Jan. 1989. Rpt. *London Theatre Record* 8:
    1727-28.
Nathan, David. *Jewish Chronicle* 23 Dec. 1988. Rpt.
    London Theatre Record 8: 1728.
Osborne, Charles. *London Daily Telegraph* 15 Dec. 1988.
    Rpt. *London Theatre Record* 8: 1733.
Paton, Maureen. *London Daily Express* 14 Dec. 1988.
    Rpt. *London Theatre Record* 8: 1731.
Rich, Frank. *New York Times* 15 Dec. 1988, sec. 3: 15.
Shulman, Milton. *London Evening Standard* 14 Dec. 1988.
    Rpt. *London Theatre Record* 8: 1730.
Tinker, Jack. *London Daily Mail* 14 Dec. 1988. Rpt.
    London Theatre Record 8: 1732-33.
Wardle, Irving. *Times* (London) 18 Nov. 1988: 19.
---. *Times* (London) 4 Dec. 1988: 20.

Orpheus Descending. Peter Hall Company. New York: Neil
Simon Theatre, 24 Sept. 1989. Peter Hall, dir. Alison
Chitty, Paul Pyant, design. Stephen Edwards, music.
With Kevin Anderson (Val), Vanessa Redgrave (Lady), Anne
Twomey (Carol), Tammy Grimes (Vee). Reviews:

Barnes, Clive. *New York Post* 25 Sept. 1989. Rpt. *New
    York Theatre Critics' Reviews* 50: 231-32.
Beaufort, John. *Christian Science Monitor* 3 Oct. 1989.
    Rpt. *New York Theatre Critics' Reviews* 50: 234.
Brustein, Robert. *New Republic* 30 Oct. 1989: 25-27.
Disch, Thomas M. *Nation* 249 (20 Nov. 1989): 609-11.
Henry, William A. III. *Time* 9 Oct. 1989: 109, 112.
Holditch, W. Kenneth. *Tennessee Williams Literary
    Journal* 1.2 (Winter 1989-90): 65-67.
Kerr, Walter. *New York Times* 19 Nov. 1989, sec. 2: 38.
Kissel, Howard. *New York Daily News* 25 Sept. 1989.
    Rpt. *New York Theatre Critics' Reviews* 50: 229-30.
Kroll, Jack. *Newsweek* 9 Oct. 1989: 86.

Nightingale, Benedict. *New York Times* 17 Sept. 1989,
    sec. 2: 1. [On Redgrave]
Oliver, Edith. *New Yorker* 9 Oct. 1989: 125.
Raymond, Gerard. *Advocate* 12 Feb. 1991: 62-64.
    [Interview with Redgrave]
Rich, Frank. *New York Times* 25 Sept. 1989, sec. 3: 15.
Siegel, Joel. WABC-TV, 24 Sept. 1989. Rpt. *New York
    Theatre Critics' Reviews* 50: 236.
Simon, John. *New York* 9 Oct. 1989: 86-87.
Stearns, David Patrick. *USA Today* 25 Sept. 1989. Rpt.
    in part *New York Theatre Critics' Reviews* 50: 230.
Watt, Douglas. *New York Daily News* 6 Oct. 1989. Rpt.
    New York Theatre Critics' Reviews 50: 230.
Weales, Gerald. *Commonweal* 116 (17 Nov. 1989): 642-43.
Wilson, Edwin. *Wall Street Journal* 27 Sept. 1989.
    Rpt. *New York Theatre Critics' Reviews* 50: 233.
Winer, Linda. *New York Newsday* 25 Sept. 1989. Rpt.
    New York Theatre Critics Reviews 50: 232-33.

Orpheus Descending. Adaptation by Peter Hall. Neder-
lander Film. TNT-TV, 24 Sept. 1990. Peter Hall, dir.
Tom H. John, design. Michael Fash, camera. Stephen
Edwards, music. With Kevin Anderson (Val), Vanessa
Redgrave (Lady), Anne Twomey (Carol), Miriam Margolyes
(Vee). Reviews:
    Tennessee Williams Literary Journal 2.1 (Winter 1990-
    91): 66-67.
O'Connor, John J. *New York Times* 24 Sept. 1990: 83.
Roush, Matt. *USA Today* 24 Sept. 1990, sec. D: 3.

OUT CRY: see *The Two-Character Play*

"A PERFECT ANALYSIS GIVEN BY A PARROT": Comedy set in St.
Louis, about two lonely women whose lives have been
shaped by their relations with men. Ms., Texas (G).
    The characters and some of their dialogue appear in Act
1, scene 5, of *The Rose Tattoo*. But their names are
reversed (as they are in the movie version of *Tattoo*).

Esquire 50 (Oct. 1958): 131-34.

*A Perfect Analysis Given by a Parrot...: Comedy in One
Act*. New York: Dramatists Play Service, n.d. 18 pp.
Il. Contents: play, 3-16.

Dragon Country, 1969: 263-78 (A 2).

Esquire 80 (Oct. 1973): 288-90, 486-88.

Esquire: The Best of Forty Years. New York: McKay, 1973.
   169-72.

Theatre, Vol. 7, 1981: 263-78 (A 2).

Trans. (H):   French, Spanish.

Productions

"A Perfect Analysis Given by a Parrot." Key West
Players. Key West, FL: Waterfront Playhouse, 1 May 1970.
Tennessee Williams, dir.

Tennessee Laughs: Three 1-Act Plays. Chicago: Goodman
Theatre, 8-23 Nov. 1980. Gary Tucker, dir. With Rachel
Stephens (Flora), Muriel Moore (Bessie). See "Frosted
Glass Coffin."

Ten by Tennessee. New York: Lucille Lortel Theatre, 11
May-29 June 1986. Michael Kahn, dir. With Lisa Banes
(Flora), Mary Lou Rosato (Bessie). See "Auto-da-Fé."

PERIOD OF ADJUSTMENT: Dark comedy about the marital problems of two couples, set in a Southern city at Christmas.
   Mss., Delaware, Harvard, Princeton, Texas (G).
      Begun 1957-58, with each successive published script the
   dialogue and the action were tightened and the satire
   sharpened.   The pre-opening essay was "Prelude to a Comedy" (D 1).   The unpublished 1962 screenplay was by Isobel Lennart.

Publication: First Version

*Period of Adjustment (or High Point Is Built on a Cavern:
   A Serious Comedy)*. *Esquire* 54 (Dec. 1960): 210-76.

Publication: Second Version

*Period of Adjustment: High Point over a Cavern: A Serious
   Comedy*. New York: New Directions, 1960. viii, 120 pp.
   Contents: play, 3-120. Review:
      Freedley, George. *New York Morning Telegraph* 27
      Dec. 1960: 2.

The Best Plays of 1960-1961.... Ed. Louis Kroneberger.
   New York: Dodd, Mead, 1961. 115-32. Excerpts.

*Period of Adjustment: High Point over a Cavern: A Serious
   Comedy*. London: Secker & Warburg, 1961. 95 pp.

*Period of Adjustment: High Point over a Cavern: A Serious
Comedy.* Signet Book. New York: New American Library,
1962; Toronto: New American Library of Canada, 1962.
127 pp. Ils.

Period of Adjustment, etc., 1963 (A 2).

Theatre, Vol. 4, 1972: 125–246.

Four Plays, 1976: 3–127 (A 2).

Period of Adjustment, etc., 1982: 7–94 (A 2).

Trans. (H):   Arabic, Czech, Dutch, German, Greek,
Hungarian, Japanese, Spanish.

Publication: Third Version

*Period of Adjustment, or High Point Is Built on a Cavern:
A Serious Comedy.* New York: Dramatists Play Service,
1961. 78 pp. Il. Contents: play, 5–71.

Criticism

Goldfarb, Alvin.   *"Period of Adjustment* and the New Tennessee Williams." Tharpe (A 3): 310–17.

Productions

Period of Adjustment. Miami: Coconut Grove Playhouse, 29
Dec. 1958–3 Jan. 1959 (première). Tennessee Williams,
Owen Phillips, dirs. Leon Munier Jr., design. With
James Daly (Ralph), Robert Webber (George), Barbara Bax-
ley (Isabel), Martine Bartlett (Dorothea). Review:
   Time 12 Jan. 1959: 54–56.

Period of Adjustment. Previews: Philadelphia, Wilming-
ton, New Haven. New York: Helen Hayes Theatre, 10 Nov.
1960–4 Mar. 1961 (132). George Roy Hill, dir. Jo Miel-
ziner, Patricia Zipprodt, design. With James Daly
(Ralph), Robert Webber (George), Barbara Baxley (Isabel),
Rosemary Murphy (Dorothea). Reviews, Prod. Notes:
   Newsweek 21 Nov. 1960: 79.
   Theatre Arts Oct. 1960: 16.
   Time 21 Nov. 1960: 75.
   Times (London) 23 Nov. 1960: 15.
   Variety 19 Oct. 1960: 60. [Wilmington preview]
   Variety 16 Nov. 1960: 70.
   Variety 22 Feb. 1961: 71, 76. [Receipts]

Aston, Frank. *New York World-Telegram* 11 Nov. 1960.
    Rpt. *New York Theatre Critics' Reviews* 21: 177; Van
    Antwerp (F 1): 213-15.
Bolton, Whitney. *New York Morning Telegraph* 12 Nov.
    1960: 2.
---. *New York Morning Telegraph* 28 Nov. 1960: 2.
Brustein, Robert. *New Republic* 28 Nov. 1960: 38-39.
    Rpt. *Seasons of Discontent...* (New York: Simon,
    1965): 117-19.
Chapman, John. *New York Daily News* 11 Nov. 1960: 60.
    Rpt. *New York Theatre Critics' Reviews* 21: 176.
---. *New York Sunday News* 20 Nov. 1960, sec. 2: 1.
Clurman, Harold *Nation* 191 (3 Dec. 1960): 443-44.
Coleman, Robert. *New York Mirror* 11 Nov. 1960, sec. A:
    1. Rpt. *New York Theatre Critics' Reviews* 21: 179.
Driver, Tom F. *Christian Century* 77 (28 Dec. 1960):
    1536.
Duprey, Richard A. *Catholic World* 192 (Jan. 1961):
    255-56.
Gassner, John. *Educational Theatre Journal* 13 (Mar.
    1961): 51-53. Rpt. *Dramatic Soundings...*, ed.
    Glenn Loncy (New York: Crown, 1968): 586-87.
Gelb, Arthur. *New York Times* 1 May 1960, sec. 2: 1, 3.
    Rpt. Van Antwerp (F 1): 205-07. [Elia Kazan's re-
    fusal to direct]
Griffin, John. *Theatre* Dec. 1960: 18, 45.
Hatch, Robert. *Horizon* Mar. 1961: 102-03.
Hayes, Richard. *Commonweal* 74 (2 June 1961): 255.
Hewes, Henry. *Saturday Review* 26 Nov. 1960: 28.
Kazan, Elia. *A Life* (F 1): 595-96.
Kerr, Walter. *New York Herald Tribune* 11 Nov. 1960:
    10. Rpt. *New York Theatre Critics' Reviews* 21: 176;
    Van Antwerp (F 1): 211-13.
---. *New York Herald Tribune* 20 Nov. 1960, sec. 4: 2.
Lewis, Theophilus. *America* 104 (17 Dec. 1960): 410-11.
Mannes, Marya. *Reporter* 22 Dec. 1960: 35.
McCarten, John. *New Yorker* 19 Nov. 1960: 93-94.
McClain, John. *New York Journal-American* 11 Nov. 1960:
    11. Rpt. *New York Theatre Critics' Reviews* 21: 177.
Pryce-Jones, Alan. *Theatre Arts* Jan. 1961: 57-58.
Richards, Stanley. *Players* 37 (Apr. 1961): 161.
Simon, John. *Hudson Review* 14 (Spring 1961): 83-84.
Tallmer, Jerry. *Village Voice* 24 Nov. 1960: 9.
Taubman, Howard. *New York Times* 11 Nov. 1960: 34.
    Rpt. *New York Times Theatre Reviews; New York
    Theatre Critics' Reviews* 21: 178.
---. *New York Times* 20 Nov. 1960, sec. 2: 1. Rpt. *New
    York Times Theatre Reviews*.
Watts, Richard Jr. *New York Post* 11 Nov. 1960: 54.
    Rpt. *New York Theatre Critics' Reviews* 21: 178.

Zolotow, Sam. *New York Times* 11 Mar. 1960: 19.
   [Plans]
---. *New York Times* 28 Apr. 1960: 29. [Kazan's
   refusal to direct]

Period of Adjustment. Bristol: Theatre Royal, 4 Sept.
1961. Val May, dir. Graham Barlow, design. With Harry
H. Corbett (Ralph), John Franklyn Robbins (George),
Elizabeth Shepherd (Isabel), Rhoda Lewis (Dorothea).
Reviews:
   Times (London) 5 Sept. 1961: 15.
   Tynan, Kenneth. *London Observer* 17 Sept. 1961: 26.

Period of Adjustment. London: Royal Court Theatre, 13
June 1962; Wyndham Theatre 10 July-3 Nov. 1962. Roger
Graef, dir. With Bernard Braden (Ralph), Neill McGallum
(George), Collin Wincox (Isabel), Betty McDowall (Doro-
thea). Reviews:
   New York Times 14 June 1962: 24. Rpt. *New York Times*
      Theatre Reviews.
   Times (London) 14 June 1962: 6.
   Times (London) 11 July 1962: 13.
   Times (London) 2 Oct. 1962: 18. [Cast change]
   Clurman, Harold. *Nation* 11 Aug. 1962: 59.
   Foreman, Carl. *New Statesman* 63 (22 June 1962): 917.
   Gascoigne, Bamber. *Spectator* 108 (22 June 1962): 823,
      826.
   Tynan, Kenneth. *London Observer* 17 June 1962: 23.

Period of Adjustment. Screenplay by Isobel Lennart.
MGM, 31 Oct. 1962 (première). George Roy Hill, dir.
Paul C. Vogel, camera. George W. Davis, Edward Carfagne,
design. Lyn Murray, music. With Tony Franciosa (Ralph),
Jim Hutton (George), Jane Fonda (Isabel), Lois Nettleton
(Dorothea). Reviews, Prod. Notes:
   Filmfacts 5 (1962): 280.
   Newsweek 12 Nov. 1962: 96.
   Time 16 Nov. 1962: 97.
   Variety 31 Oct. 1962: 6.
   Beckley, Paul V. *New York Herald Tribune* 1 Mar. 1962:
      13.
   Coleman, John. *New Statesman* 65 (25 Jan. 1963): 134.
   Comerford, Adelaide. *Films in Review* 8 (Dec. 1962):
      627.
   Crowther, Bosley. *New York Times* 1 Nov. 1962: 34.
      Rpt. *New York Times Film Reviews*.
   Davies, Brenda. *Sight and Sound* 32 (Spring 1963): 93.
   Gill, Brendan. *New Yorker* 10 Nov. 1962: 234-35.
   Gilliatt, Penelope. *London Observer* 20 Jan. 1963: 25.
   Hartung, Philip T. *Commonweal* 77 (14 Dec. 1962): 315.
   Knight, Arthur. *Saturday Review* 10 Nov. 1962: 77.

Walsh, Moira. *America* 108 (19 Jan. 1963): 119-20.
Whitehall, Richard. *Films and Filming* Mar. 1963: 38.
Winsten, Archer. *New York Post* 1 Nov. 1962: 20.

"PORTRAIT OF A MADONNA": Drama about a woman living in a world of illusions as self-defense.

27 Wagons Full of Cotton, 1945, 1953: 87-104 (A 2).

27 Wagons Full of Cotton, 1949: 85-100 (A 2).

Twenty One-Act Plays: An Anthology for Amateur Performing Groups. Ed. Stanley Richards. Dolphin Books. Garden City: Doubleday, 1978. 61-79.

Theatre, Vol. 6, 1981: 107-27 (A 2).

Trans. (H): French, German, Greek, Italian.

Inclusion in Textbooks

Lauter, Paul, et al., eds. *The Heath Anthology of American Literature.* Lexington, MA: Heath, 1990. Vol. 2: 2190-2201.

McQuade, Donald, et al., eds. *The Harper American Literature.* New York: Harper, 1987. Vol. 2: 1816-28. Compact ed.: 1993-2005.

Miller, James E. Jr. *Heritage of American Literature.* San Diego: Harcourt, 1991.

Productions

4 Short Plays. Los Angeles: Las Palmas Theatre, 13 Jan. 1947. Hume Cronyn, dir. With Jessica Tandy (Miss Collins). Playbill: Van Antwerp (F 1): 78. See "Last of My Solid Gold Watches."

Trilogy of One Act Plays. Dallas: Gulf Oil Playhouse, Sept. 1947. Margo Jones, dir. With Katharine Squires (Miss Collins). See "Last of My Solid Gold Watches."

"Portrait of a Madonna." Actor's Studio. ABC-TV, Sept. 1948. Hume Cronyn, dir. With Jessica Tandy (Miss Collins).

Triple Plays. Theatre Guild. New York: Playhouse Theatre, 15 Apr. 1959. Hume Cronyn, dir. David Hayes, Anna

Hill Johnstone, design. With Jessica Tandy (Miss Col-
lins), Hume Cronyn (Doctor). Reviews:
  Theatre Arts June 1959: 9.
  Variety 22 Apr. 1959: 78.
  Village Voice 6 May 1959: 8.
  Aston, Frank. *New York World-Telegram* 16 Apr. 1959:
    22. Rpt. *New York Theatre Critics' Reviews* 20: 321.
  Atkinson, Brooks. *New York Times* 16 Apr. 1959: 28.
    Rpt. *New York Times Theatre Reviews; New York
    Theatre Critics' Reviews* 20: 322.
  ---. *New York Times* 26 Apr. 1959, sec. 2: 1. Rpt. *New
    York Times Theatre Reviews.*
  Chapman, John. *New York Daily News* 16 Apr. 1959: 77.
    Rpt. *New York Theatre Critics' Reviews* 20: 320.
  Coleman, Robert. *New York Daily Mirror* 16 Apr. 1959:
    25. Rpt. *New York Theatre Critics' Reviews* 20: 320.
  Kerr, Walter. *New York Herald Tribune* 16 Apr. 1959:
    14. Rpt. *New York Theatre Critics' Reviews* 20: 323.
  McClain, John. *New York Journal-American* 16 Apr. 1959:
    20. Rpt. *New York Theatre Critics' Reviews* 20: 321.
  Tynan, Kenneth. *New Yorker* 25 Apr. 1959: 82-85.
  Watts, Richard Jr. *New York Post* 16 Apr. 1959: 26.
    Rpt. *New York Theatre Critics' Reviews* 20: 322.
  ---. *New York Post* 26 Apr. 1959: 14.

Ten by Tennessee. New York: Lucille Lortel Theatre, 11
May-29 June 1986. Michael Kahn, dir. With Lisa Banes
(Miss Collins), Richard Howard (Elevator Boy), Anderson
Matthews (Porter), Derek D. Smith (Doctor). See "Auto-
da-Fé."

Other Productions:
  Atkinson, Brooks. *New York Times* 1 Apr. 1957: 21.
    Rpt. *New York Times Theatre Reviews.* [Washington]

"THE PURIFICATION": Poetic drama set in New Mexico about a
  brother's trial for incest. Ms., Harvard (G).

  "Dos Ranchos, or The Purification." *New Directions 1944*
  (# 8). New York: New Directions, 1944. 230-56.

  27 Wagons Full of Cotton, 1945, 1953: 29-62 (A 2).

  27 Wagons Full of Cotton, 1949: 33-64 (A 2).

  Theatre, Vol. 6, 1981: 39-77 (A 2).

Productions

"The Purification or (Song for Guitar)." Pasadena Labo-
ratory Theatre. Pasadena, CA: Pasadena Playbox, 27-29
July 1944 (première). Margo Jones, dir.

"The Purification." Dallas: Theatre '54, May 1954. Mar-
go Jones, dir. Sarah Cabell Massey, design. Reviews:
  Atkinson, Brooks. *New York Times* 29 May 1954: 12.
  Rpt. *New York Times Theatre Reviews.*
  ---. *New York Times* 6 June 1954, sec. 2: 1. Rpt. *New
  York Times Theatre Reviews.*

"The Purification." ANTA Matinee Theatre Series. New
York: Theatre de Lys, 8 Nov. 1959. Tom Brennan, dir.
Sharon Young, Michael Childs, music, choreography. With
Ted Von Briethaysen (Son), John Cunningham (Judge), Mary
Hara (Mother), Stan Kahn (Father), Eva Stern (Elena).
Reviews:
  Gelb, Arthur. *New York Times* 9 Dec. 1959: 57. Rpt.
  New York Times Theatre Reviews.
  Tallmer, Jerry. *Village Voice* 16 Dec. 1959: 8.

Four by Tennessee. Play of the Week. PBS-TV, 6 Feb.
1961. With Mike Kellin, Thomas Chambers, Eileen Heckart,
Salome Jens, Anne Revere. See "Hello from Bertha."

Other Productions:
  Gussow, Mel. *New York Times* 10 Dec. 1975: 56. [Mama
  Gails, New York]

Production: Ballet

"The Purification." Mary Anthony Dance Theatre. Westport, CT: White Barn Theatre, 4 Aug. 1957. Mary Anthony,
choreography. Louis Calabro, music. Eugene Van Hekle,
guitar. With Cameron McCash (Son), Paul Berensohn
(Judge), Judith Spector (Mother), John Starkweather
(Father), Mary Anthony (Elena).

THE RED DEVIL BATTERY SIGN: Drama about a Dallas mariachi
  player pulled into political intrigues. Ms., Columbia,
  Delaware (G)
    Begun about 1959, largely written 1973, and extensively
  revised after its stage failure, the play has distant
  connections to the novella "The Knightly Quest" (B 1).
  The first version was set on the day of Kennedy's assas-
  sination; all references were removed from the published
  version, a 1979 revison based on the 1977 production.

The Red Devil Battery Sign. New York: New Directions,
1988; Markham, Ont.: Penguin Books, 1988. xii, 94 pp.
Also New Directions Paperbook. Contents: play, 1-94.
Review:
   Speirs, Logan. *English Studies* Feb. 1990: 55.

Criticism

Tennessee Williams: Theatre in Process. Chicago: Encyclopedia Britannica, 1976. Videocassette.

Productions

The Red Devil Battery Sign. Boston: Schubert Theatre,
18-28 June 1975 (première). Edwin Sherin, dir. Robin
Wagner, Ruth Wagner, Marilyn Rennagel, design. Sidney
Lippman, music. With Anthony Quinn (King Del Rey),
Claire Bloom (Woman Downtown), Katy Jurado (Perla),
Annette Cardona (Nina). Reviews, Prod. Notes:
   New York Times 26 June 1975: 35. [Closing]
   Time 26 May 1975: 38-39.
   Time 7 July 1975: 29.
   Buckley, Tom. *New York Times* 16 June 1975: 19.
   Calta, Louis. *New York Times* 7 Oct. 1973: 79.
   Clay, Carolyn. *Boston Phoenix* 24 June 1975: 6. Rpt.
      Van Antwerp (F 1): 297-98.
   Kelly, Kevin. *Boston Globe* 19 June 1975: 25.
   Norton, Elliot. *Boston Herald American* 19 June 1975:
      14.

The Red Devil Battery Sign. Vienna: English Theatre, 17
Jan. 1976. Franz Schafranek, dir. With Keith Baxter
(King Del Rey), Ruth Brinkmann (Woman Downtown), Maria
Britneva (Perla), Lois Baxter (Nina). Reviews:
   Curtiss, Thomas Quinn. *International Herald Tribune* 21
      Jan. 1976.
   Elwood, William R. *Educational Theatre Journal* Mar.
      1978: 116-17.
   Kahn, Sy. Stanton (A 3): 175-78.
   ---. Tharpe (A 3): 362-71.

The Red Devil Battery Sign. London: Round House, 8 June
1977; Phoenix Theatre 7-23 July 1977. Keith Baxter,
David Leland, dirs. Bob Ringwood, Kate Owen, David Her-
sey, design. Mario Ramos, music. With Keith Baxter
(King Del Rey), Estelle Kohler (Woman Downtown), Maria
Britneva (Perla), Nitzu Saul (Nina), Ken Shorter (Wolf).
Reviews:
   Times (London) 9 May 1977: 9.
   Levin, Bernard. *Sunday Times* (London) 12 June 1977:
      37.

Marowitz, Charles. *Plays and Players* Sept. 1977: 26-
27.
Radin, Victoria. *London Observer* 12 June 1977: 26.
Wardle, Irving. *Times* (London) 9 June 1977: 13.

The Red Devil Battery Sign. Vancouver: Playhouse The-
atre, 18 Oct.-15 Nov. 1980. Roger Hodgman, dir. Cameron
Porteous, Jeffrey Dallas, design. With Richard Donat
(King Del Rey), Diane D'Aquila (Woman Downtown), Joyce
Campion (Perla), Nicola Cavendish (Nina). Reviews:
Czarnecki, Mark. *Maclean's* 3 Nov. 1980: 70.
Edmonstone, Wayne. *Vancouver Sun* 20 Oct. 1980, sec. C:
6.

"THE REMARKABLE ROOMING-HOUSE OF MME. LE MONDE": Macabre
comedy about the events prior to a London landlady's
destruction of her lecherous son, a crippled homosexual
boarder, and a flashy operator.

The Remarkable Rooming-House of Mme. Le Monde: A Play.
New York: Albondocani, 1984. Unpaged. Limited edition.

THE ROMAN SPRING OF MRS. STONE: see B 1

THE ROSE TATTOO: Comedy about a Sicilian widow, living on
the Gulf coast, who is brought back to life by a truck
driver clown. Mss., Columbia, Delaware, New York Public,
Texas (G).
Begun 1948 as a result of Williams's trip to Italy, it
is one of the few early plays for which only one published version seems to exist, and according to the copy-
right page that was put together by Paul Bigelow. See
Williams's essays "The Timeless World of a Play" (D 1 and
below) and "The Meaning of *The Rose Tattoo* (D 1). Williams also wrote the unpublished 1955 screenplay; it was
adapted by Hal Kantor. See also his essay on "Anna Magnani" (D 1).
The one-act comedy "A Perfect Analysis Given by a Parrot" (above) relates to Act 1, scene 5.

The Rose Tattoo. New York: New Directions, 1951. Lon-
don: Secker & Warburg, 1954. xvi, 144 pp. Il. Con-
tents: "The Timeless World of a Play" (D 1), vi-xi;
Author's Production Notes, xiii-xiv; play, 1-144.
Review:
Times Literary Supplement 4 Mar. 1955: 130.

The Best Plays of 1950-1951.... Ed. John Chapman. New
York: Dodd, Mead, 1951. 210-36. Excerpts.

Theatre Arts 39 (May 1955): 32-64, 96.

The Rose Tattoo. Signet Book. New York: New American
Library, 1955. 128 pp. Ils.

Best American Plays, Fourth Series, *1951-1957.* Ed. John
Gassner. New York: Crown, 1958. 91-132.

Rose Tattoo, etc., 1958, 1976: 9-113 (A 2).

Five Plays, 1962: 125-213 (A 2).

Three Plays, 1964: 1-156 (A 2).

The Rose Tattoo...: Play in Three Acts. New York: Dramatists Play Service, [1965]. 94 pp. Il.

Three by Tennessee, 1976 (A 2).

The Tony Winners: A Collection of Ten Exceptional Plays
.... Ed. Stanley Richards. Garden City: Doubleday,
1977. 111-214.

Theatre, Vol 2, 1971: 257-415 (A 2).

Selected Plays, 1977: 183-278 (A 2).

Eight Plays, 1979: 297-398 (A 2).

Trans. (H):   Arabic, Chinese, Czech, Danish, French,
German, Greek, Japanese, Norwegian, Portuguese, Slovak,
Spanish.

Inclusion in Textbooks

Clayes, Stanley A., and David G. Spencer, eds. *Contemporary Drama.* New York: Scribner's, 1962.

Corrigan, Robert W., and James L. Rosenberg, eds. *The
Art of the Theatre: A Critical Anthology of Drama.* San
Francisco: Chandler, 1964. 475-568.

Grebanier, Bernard D., and Seymour Reiter, eds. *Introduction to Imaginative Literature.* New York: Crowell,
1960.

Criticism

Gómez García, Ascensión. *"The Rose Tattoo y The Roman
Spring of Mrs. Stone*: Cara y cruz de una misma moneda."
Revista Canaria de Estudios Ingleses 16 (Apr. 1988):
183-92.

Kolin, Philip C. "'Sentiment and humor in equal mea-
sure': Comic Forms in *The Rose Tattoo*." Tharpe (A 3):
214-31.

Lal, P. N. "Christopher Fry and Tennessee Williams: A
Comparative Study of *A Phoenix Too Frequent* and *The
Rose Tattoo*." *Indian Journal of English Studies* 19
(1979): 81-91.

Munro, C. Lynn. "The Tattooed Heart and the Serpentine
Eye: Morrison's Choice of Epigraph for *Sula*." *Black
American Literature Forum* 18.4 (1984): 150-54.

Schwanitz, Dietrich. "Der Vorganger und sein Nachfolger:
Vorschlage zu einer Methode der literarischen Vater-
schaftsbestimmung." *Die amerikanische Literatur in der
Weltliteratur: Themen und Aspekte*. Ed. Claus Uhlig
and Volker Bischoff. Berlin: Schmidt, 1982. 14-33.

Starnes, Leland. "The Grotesque Children of *The Rose
Tattoo*." *Modern Drama* 12 (Feb. 1970): 357-69. Rpt. D.
Parker (A 3): 39-51.

Weldon, Roberta F. *"The Rose Tattoo*: A Modern Version of
The Scarlet Letter." *Interpretations* 15 (Fall 1983):
70-77.

Productions

The Rose Tattoo. Chicago: Erlanger Theatre, 29 Dec. 1950
(première); New York: Martin Beck Theatre, 3 Feb.-27 Oct.
1951 (306). Daniel Mann, dir. Boris Aronson, design.
David Diamond, music. With Maureen Stapleton (Serafina),
Eli Wallach (Alvaro), Phyllis Love (Rosa), Don Murray
(Jack), Sal Mineo (Salvatore). Program: Leavitt (F 1):
95. Winner Antoinette Perry (Tony) Award. Reviews,
Prod. Notes:
   Life 26 Feb. 1951: 80-84.
   New York Times 26 Mar. 1951: 20. [Tony Award]
   Newsweek 12 Feb. 1951: 72.
   Theatre Arts 35 (April 1951): 16.
   Time 12 Feb. 1951: 53-54.
   Variety 10 Jan. 1951: 60. [Chicago]

Atkinson, Brooks. *New York Times* 5 Feb. 1951: 19.
    Rpt. *New York Times Theatre Reviews; New York
    Theatre Critics' Reviews* 12: 365.
---. *New York Times* 11 Feb. 1951, sec. 2: 1. Rpt. *New
    York Times Theatre Reviews.* Response: *New York
    Times* 25 Mar. 1951, sec. 2: 3; *New York Times* 1 Apr.
    1951, sec. 2: 3.
---. *New York Times* 27 May 1950, sec. 2: 1.
---. *New York Times* 3 June 1951, sec. 2: 1. [Changes]
Barnes, Howard. *New York Herald Tribune* 11 Feb. 1950,
    sec. 4: 1.
Beyer, William H. *School and Society* 73 (24 Mar.
    1951): 181-83.
Bolton, Whitney. *New York Morning Telegraph* 6 Feb.
    1950: 2.
Brown, John Mason. *Saturday Review* 10 Mar. 1951: 22-
    24. Rpt. *As They Appear* (New York: McGraw-Hill,
    1952): 161-66.
Chapman, John. *New York Daily News* 5 Feb. 1951: 37.
    Rpt. *New York Theatre Critics' Reviews* 12: 365.
Clurman, Harold. *New Republic* 19 Feb. 1951: 22.
Coleman, Robert. *New York Daily Mirror* 5 Feb. 1951:
    23. Rpt. *New York Theatre Critics' Reviews* 12: 364.
Dupree, F. W. *Partisan Review* 18 (Mar.-June 1951):
    333-34.
Funke, Lewis. *New York Times* 29 Oct. 1950, sec. 2: 1.
    [Casting]
Gibbs, Wolcott. *New Yorker* 10 Feb. 1951: 54.
Gilroy, Harry. *New York Times* 28 Jan. 1951, sec. 2: 1,
    3.
Guernsey, Otis L. *New York Herald Tribune* 5 Feb. 1951.
    Rpt. *New York Theatre Critics' Reviews* 12: 363-64.
    Van Antwerp (F 1): 130-31.
Hawkins, William. *New York World-Telegram* 5 Feb. 1951.
    Rpt. *New York Theatre Critics' Reviews* 12: 366.
Kerr, Walter. *Commonweal* 53 (23 Feb. 1951): 492-94.
Marshall, Margaret. *Nation* 172 (17 Feb. 1951): 161-62.
McClain, John. *New York Journal-American* 5 Feb. 1951:
    8. Rpt. *New York Theatre Critics' Reviews* 12: 364.
Nathan, George Jean. *New York Journal-American* 12 Feb.
    1951: 12.
---. *Theatre Book of the Year 1950-1951.* New York:
    Knopf, 1951. 209-12.
Rice, Vernon. *New York Post* 1 Feb. 1951: 36.
Shanley, J. P. *New York Times* 3 Feb. 1951: 9.
    [Opening]
Sheaffer, Louis. *Brooklyn Daily Eagle* 5 Feb. 1951: 7.
Shipley, Joseph T. *New Leader* 19 Feb. 1951: 27.
Watts, Richard Jr. *New York Post* 5 Feb. 1951: 26.
    Rpt. *New York Theatre Critics' Reviews* 12: 366; Van
    Antwerp (F 1): 131-32.

---. *New York Post* 18 Feb. 1951, amus. sec.: 12.
Wyatt, Euphemia Van Rennsselaer. *Catholic World* 172
   (Mar. 1951): 467-68.
Zolotow, Sam. *New York Times* 27 Aug. 1951: 16. [Tour]

The Rose Tattoo. Paramont, 12 Dec. 1955 (première).
Daniel Mann, dir. James Wong Howe, camera. Hal Pereira,
Tambia Larsen, design. Alex North, music. With Anna
Magnani (Serafina), Burt Lancaster (Alvaro), Marisa Pavan
(Rosa), Ben Cooper (Jack), Jo Van Fleet (Bessie), Vir-
ginia Grey (Estelle). Music soundtrack: Columbia
Records, 1955; excerpts, *North of Hollywood*, RCA Victor
Records, 1958. Reviews, Prod. Notes:
   Harper's Bazaar Feb. 1955: 124-25.
   Life 28 Nov. 1955: 139-44.
   Look 27 Dec. 1955: 90.
   National Parent-Teacher Dec. 1955: 40.
   New York Times Magazine 10 Apr. 1955: 47.
   New York Times Magazine 30 Oct. 1955: 29.
   Newsweek 26 Dec. 1955: 65-66.
   Spectator 198 (21 June 1956): 814.
   Time 19 Dec. 1955: 94-95.
   Variety 2 Nov. 1955: 6.
   Baker, Peter G. *Films and Filming* Mar. 1956: 16.
   Bingham, Robert. *Reporter* 29 Dec. 1955: 36-37.
   Burles, Kenneth T. *Magill's Survey of Cinema: English
      Language Films*. Ed. Frank N. Magill. Englewood
      Cliffs, NJ: Salem, 1980. 1472-75.
   Cahoon, Herbert. *Library Journal* 80 (1 Nov. 1955):
      2478.
   Crowther, Bosley. *New York Times* 13 Dec. 1955: 55.
      Rpt. *New York Times Film Reviews*.
   ---. *New York Times* 18 Dec. 1955, sec. 2: 3.
   Downing, Robert. *Films in Review* 6 (Dec. 1955): 527-
      28.
   Hartung, Philip T. *Commonweal* 63 (23 Dec. 1955): 305-
      06.
   Hatch, Robert. *Nation* 182 (7 Jan. 1956): 18.
   Johnson, Grady. *New York Times* 5 Dec. 1954, sec. 2: 9.
      [Filming]
   Kass, Robert. *Catholic World* 182 (1 Dec. 1955): 218.
   Knight, Arthur. *Saturday Review* 10 Dec. 1955: 25-26.
      Rpt. Van Antwerp (F 1): 155-57.
   McCarten, John. *New Yorker* 24 Dec. 1955: 52.
   Pratley, Gerald. *Films in Review* 7 (Apr. 1956): 782-
      83.
   Prouse, Derek. *Sight and Sound* 25 (Spring 1956): 194-
      96.
   Sarris, Andrew. *Film Culture* 5/6 (Winter 1955). Rpt.
      Confessions of a Cultist... (New York: Simon, 1970):
      19-20.

Walsh, Moira. *America* 94 (Dec. 1955): 362.
Weiler, A. H. *New York Times* 3 May 1954, sec. 2: 5.
   [Film rights]
Whitebait, William. *New Statesman* 51 (3 Mar. 1956):
   192-93.
Wood, Thomas. *New York Herald Tribune* 23 Jan. 1955,
   sec. 4: 3. [Filming]
Zinsser, William K. *New York Herald Tribune* 13 Dec.
   1955: 20.

The Rose Tattoo. Dublin Theatre Festival. Dublin: 13-27
May 1957. Alan Simpson, dir. With Anna Manahan (Sera-
fina), Pat Nolan (Alvaro), Kate Binchy (Rosa). Reviews,
Prod. Notes:
   New York Times 24 May 1957: 31. [Arrest]
   New York Times 25 May 1957: 24.
   New York Times 31 Aug. 1958, sec. 2: 3.
   Times (London) 14 May 1957: 3.
   Times (London) 24 May 1957: 10. [Simpson's arrest]
   Times (London) 25 May 1957: 4.
   Times (London) 27 May 1957: 6.
   Times (London) 5 July 1957: 14. [Trial]
   Times (London) 9 July 1957: 6.
   Times (London) 10 June 1958: 6. [Judgment]

The Rose Tattoo. Liverpool: New Shakespeare Theatrical
Club, 4 Nov. 1958; London: New Theatre, 15 Jan. 1959.
Sam Wanamaker, dir. With Lea Padovani (Serafina), Sam
Wanamaker (Alvaro). Reviews, Prod. Notes:
   English 12 (Summer 1959): 184.
   Times (London) 3 Nov. 1958: 7.
   Times (London) 21 Nov. 1958: 16.
   Times (London) 18 Dec. 1958: 14.
   Brien, Alan. *Spectator* 202 (23 Jan. 1959): 103-05.
   Sim, David. *Theatre World* Mar. 1959: 13-18.
   Worsley, T. C. *New Statesman* 57 (24 Jan. 1959): 104.

The Rose Tattoo. New York: City Center Theatre, 20 Oct.
1966; New York: Billy Rose Theatre, 9 Nov.-31 Dec. 1966
(76). Milton Katselas, dir. With Maureen Stapleton
(Serafina), Harry Guardino (Alvaro), Maria Tucci (Rosa),
Christopher Walken (Jack). Recording: Caedmon Records,
1967. [In record container: "Facts about Me" (D 1),
Robert W. Corrigan, "The World of Tennessee Williams."]
Reviews:
   Time 18 Nov. 1966: 80.
   Chapman, John. *New York Daily News* 21 Oct. 1966: 70.
   Clurman, Harold. *Nation* 203 (7 Nov. 1966): 493.
   Croce, Arlene. *National Review* 24 Jan. 1967: 99.
   Hewes, Henry. *Saturday Review* 26 Nov. 1966: 60.

Kerr, Walter. *New York Times* 20 Nov. 1966, sec. 2: 1.
Rpt. *New York Times Theatre Reviews*.

Lewis, Theophilus. *America* 115 (10 Dec. 1966): 786.

Mishkin, Leo. *New York Morning Telegraph* 22 Oct. 1966:
3.

Nadel, Norman. *New York World-Telegram* 21 Oct. 1966:
33.

Sullivan, Dan. *New York Times* 21 Oct. 1966: 36.   Rpt.
New York Times Theatre Reviews.

Tallmer, Jerry. *New York Post* 21 Oct. 1966: 56.

Zolotow, Sam. *New York Times* 26 Oct. 1966: 40.

Other Productions:

New York Times 22 July 1958: 21.   [Canceled Salisbury,
Southern Rhodesia]

Newsweek 18 June 1984.   [Canceled Broadway prod. with
Gina Lollobrigida, Christopher Atkins]

Tennessee Williams Literary Journal 1.2 (Winter 1989–
90): 61.   [Williamstown, MA, with Maria Tucci, James
Naughton]

Conway, Mary L.   *Drama Critique* 11 (Winter 1968): 58–
60.   [Cleveland]

Frank, Leah D.   *New York Times* 6 Apr. 1986, sec. 21:
15.   [New York]

Hampton, Wilborn.   *New York Times* 28 Feb. 1989, sec. 3:
3.   [Williamstown, MA]

Morley, Sheridan.   *International Herald Tribune* 19 June
1991: 8.   [Peter Hall prod. with Julie Walters and
Ken Stott]

Webster, Ivan.   *Encore* 4 Sept. 1979: 40–41.   [Stock-
bridge, Ma., with Cicely Tyson; Craig Anderson,
dir.]

"SECRET PLACES OF THE HEART":   Unpublished and unfinished
script.
A note in *Family Weekly* 24 Apr. 1983, says, "Williams's
last screenplay ... has been bought by director Keith
David Hack and will be set in contemporary St. Louis...."

"Secret Places of the Heart."   BBC-Radio, 4 Nov. 1988
(première).   Note:
Tennessee Williams Literary Journal 1.1 (Spring 1989):
78.

SENSO: Unpublished dialogue with Paul Bowles: based on
screenplay by Camillo Alianello, Giorgio Bissani, Giorgio
Prosperi; adapted by Luchino Visconti and Suso Cecchi
d'Amico, 1953.

The screenplay grew out of a story by Camillo Boito concerning an 1866 affair between a love-mad Venetian countess and an Austrian officer; abandoned during the war
between the two countries, she denounces him as a deser-
ter, and he is executed. The film was released in England, 1957, as *The Wanton Countess*.

Senso. Ed. Giovanni Battista Cavallaro. Bologna: Cap-
    pelli, 1955. 212 pp. Trans. Judith Green: *Two
    Screenplays.* New York: Orion, 1970.

Film

Senso. Lux, 1954. Luchino Visconti, dir. G. R. Aldo,
B. Krasker, camera. Ottavio Scotti, Marcel Escoffier,
Pietro Tosi, design. With Alida Valli (Countess Licia
Serpieri), Farley Granger (Lt. Franz Mahler), Massimo
Girotti (Marquis Ussoni), Heinz Moog (Count Serpieri).
Reviews, Prod. Notes:
    Filmfacts 9 (1968): 328.
    Baker, Peter G. *Films and Filming* 4 (Oct. 1957): 25.
    Nowell-Smith, Geoffrey. *Luchino Visconti.* London:
        Secker, 1967. 79-99.
    Tanner, Alain. *Sight and Sound* 27 (Autumn 1957): 92-
        93.
    Villien, Bruno. *Visconti.* Paris: Calmann-Levy, 1986.
    Weiler, A. H. *New York Times* 9 July 1968: 31. Rpt.
    New York Times Film Review.

THE SEVEN DESCENTS OF MYRTLE: see *Kingdom of Earth*

SLAPSTICK TRAGEDY: see "The Gnadiges Fraulein" and "The Mu-
    ilated"

SMALL CRAFT WARNINGS/"CONFESSIONAL": Revelations of the
lives and desires of several persons in a southern California bar. Mss., Congress, Delaware, Texas (G).
    Small Craft Warnings is more an expansion than a rewrite
of "Confessional," but the character of Bobby is quite
changed. Several pertinent essays and letters were published with *Small Craft Warnings*.

Publication: "Confessional"

Dragon Country, 1969: 151-96 (A 2).

Best Short Plays of the World Theatre 1968-1973. Ed.
    Stanley Richards. New York: Crown, 1973. 1-21.

Theatre, Vol. 7, 1981: 151-96 (A 2).

Trans. (H): Spanish.

Publication: *Small Craft Warnings*

Small Craft Warnings. New York: New Directions, 1972;
Toronto: McClelland & Stewart, 1972. Also New Directions
Paperbook. London: Secker & Warburg, 1973. vi, 86 pp.
Il. Contents: "Too Personal?" 3-6; play, 11-73; "Notes
after the Second Invited Audience: (And a Troubled
Sleep)," 74-78; "*Small Craft Warnings*: Genesis and Evolu-
tion" [letters], 79-86. Reviews:
    Choice 9 (Feb. 1973): 1594.
    Wimble, B. L. *Library Journal* 97 (1 Sept. 1972): 2748.

Another edition: 92 pp. [book club?].

The Best Plays of 1971-1972.... Ed. Otis L. Guernsey.
New York: Dodd, Mead, 1972. 276-90. Excerpts.

Plays and Players 20 (Apr. 1973): i-xiii.

Theatre, Vol. 5, 1976: 215-300 (A 2).

Period of Adjustment, etc., 1982: 177-235 (A 2).

Trans. (H): German, Norwegian, Spanish.

Productions

"Confessional." Maine Theatre Arts Festival. Bar Har-
bour, ME: July 1971 (première). William E. Hunt, dir.
Prod. Notes:
    Funke, Lewis. *New York Times* 19 Dec. 1971, sec. 2: 3,
    43.

Small Craft Warnings. New York: Truck and Warehouse
Theatre, 2 Apr. 1972; New Theatre, 6 June-17 Sept. 1972
(première: 200). Richard Altman, dir. Fred Voelpel,
John Gleason, design. With Helena Carroll, later Peg
Murray (Leona), Gene Fanning (Monk), David Hooks, some-
times Tennessee Williams (Doc), Cherry Davis, later Candy
Darling (Violet), Alan Mixon (Quentin), William Hickey
(Steve), Brad Sullivan (Bill). Reviews, Prod. Notes:
    New York Daily News 6 June 1972: 52. [Williams on
    stage]
    New York Post 6 June 1972: 65. [Williams on stage]
    New York Times 7 Mar. 1972: 45.
    New York Times 2 June 1972: 24.
    New York Times 6 June 1972: 48. [Williams on stage]

Variety 6 Apr. 1972: 60.
Variety 12 Apr. 1972: 98.
Variety 7 June 1972: 1, 60. [Williams on stage]
Village Voice 22 June 1972: 55. [Williams on stage]
Barnes, Clive. *New York Times* 3 Apr. 1972: 50.
---. *Times* (London) 6 April 1972: 10.
---. *Times* (London) 13 May 1972: 10.
Bell, Arthur. *Village Voice* 24 Feb. 1972: 58. Rpt.
    Leavitt (H): 154. [Casting]
Brustein, Robert. *New Republic* 17 Mar. 1973: 23.
Calta, Louis. *New York Times* 6 June 1972: 48.
Clurman, Harold. *Nation* 214 (24 Apr. 1972): 540-41.
    Rpt. Van Antwerp (F 1): 283-84, 286.
Funke, Lewis. *New York Times* 19 Dec. 1971, sec. 2: 3,
    43.
Gottfried, Martin. *Women's Wear Daily* 4 Apr. 1972.
    Rpt. *New York Theatre Critics' Reviews* 33: 273.
Harris, Leonard. CBS-TV, 2 Apr. 1972. Rpt. *New York
    Theatre Critics' Reviews* 33: 274.
Hewes, Henry. *Saturday Review* 22 Apr. 1972: 22-24.
Hughes, Catherine. *America* 126 (29 Apr. 1972): 462.
Kalem, T. E. *Time* 17 Apr. 1972: 72-73.
Kauffmann, Stanley. *New Republic* 29 Apr. 1972: 24.
    Rpt. *Persons of the Drama...* (New York: Harper,
    1976): 168-71.
Kerr, Walter. *New York Times* 6 Apr. 1972, sec. 2: 8,
    29.
McMorrow, Tom. *New York Daily News* 8 June 1972: 116.
    [Williams on stage]
O'Haire, Patricia. *New York Sunday News* 2 Apr. 1972:
    25.
Oliver, Edith. *New Yorker* 15 Apr. 1972: 110.
Rollin, Betty. NBC, 2 Apr. 1972. Rpt. *New York
    Theatre Critics' Reviews* 33: 273.
Simon, John. *New York* 17 Apr. 1972: 84.
Smith, Michael. *Village Voice* 6 Apr. 1972: 61.
Wasserman, Debbi. *Show Business* 7 Sept. 1972: 11.
Watt, Douglas. *New York Daily News* 3 Apr. 1972: 52.
    Rpt. *New York Theatre Critics' Reviews* 33: 271-72.
Watts, Richard. *New York Post* 3 Apr. 1972: 23. Rpt.
    New York Theatre Critics' Reviews 33: 272.
Weales, Gerald. *Commonweal* 96 (5 May 1972): 214-16.

Small Craft Warnings. London: Hampstead Theatre Club, 29
Jan. 1973; Comedy Theatre, 13 Mar. 1973. Vivian Matalon,
dir. Saul Rodomsky, Robert Ornbo, design. With Elaine
Strich (Leona), Peter Jones (Monk), George Pravda (Doc),
Frances de la Tour (Violet), Tony Beckley (Quentin),
James Berwick (Steve), Edward Judd (Bill). Reviews:
    Plays and Players Apr. 1973: xiv-xv. [Interview with
    Matalon]

Variety 28 Mar. 1973: 74, 79.
Brustein, Robert. *New Republic* 17 Mar. 1973: 23.
Hayman, Ronald. *Sunday Times* (London) 10 Mar. 1973:
  11. [Interview with De la Tour]
Hobson, Harold. *Sunday Times* (London) 4 Feb. 1973: 36.
Nightingale, Benedict. *New Statesman* 85 (9 Feb. 1973):
  208-09.
Walker, John. *International Herald Tribune* 3 Feb.
  1973.
---. *International Herald Tribune* 30 Mar. 1973.
Wardle, Irving. *Times* (London) 30 Jan. 1973: 9.

"SOME PROBLEMS FOR THE MOOSE LODGE":   see *A House Not Meant
  to Stand*

SOMETHING CLOUDY, SOMETHING CLEAR: Unpublished semi-auto-
  biogaphical drama about a triangular love relationship in
  Provincetown in 1940.
    This was Williams's next-to-last new play to open, and
  his last in New York.

  Something Cloudy, Something Clear. Jean Cocteau Repertory Company. New York: Bouwerie Lane Theatre, 24 Aug.
  1981-13 Mar. 1982 (première: 51). Eve Adamson, dir.
  Douglas McKeown, Giles Hogye, design. Richard Peck,
  dance. With Craig Smith (August), Elton Cermier (Kip),
  Dominique Cieri (Clare). Program: Van Antwerp (F 1):
  378. Reviews:
    New York Times 25 Aug. 1981, sec. C: 8.
    Barnes, Clive. *New York Post* 14 Sept. 1981: 25.
    Clarke, Gerald. *Time* 21 Sept. 1981: 65.
    Feingold, Michael. *Village Voice* 16 Sept. 1981.
    Grumley, Michael. *New York Native* 5 Oct. 1981: 33.
    Hughes, Catherine. *America* 145 (10 Oct. 1981): 202.
    ---. *Plays and Players* Nov. 1981: 58-59.
    Isaac, Dan. *Other Stages* 17 Dec. 1981: 6-8.
    Kakutani, Michiko. *New York Times* 13 Aug. 1981.
    Kerr, Walter. *New York Times* 27 Sept. 1981, sec. 2: 3.
    Rich, Frank. *New York Times* 11 Sept. 1981, sec. C: 3.

"SOMETHING UNSPOKEN": Drama about two New Orleans women
  caught in a charged lesbian atmosphere. Ms., Texas (G).
    The play has been produced separately and, together with
  Suddenly Last Summer, under the collective title *Garden
  District.*

  27 Wagons Full of Cotton, 1953: 219-38 (A 2).

The Best Short Plays of 1955-1956.   Ed. Margaret Mayorga.
Boston: Beacon, 1956.   83-110.

Garden District, 1959: 7-25 (see *Suddenly Last Summer*
below).

Orpheus Descending, etc., 1961 (A 2).

Five Plays, 1962: 217-35 (A 2).

Ten Great One-Act Plays. Ed. Morris Sweetkind.   New
York: Bantam, 1968.   123-41.

Baby Doll, etc. 1968: 97-112 (A 2).

Theatre, Vol. 6, 1981: 273-96 (A 2).

Trans. (H): German, Greek, Spanish.

Inclusion in Textbooks

Cox, R. David, and Shirley S. Cox, eds.   *Themes in the
One-Act Play.* New York: McGraw-Hill, 1971. 167-79.

Summers, Hollis Spurgeon, and Edgar Whan, eds.   *Literature: An Introduction.* New York: McGraw-Hill, 1960.

Productions

"Something Unspoken."   Lake Hopatcong, NJ: Lakeside Sum-
mer Theatre, 22 June 1955.   Herbert Machiz, dir.   Paul
Georges, Jack Haupman, design.   With Patricia Ripley
(Cornelia), Hortense Alden (Grace).

Garden District. New York: York Theatre, 7 Jan. 1958.
Herbert Machiz, dir.   With Eleanor Phelps (Cornelia),
Hortense Alden (Grace).   Program: Leavitt (F 1): 120.
See *Suddenly Last Summer.*

Garden District. London: Arts Theatre, 16 Sept. 1958.
Herbert Machiz, dir.   With Beryl Measor (Cornelia),
Beatrix Lehmann (Grace).   See *Suddenly Last Summer.*

Other Productions:
  Times (London) 3 Nov. 1960: 16. [London Univ.]
  Peter, John. *Sunday Times* (London) 13 Oct. 1974: 31.
    [Dublin]

STAIRS TO THE ROOF: Unpublished fantasy set in a shirt-maker's factory; described by Nelson (A 3): 67-74. Mss., California-Los Angeles, Texas (G).

Stairs to the Roof: A Prayer for the Wild of Heart That Are Kept in Cages. Pasadena, CA: Playbox, 25 Mar.- Apr. 1945 (première). Gilmor Brown, dir. Program: Van Antwerp (F 1): 81.

Stairs to the Roof. Pasadena, CA.: Playhouse, 26 Feb. 1947. Gilmor Brown, Rita Glover, dirs. Reviews:
    New York Times 26 Feb. 1947: 35.
    Theatre Arts 31 (July 1947): 12.
    Variety 28 Feb. 1947: 6. Rpt. Van Antwerp (F 1): 81-
    82.

"STEPS MUST BE GENTLE": Conversation between the ghosts of Hart Crane and his mother.

Steps Must Be Gentle: A Dramatic Reading for Two Perform-ers. New York: William Targ, 1980. 22 pp. Limited edition.

Theatre, Vol. 6, 1981: 315-27 (A 2).

Criticism

Stanton, Stephen S. "Some Thoughts about *Steps Must Be Gentle*." *Tennessee Williams Review* 4.1 (1983): 48-53.

Production

"Steps Must Be Gentle." Ann Arbor, MI: Trueblood Arena Theatre (Univ. of Michigan), 15-18 Mar. 1983 (première). Christopher Connelly, dir. With Mary Jeffries (Grace), Timothy Hopper (Hart).

STOPPED ROCKING: Screenplay written mid-1970s: a triangular love relationship, one member of whom is in a psychiatric ward, set in contemporary St. Louis and the Ozarks.

Stopped Rocking and Other Screenplays, 1984: 293-384 (A 2).

"THE STRANGEST KIND OF ROMANCE: A LYRIC PLAY IN FOUR SCENES": Drama written 1942, set in a Midwestern indus-

trial city: a little man's stand against inhumaneness.
Ms., Texas (G).
  The play grew out of the short story "The Malediction"
(B 1).

27 Wagons Full of Cotton, 1945, 1953: 133–58 (A 2).

27 Wagons Full of Cotton, 1949: 127–48 (A 2).

Theatre, Vol. 6, 1981: 169–200 (A 2).

Trans. (H):   French, Swedish.

Production

Ten by Tennessee. New York: Lucille Lortel Theatre, 11
May–29 June 1986. Michael Kahn, dir. With Derek D.
Smith (Little Man), Mary Lou Rosato (Landlady). See
"Auto-da-Fé."

A *STREETCAR NAMED DESIRE*: Tragedy of the contest between a
Mississippi aristocrat seeking security in her sister's
home in New Orleans and her Polish-American brother-in-
law. Mss., Columbia, Delaware, Harvard, Illinois-Urbana,
New York Public, Texas (G).
  The play was written 1945–47 and revised after performance. Several versions have been published. According
to George Miller (I: Gunn) the second American edition
appeared 1950. Williams also wrote the 1950 screenplay;
adapted by Oscar Saul, it was nominated for an Academy
Award and has been filmed twice. See Williams's essays
"The Catastrope of Success" and "Let Me Hang It All Out"
(D 1).
  Thomas Hart Benton painted a scene from the New York
production: "The Polker Night" (reproduced on Signet edition cover [below] and in Lewitt [F 1]: 76; sketch, in
Van Antwerp [F 1]: 106). Valerie Bettis choreographed
the 1952 ballet version to Alex North's film music; John
Neumier choreographed another version to different music.
There has even been a deliberate parody version.

Publication: First American Version

A *Streetcar Named Desire.* New York: New Directions,
    1947. 171 pp. Contents: play, 9–171. Reviews:
        Booklist 44 (15 Feb. 1948): 214.
        Library Journal 73 (1 Mar. 1948): 399.
        Eaton, W. P.. *New York Herald Tribune Weekly Book
            Review* 29 Feb. 1948: 14.

       Freedley, George. *Library Journal* 73 (1 Mar. 1948):
       399.
       Terry, C. V. *New York Times Book Review* 1 Feb.
       1948: 17.

The Burns Mantle Best Plays of 1947-48....   Ed. John
  Chapman.   New York: Dodd, Mead, 1948.   32-62.   Excerpts.

Publication: British Version

A Streetcar Named Desire: A Play.   London: John Lehmann,
  1949.   112 pp.   Contents: play, 9-112.

London Evening Standard 24 Oct.-early Nov. 1949.

Four Plays, 1956: 65-154 (A 2).

A Streetcar Named Desire.   London: Secker & Warburg,
  1957.   96 pp.

Streetcar Named Desire, etc., 1959 (A 2).

Sweet Bird of Youth, etc., 1962: 113-226 (A 2).

14 Great Plays.   London: Heineman/Octopus, 1977.   547-
  625.

Publication: Second American Version

A Streetcar Named Desire.   New York: New Directions, n.d.
  166 pp.   Fifth Printing.

A Streetcar Named Desire...with an Introduction by the
  Author.   Signet Book.   New York: New American Library,
  1951.   142 pp.   Ils.   New ils., 1984.   Contents: "On a
  Streetcar Named Success" (D 1), 7-10; play, 13-142.

Best American Plays, Third Series, *1945-1951.*   Ed. John
  Gassner.   New York: Crown, 1952.   49-93.

*Critics' Choice: New York Drama Critics' Circle Prize
  Plays 1935-1955.*   Ed. Jack Gaver.   New York: Hawthorn,
  1955.   366-408.

New Voices in the American Theatre.   New York: Modern
  Library, 1955.   1-110.

A Streetcar Named Desire.   Louisville, KY: American
  Printing House for the Blind, 1966.

Plays of Our Times. Ed. Bennett Cerf.   New York: Random
   House, 1967. 145-237.

50 Best Plays of the American Theatre. Ed. Clive Barnes.
   New York: Crown, 1969. 3: 339-83.

Theatre, Vol. 1, 1971: 239-419 (A 2).

Selected Plays, 1977: 79-181; *Selected Plays*, 1980: 79-
   179 (A 2).

Eight Plays, 1979: 91-197 (A 2).

A Streetcar Named Desire. New Directions Paperbook. New
   York: New Directions, 1980; Toronto: George J. MacLeod,
   1980. viii, 179 pp.

A Streetcar Named Desire with a Foreword by Jessica Tandy
   and an Introduction by the Author. New York: Limited
   Editions Club, 1982. Unpaged. Ils., Al Hirschfeld.
   Limited edition. Contents: Jessica Tandy, Foreword:
   "On Playing Blanche DuBois"; Williams, Introduction:
   "On a Streetcar Named Success" (D 1); play.

Trans. (H): Arabic, Bengali, Bulgarian, Chinese, French,
   German, Hungarian, Italian, Japanese, Korean, Marathi,
   Norwegian, Polish, Romanian, Russian, Slovak, Spanish,
   Swedish, Turkish (version uncertain).

            Publication: Third American Version

A Streetcar Named Desire: Acting Edition: *Play in Three
   Acts*. New York: Dramatists Play Service, 1953.   107
   pp. Il. Contents; play, 5-103.

            Publication: Student Editions

A Streetcar Named Desire.   Foreign Language Series.
   Tokyo: Hoko-Shobo, 1964. 163 pp.

A Streetcar Named Desire. Methuen Student Edition. Ed.
   Patricia Hern. London: Methuen, 1984. 1, 126 pp.
   Ils. Contents: Commentary, xiv-1; play, 1-90; Notes,
   91-113.

A Streetcar Named Desire. Ed. Helmut Wolf. Diesterweg,
   19--. 115 pp.

A Streetcar Named Desire. Hereford Plays. Ed. Ray
   Speakman. London: Methuen, 1984; Oxford: Heinemann
   Methuen, 1989. vii, 148 pp. Review:

Self, David. *Times Educational Supplement* 25 May
    1990, sec. B: 17.

Inclusion in Textbooks (Second
American Version)

Bain, Carl E., et al., eds. *The Norton Introduction to
    Literature*. 5th ed. New York: Norton, 1991.

Barnett, Sylvan, et al., eds. *Tragedy and Comedy: An An-
    thology of Drama*. Boston: Little, Brown, 1967.   281–
    368.

Baym, Nina, et al., eds. *The Norton Anthology of Amer-
    ican Literature*. 2nd ed. New York: Norton, 1985.
    1771–1841.   2nd shorter ed.: 2207–77.

Clayes, Stanley A., ed. *Drama & Discussion*.   New York:
    Appleton, 1967.   532–83.

Goodman, Randolph, ed. *Drama on Stage*. New York: Holt,
    1961.

Tucker, S. Marion, and Alan S. Downer, eds. *Twenty-Five
    Modern Plays*. 3rd. ed. New York: Harper, 1953.

Publication: Screenplay

Sight and Sound 21 (Apr.-June 1952). Excerpts.

Film Scripts: One. Ed. George P. Garrett et al.   New
    York: Appleton-Century-Crofts, 1971.   330–484.

Criticism

Because of the interest in specific productions, one
should also regard the production record below.

Adler, Thomas P. *A Streetcar Named Desire: The Moth and
    the Lantern*. Boston: Twayne, 1990. 99 pp. Review:
        Holditch, W. Kenneth. *Tennessee Williams Literary
        Journal* 2.1 (Winter 1990-91): 55–56.

Barranger, Milly S. *Theatre Past and Present....* Bel-
    mont, CA: Wadsworth, 1984.   434–43.

Barry, Jackson G. "The Action as Unit in the Semiotic
    Analysis of Drama." *Semiotics 1985* (1986): 107–15.

———. *Dramatic Structure: The Shaping of Experience*.
    Berkeley: Univ. of California Pr., 1970.   53–55.

Berkman, Leonard. "The Tragic Downfall of Blanche Du-
    Bois." *Modern Drama* 10 (Dec. 1967): 249-57. Rpt.
    Bloom (below): 33-40.

Berlin, Normand. "Complementarity in A *Streetcar Named
    Desire*." Tharpe (A 3): 97-103.

Bernard, Kenneth. "The Mercantile Mr. Kowalski." *Dis-
    course* 7 (Summer 1964): 337-40.

Bianco, Patricia Stevens. "Analyzing Relationships among
    Characters in Drama: A Combination of Precepts from
    Constantin Stanislavski's System of Acting and Eric
    Berne's System of Transactional Analysis." Diss.,
    Florida State Univ., 1984. *Dissertation Abstracts
    International* 45 (1984): 986 A.

Bigsby, C. W. E. "Tennessee Williams' Streetcar to Glo-
    ry." *The Forties: Fiction, Poetry, Drama*. Ed. Warren
    French. DeLand, FL: Everett/Edwards, 1969. Rpt. Bloom
    (below): 41-47; Miller (below): 103-08 (excerpts).

Bloom, Harold, ed. *Tennessee Williams's A Streetcar
    Named Desire*. New York: Chelsea House, 1988. viii,
    136 pp.

Bodis, Klara. "Blanche: A Complexity of Attitudes."
    *Acta Universitatis Szegediensis de Attila Jozsef
    Nominatae...* 2 (1982): 143-51.

Cardullo, Bert. "The Blind Mexican Woman in Williams' A
    Streetcar Named Desire." *Notes on Modern American Lit-
    erature* 7.2 (1983): item 14.

---. "Drama of Intimacy and Tragedy of Incomprehension:
    A *Streetcar Named Desire* Reconsidered." Tharpe (A 3):
    137-53. Rpt. Bloom (above): 79-92.

---. "The 'Paper Moon' Song in A *Streetcar Named De-
    sire*." *Notes on Contemporary Literature* 13.3 (1983):
    11-12.

---. "The Role of the Baby in A *Streetcar Named Desire*."
    Notes on Contemporary Literature 14.2 (1984): 4-5.

---. "Williams' A *Streetcar Named Desire*." *Explicator*
    43.2 (1985): 44-45.

Casey, Constance. "Literary New Orleans." *Publishers
    Weekly* 9 May 1986: 154-55.

Chesler, S. Alan.   "A *Streetcar Named Desire*: Twenty-Five
Years of Criticism."   *Notes on Mississippi Writers* 7
(1974): 44-53.

Copeland, Roger.   "The British Always Have a Word for
It."   *New York Times* 3 Aug. 1980, sec. 2: 1, 3.

Corrigan, Mary Ann.   "Realism and Theatricalism in *A
Streetcar Named Desire*."   *Modern Drama* 19 (Dec. 1976):
385-96.   Rpt. Bloom (above): 49-60; D. Parker (A 3):
27-38.

Debusscher, Gilbert.   "Trois images de la modernité chez
Tennessee Williams: Une micro-analyse d'*Un tramway
nommé Désir*."   *Journal of Dramatic Theory and Criticism*
3.1 (1988): 143-55.

Dickinson, Vivienne.   "A *Streetcar Named Desire*: Its Development through the Manuscripts."   Tharpe (A 3): 154-
71.

Dowling, Ellen.   "The Derailment of *A Streetcar Named Desire*."   *Literature/Film Quarterly* 9 (1981): 233-40.

---, and Nancy Pride.   "Three Approaches to Directing *A
Streetcar Named Desire*."   *Tennessee Williams Newsletter*
2.2 (Fall 1980): 16-20.

Drake, Constance.   "Blanche Dubois: A Re-evaluation."
Theatre Annual 24 (1969): 58-69.

Durbach, Errol.   "Form and Vision in Erotic Tragedy: From
Aprhodite to Freud."   *Mosaic* 1 (July 1968): 35-52.

Efstate, Ileana.   "Tennessee Williams - A Few Considera-
tions on *A Streetcar Named Desire*."   *Analele Universi-
tatii Bueuresti, Limbi Germanice* 21 (1972): 107-13.

Ehrlich, Alan.   "A Streetcar Named Desire under the Elms:
A Study of Dramatic Space in *A Streetcar Named Desire*
and *Desire under the Elms*."   Tharpe (A 3): 126-36.

Evans, Gareth L.   *The Language of Modern Drama*.   London:
Dent, 1977.   190-98.

Farnsworth, T. A.   "The Same Old *Streetcar*: Sex Plays Are
Becoming as Stodgy as Puritanism."   *Forum* (South Afri-
ca) 9 (Feb. 1961): 23-24.

Freedman, Morris. *The Moral Impulse: Modern Drama from Ibsen to the Present.* Carbondale: Southern Illinois Univ. Pr., 1967. 115-16.

Funatsu, Tatsumi. "Blanche's Loneliness in *A Streetcar Named Desire.*" *Kyushu American Literature* (Fukuoka, Japan) 5 (Apr. 1962): 36-41.

Gardner, R. H. *The Splintered Stage: The Decline of the American Theatre.* New York: Macmillan, 1965. 111-21.

Garzilli, Enrico F. "*Long Day's Journey into Night* (Mary) and *Streetcar Named Desire* (Blanche): An Inquiry in Compassion." *Theatre Annual* 33 (1977): 7-23.

Gassner, John. *The Theatre in Our Times* New York: Crown, 1954. 355-63.

Gazolla, Ana Lucia Almeida. "*A Streetcar Named Desire*: Myth, Riutal and Ideology." *Ritual in the United States....* Ed. Don Harkness. Tampa, FL: American Studies, 1985.

Gray, Paul. "The Theatre of the Marvelous." *Tulane Drama Review* 7 (Summer 1963): 143-45.

Hall, Joan W. "'Gaudy Seedbearers': Shakespeare, Pater, and *A Streetcar Named Desire.*" *Notes on Contemporary Literature* 20.4 (1990): 9-11.

Hanks, Pamela Anne. "Must We Acknowledge What We Mean? The Viewer's Role in Filmed Versions of *A Streetcar Named Desire.*" *Journal of Popular Film & Television* 14.3 (1986): 114-22.

Harwood, Britton J. "Tragedy as Habit: *A Streetcar Named Desire.* Tharpe (A 3): 104-15.

Homan, Sydney. *The Audience as Actor and Character: The Modern Theater of Beckett, Brecht, Genet, Ionesco, Pinter, Stoppard, and Williams.* Lewisburg, PA: Bucknell Univ. Pr., 1989. 123-33.

Hornby, Richard. "O'Neill's 'Death of a Salesman.'" *Journal of Dramatic Theory and Criticism* 2.2 (1988): 53-59.

Hulley, Kathleen. "The Fate of the Symbolic in *A Streetcar Named Desire.*" *Drama and Symbols.* Cambridge: Cambridge Univ. Pr., 1982. 89-99. Rpt. Bloom (above): 111-22.

Hurrell, John D., ed. *Two Modern American Tragedies:*
Reviews and Criticism of Death pf a Salesman and A
Streetcar Named Desire. New York: Scribner's, 1961.

Isaac, Dan. "A Streetcar Named Desire - or Death?" *New*
York Times 18 Feb. 1968, sec. 2: 1,7.

Johns, Sarah Boyd. "Williams' Journey to *Streetcar*: An
Analysis of Pre-Production Manuscripts of A *Streetcar*
Named Desire." Diss., Univ. of South Carolina, 1980.
Dissertation Abstracts International 41 (1981): 3107-08
A.

Kahn, Sy. *A Streetcar Named Desire (Tennessee Williams).*
Audiocassette. DeLand, FL: Everett/Edwards, 197-.

Kolin, Philip C.   "'Red-Hot!' in A *Streetcar Named De-*
sire." *Notes on Contemporary Literature* 19.4 (1989):
6-8.

---. "Why Stanley and His Friends Drink Jax Beer in Tennessee Williams's A *Streetcr Named Desire.*" *Notes on*
Contemporary Literature 20.4 (1990): 2-3.

---, ed. "A *Streetcar Named Desire*: A Playwrights'
Forum." *Michigan Quarterly Review* 29 (1990): 173-203.
Collective essays by Kolin, Robert Anderson, Thomas
Babe, Kenneth Bernard, Kenneth H. Brown, Christopher
Durang, Horton Foote, Mario Fratti, Jack Gelber,
Charles Gordone, Amlin Gray, A. R. Gurney, William
Hauptman, Israel Horovitz, Tina Howe, Garson Kanin,
Adrienne Kennedy, Jerome Lawrence, Robert E. Lee,
Romulus Linney, Emily Mann, Terrence McNally, Rochelle
Owens, John Patrick, Dennis J. Reardon, Arthur Sainer,
Joan Schenkar, James Schevill, Michael T. Smith, Barrie
Stavis, Megan Terry, Alfred Uhry, Jean-Claude van Ital-
lie, Wendy Wasserstein, Robert Wilson, Susan Yankowitz,
Paul Zindel.

Kronfeld, David Allen.   "The Mad Character in Modern Literature." Diss., Brown Univ., 1978. *Dissertation Ab-*
stracts International 39 (1979): 6114 A.

Law, Richard A.   "A *Streetcar Named Desire* as Melodrama."
English Record 14 (Feb. 1964): 2-8.

Lewis, Allan. *The Contemporary Theatre: The Significant*
Playwrights of Our Time. New York: Crown, 1962. Chap.
19.

Lewis, Theophilus. "Freud and the Split-Level Drama."
    Catholic World 187 (May 1958): 98-103.

Melman, Lindy. "A Captive Maid: Blanche DuBois in *A
    Streetcar Named Desire*." *Dutch Quarterly Review* 16
    (1986): 125-44.

Miller, Jordan Y., ed. *Twentieth Century Interpretations
    of A Streetcar Named Desire: A Collection of Critical
    Essays*. Englewood Cliffs, NJ: Prentice-Hall, 1971.
    vi, 119 pp.

Mood, John J. "The Structure of *A Streetcar Named De-
    sire*." *Ball State University Forum* 14.3 (Summer 1973):
    9-10.

Morse, Donald E. "The 'Life Lie' in Three Plays by
    O'Neill, Williams, and Miller." *Cross-Cultural
    Studies: American, Canadian, and European Literature
    1945-1985*. Ed. Mirko Jurak. Ljubljana: Edvard Kardelj
    Univ., 1988. 273-77.

On the Scene Nov.-Dec. 1972. [Entire issue]

Oppel, Horst. "'Every Man Is a King!': Zur Funktion der
    lokalhistorischen Elements in *A Streetcar Named De-
    sire*." *Studien zur englischen und amerikanischen
    Sprache und Literatur*.... Ed. Paul G. Buchloh et al.
    Neumunster: Wacholtz, 1974. 507-22.

---. "Tennessee Williams: *A Streetcar Named Desire*."
    Das amerikanische Drama. Ed. Paul Goetsch. Dus-
    seldorf: Bagel, 1974. 183-207.

Pitavy, Danièle. "L'intruse: Stratège du désir dans *De-
    sire under the Elms* and *A Streetcar Named Desire*."
    Coup de Théâtre 3 (1983): 17-27.

Porter, Thomas E. *Myth and Modern American Drama*. De-
    troit: Wayne State Univ. Pr., 1969. 153-76.

Quijano, Margarita. "El simbolismo del *Tranvía llamado
    Deseo*." *Cuadernos Americanos* 159 (July 1968): 228-35.

Quintus, John Allen. "The Loss of Dear Things: Chekhov
    and Williams in Perspective." *English Language Notes*
    18 (1981): 201-06.

Quirino, Leonard. "The Cards Indicate a Voyage on *A
    Streetcar Named Desire*." Tharpe (A 3): 77-96; short
    ed. (A 3): 29-48. Rpt. Bloom (above): 61-77.

Rathbun, Gilbert L. *Tennessee Williams' A Streetcar
    Named Desire*. New York: Monarch, 1967. 75 pp.

Riddel, Joseph N. "*A Streetcar Named Desire* - Nietzsche
    Descending." *Modern Drama* 5 (Feb. 1963): 421-30. Rpt.
    Bloom (above): 21-31; Bloom (A 3): 13-22; Miller
    (above): 80-89.

Roberts, James L.: see *Glass* Criticism (above).

Roderick, John M. "From 'Tarantula Arms' to 'Della Rob-
    bia Blue': The Tennessee Williams Tragicomic Transit
    Authority." Tharpe (A 3): 116-25. Rpt. Bloom (above):
    93-101.

Rosenberg, Joseph. "The Syntax of Dialogue: A Problem in
    Scholarship and Translation." *Theatre Southwest* 6 (May
    1980): 12-18.

Schvey, Henry I. "Madonna at the Poker Night: Pictorial
    Elements in Tennessee Williams's *A Streetcar Named De-
    sire*." *From Cooper to Philip Roth*.... Ed. J. Bakker
    and D. R. M. Wilkinson. Amsterdam: Rodopi, 1980. 71-
    77. Rpt. Bloom (above): 103-09.

Simon, John. "Brothers under the Skin: O'Neill and Wil-
    liams." *Hudson Review* 39 (1987): 553-65. Rpt. *The
    Sheep from the Goats*... (New York: Weidenfeld, 1989):
    62-76.

Sion, Georges. "Tennessee Williams: *Un Tramway nommé
    Départ*." *Bulletin de l'Académie Royal de Langue et
    Littérature Françaises* 61 (1983): 141-50.

Stavrou, Constantine N. "Blanche DuBois and Emma Bo-
    vary." *Four Quarters* 7 (May 1958): 10-13.

Steppat, Michael P. "Self-Choice and Aesthetic Dispair
    in Arthur Miller and Tennessee Williams." *Literary
    Criterion* 20.3 (1985): 49-59.

Taylor, Jo Beth. "*A Streetcar Named Desire*: Evolution of
    Blanche and Stanley." *Publications of the Mississippi
    Philological Association* 1986: 63-66.

Templeton, Joan. "*A Streetcar Named Desire*: Blanche Du-
    Bois and the Old South." *Trames...Collection Anglais*
    (Limoges) 2 (1979): 27-34.

Thomas, E. A. "A Streetcar to Where?" *Wingover* 1 (Fall-
    Winter 1958-59): 30-31.

Tillich, Paul *The Courage to Be.* New York: Yale Univ.
    Pr., 1952. 145-46.

Vlasopolos, Anca. "Authorizing History: Victimization in
    A Streetcar Named Desire." *Theatre Journal* 38 (Oct.
    1986): 322-38.

Vogel, Dan. *The Three Masks of American Tragedy.* Baton
    Rouge: Louisiana State Univ. Pr., 1974. 83-90.

Von Szeliski, John. "Tennessee Williams and the Tragedy
    of Sensitivity." *Western Humanities Review* 20 (Summer
    1966): 203-11. Rpt. Miller (above): 65-72 (excerpts).

---. *Tragedy and Fear: Why Modern Drama Fails.* Chapel
    Hill: Univ. of North Carolina Pr., 1971. 168-72.

Productions

A Streetcar Named Desire. Previews: New Haven, Boston,
Philadelphia. New York: Barrymore Theatre, 3 Dec. 1947-
17 Dec. 1949 (première: 855); City Center, 23 May 1950.
Elia Kazan, dir. Jo Mielziner, Lucinda Ballard, design.
Max Marlin, incidental music. With Jessica Tandy, later
Uta Hagen (Blanche); Marlon Brando, later Anthony Quinn
(Stan); Kim Hunter, later Jorja Cartright (Stella); Karl
Malden, later George Matthews (Mitch). Program: Leavitt
(F 1): 81. Winner Pulitzer Prize, New York Drama
Critics' Circle Award, Donaldson Award. Recording: *Ten-
nessee Williams'* A Streetcar Named Desire (Mark 56
Record, 1974 [4 Apr. 1948 radio broadcast presenting
Drama Critics' Circle Award, followed by scenes from
orig. prod.]). Reviews, Prod. Notes:
    Life 15 Dec. 1947: 101-04.
    Look 28 July 1948. [Irene M. Selznick]
    Look 1 Feb. 1949: 79. [Benton's painting]
    New York Times 1 Apr. 1948: 29. [Drama Critics' Circle
        Award]
    New York Times 4 Dec. 1947: 41. [Benefit performance]
    New York Times 18 May 1948: 27.
    New York Times 18 July 1948: 46. [Donaldson Award]
    New York Times Magazine 23 Nov. 1947: 14.
    Newsweek 15 Dec. 1947: 82-83.
    Theatre Arts Feb. 1948: 35.
    Time 14 Dec. 1947: 85.
    Time 12 Apr. 1948: 75. Rpt. Van Antwerp (F 1): 105.
    Variety 5 Nov. 1947: 60.
    Variety 10 Nov. 1947: 68.
    Variety 3 Dec. 1947: 1, 7.
    Variety 8 Mar. 1950: 37.

Adams, Frank S. *New York Times* 4 May 1948: 1, 22.
[Pulitzer Prize]

Atkinson, Brooks. *New York Times* 4 Dec. 1947: 42.
Rpt. *New York Times Theatre Reviews; New York
Theatre Critics' Reviews* 8: 252; Van Antwerp (F 1):
92–93.

---. *New York Times* 14 Dec. 1947, sec. 2: 3. Rpt. *New
York Times Theatre Reviews;* Miller (Criticism
above): 32–34.

---. *New York Times* 6 June 1948, sec. 2: 1.   Response:
New York Times 13 June 1948, sec. 2: 2.

---. *New York Times* 12 June 1949, sec. 2: 1. Rpt. *New
York Times Theatre Reviews.* [Cast changes; interview with Malden]

---. *New York Times* 24 May 1950: 36. Rpt. *New York
Times Theatre Reviews.*

Barnes, Howard. *New York Herald Tribune* 4 Dec. 1947:
25. Rpt. *New York Theatre Critics' Reviews* 8: 252;
Miller (Criticism above): 34–36.

---. *New York Herald Tribune* 14 Dec. 1947, sec. 5: 1.

Barranger, Milly S.   "Three Women Called Blanche."
Tennessee Williams Literary Journal 1.1 (Spring
1989): 15–30.

Bentley, Eric.   *Theatre Arts* Nov. 1949: 14.   Rpt. *In
Search of Theatre* (New York: Knopf, 1953): 31–34.

Beyer, William.   *School and Society* 67 (27 Mar. 1948):
241–43.

Brown, John Mason.   *Saturday Review* 27 Dec. 1947: 22–
24.   Rpt. *Seeing More Things* (New York: McGraw-Hill,
1948): 266–72; *Dramatic Personae...* (New York:
Viking, 1963): 89–94; Miller (Criticism above): 41–
45.

Brustein, Robert.   "America's New Culture Hero: Feel-
ings without Words." *Commentary* 25 (Feb. 1958):
123–29.   Rpt. *The Third Theatre* (New York: Knopf,
1969): 104–17; Bloom (above): 7–16.

Burks, Deborah G.   "'Treatment is everything': The Creation and Casting of Blanche and Stanley in Tennessee Williams' *A Streetcar Named Desire.*" *Library
Chronicle of the University of Texas* 41 (1987): 16–
39.

Calta, Louis.   *New York Times* 18 Aug. 1947: 13.   [John
Garfield dropped from consideration]

---. *New York Times* 3 Dec. 1949: 9.

Chapman, John.   *New York Daily News* 4 Dec. 1947: 8.
Rpt. *New York Theatre Critics' Reviews* 8: 249; Miller (Criticism above): 29–30.

---. *New York Daily News* 24 May 1950: 73.

Clurman, Harold.   *Tomorrow* Feb. 1948: 51–54.   Rpt. *Lies
like Truth* (New York: Macmillan, 1958).

Coleman, Robert. *New York Daily Mirror* 4 Dec. 1947:
    38. Rpt. *New York Theatre Critics' Reviews* 8: 252.
---. *New York Daily Mirror* 24 May 1950: 39.
Currie, George. *Brooklyn Daily Eagle* 4 Dec. 1947: 8.
Downing, Robert. "Streetcar Conductor: Some Notes from
    Backstage." *Theatre Annual* 9 (1950): 25-33. Rpt.
    Van Antwerp (F 1): 107, 109-11.
Drutman, Irving. *New York Herald Tribune* 29 Feb. 1948,
    sec. 5: 4. [Interview with Malden]
Durgin, Cyrus. *Boston Daily Globe* 4 Nov. 1947: 7.
    [Boston tryout]
Freedley, George. *New York Morning Telegraph* 5 Dec.
    1947: 2.
Funke, Lewis. *New York Times* 4 Apr. 1948, sec. 2: 1.
    [Drama Critics' Circle Award]
Gabriel, Gilbert W. *Theatre Arts* Apr.-May 1948: 30.
Garland, Robert. *New York Journal-American* 4 Dec.
    1947. Rpt. *New York Theatre Critics' Reviews* 8:
    251; Miller (Criticism above): 36-38.
---. *New York Journal American* 6 July 1948: 12. [Cast
    changes]
---. *New York Journal American* 14 May 1950: 22.
Gassner, John. *Forum* 109 (Feb. 1948): 86-88.
Gibbs, Wolcott. *New Yorker* 13 Dec. 1947: 50-54.
Gilder, Rosamund. *Theatre Arts* Jan. 1948: 10-13.
Hawkins, William. *New York World-Telegram* 4 Dec. 1947:
    36. Rpt. *New York Theatre Critics' Reviews* 8: 251.
---. *New York World-Telegram* 24 May 1950: 40.
Higham, Charles. *Brando....* New York: New American
    Library, 1987. 76-99.
Hughes, Elinor. *Boston Herald* 4 Nov. 1947. Rpt. Mil-
    ler (Criticism above): 27-29. [Boston preview]
Jones, David R. "Elia Kazan and *A Streetcar Named
    Desire*: A Director at Work." *Great Directors at
    Work....* Berkeley: California Univ. Pr., 1986.
    138-99.
Kazan, Elia. *A Life* (F 1): 326-31, 334-53.
---. "Notebook for *A Streetcar Named Desire*." *Direct-
    ing the Play*. Ed. Toby Cole and Helen Krich Chinoy.
    Indianapolis: Bobbs-Merrill, 1953. 296-310. Rpt.
    Toby Cole and Helen Chinoy, eds, *Directors on
    Directing* (Indianapolis: Bobbs-Merrill, 1963): 364-
    79; George Oppenheimer, ed. *The Passionate
    Playgoer...* (New York: Viking, 1958): 342-56; Miller
    (Criticism above): 21-29; Van Antwerp (F 1): 85-92.
Kronenberger, Louis. *New York PM* 5 Dec. 1947. Rpt.
    New York Theatre Critics' Reviews 8: 250.
Krutch, Joseph Wood. *Nation* 165 (20 Dec. 1947): 686-
    87. Rpt. Miller (Criticism above): 38-40; Van
    Antwerp (F 1): 95-96.

McCarthy, Mary. *Partisan Review* 25 (Mar. 1948): 357–
    60. Rpt. *Sights and Spectacles 1937-1956* (New York:
    Farrar, 1956): 131-35; *Theatre Chronicles 1937-1962*
    (New York: Farrar, 1963): 131-35.
Morehouse, Ward. *New York Sun* 4 Dec. 1947: 44. Rpt.
    New York Theatre Critics' Reviews 8: 250.
Nathan, George Jean. *New York Journal American* 15 Dec.
    1947: 14. Rpt. Miller (above).
---. *Theatre Book of the Year 1947-1948*. New York:
    Knopf, 1948. 163-66. Rpt. *The Magic Mirror...*, ed.
    Thomas Quinn Curtiss (New York: Knopf, 1960): 238–
    42; Hurrell (Criticism above): 89-91.
Norton, Elliot. *Boston Globe* 4 Nov. 1947: 6. [Boston
    preview]
Phelan, Kappo. *Commonweal* 47 (19 Dec. 1947): 254-55.
Saroyan, William. *Theatre Arts* Oct. 1948: 21.
Selznick, Irene Mayer. *A Private View* (F 1).
Shaw, Irwin. *New Republic* 22 Dec. 1947: 34-35. Rpt.
    Miller (Criticism above): 29-30.
Sheaffer, Louis. *Brooklyn Daily Eagle* 24 May 1950: 12.
Spector, Susan. "Alternative Visions of Blanche
    DuBois: Uta Hagen and Jessica Tandy in *A Streetcar
    Named Desire*." *Modern Drama* 32 (Dec. 1989): 545-61.
Stevens, Virginia. *Theatre Arts* Dec. 1947: 18-22.
Tandy, Jessica. "One Year of Blanche du Bois." *New
    York Times* 28 Nov. 1948, sec. 2: 1, 3. Rpt. Van
    Antwerp (F 1): 99-100.
Taylor, Harry. *Masses and Mainstream* 1 (Apr. 1948):
    51-56. Rpt. Hurrell (Criticism above): 96-99'.
Thomas, Bob. *Marlon...*. New York: Random House, 1973.
    38-49.
Watts, Richard Jr. *New York Post* 4 Dec. 1947: 43.
    Rpt. *New York Theatre Critics' Reviews* 8: 249; Mil-
    ler (Criticism above): 20-31.
---. *New York Post* 24 May 1950: 71.
Wyatt, Euphemia Van Rensselaer. *Catholic World* 166
    (Jan. 1948): 558.
Zolotow, Sam. *New York Times* 3 Dec. 1948: 32.
    [Opening]

A Streetcar Named Desire. Manchester: 27 Sept. 1949;
London: Aldwych Theatre, 12 Oct. 1949. Laurence Olivier,
dir. Jo Mielziner, Beatrice Dawson, design. With Vivien
Leigh (Blanche), Bonar Colleano (Stan), Renee Asherson
(Stella), Bernard Braden (Mitch). Reviews, Prod. Notes:
    New York Times 29 Sept. 1949: 38. Rpt. *New York Times
    Theatre Reviews*.
    New York Times 13 Oct. 1949: 33. Rpt. *New York Times
    Theatre Reviews*.
    New York Times 1 Dec. 1949: 42.
    New York Times 11 Dec. 1949: 84.

Theatre Arts Jan. 1950: 35.

Time 31 Oct. 1949: 54.

Atkinson, Brooks. *New York Times* 11 Dec. 1949, sec. 2:
   3. Rpt. *New York Times Theatre Reviews.*

Barranger, Milly S.: see prod. above.

Dent, Alan. *Vivien Leigh....* London: Hamilton, 1969.

Edwards, Anne. *Vivien Leigh....* New York: Simon,
   1977. 170-72.

Fleming, Peter. *Spectator* 183 (21 Oct. 1949): 533.

Hobson, Harold. *Times* (London) 13 Nov. 1949: 2. Rpt.
   Miller (Criticism above): 47-49.

---. *Christian Science Monitor* 3 Dec. 1949: 4.

Johns, Eric. *Theatre World* Dec. 1949: 9-10.

Robyns, Gwen. *Vivien Leigh.* London: Frewin, 1986.

Smith, R. D. *New Statesman* 38 (22 Oct. 1949): 451.

Taylor, John Russell. *Vivien Leigh.* London: Elm Tree,
   1984.

Trewin, J. C. *Illustrated London News* 215 (5 Nov.
   1949): 712.

Walker, Alexander. *Vivien....* New York: Weidenfeld,
   1987.

Worsley, T. C. *New Statesman* 38 (17 Dec. 1949): 723-
   24. Rpt. Von Antwerp (F 1): 122-25.

A *Streetcar Named Desire.* Group Production. Warner
Brothers, 19 Sept. 1951 (première). Elia Kazan, dir.
Harold Stradling, camera. Richard Day, design. Alex
North, music. With Vivien Leigh (Blanche), Marlon Brando
(Stan), Kim Hunter (Stella), Karl Malden (Mitch). Winner
New York Film Critics' Circle Award. Music soundtrack:
Capitol Records, 1951; excerpts: *North of Hollywood*, RCA
Victor Records, 1958. Reviews, Prod. Notes, Criticism:

Christian Century 68 (28 Nov. 1951): 1397.

Life 24 Sept. 1951: 91-95.

Mercure de France 315 (June 1952): 329-31.

New York Times Magazine 22 July 1951: 34-35.

Newsweek 10 Oct. 1951: 87-88.

Time 17 Sept. 1951: 105-06.

Variety 20 June 1951: 6.

Alpert, Hollis. *Saturday Review* 1 Sept. 1951: 30-31.

Bauer, Leda. *Theatre Arts* July 1951: 35, 88.

Brady, Thomas H. *New York Times* 28 May 1950, sec. 2:
   3. [Filming]

---. *New York Times* 27 Aug. 1950, sec. 2: 5.

Burles, Kenneth T. *Magill's Survey of Cinema: English
   Language Films.* Ed. Frank N. Magill. Englewood
   Cliffs, NJ: Salem, 1980. 1641-44.

Calta, Louis. *New York Times* 13 Oct. 1949: 33. [Film
   rights]

Ciment, Michel, ed. *Kazan on Kazan.* London: Secker,
   1973. 66-71.

Corliss, Richard. *Film Comment* 4 (Summer 1968): 44-47.
Creelman, Eileen. *New York World-Telegram* 9 Sept.
     1950: 4. [Censorship]
Crowther, Bosley. *New York Times* 20 Sept. 1951: 37.
     Rpt. *New York Times Film Reviews*.
---. *New York Times* 23 Sept. 1951, sec. 2: 1.
Dent, Alan. *Illustrated London News* 220 (22 Mar.
     1952): 502.
Edwards, Anne. *Vivien Leigh* (above): 172, 176-81.
Farber, Manny. *Nation* 173 (20 Oct. 1951): 334.
Fulton, A. R. *Theatre Arts* Mar. 1953: 78-83.
Guernsey, Otis L. Jr. *New York Herald-Tribune* 20 Dec.
     1951: 20.
Hartung, Philip T. *Commonweal* 54 (28 Sept. 1950): 596-
     97.
Hatch, Robert. *New Republic* 8 Oct. 1951: 21.
Higham, Charles. *Brando* (above): 114-19.
Hine, Al. *Holiday* Oct. 1951: 25-28.
Isaacs, Hermine Rich, et al. *Films in Review* 2 (Dec.
     1951): 51-55.
Jordan, Rene. *Marlon Brando*. New York: Galahad, 1973.
     33-42.
Kazan, Elia. *A Life* (F 1): 383-87, 416-17.
---. *New York Times* 21 Oct. 1951: 28.
McCarten, John. *New Yorker* 29 Sept. 1951: 111-12.
McDonald, Gerald B. *Library Journal* 76 (15 Oct. 1951):
     1722-23.
Mitgang, Herbert. *New York Times* 9 Sept. 1951, sec. 2:
     5. [Malden]
Reisz, Karel. *Sight and Sound* 21 (Apr.-June 1952):
     170-71.
Schnathmeier, Susanne. "The Unity of Place in Elia
     Kazan's Film Version of *A Streetcar Named Desire* by
     Tennessee Williams: A Traditional Dramatic Category
     Seen from a Semiotic Point of View." *Kodikas/Code*
     10 (1987): 83-93.
Schröder, Ralf J. *Vom Drama zum Film: Aussersprach-
     liche Zeichen in Tennessee Williams' A Streetcar
     Named Desire*. Würzburg: Königshausen, 1983. 302
     pp. Ils.
Thomas, Bob. *Marlon* (above): 58-62.
Thomas, Tony. *The Films of Marlon Brando*. Secaucus,
     NJ: Citadel, 1973. 34-45.
Whitebait, William. *New Statesman* 43 (8 Mar. 1952):
     274.

A Streetcar Named Desire. Adpt. Helen Jerome. Omnibus.
CBS-TV, 30 Oct. 1955. Elliot Silverstein, dir. Max Mer-
lin, music. With Jessica Tandy, Hume Cronyn.

A Streetcar Named Desire. Miami: Coconut Grove Play-
house, 16 Jan.-4 Feb. 1956; New York: City Center The-
atre, 15 Feb. 1956. Herbert Machiz, dir. Watson Bar-
rett, design. With Tallulah Bankhead (Blanche), Gerald
O'Laughlin (Stan), Frances Heflin (Stella), Rudy Bond
(Mitch). Reviews, Prod. Notes:
  Theatre Arts Apr. 1956: 24.
  Time 13 Feb. 1956: 32.
  Time 27 Feb. 1956: 61.
  Atkinson, Brooks. *New York Times* 16 Feb. 1956: 24.
    Rpt. *New York Times Theatre Reviews; New York
    Theatre Critics' Reviews* 17: 362. Response: *New
    York Times* 11 Mar. 1956, sec. 2: 3.
  Campbell, Sandy. *B: Thirty-Nine Letters from Coconut
    Grove.* Verona: Stamperia Valdonega, 1974. 59 pp.
    ils. Limited edition.
  Chapman, John. *New York Daily News* 16 Feb. 1956: 46.
    Rpt. *New York Theatre Critics' Reviews* 17: 365.
  Coleman, Robert. *New York Daily Mirror* 16 Feb. 1956:
    30. Rpt. *New York Theatre Critics' Reviews* 17: 364.
  Gibbs, Wolcott. *New Yorker* 25 Feb. 1956: 90-93.
  Hawkins, William. *New York World-Telegram* 11 Feb.
    1956: 9. [Interview with Bankhead]
  ---. *New York World-Telegram* 16 Feb. 1956: 20. Rpt.
    New York Theatre Critics' Reviews 17: 362.
  Hewes, Henry. *Saturday Review* 3 Mar. 1956: 22.
  Kerr, Walter F. *New York Herald Tribune* 16 Feb. 1956:
    14. Rpt. *New York Theatre Critics' Reviews* 17: 364.
  McClain, John. *New York Journal American* 16 Feb. 1956:
    18. Rpt. *New York Theatre Critics' Reviews* 17: 363.
  Watts, Richard Jr. *New York Post* 16 Feb. 1956: 15.
    Rpt. *New York Theatre Critics' Reviews* 17: 363.
  Wyatt, Euphemia Van Rensselaer. *Catholic World* 183
    (Apr. 1956): 67.

A Streetcar Named Desire. Los Angeles: Ahmanson Theatre,
Mar.-28 Apr. 1973. James Bridges, dir. With Faye Duna-
way (Blanche), Jon Voight (Stan), Lee McCain (Stella),
Earl Holliman (Mitch). Partial playbill: Leavitt (F 1).
Reviews:
  Newsweek 2 Apr. 1973: 44.
  Farber, Stephen. *New York Times* 1 Apr. 1973, sec. 2:
    1, 15.
  Jacobs, Jody. *Los Angeles Times* 22 Mar. 1973, sec. 4:
    4, 15.
  Loynd, Ray. *Los Angeles Herald-Examiner* 18 Mar. 1973,
    sec. G: 1.
  ---. *Los Angeles Herald-Examiner* 21 Mar. 1973, sec. D:
    2.
  Sullivan, Dan. *Los Angeles Times* 21 Mar. 1973, sec. 4:
    1, 10.

A *Streetcar Named Desire*. Lincoln Center Repertory Com-
pany. New York: Vivian Beaumont Theatre, 26 Apr.-29 July
1973 (110). Elias Rabb, dir. Douglas W. Schmidt, John
Gleason, Nancy Potts, design. Cathy McDonald, music.
With Rosemary Harris (Blanche), James Farentino (Stan),
Patricia Connally (Stella), Philip Bosco (Mitch).
Recording: Caedmon Records, 1973. [On cover of record-
ing: Marianne Mantell, Note.] Reviews, Prod. Notes:
    Variety 2 May 1973: 66.
    Barnes, Clive. *New York Times* 27 Apr. 1973: 31.
    Clurman, Harold. *Nation* 216 (14 May 1973): 635-36.
    Gill, Brendan. *New Yorker* 5 May 1973: 81.
    Gottfried, Martin. *Women's Wear Daily* 30 Apr. 1973.
        Rpt. *New York Theatre Critics' Reviews* 34: 282.
    Harris, Leonard. CBS-TV, 26 Apr. 1973. Rpt. *New York
        Theatre Critics' Reviews* 34: 284.
    Hirsch, Foster. *New York Times* 15 Apr. 1973, sec. 2:
        1-3. Response: *New York Times* 10 June 1973, sec. 2:
        4.
    Hughes, Catherine. *America* 128 (26 May 1973): 495.
    Kalem, T. E. *Time* 7 May 1973: 88-90. Rpt. *New York
        Theatre Critics' Reviews* 34: 283.
    Kerr, Walter. *New York Times* 6 May 1973, sec. D: 1,
        10.
    Klemesrud, Judy. *New York Times* 10 June 1973, sec. 2:
        1, 3. [Interview with Farentino]
    Kroll, Jack. *Newsweek* 7 May 973: 109-10. Rpt. *New
        York Theatre Critics' Reviews* 34: 283.
    Novick, Julius. *Village Voice* 3 May 1973: 68, 86.
    Reed, Rex. *New York Sunday News* 13 May 1973, sec. 3:
        5.
    Sanders, Kevin. ABC-TV, 26 Apr. 1973. Rpt. *New York
        Theatre Critics' Reviews* 34: 284.
    Simon, John. *New York* 14 May 1973: 97.
    Watt, Douglas. *New York Daily News* 27 Apr. 1973: 66.
        Rpt. *New York Theatre Critics' Reviews* 34: 281.
    ---. *New York Daily News* 6 May 1973, sec. 3: 3.
    Watts, Richard. *New York Post* 27 Apr. 1973: 27. Rpt.
        New York Theatre Critics' Reviews 34: 281.
    Wilson, Edwin. *Wall Street Journal* 14 May 1973. Rpt.
        New York Theatre Critics' Reviews 34: 282-83.

A *Streetcar Named Desire*. New York: St. James Theatre, 4
Oct.-18 Nov 1973. Jules Irving, dir. Same prod. staff
as above. With Lois Nettleton (Blanche), Alan Feinstein
(Stan), Barbara Eda-Young (Stella), Biff McGuire (Mitch).
Reviews, Prod. Notes:
    Women's Wear Daily 8 Oct. 1973. Rpt. *New York Theatre
        Critics' Reviews* 34: 225.
    Barnes, Clive. *New York Times* 5 Oct. 1973: 19.
    Calta, Louis. *New York Times* 29 July 1973: 40.

Probst, Leonard. NBC, 4 Oct. 1973. Rpt. *New York
  Theatre Critics' Reviews* 34: 225.
Watt, Douglas. *New York Daily News* 5 Oct. 1973: 54.
  Rpt. *New York Theatre Critics' Reviews* 34: 224.
Watts, Richard. *New York Post* 5 Oct. 1973: 18. Rpt.
  New York Theatre Critics' Reviews 34: 224.

A Streetcar Named Desire. London: Piccadilly Theatre, 14
Mar. 1974 (100+). Edwin Sherwin, dir. Patrick Robert-
son, Beatrice Dawson, Richard Pilbrow, Molly Friedel,
design. With Claire Bloom (Blanche), Martin Shaw (Stan),
Morag Hood (Stella), Joss Ackland (Mitch). Playbill:
Leavitt (F 1). Reviews, Prod. Notes:
  Guardian 27 June 1973: 7.
  New York Times 27 June 1973: 37.
  Variety 27 Mar. 1974: 72.
  Barnes, Clive. *New York Times* 17 Aug. 1974: 16.
  Batchelor, Ruth. *Miss London* 25 Mar. 1974: 8.
  Dawson, Helen. *Plays and Players* 21 (May 1974): 28-31.
  Kingston, Jeremy. *Punch* 266 (27 Mar. 1974): 519.
  Lambert, J. W. *Drama* Summer 1974: 45-46.
  Walker, John. *International Herald Tribune* 23-24 Mar.
    1974: 7.

A Streetcar Named Desire. Academy Festival Theatre.
Lake Forest (Chicago): Drake Theatre, 8 June 1975. Jack
Gelber, dir. With Geraldine Page (Blanche), Rip Torn
(Stan), Flora Elkins (Stella), Jack Hollander (Mitch).

A Streetcar Named Desire. London: Greenwich, 12 Sept.-22
Oct. 1983; Mermaid, 28 Feb.-25 May 1984. Alen Strachan,
dir. Bernard Culshaw, John A. Williams, design. With
Sheila Gish (Blanche), Paul Herzberg (Stan), Claire Hig-
gins (Stella), Duncan Preston (Mitch). Reviews:
  Barber, John. *London Daily Telegraph* 1 Mar. 1984.
    Rpt. *London Theatre Record* 4: 151-52.
  Barkley, Richard. *London Sunday Express* 4 Mar. 1984.
    Rpt. *London Theatre Record* 4: 153-54.
  Billington, Michael. *Guardian* 1 Mar. 1984. Rpt.
    London Theatre Record 4: 152.
  Coveney, Michael. *London Financial Times* 1 Mar. 1984.
    Rpt. *London Theatre Record* 4: 151.
  De Jongh, Nicholas. *Guardian*. Rpt. *London Theatre
    Record* 3: 797.
  Gordon, Giles. *Specator*. Rpt. *London Theatre Record*
    3: 798.
  ---. *Spectator* 10 Mar. 1984. Rpt. *London Theatre
    Record* 4: 153.
  Hirschhorn, Clive. *London Sunday Express*. Rpt. *London
    Theatre Record* 3: 798.

Hoyle, Martin. *London Financial Times*. Rpt. *London
    Theatre Record* 3: 799.
Hurren, Kenneth. *London Mail on Sunday* 4 Mar. 1984.
    Rpt. *London Theatre Record* 4: 153.
King, Francis. *London Sunday Telegraph*. Rpt. *London
    Theatre Record* 3: 798-99.
Morley, Sheridan. *Punch*. Rpt. *London Theatre Record*
    3: 797.
---. *Punch* 14 Mar. 1984. Rpt. *London Theatre Record*
    4: 152.
Pontac, Perry. *Plays and Players* Nov. 1983: 24-25.
Radin, Victoria. *London Observer* 4 Mar. 1984. Rpt.
    London Theatre Record 4: 153.
Say, Rosemary. *London Sunday Telegraph* 4 Mar. 1984.
    Rpt. *London Theatre Record* 4: 153.
Shorter, Eric. *London Daily Telegraph*. Rpt. *London
    Theatre Record* 3: 798.

A Streetcar Named Desire. Keith Barish Productions.
ABC-TV, 4 Mar. 1984. John Erman, dir. Marvin Hamlisch,
music. With Ann-Margret (Blanche), Treat Williams
(Stan), Beverly D'Angelo (Stella), Randy Quaid (Mitch).
Music soundtrack: Allegiance Records, 1984. Reviews,
Prod. Notes, Criticism:
Life Mar. 1984: 73-76.
Newsweek 27 June 1983: 65.
Brown, Arch. *New York Native* 26 Mar. 1984: 14.
Curry, Jack. *USA Today* 2 Mar. 1984, sec. D: 1.
Hodges, Ann. *TV Chronilog (Houston Post)* 4-10 Mar.
    1984: 4-5. [Interview with Ann-Margret]
Leonard, John. *New York* 5 Mar. 1984: 98+.
O'Connor, John J. *New York Times*
Schlueter, June. "Imitating an Icon: John Erman's
    Remake of Tennessee Williams' *A Streetcar Named
    Desire*." *Modern Drama* 28 (1985): 139-47.
Simon, John. *Vogue* Feb. 1984: 71.
Sragow, Michael. *American Film* Nov. 1985: 67.
Turan, Kenneth. *TV Guide* 3-9 Mar. 1984: 27-28, 31-34.
    [Interview with Ann-Margret]
Waters, Harry F. *Newsweek* 5 Mar. 1984: 91.

A Streetcar Named Desire. Williamstown Theatre Festival.
Williamstown, MA: summer 1986. Nikos Psacharopoulos,
dir. With Blythe Danner (Blanche), Christopher Walken
(Stan), Sigourney Weaver (Stella), James Naughton
(Mitch). Reviews:
Gussow, Mel. *New York Times* 22 Aug. 1986, sec. 3: 3.
Story, Richard David. *USA Today* 22 Aug. 1986.
Stuart, Otis. *New York Native* 15 Sept. 1986: 40.
Vineberg, Steve. *Theatre Journal* 39 (May 1987): 235-
    36.

A *Streetcar Named Desire*. New York: Circle-in-the-
Square, 10 Mar.–22 May 1988. Nikos Psacharopoulos, dir.
John Conklin, Jess Goldstein, Curt Ostermann, design.
Michael O'Flaherty, music. With Blythe Danner (Blanche),
Aidan Quinn (Stanley), Frances McDormond (Stella), Frank
Converse (Mitch). Reviews:

   New York Times 16 Apr. 1988: 18. [Cast changes]
   Barnes, Clive. *New York Post* 11 Mar. 1988. Rpt. *New
      York Theatre Critics' Reviews* 49: 341–42.
   Beaufort, John. *Christian Science Monitor* 14 Mar.
      1988. Rpt. *New York Theatre Critics' Reviews* 49:
      343.
   Gussow, Mel. *New York Times* 14 Mar. 1988, sec. 3: 13.
   Hodgson, Moira. *Nation* 246 (16 Apr. 1988): 547–48.
   James, Caryn. *New York Times* 6 Mar. 1988, sec. 2: 1,
      24. [Interview with Psacharopoulos]
   Kissel, Howard. *New York Daily News* 11 Mar. 1988.
      Rpt. *New York Theatre Critics' Reviews* 49: 340–41.
   Kramer, Mimi. *New Yorker* 28 Mar. 1988: 81–82.
   Lida, David. *Women's Wear Daily* 11 Mar. 1988. Rpt.
      New York Theatre Critics' Reviews 49: 340.
   Rich, Frank. *New York Times* 11 Mar. 1988, sec. 3: 3.
      Rpt. *New York Theatre Critics' Reviews* 49: 339–40.
   Siegel, Joel. WABC-TV, 10 Mar. 1988. Rpt. *New York
      Theatre Critics' Reviews* 49: 342–43.
   Simon, John. *New York* 21 Mar. 1988: 88+.
   Stearns, David Patrick. *USA Today* 18 Mar. 1988. Rpt.
      New York Theatre Critics' Reviews 49: 344.
   Watt, Douglas. *New York Daily News* 18 Mar. 1988. Rpt.
      New York Theatre Critics' Reviews 49: 341.
   Winer, Linda. *New York Newsday* 11 Mar. 1988. Rpt. *New
      York Theatre Critics' Reviews* 49: 344.

   Other Productions:
   Atkinson, Brooks. *New York Times* 4 Mar. 1955: 18.
      Rpt. *New York Times Theatre Reviews*. [New York]
   Berkowitz, Gerald M. *Tennessee Williams Review* 3.2
      (1982): 55–56. [Edinburgh]
   Calta, Louis. *New York Times* 25 Sept. 1958: 30. [Pro-
      posed New York prod. with Negro cast]
   Garebien, Keith. *Journal of Canadian Studies* 19.4
      (Winter 1984–85): 141–42. [Stratford, Ont.]
   Gelb, Arthur. *New York Times* 14 July 1958: 16. [Pro-
      posed New York prod. with Negro cast]
   Gussow, Mel. *New York Times* 11 Oct. 1976: 34.
      [Princeton with Shirley Knight, Glenn Close]
   Homan, Richard L. *Educational Theatre Journal* 27 (Dec.
      1975): 552–53. [Minneapolis]
   Hughes, Catherine. *American* 134 (26 May 1976): 495.
   John, Mary. *Drama Critique* 11 (Winter 1968): 56–58.
      [Cincinnati]

Stuart, Roxana (F 1). [Key West]

Productions: Ballets

A *Streetcar Named Desire*. Choreography by Valerie
Bettis. Music by Alex North, arr. Rayburn Wright. Sla-
venska-Franklin Ballet Company. Montreal: Her Majesty's
Theatre, 9 Oct. 1952 (première); New York: Century The-
atre, 8 Dec. 1952. Otto Frolich, cond. Peter Larkin,
Saul Bolasni, design. With Mia Slavenska (Blanche),
Frederic Franklin (Stan), Lois Ellyn (Stella), Marvin
Kauter (Mitch). Reviews:
  New York Times Magazine 7 Dec. 1952: 63.
  Newsweek 22 Dec. 1952: 71.
  Time 22 Dec. 1952: 43.
  Biancolli, Louis. *New York World Telegram* 9 Dec. 1952.
  Martin, John. *New York Times* 9 Dec. 1952: 42.
  Watt, Douglas. *New Yorker* 20 Dec. 1952: 103-04.

A *Streetcar Named Desire*. Choreography by Valerie Bet-
tis. Dance Theatre of Harlem. New York: City Center
Theatre, 14 Jan. 1982. Peter Larkin, design. With Vir-
ginia Johnson (Blanche), Lowell Smith (Stanley), Elena
Carter (Stella), Donald Williams (Mitch). Reviews:
  Aloff, Mindy. *Dance Magazine* May 1982: 20.
  Kisselgoff, Anna. *New York Times* 16 Jan. 1982: 11.
  Maskey, Jacqueline. *High Fidelity* May 1982: MA 11.
  Tobias, Tobi. *New York* 8 Feb. 1982: 46-47.

A *Streetcar Named Desire*. Choreography by John Neumeier.
Music by Sergei Prokofiev and Alfred Schnittke. Stutt-
gart Ballet. Washington: Kennedy Center, 27 May-8 June
1986; San Antonio: Municipal Auditorium, 15 June 1986.
John Neumeier, design. With Marcia Haydee (Blanche),
Tamas Detrich (Allan Grey), Richard Cragun (Stan), Lisi
Grether (Stella), Valdimir Klos (Mitch). Reviews:
  Holmes, Ann. *Houston Chronicle* 16 June 1986, sec. 4:
    1, 6.
  Zimmer, Elisabeth. *Dance Magazine* Dec. 1986: 25.

A *Streetcar Named Desire*. Choreography by John Neumeier.
Stuttgart Ballet. Festival of Two Worlds. Spoleto,
Italy: 24 June 1987.

Production: Parody

Belle Reprieve. Bloolips and Split Britches. London:
Drill Hall Arts Center, winter 1991; New York: One Dream
Theater, 14 Feb. 1991; Boston: Double Edge Theater, 3-7
Apr. 1991. Lois Weaver, dir. With Lois Weaver, Peggy
Shaw, Bette Boume, Precious Pearle. Reviews:

    American Theatre Mar. 1991: 14.
    Caldwell, Ron. *Gay Community News* 2-8 Apr. 1991: 16,
      7.

SUDDENLY LAST SUMMER: Tragedy set in New Orleans narrating
the destruction, a year earlier, of a homosexual poet.
Mss., Columbia, Princeton, Texas (G).
  The play was produced together with "Something Unspoken"
under the collective title *Garden District*. Some dialogue from the first printing (pp. 20-23) was cut and
rewritten for the second printing (pp. 20-21). Williams
revised the ending for a 1976 unpublished version. His
name is on the unpublished 1959 screenplay, but Gore
Vidal has several times insisted that only he wrote it.

Publication: First Version

Suddenly Last Summer. New York: New Directions, 1958.
    90 pp. Il. Contents: play, 13-90. Review:
      New York Times 25 May 1958, sec 2: 1.
      Freedley, George. *New York Morning Telegraph* 20 May
        1958: 2.
      Justice, Donald. *Poetry* 93 (Mar. 1959): 402-03.

*Garden District: Two Plays...: Something Unspoken; Sud-
    denly Last Summer*. London: Secker & Warburg, 1959.   72
    pp. Contents: "Something Unspoken," 7-25; *Suddenly
    Last Summer*, 27-72. Review:
      Times Literary Supplement 19 June 1959: 370.

Orpheus Descending, etc., 1961 (A 2).

Five Plays, 1962: 237-82 (A 2).

Baby Doll, etc., 1968: 113-59 (A 2).

Publication: Second Version

Suddenly Last Summer. New York: Dramatists Play Service,
    1958. 45 pp. Contents: play, 5-44.

Suddenly Last Summer. New York: New Directions, 1958.
    Second printing. 88 pp. Il. Contents: play, 13-88.

Suddenly Last Summer. Signet Book. New York: New Amer-
    ican Library, 1960. 93 pp. Ils.

Theatre, Vol. 3, 1971: 343-423 (A 2).

Four Plays, 1976: 3-93 (A 2).

Trans. (H):   French, German, Greek, Hungarian, Japanese,
Polish, Portuguese, Spanish (version uncertain).

Publication: Student Edition

Suddenly Last Summer. Modern English Series. Tokyo:
Kinseido, 1967. 112 pp.

Inclusion in Textbooks (Second Version)

Lief, Leonard, and James F. Light, eds. *The Modern Age:*
Literature. New York: Holt, 1969.

Messner, Nancy Shingler, et al., eds. *Collection: Liter-*
ature for the Seventies. Lexington, MA: Heath, 1972.

Criticism

Debusscher, Gilbert.   "Oedipus in New Orleans: Myth in
Suddenly Last Summer." *Revue des Langues Vivantes*
Bicentennial Issue (1971): 53-63.

Farman, Robert J. *Masterplots II: Drama Series*.   Ed.
Frank N. Magill. Pasadena, CA: Salem, 1990.   1508-13.

Funatsu, Tatsumi.   "A Study of *Suddenly Last Summer*."
Fukuoka University Review of Literature and Science 7
(Mar. 1963): 341-62.

Houston, Neal B.   "Meaning by Analogy in *Suddenly Last*
Summer." *Notes on Modern American Literature* 1980:
item 24.

Hurley, Paul J.   "*Suddenly Last Summer* as 'Morality
Play.'" *Modern Drama* 8 (Feb. 1966): 392-98.

Hurt, James R.   "*Suddenly Last Summer*: Williams and Melville." *Modern Drama* 3 (Feb. 1961): 396-400.

Johnson, Mary Lynn.   "Williams's *Suddenly Last Summer*,
Scene One." *Explicator* 21 (Apr. 1963): item 66.

Oetjens, Carola. *Psychoanalyse als Methode der Litera-*
turinterpretation: Dargestellt am Beispiel von Tennes-
see Williams' Suddenly Last Summer. Frankfurt: Lang,
1982.   151 pp.

Reppert, Carol F.   "*Suddenly Last Summer*: A Re-evaluation
of Catherine Holly in Light of Melville's Chola Widow."
Tennessee Williams Newsletter 1.2 (Fall 1979): 8-11.

Russo, Vito. *The Celluloid Closet: Homosexuality in the Movies*. New York: Harper, 1981. 2nd ed., 1987. 115-18.

Satterfield, John. "Williams's *Suddenly Last Summer*: The Eye of the Needle." *Markham Review* 6 (1977): 27-33.

Welsh, James M. "Dream Doctors as Healers in Drama and Film: A Pardigm, an Antecedent, and an Imitation." *Literature and Medicine* 6 (1987): 117-27.

Productions

Garden District. New York: York Theatre, 7 Jan. 1958 (première, 216?). Herbert Machiz, dir. Robert Soule, Stanley Simmons, Lee Watson, design. Ned Rorem, music. With Anne Meacham (Catherine), Hortense Alden (Mrs. Venable), Robert Lansing (Dr. Cukrowicz). Program: Leavitt (F 1): 120. Reviews:
  Newsweek 20 Jan. 1958: 84.
  Theatre Arts Mar. 1958: 13.
  Theatre Arts May 1958: 10.
  Time 20 Jan. 1958: 42.
  Variety 15 Jan. 1958: 74, 79.
  Aston, Frank. *New York World-Telegram* 8 Jan. 1958: 32.
  Atkinson, Brooks. *New York Times* 8 Jan. 1958: 23.
    Rpt. *New York Times Theatre Reviews*.

  ---. *New York Times* 19 Jan. 1958, sec. 2: 1. Rpt. *New York Times Theatre Reviews*.
  Bolton, Whitney. *New York Morning Telegraph* 9 Jan. 1958: 2.
  Calta, Louis. *New York Times* 22 Feb. 1958: 8. [Script changes]
  Chapman, John. *New York Daily News* 8 Jan. 1958: 52.
  Clurman, Harold. *Nation* 186 (25 Jan. 1958): 86-87. Rpt. Van Antwerp (F 1): 184-85.
  Dennis, Patrick. *New Republic* 27 Jan. 1958: 20.
  Driver, Tom F. *Christian Century* 75 (29 Jan. 1958): 136-37.
  Freedley, George. *New York Morning Telegraph* 16 Jan. 1958: 2.
  Gassner, John. *Theatre at the Crossroads* (A 3): 226-28.
  Gibbs, Wolcott. *New Yorker* 18 Jan. 1958: 64-66.
  Hardwick, Elizabeth. *Partisan Review* 25 (Spring 1958): 283-84.
  Hayes, Richard. *Commonweal* 68 (30 May 1958): 232-33.
  Hewes, Henry. *Saturday Review* 25 Jan. 1958: 26. Rpt. George Openheimer, ed. *The Passionate Playgoer...* (New York: Viking, 1958): 250-54.

Kerr, Walter. *New York Herald Tribune* 8 Jan. 1958: 16.
---. *New York Herald Tribune* 19 Jan. 1958, sec 4: 1,
    4.
Mannes, Marya. *Reporter* 6 Feb. 1958: 42-43. Rpt. Van
    Antwerp (F 1): 185-87.
Richards, Stanley. *Players* 34 (Mar. 1958): 136-37.
Robinson, Robert. *Spectator* 200 (28 Mar. 1958): 389-
    90.
Rorem, Ned. *The Later Diaries* (F 1): 75.
Watts, Richard Jr. *New York Post* 8 Jan. 1958: 64.
Wyatt, Euphemia Van Rensselaer. *Catholic World* 186
    (Mar. 1958): 469-70.
Zolotow, Sam. *New York Times* 14 May 1958: 37. [Cast
    changes]

Garden District. London: Arts Theatre, 16 Sept. 1958.
Herbert Machiz, dir. With Patricia Neal (Catherine),
Beatrix Lehmann (Mrs. Venable), David Cameron (Dr. Cuk-
rowicz). Reviews:
New York Times 17 Sept. 1958: 44.
Stage 18 Sept. 1958: 11.
Times (London) 4 Aug. 1958: 10. [Interview with
    Machiz]
Brien, Alan. *Spectator* 201 (26 Sept. 1958): 401-02.
Robinson, Robert. *New Statesman* 56 (27 Sept. 1958):
    407-08.
Tynan, Kenneth. *London Observer* 2 Sept. 1958. Rpt.
    Curtains... (New York: Atheneum, 1961): 278-80.
Weightman, J. G. *Twentieth Century* 164 (Nov. 1958):
    461-63.

Garden District. American tour, 11 Mar.-30 May 1959.
Herbert Machiz, dir.   Robert Soule, Lee Watson, Alice
Gibson, design. With Diana Barrymore (Catherine),
Cathleen Nesbitt (Mrs. Venable), Richard Gardner (Dr.
Cukrowicz).

Suddenly Last Summer. Screenplay by Gore Vidal. Colum-
bia, 11 Dec. 1959 (première). Joseph Mankiewicz, dir.
Jack Hildyard, camera. William Keller, design. Burton
Orr, Malcolm Arnold, music. With Elizabeth Taylor (Cath-
erine), Katharine Hepburn (Mrs. Venable), Montgomery
Clift (Dr. Cukrowicz). Reviews, Prod. Notes:
Filmfacts 2 (1959): 319.
New York Times 4 Dec. 1959: 36. [Rating]
Newsweek 28 Dec. 1959: 64.
Time 11 Jan. 1960: 64-66.
Variety 16 Dec. 1959: 6.
Alpert, Hollis. *Films and Filming* June 1960: 8, 32.
Baker, Peter. *Films and Filming* June 1960: 21.

Bosworth, Patricia. *Montgomery Clift....* New York:
    Harcourt, 1978. 306-07.
Crowther, Bosley. *New York Times* 23 Dec. 1959: 22.
    Rpt. *New York Times Film Reviews.*
Edwards, Anne. *A Remarkable Woman....* New York: Mor-
    row, 1985. 211-22. [Hepburn]
Hart, Henry. *Films in Review* Jan. 1960: 39-41.
Hartung, Philip T. *Commonweal* 71 (1 Jan. 1960): 396.
Hatch, Robert. *Nation* 190 (16 Jan. 1960): 59. Rpt.
    Van Antwerp (F 1): 204-05.
Jacobs, Jay. *Reporter* 4 Feb. 1960: 37-38.
Johnson, Albert. *Film Quarterly* 13 (Spring 1960); 40-
    42.
Kauffmann, Stanley. *New Republic* 18 Jan. 1960: 20-21.
    Rpt. *A World on Film...* (New York: Harper, 1966):
    81-82.
Knight, Arthur. *Saturday Review* 2 Jan. 1960: 31.
LaGuardia, Robert. *Monty....* New York: Arbor House,
    1977. 198-204. [Clift]
Lejeune, C. A. *London Observer* 15 May 1960: 21.
Macdonald, Dwight. *Esquire* Apr. 1960. Rpt. *Dwight
    Macdonald on Movies* (Englewood Cliffs, NJ: Prentice-
    Hall, 1969): 145-46.
Marek, Richard. *McCalls* Feb. 1960: 8.
Marill, Alvin H. *Katharine Hepburn.* New York:
    Galahad, 1973. 110-17.
McCarten, John. *New Yorker* 9 Jan. 1960: 74-75.
Pryor, Thomas M. *New York Times* 31 Oct. 1958: 33.
    [Casting]
Quigly, Isabel. *Spectator* 204 (20 May 1960): 736-38.
Walsh, Moira. *America* 102 (9 Jan. 1960): 428-29.
Whitebait, William. *New Statesman* 59 (21 May 1960):
    753.

Suddenly Last Summer. Key West: Greene Street Theatre,
April 1976 (première). William Prosser, dir. With
Roxana Stuart (Catherine), Janice White (Mrs. Venable),
Jay Drury (Dr. Cukrowicz). Program: Leavitt (F 1): 158.
Review:
New York Times 27 Apr. 1976: 28.

Other Productions:
    New York Times 21 Aug. 1961: 18. [South American tour]
    Burks, Edward C. *New York Times* 29 July 1961: 8.
        [South American tour]
    De Jongh, Nicholas. *Guardian.* Rpt. *London Theatre
        Record* 3: 582. [London New End prod., 28 June-17
        July 1983]

SUMMER AND SMOKE: Quasi-allegorical contest between the body
and the soul, set in Mississippi near the beginning of
the century. Mss., Columbia, Delaware, Princeton, Texas
(G).
    Summer and Smoke, begun 1945, has a passing relationship
with the short story "The Yellow Bird" (B 1). Williams
revised the text several times. Another version is entitled *The Eccentricities of a Nightingale* (A 1 above).
The relationship among the various published texts poses
an interesting problem. His essay for the New York opening was "Questions without Answers" (D 1).
    James Poe and Meade Roberts provided a free adaptation
for the unpublished 1961 screenplay. Lanford Wilson
wrote the libretto for the 1971 opera version; it was set
to music by Lee Hoiby.

Publication: First American Version

Summer and Smoke. New York: New Directions, 1948. xii,
    130 pp. Ils. Contents: Author's Production Notes,
    vii-x; play, xi-130. Reviews:
      Booklist 45 (15 Mar. 1949): 239.
      Clurman, Harold. *New Republic* 15 Nov. 1948: 28.
      Freedley, George. *Library Journal* 74 (15 Jan.
        1949): 129.
      Funke, Lewis. *New York Times Books Review* 16 Jan.
        1949: 20.

Best American Plays, Third Series, *1945-1951*.   Ed. John
    Gassner. New York: Crown, 1952. 665-701.

Summer and Smoke. Signet Book. New York: New American
    Library, 1961. 127 pp. Ils.

Period of Adjustment, etc., 1963 (A 2).

Eccentricities of a Nightingale, 1964: 109-248 (above).

Theatre, Vol. 2, 1971: 113-256 (A 2).

Four Plays, 1976: 3-127 (A 2).

Eight Plays, 1979: 199-296 (A 2).

Publication: Second American Version

Summer and Smoke: Acting Version: Play in Two Parts. New
    York: Dramatists Play Service, 1950. 82 pp. Contents:
    Author's Note on the Setting, 4-5; Author's Description
    of Set Interiors, 6; play, 7-79.

Publication: British Version

Summer and Smoke: A Play. London: John Lehmann, 1952.
95 pp. Contents: Author's Production Notes, 9-10;
play, 11-95.

Four Plays, 1956: 155-228 (A 2).

Summer and Smoke. London: Secker & Warburg, 1957. 96
pp.

Period of Adjustment, etc., 1982: 95-175 (A 2).

Trans. (H): Arabic, Bengali, Czech, French, German,
Greek, Hungarian, Italian, Japanese, Norwegian, Portuguese, Spanish (version uncertain).

Publication: Student Edition

Summer and Smoke. Contemporary Library. Tokyo: Nan-un-
Do, 1964. 148 pp.

Inclusion in Textbooks (First Version)

Collection of Contemporary American Literature 13.
Tokyo: 1959. 235-313.

Goldstone, Richard, ed. *Contexts of the Drama*. New
York: McGraw-Hill, 1968. 603-64.

Hatcher, Harlan, ed. *A Modern Repertory*. New York: Harcourt, 1953.

Taylor, John Chesley, and Gary Richard Thompson, eds.
*Ritual, Realism, and Revolt: Major Traditions in the
Drama*. New York: Scribner's, 1972.

Criticism

Brooking, Jack. "Directing *Summer and Smoke*: An Exist-
entialist Approach." *Modern Drama* 2 (Feb. 1960): 377-
85.

Moody, R. Bruce, and Beckman H. Cottrell. "Two Views of
Summer and Smoke." *Contexts of the Drama* (see above):
664-70.

Rost, Maria. *Masterplots II: Drama Series*. Ed. Frank N.
Magill. Pasadena, CA: Salem, 1990. 1514-19.

Productions

Summer and Smoke. Theatre '47. Dallas: Gulf Oil Play-
house, 8 July 1947 (première). Margo Jones, dir. With
Katherine Balfour (Alma), Tod Andrews (John). Reviews:
  New York Times 1 Aug. 1947: 21.
  Theatre Arts Sept. 1947: 11.
  Atkinson, Brooks. *New York Times* 10 Aug. 1947, sec. 2:
    1. Rpt. *New York Times Theatre Reviews*.
  Jones, Margo. *Theatre-in-the-Round*. New York: McGraw-
    Hill, 1965. 142–46.
  Rosenfield, John. *New York Times* 9 July 1947: 18.
    Rpt. *New York Times Theatre Reviews*.

Summer and Smoke. Previews: Buffalo, Detroit, Cleveland.
New York: Music Box Theatre, 6 Oct. 1948–1 Jan. 1949
(100). Margo Jones, dir. Jo Mielziner, design. Paul
Bowles, music. With Margaret Philipps (Alma), Tod
Andrews (John). Recording of music: Dramatists Play
Service. Reviews, Prod. Notes:
  Life 25 Oct. 1948: 102–03.
  New York Times 26 Sept. 1948: 66–67.
  New York Times 3 Oct. 1948, sec. 2: 1, 3.
  New York Times 5 Dec. 1948, sec. 2: 7. [Lighting]
  New York Times Magazine 26 Sept. 1948: 66–67.
  Newsweek 18 Oct. 1948: 88.
  Time 18 Oct. 1948: 82–83.
  Variety 22 Sept. 1948: 47. [Detroit tryout]
  Variety 13 Oct. 1948: 50.
  Atkinson, Brooks. *New York Times* 7 Oct. 1948: 33.
    Rpt. *New York Times Theatre Reviews; New York The-
    atre Critics' Reviews* 9: 205–06.
  ———. *New York Times* 17 Oct. 1948, sec. 2: 1. Rpt. *New
    York Times Theatre Reviews*.
  Barnes, Howard. *New York Herald Tribune* 7 Oct. 1948:
    16. Rpt. *New York Theatre Critics' Reviews* 9: 205.
  Beyer, William. *School and Society* 68 (30 Oct. 1948):
    303–04.
  Brown, John Mason. *Saturday Review* 30 Oct. 1948: 31–
    33. Rpt. Van Antwerp (F 1): 116, 118–20.
  Chapman, John. *New York Daily News* 7 Oct. 1948: 81.
    Rpt. *New York Theatre Critics' Reviews* 9: 206.
  Clurman, Harold. *New Republic* 25 Oct. 1948: 25–26.
    Rpt. *Lies like Truth*... (New York: Macmillan, 1958):
    80–83; *The Divine Pastime*... (New York: Macmillan,
    1974): 18–20.
  ———. *New Republic* 15 Nov. 1948: 27–28.
  Coleman, Robert. *New York Daily Mirror* 7 Oct. 1948:
    36. Rpt. *New York Theatre Critics' Reviews* 9: 208.
  Currie, George. *Brooklyn Daily Eagle* 7 Oct. 1948: 6.

Freedley, George. *New York Morning Telegraph* 8 Oct.
     1948: 2.
Gabriel, Gilbert W. *Theatre Arts* Jan. 1949: 10-11.
Garland, Robert. *New York Journal American* 7 Oct.
     1948: 21. Rpt. *New York Theatre Critics' Reviews* 9:
     206-07.
Gassner, John. *Forum* 110 (Dec. 1948): 351-53.
---. *Theatre Time* Spring 1949: 5-11.
Gibbs, Wolcott. *New Yorker* 16 Oct. 1948: 51-52.
Hawkins, William. *New York World-Telegram* 7 Oct. 1948:
     14. Rpt. *New York Theatre Critics' Reviews* 9: 207.
Krutch, Joseph Wood. *Nation* 167 (23 Oct. 1948): 473-
     74.
Lardner, John. *New York Star* 8 Oct. 1948. Rpt. *New
     York Theatre Critics' Reviews* 9: 208-09.
Morehouse, Ward. *New York Sun* 7 Oct. 1948: 28. Rpt.
     New York Theatre Critics' Reviews 9: 208.
Nathan, George Jean. *New York Journal American* 18 Oct.
     1948: 12. Rpt. *The Magic Mirror...*, ed. Thomas
     Quinn Curtiss (New York: Knopf, 1960): 238-42.
---. *Theatre Book of the Year 1948-1949*. New York:
     Knopf, 1949. 114-21.
Phelan, Kappo. *Commonweal* 49 (29 Oct. 1948): 68-69.
Watts, Richard Jr. *New York Post* 7 Oct. 1984: 33.
     Rpt. *New York Theatre Critics' Reviews* 9: 207.
Wyatt, Euphemia Van Rensselaer. *Catholic World* 168
     (Nov. 1948): 161.

Summer and Smoke. Previews: Cambridge, Brighton. Lon-
don: Lyric Theatre, Hammersmith, 22 Nov. 1951; Duchess
Theatre, 24 Jan. 1952. Peter Glenville, dir. Reece Pem-
berton, William Chappell, design. Paul Bowles, music.
With Margaret Johnston (Alma), William Sylvester (John),
Maria Britneva (Rosemary). Reviews:
     New York Times 25 Jan. 1952: 13. Rpt. *New York Times
          Theatre Reviews*.
     Times (London) 23 Nov. 1951: 2.
     Darlington, W. A. *New York Times* 10 Feb. 1952: 3.
          Rpt. *New York Times Theatre Reviews*.
     Tynan, Kenneth. *Spectator* 187 (7 Dec. 1951): 772.
     Worsley, T. C. *New Statesman* 42 (8 Dec. 1951): 664.
     Zolotow, Sam. *New York Times* 23 Nov. 1951: 32.

Summer and Smoke. New York: Circle-in-the-Square Theatre, 24 Apr. 1952. José Quintero, dir. Keith Cuerden,
design. With Geraldine Page (Alma), Lee Richard (John).
Reviews, Prod. Notes:
     Atkinson, Brooks. *New York Times* 25 Apr. 1952: 19.
          Rpt. *New York Times Theatre Reviews*.
     ---. *New York Times* 4 May 1952, sec. 2: 1. Rpt. *New
          York Times Theatre Reviews*.

Gassner, John. *Theatre at the Crossroads* (A 3): 218-
23.
Hawkins, William. *New York World-Telegram* 7 May 1952:
32.
Hewes, Henry. *Saturday Review* 10 May 1952: 28.
Little, Stuart W. *Off-Broadway: The Prophetic Theater.*
New York: Coward, 1972. 13-27.
Quintero, Jose. *If You Don't Dance They Beat You.*
Boston: Little, Brown, 1974. 111-22.
Sheaffer, Louis. *Brooklyn Eagle* 28 Apr. 1952: 8.
Wyatt, Euphemia Van Rennselaer. *Catholic World* 176
(Nov. 1952): 148-49.

Summer and Smoke. Screenplay by James Poe and Meade
Roberts. Paramount, 15 Nov. 1961 (première). Peter
Glenville, dir. Charles Lange, Jr., camera. Walter
Tyler, Hal Pereira, design. Elmer Bernstein, music.
With Geraldine Page (Alma), Laurence Harvey (John), Rita
Moreno (Rosa), Una Merkel (Mrs. Winemiller). Music
soundtrack: RCA Victor Records, 1962; later Entr'acte
Records. Reviews, Prod. Notes:
Filmfacts 4 (1961): 275.
Illustrated London News 240 (28 Apr. 1962): 676.
Newsweek 20 Nov. 1961: 106.
Redbook Dec. 1961: 16.
Time 1 Dec. 1961: 76.
Variety 6 Sept. 1961: 6.
Armitage, Peter. *Film* 32 (Summer 1962): 22.
Baker, Peter. *Films and Filming* May 1962: 31-32.
Beckley, Paul V. *New York Herald Tribune* 17 Nov. 1961:
15.
---. *New York Herald Tribune* 19 Nov. 1961, sec. 4: 4.
Cameron, Kate. *New York Daily News* 17 Nov. 1961: 66.
Coleman, John. *New Statesman* 63 (20 Apr. 1962): 570-
71.
Crowther, Bosley. *New York Times* 17 Nov. 1961: 41.
Rpt. *New York Times Film Reviews.*
---. *New York Times* 19 Nov. 1961, sec. 2: 1.
Finkelstein, Sidney. *Mainstream* 15 (May 1962): 59-60.
Gill, Brendan. *New Yorker* 25 Nov. 1961: 205-06.
Hartung, Philip T. *Commonweal* 75 (1 Dec. 1961): 259.
Kauffmann, Stanley. *New Republic* 27 Nov. 1961: 18-20.
Knight, Arthur. *Saturday Review* 11 Nov. 1961: 32.
Pryor, Thomas. *New York Times* 13 Dec. 1954: 34.
[Plans]
Rhode, Eric. *Sight and Sound* 31 (Spring 1962): 95.
Schlesinger, Arthur Jr. *Show* Mar. 1962: 98.
Schumach, Murray. *New York Times* 29 Jan. 1961, sec. 2:
7.
Smith, Milburn. *Theatre* Sept. 1961: 20-21.
Walsh, Moira. *America* 106 (25 Nov. 1961): 308-10.

Wharton, Flavia. *Films in Review* 12 (Dec. 1961): 621.
Winsten, Archer. *New York Post* 17 Nov. 1961: 59.

Summer and Smoke. BBC-TV, 23 Jan. 1972. With Lee Remick
(Alma), David Hedison (John), Betsy Blair (Mrs. Winemil-
ler). Review:
   Buckley, Leonard. *Times* (London) 24 Jan. 1972.

Other Productions:
   Goodman, John. *New York Times* 29 Oct. 1950, sec. 2: 3.
     Rpt. *New York Times Theatre Reviews.* [Western tour
     with Dorothy McGuire, John Ireland, Una Merkel]
   Gussow, Mel. *New York Times* 31 July 1986, sec 3: 17.
     [Williamstown, MA]
   Hughes, Catherine. *America* 133 (15 Nov. 1975): 340-41.
     [New York]
   Kerr, Walter. *New York Times* 19 Oct. 1975, sec. 2: 1,
     5. [New York]
   Shanley, J. P. *New York Times* 9 Aug. 1949: 21. [PA]
   Spillman, Susan. *USA Today* 24 Feb. 1988. [Los Angeles
     with Christine Lahti, Christopher Reeve]
   Wilkerson, Jo Norman. *Tennessee Williams Review* 3.1
     (1981): 14-18. [Bangor, ME]

Publication: Opera

Summer and Smoke: Opera in Two Acts. Music by Lee Hoiby;
Libretto by Lanford Wilson. New York: Belwin-Mills,
1972. 66 pp. Vocal Score, 1976. 332 pp.

Productions: Opera

Summer and Smoke. Libretto by Lanford Wilson; music by
Lee Hoiby. St. Paul, MI: St. Paul Opera, 19 June 1971
(première). Frank Corsaro, dir. Lloyd Evans, Hans Sand-
heimer, design. Julius Rudel, cond. With Mary Beth Peil
(Alma), John Reardon (John). Reviews, Prod. Notes:
   Ericson, Raymond. *New York Times* 25 June 1971: 18.
   Feldman, Mary Ann. *Opera News* Sept. 1971: 18-20.
   Gerstel, Judith. *High Fidelity & Musical America* 21
     (Sept. 1971): MA 20.
   Hoiby, Lee. "Making Tennessee Williams Sing." *New
     York Times* 13 June 1971, sec. 2: 17, 20.
   Little, Stuart W. *New York Herald Tribune* 23 Feb.
     1966: 19. [Plans]

Summer and Smoke. New York City Opera Company. New
York: State Theatre, 19 Mar. 1972. Frank Corsaro, dir.
Lloyd Evans, Hans Sandheimer, design. Julius Rudel,
cond. With Mary Beth Peil (Alma), John Reardon (John).
Reviews:

Kolodin, Irving. *Saturday Review* 8 Apr. 1972: 18.
Mayer, Martin. *High Fidelity & Musical America* 22
(July 1972): MA 10.
Rorem, Ned. *New Republic* 8 Apr. 1972: 19.
Schonberg, Harold G. *New York Times* 21 Mar. 1972: 34.
Rpt. Van Antwerp (F 1): 282-83.

Summer and Smoke. Chicago: Chicago Opera Theatre, 23 May
1980. Frank Galati, dir. PBS-TV, 23 June 1982. Kirk
Browning, dir. David Emmons, Kate Bergh, Geoffrey
Bushor, design. Robert Frisbie, cond. With Mary Beth
Peil (Alma), Robert Orth (John). Reviews:
  Opera News June 1982: 22.
  Davis, Peter. *New York* 21 June 1982: 61.
  O'Connor, John J. *New York Times* 23 June 1982, sec. C:
  27.
  Von Rhein, John. *Opera News* Sept. 1980: 56.

American Girl. Eb-Sko Records, 198-. Helen-Kay Eberley
(Alma). "No, I haven't been well."

American Song Recital. New World Records, 198-. William
Parker (John). "Anatomy Lesson" and Scene.

SWEET BIRD OF YOUTH: Tragedy of a would-be actor trying to
recapture his youth spent in a town on the Gulf coast.
Mss., California-Los Angeles, Columbia, Congress, Delaware, Houston, New York Public, Texas (G).
   The play began 1948-49 as a number of sketches, including "The Enemy: Time," 1952. The full-length version was
produced in Miami in 1956; see Leavitt (F 1): 114. This
script was revised 1956-58. Then under Elia Kazan's influence the play was profoundly altered in 1959 for its
New York production. The *Esquire* in-progress version is
already far changed from the text handed to Kazan, but it
is the closest the reader can presently get to Williams's
original conception since the New Directions text reflects this production. The Dramatists Play Service text
is strange, but some pre-1959 elements were restored.
Williams spoke of rewriting the play to make the actress
more central. The pre-opening essay was entitled "Williams' Wells of Violence" (D 1), reprinted as a Foreword
(below).
   Richard Brooks prepared the unpublished 1961 screenplay,
a loose adaptation, and Gavin Lambert prepared the 1989
television adaptation.

Publication: One-Act Sketch

"The Enemy: Time." *Theatre* 1 (Mar. 1959): 14-17.

Publication: Early Version

Sweet Bird of Youth. *Esquire* 51 (Apr. 1959): 114-55.
  Note: "... In Unmeditated Flight": 24.

Publication: Revised Version

Sweet Bird of Youth. New York: New Directions, 1959.
  New York: New Directions, 1975; Toronto: McClelland &
  Stewart, 1975. New Directions Paperbook. xiv, 114 pp.
  Il. Contents: Foreword (D 1), vii-xi; Synopsis of
  Scenes, 2; play, 3-114. Reviews:
    Theatre Arts Feb. 1960: 91.
    Variety 2 Dec. 1959: 77.
    Freedley, George. *Library Journal* 85 (15 Jan.
      1960): 299.

The Best Plays of 1958-1959.... Ed. Louis Kronenberger.
  New York: Dodd, Mead, 1959. 209-31. Excerpts.

Sweet Bird of Youth: A Play. London: Secker & Warburg,
  1961. 93 pp. Contents: Foreword, 7-10; play, 15-93.
  Review:
    Times Literary Supplement 13 Jan. 1961: 23.

Sweet Bird of Youth...with a Foreword by the Author.
  Signet Book. New York: New American Library, 1962;
  Toronto: New American Library of Canada, 1962. 124 pp.
  Ils.

Sweet Bird of Youth, etc. 1962: 7-111 (A 2).

Three Plays, 1964: 331-452 (A 2).

Theatre, Vol. 4, 1972: 1-124 (A 2).

Three by Tennessee, 1976 (A 2).

Selected Plays, 1977: 475-560; *Selected Plays*, 1980: 377-
  460 (A 2).

Eight Plays, 1979: 643-735 (A 2).

Trans. (H): Chinese, Czech, French, German, Greek, Hungarian, Norwegian, Russian, Slovak, Spanish.

Publication: Second Revised Version

Sweet Bird of Youth. New York: Dramatists Play Service,
  1962. 72 pp. Contents: play, 5-60; Alternate Ending,
  60-61.

Criticism

Chase, Nan. *Masterplots II: Drama Series*. Ed. Frank N.
Magill. Pasadena, CA: Salem, 1990. 1524-28.

Debusscher, Gilbert. "And the Sailor Turned into a Princess: New Light on the Genesis of *Sweet Bird of Youth*."
Studies in American Drama 1 (1986): 25-31.

Dukore, Bernard F. "American Abelard: A Footnote to
Sweet Bird of Youth." *College English* 26 (May 1965):
630-34.

Gunn, Drewey Wayne. "The Troubled Flight of Tennessee
Williams's *Sweet Bird*: From Manuscript through Published Texts." *Modern Drama* 24 (Mar. 1981): 26-35.

Hays, Peter L. "Tennessee Williams' Use of Myth in *Sweet
Bird of Youth*," *Educational Theatre Journal* 18 (Oct.
1966): 255-58.

Kolin, Philip C. "Parallels between *Desire under the
Elms* and *Sweet Bird of Youth*." *Eugene O'Neill Review*
13.2 (1989): 23-35.

Roulet, W. M. "*Sweet Bird of Youth*: Williams' Redemptive
Ethic." *Cithara* 3 (1964): 31-36.

Productions

Sweet Bird of Youth. Coral Gables, FL: Studio M Play-
house, 16 Apr. 1956 (première). George Keathley, dir.,
design. With Alan Mixon (Phil), Margrit Wyler (Prin-
cess), Ruth Martin (Valerie), James Reese (Boss Finley),
Blanche Kelly (Aunt Nonnie), Eleanor Sherman (Miss Lucy),
Robert Choromokos (Fred Finley). Program: Leavitt (F
1): 114. Reviews:
  New York Times 17 Apr. 1956: 27. Rpt. *New York Times
    Theatre Reviews*.
  Theatre Arts Aug. 1956: 66-67.
  Zolotow, Sam. *New York Times* 13 Apr. 1956: 21.

Sweet Bird of Youth. Previews: Philadelphia. New York:
Martin Beck Theatre, 10 Mar. 1959-30 Jan. 1960 (première:
383). Tour: 1 Feb.-21 May 1960. Elia Kazan, dir. Jo
Mielziner, Anna Hill Johnstone, design. Paul Bowles,
music. With Paul Newman, later Rip Torn (Chance), Geral-
dine Page (Princess), Diana Hyland (Heavenly), Sidney
Blackmer (Boss Finley), Madeleine Sherwood (Miss Lucy),
Rip Torn (Tom). Program: Leavitt (F 1): 125. Reviews,
Prod. Notes:

Life 20 Apr. 1959: 71-73.

Newsweek 23 Mar. 1959: 75.

Theatre Arts May 1959: 21-22.

Time 23 Mar. 1959: 58.

Times (London) 10 Apr. 1959: 4.

Variety 18 Mar. 1959: 90.

Variety 23 Dec. 1959: 56.

Aston, Frank. *New York World-Telegram* 11 Mar. 1959:
   30. Rpt. *New York Theatre Critics' Reviews* 20: 348.

Atkinson, Brooks. *New York Times* 11 Mar. 1959: 39.
   Rpt. *New York Times Theatre Reviews; New York Theatre Critics' Reviews* 20: 350.

---. *New York Times* 22 Mar. 1959, sec. 2: 1.

Balch, Jack. *Theatre* Mar. 1959: 22-23. [Rehearsals]

Bolton, Whitney. *New York Morning Telegraph* 12 Mar.
   1959: 2.

---. *New York Morning Telegraph* 16 Mar. 1959: 1-2.

Brustein, Robert. *Encounter* June 1959: 59-60.

---. *Hudson Review* 12 (Summer 1959): 155-60.

Chapman, John. *New York Daily News* 11 Mar. 1959: 65.
   Rpt. *New York Theatre Critics' Reviews* 20: 349; Van
   Antwerp (F 1): 196-98.

Clurman, Harold. *Nation* 188 (28 Mar. 1959): 281-83.
   Rpt. *The Naked Image...* (New York: Macmillan, 1966):
   123-26.

Coleman, Robert. *New York Daily Mirror* 11 Mar. 1959,
   sec. A: 1. Rpt. *New York Theatre Critics' Reviews*
   20: 349; Van Antwerp (F 1): 195-96.

Cotter, Jerry. *Sign* May 1959: 55.

Driver, Tom F. *Christian Century* 76 (15 Apr. 1959)
   455.

---. *Christian Century* 76 (17 June 1959): 726. Rpt.
   Christian Century 101 (11 July 1984): 690-92.
   Response: *Christian Century* 76 (22 July 1959) 854-
   55.

---. *New Republic* 20 Apr. 1959: 21-22.

Duprey, Richard A. *Catholic World* 189 (June 1959):
   191-94.

Gallaway, Marian. *Players* Nov. 1960: 42-43.

Gassel, Sylvia. *Village Voice* 24 June 1959: 8-9.

Gassner, John. *Educational Theatre Journal* 11 (May
   1959); 122-24.

---. *Theatre at the Crossroads* (A 3): 228-31.

Gelb, Arthur. *New York Times* 30 June 1958: 23. [Re-
   write]

Hayes, Richard. *Commonweal* 70 (24 Apr. 1959): 102.

Herridge, Frances. *New York Post* 17 May 1960: 66.
   [Cast changes]

Hewes, Henry. *Saturday Review* 28 Mar. 1959: 26.
   Response: *Saturday Review* 18 Apr. 1959: 29.

Kazan, Elia. *A Life* (F 1): 544-46.

Kerr, Walter. *New York Herald Tribune* 11 Mar. 1959:
    16. Rpt. *The Theatre in Spite of Itself* (New York:
    Simon, 1963): 247-55.
---. *New York Herald Tribune* 22 Mar. 1959, sec. 4: 1-
    2.
---. *New York Herald Tribune* 17 May 1959, sec. 4: 1-2.
---. *New York Herald Tribune* 6 Sept. 1959, sec. 4: 1.
Lewis, Theophilus. *America* 101 (4 Apr. 1959): 55-56.
Mannes, Marya. *Reporter* 16 Apr. 1959: 34.
McClain, John. *New York Journal-American* 8 Mar. 1959,
    sec. 2: 27.
---. *New York Journal-American* 11 Mar. 1959: 21. Rpt.
    New York Theatre Critics' Reviews 20: 350.
Michelfelder, William F. *New York World-Telegram* 11
    Mar. 1959: 17.
Morella, Joe, and Edward Z. Epstein. *Paul and Joanne*.
    New York: Delacourte, 1988. 77-80. [Newman]
Real, Jere. *Advocate* 27 May 1986: 46. [Interview with
    James Baldwin, Kazan's "script boy"]
Shipley, Joseph T. *New Leader* 30 Mar. 1959: 26.
Tallmer, Jerry. *Village Voice* 18 Mar. 1959: 9.
Tynan, Kenneth. *New Yorker* 21 Mar. 1959: 98-100. Rpt.
    Curtains... (New York: Atheneum, 1961): 306-07.
Watts, Richard Jr. *New York Post* 11 Mar. 1959: 78.
    Rpt. *New York Theatre Critics' Reviews* 20: 348-49.
---. *New York Post* 22 May 1959: 11.
Wyatt, Euphemia Van Rensselaer. *Catholic World* 189
    (May 1959): 158-59.
Zolotow, Sam. *New York Times* 12 Mar. 1959: 26.

Sweet Bird of Youth. Hollywood (Los Angeles): Civic
Playhouse, 1 Nov. 1961 (première). Edward Ludlom, dir.
Prod. Notes:
Schumach, Murray. *New York Times* 27 Oct. 1961: 27.
    [Rewrite]

Sweet Bird of Youth. Screenplay by Richard Brooks. MGM,
20 Feb. 1962 (première). Richard Brooks, dir. Milton
Krasner, camera. George W. Davis, Urie McCleary, design.
Harold Gelman, music. With Paul Newman (Chance), Geral-
dine Page (Princess), Shirley Knight (Heavenly), Ed Beg-
ley (Boss Finley), Madeleine Sherwood (Miss Lucy), Rip
Torn (Tom). Reviews, Prod. Notes:
Filmfacts 5 (1962): 65.
Illustrated London News 240 (12 May 1962): 770.
New York Times Magazine 14 Jan. 1962: 62-65.
Newsweek 2 Apr. 1962: 86.
Time 30 Mar. 1962: 83.
Variety 28 Feb. 1962: 6.
Alpert, Hollis. *Saturday Review* 30 Mar. 1962: 26.

Beckley, Paul V. *New York Herald Tribune* 29 Mar. 1962:
    15.
Coleman, John. *New Statesman* 63 (11 May 1962): 688.
Cronin, Morton. *National Review* 12 (27 Feb. 1962):
    137-38.
Crowther, Bosley. *New York Times* 29 Mar. 1962: 28.
    Rpt. *New York Times Film Reviews*.
Cutts, John. *Films and Filming* June 1962: 35.
Gill, Brendan. *New Yorker* 7 Apr. 1962: 148-50.
Hartung, Philip T. *Commonweal* 76 (30 Mar. 1962): 18.
Hodgens, R. M. *Film Quarterly* 15 (Summer 1962): 64.
Kauffmann, Stanley. *New Republic* 16 Apr. 1962: 28.
    Rpt. *A World on Film*... (New York: Harper, 1966):
    85-87.
LaBadie, Donald W. *Show* Mar. 1962: 30.
Macdonald, Dwight. *Esquire* June 1962: 56-58. Rpt.
    Dwight Macdonald on Movies (Englewood Cliffs, NJ:
    Prentice-Hall, 1969): 148-49.
Rothschild, Elaine. *Films in Review* 8 (Apr. 1962):
    233-34.
Schumach, Murray. *New York Times* 27 Aug. 1961, sec. 2:
    7. [Filming]
Winsten, Archer. *New York Post* 29 Mar. 1962: 26.
Zolotow, Sam. *New York Times* 12 Mar. 1959: 26. [Film
    rights]

Sweet Bird of Youth. Manchester: Experimental Club, Feb.
1964. With Ron Skinner (Chance), Irene Rostron (Princess).

Sweet Bird of Youth. Watford, Eng.: Palace Theatre, 19
Nov. 1968. Giles Havergal, dir. With Christopher Gable
(Chance), Vivien Merchant (Princess), John Savident (Boss
Finley). Reviews:
    Nightingale, Benedict. *New Statesman* 76 (29 Nov.
        1968): 765.
    Wardle, Irving. *Times* (London) 19 Nov. 1968: 9.

Sweet Bird of Youth. Washington: Kennedy Center, 8 Oct.
1975 (97); New York: Brooklyn Academy of Music, 3-14 Dec.
1975 (15); Harkness Theatre, 29 Dec. 1975-7 Feb. 1976
(48). Edwin Sherwin, dir. Karl Eigst, Ken Billington,
Laura Cross, design. With Christopher Walken (Chance),
Irene Worth (Princess), Pat Corley (Boss Finley). Playbill: Leavitt (F 1). Reviews:
    Barnes, Clive. *New York Times* 4 Dec. 1975: 53. Rpt.
        New York Theatre Critics' Reviews 36: 113-14.
    Beaufort, John. *Christian Science Monitor* 10 Dec.
        1975. Rpt. *New York Theatre Critics' Reviews* 36:
        116-17.
    Clurman, Harold. *Nation* 221 (27 Dec. 1975): 700.

Gottfried, Martin. *New York Post* 4 Dec. 1975. Rpt.
   New York Theatre Critics' Reviews 36: 115-16.
Hughes, Catherine. *America* 134 (31 Jan. 1976): 75.
Kauffmann, Stanley. *New Republic* 17 Jan. 1976: 28-29.
Kerr, Walter. *New York Times* 21 Dec. 1975, sec. 2: 5.
Kissel, Howard. *Women's Wear Daily* 31 Dec. 1975. Rpt.
   New York Theatre Critics' Reviews 36: 116.
Mallet, Gina. *Time* 15 Dec. 1975: 71.
Watt, Douglas. *New York Daily News* 4 Dec. 1975. Rpt.
   New York Theatre Critics' Reviews 36: 115.
Wilson, Edwin. *Wall Street Journal* 8 Dec. 1975. Rpt.
   New York Theatre Critics' Reviews 36: 114.

Sweet Bird of Youth. London: Haymarket Theatre, 9 July-
16 Nov. 1985. Harold Pinter, dir. Eileen Diss, Robin
Fraser, Mick Hughes, design. With Michael Beck (Chance),
Lauren Bacall (Princes), Geraldine Alexander (Heavenly),
James Grant (Boss Finley), Frances Cuka (Miss Lucy).
Reviews:
Asquith, Ros. *London Observer* 14 July 1985. Rpt. *Lon-
   don Theatre Record* 5: 660-61.
Barber, John. *London Daily Telegraph* 11 July 1985.
   Rpt. *London Theatre Record* 5: 643, 659.
Billington, Michael. *Guardian* 11 July 1985. Rpt. *Lon-
   don Threatre Record* 5: 653.
Coveney, Michael. *London Financial Times* 10 July 1985.
   Rpt. *London Theatre Record* 5: 653.
Croppe, Martin. *Times* (London) 11 July 1985.
Edwards, Christopher. *Spectator* 20 July 1985. Rpt.
   London Theatre Record 5: 661-62.
Gussow, Mel. *New York Times* 1 Aug. 1985, sec. 3: 16.
Hirschhorn, Clive. *London Sunday Express* 14 July 1985.
   Rpt. *London Theatre Record* 5: 659.
Hoyle, Martin. *Plays and Players* Sept. 1985: 18-19.
Hurren, Kenneth. *London Mail on Sunday* 14 July 1985.
   Rpt. *London Theatre Record* 5: 653.
King, Francis. *London Sunday Telegraph* 14 July 1985.
   Rpt. *London Theatre Record* 5: 660.
Morley, Sheridan. *Punch* 17 July 1985. Rpt. *London
   Theatre Record* 5: 660.
Nathan, David. *Jewish Chronicle* 19 July 1985. Rpt.
   London Theatre Record 5: 659.
Nightingale, Benedict. *New Statesman* 19 July 1985: 32.
   Rpt. *London Theatre Record* 5: 662.
Shulman, Milton. *London Standard* 10 July 1985. Rpt.
   London Theatre Record 5: 661.

Sweet Bird of Youth. Western tour: Denver Center, 19
Nov. 1986-Los Angeles Ahmanson Theatre, 25 Jan. 1987.
Michael Blakemore, dir. Michael Annals, Carrie Robbins,
Martin Aronstein, Michael Vale, design. Barrington Phe-

loung, music. With Mark Soper (Chance), Lauren Bacall
(Princess), Henderson Forsythe (Boss Finley). Review:
Curry, Jack. *USA Today* 9 Dec. 1986.

Sweet Bird of Youth. Adaptation by Gavin Lambert. NBC-
TV, 1 Oct. 1989. Nicholas Roeg, dir. With Mark Harmon
(Chance), Elizabeth Taylor (Princess), Rip Torn (Boss
Finley), Valerie Perrine (Miss Lucy), Cheryl Paris (Hea-
venly). Reviews, Prod. Notes:
  Newsweek 11 Sept. 1989: 48.
  Tennessee Williams Literary Journal 1.2 (Winter 1989–
    90): 63–65.
  Buck, Jerry. AP. *Corpus Christi Caller* 1 Oct. 1989,
    sec. H: 12–13.
  Farber, Stephen. *New York Times* 30 July 1989, sec. 2:
    27. [Filming]
  Green, Tom. *USA Today* 29 Sept. 1989, sec. D: 3.
    [Interview with Harmon]
  Hodges, Ann. *TV Chronolog (Houston Post* 1–7 Oct. 1989:
    4–5. [Interviews]
  Leonard, John. *New York* 2 Oct. 1989: 76.
  O'Connor, John J. *New York Times* 29 Sept. 1989, sec.
    C: 34.
  Roush, Matt. *USA Today* 29 Sept. 1989, sec. A: 1.
  Warren, Elaine. *TV Guide* 30 Sept. 1989: 10–12. [In-
    terviews]

Other Productions:
  New York Times 21 Aug. 1961: 18. [South American tour]
  Time 1 Sept. 1961: 52. [South American tour]
  Barks, Edward C. *New York Times* 29 July 1961: 8.
    [South American tour]
  Bemrose, John. *Maclean's* 101 (2 May 1988): 66. [To-
    ronto with Joanne Woodward, Charles Durning]

"TALK TO ME LIKE THE RAIN AND LET ME LISTEN...": Dialogue
between two lost persons in New York. Ms., Texas (G).

27 Wagons Full of Cotton, 1953: 209–18 (A 2).

The Disinherited: Plays. Ed. Abe C. Ravitz. Encino, CA:
Dickensen, 1974.

Theatre, Vol. 6, 1981: 263–72 (A 2).

Trans. (H): Czech, French, German, Greek, Hungarian,
Italian.

Productions

"Talk to Me like the Rain and Let Me Listen." Westport, CT: White Barn Theatre, 26-27 July 1958. Sherwood Arthur, dir. With Norma Cates (Woman), John Napier (Man).

"Talk to Me like the Rain and Let Me Listen." PBS-TV, 3 Dec. 1970. Glenn Jordan, dir. With Lois Smith (Woman), William Mixon (Man). See "I Can't Imagine Tomorrow."

Ten by Tennessee. New York: Lucille Lortel Theatre, 11 May-29 June 1986. Michael Kahn, dir. With Laura Hicks (Woman), Derek D. Smith (Man). See "Auto-da-Fé."

***THIS IS (AN ENTERTAINMENT)*:** Unpublished fantasy set in an imaginary mid-European country, examining the nature of sexuality and of fear. Ms., Columbia, Delaware (G).

This Is (An Entertainment). American Conservatory Theatre. San Francisco: Geary Theatre, 20 Jan. 1976 (première, 21). Allen Fletcher, dir. John Jensen, F. Mitchell Dana, Robert Morgan, design. Conrad Susa, music. With Elizabeth Huddle (Countess), Ray Reinhardt (Count), Nicholas Cortland, Anne Lawder, Marian Wal-ters, Sydney Walker. Reviews:
  Performing Arts Feb. 1976: 29.
  Variety 4 Feb. 1976.
  Armstrong, James. *After Dark* June 1976: 28-31. Rpt.
    Van Antwerp (F 1): 315-18.
  Clark, Judith Hersh. Stanton (A 3): 179-81.
  Cohn, Ruby. *Educational Theatre Journal* 28 (Oct.
    1976): 406-07.
  Eichelbaum, Stanley. *San Francisco Examiner* 21 Jan.
    1976. Rpt. *New York Times* 12 Feb. 1976, sec. 2: 5.
  Sullivan, Dan. *Los Angeles Times* 22 Jan. 1976.
  Weiner, Bernard. *San Francisco Chronicle* 22 Jan. 1976.

"THIS IS THE PEACEFUL KINGDOM, OR GOOD LUCK GOD": Absurd drama about faith, compassion, and prejudice - both religious and ethnic - in a Queens (NY) nursing home during a 1978 strike.

Theatre, Vol. 7, 1981 (A 2): 331-65 (A 2).

"THIS PROPERTY IS CONDEMNED": A doomed Mississippi girl's conversation with a boy, revealing the heritage that has created her. Mss., Columbia, Texas (G).

Landscape with Figures, 1941: 173-93 (see "At Liberty," above).

27 Wagons Full of Cotton, 1945, 1953: 195-207 (A 2).

27 Wagons Full of Cotton, 1949: 181-92 (A 2).

Perspectives USA 1 Jan. 1952: 95-105.

Theatre, Vol. 6, 1981: 245-61 (A 2).

Trans. (H): French, Greek, Hungarian, Italian.

Productions: Play and Film Version

"This Property Is Condemned." New York: New School for Social Research, 2 June 1942 (première).

Trilogy of One Act Plays. Dallas: Gulf Oil Playhouse, Sept. 1947. Margo Jones, dir. With Rebecca Hargis (Willie), Charles Taliaferro (Tom). See "Last of My Solid Gold Watches."

Three premières. New York: Cherry Lane Theatre, 28 Oct 1956. Charles Olsen, dir. With Sandra Kolb (Willie), Billy James (Tom). Reviews:
   Variety 14 Nov. 1956: 74. Rpt. Van Antwerp (F 1): 164.
   Beckley, Paul V. *New York Herald Tribune* 29 Oct. 1956:
      10. Rpt. Van Antwerp (F 1): 163-164.
   Bolton, Whitney. *New York Morning Telegraph* 30 Oct.
      1956: 2.
   Funke, Lewis. *New York Times* 29 Oct. 1956: 34. Rpt.
      New York Times Theatre Reviews.
   McClain, John. *New York Journal-American* 29 Oct. 1956:
      10.

Three by Tennessee. Kraft Television Theatre. NBC-TV, 16 Apr. 1958. Sidney Lumet, dir. With Zina Bethune (Willie), Martin Huston (Tom). See "Last of My Solid Gold Watches."

This Property Is Condemned. Screenplay by Francis Ford Coppola, Fred Coe, Edith Sommer. Seven Arts/Ray Stark, June 1966 (première). Sydney Pollack, dir. James Wong Howe, camera. Hal Pereira, Stephen Grimes, Phil Jeffries, design. With Natalie Wood (Alva), Robert Redford (Owen), Mary Badham (Willie), Jon Provost (Tom), Kate Reid (Hazel), Charles Bronson (Nichols). Music sound track: Verve Records, 1966. Reviews, Prod. Notes:
   Filmfacts 9 (1966): 206.
   Newsweek 1 Aug. 1966: 83-84.

Time 22 July 1966: 62.
Variety 11 May 1966: 1.
Variety 15 June 1966: 6.
Adler, Renata. *New Yorker* 27 Aug. 1966: 88-90.
Alpert, Hollis. *Saturday Review* 25 June 1966: 40.
Carroll, Kathleen. *New York Daily News* 4 Aug. 1966:
   67.
Crowther, Bosley. *New York Times* 4 Aug. 1966: 24.
   Rpt. *New York Times Film Reviews.*
Durgnat, Raymond. *Films and Filming* Nov. 1966: 68.
Farber, Stephen. *Film Quarterly* 20 (Winter 1966-67):
   61.
Guy, Rory. *Cinema* July 1966: 47.
Hale, Wanda. *New York Sunday News* 31 July 1966: 57.
Hartung, Philip T. *Commonweal* 84 (19 Aug. 1966): 533-
   34.
Mishkin, Leo. *New York Morning Telegraph* 4 Aug. 1966:
   3.
Reed, Rex. *New York Times* 16 Jan. 1966, sec. 2: 13.
   Rpt. *Conversations in the Raw...* (New York: World,
   1969): 235-40; Van Antwerp (F 1): 238-40.
Weiler, A. H. *New York Times* 11 Feb. 1963, sec. 2: 7.
   [Film rights]
Williams, Hugo. *New Statesman* 7 June 1985: 41.
Winsten, Alfred. *New York Post* 4 Aug. 1966: 18.

Ten by Tennessee. New York: Lucille Lortel Theatre, 11
May-29 June 1986. Michael Kahn, dir. With Laura Hicks
(Willie), Richard Howard (Tom). See "Auto-da-Fé."

Other Productions:
   Times (London) 21 Sept. 1953: 10.
   Times (London) 27 Oct. 1953: 10. [London]
   Times (London) 26 Aug. 1960: 5. [London]

Production: Ballet

"This Property Is Condemned." Ballet Theatre Workshop.
New York: Phoenix Theatre, 13 May 1957 (première).
Donald Saddler, choreography. Genevieve Pitot, music.
Stanley Simmons, costumes. With Ruth Ann Koesun (Wil-
lie), Ralph McWilliams (Tom), Beverly Barsanti (Alva).

"THREE PLAYERS OF A SUMMER GAME": Unpublished staged version of the short story (B 1). Ms., Texas (G).

"Three Players of a Summer Game." Westport, CT: White
Barn Theatre, 19 July 1955 (première). Henry Hewes, dir.
Alfred Chadbourn, design. With Albert Salmi (Brick Pol-

litt), David Stewart (Southern Gentleman), Loretta Lever-
see (Mary Louise Grey), Margaret Feury (Isabel Grey).

TIGER TAIL: see *Baby Doll*

"THE TRAVELLING COMPANION": Dialogue in a New York hotel
between an aging gay and the young but uncooperative
hustler with whom he is travelling. Ms. Delaware (G).

Christopher Street 58 (Dec. 1981): 32-40.

"27 WAGONS FULL OF COTTON: A MISSISSIPPI DELTA COMEDY:
Tragicomedy about an immature Mississippi woman being
used by two men. Mss., Congress, Texas (G).
  The play grew out of the short story of the same title
(B 1). It was largely the basis for the screenplay *Baby
Doll* (above).

The Best One-Act Plays of 1944. Ed. Margaret Mayorga.
New York: Dodd, Mead, 1945. 155-83.

27 Wagons Full of Cotton, 1945, 1953: 1-28 (A 2).

Spearhead: 10 Years' Experimental Writing in America.
New York: New Directions, 1947.

27 Wagons Full of Cotton, 1949: 7-32 (A 2).

Baby Doll, 1956: 143-90 (above).

The Best Short Plays, 20th Anniversary Edition. Ed. Margaret Mayorga. Boston: Beacon, 1957. 381-404.

24 Favorite One-Act Plays. Ed. Bennett Cerf and Van H.
Cartmell. New York: Doubleday, 1958. 95-116.

One Act: Short Plays of the Modern Theatre. Ed. Samuel
Moon. New York: Grove, 1961. 113-43.

Pulitzer Prize Reader. Ed. Leo Hamalian and Edmond L.
Volpe. New York: Popular Library, 1961.

Theatre, Vol. 6, 1981: 1-38 (A 2)

Trans. (H): Czech, French, Greek, Italian.

Inclusion in Textbook

Drabeck, Bernard A., et al., eds. *Exploring Literature
    through Reading and Writing.* Boston: Houghton Mifflin,
    1982. 142-60.

Criticism

Bray, Robert. *Masterplots II: Drama Series.* Ed. Frank
    N. Magill. Pasadena, CA: Salem, 1990. 1665-69.

Productions

"27 Wagons Full of Cotton." New Orleans: Dixon Hall
(Tulane Univ.), 17 Jan. 1955. Edward Ludlam, dir.
George Hendrickson, Homer Pouport, design. With Maureen
Stapleton (Flora), Felice Orlandi (Silva), Paul Ballen-
tyne (Jake). Review:
    Atkinson, Brooks. *New York Times* 19 Jan. 1955: 23.
    Rpt. *New York Times Theatre Reviews.*

All in One. New York: Playhouse Theatre, 19 Apr. 1955.
Vincent J. Donehue, dir. Eldon Elder, Pat Campbell, de-
sign. With Maureen Stapleton (Flora), Felice Orlandi
(Silva), Myron McCormick (Jake). Reviews:
    Theatre Arts July 1955: 17.
    Time 2 May 1955: 78.
    Variety 27 Apr. 1955: 64, 70.
    Atkinson, Brooks. *New York Times* 20 Apr. 1955: 40.
        Rpt. *New York Times Theatre Reviews.*
    ---. *New York Times* 24 Apr. 1955, sec. 2: 1. Rpt. *New
        York Times Theatre Reviews.*
    Bentley, Eric. *New Republic* 2 May 1955: 22.
    Bolton, Whitney. *New York Morning Telegraph* 21 Apr.
        1955: 3.
    Calta, Louis. *New York Times* 19 Apr. 1955: 28.
    Chapman, John. *New York Daily News* 20 Apr. 1955. Rpt.
        New York Theatre Critics' Reviews 16: 328.
    Coleman, Robert. *New York Daily Mirror* 20 Apr. 1955.
        Rpt. *New York Theatre Critics' Reviews* 16: 326.
    Freedley, George. *New York Morning Telegraph* 6 May
        1955: 2.
    Gibbs, Wolcott. *New Yorker* 30 Apr. 1955: 69-71.
    Hawkins, William. *New York World-Telegram* 20 Apr.
        1955. Rpt. *New York Theatre Critics' Reviews* 16:
        325.
    Hayes, Richard. *Commonweal* 62 (10 June 1955); 255.
    Hewes, Henry. *Saturday Review* 14 May 1955: 26.
    Kerr, Walter F. *New York Herald Tribune* 20 Apr. 1955.
        Rpt. *New York Theatre Critics' Reviews* 16: 327.
    Lewis, Theophilus. *America* 93 (15 May 1955): 193.

McClain, John. *New York Journal-American* 20 Apr. 1955.
    Rpt. *New York Theatre Critics' Reviews* 16: 326.
Watts, Richard Jr. *New York Post* 20 Apr. 1955. Rpt.
    New York Theatre Critics' Reviews 16: 327.
Wyatt, Euphemia Van Rensselaer. *Catholic World* 181
    (June 1955): 227.

"27 Wagons Full of Cotton." New York: Phoenix Theatre,
26 Jan. 1976 (33). Arvin Brown, dir. James Tilton,
Albert Wolsky, design. With Meryl Streep (Flora), Tony
Musante (Silva), Roy Pople (Jake). Videotaped. Reviews:
    Barnes, Clive. *New York Times* 27 Jan. 1976: 26. Rpt.
        New York Theatre Critics' Reviews 47: 382-83.
    Beaufort, John. *Christian Science Monitor* 4 Feb. 1976.
        Rpt. *New York Theatre Critics' Reviews* 47: 384.
    Clurman, Harold. *Nation* 222 (14 Feb. 1976): 189-90.
    Gill, Brendan. *New Yorker* 9 Feb. 1976: 78.
    Gottfried, Martin. *New York Post* 27 Jan. 1976: 16.
        Rpt. *New York Theatre Critics' Reviews* 47: 382.
    Kerr, Walter. *New York Times* 8 Feb. 1976, sec. 2: 5.
    Probst, Leonard. NBC, 27 Jan. 1976. Rpt. *New York
        Theatre Critics' Reviews* 47: 385.
    Watt, Douglas. *New York Daily News* 27 Jan. 1976: 44.
        Rpt. *New York Theatre Critics' Reviews* 47: 383.
    Wilson, Edwin. *Wall Street Journal* 2 Feb. 1976. Rpt.
        New York Theatre Critics' Reviews 47: 384.

27 Wagons Full of Cotton. American Playwrights Theatre.
A&E-TV, 1 Feb. 1990. Don Scardino, dir. Tom H. John,
Ingrid Price, Michael Franks, design. Brian Keane,
music. With Lesley Ann Warren (Flora), Ray Starkey
(Silva), Peter Boyle (Jake). Review:
    O'Connor, John J. *New York Times* 1 Feb. 1990, sec. C:
        22.

THE TWO-CHARACTER PLAY/OUT CRY: Drama written 1959-75 (or
    later) about two actors locked in an abandoned theatre in
    a foreign country much as they are locked in their mem-
    ories of their Mississippi childhood. Ms., Columbia (G).
    Three versions of this play were published (and more
    produced). In general those entitled *The Two-Character
    Play* are among the most interesting of Williams' final
    period; that entitled *Out Cry* is among the worst. In
    both the play within a play remains almost the same; it
    is the nature of the actors and their response to their
    fate which changed so radically. The pre-Broadway open-
    ing essay was "Let Me Hang It All Out" (D 1). See also
    "Notes for *The Two-Character Play*" (D 1).

Publication: First Version

The Two-Character Play.   New York: New Directions, 1969.
    iv, 96 pp.   Contents: play, 1-96.   Limited edition.

Publication: Second Version

Out Cry.   New York: New Directions, 1973; Toronto:
    McClelland & Stewart, 1973.   vi, 72 pp.   Ils.   Also New
    Directions Paperbook.   Contents: A Dispensable Fore-
    word, 3; Synopsis of Scenes, 6; play, 7-72.   Review:
    Virginia Quarterly 49 (Winter 1974): vi.

Another edition: 86 pp. [book club?].

Publication: Third Version

Theatre, Vol. 5, 1976: 301-70 (A 2)

The Two-Character Play.   New Directions Paperbook.   New
    York: New Directions, 1979; Toronto: George J. McLeod,
    1979.   xii, 63 pp.

Criticism

Amor, Edward, et al.   "The *Out Cry* Questionnaire."   *Ten-
    nessee Williams Review* 3.2 (1982): 21-26.

Colt, Jay Leo.   "Dancing in Red Hot Shoes."   *Tennessee
    Williams Review* 3.2 (1982): 6-8.

Devlin, Albert J.   "The Later Career of Tennessee Wil-
    liams."   *Tennessee Williams Literary Journal* 1.2
    (Winter 1989-90): 7-17.

Gillen, Francis.   "Horror Shows, Inside and Outside My
    Skull: Theater and Life in Tennessee Williams's *Two-
    Character Play*."   *Forms of the Fantastic: Selected
    Essays from the Third International Conference on the
    Fantastic in Literature and Film*.   New York: Greenwood,
    1986.   227-31.

Ishida, Akira.   [Tennessee Williams's *The Two-Character
    Play*.   *Annual Report of Studies*] (Kyoto, Japan) 21
    (1970): 399-426.

Jackson, Esther M.   "Tennessee Williams' *Out Cry*: Studies
    in Dramatic Form at the University of Wisconsin,
    Madison."   *Tennessee Williams Newsletter* 2.2 (Fall
    1980): 6-12.

Jones, Betty Jean. "Tennessee Williams' *Out Cry*: Studies
in Production Form at the University of Wisconsin-
Madison, Part II." *Tennessee Williams Review* 3.2
(1982): 9-16.

Kahn, Sy M. "Listening to *Out Cry*: Bird of Paradox in a
Gilded Cage." *New Essays on American Drama*. Ed. Gil-
bert Debusscher and Henry I. Schvey. Amsterdam:
Rodopi, 1989. 41-62.

Stamper, Rexford. "*The Two-Character Play*: Psychic Indi-
viduation." Tharpe (A 3): 354-61.

Stauffacher, Paul K. "Designing Tennessee Williams' *Out
Cry*." *Tennessee Williams Review* 3.2 (1982): 17-20.

Taylor, Lyle. "*The Two-Character Play*: A Producer's
View." *Tennessee Williams Newsletter* 1.2 (Fall 1979):
20-23.

Productions

The Two-Character Play. London: Hampstead Theatre Club,
12 Dec. 1967 (première). James Rosse-Evans, dir. With
Peter Wyngarde (Felice), Mary Ure (Claire). Reviews:
  New York Times 13 Dec. 1967: 54. Rpt. *New York Times
    Theatre Reviews*.
  New York World-Journal Tribune 16 Nov. 1966: 43.
  Time 22 Dec. 1967: 63.
  Bolton, Whitney. *New York Morning Telegraph* 14 Dec.
    1967: 3.
  French, Philip. *New Statesman* 74 (22 Dec. 1967): 886-
    87.
  Kretzmer, Herbert. *London Daily Express* 13 Dec. 1967.
  Marowitz, Charles. *Village Voice* 21 Dec. 1967: 35.
  Nathan, David. *London Sun* 12 Dec. 1967: 7.
  Wade, David. *Times* (London) 13 Dec. 1967.

Out Cry. Chicago: Ivanhoe Theatre, 8 July 1971 (pre-
mière). George Keathley, dir. With Donald Madden
(Felice), Eileen Herlie (Claire). Prod. Notes:
  New York Times 10 March 1971: 33.
  Variety 3 Mar. 1971: 1, 54.
  Funke, Lewis. *New York Times* 2 May 1971, sec. 2: 1,
    24.
  Winakor, Bess. *Women's Wear Daily* 28 June 1971.

Out Cry. Previews: New Haven, Philadelphia, Washington.
New York: Lyceum Theatre, 1-10 Mar. 1973 (12). Peter
Glenville, dir. Jo Mielziner, Sandy Cole, design. With

Michael York (Felice), Cara Duff-MacCormick (Claire).
Program: Van Antwerp (F 1): 288. Reviews, Prod. Notes:
   Variety 7 Mar. 1973: 70.
   Barnes, Clive. *New York Times* 2 Mar. 1973: 18.
   Clurman, Harold. *Nation* 216 (19 Mar. 1973): 380.
   Funke, Lewis. *New York Times* 3 Dec. 1972, sec. 2: 1,
      27.
   Gill, Brendan. *New Yorker* 10 Mar. 1973: 104.
   Gottfried, Martin. *Women's Wear Daily* 5 Mar. 1973.
      Rpt. *New York Theatre Critics' Reviews* 34: 344.
   Gussow, Mel. *New York Times* 11 Mar. 1973, sec. 2: 1,
      5. Response: *New York Times* 8 Apr. 1973, sec. 2:
      6.
   Harris, Leonard. CBS-TV, 1 Mar. 1973. Rpt. *New York
      Theatre Critics' Reviews* 34: 346.
   Hughes, Catherine. *America* 128 (17 Mar. 1973): 242.
   Kalem, T. E. *Time* 12 Mar. 1973: 89. Rpt. *New York
      Theatre Critics' Reviews* 34: 344.
   Kauffmann, Stanley. *New Republic* 24 Mar. 1973: 22.
   Kroll, Jack. *Newsweek* 12 Mar. 1973: 88. Rpt. *New York
      Theatre Critics' Reviews* 34: 344.
   Novick, Julius. *Village Voice* 8 Mar. 1973: 58.
   Probst, Leonard. NBC, 1 Mar. 1973. Rpt. *New York The-
      atre Critics' Reviews* 34: 346.
   Reed, Rex. *New York Sunday News* 11 Mar. 1973, sec. 3:
      5. Rpt. Van Antwerp (F 1): 287-89.
   Simon, John. *New York* 19 Mar. 1973: 66.
   Tolliver, Melba. ABC-TV, 1 Mar. 1973. Rpt. *New York
      Theatre Critics' Reviews* 34: 346.
   Watt, Douglas. *New York Daily News* 2 Mar. 1973: 50..
      Rpt. *New York Theatre Critics' Reviews* 34: 343.
   Watts, Richard. *New York Post* 2 Mar. 1973. Rpt. *New
      York Theatre Critics' Reviews* 34: 345-46.
   ---. *New York Post* 17 Mar. 1973: 16.
   Wilson, Edwin. *Wall Street Journal* 6 Mar. 1973: 30.
      Rpt. *New York Theatre Critics' Reviews* 34: 345.
   York, Michael. "Tennessee Williams in Rehearsal."
      Theatre 73 (London): 154-62.

The Two-Character Play. New York: Quaigh Theatre, 14
Aug. 1975 (première). Bill Lentsch, dir. Greg Huskinko,
Isabelle Harris, design. With Robert Stattel (Felice),
Mayellen Flynn (Claire). Review:
   Van Gelder, Lawrence. *New York Times* 22 Aug. 1975: 16.

The Two-Character Play. Los Angeles: Callboard Theatre,
22 Feb. 1977 (24). John Hancock, dir. Stephen Roberts,
Robert LaVigne, Alan Blacher, design. Fred Karlin,
music. With Scott Wilson (Felice), Dorothy Tristan
(Claire).

The Two-Character Play. New York: Harold Clurman The-
atre, 27 Sept.-19 Oct. 1980 (17). Alfred Ryder, dir.
Tom Schwinn, Beba Shamash, Adam Gross, design. With
Alfred Ryder (Felix), Olive Deering (Claire).

Other Productions:
    Iachetta, Michael. *New York Daily News* 26 June 1974:
        38. [Off-Broadway]

"THE UNSATISFACTORY SUPPER, OR THE LONG STAY CUT SHORT":
Drama about an unwanted Mississippi relative.
    The play was combined with "27 Wagons Full of Cotton" to
become the basis for the screenplay *Baby Doll* (above).
It has been published under two different titles.

"The Unsatisfactory Supper." *The Best One-Act Plays of
    1945*. Ed. Margaret Mayorga. New York: Dodd, Mead,
    1945. 235-49.

"The Long Stay Cut Short, or The Unsatisfactory Supper."
    American Blues, 1948: 33-42 (A 2).

Same. *Perspectives USA* 8 (Summer 1954): 104-14.

Same. *Baby Doll*, 1956: 191-208 (A 1 above).

Same. *An Anthology of Mississippi Writers*. Ed. Noel E.
    Polk and James R. Seafidel. Jackson: Univ. Pr. of Mis-
    sissippi, 1979. 278-89.

"The Unsatisfactory Supper, or The Long Stay Cut Short."
    Theatre, Vol. 6, 1981: 297-313 (A 2).

Trans. (H): French, German, Italian.

Production

Ten by Tennessee. New York: Lucille Lortel Theatre, 11
May-29 June 1986. Michael Kahn, dir. With Laura Hicks
(Aunt Rose), Mary Lou Rosato (Baby Doll), Anderson Mat-
thews (Archie Lee). See "Auto-da-Fé."

VIEUX CARRÉ: Semi-autobiographical drama about the problems
of several people in a New Orleans rooming house just before World War II. Mss., Columbia (G).
    In the first, unpublished, version the first act was
called "The Angel in the Alcove" after the short story (B
1); the second act was called "I Never Get Dressed until
after Dark on Sundays." See also "The Lady of Larkspur

Lotion" (A 1 above). The pre-opening essay was entitled
"I Am Widely Regarded as the Ghost of a Writer" (D 1).
After the failure of the play, Williams revised it, and
this version, first produced in England, 1978, was published.

Vieux Carré. New York: New Directions, 1979; Toronto:
   George J. McLeod, 1979. viii, 116 pp. Il. Also New
   Directions Paperbook. Contents: Note on setting, 4;
   play, 5-116. Reviews
      Choice 16 (Nov. 1979): 1178.
      Witham, Barry B. *Library Journal* 104 (15 May 1979);
      1156.

Trans. (H): German.

Criticism

Prosser, William. "*Vieux Carré*: The Education of an Artist." *Tennessee Williams Review* 4.1 (1983): 54-58.

Simard, Rodney. "The Uses of Experience: Tennessee Williams in *Vieux Carré*." *Southern Literary Journal* 17
   (Spring 1985): 67-78.

Productions

Vieux Carré. New York: St. James Theatre, 11-15 May 1977
(première, 5). Arthur Allan Seidelman, dir. James Til-
ton, Jane Greenwood, design. Galt MacDermott, music.
With Richard Alfieri (Writer), Sylvia Sidney (Mrs. Wire),
Tom Aldredge (Painter), John William Reilly (Tye), Diane
Kagan (Jane). Playbills: Van Antwerp (F 1): 328;
Leavitt (F 1). Reviews:
   New Leader 20 June 1977: 21.
   New York Theatre Annual 1976-77 1 (1978): 37.
   New York Times 27 Dec. 1976, sec. C: 21.
   New York Times 9 Mar. 1977, sec. C: 24.
   Variety 18 May 1977: 124.
   Barnes, Clive. *New York Times* 12 May 1977, sec. C: 22.
      Rpt. *New York Theatre Critics' Reviews* 38: 244.
   Beaufort, John. *Christian Science Monitor* 23 May 1977.
      Rpt. *New York Theatre Critics' Reviews* 38: 247.
   Clurman, Harold. *Nation* 224 (28 May 1977): 669.
   Feingold, Michael. *Village Voice* 30 May 1977: 87.
   Gill, Brendan. *New Yorker* 23 May 1977: 83.
   Gottfried, Martin. *New York Post* 12 May 1977: 27.
      Rpt. *New York Theatre Critics' Reviews* 38: 245.
   Kalem, T. E. *Time* 23 May 1977: 108. Rpt. *New York
      Theatre Critics' Reviews* 38: 246.

Kerr, Walter. *New York Times* 22 May 1977, sec. 2: 5,
    30.
Kissel, Howard. *Women's Wear Daily* 12 May 1977. Rpt.
    New York Theatre Critics' Reviews 38: 246.
Probst, Leonard. NBC, 11 May 1977. Rpt. *New York
    Theatre Critics' Reviews* 38: 246-47.
Raidy, William A. *New Orleans Times-Picayune* 13 May
    1977. Rpt. Van Antwerp (F 1): 330-31.
Rich, Alan. *Village Voice* 30 May 1977: 92.
Simon, John. *New Leader* 60 (20 June 1977): 21-27.
Watt, Douglas. *New York Daily News* 12 May 1977: 83.
    Rpt. *New York Theatre Critics' Reviews* 38: 244-45.
---. *New York Daily News* 22 May 1977, leisure sec.:
    15.

Vieux Carré. Nottingham, Eng.: Playhouse Theatre, 16 May
1978 (première); London: Picadilly Theatre, 9 Aug. 1978.
Keith Hack, dir. Voytek, Francis Reid, Maria Bjornson,
design. Jeremy Nicholas, music. With Karl Johnson
(Writer), Sylvia Miles (Mrs. Wire), Richard Kane (Nightingale), Jonathan Kent (Tye), Di Trevis, later Sheila
Gish (Jane). Reviews, Prod. Notes:
    Variety 23 Aug. 1978: 90.
    Aire, S. *Plays and Players* July 1978: 20-21.
    Curtis, Anthony. *Drama* 130 (Autumn 1978): 52-53.
    Cushman, Robert. *London Observer* 20 Aug. 1978: 21.
    Dean, Joan F. *Tennessee Williams Newsletter* 1.1
        (Spring 1979): 26-27.
    Hamilton, Ian. *New Statesman* 96 (25 Aug. 1978): 251-
        52.
    Hobson, Harold. *Drama* 130 (Autumn 1978): 45.
    Jenkins, Peter. *Spectator* 26 Aug. 1978: 20-21.
    Nightingale, Benedict. *New Statesman* 95 (10 May 1978):
        688.
    Robson, David. *Sunday Times* (London) 20 Aug. 1978: 41.
        [Interview with Miles]
    Shorter, Eric. *Drama* 129 (Summer 1978): 68-69.
    Shrimpton, Nick. *Plays and Players* May 1978: 39.

Vieux Carré. New York: WPA Theatre, 31 Mar.-24 Apr.
1983. Stephen Zuckerman, dir. James Fenhagen, Charles
Cosler, Mimi Maxmen, design. With Mark Soper (Writer),
Jacqueline Brooks (Mrs. Wire), Tom Klunis (Nightingale),
John Bedford-Lloyd (Tye), Anne Twoney (Jane). Review:
    Gussow, Mel. *New York Times* 5 Apr. 1983, sec. 3: 13.

Other Productions:
    Tennessee Williams Review 3.1 (1981): 31-33. [Shreve-
        port, LA]
    Anderson, Scott P. *Advocate* 4 Aug. 1983. [Los Ange-
        les]

Spunberg, Bernard. *Advocate* 8 Dec. 1983. [San Fran-
cisco]

Young, Michael Cochise. *Tennessee Williams Review* 3.1
(1981): 22-23. [Philadelphia]

THE WANTON COUNTESS: see *Senso*

WILL MR. MERRIWETHER RETURN FROM MEMPHIS?: Unpublished surrealistic drama written in 1969 about lonely women coping
with their sexual drives by conjuring up apparitions.

Will Mr. Merriwether Return from Memphis? Key West: Ten-
nessee Williams Fine Arts Center (Florida Keys Community
College), 24 Jan. 1980 (première). William Prosser, dir.
Peggy Kellner, Michael Orris Watson, design. Ronald Mal-
tais, music. Mimi McDonald, dance. With Roxana Stuart
(Louise), Melissa Leo (Gloria), Naomi Riseman (Nora).
Program: Van Antwerp (F 1): 358. Videotaped. Reviews:
  New York Times 26 Jan. 1980.
    Kalem, T. E. *Time* 4 Feb. 1980: 61. Resume: *Tennessee
    Williams Newsletter* 2.1 (Spring 1980): 45-46.
    Prosser, William. "Loneliness, Apparitions, and the
    Saving Grace of the Imagination." *Tennessee Wil-
    liams Newsletter* 2.2 (Fall 1980): 13-15.
    Tucci, Jim. *Key West Citizen* 25 Jan. 1980: 2. Rpt.
    Van Antwerp (F 1): 357-359.

YOU TOUCHED ME: Romantic comedy written with Donald Windham, a loose adaptation of the D. H. Lawrence short story
(with touches of Lawrence's other works, particularly *The
Fox*). Mss., Columbia, Texas (G).

Montgomery Clift hoped to turn out a screenplay, but he
never succeeded.

You Touched Me! A Romantic Comedy in Three Acts... Suggested by a short story of the same name by D. H. Lawrence. New York: Samuel French, 1947. 116 pp. Contents: play, 3-114; Story of the Play, 116.

Trans. (H): Greek.

Criticism

Weales, Gerald C. "Tennessee Williams Borrows a Little
Shaw." *Shaw Review* 8 (May 1965): 63-64.

Productions

You Touched Me. Cleveland: Playhouse, 13 Oct. 1943 (pre-
mière). Margo Jones, dir. Review:
  New York Times 17 Oct. 1943, sec. 2: 2. Rpt. *New York
  Times Theatre Reviews).*

You Touched Me! Previews: Boston, Washington. New York:
Booth Theatre, 25 Sept. 1945–5 Jan. 1946 (109). Guthrie
McClintie, Lee Schubert, dirs. With Montgomery Clift
(Hadrian), Marianne Stewart (Matilda), Edmund Gwenn (Cap-
tain). Reviews, Prod. Notes:
  New York Times Magazine 23 Sept. 1945: 28–29.
  Theatre Arts 29 (Dec. 1945): 680.
  Time 8 Oct. 1945: 77
  Variety 19 Sept. 1945: 52. [Boston tryout]
  Variety 3 Oct. 1945: 52.
  Barnes, Howard. *New York Herald Tribune* 26 Sept. 1945:
    18. Rpt. *New York Theatre Critics' Reviews* 6: 167.
  Bentley, Eric. *Sewanee Review* 54 (Jan.–Mar. 1946):
    315.
  Bosworth, Patricia. *Montgomery Clift....* New York:
    Harcourt, 1978. 101–03 (also 151–52).
  Chapman, John. *New York Daily News* 26 Sept. 1945.
    Rpt. *New York Theatre Critics' Reviews* 6: 164.
  Freedley, George. *New York Morning Telegraph* 27 Sept.
    1948: 2.
  ---. *New York Morning Telegraph* 26 Oct. 1945: 2.
  Garland, Robert. *New York Journal-American* 26 Sept.
    1945: 10. Rpt. *New York Theatre Critics' Reviews* 6:
    166.
  Gibbs, Wolcott. *New Yorker* 6 Oct. 1945: 48.
  Gilder, Rosamond. *Theatre Arts* 29 (Nov. 1945): 618–21,
  Houghton, Norris, *Free World* 10 (Nov. 1945): 87–88.
  Kronenberger, Louis. *New York PM* 26 Sept. 1945. Rpt.
    New York Theatre Critics' Reviews 6: 165.
  Krutch, Joseph Wood. *Nation* 161 (6 Oct. 1945): 349–50.
  Morehouse, Ward. *New York Sun* 26 Sept. 1945: 28. Rpt.
    New York Theatre Critics' Reviews 6: 167.
  Nathan, George Jean. *Theatre Book of the Year 1945–
    1946.* New York: Knopf, 1946. 87–96.
  Nichols, Lewis. *New York Times* 26 Sept. 1945: 27.
    Rpt. *New York Times Theatre Reviews; New York The-
    atre Critics' Reviews* 6: 167.
  ---. *New York Times* 30 Sept. 1945, sec. 2: 1. Rpt.
    New York Times Theatre Reviews.
  Phelan, Kappo. *Commonweal* 42 (12 Oct. 1945): 623–24.
  Rascoe, Burton. *New York World-Telegram* 26 Sept. 1945:
    34. Rpt. *New York Theatre Critics' Reviews* 6: 165;
    Leavitt (F 1): 68.

Waldorf, Willela. *New York Post* 26 Sept. 1945: 38.
    Rpt. *New York Theatre Critics' Review* 6: 166.
Wyatt, Euphemia Van Rensselaer. *Catholic World* 162
    (Nov. 1945): 166-67.
Young, Stark. *New Republic* 112 (8 Oct. 1945): 469.

Other Productions:
    Times (London) 1 Sept. 1956: 8.   [BBC-TV, 9 Sept. 1956]
    Richards, David. *New York Times* 31 Mar. 1991, sec. 2H:
        5, 24.   [Cleveland Playhouse]

2.   COLLECTIONS

American Blues: Five Short Plays...: Acting Edition.   New
    York: Dramatists Play Service, 1948.   80 pp.   Contents:
    Publisher's Note, 3; "Moony's Kid Don't Cry," 5-14; "The
    Dark Room," 15-21; "The Case of the Crushed Petunias: A
    Lyrical Fantasy," 22-32; "The Long Stay Cut Short, or The
    Unsatisfactory Supper," 33-42; "Ten Blocks on the Camino
    Real: A Fantasy," 43-77.   Review:
        Freedley, George. *Library Journal* 74 (15 Jan. 1949):
        129.

Baby Doll & Tiger Tail...:   see A 1

*Baby Doll...Incorporating the Two One-Act Plays Which Sug-
    gested It*...:   see A 1

*Baby Doll: The Script for the Film; Something Unspoken; Sud-
    denly Last Summer*.   Penguin Plays.   Harmondsworth: Pen-
    guin Books, 1968.   159 pp.   On spine: *Three Plays*.

*Cat on a Hot Tin Roof; The Milk Train Doesn't Stop Here
    Anymore; The Night of the Iguana*.   Penguin Plays.   Har-
    mondsworth: Penguin Books, 1976.   329 pp.

Dragon Country: A Book of Plays.   New York: New Directions,
    1969; Toronto: McClelland & Stewart, 1969 (c 1970).   iv,
    278 pp.   Also New Directions Paperbook.   Contents: *In
    the Bar of a Tokyo Hotel*, 1-53; "I Rise in Flame, Cried
    the Phoenix: A Play in One Act about D. H. Lawrence," 55-
    75; "The Mutilated," 77-130; "I Can't Imagine Tomorrow,"
    131-50; "Confessional," 151-96; "The Frosted Glass Cof-
    fin," 197-314; "The Gnädiges Fräulein," 215-62; "A Per-
    fect Analysis Given by a Parrot," 263-78.

The Eccentricities of a Nightingale and Summer and Smoke:
    see A 1

Eight Plays. Garden City: Doubleday, 1979. 843 pp. Con-
    tents: Harold Clurman, Introduction, ix-xiv; *The Glass
    Menagerie*, 1-90; *A Streetcar Named Desire*, 91-197; *Summer
    and Smoke*, 199-296; *The Rose Tattoo*, 297-398; *Cat on a
    Hot Tin Roof*, 399-536; *Orpheus Descending*, 537-641; *Sweet
    Bird of Youth*, 643-735; *The Night of the Iguana*, 737-843.

Five Plays...: *Cat on a Hot Tin Roof; The Rose Tattoo; Gar-
    den District: Something Unspoken, Suddenly Last Summer;
    Orpheus Descending*. London: Secker & Warburg, 1962.
    xvi, 374 pp. Review:
        Whiting, John. *Spectator* 206 (30 Mar. 1962): 418.

Four Plays...: *The Glass Menagerie; A Streetcar Named De-
    sire; Summer and Smoke; Camino Real*. London: Secker &
    Warburg, 1956. xii, 320 pp. Review:
        Hartby, Anthony. *Spectator* 197 (14 Dec. 1956): 879.

*Four Plays: Summer and Smoke; Orpheus Descending; Suddenly
    Last Summer; Period of Adjustment*. Signet Modern Clas-
    sic. New York: New American Library, 1976. 496 pp.

*The Milk Train Doesn't Stop Here Anymore; Cat on a Hot Tin
    Roof*. Penguin Plays. Harmondsworth: Penguin Books,
    1969. 224 pp.

The Night of the Iguana; Orpheus Descending. Penguin Plays.
    Harmondsworth: Penguin Books, 1968. 224 pp. On spine:
    Two Plays.

*Orpheus Descending; Something Unspoken; Suddenly Last Sum-
    mer*. Penguin Plays. Harmondsworth: Penguin Books, 1961.
    188 pp.

Orpheus Descending, with Battle of Angels: see A 1

Period of Adjustment/Summer and Smoke. Four Square Books.
    London: New English Library, 1963. 255 pp.

*Period of Adjustment; Summer and Smoke; Small Craft Warn-
    ings*. Penguin Plays. Harmondsworth: Penguin Books,
    1982. 235 pp. On spine: *Period of Adjustment & Other
    Plays*.

The Rose Tattoo; Camino Real. Ed. E. Martin Browne. Pen-
    guin Plays. Harmondsworth: Penguin Books, 1958. 233 pp.
    Includes E. Martin Browne, Introduction, 7-8; and John
    Whiting, "*Camino Real*: An Appreciation," 117-18.

The Rose Tattoo; Camino Real; Orpheus Descending.   Penguin
   Plays. Harmondsworth: Penguin Books, 1976. 347 pp. Includes same essays as above.

Selected Plays. Franklin Center, PA: Franklin Library,
   1977. 665 pp. Ils., Jerry Pinkney. Limited edition.
   Contents: *The Glass Menagerie*, 1-78; *A Streetcar Named
   Desire*, 79-181; *The Rose Tattoo*, 183-278; *Camino Real*,
   279-387; *Cat on a Hot Tin Roof*, 383-474; *Sweet Bird of
   Youth*, 475-560; *The Night of the Iguana*, 561-665.

Selected Plays. Franklin Center, PA: Franklin Library,
   1980. viii, 565 pp. Ils., Herbert Tauss. Limited edition. Contents: A Special Message to Subscribers from
   Tennessee Williams, iv-vii; *The Glass Menagerie*, 1-76; *A
   Streetcar Named Desire*, 79-179; *Camino Real*, 181-282; *Cat
   on a Hot Tin Roof*, 285-374; *Sweet Bird of Youth*, 377-460;
   The Night of the Iguana, 463-565.

Stopped Rocking and Other Screenplays. New York New Direc-
   tions, 1984; Toronto: George J. McLeod, 1984. xii, 384
   pp. Also New Directions Paperbook. Contents: Richard
   Gilman, Introduction, vii-xii; *All Gaul Is Divided*, 1-93;
   The Loss of a Teardrop Diamond, 95-192; *One Arm*, 193-291;
   Stopped Rocking, 293-384. Reviews:
      Booklist 80 (Aug. 1984): 1589.
      Caltabiano, Frank P. *World Literature Today* 59 (Summer
         1985): 428.
      Hafley, J. *Choice* 22 (Feb. 1985): 821.
      Real, Jere. *Advocate* 27 Nov. 1984: 54.
      Wohlsen, Theodore O. *Library Journal* 109 (1 Sept.
         1984): 1684.

A *Streetcar Named Desire; The Glass Menagerie.* Ed. E. Martin Browne. Penguin Plays. Harmondsworth: Penguin
   Books, 1959. 207 pp. Includes E. Martin Browne, Introduction, 7-8.

*Sweet Bird of Youth; A Streetcar Named Desire; The Glass
   Menagerie.* Ed. E. Martin Browne. Penguin Plays. Har-
   mondsworth: Penguin Books, 1962. 313 pp. On spine:
   Sweet Bird of Youth and Other Plays.

The Theatre of Tennessee Williams. Volume I: *Battle of
   Angels; The Glass Menagerie; A Streetcar Named Desire.*
   New York: New Directions, 1971; Toronto: McClelland &
   Stewart, 1971. New York: New Directions, 1990. New
   Directions Paperbook. viii, 419 pp.

The Theatre of Tennessee Williams. Volume II: *The Eccentricities of a Nightingale; Summer and Smoke; The Rose*

Tattoo; Camino Real. New York: New Directions, 1971;
Toronto: McClelland & Stewart, 1971. New York: New
Directions, 1990. New Directions Paperbook. viii, 591
pp. Ils.

The Theatre of Tennessee Williams. Volume III: *Cat on a Hot
Tin Roof; Orpheus Descending; Suddenly Last Summer.* New
York: New Directions, 1971; Toronto: McClelland & Stew-
art, 1971. viii, 376 pp. Il.

The Theatre of Tennessee Williams. Volume IV: *Sweet Bird of
Youth; Period of Adjustment; The Night of the Iguana.*
New York: New Directions, 1972; Toronto: McClelland &
Stewart, 1972. viii, 376 pp. Ils.

The Theatre of Tennessee Williams. Volume V: *The Milk Train
Doesn't Stop Here Anymore; Kingdom of Earth (The Seven
Descents of Myrtle); Small Craft Warnings; The Two-Char-
acter Play.* New York: New Directions, 1976; Toronto:
McClelland & Stewart, 1976. New York: New Direction,
1990. New Directions Paperbook. viii, 370 pp. Ils.
Contents inc. revised *Kingdom of Earth,* 121-214; revised
The Two-Character Play, 299-370.

The Theatre of Tennessee Williams. Volume VI: *27 Wagons
Full of Cotton and Other Short Plays.* New York: New
Directions, 1981; Toronto: George J. McLeod, 1981. x,
358 pp. Contents: *27 Wagons Full of Cotton* (2nd Amer.
ed. [below] reset), plus "The Unsatisfactory Supper, or
The Long Stay Cut Short," 297-313; "Steps Must Be Gentle," 315-27; "The Demolition Downtown," 329-58.

The Theatre of Tennessee Williams. Volume VII: *In the Bar
of a Tokyo Hotel and Other Plays.* New York: New Directions, 1981; Toronto: George J. McLeod, 1981. viii, 365
pp. Contents: *Dragon Country* (above), plus "Lifeboat
Drill," 279-96; "Now the Cat with Jewelled Claws," 297-
330; "This Is the Peaceful Kingdom, or Good Luck God,"
331-65.

*Three by Tennessee: Sweet Bird of Youth; The Rose Tattoo;
The Night of the Iguana.* Signet Modern Classic. New
York: New American Library, 1976. 508 pp.

*Three Plays of Tennessee Williams: The Rose Tattoo; Camino
Real; Sweet Bird of Youth.* New York: New Directions,
1964. 452 pp.

27 Wagons Full of Cotton and Other One-Act Plays. Norfolk,
CT: New Directions, 1945. vi, 207 pp. On spine: *Tennessee Williams' One-Act Plays.* Contents: "27 Wagons

Full of Cotton: A Mississippi Delta Comedy," 1-28; "The
Purification," 29-62; "The Lady of Larkspur Lotion," 63-
72; "The Last of My Solid Gold Watches," 73-85; "Portrait
of a Madonna," 87-104; "Auto-da-Fé: A Tragedy in One
Act," 105-20; "Lord Byron's Love Letter," 121-32; "The
Strangest Kind of Romance: A Lyric Play in Four Scenes,"
133-58; "The Long Goodbye," 159-79; "Hello from Bertha,"
181-93; "This Property Is Condemned," 195-207. Reviews
   Theatre Arts 30 (Sept. 1946): 557.
   Eaton, W. P. *New York Herald Tribune Weekly Book Re-
      view* 19 May 1946: 24.
   Freedley, George. *Library Journal* 71 (15 Mar. 1946):
      407.
   Kennedy, Leo. *Book Week* 3 Feb. 1946: 3.
   Krutch, Joseph Wood. *Nation* 162 (2 Mar. 1946): 267.
   Sutcliffe, Denham. *New York Times Book Review* 24 Feb.
      1946: 8. Rpt. Van Antwerp [F 1]: 74-75.

27 Wagons Full of Cotton and Other One-Act Plays. London:
   John Lehmann, 1949. 192 pp. Contents: "27 Wagons Full
   of Cotton," 7-32; "The Purification," 33-64; "The Lady of
   Larkspur Lotion," 65-72; "The Last of My Solid Gold
   Watches," 73-84; "Portrait of a Madonna," 85-100; "Auto-
   da-Fé," 101-14; "Lord Byron's Love Letter," 115-26; "The
   Strangest Kind of Romance," 127-48; "The Long Goodbye,"
   149-67; "Hello from Bertha," 169-80; "This Property Is
   Condemned," 181-92.

27 Wagons Full of Cotton and Other One-Act Plays. Norfolk,
   CT: New Directions, 1953. New York: New Directions,
   1966; Toronto: McClelland & Stewart, 1966. New Directions Paperbook. xii, 238 pp. Contents: same as 1945,
   plus "Something Wild..." (D 1), vii-xii, "Talk to Me like
   the Rain and Let Me Listen...," 209-18; "Something Unspoken," 219-38.

3. CRITICISM

See also individual plays (A 1).

Abbott, Anthony S. *The Vital Lie: Reality and Illusion in
   Modern Drama*. Tuscaloosa: Univ. of Alabama Pr., 1989.
   139-47.

Adams, Julie. "Visions of Heroism in Modern American Drama:
   Selected Plays by Miller, Williams, Anderson, and
   O'Neill." Diss., Univ. of Toronto, 1988. *Dissertation
   Abstracts International* 49 (1989): 2655 A.

Adler, Jacob H. "Modern Southern Drama." *The History of
    Southern Literature*. Ed. Louis D. Rubin et al. Baton
    Rouge: Louisiana State Univ. Pr., 1985. 439-42.

---. "The Rose and the Fox: Notes on the Southern Drama."
    South.... Ed. Louis D. Rubin, Jr., and Robert D. Jacobs.
    Garden City: Doubleday, 1961. 347-75. Revision: "Ten-
    nessee Williams' South: The Culture and the Power,"
    Tharpe (below): 30-52.

---. "Tennessee Williams." *Critical Survey of Drama*. Eng-
    lish Language Series 5. Ed. Frank M. Magill. Englewood
    Cliffs, NJ: Salem, 1985.

---. "Williams and the Bard." *Tennessee Williams Literary
    Journal* 2.1 (Winter 1990-91): 37-49.

Adler, Thomas P. "The Dialogue of Incompletion: Language in
    Tennessee Williams' Later Plays." *Quarterly Journal of
    Speech* 61 (Feb. 1975): 48-58. Rpt. (excerpt) Stanton
    (below): 74-85.

---. "Images of Entrapment in Tennessee Williams's Later
    Plays." *Notes on Modern American Literature* 5 (Spring
    1981): item 11.

---. *Mirror on the Stage: The Pulitzer Plays as an Approach
    to American Drama*. West Lafayette, IN: Purdue Univ. Pr.,
    1987. 17-20, 33-35.

---. "The Search for God in the Plays of Tennessee Wil-
    liams." *Renascence* 26 (Autumn 1973): 48-56. Rpt. Stan-
    ton (below): 138-48.

---. "Theatre Looking at Theatre: A Self-Image of the Post-
    World War II American Drama." *Claudel Studies* 9.1
    (1982): 31-42.

---. "The (Un)reliability of the Narrator in *The Glass
    Menagerie* and *Vieux Carré*." *Tennessee Williams Review*
    3.2 (1982): 6-9.

"American Drama since 1940: The Search for an Ideal." *Books
    U.S.A.* 4 (April 1963): 2-8.

Antonini, Giacomo. "Assillo ed ortifizio in Tennessee Wil-
    liams." *Fiera Letteraria* 29 June 1958: 8.

Archer, Mark. "Tennessee Williams." *Drama* 168 (1988): 15-
    16.

Armato, Philip M. "Tennessee Williams' Meditations of Life
    and Death in *Suddenly Last Summer, The Night of the
    Iguana*, and *The Milk Train Doesn't Stop Here Anymore*."
    Tharpe (below): 558-70.

Asibong, Emmanuel B. *Tennessee Williams, the Tragic Ten-
    sion: A Study of the Plays of Tennessee Williams from The
    Glass Menagerie (1944) to The Milk Train Doesn't Stop
    Here Anymore (1966)*. Ilfracombe: Stockwell, 1978. 71
    pp.

Asral, Ertem. "Tennessee Williams on Stage and Screen."
    Diss., Univ. of Pennsylvania, 1960. *Dissertation Ab-
    stracts* 22 (1961): 1169-70.

Asselineau, Roger. "Tennessee Williams, ou la Nostalgie de
    la pureté." *Études Anglaises* 10 (Oct.-Dec. 1957): 431-
    43. Rpt. *Das amerikanische Drama von den Anfangen bis
    zur Gegenwart*, ed. Hans Itschert (Darmstadt: Wissens-
    chaftliche Buchgesellschaft, 1972): 276-92.

---. *The Transcendentalist Constant in American Literature*.
    New York: New York Univ. Pr., 1980. 153-62.

Atkinson, Brooks. *Broadway*. New York: Macmillan, 1970.
    394-402, 429-32.

---. "His Bizarre Images Can't Be Denied." *New York Times*
    26 Nov. 1961, sec. 2: 1, 36.

---, and Albert Hirschfeld. *The Lively Years, 1920-1973*.
    New York: Association, 1973. 191-94, 227-31.

Aubriant, Michel. "Tennessee Williams a mis la femme en
    accusation." *Paris Théâtre* 11 (1958): 6-10.

Babuscio, Jack. "The Cinema of Camp." *Gay Sunshine* Winter
    1978: 21-22.

Balachandran, K. "Marriage and Family Life in Tennessee
    Williams." *Notes on Mississippi Writers* 21.2 (1989): 69-
    76.

Barker, Stephen. *Tennessee Williams*. Videocassette. Wash-
    ington: Tapes for Readers, 1978.

Barksdale, Richard K. "Social Background in the Plays of
    Miller and Williams." *College Language Association Jour-
    nal* 6 (Mar. 1963): 161-69.

Barranger, Milly S. "New Orleans as Theatrical Image in Plays by Tennessee Williams." *Southern Quarterly* 23.2 (1985): 38–54.

Barton, Lee. "Why Do Homosexual Playwrights Hide Their Homosexuality?" *New York Times* 23 Jan. 1972, sec. 2: 1, 3. Response: *New York Times* 13 Feb. 1972, sec. 2: 5 (inc. Eric Bentley).

Baumgart, Wolfgang. "Die Gegenwart des Barocktheaters." *Archiv für das Studium der neueren Sprachen und Literaturen* 1961: 65–76.

Beasley, Henry R. "An Interpretative Study of the Religious Element in the Work of Tennessee Williams." Diss., Louisiana State Univ., 1973. *Dissertation Abstracts International* 34 (1974): 5954–55 A.

Beaton, Cecil, and Kenneth Tynan. *Persona Grata.* New York: Putnam's, 1954. 96–97.

Beltzer, Lee. "The Plays of Eugene O'Neill, Thornton Wilder, Arthur Miller, and Tennessee Williams on the London Stage 1945–1960." Diss., Univ. of Wisconsin, 1965.

Bennett, Beate Hein. "Williams and European Drama: Infernalists and Forgers of Modern Myths." Tharpe (below): 429–59.

Berkman, Leonard. "Intimate Relations in Tennessee Williams' Plays." Diss., Yale Univ., 1970. *Dissertation Abstracts International* 40 (1980): 5249–50 A.

Berkowitz, Gerald M. *New Broadways: Theatre across America 1950–1980.* Titowa, NJ: Rowman, 1982. 145–49 and passim.

———. "Williams' 'Other Places' – A Theatrical Metaphor in the Plays." Tharpe (below): 712–19.

Bier, Charles Richard. "The One-Act Plays of Tennessee Williams." Diss., Univ. of Southwestern Louisiana, 1979. *Dissertation Abstracts International* 41 (1980): 2101–02 A.

Bigsby, C. W. E. *A Critical Introduction to Twentieth Century American Drama.* Cambridge: Cambridge Univ. Pr., 1984. 2: 1–134. Rpt. (excerpt) Bloom (A 1: *Glass*): 89–99; Bloom (below): 131–49.

Birney, Earle.   "North American Drama Today: A Popular Art?"
Transactions of the Royal Society of Canada 51 (June
1957): 31-42.

Blackwell, Louise.   "Tennessee Williams and the Predicament
of Women."   *South Atlantic Bulletin* 35 (Mar. 1970): 9-14.
Rpt. (revised) Stanton (below): 100-06.

Blades, Larry T.   "Williams, Miller, and Albee: A Comparative Study."   Diss., St. Louis Univ., 1971.   *Dissertation
Abstracts International* 32 (1972): 4600 A.

Blanke, Gustav H.   "Das Bild des Menschen im modernen amerikanischen Drama."   *Neueren Sprachen* 18 (Mar. 1969): 117-
29.

Blitgen, M. Carol.   "Tennessee Williams: Modern Idolator."
Renascence 22 (Summer 1970): 192-97.

Bloom, Harold, ed.   *Tennessee Williams*.   Modern Critical
Views Series.   New York: Chelsea, 1987.   viii, 168 pp.

Blumstein, Glenn J.   "The Troubled Cinema of Tennessee."
Playbill (Univ. of Iowa) 63 (June 1984): 33-34.

Bock, Hedwig.   "Tennessee Williams: Southern Playwright."
Essays on Contemporary American Drama.   Ed. with Albert
Wertheim.   Munich: Hueber, 1981.   5-18.

Bolton, Whitney.   "Bringing Up a Point about Mr. Williams."
New York Morning Telegraph 28 Apr. 1955: 2.   [Alleged
obscenity]

Bonin, Jane F.   *Major Themes in Prize-Winning American
Drama*.   Metuchen, NJ: Scarecrow, 1975.   Passim.

Bonner, Thomas Jr.   "On Stage in New Orleans: A Photo Essay
on Tennessee Williams's Plays."   *Studies in American
Drama* 3 (1988): 79-98.

Borny, Geoffrey.   "Williams and Kazan: The Creative Syn-
thesis."   *Australian Drama Studies* 8 (1986): 33-47.

Boxill, Roger.   *Tennessee Williams*.   New York: St. Martin's,
1987; London: Macmillan, 1987.   xvi, 186 pp.   Ils.   Review:
    Parker, R. B.   *Modern Drama* 31 (Mar. 1988): 119.

Boyle, Robert.   "Williams and Myopia."   *America* 104 (19 Nov.
1960): 263-65.   [Reply to Gardiner (below)]

Bradbury, John M. *Renaissance in the South: A Critical History of the Literature 1920-1960.* Chapel Hill: Univ. of North Carolina Pr., 1963. 192-95.

Brady, Leo. "The Showcase." *Critic* Aug.-Sept. 1960: 61, 78. [Reply to Mannes (below)]

Brandt, George. "Cinematic Structure in the Work of Tennessee Williams." *American Theatre.* Ed. John R. Brown and Bernard Harris. London: Arnold, 1967. 163-87.

Bray, Robert. "The Burden of the Past in the Major and Minor Plays of Tennessee Williams." Diss., Univ. of Mississippi, 1983. *Dissertation Abstracts International* 44 (1984): 3382 A.

---. "The Burden of the Past in the Plays of Tennessee Williams." *The Many Forms of Drama.* Ed. Karelisa V. Hartigan. Lanham, MD: Univ. Pr. of America, 1985. 1-9.

---. "Time as Enemy in the Short Plays of Tennessee Williams." *Tennessee Williams Literary Journal* 1.1 (Spring 1989): 51-60.

Brockett, Oscar G., and Robert R. Findlay. *Century of Innovation: A History of European and American Theatre and Drama since 1870.* Englewood Cliffs, NJ: Prentice-Hall, 1973. 568-70.

Brooks, Charles B. "The Comic Tennessee Williams." *Quarterly Journal of Speech* 44 (Oct. 1958): 275-81.

---. "The Multiple Set in American Drama." *Tulane Drama Review* 3 (Dec. 1958): 35-37.

---. "Williams' Comedy." Tharpe (below): 720-35; short ed. (below): 173-88.

Brown, Ray C. B. "Tennessee Williams: The Poetry of Stagecraft." *Voices* 138 (Summer 1949): 4-8.

Buchloh, Paul G. "Gesellschaft, Individuum und Gemeinschaft bei Tennessee Williams." *Studium Generale* 21 (1968): 49-73. Rpt. (revised) Itschert (below): 307-40.

---. "Tennessee Williams: Assoziationschriften." *Studien zur englischen und amerikanischen Sprache und Literatur* .... Neumunster: Wacholtz, 1974. 405-39.

Bukoski, Anthony. "The Lady and Her Business of Love in Selected Southern Fiction." *Studies in the Humanities* 5 (Jan. 1976): 14-18.

Byun, Chang-ku. "Impasse of the Romantic Imagination in the Plays of Tennessee Williams." Diss., Univ. of Tulsa, 1988. *Dissertation Abstracts International* 49 (1988): 816-17 A.

Cahalan, Thomas L, and Paul A. Doyle. *Modern American Drama.* Boston: Student Outlines, 1960. 133-43.

Cain, Bernice P. "The Fugitive Pattern in Selected Plays by Tennessee Williams." Diss., Bowling Green State Univ., 1983. *Dissertation Abstracts International* 45 (1984): 1574 A.

Calandra, Denis Michael. "Comic Elements in the Plays of Tennessee Williams." Diss., Univ. of Nebraska, 1970. *Dissertation Abstracts International* 31 (1971): 5390-91 A.

Callahan, Edward F. "Tennessee Williams' Two Worlds." *North Dakota Quarterly* 25 (Summer 1957): 61-67.

Calvery, Catherine Ann. "Illusion in Modern American Drama: A Study of Selected Plays by Arthur Miller, Tennessee Williams, and Eugene O'Neill." Diss., Tulane Univ., 1964. *Dissertation Abstracts* 25 (1965): 6111-12.

Cao, Guochen. [The artistry of Tennessee Williams's drama.] *Foreign Literature Studies* 34 (Dec. 1986): 86-91.

Capellan, Angel. "Tennessee Williams, tridimensional: Dramaturgo, poeta, memorialista." *Arbor* 401 (1979): 91-98.

Casper, Leonard. "Triangles of Transaction in Tennessee Williams." Tharpe (below): 736-52; short ed. (below): 189-205.

Castro, Donald Frank. "A Phenomenological Approach to the Concept of Genre." Diss., Washington State Univ., 1978. *Dissertation Abstracts International* 39 (1978): 859 A.

Chaillet, Jean-Paul. "Un cinéma de libération." Sarotte (below): 75-81.

Chesler, S(tanley) Alan. "Tennessee Williams' Literary Reputation in the United States." Diss., Kent State Univ., 1971. *Dissertation Abstracts International* 32 (1972): 6418 A.

---. "Tennessee Williams: Reassessment and Assessment."
    Tharpe (below): 848-80.

Clayton, John S. "The Sister Figure in the Works of Tennes-
    see Williams." *Carolina Quarterly* 11 (Summer 1960): 47-
    60. Rpt. Parker (A 1: *Glass* Criticism): 109-19; Gene-
    vieve Faber, ed., *Le theatre noir aux Etats-Unis* (Paris:
    CNRS, 1982): 109-19.

---. "Themes of Tennessee Williams." Diss., Yale Univ.,
    1960. *Dissertation Abstracts* 30 (1969): 718 A.

Cluck, Nancy Anne. "Showing or Telling: Narrators in the
    Drama of Tennessee Williams." *American Literature* 51
    (Mar. 1979): 84-93.

Clum, John M. "'Something Cloudy, Something Clear': Homo-
    phobic Discourse in Tennessee Williams." *South Atlantic
    Quarterly* 88 (Winter 1989): 161-79.

Clurman, Harold. "Tennessee Williams: Poet and Puritan."
    New York Times 29 Mar. 1970, sec. 2: 5, 11. Rpt. *The
    Divine Pastime...* (New York: Macmillan, 1974): 227-31.

Codignola, Luciano. "Il dramma a soggetto in America." *Il
    teatro della guerra fredda e altre cose*. Urbino: Arga-
    lia, 1969. 123-40.

Coffey, Warren. "Tennessee Williams: The Playwright as
    Analysand." *Ramparts* Nov. 1962: 51-58.

Cohn, Ruby. *Dialogue in American Drama*. Bloomington: Indi-
    ana Univ. Pr., 1971. 97-129. Rpt. Bloom (above): 55-70;
    Stanton (below): 45-60.

---. "Twentieth-Century Drama." *Columbia Literary History
    of the United States*. Ed. Emory Elliott. New York:
    Columbia Univ. Pr., 1988. 1103-05.

---. "The Late Tennessee Williams." *Modern Drama* 27
    (1984): 336-44.

---. "Tributes to Wives." *Tennessee Williams Review* 4.1
    (1983): 12-17.

Colanzi, Rita Mary. "'A Flame Burning Nothing': Tennessee
    Williams' Existential Drama." Diss., Temple Univ., 1990.
    Dissertation Abstracts International 51 (1990): 3741 A.

Cole, Charles W., and Carol I. Franco. "Critical Reaction
    to Tennessee Williams in the Mid-1960's." *Players* 49
    (Fall-Winter 1974): 18-23.

Coronis, Athena. "Tennessee Williams and Greek Culture
    (with Special Emphasis on Euripides)." Diss., Univ. of
    California-Riverside, 1986. *Dissertation Abstracts
    International* 47 (1987): 2573 A.

Corrigan, Mary Ann (Roman). "Beyond Verisimilitude: Echoes
    of Expressionism in Williams' Plays." Tharpe (below):
    375-412.

---. "Expressionism in the Early Plays of Tennessee Wil-
    liams." Diss., Univ. of Michigan, 1975. *Dissertation
    Abstracts International* 36 (1976): 6681 A.

---. "Memory, Dream, and Myth in the Plays of Tennessee
    Williams." *Renascence* 28 (Spring 1976): 155-67.

Corrigan, Robert W. "The American Theatre 1960-1965." *Arts
    and Sciences* (New York Univ.) 66 (Spring 1966): 10-15.

---. "The Soulscape of Contemporary American Drama." *World
    Theatre* 11 (Winter 1962-63): 316-28.

Costello, Donald P. "Tennessee Williams' Fugitive Kind."
    Modern Drama 15 (May 1972): 26-43. Rpt. (abr.) Stanton
    (below): 107-22.

Coulon, Georges. "Tennessee Williams, ou les voies de la
    transcendance de *Suddenly Last Summer* à *The Night of the
    Iguana*." *Études Anglaises* 78 (1978): 107-15.

---. "Tennessee Williams: Tragique et Tragédie." Sarotte
    (below): 19-24.

Cowser, R. L. Jr. "Symbolic Names in the Plays of Tennessee
    Williams." *Of Edsels and Marauders*. Ed. Fred Tarpley
    and Ann Moseley. Commerce, TX: Names Institute, 1971.
    89-93.

Crowther, Bosley. "Wronging Writing." *New York Times* 8
    Apr. 1962, sec. 2: 1.

Curley, Dorothy Nyren, et al., eds. *A Library of Literary
    Criticism: Modern American Literature*. New York: Ungar,
    1969. 3: 373-79.

Da Ponte, Durant. "Tennessee Williams' Gallery of Feminine
    Characters." *Tennessee Studies in Literature* 10 (1965):
    7-26. Rpt. (excerpt) Miller (A 1: *Streetcar*): 53-56.

Davidson, Peter. "Tennessee Williams, Arthur Miller, and
    Edward Albee." *The New Pelican Guide to English Litera-
    ture*. Ed. Boris Ford. Harmondsworth: Penguin, 1988. 9:
    553-58.

Davis, Joseph K. "The American South as Mediating Image in
    the Plays of Tennessee Williams." *Amerikanisches Drama
    und Theater im 20. Jahrhundert*. Ed. Alfred Weber and
    Siegfried Neuweiler. Gottingen: Vandenhoeck, 1976. 171-
    89.

Davis, Ronald L. "All the New Vibrations: Romanticism in
    20th-Century America." *Southern Review* 5 (Summer 1969):
    156-70.

Dawson, William Meredith. "The Female Characters of August
    Strindberg, Eugene O'Neill, and Tennessee Williams."
    Diss., Univ. of Wisconsin, 1964. *Dissertation Abstracts*
    25 (1964): 2663.

Debusscher, Gilbert. "The Artistry of Tennessee Williams's
    Personal Nomenclature." *Handelinger von het Tweeender-
    tigste Nederlands Filologencongres*. Amsterdam: Univ.
    Pr., 1974. 234-44.

---. "'Minting Their Separate Wills': Tennessee Williams
    and Hart Crane." *Modern Drama* 26 (1983): 455-76. Rpt.
    Bloom (above): 113-30; Parker (A 1: *Glass*): 31-43.

---. "Tennessee Williams as Hagiographer: An Aspect of
    Obliquity in Drama." *Revue des Langues Vivantes* 40
    (1974): 449-56. Rpt. Stanton (below): 149-57.

---. "Tennessee Williams's Black Nativity: An Unpublished
    Libretto." *American Literature in Belgium*. Amsterdam:
    Rodopi, 1988. 127-33. ["Heavenly Grass]

Deniger, Timothy. "From the Plays of Tennessee Williams: A
    Defense of One-Night Stands." *Advocate* 17 Mar. 1983: 28-
    30.

Dersnah, James Louis. "The Gothic World of Tennessee Wil-
    liams." Diss., Univ. of Wisconsin-Madison, 1984. *Dis-
    sertation Abstracts International* 45 (1985): 3131 A.

Dervin, Daniel A.   "The Spook in the Rainforest: The
    Incestuous Structure of Tennessee Williams's Plays."
    Psychocultural Review 3 (Summer-Fall 1979): 153-83.

Devi, K. Lakshmi.   "The World of Tennessee Williams."   *An-
    dhra University Magazine* 20 (1959-60): 86-92.

Dietrich, Margret.   "Der Dramatiker Tennessee Williams und
    sein Werk für das heutige Theater."   *Universitas* (Stutt-
    gart) 23 (May 1968): 511-16.

Dillard, Robert Lee.   "The Tennessee Williams Hero: An Ana-
    lytic Survey."   Diss., Univ. of Missouri, 1965.   *Diserta-
    tion Abstracts* 26 (1966): 5592-93 A.

Dommergues, Pierre.   *Les écrivains d'aujourd'hui.*   Paris:
    Pr. Univ., 1967.

---.   "Le théâtre entre deux alienations."   *Les U.S.A. à la
    recherche de leur identité: Rencontres avec quarante
    écrivains américans.*   Paris: Grasset, 1967.   329-76.

Donahue, Francis.   *The Dramatic World of Tennessee Williams.*
    New York: Ungar, 1964.   243 pp.

---.   "Dramaturgos del norte."   *Cuadernos Americanos* 157
    (1968): 254-66.

---.   "Tennessee Williams y su teatro."   *Atenea* 447 (1983):
    171-90.

Downer, Alan S.   *Fifty Years of American Drama 1900-1950.*
    Chicago: Regnery, 1951.   102-05, 145-47.

---.   "Mr. Williams and Mr. Miller."   *Furioso* 4 (Summer
    1949): 66-70.

---.   *Recent American Drama.*   Minneapolis: Univ. of Minne-
    sota Pr., 1961.   28-33.

---.   "The Two Worlds of Arthur Miller and Tennessee Wil-
    liams."   *Princeton Alumni Weekly* 20 Oct. 1961: 8-11, 17,
    20.

Drake, Constance M.   "Six Plays by Tennessee Williams: Myth
    in the Modern World."   Diss., Ohio State Univ., 1970.
    Dissertation Abstracts International 32 (1971): 426 A.

Draya, Ren.   "The Frightened Heart: A Study of Character and
    Theme in the Fiction, Poetry, Short Plays and Recent
    Drama of Tennessee Williams."   Diss., Univ. of Colorado,

1977. *Dissertation Abstracts International* 38 (1977): 2773 A.

Driver, Tom F. *Romantic Quest and Modern Query: A History of the Modern Theater.* New York: Delacorte, 1970. 309–10, 313.

Duprey, Richard A. "The Battle for the American Stage." *Catholic World* 197 (July 1963): 246–51.

———. "Where Are Our Playwrights?" *America* 108 (5 Jan. 1963): 10–12.

Dusenbury, Winifred. *The Theme of Loneliness in Modern American Drama.* Gainesville: Univ. of Florida Pr., 1960. 134–54.

Egri, Peter. "A nouvella- es dramaforma osszefuggese Tennesee Williams muveszeteben (Uvegkisasszony arckepe - Uvegfigurak)." *Filologiai Kozlony* 20 (1974): 396–414.

Ehrenpries, Irwin. "Readable Americans." *Revue des Langues Vivantes* 25 (1959): 416–19.

Embry, Glenn Thomas. "Sexual Confusion in the Major Plays of Tennessee Williams." Diss., Univ. of California-Los Angeles, 1975. *Dissertation Abstracts International* 36 (1975): 309 A.

Enck, John Jacob. "Memory and Desire and Tennessee Williams' Plays." *Transactions of the Wisconsin Academy of Sciences, Arts, Letters* 42 (1953): 249–56.

Evans, Gareth L. "American Connections: O'Neill, Miller, Williams, and Albee." *The Language of Modern Drama.* London: Dent, 1977. 177–204 (esp. 190–98).

Falk, Signi Lenea. "The Profitable World of Tennessee Williams." *Modern Drama* 1 (Dec. 1958): 172–80. Rpt. Hurrell (A 1: *Streetcar*) 117–23.

———. *Tennessee Williams.* New York: Twayne, 1962. 224 pp. Rpt. (excerpt) Miller (A 1: *Streetcar* Criticism): 94–102. Reviews:
  Booklist 58 (15 Mar. 1962): 471.
  Times Literary Supplement 8 June 1962: 428.
  New York Herald Tribune Books 4 Mar. 1962: 12.

———. *Tennessee Williams.* 2nd ed. New York: Twayne, 1978. 194 pp. Rpt. (excerpt) Bloom (A 1: *Glass* Criticism): 79–87. Reviews:

Choice 15 (Dec. 1978): 1366.
   Kalson, Albert E. *Southern Quarterly* 19 (Winter 1981):
     81-84.

Fayard, Jeanne. *Tennessee Williams.* Paris: Seghers, 1972.
   190 pp. Ils.

Fedder, Norman J(oseph). "The Influence of D. H. Lawrence
   on Tennessee Williams." Diss., State Univ. of New York,
   1962. *Dissertation Abstracts* 24 (1963): 742-43.

---. *The Influence of D. H. Lawrence on Tennessee Williams.*
   The Hague: Mouton, 1966. 131 pp.

---. "Tennessee Williams' Dramatic Technique." Tharpe
   (below): 795-812; short ed. (below): 119-46.

Fischer-Seidel, Therese. *Mythenparodie im modernen englischen und amerikanischen Drama: Tradition und Kommunika-
   tion bei Tennessee Williams, Edward Albee, Samuel Bek-
   kett, und Harold Pinter.* Heidelberg: Winter, 1986. 49-
   83.

Fisher, William J. "Trends in Post-Depression American
   Drama: A Study of the Works of William Saroyan, Tennessee
   Williams, Irwin Shaw, Arthur Miller." Diss., State Univ.
   of New York, 1952.

Fitch, Robert E. "Le Mystique de la Merde." *New Republic* 3
   Sept. 1956: 17-18. Report: *Time* Oct. 1956: 94-95.

Flaxman, Seymour L. "The Debt of Williams and Miller to
   Ibsen and Strindberg." *Comparative Literature Studies*
   special advance issue (1963): 51-60.

Flèche, Anne. "Counter Realism in U. S. Drama: O'Neill and
   Williams." Diss., Rutgers Univ., 1989. *Dissertation
   Abstracts International* 50 (1990): 3951 A.

Fleit, Muriel. "The Application of Interaction Process
   Analysis to Selected Plays of Tennessee Williams."
   Diss., New York Univ., 1978. *Dissertation Abstracts
   International* 39 (1978): 1931 A.

Fleming, William P. Jr. "Tragedy in American Drama: The
   Tragic Views of Eugene O'Neill, Tennessee Williams, Arthur Miller, and Edward Albee." Diss., Univ. of Toledo,
   1972. *Dissertation Abstracts International* 33 (1972):
   308 A.

192   Plays and Screenplays

Forsythe, Ronald. "Why Can't 'We' Live Happily Ever After, Too?" *New York Times* 23 Feb. 1969, sec. 2: 1. [Gays]

Free, William J. "Camp Elements in the Plays of Tennessee Williams." *Southern Quarterly* 21.2 (1983): 16-23.

---. "Williams in the Seventies: Directions and Discontents." Tharpe (below): 815-28; short ed. (below): 247-60.

Freedley, George. "Freudians Both." *Players* 32 (Mar. 1956): 235-49. [O'Neill]

Freedman, Morris. *American Drama in Social Context.* Carbondale: Southern Illinois Univ. Pr., 1971. 779-80.

Friedrich, Jutta. "Individuum und Gesellschaft in den Dramen von Tennessee Williams." *Zeitschrift für Anglistik und Amerikanistik* (Jena) 13 (1965): 45-60.

Fritscher, John J. "Popular Culture as Cyclic Phenomenon in the Evolution of Tennessee Williams." *Challenges in American Culture.* Ed. Ray B. Browne et al. Bowling Green: Popular Pr., 1970. 258-64.

---. "Some Attitudes and a Posture: Religious Metaphor and Ritual in Tennessee Williams' Query of the American God." *Modern Drama* 13 (Sept. 1970): 201-15.

Ganz, Arthur. "The Desperate Morality of the Plays of Tennessee Williams." *American Scholar* 31 (Spring 1962): 178-94. Rpt. *American Drama and Its Critics...* (Chicago: Univ. of Chicago Pr., 1965): 203-217; *Readers of the Self* ... (New York: New York Univ. Pr., 1980): 107-22; Bloom (above): 99-111; Stanton (below): 123-37 (revised).

Gardiner, Harold C. "Is Williams' Vision Myopic?" *America* 103 (30 July 1960): 495-96. [Reply to Mannes (below)] Reply to Gardiner: see Boyle (above).

Gardner, Peter. "An Essay on Tennessee Williams." *Kyushu American Literature* (Japan) 1 (June 1958): 2-8.

Gassner, John. "Anchors Aweigh: Maxwell Anderson and Tennessee Williams." *Theatre Time* Spring 1949. Rpt. *Dramatic Soundings...*, ed. Glenn Loncy (New York: Crown, 1968): 304-13.

---. "The Influence of Strindberg in the United States." *World Theatre* 11 (Spring 1962): 21-29.

---. "Realism and Poetry in New American Playwrighting."
World Theatre 2 (Spring 1953): 19-20.

---. "Tennessee Williams: Dramatist of Frustration." *College English* 10 (Oct. 1946): 1-7.

---. *Theatre at the Crossroads.* New York: Holt, 1960. 77-91, 218-31.

---. *The Theatre in Our Times.* New York: Crown, 1954.
342-54. Rpt. (abr.) *On Contemporary Literature*, ed.
Richard Kostelanetz (Freeport, NY: Books for Libraries,
1964): 48-63.

Geier, Woodrow Augustus. "Images of Man in Five American
Dramatists: A Theological Critique." Diss., Vanderbilt
Univ., 1959. *Dissertation Abstracts* 20 (1959): 1463-64.

Gellert, Roger. "A Survey of the Homosexual in Some Plays."
Encore 8 (Jan.-Feb. 1961): 34-35.

Gilman, Richard. "The Drama Is Coming Now." *Tulane Drama
Review* 7 (Summer 1963): 27-42.

Giuliani, Maria T. "Tennessee Williams." *I contemporanei:
Novecento americano.* Ed. Elemire Zolla. Rome: Lucarini,
1982. 2: 485-505.

Glantz Shapiro, Margarita. *Tennessee Williams y el teatro
norteamericano.* Mexico: Univ. de Mexique, 1963.

Glicksberg, Charles I. "Depersonalization in the Modern
Drama." *Personalist* 39 (Spring 1958): 158-69.

---. "The Lost Self in Modern Literature." *Personalist* 43
(Autumn 1962): 527-38.

---. "The Modern Playwright and the Absolute." *Queen's
Quarterly* 65 (Autumn 1958): 459-71.

Goetsch, Paul. "Vom psychologisch-sozialkritischen zum
absurden Drama: Williams, Miller, Albee." *Das amerikanische Drama.* Ed. Gerhard Hoffmann. Bern: Francke,
1984. 202-39.

Golden, Joseph. *The Death of Tinkerbell.* Syracuse: Syracuse Univ. Pr., 1967. 123-31.

Goldstein, Malcolm. "Body and Soul on Broadway." *Modern
Drama* 7 (Feb. 1965): 411-21.

194   Plays and Screenplays

Gorowara, Krishna. "The Fire Symbol in Tennessee Williams."
   Literary Half-Yearly 8 (Jan.-July 1967): 57-73.

Gottfried, Martin. *A Theater Divided: The Postwar American
   Stage.* Boston: Little, Brown, 1967. 248-57.

Gould, Jean R. *Modern American Playwrights.* New York:
   Dodd, Mead, 1966. 225-46.

Gray, Richard. *The Literature of Memory: Modern Writers of
   the American South.* Baltimore: Johns Hopkins Univ. Pr.,
   1977. 258-64.

Green, William. "Significant Trends in the Modern American
   Theatre." *Manchester Review* 8 (Autumn 1957): 65-78.

Gresset, Michel. "Orphée sous les tropiques, ou les thèmes
   dans le théâtre recent de Tennessee Williams." *Le théâtre moderne.* Ed. Jean Jacquot. Paris: Centre National,
   1967. 2.: 163-76. Rpt. Sarrotte (below): 91-103.

Groff, Edward. "Point of View in Modern Drama." *Modern
   Drama* 2 (Dec. 1959): 268-82.

Guerrero Zamora, Juan. *Historia del teatro contemporáneo.*
   Barcelona: Flores, 1967. 4: 125-37.

Hafley, James. "Abstraction and Order in the Language of
   Tennessee Williams." Tharpe (below): 753-62.

Hagopian, John V., and Martin Dolch. "Tennessee Williams."
   Insight: Analysis of American Literature. Frankfurt:
   Hirschgraben, 1967. 1: 271-81.

Hagy, Boyd Frederick. "A Study of the Changing Patterns of
   Melodrama as They Contributed to American Playwriting
   from 1920-1950." Diss., Catholic Univ. of America, 1978.
   Dissertation Abstracts International 39 (1978): 1548-49
   A.

Hainsworth, J. D. "Tennessee Williams: Playwright on a Hot
   Tin Roof?" *Études Anglaises* 20 (July-Sept. 1967): 225-
   32.

Hairi, Salahuddin. "The Conflict between the Physical and
   the Ideal in the Plays of Tennessee Williams." Diss.,
   Southern Illinois Univ., 1979. *Dissertation Abstracts
   International* 40 (1980): 4595 A.

Hale, Allean. "Tennessee's Long Trip." *Missouri Review* 7
   (1984): 201-12. [Noh influence]

Hall, Peter. "Tennessee Williams: Notes on the Moralist."
    Encore 4 (Sept.-Oct. 1957): 16-19.

Hardaway, Elizabeth Hamilton. "Segmentation, Semiotization,
    and Stagecraft: An Analysis of the Dramatic Tensions That
    Determine the Success or Failure of Selected Plays by
    Tennessee Williams." Diss., Univ. of Georgia, 1987.
    Dissertation Abstracts International 48 (1988): 2871 A.

Hardwick, Elizabeth. "Tennessee Williams' Women and All
    Their Sad Young Men." *Vogue* Nov. 1983: 124, 126, 130.

Hashim, James. "Violence in the Drama of Tennessee Wil-
    liams." *Players* 45 (Feb.-Mar. 1970): 125-28.

Haskell, Molly. *From Reverence to Rape: The Treatment of
    Women in the Movies.* New York: Holt, 1974. New York:
    Penguin, 1974. 248-53.

Hauptman, Robert. *The Pathological Vision: Jean Genet,
    Louis-Ferdinand Celine, and Tennessee Williams.* New
    York: Lang, 1984. 95-122.

---. "The Pathological Vision - Three Studies: Jean Genet,
    Louis-Ferdinand Celine, Tennessee Williams." Diss., Ohio
    State Univ., 1971. *Dissertation Abstracts International*
    32 (1972): 5229 A.

Hays, Peter L. *The Limping Hero: Grotesques in Literature.*
    New York: New York Univ. Pr., 1971. 39-42, 86-88, 173-
    76.

Heal, Edith. "Words about Williams." *Columbia University
    Forum* 10 (Spring 1967): 45-47.

Heilman, Robert B. "Tennessee Williams: Approaches to Trag-
    edy." *Southern Review* 1 (August 1965): 770-90. Rpt. *The
    Iceman, the Arsonist, and the Troubled Agent...* (Seattle:
    Univ. of Washington Pr., 1973): 115-41; Stanton (below):
    17-35 (excerpt).

---. *Tragedy and Melodrama: Versions of Exprience.* Seat-
    tle: Univ. of Washington Pr., 1968. 120-22.

Heiney, Donald. *Recent American Literature.* Woodbury, NY:
    Barron's, 1958. 406-15.

Henshaw, Marjorie. "El 'motif' del sur en la obra de Ten-
    nessee Williams." *Anglia* (México) 2 (1969): 131-37.

Hernlund, Bengt. "Tennessee Williams's enaktare." *Roster i Radio* 20 (1953): 9, 36.

Herron, Ima H. *The Small Town in American Drama*. Dallas: Southern Methodist Univ. Pr., 1969. 344-77.

Hirsch, Foster. *A Portrait of the Artist: The Plays of Tennessee Williams*. Port Washington, NY: Kennikat, 1978. 121 pp. Reviews:
    Kalson, Albert E. *Southern Quarterly* 19 (Winter 1981): 81-84.
    Tischler, Nancy M. *Tennessee Williams Newsletter* 1.2 (Fall 1979): 15-16.

---. "Tennessee Williams." *Cinema* 8 (Spring 1973).

Holditch, W. Kenneth. "Tennessee Williams: Poet as Playwright." *Xavier Review* 3.2 (1983): 21-27.

Hughes, Catharine. *American Playwrights 1945-1975*. London: Pitman, 1976. 15-31.

Hunningher, Benjamin. "Tennessee Williams tegenover de vijand Tijd." *Gids* 123 (Jan. 1960): 38-57.

Hurley, Paul J. "The Sad Fate of Tennessee Williams." *Shenandoah* 15 (Winter 1964): 61-66.

---. "Tennessee Williams: Critic of American Society." Diss., Duke Univ., 1962. *Dissertation Abstracts* 29 (1963): 2034-35.

---. "Tennessee Williams: The Playwright as Social Critic." *Theatre Annual* 21 (1964): 40-56.

"In the Gutter." *Time* 11 Apr. 1960: 76.

Inglis, William Heard III. "Strindberg and Williams: A Study in Affinities." Diss., Univ. of Washington, 1975. *Dissertation Abstracts International* 37 (1976): 698-99 A.

Isaac, Dan. "Form and Memory in the Major Plays of Tennessee Williams." Diss., Univ. of Chicago, 1968.

---. "In Defense of Tennessee Williams." *Religious Education* 53 (Sept.-Oct. 1958): 452-53.

Ishida, Akira. "Kage of Ikita Gekisakka." *Eigo Seinen* 1983: 129, 168-69.

244444

---. [Some ideas of Tennessee Williams's theatre. *Annual Report of Studies*] (Doshisha Women's College, Kyoto) 24 (1973): 138-62.

---. ["Spring Storm" and "Not about Nightingales," two unpublished plays by Tennessee Williams. *Annual Report of Studies*] 35 (1984): 113-38.

Itschert, Hans, ed. *Das amerikanische Drama von den Anfängen zur Gegenwart.* Darmstadt: Wissenschaftliche Buchgesellschaft, 1972. 265-92.

Iwamoto, Iwao. [Truth and illusion in Tennessee Williams's plays. *Studies in English Literature*] (Tokyo) 41 (Aug. 1964): 73-86.

Jackson, Esther Merle. *The Broken World of Tennessee Williams.* Madison: Univ. of Wisconsin Pr., 1965. xxiv, 179 pp. Ils. Rpt. (excerpts) *The American Theatre Today*, ed. Alan S. Downer (New York: Basic Books, 1967): 73-84; Bloom (above): 71-84. Reviews:
   American Literature 37 (Nov. 1965): 362.
   Lee, D. A. *Canadian Forum* 45 (Dec. 1965): 208.

---. "The Emergence of a Characteristic Contemporary Form in the Drama of Tennessee Williams." Diss., Ohio State Univ., 1958. *Dissertation Abstracts* 19 (1959): 3053-54.

---. "The Emergence of the Anti-Hero in the Contemporary Drama." *Central States Speech Journal* 12 (1960-61): 92-99. Rpt. (excerpts) Stanton (below): 87-90.

---. "Music and Dance as Elements of Form in the Drama of Tennessee Williams." *Revue d'Histoire du Theatre* 15 (1963): 294-301. Rpt. Ischert (above): 265-75.

---. "The Problem of Form in the Drama of Tennessee Williams." *College Language Association Journal* 4 (Sept. 1960): 8-12.

---. "Tennessee Williams: Poetic Consciousness in Crisis." Tharpe (below): 53-72.

Jackson, Joe, and Kim Connell. "Gigolos: The Last of the Courtly Lovers." *Journal of Popular Culture* 15.2 (1981): 130-41.

Jan-Orn, Charlemarie. "The Characterization of Women in Tennessee Williams' Work." Diss., Univ. of Nebraska-Lincoln, 1979. *Dissertation Abstracts International* 40 (1980): 4037-38 A.

198   Plays and Screenplays

Jauslin, Christian. *Tennessee Williams*. Hannover: Friedrich, 1969. 154 pp. Ils.

---. *Tennessee Williams - Dramatiker Welttheaters*. Munich: Friedrich, 1976.

Johnson, Kenneth E. "Memory Plays in American Drama." *Within the Dramatic Spectrum*. Ed. Karelisa V. Hartigan. Landhan, MD: Univ. Pr. of America, 1986. 115-23.

Johnstone, Monica Carolyn. "Tennessee Williams and American Realism." Diss., Univ. of California-Berkeley, 1987. *Dissertation Abstracts International* 49 (1988): 1314 A.

Jones, Robert Emmet. "Sexual Roles in the Works of Tennessee Williams." Tharpe (below): 545-57.

---. "Tennessee Williams's Early Heroines." *Modern Drama* 2 (Dec. 1959): 211-19. Rpt. Hurrell (A 1: *Streetcar*): 111-16.

Josephson, Lennart. "Tennessee Williams, Dramatik." *Bonniers Litterara Magasin* (Stockholm) 18 (Mar. 1949): 207-11.

Joshi, B. D. "Pangs of Modernity: The Diminishing Tragic Image of Man in the Plays of Miller, Williams, and Albee." *Indian Scholar* 5 (1983): 111-20.

Jotterand, Frank. *Le nouveau théâtre américain*. Paris: Seuil, 1970. 34-38.

Kahn, Sy. "Through a Glass Menagerie Darkly: The World of Tennessee Williams. *Modern American Drama: Essays in Criticism*. Ed. William E. Taylor. DeLand, FL: Everett/Edwards, 1968. 71-89.

Kalson, Albert E. "Tennessee Williams at the Delta Brillant." Tharpe (below): 774-94; short ed. (below): 107-27.

---. "Tennessee Williams Enters *Dragon Country*." *Modern Drama* 16 (June 1973): 61-67.

Keating, Edward M. "Mildew on the Old Magnolia." *Ramparts* Nov. 1962: 69-74.

Kerjan, Lilane. "La postérité de Tennessee Williams." Sarotte (below): 83-89.

Kernan, Alvin B.   "Truth and Dramatic Mode in the Modern
   Theatre: Chekhov, Pirandello, and Williams." *Modern
   Drama* 1 (Sept. 1958): 111-14. Rpt. (excerpt) Bloom
   (above): 9-11.

Kerr, Walter. "Failures of Williams." *Pieces at Eight*.
   New York: Simon, 1957. 125-34.

Kesting, Marianne. "Tennessee Williams." *Hochland* 50 (Dec.
   1957): 171-74.

Kienzle, Siegfried. *Modernes Welttheater*. Stuttgart:
   Kroner, 196-. Trans. Alexander Henderson and Elizabeth
   Henderson: *Modern World Theater*.... New York: Ungar,
   1970. 476-84.

King, Kimball. *The Works of Tennessee Williams*. Audiocassette. DeLand, FL: Everett/Edwards, 1976.

Kinney, Harry Alexander. "Tennessee Williams and the Fugitive Kind." Diss., Univ. of California-Berkeley, 1983.
   Dissertation Abstracts International 44 (1984): 2294 A.

Kleinfield, H. E. "Tennessee Williams: Psychology and Sin:
   Thoughts on a People's Theatre." *Chrysalis* 9.1-2 (1956).

Klinger, Kurt. "Zwischenruf zum Toleranz: Zun Werk von Tennessee Williams nach dessen 50. Geburtstag." *Forum* 11
   (1964): 266-68.

Koepsel, Jürgen. *Der amerikanische Süden und seine Funk-
   tionen im dramatischen Werk von Tennessee Williams*.
   Bern: Herbert Lang, 1974; Frankfurt: Peter Lang, 1974.
   263 pp.

Kohler, Klaus. "Psychodiagnose und Gesellschaftsanalyse im
   Bühnenwerk von Tennessee Williams." *Studien zum ameri-
   kanischen Drama nach dem zweiten Weltkrieg*. Ed. Eberhard
   Bruning et al. Berlin: Rutten, 1977. 54-104.

Koljevic, Nikola. "Tri relikana americke drame." *Poz* 25
   (1983): 437-55.

Koreneva, Maya M. *Contemporary American Drama 1945-70*.
   Moscow: Gorky Institute of World Literature, 1975.

Kourilsky, Francoise. *Le théâtre aux U.S.A.* Paris: Renaissance du Livre, 1967.

Koutsoudaki, Mary. "The Use and Meaning of the Dionysiac
   Myth in Selected Plays of Albert Camus and Tennessee Wil-

liams." Diss., State Univ. of New York—Buffalo, 1983.
Dissertation Abstracts International 44 (1984): 3058 A.

Kramer, Victor. "Memoirs of Self-Indictment: The Solitude
of Tennessee Williams." Tharpe (below): 663-75.

Krutch, Joseph Wood. *The American Drama since 1918: An
Informal History.* New York: Braziller, 1957. 324-32.

———. *"Modernism" in Modern Drama.* Ithaca: Cornell Univ.
Pr., 1953. 126-30.

———. "Why the O'Neill Star Is Rising." *New York Times Magazine* 19 Mar. 1961: 36-37, 108-11.

Kunkel, Francis L. "Tennessee Williams and the Death of
God." *Commonweal* 87 (23 Feb. 1968): 614-17. Rpt. *Passion and the Passion...* (Philadelphia: Westminster,
1975): 99-107.

Lal, P. N. "The Poetic Use of the Theatre in the Plays of
Tennessee Williams." *Indian Journal of English Studies*
13 (1972): 132-47.

Langsam, Paula A. "A Study of the Major Characters in
Selected Plays of Tennessee Williams." Diss., State
Univ. of New York, 1966. *Dissertation Abstracts* 27
(1967): 3972 A.

Lapole, Nick. "Williams Built Actors." *New York Journal-
American* 20 Feb. 1966, sec. L: 35.

Larsen, June Bennett. "Tennessee Williams: Optimistic Sym-
bolist." Tharpe (below): 413-28.

Lasko, Joanne Zunzer. "'The Fiddle in the Wings': An Approach to Music in Drama." Diss., American Univ., 1977.
Dissertation Abstracts International 38 (1977): 1391 A.

Laufe, Abe. *Anatomy of a Hit.* New York: Hawthorn, 1966.
169-72, 180-85, 308-13.

Lawrence, Elaine Louise. "Four Defeated Heroines: Tennessee
Williams' Southern Gentlewomen." *Lit* 7 (Spring 1966): 7-
39.

Lawson, John Howard. "Modern U.S. Dramaturgy." *Inostran-
nava Literatura* 8 (Aug. 1962): 186-96.

Lee, Hyuy-ok. [A study of Tennessee Williams's fugitive
kind.] *Yonsei Review* (Seoul) 5 (1978): 167-78.

Levy, Valerie B. "Violence as Drama: A Study of the Development of the Use of Violence on the American Stage."
Diss., Claremont Grad. School, 1970. *Dissertation Abstracts International* 31 (1971): 6618-19 A.

Lewis, Allan. *American Plays and Playwrights of the Contemporary Theatre.* New York: Crown, 1965. 2nd ed., 1970.
53-65.

Leyburn, Ellen Douglass. "Comedy and Tragedy Transposed."
Yale Review 53 (Summer 1964): 553-62.

Link, Franz H. *Tennessee Williams' Dramen: Einsamkeit und
Liebe.* Darmstadt: Thesen, 1974. 144 pp.

Londré, Felicia Hardison. *Tennessee Williams.* New York:
Ungar, 1979. vi, 213 pp. Ils. Reviews:
   Kalson, Albert E.: see Hirsch (above).
   Pilkinton, Mark C. *Tennessee Williams Newsletter* 2.2
   (Fall 1980): 23-25.
   Yacowar, Maurice. *Modern Drama* 24 (Mar. 1981): 112-13.

---. *Tennessee Williams: Life, Work, Criticism.* Frederic-
ton, NB: York, 1989. 42 pp.

---: see Section I.

Loney, Glen. "Tennessee Williams, the Castastrophe of Success: 'You Can't Retire from Being an Artist.'" *Performing Arts Journal* 7 (1983): 73-87.

Lopez, C. J. "El teatro de Tennessee Williams." *Cuadernos
Hispanoamericanos* (Madrid) 29 (May 1952): 208-12.

Lotersztein, S. *Tennessee Williams: Poeta del naufragio.*
Buenos Aires: Instituto Amigos de Libro Argentino, 1965.
101 pp.

Lubbers, Klaus. "Tennessee Williams." *Amerikanische Literatur der Gegenwart.* Ed. Martin Christadler. Stuttgart:
Kroner, 1973. 425-49.

Lumley, Frederick. *New Trends in 20th Century Drama: A Survey since Ibsen and Shaw.* 4th ed. New York: Oxford
Univ. Pr., 1972. 182-99.

Lygizos, Mitsos. *To Neoellinkio plaisto pangosmio teatro.*
Athens: Saliveros, 1958.

Macey, Samuel L.   "Nonheroic Tragedy: A Pedigree for Amer-
    ican Tragic Drama." *Comparative Literature Studies* 6
    (Mar. 1969): 1-19.

Machts, Walter. "Das Menschenbild in den Dramen Tennessee
    Williams." *Neueren Spachen* 10 (Oct. 1961): 445-55. Rpt.
    Itschert (above): 293-306.

MacNicholas, John.   "Williams' Power of the Keys." Tharpe
    (below): 581-605; short ed. (below): 113-37.

Magid, Marion.   "The Innocence of Tennessee Williams." *Com-
    mentary* 35 (Jan. 1963): 34-43. Rpt. *Essays in the Modern
    Drama* (Boston: Heath, 1964): 280-93; Miller (A 1: *Street-
    car*): 73-79.

Magill, Frank N., ed. *Masterplots*. Englewood Cliffs, NJ:
    Salem, 1976. 845-47, 2270-71, 6308-10.

---, ed. *Survey of Contemporary Literature*. Englewood
    Cliffs, NJ: Salem, 1977. 1117-20, 4045-47, 5323-26,
    5656-58, 7361-64.

Mann, Bruce Joe.   "Tennessee Williams' Late Style: The Aging
    Playwright and His Imagination." Diss., Univ. of Michi-
    gan, 1984. *Dissertation Abstracts International* 45
    (1985): 2103 A.

Mannes, Marya.   "Plea for Fair Ladies." *New York Times Mag-
    azine* 29 May 1960: 16, 26-27. Responses: Boyle (above);
    Gardiner (above); Williams (D 1).

Manvell, Roger. *Theater and Film: A Comparative Study of
    the Two Forms of Dramatic Art and of the Problems of
    Adaptation of Stage Plays into Film*. Rutherford, NJ:
    Fairleigh Dickinson Univ. Pr., 1979.

Martynova, Anna.   "Prigovor zhestokosti." *Literaturnaia
    Gazeta* 16 (20 Apr. 1983): 11.

Matthew, David Charles Cameron.   "The Ritual of Self-
    Assassination in the Drama of Tennessee Williams."
    Diss., Columbia Univ., 1974. *Dissertation Abstracts
    International* 35 (1975): 6147 A.

McCarthy, Mary.   "American Realists, Playwrights." *Encoun-
    ter* 17 (July 1961): 24-31. Rpt. *Theatre Chronicles 1937-
    1962*. New York: Farrar, 1963. 209-29.

---.   "Realism in the American Theater." *Harper's* July
    1961: 45-52.

McClelland, Charles E. "Tennessee Williams' Plays as Films:
An Unhappy Medium" *Media History Digest* 3 (Summer 1983):
53-57, 59.

McGlinn, Jeanne M. "Tennessee Williams' Women: Illusion and
Reality, Sexuality and Love." Tharpe (below): 510-24.

McHughes, William Francis. "A Psychological Script Analysis
of the Later Plays of Tennessee Williams 1960-1980."
Diss., Southern Illinois Univ.-Carbondale, 1980. *Dissertation Abstracts International* 41 (1981): 3328-29 A.

McRae, Russell Williams. "Tennessee Williams: An Artifice
of Mirrors." Diss., York Univ. (Canada), 1975. *Dissertation Abstracts International* 36 (1976): 311-12 A.

Mennemeier, Franz N. *Das moderne Drama des Auslandes.* 3rd
ed. Dusseldorf: Bagel, 1976. 66-80.

Miller, Arthur. "Morality and Modern Drama." *Educational
Theatre Journal* 10 (Oct. 1958): 190-202. Rpt. *The The-
ater Essays of Arthur Miller*, ed. Robert A. Martin (New
York: Viking, 1978): 195-214.

---. "The Shadow of the Gods: A Critical View of the Amer-
ican Theater." *Harper's* Aug. 1958: 46-51. Rpt. *American
Playwrights on Drama*, ed. Horst Frenz (New York: Hill &
Wang, 1965): 147-50; *Theater Essays* (above): 175-94.

Miller, J. William. *Modern Playwrights at Work.* New York:
French, 1968. 1: 335-85.

Miller, Jordan Y. "Myth and the American Dream: O'Neill to
Albee." *Modern Drama* 7 (Sept. 1964): 190-98.

Miller, Robert Royce. "Tragedy in Modern American Drama:
The Psychological, Social, and Absurdist Conditions in
Historical Perspective." Diss., Middle Tennessee State
Univ., 1975. *Dissertation Abstracts International* 36
(1975): 3717 A.

Milstead, John. "The Structure of Modern Tragedy." *Western
Humanities Review* 12 (Aug. 1958): 365-69.

Minyard, John Douglas. "Classical Motivations in Tennessee
Williams." *Classical and Modern Literature* 6 (1986):
287-303.

Mishoe, Billy. "Time as Antagonist in the Dramas of Tennessee Williams." Diss., Florida State Univ., 1972. *Dissertation Abstracts International* 33 (1972): 2944-45 A.

Mitchell, John D.   "Applied Psychoanalysis in the Drama."
    American Imago 14 (Fall 1953): 272-73.

Mraz, Doyne Joseph.   "The Changing Image of the Female Char-
    acters in the Works of Tennessee Williams."   Diss., Univ.
    of Southern California, 1967.   *Dissertation Abstracts* 28
    (1968): 4304.

Mueller, W. R.   "Tennessee Williams: A New Direction?"
    Christian Century 81 (14 Oct. 1964): 1271-72.

Murray, Edward.   "Tennessee Williams - After 'The Celluloid
    Brassiere.'"   *The Cinematic Imagination: Writers and the
    Motion Pictures*.   New York: Ungar, 1972.   46-72.

Nardin, James T.   "What Tennessee Williams Didn't Write."
    Essays in Honor of Esmond Linworth Marilla.   Ed. Thomas
    A. Kirby and William J. Olive.   Baton Rouge: Louisiana
    State Univ. Pr., 1970.   331-41.

Narumi, Hiroshi.   [Tennessee Williams's black plays.]   *Rik-
    kyo Review of Arts and Letters* (Tokyo) 24 (Mar. 1963):
    26-51.

Navone, John.   "The Myth and Dream of Paradise."   *Studies in
    Religion* 5 (1975): 152-61.

Nelson, Benjamin.   "Avant Garde Dramatists from Ibsen to
    Ionesco."   *Psychoanalytic Review* 55 (1968): 505-12.

---.   *The Plays of Tennessee Williams: Cat on a Hot Tin
    Roof, The Glass Menagerie, Orpheus Descending, A Street-
    car Named Desire, and Others*.   New York: Monarch, 1965.
    96 pp.

---.   *Tennessee Williams: The Man and His Work*.   New York:
    Obolensky, 1961.   304 pp.   *Tennessee Williams: His Life
    and Work*.   London: Peter Owens, 1961.   Rpt. (excerpt)
    Parker (A 1: *Glass* Criticism): 87-95.   262 pp.   Reviews:
    Booklist 58 (1 Apr. 1962): 516.
    Kirkus 29 (15 Oct. 1961): 962.
    New York Herald Tribune Books 28 Jan. 1962: 13.
    Times Literary Supplement 8 June 1972: 428.
    Atkinson, Brooks.   *New York Times Book Review* 26 Nov.
        1961: 1, 36.
    Gascoigne, Bamber.   *Spectator* 207 (22 Dec. 1961): 933.
    Pine, J. C.   *Library Journal* 87 (15 Jan. 1962): 117.
    Walsh, Moira.   *Catholic World* 195 (May 1962): 121.
    Weatherby, W. J.   *Manchester Guardian* 13 Oct. 1961: 7.

Niesen, George. "The Artist against the Reality in the
     Plays of Tennessee Williams." Tharpe (below): 463-93;
     short ed. (below): 81-111.

Normand, Jean. "Le poète, image de l'étranger: l'Orphée de
     Tennessee Williams." *Revue Française d'Études Améri-
     caines* 9 (1980): 117-25.

Okada, Haruma. *Tennessee Williams: Sakuhin ni miru Genso to
     Shinjitsu.* Tokyo: Yashio, 1983. 202 pp. [Illusion]

Orr, John. *Tragic Drama and Modern Society: Studies in the
     Social and Literary Theory of Drama from 1870 to the Pre-
     sent.* London: Macmillan, 1981. 206-40.

Osada, Mitsunobu. "The Metamorphosis of Tennessee Williams
     in the Sixties and After." *Eigo-Eibel-Bungaku* 24 (Mar.
     1984): 203-25.

Ott, Volker. *Homotrophic und die Figur des Homotropen in
     der Literatur des zwanzigsten Jahrhunderts.* Frankfurt:
     Lang, 1979. 206-15.

Packard, William. "Poetry in the Theatre - V." *Trace* 16
     (1967): 452-55.

Pagan, Nicholas Osborne. "Tennessee Williams' Kind of
     Theater: Signature and Biography." Diss., Univ. of
     Florida, 1989. *Dissertation Abstracts International* 51
     (1990): 854 A.

Palffy, Istvan. "'Otherness' as a Salient Feature in Ten-
     nessee Williams' Plays." *The Origins and Originality of
     American Culture.* Ed. Frank Tibor. Budapest: Akademiai
     Kiado, 1984. 423-29.

---. "Tennessee Williams es a dramai ember massaga." *Filo-
     logiai Kozlony* 27 (1981): 99-104.

Pamfil-Popovici, Liliana. "Aspecte contradictorii ale tea-
     trului lui Tennessee Williams." *Analele Universitatii
     Bucuresti* 17 (1968): 331-45.

Parker, Dorothy, ed. *Essays on Modern American Drama: Wil-
     liams, Miller, Albee, and Shepherd.* Toronto: Univ. of
     Toronto Pr., 1987. 1-51.

Parker, R. B. "The Circle Closed: A Psychological Reading
     of *The Glass Menagerie* and *The Two-Character Play.*" *Mod-
     ern Drama* 28 (1985): 517-34. Rpt. Bloom (A 1: *Glass*):
     119-36.

Pasquier, Marie-Claire. "Mortal Ladies Possessed." Sarotte
    (below): 109-13. [Women in the plays]

Patsalidis, Savas. "E Doxologia ke o Anathematismos tu
    Eroticu Logu ston T. Williams." *Diavazo* 139 (3 Mar.
    1986): 16-22.

Patterson, Nancy Marie. "Patterns of Imagery in the Major
    Plays of Tennessee Williams." Diss., Univ. of Arkansas,
    1957. *Dissertation Abstracts* 17 (Sept. 1957): 2014.

Pauly, Thomas A. *An American Odyssey: Elia Kazan and Amer-
    ican Culture*. Philadelphia: Temple Univ. Pr., 1983.

Pavlov, Grigor. *Blood and Mustard: A Brief Look at Tennes-
    see Williams' Major Theses and Techniques*. Sofia: 1971.
    16 pp.

Pearson, Kenneth. "Worlds of Violence." *Sunday Times Maga-
    zine* (London) 26 June 1960: 40.

Pease, Donald. "Reflections on Moon Lake: The Presence of
    the Playwright." Tharpe (below): 829-47; short ed. (be-
    low): 261-79.

Perrier, Ronald Gordon. "A Study of the Dramatic Works of
    Tennessee Williams from 1963 to 1971." Diss., Univ. of
    Minnesota, 1972. *Dissertation Abstracts International* 33
    (1972): 1879 A.

Peterson, Carol. *Tennessee Williams*. Berlin: Colloquium,
    1975. 95 pp.

Pettinelli, Frances. "Tennessee Williams: A Study of the
    Dramaturgical Evolution of Three Later Plays 1969-78."
    Diss., City Univ. of New York, 1988. *Dissertation Ab-
    stracts International* 49 (1989): 2028 A.

Phillips, Gene D. *The Films of Tennessee Williams*. Phila-
    delphia: Art Alliance, 1980; London/Toronto: Associated
    Univ. Pr., 1980. 336 pp. Ils. Review:
        Yacowar, Maurice. *Tennessee Williams Review* 3.1
            (1981): 10-11.

---. "Underrated Williams: A Reconsideration of *The Seven
    Descents of Myrtle* and *The Milk Train Doesn't Stop Here
    Anymore*." *Tennessee Williams Literary Journal* 1.1
    (Spring 1989): 45-50.

Ploritis, Marios. *Prosopa tou neoterou dramatos*. Athens:
    Galaxias-Ermias, 1978. 124-44.

Popkin, Henry. "The Plays of Tennessee Williams." *Tulane Drama Review* 4 (Mar. 1960): 45-64.

---. "Realism in the U.S.A." *World Theatre* 14 (Mar.-Apr. 1965): 119-26.

---. "Tennessee Williams Reexamined." *Arts in Virginia* 11 (Spring 1971): 2-5.

---. "Williams, Osborne, or Beckett?" *New York Times Magazine* 13 Nov. 1960: 32-33, 119-21. Rpt. *Essays in the Modern Drama* (Boston: Heath, 1964): 235-42.

Postlewait, Thomas. "Simultaneous Design on the American Stage: The Achievement of Tennessee Williams." *40 Years of Mise en Scene, 1945-1985....* Dundee: Lochee, 1986. 95-101.

Pradhan, N. S. *Modern American Drama: A Study in Myth and Tradition.* London: Arnold/Heinemann, 1978. Passim.

Prasad, Hari M. "Plastic Theatre of Tennessee Williams." *Indian Scholar* 2.1 (1980): 51-56.

Prenshaw, Peggy W. "The Paradoxical Southern World of Tennessee Williams." Tharpe (below): 5-29.

Presley, Delma Eugene. "Little Acts of Grace." Tharpe (below): 571-80.

---. "The Moral Function of Distortion in Southern Grotesque." *South Atlantic Bulletin* 37 (Spring 1973): 37-46.

---. "The Search for Hope in the Plays of Tennessee Williams." *Mississippi Quarterly* 25 (Winter 1971-72): 31-43.

---. "The Theological Dimensions of Tennessee Williams: A Study of Eight Major Plays." Diss., Emory Univ., 1969. *Dissertation Abstracts* 30 (1969): 2038.

---, and Hari Singh. "Epigraphs to the Plays of Tennessee Williams." *Notes on Mississippi Writers* 3 (Spring 1970): 2-12.

Quinby, Lee. "Tennessee Williams: Hermaphroditic Symbolism in *The Rose Tattoo, Orpheus Descending, The Night of the Iguana,* and *Kingdom of Earth.*" *Tennessee Williams Newsletter* 1.2 (Fall 1979): 12-14.

Quirino, Leonard Salvator. "The Darkest Celebrations of
Tenneseee Williams: A Study of *Battle of Angels, A
Streetcar Named Desire, Orpheus Descending, Camino Real,
Cat on a Hot Tin Roof,* and *Suddenly Last Summer*." Diss.,
Brown Univ., 1964. *Dissertation Abstracts* 25 (1965):
4706.

Ralfailovich, Pnina. "Tennessee Williams's South." *Southern Studies* 23.2 (1984): 191-97.

Ramaswamy, S. "The Heroines of Tennessee Williams's Plays."
Journal of the Karnatak University: Humanties 14 (1970):
79-90.

---. "Tennessee Williams as a Man of the Theatre." *Indian
Journal of American Studies* 13.1 (1983): 97-105.

Rebora, Robert. "Estate fumo di Tennessee Williams: Ritagli
crepuscolari decadenti." *Fiera Letteratia* 29 Oct. 1950:
8.

Reid, Desmond. "Tennessee Williams." *Studies* (Dublin): 46
(Winter 1957): 431-46. Rpt. Hurrell (A 1: *Streetcar*):
100-10.

Renaux, Sigrid. "Tennessee Williams: Attitudes toward Love
and Decay in Blanche DuBois and Mrs. Stone." *Revista
Letras* (Curitiba) 28 (1979): 81-91.

Richardson, Thomas J. "The City of Day and the City of
Night: New Orleans and the Exotic Unreality of Tennessee
Williams." Tharpe (below): 631-46.

Rios, Charlotte Rose. "Violence in Contemporary Drama: Antonio Artaud's *Theatre of Cruelty* and Selected Drama of
Genet, Williams, Albee, Bond, and Pinter." Diss., Univ.
of Notre Dame, 1981. *Dissertation Abstracts International* 41 (1981): 4710-11 A.

Roberts, Preston T. Jr. "Bringing Pathos into Focus." *University of Chicago Magazine* 47 (Feb. 1954): 7-11, 18.

Rogers, Ingrid. *Tennessee Williams: A Moralist's Answer to
the Perils of Life.* Frankfurt: Peter Lang, 1976; Bern:
Herbert Lang, 1976. 267 pp.

Rogoff, Gordon. "The Restless Intelligence of Tennessee
Williams." *Tulane Drama Review* 10 (Summer 1966): 78-92.

---. *Theatre Is Not Safe: Theatre Criticism 1962-1986.*
Evanston, IL: Northwestern Univ. Pr., 1987. 80-91.

Ross, Marlon B.   "The Making of Tennessee Williams: Imagining a Life of the Imagination." *Southern Humanities Re-*
view 21 (1987): 117-31.

Sagar, K. M.   "What Mr. Williams Has Made of D. H. Lawrence." *Twentieth Century* 168 (Aug. 1960): 143-53.

Samuels, Charles Thomas.   "Sex, Dreams, and Tennessee Williams." *Syracuse Review* 2 (Jan. 1957): 12-19. Response:
Williams (D 3).

Sarotte, Georges-Michel.   *Comme un frère, comme un amant:*
L'homosexualité masculine dans le roman et le théâtre
américains de Herman Melville à James Baldwin. Paris:
Flammarion, 1976. 127-42. Rpt. (excerpt) Sarotte (be-
low): 130-39. Trans. Richard Miller: *Like a Brother,*
Like a Lover... (Garden City: Anchor, 1978): 107-20.

---.   "Tennessee Williams, ou l'Intelligence du coeur."
Sarotte (below): 5-7.

---, ed. *Tennessee Williams.* L'Album Masques. Paris:
Association Masques, 1986. 154 pp. Ils.

Savery, Pancho.   "The Faded and Frightened and Different and
Odd and Lonely: Psychological Realism, Polarity, Morality, and Identification in the Theatre of Tennessee Williams." Diss., Cornell Univ., 1980. *Dissertation Ab-*
stracts International 40 (1981): 4035 A.

Scanlon, Tom.   "The American Family and Family Dilemmas in
American Drama." Diss., Univ. of Minnesota, 1970. *Dis-*
sertation Abstracts International 32 (1971): 1529 A.

---.   *Family, Drama, and American Dreams.* Westport, CT:
Greenwood, 1978. 156-79. Rpt. Parker (A 1: *Glass* Criticism): 96-108.

Schaefer, Hans Joachim.   "Zum Verstandius amerikanischer
Dramatik." *Begebnung* 18 (Nov. 1963): 318-22.

Schafer, Jurgen. *Geschichte des amerikanischen Dramas im*
20. Jahrhundert. Stuttgart: Kohlhamer, 1982. 102-14.

Scheick, William J.   "An Intercourse Not Well Designed: Talk
and Touch in the Plays of Tennessee Williams." Tharpe
(below): 763-73.

Schneiderman, Leo.   "Tennessee Williams: The Incest-Motif
and Fictional Love Relationships." *Psychoanalytic Review*
73 (1986): 97-110.

Schroeder, Patricia R. *The Presence of the Past in Modern
American Drama*. Rutherford, NJ: Fairleigh Dickinson
Univ. Pr., 1989. 105-24.

Sharma, P. P. "The Predicament of the 'Outsiders' in Tennessee Williams' Plays." *Indian Journal of American
Studies* 5 (Jan.-July 1975): 69-75.

Sharp, William. "An Unfashionable View of Tennessee Williams." *Tulane Drama Review* 6 (Mar. 1962): 160-71.

Shaughnessy, Mary Ellen. "Incomplete Sentences: A Study of
Tennessee Williams since 1960." Diss., State Univ. of
New York-Buffalo, 1977. *Dissertation Abstracts Interna-
tional* 38 (1978): 5485 A.

Sievers, W. David. *Freud on Broadway: A History of Psycho-
anlaysis and the American Drama*. New York: Hermitage,
1955; Toronto: McLeod, 1955. 370-88. Rpt. Miller (A 1:
Streetcar): 90-93.

Silvestru, Valentin. "Tennessee Williams si repulsia fata
de cruzime." *Prezenta Teatrului: Studii Critice*. Bucharest: Meridiane, 1968. 227-36.

Simons, Piet. "De bonte geitebok of de verwelkte roos."
Ons Erfdeel 18.3 (1975): 443-44.

Skloot, Robert. "Submitting Self to Flame: The Artist's
Quest in Tennessee Williams 1935-1954." *Educational Theatre Journal* 25 (May 1973): 199-206.

Smith, Harry Willard Jr. "Mielziner and Williams: A Concept
of Style." Diss., Tulane Univ., 1966. *Dissertation Abstracts* 27 (1966): 552.

---. "Tennessee Williams and Jo Mielziner: The Memory
Plays." *Theatre Survey* 23 (1982): 223-35.

Sorell, Walter. "The Case of Tennessee Williams." *Cresset*
36.8 (1973): 26-27.

Spero, Richard Henry. "The Jungian World of Tennessee Williams." Diss., Univ. of Wisconsin, 1970. *Dissertation
Abstracts International* 31 (1971): 6205 A.

Spevack, Marvin. "Tennessee Williams: The Idea of the Theatre." *Jahrbuch fur Amerikastudien* 10 (1965): 221-31.
Rpt. Itschert (above): 249-64.

Spivey, Ted R.   "Tennessee Williams: Desire and Impotence in
New Orleans." *Revival: Southern Writers in the Modern
City*. Gainesville: Univ. of Florida Pr., 1986.   122-38.

Stanton, Stephen S., ed. *Tennessee Williams: A Collection
of Critical Essays*. Englewood Cliffs, NJ: Prentice-Hall,
1977.   x, 194 pp. Reviews:
   Choice 15 (May 1978): 403.
   Times Educational Supplement 19 May 1978: 32.

Starnes, R. Leland.   "Comedy and Tennessee Williams."
Diss., Yale Univ., 1965. *Dissertation Abstracts International* 41 (1980): 2359 A.

Stasio, Marilyn.   "An Updated Look at Tennessee Williams'
'Fugitives.'"   *Cue* 7 Feb. 1970: 7.

Stavrou, Constantine N.   "The Neurotic Heroine in Tennessee
Williams." *Literarature and Psychology* 5 (May 1955): 26-
34.

Steiner, Robert J.   "Toward an Integrated Personality: A
Study of the Dramas of Tennessee Williams." Diss., St.
John's Univ., 1965.

Stephens, Suzanne Schaddelee.   "The Dual Influence: A Dramatic Study of the Plays of Edward Albee and the Specific
Dramatic Forms and Themes Which Influenced Them." Diss.,
Univ. of Miami, 1972. *Dissertation Abstracts International* 34 (1973): 342 A.

Steppat, Michael.   "The Inescapable Self in Modern American
Drama." *Literatur in Wissenschaft und Unterricht* 22
(1989): 313-25.

Stutzman, Ralph W.   "The Sting of Reality: The Theology of
Tennessee Williams." *Unitarian Universalist Register-
Leader* Apr. 1963: 11-13.

Styan, John L. *The Dark Comedy*.   Cambridge: Cambridge Univ.
Pr., 1968.   217-26.

---.   "Tennessee Williams: America's Chekhov." *Tennessee
Williams Review* 4.1 (1983): 8-11.

Sweeney, Patricia. *Women in Southern Literature: An Index*.
New York: Greenwood, 1986. Passim.

Taylor, William E.   "Tennessee Williams: Academia on Broadway." *Essays in Modern American Literature*. Ed. Richard

E. Langford et al. DeLand, FL: Stetson Univ. Pr., 1963.
90-96.

Tennessee Williams. Filmstrip. Peoria, IL: Klise, 197-.

"Tennessee Williams - Retrospective." *WPAT Gaslight Review*
Mar. 1966: 13, 10-49.

Tharpe, Jac, ed. *Tennessee Williams: A Tribute*. Jackson:
Univ. Pr. of Mississippi, 1977. 896 pp. Reviews:
   Book Forum 3 (Summer 1977): 420.
   Choice 14 (Feb. 1978): 1649.
   Bone, Larry Earl. *Library Journal* 102 (1 Nov. 1977):
   2263.
   Holditch, W. Kenneth. *Southern Review* 16 (Jan. 1978):
   167-69.
   Stanton, Stephen S. *Tennessee Williams Newsletter* 1.2
   (Fall 1979): 36-37.
   Young, Thomas Daniel. *Southern Quarterly* 16 (Jan.
   1978): 167-68.

---. *Tennessee Williams: 13 Essays*.... Jackson: Univ. Pr.
of Mississippi, 1980. xiv, 287 pp.

Theim, Willy H. *Tennessee Williams*. Dusseldorf: Girardet,
1956. 152 pp.

Thompson, Judith J. "The Significance of Memory, Myth, and
Symbol in the Plays of Tennessee Williams: A Recurrent
Structural Pattern." Diss., Univ. of Kansas, 1982. *Dis-
sertation Abstracts International* 43 (1983): 2671-72 A.

---. *Tennessee Williams' Plays: Memory, Myth, and Symbol*.
New York: Peter Lang, 1987. xi, 253 pp.

---. "Symbol, Myth, and Ritual in *The Glass Menagerie*, *The
Rose Tattoo*, and *Orpheus Descending*." Tharpe (above):
679-711; short ed. (above): 139-71.

Tischler, Nancy M. "The Distorted Mirror: Tennessee Williams' Self-Portraits." *Mississippi Quarterly* 25 (1972):
389-403. Rpt. Stanton (above): 158-70.

---. "A Gallery of Witches." Tharpe (above): 494-509.

---. "The South Stage Center: Hellman and Williams." *The
American South*.... Ed. Louis D. Rubin, Jr. Baton Rouge:
Louisiana State Univ. Pr., 1980. 323-33.

---. *Tennessee Williams*. Austin, TX: Steck-Vaughn, 1969.
42 pp.

---. "Tennessee Williams' Bohemian Revision of Christianity." *Susquehanna University Studies* 7 (June 1963): 103-
08.

---. *Tennessee Williams: Rebellious Puritan.* New York:
Citadel, 1961. 319 pp. Rpt. (excerpt) Bloom (A 1: *Glass
Criticism*): 91-116. Reviews:
  Booklist: see Nelson (above).
  New York Herald Tribune Books: see Nelson (above).
  Atkinson, Brooks: see Nelson (above).
  Freedley, George. *Theatre Arts* Apr. 1962: 8.
  Pine, J. C.: see Nelson (above).

Toohey, John L. *A History of the Pulitzer Prize Plays.* New
York: Citadel, 1967. 212-19, 266-75.

Toschi, Gastone. "La morbida e diabolica magia de Tennessee
Williams." *Letture* 19 (1964): 563-82.

True, Warren Roberts. "Chekhovian Dramaturgy in the Plays
of Tennessee Williams, Harold Pinter, and Ed Bullins."
Diss., Univ. of Tennessee, 1976. *Dissertation Abstracts
International* 37 (1977): 5131 A.

Tynan, Kenneth. "American Blues: The Plays of Arthur Miller
and Tennessee Williams." *Encounter* 2 (May 1954): 13-19.
Rpt. *Curtains...* (below): 257-66; Hurrell (A 1: *Streetcar*): 124-30; *The Modern American Theatre...* (Englewood
Cliffs, NJ: Prentice-Hall, 1967): 34-44.

---. "The Broadway Dilemma." *Curtains: Selections from the
Drama Criticism and Other Writings.* New York: Atheneum,
1961. 365-75.

Ulanov, Barry. *The Two Worlds of American Art: The Private
and the Popular.* New York: Macmillan, 1965. 348-54.

Usui, Yoshitaka. "Tennessee Williams, Rebel and Martyr."
English Literature (Waseda) 20 (Jan. 1962): 59-70; 21
(Mar. 1962): 42-53.

Vahland, Barbara. *Der Held als Opfer: Aspekte des Melo-
dramatischen bei Tennessee Williams.* Bern: Herbert Lang,
1976. 188 pp.

Van Decker, Lori. "A World of Light and Shadow: The Plays
of Tennessee Williams." *Columns* (Columbia Univ.) 38
(Feb. 1989): 13-21.

Van Laan, Thomas F. "'Shut Up!' 'Be Quiet!' 'Hush!' Talk
and Its Suppression in Three Plays by Tennessee Williams." *Comparative Drama* 22 (1988): 244-65.

Verkein, Lea. "Von Broadway naar Picadilly." *Vlaamse Gide*
45 (July 1961): 492-95.

Vidal, Gore. "Love, Love, Love." *Partisan Review* 26 (Fall
1959): 613-20. Rpt. *Rocking the Boat* (Boston: Little,
1962): 73-87; *Homage to Daniel Shays...* (New York: Random
House, 1972): 47-57.

Villard, Leonie. *Panorama du théâtre américain du renouveau*
1915-1962. Paris: Seghers, 1964. 251-59.

Villarino, Maria de. "La mujer en tres expresiones del teatro contemporáneo." *Revista de Estudios de Teatro* 11
(1970): 57-64.

Von Dornum, John Howard. "The Major Plays of Tennessee Williams." Diss., Univ. of Southern California, 1962. *Dissertation Abstracts* 23 (1962): 1371-72.

Vos, Nelvin. "A Kingdom Not of This Earth: The Plays of
Tennessee Williams." *Christian Scholar's Review* 13
(1984): 373-77.

Vowles, Richard B. "Tennessee Williams and Strindberg."
Modern Drama 1 (Dec. 1958): 166-71.

---. "Tennessee Williams: The World of His Imagery." *Tulane Drama Review* 3 (Dec. 1958): 51-56.

Wang, Qun. "On the Dramatization of the Illusory World in
Tennessee Williams, Arthur Miller, and Edward Albee's
Major Plays." Diss., Univ. of Oregon, 1990. *Disserta-
tion Abstracts International* 51 (1991): 2569 A.

Warren, Clifton Lanier. "Tennessee Williams as a Cinematic
Writer." Diss., Indiana Univ., 1963. *Dissertation Abstracts* 25 (1964): 489-90.

Watson, Ray A. "The Archetype of the Family in the Drama of
Tennessee Williams." Diss., Univ. of Tulsa, 1973. *Dissertation Abstracts International* 34 (1973): 1299 A.

Watts, Richard Jr. "The Magic of Tennessee Williams." *New
York Post* 19 Jan. 1958: 21.

Weales, Gerald C. *American Drama since World War II.* New
York: Harcourt, 1962. 18-39.

---. "Clifford's Children: Or It's a Wise Playwright Who
Knows His Own Father." *Studies in American Drama* 2
(1987): 3-18. [Odetts]

---. "Drama." *Harvard Guide to Contemporary American Writing.* Ed. Daniel Hoffman. Cambridge: Harvard Univ. Pr.,
1979.

---. "Drama." *Literary History of the United States.* 4th
ed. Ed. Robert E. Spiller et al. New York: Macmillan,
1974; London: Collier Macmillan, 1974. 1447-49.

---. *The Jumping-Off Place: American Drama in the 1960's.*
New York: Macmillan, 1969; London: Collier Macmillan,
1969. 3-14. Rpt. (excerpt) Stanton (above): 61-70.

---. *Tennessee Williams.* Minneapolis: Univ. of Minnesota
Pr., 1965. Revision: *American Writers...,* ed. Leonard
Ungar (New York: Scribner's, 1974), 4: 378-401.

Weissman, Philip. "Psychopathological Characters in Current
Drama: A Study of a Trio of Heroines." *American Imago* 17
(Fall 1960): 271-78. Rpt. (excerpt) *Creativity in the
Theater...* (New York: Basic, 1965.); Miller (A 1:
Streetcar): 57-64.

Wilhelm, Nancy Olivia. "Under One Roof: The Language of the
Power Struggles in Five Tennessee Williams' Plays."
Diss., Univ. of Arkansas, 1986. *Dissertation Abstracts
International* 47 (1986): 1725 A.

Willett, Ralph W. "The Ideas of Miller and Williams." *Theatre Annual* 22 (1965-66): 31-40.

Williams, Robert. *Modern Tragedy.* Stanford: Stanford Univ.
Pr., 1966; London: Chatto, 1966. 106-20.

Yacowar, Maurice. *Tennessee Williams and Film.* New York:
Ungar, 1977. viii, 168 pp. Rpt. (excerpt) Parker (A 1:
Glass Criticism): 9-14. Reviews:
    Booklist 74 (15 Dec. 1977): 654.
    Choice 15 (Mar. 1978): 82.
    West Coast Review of Books 4 (May 1977): 531.
    Deutelbaum, Marshall. *Library Journal* 102 (July 1977):
        1521.
    Kalson, Albert. *Tennessee Williams Newsletter* 1.1
        (Spring 1979): 14-15.

Zaman, Niaz. "The Confessional Art of Tennessee Williams."
Diss., George Washington Univ., 1987. *Disertation Abstracts International* 48 (1988): 2875 A.

Zlobin, G. "On the Stage and Behind the Scenes." *Inostran-
    naja Literature* 7 (July 1960): 199-210.

4. REPORTS ON CONFERENCES

Barranger, Milly S.; Dennis Vannatta; Richard Leavitt; Ken-
    neth Holditch; Virginia Carr. "The 1989 Festival's Scho-
    lars Panel." *Tennessee Williams Literary Journal* 1.2
    (Winter 1989-90): 42-54.

Clark, Judith Hersh; Lyle Taylor; Thomas P. Adler; Esther M.
    Jackson; Sy M. Kahn. "MLA Meeting." *Tennessee Williams
    Newsletter* 2.1 (Spring 1980): 46-56.

Phillips, Gene D.; S. Alan Chesler; Esther M. Jackson; Don-
    ald E. Pease, Jr. "Tennessee Williams: A Re-evaluation
    (ATA Convention)." *Tennessee Williams Newsletter* 2.2
    (Fall 1980): 53-60.

Pierson, Clare Beth. "A Persistent Dream: The Tennessee
    Williams/New Orleans Literary Festival." *Tennessee Wil-
    liams Literary Journal* 1.1 (Spring 1989): 61-64.

---. "The Tennessee Williams/New Orleans Literary Festival
    - 1989." *Tennessee Williams Literary Journal* 1.2 (Winter
    1989-90): 55-59.

"Tennessee Williams Discussed." *Stage* 16 Oct. 1958: 14.
    [Henry Adler, Ellen Pollock, Charles Marowitz on *Glass
    Menagerie*]

"The Tennessee Williams/New Orleans Literary Festival."
    Tennessee Williams Literary Journal 2.1 (Winter 1990-91):
    74-75.

5. PARODIES AND ADMONISHMENTS

Carter, Hodding. "Yes, Tennessee, There Are Southern
    Belles." *New York Times Magazine* 7 Oct. 1962: 32-33, 93.

Caruso, Joseph S. *News for Tennessee.* Unpublished play,
    1979. [Performed, Los Angeles Pilot Theatre, 1979, with
    Fred Halsted, Joseph Yale]

Duff, Jo. "It Is Easter Sunday and I Am in St. Cloud: A
    Passion Play." *National Lampoon* July 1976: 44-45. [Par-
    ody}

Highet, Gilbert. "A Memorandum." *Horizon* 1 (May 1959): 54-55.

Jacobs, Will, and Gerard Jones. *The Beaver Papers: The Story of the "Lost Season."* New York: Crown, 1983. [Parody]

Lemon, Richard. "Cinderella Descending." *Saturday Review* 16 Sept 1961: 6. [Parody]

Letter to the Editor. *National Lampoon* Nov. 1979: 8. [Parody]

"No Time like the Present: Excerpts from Issues of *Time* Magazine." *Esquire* Apr. 1963: 58-59. [Survey of criticism]

Mannes, Marya. "Something Unspeakable." *Reporter* 18 (6 Feb. 1958): 42-43. Rpt. Van Antwerp (F 1): 185-87. [Parody]

Russell, Ray. "My Gorge Rises in Flame, Cried the Phoenix." *The Little Lexicon of Love.* Los Angeles: Sherbourne, 1966. 157-70. [Parody]

"Sin-Doll Ella." *The Worst from Mad.* 2nd annual edition. New York: E.C., 1959. [Parody]

Wallach, Ira. "A Tattooed Streetcar Named Rose." *Twentieth Century Parody, American and British.* Ed. Burling Lowrey. New York: Harcourt, 1960. 204-12. [Parody]

Weaver, Lois, et al. *Belle Reprieve.* Unpublished play, 1991: see A 1 (*Streetcar*: Productions).

Welles, Joel. "Goldilocks and the Three Bears." *Grim Fairy Tales for Adults.* New York: Macmillan, 1967; London: Collier Macmillan, 1967. 21-30. [Parody]

Wilson, Albert Edward. *Playwrights in Aspic.* Denver: Univ. of Denver Pr., 1960. 118-24. [Parody]

B. SHORT STORIES AND NOVELS

This section is arranged in the same way as Section A but is much less complex. B 1 lists Williams's fiction alphabetically by title. For each title there appears its publication history in chronological order, followed by any criticism, listed alphabetically by author. Two film adaptations are also noted. Three stories that were published before 1939 appeared under the name Thomas Lanier or Tom Williams. B 2 lists collections of short stories alphabetically by title. B 3 lists general criticism alphabetically by author. One should also regard criticism listed in A 3. Reviews are entered at the appropriate places.

Williams published four collections: *One Arm*, 1948; *Hard Candy*, 1954; *The Knightly Quest*, 1966; and *Eight Mortal Ladies Possessed*, 1974. The posthumous *Collected Stories* contains 50 works (including two memoirs disguised as stories). Two other works were left uncollected. Several of these stories are works of great power and beauty. Three were chosen for inclusion in the *Best American Short Story* series. Twelve of the stories have a relationship to later plays and screenplays. And other short story treatments of materials that later appeared in play form remain in manuscript.

There were also two novels: *The Roman Spring of Mrs. Stone*, 1950, and *Moise and the World of Reason*, 1975. The former would seem, on the basis of sheer number of English editions and translations, to be Williams's most popular non-dramatic work. It even appeared briefly on the *New York Times* best seller list when it was first published. Turned into a film in 1961, the screenplay was by another writer.

1. INDIVIDUAL TITLES, WITH ADAPTATIONS

"THE ACCENT OF A COMING FOOT": Pensive story written 1935 about a couple fated to go their separate ways. Ms., Texas (G).

Collected Stories, 1985: 32-42; 1986: 34-44 (B 2).

Trans. (H): French.

"THE ANGEL IN THE ALCOVE": Autobiographical fantasy written 1943, set in a New Orleans boardinghouse. Ms, Texas (G). The story is related to the play *Vieux Carre* (A 1).

One Arm, 1948, 1954: 135-49 (B 2).

Three Players of a Summer Game, 1960: 171-81; 1965: 147-56 (B 2).

Collected Stories, 1985: 120-27; 1986: 125-32 (B 2).

The Signet Classic Book of Southern Short Stories. Ed. Dorothy Abbott and Susan Koppelman. New York: New American Library, 1990.

Trans. (H): Danish, French, German, Greek, Italian, Japanese, Spanish.

"BIG BLACK: A MISSISSIPPI IDYLL": Variation on the theme of Beauty and the Beast, set in the South. Ms., Missouri, copy Texas (G).
It won honorable mention in the 1931-32 University of Missouri short story contest.

Collected Stories, 1985: 26-31; 1986: 28-33 (B 2).

Trans. (H): French.

"CHRONICLE OF A DEMISE": Satiric story of a saint's last days in New York, written in the style of magic realism. Mss., Delaware, Texas (G).

One Arm, 1949, 1954: 71-80 (B 2).

Knightly Quest, 1968: 99-105 (B 2).

Collected Stories, 1985: 252-56; 1986: 264-68 (B 2).

Trans. (H): Danish, French, German, Greek, Italian, Japanese, Spanish.

"THE COMING OF SOMETHING TO THE WIDOW HOLLY": Quasi-science fiction story about the death of a New Orleans landlady, written 1943-53. Mss., Delaware, Texas (G).

New Directions in Prose and Poetry 14. New York: New Directions, 1953. 194-20. Review:

Poore, Charles. *New York Times* 14 Feb. 1953: 15.

Hard Candy, 1954: 163-77 (B 2).

Three Players of A Summer Game, 1960: 88-99; 1965: 75-84 (B 2).

A *New Directions Reader*. Ed. Hayden Carruth and John Laughlin. New York: New Directions, 1964. 164-73.

Collected Stories, 1985: 326-34; 1986: 344-52 (B 2).

Trans. (H): French, German, Greek, Italian, Japanese, Spanish.

"COMPLETED": Story written 1973 about an emotionally arrested Mississippi woman who retreats from the world.

Eight Mortal Ladies Possessed, 1974: 79-90 (B 2).

Collected Stories, 1985: 519-26; 1986: 551-59 (B 2).

Trans. (H): French, German, Japanese, Spanish.

"THE DARK ROOM": Dialogue between an Italian immigrant and a social worker about the plight of the woman's daughter. Ms., Texas (G).
  The work is related to the one-act play of the same title (A 1).

Collected Stories, 1985: 93-98; 1986: 97-102 (B 2).

Trans. (H): French.

"DESIRE AND THE BLACK MASSEUR": Story written 1942-46 about the murder of a closeted, masochistic homosexual. Mss., Columbia, Texas (G).

New Directions in Prose and Poetry 10. New York: New Directions, 1948. 239-46. Reviews:
    Poore, Charles. *New York Times* 9 Dec. 1948: 31.
    Smith, Harrison. *Saturday Review* 25 Dec. 1948: 9-10.

One Arm, 1948, 1954: 81-94 (B 2).

Knightly Quest, 1968: 106-15 (B 2).

Collected Stories, 1985: 205-12; 1986: 216-23 (B 2).

Trans. (H): Danish, French (inc. film version *Noir et
Blanc*), German, Greek, Italian, Japanese, Spanish.

Inclusion in Textbook

Evans, Oliver, and Harry Finestone, eds. *The World of
the Short Story: Archetypes in Action.* New York:
Knopf, 1971. 535-40.

Criticism

Hurley, Paul J. "Williams's 'Desire and the Black Masseur': An Analysis." *Studies in Short Fiction* 2 (Fall
1964): 51-55.

Schubert, Karl. "Tennessee Williams: 'Desire and the
Black Masseur' (1948)." *Die amerikanische Short Story
der Gegenwart: Interpretationen.* Ed. Peter Freese.
Berlin: Schmidt, 1976. 119-28.

"THE DONSINGER WOMAN AND THEIR HANDY MAN JACK": see E 1

"THE FIELD OF BLUE CHILDREN": Story written 1937 about a
young college girl's encounter with another student, a
would-be poet. Ms., Texas (G).
  This was Williams's first work to be published under the
name Tennessee Williams.

Story 15 (Sept.-Oct. 1939): 66-72.

One Arm, 1948, 1954: 151-66 (B 2).

Housewife 14 (Oct. 1952): 38, 83-86.

Dude 1 (Aug. 1956): 38-40, 66-67.

Three Players of a Summer Game, 1960: 138-49; 1965: 119-
28 (B 2).

Firsts of the Famous. Ed. Whit Burnett. New York: Ballantine, 1962. 224-34.

Twenty-Three Modern Stories. Ed. Barbara Hewes. New
York: Vintage, 1963. 92-102.

Mississippi Writers: Reflections of Childhood and Youth.
   Ed. Dorothy Abbott. Jackson: Univ. Pr. of Mississippi,
   1985. 1: 675-83.

Collected Stories. 1985: 70-78; 1986: 73-81 (B 2).

Trans. (H): Danish, Dutch, French, German, Greek, Italian, Japanese, Polish, Spanish.

"GIFT OF AN APPLE": Story written c. 1936 about a hitch-
   hiker's encounter with a woman living in a trailer in the
   Southwest. Ms., Texas (G).

Collected Stories, 1985: 63-69; 1986: 66-72. (B 2).

Trans. (H): French.

"GRAND": see D 1

"HAPPY AUGUST THE TENTH": Story written 1970 about two Manhattan women living in a charged lesbian atmosphere.
   Ms., California-Los Angeles (G).

Antaeus 4 (Winter 1971): 22-33.

Esquire Dec. 1972: 256-60.

The Best American Short Stories 1973.... Ed. Martha
   Foley. Boston: Houghton Mifflin, 1973. 276-88.

Eight Mortal Ladies Possessed, 1974: 1-18 (B 2).

Collected Stories, 1985: 464-76; 1986: 493-505 (B 2).

Trans. (H): French, German, Japanese, Spanish.

                              Criticism

Shuman, R. Baird. *Masterplots II: Short Story Series.*
   Ed. Frank N. Magill. Pasadena, CA: Salem, 1986. 981-
   84.

"HARD CANDY": Story written 1949-53 about an aged, un-
   attractive gay finding pleasure and death in the balcony
   of a movie theate. Mss., Columbia, Delaware, Texas (G).
   The story is a variation on the earlier story "The
   Mysteries of the Joy Rio" (below).

Hard Candy, 1954, 1959: 101-21 (B 2).

Knightly Quest, 1968: 116-31 (B 2).

Collected Stories, 1985: 335-46; 1986: 353-65 (B 2).

Trans. (H): French, German, Italian, Japanese, Spanish.

"THE IMPORTANT THING": Story of a college student's encounter with a young woman, a social misfit. Mss., Delaware, Texas (G).
   In the first version Flora was called Laura. Some editorial changes of a minor type are also found.

Story 27 (Nov.-Dec. 1945): 17-25.

One Arm, 1948, 1954: 113-24 (B 2).

Story: The Fiction of the Forties. Ed. Whit and Hallie Burnett. New York: Dutton, 1949. 38-51.

Three Players of a Summer Game, 1960: 39-55; 1965: 33-46 (B 2).

The Modern Short Story in the Making. Ed. Whit and Hallie Burnett. New York: Hawthorne, 1964. 125-39.

Story Jubilee. Ed. Whit and Hallie Burnett. Garden City: Doubleday, 1965.

Collected Stories, 1985: 163-74; 1986: 171-83 (B 2).

Trans. (H): Danish, French, German, Greek, Italian, Japanese, Spanish.

Screen Production

The Important Thing. Screenplay by Anne Borin and Peter Parnell. Anne Borin Productions, 1981. Anne Borin, dir. Cathy Dorsey, camera. With Mark Kaplan, Jackie Jacobus, Mark Bowen.

"IN MEMORY OF AN ARISTOCRAT": Portrait written 1940 about an unappreciated New Orleans artist. Ms., Texas (G).
   It was adapted to the stage by Sandra Kersten, 1991, with "Two on a Party" and "Grand" under the collective title *The Glorious Bird*.

Collected Stories, 1985: 79-92; 1986: 82-96 (B 2).

Trans. (H): French.

"THE INTERVAL": Story written 1945 about a stolid Midwestern teacher's three-year relationship with a failed
actor. Ms., Texas (G).
  The story bears some comparison with *Sweet Bird of Youth*
(A 1).

Collected Stories, 1985: 189-99; 1986: 199-210 (B 2).

Trans. (H): French.

"THE INVENTORY AT FONTANA BELLA": Story written 1972 about
the final hours of a senile Italian principessa.

Playboy 20 (Mar. 1973): 77-78, 172.

Eight Mortal Ladies Possessed, 1974: 19-29 (B 2).

Collected Stories, 1985: 477-83; 1986: 506-12 (B 2).

Trans. (H): French, German, Japanese, Spanish.

"IT HAPPENED THE DAY THE SUN ROSE": Story of sorcery and
sexual escapades in Tangier.

It Happened the Day the Sun Rose. Los Angeles: Sylvester
  & Orphanos, 1981. viii, 34 pp. Limited edition.

"THE KILLER CHICKEN AND THE CLOSET QUEEN": Comedy written
1977 about a middle-aged New York lawyer, his trying
mother, and their encounter with an amoral adolescent.

Christopher Street 3 (July 1978): 17-26.

Aphrodisiac: Fiction from Christopher Street. New York:
  Coward-McCann, 1980. 40-66.

Collected Stories, 1985: 552-70; 1986: 587-606 (B 2).

Trans. (H): French.

"THE KINGDOM OF EARTH": Story written 1942, from a first
person perspective, about a Mississippi man's supplanting
his half-brother's place. Mss., Columbia, Princeton,
Texas (G).

It was the basis for the play *Kingdom of Earth* (A 1).

The Kingdom of Earth, 1954: 223-42 (B 2).

Knightly Quest, 1966: 145-65 (B 2).

Knightly Quest, 1968: 227-41 (B 2).

Collected Stories, 1985: 268-78; 1986: 388-99 (B 2).

Trans. (H): French, German, Italian, Spanish.

"THE KNIGHTLY QUEST": Novella, partly science fiction, begun in 1949 about a gay prodigal's return to his family,
who are engaged in political manipulations.
    The work is distantly related to the play *The Red Devil
Battery Sign* (A 1).

Knightly Quest, 1966: vii-108 (B 2).

Knightly Quest, 1968: 9-90 (B 2).

Collected Stories, 1985: 398-455; 1986: 421-83 (B 2).

Trans. (H): French, German, Italian, Spanish.

"A LADY'S BEADED BAG": Social protest story about a dere-
lict's finding a rich woman's purse. Ms., Texas (G).

Columns 1 (May 1930): 11-12.

Collected Stories, 1985: 13-16; 1986: 14-17 (B 2).

Trans. (H): French.

"THE MALEDICTION": Story begun 1941 about a little man's
victimization by the mechanized world. Ms., Texas (G).
    It was the basis for the play "The Strangest Kind of
Romance" (A 1).

Town and Country 100 (June 1945): 66-67, 114-119.

One Arm, 1948, 1954: 31-57 (B 2).

Three Players of a Summer Game, 1960: 150-70; 1965: 129-
    46 (B 2).

Collected Stories, 1985: 147-62; 1986: 154-70 (B 2).

Trans. (H): Danish, French, German, Greek, Italian,
Japanese, Spanish.

"MAMA'S OLD STUCCO HOUSE": Story set in Macon, GA, about a
failed gay painter finally free of his domineering
mother. Ms., California-Los Angeles (G).

Esquire 62 (Jan. 1965): 87-90.

Esquire '65. Ed. Arnold Gingrich. New York: 1965.

London Weekend Telegraph 7 May 1965: 49-54.

Knightly Quest, 1966: 103-21 (B 2).

Knightly Quest, 1968: 197-210 (B 2).

Collected Stories, 1985: 388-97; 1986: 410-20 (B 2).

Trans. (H): French, German, Italian, Spanish.

"MAN BRING THIS UP ROAD": Story written 1953 about a failed
artist's unsuccessful encounter with a rich grimalkin in
Italy. Ms., California-Los Angeles (G).
  The story was the basis for the play *The Milk Train
Doesn't Stop Here Anymore* (A 1).

Mademoiselle 49 (July 1959): 56-61, 102.

Vogue's Gallery. London: Conde Nast, 1962. 172-84.

International (London) 1 (Spring 1965): 61-65.

Knightly Quest, 1966: 123-43 (B 2).

Knightly Quest, 1968: 211-26 (B 2).

Mayfair 2 (June 1970): 24-25, 64-67.

Collected Stories, 1985: 347-58; 1986: 366-77 (B 2).

Trans. (H): French, German, Italian, Spanish.

"THE MAN IN THE OVERSTUFFED CHAIR": see D 1

"THE MATTRESS BY THE TOMATO PATCH": Portrait of Williams's
sensual Santa Monica landlady, written 1953. Mss., Delaware, Texas (G).

London Magazine 1 (Oct. 1954): 16-24.

Hard Candy, 1954: 145-61 (B 2).

Knightly Quest, 1968: 150-62 (B 2).

American Short Stories since 1945. Ed. John Hollander.
    New York: Harper, 1968.

Collected Stories, 1985: 359-67; 1986: 378-87 (B 2).

Trans. (H): French, German, Italian, Japanese, Spanish.

"MISS COYNTE OF GREENE": Comedy written 1972 about a Mississippi woman's mission to create a new race.

Playboy 20 (Dec. 1973): 184-88, 198, 237-40.

Eight Mortal Ladies Possessed, 1974: 31-56 (B 2).

Collected Stories, 1985: 484-502; 1986: 513-33 (B 2).

Trans. (H): French, German, Japanese, Spanish.

MOISE AND THE WORLD OF REASON: Quasi-autobiographical novel
about a failed gay writer, an exhausted painter, and a
has-been playwright coming together in New York.

Moise and the World of Reason. New York: Simon &
    Schuster, 1975. Limited and trade editions. London:
    W. H. Allen, 1976. 190 pp. Reviews:
        New Yorker 26 May 1975: 118-19.
        Virginia Quarterly Review 51 (Autumn 1975): cxliv.
        Agar, John. *Library Journal* 100 (15 June 1975):
            1243.
        Barnes, Julian. *New Statesman* 91 (12 Mar. 1976):
            334.
        Blumberg, Myrna. *Times* (London) 18 Mar. 1976: 13.
        Clayton, Sylvia. *Times Literary Supplement* 12 Mar.
            1976: 283. Response: *Times Literary Supplement*:
            18 Mar. 1976: 13.
        Devere, John. *Mandate* July 1975: 8.
        Fallowell, Duncan. *Spectator* 236 (20 Mar. 1976):
            23.

Hirsch, Foster. *New Republic* 24 May 1975: 24-25.
    Rpt. Van Antwerp (F 1): 295-97.
Lehmann-Haupt, Christopher. *New York Times* 15 May
    1975: 41.
Neville, Jill. *Sunday Times* (London) 7 Mar. 1976:
    41.
Roosevelt, Karyl. *New York Times Book Review* 13
    July 1975: 26-28.
Sager, Lorna. *London Observer* 7 Mar. 1976: 27.
Thompson, R. J. *Best Sellers* 35 (Aug. 1975): 114.

Moise and the World of Reason. New York: Bantam, 1976.
    viii, 214 pp.

Trans. (H): French, German, Italian, Japanese, Portu-
    guese, Spanish.

"MOTHER YAWS": Story about a slow-minded Tennessee woman
afflicted by both a disease and an unfeeling family.

Esquire 87 (May 1977): 78-80.

Collected Stories, 1985: 544-51; 1986: 578-86 (B 2).

Trans. (H): French.

"THE MYSTERIES OF THE JOY RIO": Story written 1939-41 about
an aged gay who returns to the movie theatre that had
brought him youthful pleasures and who there finds death.
Ms., Delaware (G).
    "Hard Candy" (above) is a later variation on the same
theme.

Hard Candy, 1954: 201-20 (B 2).

Knightly Quest, 1968: 181-96 (B 2).

Collected Stories, 1985: 99-109; 1986: 103-14 (B 2).

Trans. (H): French, German, Italian, Spanish.

"THE NIGHT OF THE IGUANA": Story written 1946-48 about a
nervous painter and her encounter with two gay writers in
Mexico. Mss., Delaware, Texas (G).
    The story distantly foreshadows the play of the same
title (A 1).

One Arm, 1948, 1954: 167-96 (B 2).

Three Players of a Summer Game, 1960: 200-23; 1965: 173-93 (B 2).

Collected Stories, 1985: 229-45; 1986: 240-57 (B 2).

Trans. (H):   Danish, French, German, Greek, Italian, Japanese, Spanish.

"ONE ARM":   Story written 1942-45 about a hustler's execution in New Orleans. Ms., Texas (G).
A screenplay *One Arm* (A 1) grew out of the story.

One Arm, 1948, 1954, 1967: 5-29 (B 2).

Three Players of a Summer Game, 1960: 56-74; 1965: 47-62 (B 2).

Collected Stories, 1985: 175-88; 1986: 184-98 (B 2).

Trans. (H):   Danish, French, German, Greek, Italian, Japanese, Spanish.

"ORIFLAMME":   Symbolic story about death and anarchy, written 1937-44: a Mississippi woman's epipany in St. Louis. Ms., Texas (G).

"Red Part of a Flag, or Oriflamme." *Vogue* 163 (Mar. 1974): 124, 158-59.

"Oriflame." *Eight Mortal Ladies Possessed*, 1974: 91-100 (B 2).

Same. *Collected Stories*, 1985: 128-33; 1986: 133-39 (B 2).

Trans. (H):   French, German, Japanese, Spanish.

"THE POET":   Symbolic story about the death of a visionary. Ms., Delaware (G).

One Arm, 1948, 1954: 59-69 (B 2).

Knightly Quest, 1968: 91-98 (B 2).

Collected Stories, 1985: 246-51; 1986: 258-63 (B 2).

Trans. (H):   Danish, French, German, Greek, Italian, Japanese, Spanish.

"PORTRAIT OF A GIRL IN GLASS": Autobiographical story written 1941-43 about a young St. Louis woman living in a world of illusions. Mss., Columbia, Texas (G).
   The plot and characters are much the same as those in *The Glass Menagerie* (A 1) but with several interesting variations.

One Arm, 1948, 1954: 95-112 (B 2).

Three Players of a Summer Game, 1960: 75-87; 1965: 63-74 (B 2).

Mississippi Writers: Reflections of Childhood and Youth. Ed. Dorothy Abbott. Jackson: Univ. Pr. of Mississippi, 1985. 1: 684-93.

Collected Stories, 1985: 110-19; 1986: 115-24 (B 2).

Trans. (H): Danish, French, German, Greek, Hungarian, Italian, Japanese, Spanish, Swedish.

Inclusion in Textbooks

Gassner, John, and Ralph G. Allen, eds. *Theatre and Drama in the Making.* Boston: Houghton Mifflin, 1964. 840-48.

Meyer, Michael, ed. *The Bedford Introduction to Literature.* New York: St. Martin's, 1987. 445-52.

"A RECLUSE AND HIS GUEST": Allegorical story recounting an encounter between an androgynous traveller and a fearful hermit in central Europe. Ms., California-Los Angeles (G).

Playboy 17 (Jan. 1970): 101-02, 124, 244.

Collected Stories, 1985: 456-63; 1986: 484-92 (B 2).

Trans. (H): French.

"RED PART OF A FLAG": see "Oriflamme"

"THE RESEMBLANCE BETWEEN A VIOLIN CASE AND A COFFIN": Autobiographical story written 1949 about a Mississippi boy's and his sister's encounter with a teenage violinist. Mss., Delaware, Texas (G).

Flair 1 (Feb. 1950): 40-41, 126-28.

Penguin New Writing 40.   Harmondsworth: Penguin, 1950.
    13-28.

The Best American Short Stories 1951.   Ed. Martha Foley.
    Boston: Houghton Mifflin, 1951.   338-50.   Review:
    Peden, William.   *Saturday Review* 18 Aug. 1951: 17.

Hard Candy, 1954: 79-100 (B 2).

Three Players of a Summer Game, 1960: 182-99; 1965: 157-
    72 (B 2).

Collected Stories, 1985: 270-82; 1986: 283-96 (B 2).

Trans. (H):   French, German, Italian, Japanese, Spanish.

Criticism

Shuman, R. Baird.   *Masterplots II: Short Story Series.*
    Ed. Frank N. Magill.   Pasadena, CA: Salem, 1986.   1933-
    36.

THE ROMAN SPRING OF MRS. STONE: Novel about an aging movie
star coming to a decisive meeting with a young hustler in
Rome.   Mss., Columbia, Delaware, Princeton, Texas (G).
Gavin Lambert wrote the screenplay, 1961.

The Roman Spring of Mrs. Stone.   New York: New Direc-
    tions, 1950.   viii, 148 pp.   Limited and trade edi-
    tions.   New York: New Directions, 1969: Toronto:
    McClelland & Stewart, 1969.   New Directions Paperbook.
    Reviews:
        Atlantic Nov. 1950: 101.
        Booklist 47 (1 Oct. 1950); 62.
        Kirkus 18 (15 July 1950): 395.
        New York Herald Tribune 7 Aug. 1950: 11.
        New Yorker 25 Nov. 1950: 149-50.
        Newsweek 9 Oct. 1950: 94.
        Theatre Arts Nov. 1950: 2.
        Time 30 Oct. 1950: 109.   Rpt. Van Antwerp (F 1):
            127-28.
        Alpert, Hollis.   *Saturday Review* 30 Sept. 1950: 18.
        Crandall, Norma.   *New Republic* 22 Jan. 1951: 20.
        Freedley, George.   *Library Journal* 75 (1 Sept.
            1950): 1409.
        ---.   *New York Morning Telegraph* 14 Aug. 1950: 2.
        Gannet, Lewis.   *New York Herald Tribune* 6 Dec. 1950:
            31.

Geismar, Maxwell. *New York Post* 15 Oct. 1950, sec.
M: 16.
Hayes, Alfred. *New York Herald Tribune Book Review*
22 Oct. 1950: 14.
McLaughlin, Richard. *New Leader* 30 Oct. 1950: 23.
Miles, George. *Commonweal* 53 (3 Nov. 1950): 99-100.
Popkin, Henry. *Theatre Arts* Nov. 1950: 2-4.
Prescott, Orville. *New York Times* 29 Sept. 1950:
25.
Rolo, Charles J. *Atlantic* Nov. 1950: 101.
---. *New York Times Book Review* 1 Oct. 1950: 4.
Sheaffer, Louis. *Brooklyn Daily Eagle* 17 Oct. 1950:
8.

The Roman Spring of Mrs. Stone. London: John Lehmann,
1950. London: Secker & Warburg, 1957. 126 pp.
Review:
Shrapnel, Norman. *Manchester Guardian* 15 Dec. 1950:
5.

The Roman Spring of Mrs. Stone. Signet Book. New York:
New American Library, 1952. 141 pp.

The Roman Spring of Mrs. Stone. New York: New American
Library, 1961. Signet Book. Ils. New York: Bantam,
1976. 128 pp.

The Roman Spring of Mrs. Stone. Frogmore, St. Albans:
Panther, 1977. 111 pp.

The Roman Spring of Mrs. Stone. New York: Ballantine,
1985. 150 pp. Ils.

The Roman Spring of Mrs. Stone. Audiocassette read by
Shirley Knight. Downsview, Ont.: Listen for Pleasure,
1986.

Trans. (H): Bulgarian, Czech, Danish, Dutch, Finnish,
French, German, Greek, Hebrew, Italian, Japanese, Per-
sian, Portuguese, Russian, Serbo-Croatian, Slovak,
Slovene, Spanish, Swedish, Turkish.

Criticism

Gerard, Albert. "The Eagle and the Star: Symbolic Motifs
in *The Roman Spring of Mrs. Stone.*" *English Studies* 36
(Aug. 1955): 145-53.

Gómez García, Ascensión: see A 1 (*Rose Tattoo*: Criticism)

Hyman, Stanley Edgar.   "Some Trends in the Novel."   *College English* 20 (Oct. 1958): 2-9.

Screenplay

Lambert, Gavin.   *"The Roman Spring of Mrs. Stone*: Script Extract."   *Films and Filming* 8 (Oct. 1961): 20-21, 38.

Screen Production

The Roman Spring of Mrs. Stone.   Screenplay by Gavin Lambert. Seven Arts Production.   Warner Brothers film, 24 Nov. 1961 (première).   José Quintero, dir.   Harry Warman, camera.   Herbert Smith, design.   Richard Addinsell, Paddy Roberts, music.   With Vivien Leigh (Karen), Warren Beatty (Paolo), Lotte Lenya (Contessa).   Reviews, Prod. Notes:

   Filmfacts 4 (1961): 329.

   New York Times Magazine 16 Apr. 1961: 72.

   Newsweek 1 Jan. 1962: 53.

   Time 29 Dec. 1961: 57.

   Beckley, Paul V.   *New York Herald Tribune* 29 Dec. 1961: 9.

   Cameron, Kate.   *New York Sunday News* 17 Dec. 1961, sec. 2: 3.

   Coleman, John.   *New Statesman* 63 (23 Feb. 1962): 273.

   Crowther, Bosley.   *New York Times* 29 Dec. 1961: 11. Rpt. *New York Times Film Reviews.*

   Dent, Alan.   *Illustrated London News* 240 (3 Mar. 1962): 346.

   Edwards, Anne.   *Vivien Leigh....*   New York: Simon, 1977.   241-46.

   Fitzpatrick, Ellen.   *Films in Review* 13 (Jan. 1962): 42-43.

   Gill, Brendan.   *New Yorker* 13 Jan. 1962: 97-98.

   Gow, Gordan.   *Films and Filming* Oct. 1961: 91, 37. [Interview with Quintero]

   Hale, Wanda.   *New York Daily News* 29 Dec. 1961: 48.

   Hartung, Philip T.   *Commonweal* 75 (29 Dec. 1961): 365-66.

   Hodgens, R. M.   *Film Quarterly* 15 (Spring 1962): 72.

   Knight, Arthur.   *Saturday Review* 9 Dec. 1961: 28.

   Mekas, Jonas.   *Village Voice* 1 Feb. 1962: 11.

   Quigly, Isabel.   *Spectator* 208 (23 Feb. 1962): 242.

   Quintero, Jose.   *If You Don't Dance They Beat You.* Boston: Little, Brown, 1974.   266-76.

   Thomson, David.   *Warren Beatty and Desert Eyes.*   Garden City: Doubleday, 1987.   126-32.

   Wald, Richard C.   *New York Herald Tribune* 1 Jan. 1961, sec. 4: 9.

   Walsh, Moira.   *America* 106 (13 Jan. 1962): 481.

Watts, Stephen. *New York Times* 15 Jan. 1961, sec. 2:
   7.
Winston, Archer. *New York Post* 29 Dec. 1961: 25.
Wyndham, Francis. *Sight and Sound* 31 (Spring 1962):
   92-93.

"RUBIO Y MORENA": Story about a writer's infidelity to the
Mexican-American with whom he lives. Ms., Delaware,
Texas (G).

Partisan Review 15 (Dec. 1948): 1293-1306.

New Directions in Prose and Poetry 11. New York: New
   Directions, 1949. 459-71.

Hard Candy, 1954: 123-44 (B 2).

Knightly Quest, 1968: 132-49 (B 2).

Collected Stories, 1985: 257-69; 1986: 269-82 (B 2).

Trans. (H): French, German, Italian, Japanese, Spanish.

Criticism

Hyman, Stanley Edgar. "Some Notes on the Albertine Stra-
   tegy." *Hudson Review* 6 (Autumn 1953): 416-22.

"SABBATHA AND SOLITUDE": Story written 1973 about a poet,
now forgotten by her public.

Playgirl 1 (Sept. 1973): 49-51, 122-24, 129.

Eight Mortal Ladies Possessed, 1974: 57-78 (B 2).

Collected Stories, 1985: 503-18; 1986: 534-50 (B 2).

Trans. (H): French, German, Japanese, Spanish.

"SAND": Portrait written 1936 of an aged couple after the
husband has suffered a stroke. Ms., Texas (G).

Collected Stories, 1985: 49-53; 1986: 52-56 (B 2).

Trans. (H): French.

"SOMETHING ABOUT HIM":   Story about a Mississippi librarian
in love with a clerk whom nobody else likes.

Mademoiselle 23 (June 1946): 168-69, 135-39.

Collected Stories, 1985: 213-20; 1986: 224-31 (B 2).

Trans. (H): French.

"SOMETHING BY TOLSTOI":   Story about a wife who leaves her
husband and then returns fifteen years later to find
their former life has become for him a work of fiction.
Ms., Missouri, copy Texas (G).
    It won honorable mention in the 1930-31 University of
Missouri short story contest.

Collected Stories, 1985: 17-25; 1986: 18-27 (B 2).

Sunday Times (London) 3 Aug. 1986: 26-28. Inc. Gore
    Vidal, Introduction to *Collected Stories* (B 2).

Trans. (H): French.

"STELLA FOR STAR":   Winner of 1935 St. Louis Writers Guild
contest; apparently unpublished. Ms., Texas (G).

"TEN MINUTE STOP":   Story written 1936 about a young man who
gets off the bus in Illinois. Ms., Texas (G).

Collected Stories, 1985: 54-62; 1986: 57-65 (B 2).

Trans. (H): French.

"TENT WORMS":   Written 1945, dialogue between a woman and
her husband on Cape Cod, the man not knowing he has a
fatal disease.
    The unfinished and unpublished play "Masks Outrageous
and Austere" is related.

Esquire 93 (May 1980): 70-72.

Collected Stories, 1985: 200-04; 1986: 211-15 (B 2).

Sudden Fiction: American Short-Short Stories. Ed. Robert
    Shapard and James Thomas. Layton, UT: Gibbs M. Smith,
    1986. 96-100.

Trans. (H): French.

"THREE PLAYERS OF A SUMMER GAME": Story written 1951-52
about a Mississippi alcoholic's relationship with a young
widow and her daughter, seen through the eyes of a neigh-
boring boy. Ms., Delaware, Texas (G).
   William Hawkins (*Saturday Review*, 21 June 1952: 32) des-
cribes Williams reading the unpublished story. It is a
distant basis for *Cat on a Hot Tin Roof* (A 1) and was
itself presented in 1955 as a "staged story" (A 1).

New Yorker 28 (1 Nov. 1952): 27-36.

The Best American Short Stories 1953. Ed. Martha Foley.
   Boston: Houghton Mifflin, 1953. 363-83.

Hard Candy, 1954: 7-44 (B 2).

Perspectives USA 11 (Spring 1955): 15-39.

Three Players of a Summer Game, 1960: 7-38; 1965: 7-32;

Stories from the New Yorker, 1950-1960. New York: Simon,
   1960; London: Gollancz, 1961.

Stories of Modern America. Ed. Herbert Gold and David C.
   Stevenson. New York: St. Martin's, 1961.

Fifty Best American Short Stories 1915-1965. Ed. Martha
   Foley. Boston: Houghton Mifflin, 1965. New York:
   Avenel, 1986. 466-87.

Collected Stories, 1985: 303-25; 1986: 319-43 (B 2).

Trans. (H): Danish, Dutch, French, German, Italian,
   Greek, Japanese, Spanish.

                          Criticism

May, Charles E.: see A 1 (*Cat*, Criticism).

Reck, Tom S. "The First *Cat on a Hot Tin Roof*: Williams'
   'Three Players.'" *University Review* (Kansas City, MO)
   34 (1968): 187-92.

"TWENTY-SEVEN WAGONS FULL OF COTTON": Story written 1935
about the seduction of an Arkansas woman. Ms., Texas
(G).

It is the basis for the play "27 Wagons Full of Cotton"
(A 1), which in turn was largely the basis for the
screenplay *Baby Doll* (A 1).

Manuscript 3 (August 1936): 25–28.

Collected Stories, 1985: 43–48; 1986: 45–51 (B 2).

Trans. (H): French.

"TWO ON A PARTY": Story finished 1952 about an Alabama gay
teamed up with a Louisiana lush. Mss., Delaware, Texas
(G).
The 1952 version is considerably shorter than the 1954.
It was adapted to the stage by Sandra Kersten, 1991 (see
"In Memory of an Aristocrat" above).

Panorama Spring 1952: 31–36.

Hard Candy, 1954: 45–78 (B 2).

Three Players of a Summer Game, 1960: 100–27; 1965: 85–
108 (B 2).

*The Other Persuasion: An Anthology of Short Fiction about
Gay Men and Women*. Ed. Seymour Kleinberg. New York:
Vintage, 1977. 175–94.

Collected Stories, 1985: 283–302; 1986: 297–318 (B 2).

Trans. (H): French, German, Greek, Italian, Japanese,
Spanish.

"THE VENGEANCE OF NITOCRIS": Story written 1927 (when Williams was 16) about an Egyptian queen's revenge against
her brother's murderers, though he was killed for having
committed sacrilege.
The melodramatic story was Williams's second publication
in a national magazine.

Weird Tales 12 (Aug. 1928): 253–60, 280.

Gamma 1 (1963): 27–38.

Famous Short Stories. Ed. Kurt Singer. Minneapolis:
Denison, 1968. Vol. 1.

The Pulps: Fifty Years of American Pop Cultue. Ed. Roy
Goodstone. New York: Chelsea House, 1970. 167–72.

Masterpieces of Terror and the Supernatural.... Ed. Marvin Kaye. New York: Dorset, 1985. 448-58.

Collected Stories, 1985: 1-12; 1986: 1-13 (B 2).

Trans. (H): French, Japanese.

"THE VINE": Story written 1939-44 about the near dissolution of two New York actors' marriage. Mss., Delaware,
Texas (G).

Mademoiselle 39 (July 1954): 25-30, 93. Winner of the
Benjamin Franklin Magazine Award for Excellence.

Hard Candy, 1954: 179-200 (B 2).

40 Best Stories from Mademoiselle, 1935-1960. Ed.
Cyrilly Abels and Margarita G. Smith. New York: Harper, 1960. 296-308.

Knightly Quest, 1968: 163-80 (B 2).

Collected Stories, 1985: 134-46; 1986: 140-53 (B 2).

Trans. (H): French, German, Italian, Japanese, Spanish.

"DAS WASSER IST KALT": Story of a Georgia college teacher
facing death in Italy. Ms., Delaware (G).

Antaeus 40/41 (Winter-Spring 1981): 230-46.

Collected Stories, 1985: 527-43; 1986: 560-77 (B 2).

Trans. (H): French.

"THE YELLOW BIRD": Story of an Arkansas minister's daughter's rebellion. Ms., Delaware, Texas (G).
    After the story was collected in *One Arm*, Williams read
a slightly revised version for a recording (E 1). The
second edition of *One Arm* reflected these changes. The
work distantly foreshadows *Summer and Smoke* (A 1), a bit
more closely *The Eccentricities of a Nightingale* (A 1).

Town and Country 101 (June 1947) 40-41, 102-07.

One Arm, 1948: 198-210; 1954: 198-211 (B 2).

Best Tales of the Deep South.   Ed. Malcolm Cowley.   New
    York: Lion, 1955.   128-35.

Three Players of a Summer Game, 1960: 128-37; 1965: 109-
    18 (B 2).

Stories of the Modern South.   Ed. Ben Forkner and Patrick
    Samway.   New York: Bantam, 1978.   408-15.   New York:
    Penguin, 1981.   424-31.

Collected Stories, 1985: 221-28; 1986: 232-39 (B 2).

A *Collection of Classic Southern Humor.*   Ed. George Wil-
    liam Koon.   Atlanta: Peachtree, 1986.   2: 15-23.

Trans. (H):   Danish, French, German, Greek, Italian, Jap-
    anese, Spanish.

Inclusion in Textbook

Rehder, Jessie C, ed.   *The Story at Work....*   New York:
    Odyssey, 1963.   327-35.

2.   COLLECTIONS

Collected Stories with an Introduction by Gore Vidal.   New
    York: New Directions, 1985; Markham, Ont.: Penguin Books
    Canada, 1985; London: London: Secker & Warburg, 1986; London:
    Pen, 1988.   Picador Classic.   xviii, 574 pp.   Contents:
    Preface: "The Man in the Overstuffed Chair," vii-xvi;
    Introduction by Gore Vidal, xix-xxv; "The Vengeance of
    Nitocris," 1-12; "A Lady's Beaded Bag," 13-16; "Something
    by Tolstoi," 17-25; "Big Black: A Mississippi Idyll," 26-
    31; "The Accent of a Coming Foot," 32-42; "Twenty-Seven
    Wagons Full of Cotton," 43-48; "Sand," 49-53; "Ten Minute
    Stop," 54-62; "Gift of an Apple," 63-69; "The Field of
    Blue Children," 70-78; "In Memory of an Aristocrat," 79-
    92; "The Dark Room," 93-98; "The Mysteries of the Joy
    Rio," 99-109; "Portrait of a Girl in Glass," 110-19; "The
    Angel in the Alcove," 120-27; "Oriflamme," 128-33; "The
    Vine," 134-46; "The Malediction," 147-62; "The Important
    Thing," 163-74; "One Arm," 175-88; "The Interval," 189-
    99; "Tent Worms," 200-04; "Desire and the Black Masseur,"
    205-12; "Something about Him," 213-20; "The Yellow Bird,"
    221-28; "The Night of the Iguana," 229-45; "The Poet,"
    246-51; "Chronicle of a Demise," 252-56; "Rubio y
    Morena," 257-69; "The Resemblance between a Violin Case
    and a Coffin," 270-82; "Two on a Party," 283-302; "Three
    Players of a Summer Game," 303-25; "The Coming of Some-

thing to the Widow Holly," 326-34; "Hard Candy," 335-46;
"Man Bring This Up Road," 347-58; "The Mattress by the
Tomato Patch," 359-67; "The Kingdom of Earth," 368-78;
"'Grand,'" 379-87; "Mama's Old Stucco House," 388-97;
"The Knightly Quest," 398-455; "A Recluse and His Guest,"
456-63; "Happy August the Tenth," 464-76; "The Inventory
at Fontana Bella," 477-83; "Miss Coynte of Greene," 484-
502; "Sabbatha and Solitude," 503-18; "Completed," 519-
26; "Das Wasser ist kalt," 527-43; "Mother Yaws," 544-51;
"The Killer Chicken and the Closet Queen," 552-70; Bibli-
ographical Notes, 571- 74.   Reviews:
  Booklist 82 (1 Oct. 1985): 193.
  Kirkus Review 53 (15 Aug. 1985): 830.
  Publisher's Weekly 228 (6 Sept. 1985): 57.
  Brondoli, Michael. *USA Today* 19 Feb. 1986.
  Goldstein, W. *Publishers Weekly* 227 (7 June 1985): 66.
    [Announcement]
  Hendrick, George. *World Literature Today* 60 (Summer
    1986): 471.
  Kakutani, Michiko. *New York Times* 9 Nov. 1985, sec. 1:
    15.
  May, Charles E. *Magill's Literary Annual* 1986. Engle-
    wood Cliffs, NJ: Salem, 1986: 170-74.
  Norris, Gloria. *America* 154 (17 May 1986): 414-15.
  Phillips, Robert. *Commonweal* 113 (14 Mar. 1986): 156.
  Price, Reynolds. *New York Times Book Review* 1 Dec.
    1985: 11.
  Tischler, Nancy Marie. *Choice* 23 (1986): 1068.
  Vogel, Carl. *Library Journal* 110 (15 Oct. 1985): 104.

Collected Stories. New York: Ballantine, 1986. 611 pp.

Eight Mortal Ladies Possessed: A Book of Stories. New York:
  New Directions, 1974; Toronto: McClelland & Stewart,
  1974. Also New Directions Paperbook. London: Secker &
  Warburg, 1974. viii, 100 pp. Contents: "Happy August
  the Tenth," 1-18; "The Inventory of Fontana Bella," 19-
  29; "Miss Coynte of Greene," 31-56; "Sabbatha and Solitude," 57-78; "Completed," 79-90; "Oriflame," 91-100.
  Reviews:
    Choice 11 (Jan. 1975): 1636.
    Sunday Times (London) 29 June 1975: 31.
    Adler, Jacob H. *Southern Literary Journal* 8 (Fall
      1975): 165-69.
    Annan, Gabriele. *Times Literary Supplement* 1 Aug.
      1975: 865.
    Bailey, Paul. *New Statesman* 4 July 1975: 29.
    Barras, Leonard. *Sunday Times* (London) 29 June 1975:
      31.
    Levy, Francis. *Village Voice* 26 Sept. 1974: 33.
    Malin, Irvin. *New Republic* 14 Sept. 1974: 27-28.

O'Faolain, Julia. *London Observer* 3 Aug. 1975: 21.
Peden, William. *Sewanee Review* 82 (Fall 1974): 712-29.
Phillips, Robert. *Commonweal* 102 (11 Apr. 1975): 55-
   57.
Portis, Rowe. *Library Journal* 99 (1 Apr. 1974): 1060.
Rorem, Ned. *Saturday Review/World* 21 Sept. 1974: 24-
   26. Rpt. *London Magazine* 15 (June-July 1975): 68-
   74; *An Absolute Gift*.... (New York: Simon, 1978):
   169-77; Van Antwerp (F 1): 293-95.
White, Edmund. *New York Times Book Review* 6 Oct. 1974:
   14. Rpt. Vannatta (B 3): 115-16.

Hard Candy: A Book of Stories. New York: New Directions,
   1954. Limited edition. New York: New Directions, 1959.
   Trade edition. New York: New Directions, 1967; Toronto:
   McClelland & Stewart, 1967. New Directions Paperbook.
   220 pp. Contents: "Three Players of a Summer Game," 7-
   44; "Two on a Party," 45-78; "The Resemblance between a
   Violin Case and a Coffin," 79-100; "Hard Candy," 101-21;
   "Rubio y Morena," 123-44; "The Mattress by the Tomato
   Patch," 145-61; "The Coming of Something to the Widow
   Holly," 163-77; "The Vine," 179-200; "The Mysteries of
   the Joy Rio," 201-20.   Reviews:
      Adams, J. Donald. *New York Times Book Review* 7 Aug.
      1959: 2.
      Freedley, George. *New York Morning Telegraph* 28 Sept.
      1954: 2.

Hard Candy and Other Stories. Modern English Series. Ed.
   Motoo Takigawa & Tadamasa Shima. Tokyo: Kinseido, 1967.
   [Selection]

The Kingdom of Earth, with Hard Candy: A Book of Stories.
   New York: New Directions, 1954. 242 pp. Limited Edition, not for sale. Contents: same as *Hard Candy*, 1954,
   plus "The Kingdom of Earth," 223-42.

The Knightly Quest: A Novella and Four Short Stories. New
   York: New Directions, 1966. viii, 103 pp. Contents:
   "The Knightly Quest," vii-101; "Mama's Old Stucco House,"
   103-21; "Man Bring This Up Road," 123-43; "The Kingdom of
   Earth," 145-65; "'Grand,'" 167-83. Reviews:
      Critic 25 (June 1967): 90.
      National Observer 6 Mar. 1967: 23.
      New York Times 25 Jan. 1967: 40.
      Time 10 Mar. 1967: 102.
      Atkinson, Brooks. *Saturday Review* 25 Feb. 1967: 53.
      Rpt. Van Antwerp (F 1): 244-46.
      Gaines, Ervin J. *Library Journal* 92 (15 Apr. 1967):
      1647.

Howard, Maureen. *Partisan Review* 35 (Winter 1968):
141-52.
Pryce-Jones, Alan. *New York World-Journal Tribune* 28
Feb. 1967: 24.
Quinn, J. J. *Best Sellers* 26 (1 Mar. 1967): 440.
Sheffer, Isaiah. *New Leader* 5 June 1967: 23-24.
Wakeman, John. *New York Times Book Review* 2 Apr. 1967:
4.
Zimmerman, Paul D. *Newsweek* 27 Feb. 1967: 92-94.

The Knightly Quest: A Novella and Twelve Short Stories.
London: Secker & Warburg, 1968. 253 pp. Contents:
"The Knightly Quest," 9-90; "The Poet," 91-98; "Chronicle
of a Demise," 99-105; "Desire and the Black Masseur,"
106-15; "Hard Candy," 116-31; "Rubio y Morena," 132-49;
"The Mattress by the Tomato Patch," 150-62; "The Vine,"
163-80; "The Mysteries of the Joy Rio," 181-96; "Mama's
Old Stucco House," 197-210; "Man Bring This Up Road,"
211-26; "The Kingdom of Earth," 227-41; "'Grand,'" 242-
53. Reviews:
   Times Literary Supplement 11 July 1968: 721.
   Price, R. G. G. *Punch* 255 (24 July 1968): 135.
   Scannell, Vernon. *New Statesman* 76 (12 July 1968): 56.
   Tomalin, Claire. *London Observer* 7 July 1968: 27.

One Arm and Other Stories. New York: New Directions, 1948.
iv, 210 pp. Limited edition. Contents: "One Arm," 5-
29; "The Malediction," 31-57; "The Poet," 59-69; "Chronicle of a Demise," 71-80; "Desire and the Black Masseur,"
81-94; "Portrait of a Girl in Glass," 95-112; "The Important Thing," 113-34; "The Angel in the Alcove," 135-49;
"The Field of Blue Children," 151-66, "The Night of the
Iguana," 167-96; "The Yellow Bird," 198-210.

One Arm and Other Stories. New York: New Directions, 1954.
Trade edition. New York: New Directions, 1967; Toronto:
McClelland & Stewart, 1967. New Directions Paperbook.
iv, 211 pp. Contents: same as limited edtion except
revised "Yellow Bird," 198-211. Reviews:
   New York Times 5 June 1955: 36.
   Time 3 Jan. 1955: 76.
   Cooperman, Stanley. *Nation* 180 (18 Mar. 1955): 244.
   Engle, Paul. *New Republic* 24 Jan. 1955: 26-27.
   Freedley, George. *New York Morning Telegraph* 13 Apr.
   1955: 3.
   Kelly, James. *New York Times Book Review* 2 Jan. 1955:
   5. Rpt. Vannatta (B 3): 113-14.
   Peden, William H. *Saturday Review* 8 Jan. 1955: 11-12.
   Rpt. Van Antwerp (A 3): 112-13.
   Roth, Robert. *Chicago Review* 9 (Summer 1955): 86-94.

One Arm and Other Stories.   Ed. Motoo Takigawa and Tadamasa
Shima.   Tokyo: Eihosha, 1962.   120 pp.   [Selection]

Three Players of a Summer Game and Other Stories.   London:
Secker & Warburg, 1960.   223 pp.   London/Melbourne: J. M.
Dent, 1984.   Everyman.   Contents: "Three Players of a
Summer Game," 7-38; "The Important Thing," 39-55; "One
Arm," 56-74; "Portrait of a Girl in Glass," 75-87; "The
Coming of Something to the Widow Holly," 88-99; "Two on a
Party," 100-27; "The Yellow Bird," 128-37; "The Field of
Blue Children," 138-49; "The Malediction," 150-70; "The
Angel in the Alcove," 171-81; "The Resemblance between a
Violin Case and a Coffin," 182-99; "The Night of the
Iguana," 200-23.

Three Players of a Summer Game and Other Stories.   Harmondsworth: Penguin Books, 1965.   193 pp.

3.   CRITICISM

Adler, Thomas.   *Critical Survey of Short Fiction*.   Ed. Frank
N. Magill.   Englewood Cliffs, NJ: Salem, 1981.   2433-40.

Cherry, Grady.   "Life and Art: A Classification of the
Artist-Figure in Selected Fiction of Tennessee Williams."
Diss., Texas A&M University, 1977.   *Dissertation Ab-
stracts International* 38 (1977): 2121 A.

Clark, Judith Hersh.   "The Victims in 'A Recluse and His
Guest' and 'Mother Yaws.'"   *Tennessee Williams Newsletter*
1.1 (Spring 1979): 8-10.

Clum, John M.:   see A 3

Creff, Bernard.   "Dans l'intimité de Tennessee Williams: Ses
nouvelles."   Sarotte (A 3): 115-19.

Draya, Ren.   "The Fiction of Tennesee Williams."   Tharpe (A
3): 647-62.

---:   see A 3

Goodfarb, Rowena Davis.   "Heroic Gestures: Five Short
Stories as Sources for the Plays of Tennessee Williams."
Diss., Fordham Univ., 1988.   *Dissertation Abstracts
International* 49 (1988): 817 A.

Grande, Luke M.   "Metaphysics of Alienation in Tennessee
    Williams' Short Stories." *Drama Critique* 4 (Nov. 1961):
    118-22.

Lemaire, Marcel.   "Fiction in U.S.A. from the South." *Revue
    des Langues Vivantes* 27 (1966): 244-53.

Peden, William H.   "Mad Pilgrimage: The Short Stories of
    Tennessee Williams." *Studies in Short Fiction* 1 (Summer
    1964): 243-50. Rpt. Vannatta (below): 116-23.

Ramaswamy, S.   "The Short Stories of Tennessee Williams."
    Indian Studies in American Fiction. Ed. M. K. Naih et
    al. Delhi: Macmillan India, 1974. 263-85.

Reck, Tom S.   "The Fiction of Tennessee Williams." Diss.,
    Univ. of Texas-Austin, 1967.

---.   "The Short Stories of Tennessee Williams: Nucleus for
    His Drama." *Tennessee Studies in Literature* 16 (1971):
    141-54.

Sklepowich, Edward A.   "In Pursuit of the Lyric Quarry: The
    Image of the Homosexual in Tennessee Williams' Prose Fic-
    tion." Tharpe (A 3): 525-44. Rpt. Vannatta (below):
    124-28.

Summers, Claude J. *Gay Fictions, Wilde to Stonewall:
    Studies in Male Homosexual Literary Tradition*. New York:
    Continuum, 1990. 133-55.

Vannatta, Dennis. *Tennessee Williams: A Study of the Short
    Fiction*. Boston: Twayne, 1988. xii, 142 pp.

C. POEMS AND LYRICS

C 1 lists Williams poems and songs alphabetically by
title. Poems published through 1942 (marked *) appeared
under the name Thomas Lanier Williams or some variant. This
has been a difficult section to compile, and there are probably other titles to be found. C 2 lists collections; C 3
criticism. Productions based on the poems appear in C 4.

Altogether Williams published over 150 poems and songs.
Others have been published by friends. Williams considered
his first book to be *Five Young American Poets*, in which he
appeared in 1944 with Eve Merriam, John Frederick Nims, Jean
Garrigue, and Alejandro Carrion. Two collections followed
(one in two editions): *In the Winter of Cities*, 1956, 1964;
and *Androgyne, Mon Amour*, 1977.

Unlike the speeches in Williams's plays, few of his
poems are memorable. Nevertheless, they are an interesting aspect of his total production, and several have
attracted the attention of music composers. Critical attention, however, has been practically nill.

1. INDIVIDUAL TITLES

"ACROSS THE SPACE": Love lyric.

Voices 149 (Sept.-Dec. 1952): 7-8.

In the Winter of Cities, 1956: 104-05; 1964: 108-09 (C
2).

"AFTER A VISIT"*: Lyrical impression of a room after a person has left. Ms., Texas (G).

Voices 77 (Aug.-Sept. 1934): 40. Rpt. E. D. Williams,
1963 (F 1): 45-46.

Literary Digest 118 (1 Sept. 1934): 23.

"ANDROGYNE, MON AMOUR": Free-verse musings in San Francisco
1976 about love and loneliness.

245

Ambit 69 (1977): 2-3.

Androgyne, Mon Amour, 1977: 16-18 (C 2).

"THE ANGELS OF FRUCTIFICATION": Symbolic poem in free verse written 1942 about the creation of five strange angels. Ms., Texas (G).
   One line was changed between the 1944 and 1956 texts.

Five Young American Poets, 1944: 137-39 (C 2).

In the Winter of Cities, 1956, 1964: 32-34 (C 2).

Trans. (H): French.

"APPARITION": Lyrical portrait of a departed man.

Androgyne, Mon Amour, 1977: 22 (C 2).

"AVE ATQUE VALE"*: Lyric anticipating the loss of love.

L'Alouette 4 (Oct. 1933): 201.

"THE BEANSTALK COUNTRY": Free verse about the mentally disturbed, probably arising from a visit to his sister. Ms., Texas (G).

Five Young American Poets, 1944: 130 (C 2).

In the Winter of Cities, 1956, 1964: 25 (C 2).

Trans. (H): Italian.

"A BIG STORM BLEW": Personal lyric, written 1952, pub. St. Just (D 3): 65-66.

"BLANKET ROLL BLUES": Unpublished song set to music by Kenyon Hopkins for the film *The Fugitive Kind*, 1958 (A 1). Mss., Columbia, Texas, Virginia (G).

BLUE MOUNTAIN BALLADS: see "Heavenly Grass," "Lonesome Man," "Cabin," and "Sugar in the Cane"

"THE BLOND MEDITERRANEANS: A LITANY": Free verse memories
of handsome Italians, dated 1982.

   Christopher Street 61 (1982): 14-15.

"THE BRAIN'S DISSECTION": Free verse musings about the
smallness of present-day leaders, as symbolized by Mus-
solini, almost surely written in Italy.

   Androgyne, Mon Amour, 1977: 43-44.

"CABIN": Song of old love, set to music by Paul Bowles (see
recording C 4). Ms., Texas (G).

   Blue Mountains Ballads: Cabin. Words by Tennessee Wil-
      liams; Music by Paul Bowles. New York: G. Schirmer,
      1946. 4 pp.

   In the Winter of Cities, 1956: 99; 1964: 103 (C 2).

   *20th Century Art Songs for Medium Voice and Piano: A Col-
      lection on Contemporary Songs for Recital and Study.*
      New York: G. Schirmer, 1967. 20-21.

"CACTI"*: Lyric about survival in the midst of desolation.
Ms., Texas (G).

   Voices 77 (Aug.-Sept. 1934): 40.

"CAMINO REAL": see "The Jockeys at Hialeah"

"CAN I FORGET": Love lyrice, written 1931 and printed in
Memoirs (D 1).

"CARROUSEL TUNE": Lyric about gays.

   "Carrousel Tune (from *Camino Real*)." *Voices* 149 (Sept.-
      Dec. 1952): 10-11.

   In the Winter of Cities, 1956: 91; 1964: 95 (C 2).

   The Oxford Book of American Light Verse. Ed. William
      Harmon. New York: Oxford Univ. Pr., 1979. 462-63.

"CHANGLING"*: Lyric about the different aspects of a woman.
Ms., Texas (G).

Eliot (Washington Univ.) 4 (Nov. 1936): 2.

"THE CHRISTUS OF GUADALAJARA":   Lyrical meditation about the
birth of Christ, written 1941 after Williams's 1940 visit
to Mexico. Mss., Columbia, Texas (G).

Botteghe Obscura 4 (1949): 335-37.

In the Winter of Cities, 1956: 88-90; 1964: 92-94 (C 2).

Trans. (H):   Italian.

"CINDER HILL: A NARRATIVE POEM":   Song about a prostitute,
written 1941-44. Mss., Texas (G).
Williams thought of the poem as one of the Blue Mountain
Ballads.

Androgyne, Mon Amour, 1977: 60-63 (C 2).

"CLOVER"*: Lyric about inquietude in a meadow.

College Verse 6 (Jan. 1937): 60.

"LE COEUR A SES RAISONS"*:   Sonnet about heart and mind.
Ms., Texas (G).

Eliot (Washington Univ.) 4 (Dec. 1936): 19.

"THE COMFORTER AND THE BETRAYER":   Symbolic poem in free
verse written 1953-54. Mss., Texas (G).
A longer prose version is included in St. Just (D 3):
380-81.

In the Winter of Cities, 1964: 44-45 (C 2).

"CORTEGE": Autobiographical free verse about death in a
family, the first version written 1943. Ms., Texas (G).
There are many differences between the 1944 and 1956
versions.

Five Young American Poets, 1944: 163-66 (C 2).

In the Winter of Cities, 1956: 49-52; 1964: 53-56 (C 2).

Trans. (H): French.

"COUNSEL":   Free verse about a French house of prostitution,
written in Paris, 1949. Ms., Texas (G).
  There are minor changes between the 1949 and the 1977
versions.

New Directions in Prose and Poetry 11. New York: New
  Directions, 1949. 473-77.

Androgyne, Mon Amour, 1977: 23-28 (C 2).

"THE COUPLE":   Free verse narrative poem about a poverty-
stricken Southern couple observed in the playwright's
youth, along with other memories of childhood.

Androgyne, Mon Amour, 1977: 33-39 (C 2).

"COVENANT":   Love song.
  It was set to music by Warren Benson.

In the Winter of Cities, 1964: 124 (C 2).

Shadow Wood, 1971 (C 2): 13-16.

"CRÊPE-DE-CHINE":   Portrait in free verse of a New Orleans
fortune-teller.

New Yorker 45 (5 July 1969): 28.

The New Yorker Book of Poems. New York: Viking, 1969.
  148-49.

Androgyne, Mon Amour, 1977: 45-46 (C 2).

"CRIED THE FOX":   Lyric about a pursued fox, dedicated to
the memory of D. H. Lawrence and written in Taos, 1939.
Ms., Texas (G).
  Williams recorded the poem, 1952 (E 1).

Five Young American Poets, 1944: 149 (C 2).

In the Winter of Cities, 1956, 1964: 16 (C 2).

"CYCLOPS EYE": Lyric included in the novel *Moise and the World of Reason*, 1975 (B 1).

"THE DANGEROUS PAINTERS": Free verse about artists as revolutionists, written 1942-43. Mss., Texas (G).

Five Young American Poets, 1944: 152-57 (C 2).

In the Winter of Cities, 1956: 60-66; 1964: 64-70 (C 2).

"DARK ARM, HANGING OVER THE EDGE OF INFINITY": Free verse about a sleeping (dying?) Negro, written 1941-42. Mss., Columbia, Texas (G).
  The 1944 version is in three sections; Section 2 was omitted from the 1977 version.

Five Young American Poets, 1944: 133-35 (C 2).

Androgyne, Mon Amour, 1977: 13-14 (C 2).

"A DAYBREAK THOUGHT FOR MARIA": Lyric for Maria Britneva, about being allowed to continue living.

Androgyne, Mon Amour, 1977: 51 (C 2). Rpt. Maria St. Just (D 3): 364-65.

"THE DEATH EMBRACE": Free verse attack on the mechanized state, written 1940.

Five Young American Poets, 1944: 166-69 (C 2).

In the Winter of Cities, 1956: 84-86; 1964: 88-90 (C 2).

Trans. (H): French.

"DEATH IS HIGH": Love lyric. Ms., Texas (G).

New Directions in Prose and Poetry 12. New York: New Directions, 1950. 397.

In the Winter of Cities, 1956: 117; 1964: 121 (C 2).

"DESCENT": Symbolic free verse about a lost person.

Voices 149 (Sept.-Dec. 1952): 10.

In the Winter of Cities, 1956: 56; 1964: 60 (C 2).

"DIVER"*:   Romantic lyric.

Eliot (Washington Univ.) 4 (May 1937): 19.

"THE DIVING BELL":   Free verse about an imaginary trip undersea.

Androgyne, Mon Amour, 1977: 68-69 (C 2).

The Key West Reader: The Best of Key West's Writers 1830-1990.   Ed. George E. Murphy, Jr.   Key West: Tortugas, 1989.   229.

"EIGHT POEMS":   see "This Island Is Memorable to Us"; "Testa dell' Effebo"; "Old Men with Sticks"; "Her Head on the Pillow"; "Faint as Leaf Shadow"; "The Goths"; Death Is High"; "San Sebastino de Somoma"

"ENCHANTMENT":   see "Un saison enchanté" (below)

"LES ÉTOILES D'UN CIRQUE":   Free verse narrative about trapeze artists, dedicated to Ingmar Bergman.

Androgyne, Mon Amour, 1977: 47-49 (C 2).

"EVENING":   Symbolic free verse about two evening attractions.

Androgyne, Mon Amour, 1977: 40-42 (C 2).

"EVENTS PROCEED":   Autobiographical free verse, dated internally 1949.

Androgyne, Mon Amour, 1977: 15 (C 2).

"EVERYMAN":   Allegorical lyric.   Ms., Texas (G).

Contemporary Poetry 5 (Summer 1948): 4.

In the Winter of Cities, 1956: 53; 1964: 57 (C 2).

"THE EYES": Free verse about death or lunacy, written 1949
and dedicated to Oliver Evans. Mss., Buffalo, Columbia,
Texas (G).
Williams recorded the poem, 1952 (E 1).

New Directions in Prose and Poetry 11. New York: New
Directions, 1949. 477-78.

In the Winter of Cities, 1953, 1964: 17-18 (C 2).

Trans. (H): French.

"EYES NEAR BLIND": Free verse, 1972, pub. St. Just (D 3):
265-66.

"FAINT AS LEAF SHADOW": Lyric about lovers, written 1949.
Mss., Columbia, Texas (G).

New Directions in Prose and Poetry 12. New York: New
Directions, 1950. 396.

Voices 149 (Sept.-Dec. 1952): 6-7.

In the Winter of Cities, 1956, 1964: 19 (C 2).

Trans. (H): French.

"FEAR IS A MONSTER AS VAST AS NIGHT...": Lyric about fear
included in *The Two-Character Play*, 1969 and subsequent
versions (A 1).

Androgyne, Mon Amour, 1977: 79 (C 2).

"FROGGY HAS NOT GONE AWAY": Elegy for a dog, 1972, pub. St.
Just (D 3): 316.

"GODS PASS...": Fragment pub. St. Just (D 3): 144.

"GOING HOME": Autobiographical free verse about the South,
published as first part of "Impressions through a Pennsy
Window."

Androgyne, Mon Amour, 1977: 31 (C 2).

"GOLD TOOTH BLUES": Humorous song about a woman killed for
her gold tooth. Ms., Texas (G).
  Williams recorded the poem, 1952 (E 1). It was set to
music by Paul Bowles, but he lost his copy.

In the Winter of Cities, 1956: 102; 1964: 106 (C 2).

The Oxford Book of American Light Verse. Ed. William
  Harmon. New York: Oxford Univ. Pr., 1979. 464.

"THE GOTHS": Lyric about the Northern invaders, written
1949. Ms., Texas (G).

New Directions in Prose and Poetry 12. New York: New
  Directions, 1950: 396.

"THE HARP OF WALES": Lyric about the magic of the musical
instrument, written 1945. Ms., Texas (G).

Prairie Schooner 23 (1949): 330.

Androgyne, Mon Amour, 1977: 67 (C 2).

"HEAVENLY GRASS": Religious song written 1941-42 and set to
music by Paul Bowles (see recording C 4). Mss., Univ. of
Texas (G).
  Williams called for its use in *Orpheus Descending*, 1958,
and in *Kingdom of Earth*, 1968 (A 1). He recorded the
poem, 1952 (E 1).

Blue Mountain Ballads: Heavenly Grass. Words by Tennessee Williams; Music by Paul Bowles. New York: G.
  Schirmer, 1946. 4 pp.

In the Winter of Cities, 1956: 97; 1964: 101 (C 2). Rpt.
  Nelson, 1961 (A 3): 234.

Poetry for Pleasure: The Hallmark Book of Poetry. Garden
  City: Doubleday, 1960.

Every Child's Book of Verse. Ed. Sarah Chokla Gross.
  New York: Watts, 1968.

"HER HEAD ON THE PILLOW": Love song, set to music by Paul
Bowles. Ms., Texas (G).

   New Directions in Prose and Poetry 12. New York: New
      Directions, 1950. 395.

   In the Winter of Cities, 1956: 103; 1964: 107 (C 2).

"HIS MANNER OF RETURNING": Free verse memory of a lover.

   Androgyne, Mon Amour, 1977: 70-73 (C 2).

"HOW CALMLY DOES THE ORANGE BRANCH...": Lyric used in *The
Night of the Iguana*, 1962 (A 1).

"HOW GRIMLY DO PETUNIAS LOOK...": Song used in "The Case of
the Crushed Petunias," 1948 (A 1).

"I AM AN EXILE HERE, SOME OTHER LAND...": Sonnet of exile,
identified as an early poem.

   Voices 149 (Sept.-Dec. 1952): 9-10.

"I CONFESS I CANNOT GUESS...": Lyric about existence, identified as an early poem.

   Voices 149 (Sept.-Dec. 1952): 9.

"I SEE THEM LYING SHEETED IN THEIR GRAVES": Sonnet written
c. 1931 about women poets, printed in *Memoirs* (D 1).

"I THINK THE STRANGE, THE CRAZED, THE QUEER...": Song of
optimism written 1941, pub. Nelson, 1961 (A 3): 196-97.
Ms., Texas (G).
   This version was much expanded and used as a carol, set
to music by Lee Hoiby, between scenes of "The Mutilated,"
1965 (A 1).

"I TOOK PROVISIONS WITH ME": Song used in screenplay for
One Arm, 1984 (A 1).

"I WALK THE PATHS": Lyric about father, pub. E. D. Williams
(F 1): 40.

"THE ICE-BLUE WIND": Symbolic lyric. Mss., Columbia, Texas
(G).
   The first version was written 1941-42. Only five lines
from this version appeared in the second.

Five Young American Poets, 1944: 158-59 (C 2).

Androgyne, Mon Amour, 1977: 86-87 (C 2).

"IMPRESSIONS THROUGH A PENNSY WINDOW": see "Going Home" and
"Rival Breathers"

"IN JACK-O'-LANTERN'S WEATHER"/"THE MARVELOUS CHILDREN":
Autobiographical memory of childhood written in free
verse. Ms., Texas (G).
   The poem was extensively rewritten for the 1956 collection.

   "The Marvelous Children": *Five Young American Poets*,
   1944: 147-49 (C 2).

   "In Jack-o'-Lantern's Weather": *In the Winter of Cities*,
   1956, 1964: 11-14 (C 2).

"IN MEMORIAM TO JANE TAUSSIG"*: Eulogy.

   Eliot (Washington Univ.) 8 (May 1941): inside back cover.

"INHERITORS"*: Free verse praise of pioneers. Ms., Texas
(G).

   College Verse 6 (Apr. 1937): 127-30.

"THE INTERIOR OF THE POCKET": Free-verse portrait of a
hustler, written 1948-49. Mss., Texas (G).

   New Directions in Prose and Poetry 13. New York: New
   Directions, 1951. 530-31.

   In the Winter of Cities, 1956, 1964: 35-36 (C 2).

The Male Muse: A Gay Anthology. Ed. Ian Young. Trumansburg, NY: Crossing Press, 1973. 107-08.

"INTIMATIONS": Free verse musings about mortality, written 1941-42. Mss., Texas (G).

Five Young American Poets, 1944: 159-60 (C 2).

In the Winter of Cities, 1956: 58-59; 1964: 62-63 (C 2).

Trans. (H): French.

"IRON IS THE WINTER": Love lyric, written 1942. Ms., Texas (G).

Five Young American Poets, 1944: 157 (C 2).

In the Winter of Cities, 1956: 92; 1964: 96 (C 2)

"THE ISLAND IS MEMORABLE TO US": Love poem written in Key West, 1950, for Frank Merlo. Ms., Texas (G).

New Directions in Prose and Poetry 12. New York: New Directions, 1950. 393-94.

In the Winter of Cities, 1956: 107; 1964: 111 (C 2).

"THE JOCKEYS AT HIALEAH"/"CAMINO REAL": Surrealistic free verse impressions, written 1945 and originally dedicated to Jay. Mss., Texas (G).
   Only the title and subtitles were changed when the poem was collected. Part I was originally called "The Jockeys at Hialeah"; Part II, "The Sunshine Special"; Part III, "The Doves of Aphrodite"; and Part IV, "Brass Bed."

"Camino Real." *New Directions in Prose and Poetry* 9. New York: New Directions, 1946. 77-80.

"The Jockeys at Hialeah": *In the Winter of Cities*, 1956: 69-73; 1964: 73-77 (C 2).

"KITCHEN DOOR BLUES": Humorous song about approaching death. Ms., Texas (G).
   Williams recorded the poem, 1952 (E 1).

Maryland Quarterly 2 (1944): 58-59.

In the Winter of Cities, 1956: 101; 1964: 105 (C 2).

The Oxford Book of American Light Verse. Ed. William
  Harmon. New York: Oxford Univ. Pr., 1979. 463-64.

"LADY, ANEMONE": Free verse about sexual love, written
  1944-45. Mss., Texas (G).

New Directions in Prose and Poetry 9. New York: New
  Directions, 1946. 82-83.

In the Winter of Cities, 1956: 96; 1964: 100 (C 2).

"THE LADY WITH NO ONE AT ALL": Free verse narrative about a
  woman creating an imaginary lover with whom to console
  herself.

Androgyne, Mon Amour, 1977: 80-82 (C 2).

"LAMENT"*: Lyric about loneliness.

College Verse 6 (Jan. 1937): 60-61.

"LAMENT FOR THE MOTHS": Lyric about the destruction of the
  delicate, written 1942. Ms., Texas (G).

Five Young American Poets, 1944: 32-33 (C 2).

In the Winter of Cities, 1956, 1964: 31 (C 2).

"THE LAST WINE": Symbolic lyric, written 1940. Ms., Texas
  (G).
    It was set to music by Warren Benson.

Five Young American Poets,1944: 143 (C 2).

In the Winter of Cities, 1956: 113; 1964: 117 (C 2).

Shadow Wood, 1971: 17-19 (C 2).

"THE LEGEND": Free verse about incest, written at Taos,
  1940. Ms., Texas (G).
    The poem bears comparison with "The Purification" (A 1).

Five Young American Poets, 1944: 139-41 (C 2).

258 Poems and Lyrics

In the Winter of Cities, 1956: 77–79; 1964: 81–83 (C 2).

"LETTER TO AN OLD LOVE"*:   Sonnet.   Ms., Texas (G).

Eliot (Washington Univ.) 4 (May 1937): 19.

"LIFE STORY":   Humorous poem in free verse about a man and his sexual partner for the night.   Ms., Texas (G).

In the Winter of Cities, 1956: 80–81; 1964: 84–85 (C 2).

The Penguin Book of Homosexual Verse.   Ed. Stephen Coote. New York: Penguin, 1983.   326–27.

Gay and Lesbian Poetry in Our Time: An Anthology.   Ed. Carl Morse and Joan Larkin.   New York: St. Martin's, 1988.   382–83.

Trans. (H):   French.

"LITTLE HORSE":   Tribute to Frank Merlo.   Ms., Texas (G). Williams recorded the poem, 1952 (E 1).

In the Winter of Cities, 1956: 116; 1964: 120 (C 2). Rpt. Leavitt (F 1): 74.

Midland: Twenty-Five Years of Fiction and Poetry Selected from the Writing Workshop of the State University of Iowa.   Ed. Paul Engle.   New York: Random House, 1961. 573.

"THE LITTLE TOWN"*:   Sonnet sequence about an eighty-year-old woman.   Ms., Texas (G).

Eliot (Washington Univ.) 5 (Feb. 1938): 21.

"A LITURGY OF ROSES":   Symbolic free verse about the difficulty of letting go.   Mss., Texas (G).
    The poem was originally written 1945.   It was revised 1948 and probably subsequently.   Changes between the two published versions are extensive.

Chicago Review 1 (Summer 1946): 163–66.

Androgyne, Mon Amour, 1977: 52–55 (C 2).

"LOOK BOTH WAYS BEFORE CROSSING STREETS": Couplets about his mother, pub. E. D. Williams (F 1): 40-41. Ms., Texas (G).

"LONESOME MAN": Song about having no love, written 1942 and set to music by Paul Bowles (see recording C 4). Ms., Texas (G).

Blue Mountain Ballads: Lonesome Man. Words by Tennessee Williams; Music by Paul Bowles. New York: G. Schirmer, 1946. 4 pp.

In the Winter of Cities, 1956: 98; 1964: 102 (C 2).

LORD BYRON'S LOVE LETTER (libretto): see A 1

"LYRIC"*: Lyric in tribute to a woman. Ms., Texas (G).

College Verse 6 (Jan. 1937): 59-60.

"LYRIC"*: Nostalgic lyric. Ms., Texas (G).

Eliot (Washington Univ.) 5 (Nov. 1937): 7.

"THE MAN IN THE DINING CAR": Free verse about a man trying to escape himself. Ms., Texas (G).

Five Young American Poets, 1944: 144-45 (C 2).

In the Winter of Cities, 1956: 82-83; 1964: 86-87 (C 2).

Trans. (H): French.

"THE MARVELOUS CHILDREN": see "In Jack-o'-Lantern's Weather"

"A MENDICANT ORDER": Free verse musings about a religious sect in Jamaica.

Androgyne, Mon Amour, 1977: 58-59 (C 2).

"MICKY WENT THROUGH THE WORLD WITH A BANG": Humorous couplets about a man who did what he wanted, included in
"Survival Notes," 1972 (D 1).

"THE MIND DOES NOT FORGET"*: Sonnet about memory. Ms.,
Texas (G).

Eliot (Washington Univ.) 4 (Dec. 1936): 19.

"MISS PUMA, MISS WHO?": Humorous song.

Antaeus 11 (Autumn 1973): 23-24.

Androgyne, Mon Amour, 1977: 56-57 (C 2).

"MODUS VIVENDI"*: Sonnet about life and death.
Counterpoint 1 (July 1933): 11.

"MORGENLIED": Symbolic love song written 1941. Mss.,
Columbia, Texas (G).
    The only poem in Williams's first collection which has
not been reprinted, it was set to music by Joy Fetterman.

Five Young American Poets, 1944: 136-37 (C 2).

"MORNINGS ON BOURBON STREET": Autobiographical free verse
set in New Orleans, written 1943. Ms., Texas (G).

Five Young American Poets, 131-32 (C 2).

In the Winter of Cities, 1956: 111-12; 1964: 115-16 (C
    2).

"MUMMER'S RHYME"*: Lyric about the end of life's drama.

Eliot (Washington Univ.) 4 (Mar. 1937): 1.

"MY LITTLE ONE": Lyric to a child. Ms., Texas (G).
    Williams recorded the poem, 1952 (E 1). It was set to
music by Warren Benson.

In the Winter of Cities, 1956: 106; 1964: 110 (C 2).

Six Poems. New York: New Directions, 1957. 6.

Shadow Wood, 1971 (C 2): 6-8.

"MY LOVE WAS LIGHT"*: Lyric written 1936 concerning a man's
love for a worthless woman, published as second part of
"The Shuttle." Mss., Chicago, Texas (G).

Poetry 50 (June 1937): 143.

*The Poetry Anthology 1912-1977: Sixty-Five Years of
America's Most Distinguished Verse Magazine*. Ed. Daryl
Hine and Joseph Parisi. Boston: Houghton Mifflin,
1978. 183.

"NATURE'S THANKSGIVING"*: Lyric pub. in junior high school
paper, 1925; rpt. E. D. Williams (F 1): 43; Van Antwerp
(F 1): 11.

"NEAR THE SILENCE": Lyric, 1971, pub. St. Just (D 3): 251.

"THE NEW POET"*: Italian sonnet.

*American Prefaces: A Journal of Critical and Imaginative
Writing* (Univ. of Iowa) 2 (Apr. 1937): 105.

"NIGHT VISIT": Free verse about a visit from an old friend,
now killing herself with drugs.

Amdrogyne, Mon Amour, 1977: 74-76 (C 2).

"NO SHAKEN SEAS"*: Poem expressing certitude.

Eliot (Washington Univ.) 4 (Dec. 1936): 21.

"NOT WITHOUT KNOWLEDGE"*: Quatrain about kissing.

Savitar of 1932 (Univ. of Missouri yearbook). 249.

"OCTOBER SONG"*: Sonnet of lost love. Ms., Texas (G).

Neophyte 1 (Christmas-New Year 1932-33): 36.

"ODYSSEY"*: Symbolic lyric about a pilgrim.

   Eliot (Washington Univ.) 5 (Nov. 1937): 7.

"OF ROSES": Lyric printed by Leavitt (F 1): 21.

"OLD BEAUX AND FADED LADIES PLAY": Symbolic lyric used in
   the first version of *The Two-Character Play*, 1969, and in
   part in "Now the Cat with Jewelled Claws," 1981 (A 1).

   Androgyne, Mon Amour, 1977: 79 (C 2).

"OLD MEN ARE FOND": Poem about old age. Ms., Texas (G).
   It was set to music by Warren Benson.

   In the Winter of Cities, 1964: 122-23 (C 2).

   Shadow Wood, 1971: 9-12 (C 2).

"OLD MEN GO MAN AT NIGHT": Poem about old age.

   Androgyne, Mon Amour, 1977: 9-11 (C 2).

"OLD MEN WITH STICKS": Symbolic poem about old age, written
   1949. Ms., Texas (G).
   Three lines (21-23) of the 1950 version were changed for
   the 1956 printing.

   New Directions in Prose and Poetry 12. New York: New
   Directions, 1950. 394-95.

   In the Winter of Cities, 1956, 1964: 26 (C 2).

"OLD THINGS"*: Lyric about an attic, pub. in junior high
   school paper, 1925; rpt. E. D. Williams (F 1): 43; Van
   Antwerp (F 1): 11.

"OLE 'SEPHUS (MONOLOGUE TO A COON DOG)"*: Poem in Negro
   dialect about a departed woman. Ms., Texas (G).

   Eliot (Washington Univ.) 5 (June 1937): 7.

"ONE AND TWO":   Dialogue between a painter and his/her would-be lover. Ms., Texas (G).

Five Young American Poets, 1944: 141-42 (C 2).

Androgyne, Mon Amour, 1977: 77-78 (C 2).

"ONE HAND IN SPACE":   Lyric about subject matter, written 1942. Ms., Texas (G).

Five Young American Poets, 1944: 169-70 (C 2).

Androgyne, Mon Amour, 1977: 29-30 (C 2).

"ORPHEUS DESCENDING":   Free verse based on Orpheus's visit to Hades, written 1951. Mss., Delaware, Texas (G).
    There are significant differences between the two 1952 printings; the *Voices* version was collected. (The *Panorama* version was dedicated to Alexandra Molostvova.)

Panorama Spring 1952: 30.

Voices 149 (Sept.-Dec. 1952): 5-6.

In the Winter of Cities, 1956, 1964: 27-28 (C 2).

Trans. (H): French.

"THE PURFICATION":   see A 1.

"PART OF A HERO":   Free verse about the artist. Ms., Texas (G).

London Magazine 3 (Feb. 1956): 16-17.

In the Winter of Cities, 1956: 54-55; 1964: 58-59 (C 2).

"PENATES"*:   Lyric about the disturbance caused by small changes.

Eliot (Washington Univ.) 5 (June 1937): 19.

"PHOTOGRAPH AND PEARLS": Free verse narrative about a letter from a dead sailor to his domineering mother. Ms.,
Texas (G).

In the Winter of Cities, 1964: 42-43 (C 2).

"PROBLEM"*: Poem about the numerous dead.

Eliot (Washington Univ) 9 (Jan. 1942): 20.

"PULSE": Symbolic lyric about momentary breakthroughs to
others. Mss., Texas (G).

Five Young American Poets, 1944: 150-51 (C 2).

In the Winter of Cities, 1956, 1964: 29-30 (C 2).

Trans. (H): French.

"RECOLLECTION"*: Poem about romantic loss. Ms., Texas (G).

Eliot (Washington Univ.) 4 (Feb. 1937): 1.

"RECUERDO": Autobiographical free verse about childhood,
written 1945. Ms., Texas (G).

New Directions in Prose and Poetry 9. New York: New
Directions, 1946. 80-82.

In the Winter of Cities, 1956: 74-76; 1964: 78-80 (C 2).

*Crazy to be Alive in Such a Strange World: Poems about
People*. Ed. Nancy Larrick. New York: Evans, 1977.
(Excerpt, "The Paper Lantern")

"THE RENTED ROOM": Free verse about a man and a hustler.

Christopher Street 4 (Dec. 1979): 26-27.

"REVEILLE"*: Eulogy for war dead.

Eliot (Washington Univ.) 5 (Dec. 1937): 21.

"RIVAL BREATHERS":   Free verse about Southern vegetation, the second part of "Impressions through a Pennsy Window," proving that Williams was no botanist.

Androgyne, Mon Amour, 1977: 32 (C 2).

"RIPPING OFF THE MOTHER":   Protest poem sold 1971, according to Dotson Rader (F 1), to *Evergreen Review*.

"THE ROAD":   Ironic free verse about a traveling salesman. Ms., Texas (G).

Five Young American Poets, 1944: 135-36 (C 2).

In the Winter of Cities, 1956: 114-15; 1964: 118-19 (C 2).

"SACRE DE PRINTEMPS"*:   Lyric evoking the effects of the coming of spring on the poet.

College Verse 6 (May 1937): 158-59.

"UN SAISON ENCHANTÉ!":   Sonnet included in "Lord Byron's Love Letter," 1945 (A 1).
     The spelling is Williams's.

"SAN SEBASTIANO DE SODOMA":   Lyric about the painting of the saint. Ms., Texas (G).

New Directions in Prose and Poetry 12. New York: New Directions, 1950. 396-97.

In the Winter of Cities, 1956: 108; 1964: 112 (C 2).

"SANCTUARY"*:   Love lyric. Ms., Texas (G).

Eliot (Washington Univ.) 5 (June 1937): 19.

"A SEPARATE POEM":   Free verse about the growing strain between Williams and Frank Merlo.

In the Winter of Cities, 1964: 126-29 (C 2).

"SEVEN POEMS":   see "Orpheus Descending"; "Faint as Leaf
Shadow"; Across the Space"; Two Early Poems ("I con-
fess..."; "I am an exile..."); "Descent"; "Carrousel
Tune"

"SHADOW BOXES":   Free verse about aged women, written 1941.
Ms., Texas (G).

Five Young American Poets, 1944: 162 (C 2).

In the Winter of Cities, 1956: 57; 1964: 61 (C 2).

"SHADOW WOOD":   Lyric about tenderness.
It was set to music by Warren Benson. The final stanza,
with a changed last line, was used as the epigraph for
Period of Adjustment, 1961 (A 1).

In the Winter of Cities, 1964: 125 (C 2).

Shadow Wood, 1971 (C 2): 3-5.

"THE SHALLOW POOL"*:   Love poem. Ms., Texas (G).

Eliot (Washington Univ.) 5 (June 1937): 19.

"THE SHUTTLE":   see "My Love Was Light" and "This Hour"

"THE SIEGE":   Lyric written 1941 about the self and sexual
loneliness.

Five Young American Poets, 1944: 161; *In the Winter of
Cities*, 1956, 1964: 20 (C 2).

"THE SOFT CITY":   Free verse evocation of a city, written
1941-49. Mss., Texas (G).
Part II was substantially cut when the poem was collected in 1956.

New Directions in Prose and Poetry 11. New York: New
Directions, 1949. 472-73.

In the Winter of Cities, 1956, 1964: 21-22 (C 2).

"SONNET FOR PYGMALION"*:   Warning about bringing stone to
life. Ms., Texas (G).

Eliot (Washington Univ.) 4 (Nov. 1936): 2.

"SONNETS FOR THE SPRING (A SEQUENCE)"*:   Three sonnets –
"Signer of Darkness," "The Radiant Guest," "A Branch for
Birds" – that won first prize in the Wednesday Club
senior division poetry contest, 1936. Ms., Texas (G).

St. Louis Star-Times 26 Mar. 1936. Rpt. in full, Van
Antwerp (F 1): 23–24; poems only, E. D. Williams (F 1):
76–77

Unidentified newspaper, 26 Mar. 1936. Rpt. Leavitt (F
1): 28. ["Singer of Darkness" only]

*Wednesday Club Verse: An Anthology of Honor Poems from
the Annual and Special Poetry Contests of the Wednesday
Club of St. Louis.* St. Louis: 1946. 53–54.

"SPEECH FROM THE STAIRS":   Address written 1941 to a man
whose mother has died. Ms., Texas (G).
One word was changed from the 1944 to the 1977 version.

Five Young American Poets, 1944: 151 (C 2).

Androgyne, Mon Amour, 1977: 19 (C 2).

"THE STONECUTTER'S ANGELS":   Lyric written in New Orleans,
1941, about angels on tombstones. Mss., Texas (G).

Botteghe Obscura 4 (1949): 337–39.

Trans. (H): Italian.

"STONES ARE THROWN":   Symbolic poem about fate.

Androgyne, Mon Amour, 1977: 65–66 (C 2).

"STRANGERS PASS ME ON THE STREET":   Couplets written 1929,
included in *Memoirs* (D 1). Ms., Texas (G).

"SUGAR IN THE CANE": Song about love waiting to be released, written 1942 and set to music by Paul Bowles (see
recording C 4). Ms., Texas (G).

  Blue Mountain Ballads: Sugar in the Cane. Words by Tennessee Williams; Music by Paul Bowles. New York: G.
  Schirmer, 1946. 4 pp.

  In the Winter of Cities, 1956: 100; 1964: 104 (C 2).

  The Oxford Book of American Light Verse. Ed. William
  Harmon. New York: Oxford Univ. Pr., 1979. 463.

"THE SUMMER BELVEDERE"; Symbolic poem written 1943 about
the search for peace. Mss., Texas (G).
  Williams recorded the poem, 1952 (E 1).

  Five Young American Poets, 1944: 127-30 (C 2).

  In the Winter of Cities, 1956: 45-48; 1964: 49-52 (C 2).

  Trans. (H): French.

"SWIMMER AND FISH GROUP": Free verse about a swimmer.

  College Verse 6 (Mar. 1937): 100-01.

"TANGIER: THE SPEECHLESS SUMMER": Autobiographical free
verse including scenes with Jane and Paul Bowles.

  Antaeus 1 (Summer 1970): 43-45.

  Androgyne, Mon Amour, 1977: 89-92 (C 2).

"TENOR SAX TAKING THE BREAKS": Poem written 1939 evoking a
jazz player; pub. Nelson, 1961 (A 3): 46-48. Ms., Columbia, Texas (G).

"TESTA DELL' EFFEBO": Lyric about a sculptured youth, written 1948. Ms., Texas (G).

  "Testa dell' Efebo" [sic]. *Harper's Bazaar* 82 (Aug.
  1948): 172.

New Directions in Prose and Poetry 12.   New York: New
    Directions, 1950.   394.

In the Winter of Cities, 1956, 1964: 15 (C 2).

"THEY THAT COME LATE TO THE DANCE":   Lyric in "Now the Cat
with Jewelled Claws," 1981 (A 1).   Mss., California-Los
Angeles, Texas ["She That Comes Late"] (G).

"THIS CRYPTIC BONE"*:   Poem about loss.   Ms., Texas (G).

Eliot (Washington Univ.) 5 (Nov. 1937): 11.

"THIS HOUR"*:   Lyric about the keen awareness that comes to
a waker at dawn, probably written 1936 and published as
first part of "The Shuttle."   Mss., Chicago, Texas (G).

Poetry 50 (June 1937): 142.

"THOSE WHO IGNORE THE PROPER TIME OF THEIR GOING":   Poem
about the aged, dated 1955.   Ms., Texas (G).

Semi-Colon 1.6 (1956?): 1-2.

In the Winter of Cities, 1956, 1964: 37-41 (C 2).

Trans. (H):   French.

"THREE":   Love song written 1942 and set to music by Paul
Bowles.   Ms., Texas (G).

Three.   Music by Paul Bowles; Poem by Tennessee Williams.
New York: Hargail Music Press, 1947.   4 pp.

"THREE POEMS":   see "Camino Real"; "Recuerdo"; "Lady, Anemone"

"THREE POEMS":   see "The Soft City"; "Counsel"; "The Eyes"

"TO MARIA":   Free verse about the negative, 1982; pub. St.
Just (D 3): 387-88.

"**TOWNS BECOME JEWELS**": Impressionistic poem written in 1941. Ms., Texas (G).

Five Young American Poets, 1944: 142-43 (C 2).

In the Winter of Cities, 1956: 110; 1964: 114 (C 2).

"**TUESDAY'S CHILD**": Free verse written 1948, about the incestuous love one brother feels for another. Ms., Texas (G).

Partisan Review 16 (Apr. 1949): 367.

In the Winter of Cities, 1956: 109; 1964: 113 (C 2).

"**TURNING OUT THE BEDSIDE LAMP**": Free verse musings about death, internally dated 1976.

Androgyne, Mon Amour, 1977: 88 (C 2).

"**TWO METAPHYSICAL SONNETS**": see "Le coeur a ses raisons" and "The Mind Does Not Forget"

"**TWO POEMS FROM *THE TWO-CHARACTER PLAY***": see "Fear Is a Monster" and "Old Beaux and Fades Ladies Play"

"**UNDER THE APRIL RAIN**"*: Elegy for Sara Teasdale. The lyric was awarded first prize by readers of the issue (see Van Antwerp [F 1]: 21). Ms., Texas (G).

Inspiration 2 (Spring 1933): page not numbered.

"**VALEDICTION**"*: Lyric about a departed woman. Ms., Texas (G).

Eliot (Washington Univ.) 5 (June 1937): 7.

"**WE HAVE NOT LONG TO LOVE**": Lyric written about 1941. Ms., Texas (G).

Poetry 157 (Feb. 1991): 289.

"WHICH IS MY LITTLE BOY?": Song dedicated to Carson McCullers. Ms., Texas (G).
  Williams recorded the poem, 1952 (E 1).

  Experiment 2 (Fall 1946): 161.

  Mademoiselle 31 (July 1950): 67.

  In the Winter of Cities, 1956: 95; 1964: 99 (C 2).

  Sounds and Silences: Poems for Performing. Ed. Robert W.
    Boynton and Maynard Mack. Rochelle Park, NJ: Hayden,
    1975.

"THE WINE-DRINKERS": Free verse portrait of drug users
  drinking in a New Orleans doorway, written there 1941.
  Ms., Texas (G).
  There are several changes between the two published versions.

  Five Young American Poets, 1944: 146 (C 2).

  Androgyne, Mon Amour, 1977: 50 (C 2).

"WINTER SMOKE IS BLUE AND BITTER": Lyric.

  Androgyne, Mon Amour, 1977: 12 (C 2).

  Trans. (H): French.

"WITH MILITARY HONORS"*: Lyric about burial of war dead.

  Eliot (Washington Univ.) 5 (Dec. 1937): 21.

"WOLF'S HOUR": Free verse musings, alone in the early morning.

  Androgyne, Mon Amour, 1977: 83-85 (C 2).

"A WREATH FOR ALEXANDRA MOLOSTVOVA": Elegy written for
  Maria Britneva's cousin.

  In the Winter of Cities, 1956, 1964: 23-24 (C 2). Rpt.
    Maria St. Just (D 3): 47.

"YOU AND I": Love poem. Ms., Texas (G).

Androgyne, Mon Amour, 1977: 64 (C 2).

Gay and Lesbian Poetry in Our Time: An Anthology. Ed.
  Carl Morse and Joan Larkin. New York: St. Martin's,
  1988. 383-84.

Trans. (H): French.

"YOUNG MEN WAKING AT DAYBREAK": Free verse about a man and
his lover for the night.

Evergreen Review 50 (Dec. 1967): 29.

Androgyne, Mon Amour, 1977: 20-21 (C 2).

"YOUTH MUST BE WANTON": Poem in *The Night of the Iguana,*
1961 (A 1).

2. COLLECTIONS

Androgyne, Mon Amour: Poems. New York: New Directions,
  1977; Toronto: McClelland & Stewart, 1977. 92 pp. Lim-
  ited and trade editions. Contents: "Old Men Go Mad at
  Night," 9-11; "Winter Smoke Is Blue and Bitter," 12;
  "Dark Arm, Hanging over the Edge of Infinity," 13-14;
  "Events Proceed," 15; "Androgyne, Mon Amour," 16-18;
  "Speech from the Stairs," 19; "Young Men Waking at Day-
  break," 20-21; "Apparition," 22; "Counsel," 23-28; "One
  Hand in Space," 29-30; "Impressions through a Pennsy Win-
  dow," 31-32; "The Couple," 33-39; "Evening," 40-42; "The
  Brain's Dissection," 43-44; "Crêpe-de-Chine," 45-46; "Les
  Etoiles d'un Cirque," 47-49; "The Wine-Drinkers," 50; "A
  Daybreak Thought for Maria," 51; "A Liturgy of Roses,"
  52-55; "Miss Puma, Miss Who?" 56-57; "A Mendicant Order,"
  58-59; "Cinder Hill: A Narrative Poem," 60-63; "You and
  I," 64; "Stones Are Thrown," 65-66; "The Harp of Wales,"
  67; "The Diving Bell," 68-69; "His Manner of Returning,"
  70-73; "Night Visit," 74-76; "One and Two," 77-78; "Two
  Poems from *The Two-Character Play,*" 79; "The Lady with No
  One at All," 80-82; "Wolf's Hour," 83-85; "The Ice-Blue
  Wind," 86-87; "Turning Out the Bedside Lamp," 88; "Tangier: The Speechless Summer," 89-92. Reproduction of
  painting on dust-jacket. Reviews:
    Chicago Dec. 1977: 122.

Choice 14 (Nov. 1977): 1218.
Virginia Quarterly Review 53 (Autumn 1977): 146.
Gibson, Margaret. Library Journal 102 (15 Apr. 1977):
  929.
Kahn, Sy M. Tennessee Williams Newsletter 2.1 (Spring
  1980): 30-32.
Siconolfi, M. T. Best Sellers 37 (July 1977): 122.
Weales, Gerald. New Republic 4 June 1977: 32.

Five Young American Poets: Third Series, 1944. Norfolk, CT:
  New Directions, 1944. 122-70. Contents: The Summer
  Belvedere: "Preface to My Poems--Frivolous Version,"
  122-24; "Preface to My Poems--Serious Version," 124-26;
  "The Summer Belvedere," 127-30; "The Beanstalk Country,"
  130; "Mornings on Bourbon Street," 131-32; "Lament for
  the Moths," 132-33; "Dark Arm, Hanging over the Edge of
  Infinity," 133-35; "The Road," 135-36; "Morgenlied," 126-
  37; "The Angels of Fructication," 137-39; "The Legend,"
  139-41; "One and Two," 141-42; "Towns Become Jewels,"
  142-43; "The Last Wine," 143; "The Man in the Dining
  Car," 144-45; "The Wine Drinkers," 146; "The Marvelous
  Children," 147-49; "Cried the Fox," 149; "Pulse," 150;
  "Speech from the Stairs," 151; "The Dangerous Painters,"
  152-57; "Iron Is the Winter," 157; "The Ice Blue Wind,"
  158-59; "Intimations,"159-60; "The Siege," 161; "Shadow
  Boxes," 162; "Cortege," 163-66; "The Death Embrace," 166-
  69; "One Hand in Space," 169-70. Review:
  New York Times Book Review 17 June 1945: 10.

In the Winter of Cities: Poems. Ed. with help of William S.
  Gray. Norfolk, CT: New Directions, 1956. 117 pp. Limited and trade editions. Contents: Part I: In Jack-o'-
  Lantern's Weather: "In Jack-o'-Lantern's Weather," 11-
  14; "Testa dell' Effebo," 15; "Cried the Fox," 16; "The
  Eyes," 17-18; "Faint as Leaf Shadow," 19; "The Siege,"
  20; "The Soft City," 21-22; "A Wreath for Alexandra
  Molostvova," 23-24; "The Beanstalk Country, 25; "Old Men
  with Sticks," 26; "Orpheus Descending," 27-28; "Pulse,"
  29-30; "Lament for the Moths," 31; "The Angels of Fructification,' 32-34; "The Interior of the Pocket," 35-36;
  "Those Who Ignore the Appropriate Time of Their Going,"
  37-41. Part II: The Summer Belvedere: "The Summer Belvedere," 45-48; "Cortege," 49-52; "Everyman," 53; "Part
  of a Hero," 54-55; "Descent," 56; "Shadow Boxes," 57;
  "Intimations," 58-59; "The Dangerous Painters," 60-66.
  Part III: The Jockeys at Hialeah: "The Jockeys at Hialeah," 69-73; "Recuerdo," 74-76; "The Legend," 77-79;
  "Life Story," 80-81; "The Man in the Dining Car," 82-83;
  "The Death Embrace," 84-87; "The Christus of Guadalajara," 88-90; "Carrousel Tune," 91; "Iron Is the Winter,"
  92. Part IV: Hoofprints of a Little Horse: "Which Is My

Little Boy?" 95; "Lady, Anemone," 96; "Heavenly Grass,"
97; "Lonesome Man," 98; "Cabin," 99; "Sugar in the Cane,"
100; "Kitchen Door Blues," 101; "Gold Tooth Blues," 102;
"Her Head on the Pillow," 103; "Across the Space," 104-
05; "My Little One," 106; "The Island Is Memorable to
Us," 107; "San Sebastiano de Sodoma," 108; "Tuesday's
Child," 109; "Towns Become Jewels," 110; "Mornings on
Bourbon Street," 111-12; "The Last Wine," 113; "The
Road," 114-15; "Little Horse," 116; "Death Is High," 117.
Reviews:
  Booklist 52 (15 July 1956): 478.
  Theatre Arts Aug. 1956: 10.
  Time 25 June 1956: 94.
  Fitts, Dudley. *New York Times Book Review* 8 July 1956:
    10.
  Hall, Donald. *Yale Review* 46 (Winter 1957): 297-98.
    Rpt. Van Antwerp (F): 161-62.
  McDonald, G. D. *Library Journal* 81 (1 Oct. 1956):
    2262.
  Nordell, Rod. *Christian Science Monitor* 28 June 1956:
    11.
  Scarbrough, George. *Voices* 162 (Jan.-Apr. 1957): 45-
    46.
  Tedlock, E. W. *New Mexico Quarterly* 26 (Autumn 1956):
    302-04.
  Woods, John. *Poetry* 90 (July 1957): 256-58.

In the Winter of Cities: Poems. New Directions Paperbook.
  Norfolk, CT: New Directions, 1964. 129 pp. Contents:
  same as above with additions and consequent shifts in
  pagination: "Photographs and Pearls," 42-43; "The Comforter and the Betrayer," 44-45; "Old Men Are Fond," 122-
  23; "Covenant," 124; "Shadow Wood," 125; "A Separate
  Poem," 126-29. Review:
  Evans, Oliver. *Prairie Schooner* 39 (Fall 1965): 273-
    76.

*Shadow Wood: Five Poems of Tennessee Williams for Soprano
  and Large Wind Ensemble*. Music by Warren Benson. New
  York: MCA Music, 1971. 19 pp. Contents: "Shadow Wood,"
  3-5; "My Little One," 6-8; "Old Men Are Fond," 9-12;
  "Covenant," 13-16; "The Last Wine," 17-19.

3. CRITICISM

Ariga, Fumiyasu. "Tennessee Williams - Dokubo no Shijin."
  Sengo Amerika Engeki no Tenkai. Ed. Kuniaki Svenaga and
  Koji Ishizuka. Tokyo: Bun'eido, 1983. 131-54.

Draya, Ren: see A 3

Ower, John. "Erotic Mythology in the Poetry of Tennessee
  Williams." Tharpe (A 3): 609-23.

Taylor, William E. "Tennessee Williams: The Playwright as
  Poet." Tharpe (A 3): 624-30.

4. PRODUCTIONS

In the Winter of Cities. Ballet choreographed by Matthew
Nash with selection of poems set to music sung by New York
City Gay Men's Chorus. Note:
  Freiberg, Peter. *Advocate* 5 Mar. 1985: 14-15.

Songs by American Composers. Strand Records, 1962. Side
411 B. On record: *Songs of American Composers*. Sung by
Donald Gramn, accompanied by Richard Cumming. [*Blue
Mountain Ballads*, music by Paul Bowles]

Tennessee's Waltz. Poems dramatized by Carolina Repertory
Theatre. Raleigh, NC: Theatre in the Park, 28 Apr.-2 May
1981. Review:
  Stanton, Stephen S. *Tennessee Williams Review* 3.1
    (Spring 1981): 37.

D. OCCASIONAL PIECES, AUTOBIOGRAPHY, LETTERS

D 1 contains an alphabetical list of Williams's essays and memoirs. Items of a special kind are grouped under one of the following headings: Blurbs; Brief Comments; Introductions and Notes; Program Notes. (Note: Newspapers and some magazines use quotation marks for titles; for the sake of clarity I have italicized instead.) D 2 contains the one collection so far published. D 3 lists Williams's published letters, including two collections (see St. Just and Windham). D 4 contains information about Williams's will.

As *Variety* (31 Aug. 1960: 56) noted, Williams was in the habit of writing an essay before the opening of each new play in New York. Thus we have 19 such works dating from *The Glass Menagerie*, 1945, until *Vieux Carré*, 1977. (Bruce Smith [F 1: 126] indicates one last essay was prepared for the 1980 *Clothes for a Summer Hotel*, but it was not published.) These generally appeared in the *New York Times*; a few appeared in other city newspapers. Many were reprinted in the 1978 collection; others appear in Van Antwerp (F 1).

I have not listed essays that were an integral part of one of his publications, such as the prefaces in *Five Young American Poets* (C 2) or notes in plays (A 1). (The one exception is "Too Personal?," which was written for the *New York Times* but not used by the newspaper.) Some high school essays, 1925-29 (not listed below), about pollution and about his first European trip are on file at the University of Texas. There are unquestionably other essays to be discovered, especially program notes.

1. INDIVIDUAL TITLES

"THE AGENT AS CATALYST, PART I": Tribute to agent Audrey Wood, accompaning article with same title by David Newman (F 1).

> *Esquire* 58 (Dec. 1962): 216, 260. Rpt. Van Antwerp (F 1): 228, 230-32.

"AN ALLEGORY OF MAN AND HIS SAHARA": Review of Paul Bowles's novel *The Sheltering Sky*.

New York Times Book Review 4 Dec. 1949: 7, 38.

"ANNA MAGNANI, TIGRESS OF THE TIBER": Tribute to Italian
film star, written for the opening of the film *The Rose
Tattoo*.

New York Herald Tribune 11 Dec. 1955, sec. 4: 1, 3.

"AN APPRECIATION": Eulogy for actress Laurette Taylor.
Ms., Texas (G).

New York Times 15 Dec. 1946, sec. 2: 4.   Rpt. Leavitt (F
1): 57; Van Antwerp (F 1): 75-77.

"AN APPRECIATION": Note on painter Hans Hofmann.
The actual order of publication is probably reversed;
the first suggests a mix-up with the essay above.

Women: A Collaboration of Artists and Writers.   New York:
1948. n.p.

Derrière le Miroir 16 (Jan. 1949): 5.

"THE AUTHOR TELLS WHY IT IS CALLED *THE GLASS MENAGERIE*":
Essay written for New York opening, first of a series
Williams wrote for each Broadway opening.

New York Herald Tribune 15 Apr. 1945.   Rpt. Van Antwerp
(F 1): 68.

Inclusion in Textbook

Miller, James E., et al., eds.   *United States in Literature.* Glenview, IL: Scott, 1979.   503.

"AUTHOR AND DIRECTOR: A DELICATE SITUATION": Essay on
nature of the collaboration.

Playbill 30 Sept. 1957: 9-13.

Where I Live, 1978: 93-99 (D 2).

"BIOGRAPHY OF CARSON McCULLERS": Essay on personal relationship with her, especially during summer 1946.

"The Author." *Saturday Review* 44 (23 Sept. 1961): 14-15.

Where I Live, 1978: 133-36 (D 2).

"THE BLESSINGS AND MIXED BLESSINGS OF WORKSHOP PRODUCTIONS":
Series of notes holding that a living author should be
involved with revivals of his work.

Dramatists Guild Quarterly 13.3 (Autumn 1976): 16, 23-25.

BLURBS: Comments about the following nine authors' works.

Bowles, Jane. *Two Serious Ladies*.   London: Peter Owen,
1965. *The Collected Works*.   New York: Noonday, 1966.

Choukri, Mohammed. *For Bread Alone*.   London: Owen, 1973.
San Francisco: City Lights, 1987.

Didion, Joan. *A Book of Common Prayer*.   New York: Simon,
1977.

Funke, Lewis, and John E. Booth, ed. *Actors Talk about
Acting*.   New York: Avon, 1961.

Herlihy, James. *All Fall Down*.   New York: Dutton, 1960.

Purdy, James: *Color of Darkness*.   In *Paris Review* 26
(Summer-Fall 1961): 176.

Vidal, Gore. *Visit to a Small Planet*.   Boston: Little,
Brown, 1957.

Windham, Donald. *The Dog Star*.   Garden City: Doubleday,
1950. *Emblems of Conduct*.   New York: Scribner's, 1963.

Yates, Richard. *Eleven Kinds of Loneliness: Short
Stories*.   Boston: Little, Brown, 1962. *Revolutionary
Road*.   New York: Bantam, 1962.

BRIEF COMMENTS: A few sentences to a few paragraphs on various subjects.

"Acceptance by Mr. Williams." *Proceedings of the Amer-
ican Academy of Arts and Letters and the National
Institute of Arts and Letters* n.s. 2.20 (1970): 28.
Rpt. Van Antwerp (F 1): 255. [Joke]

"American Playwrights [sic] Self-Appraisals." *Saturday
Review* 38 (3 Sept. 1955): 18-19.

"The Arts in America." *New York Times* 29 Aug. 1976, sec.
2: 16. [Statement to Clive Barnes lamenting bad connections in the theatre]

"'As if a rose might somehow be a throat' Writes Tennessee Williams about Licia Albanese." *Words and Music:
Comments by Famous Authors about the World's Greatest
Artists.* Camden, NJ: RCA Victor, n.d. 5. [Tribute to
opera star]

"Gore Vidal." *Double Exposure.* Ed. Roddy McDowell. New
York: Delacourte, 1966. Rpt. *McCall's* 94 (Oct. 1966):
107. [On fellow writer]

"My Current Reading." *Saturday Review of Literature* 31
(6 Mar. 1948): 26. [List of ten books]

"A Playwrights' [sic] Choice of 'Perfect Plays.'" *New
York Times* 14 Jan. 1979, sec. 2: 10. [List of six
works]

Untitled. *Attacks of Taste.* Ed. Evelyn B. Byrne and
Otto M. Penzler. New York: Gotham Book Mart, 1971.
48-49. Limited edition. [Childhood reading; Hart
Crane]

Untitled. *Conjunctions* 1 (Fall 1981): 45. [Tribute to
James Laughlin]

Untitled. *Dramatists Guild Quarterly* 10.4 (Winter 1974):
39. [Response to questionnaire]

Untitled. *Film en Roman de Kim* 6/7 (1956): 14. [Quality
of a good film]

Untitled. *A Portrait of the Theatre.* Ed. Frederic
Ohringer. New York: Crown, 1979; Toronto: Merritt,
1979. 113. [Autobiographical note]

Untitled. *Working with Kazan.* Ed. Jeannie Basinger et
al. Middletown, CT: Wesleyan Univ. Pr., 1973. [Trib-
ute]

"What I Look for in a Film: A Symposium." *Films in
Review* 1 (Mar. 1950): 1-2. [Art, but esp. entertain-
ment]

"CAN A GOOD WIFE BE A GOOD SPORT?" Essay submitted to *Smart Set* contest, winning 3rd prize and becoming Williams's first publication in national magazine.

Smart Set 80 (May 1927): 9, 13. Rpt. E. D. Williams (F 1): 47-48; Van Antwerp (F 1): 13-14.

"*CANDIDA*: A COLLEGE ESSAY": College theme attacking play. Ms., Texas (G).

Shaw Review 20 (May 1977): 60-62.

"THE CATASTROPHE OF SUCCESS": see "On a Streetcar Named Success"

"CONCERNING EUGENE O'NEILL": Note about problems in general of a playwright, written for the inaugural season of Ahmanson Theatre, Los Angeles.

Playbill (Ahmanson Theatre) 12 Sept.-21 Oct. 1967: 9.

"CRITIC SAYS 'EVASION,' WRITER SAYS 'MYSTERY'": Response to Walter Kerr's review of *Cat on a Hot Tin Roof* (A 1).

New York Herald Tribune 17 Apr. 1955.

Where I Live, 1978: 70-74 (D 2).

"FACTS ABOUT ME": Autobiographical note. Ms., Texas (G). According to George Miller (I: Gunn) this essay originated as "a press release prepared in late 1947; its first known published appearance was in the Boston *Herald* ...."

Boston Herald 2 Nov. 1947.

Tennessee Williams Reading, 1952 (E 1): record jacket.

Twentieth Century Authors: First Supplement: A *Biographical Dictionary of Modern Literature*. Ed. Stanley J. Kunitz. New York: Wilson, 1955. 1087-88.

The Rose Tattoo, 1967 (A 1: Prod.): brochure with recording.

D 1: Can Good Wife Be Good Sport / Happiness Is Relevant281

Where I Live, 1978: 58-62 (D 2).

Mississippi Writers: Reflections of Childhood and Youth.
 Ed. Dorothy Abbott. Jackson: Univ. Pr. of Mississippi,
 1985. 2: 658-60.

"FIVE FIERY LADIES": Tributes written to accompany photographs of actresses Vivien Leigh, Geraldine Page, Anna
 Magnani, Katharine Hepburn, and Elizabeth Taylor.

Life 50 (3 Feb. 1961): 84-89. Rpt. Van Antwerp (F 1):
 215-18.

Where I Live, 1978: 127-32 (D 2).

FOREWORD TO *CAMINO REAL*: see "On the *Camino Real* (below)

FOREWORD TO *SWEET BIRD OF YOUTH*: see "Williams' Wells of
 Violence" (below)

"'GRAND'": Though consistently published as a short story,
 actually a memoir of Williams's grandmother Mrs. Rose
 Dakin. Ms., Columbia (G).
    It was adapted to the stage by Sandra Kersten; see "In
 Memory of an Aristocrat" (B 1).

Grand. New York: House of Books, 1964. Unpaged.
 Limited edition.

Esquire 66 (Nov. 1966): 136, 158.

Knightly Quest, 1966: 167-83 (B 2).

Knightly Quest, 1968: 242-53 (B 2).

Daily Telegraph 15 Nov. 1968.

Collected Stories, 1985: 379-87; 1986: 400-09 (B 2).

Trans. (H): French, German, Italian, Spanish.

"HAPPINESS IS RELEVANT": Series of notes on problems of the
 artist, written for New York opening of *Seven Descents of
 Myrtle*.

New York Times 24 Mar. 1968, sec. 2: 1, 3. Rpt. Van
   Antwerp (F 1): 247-49.

"THE HISTORY OF A PLAY (WITH PARENTHESES)": Essay concerning *Battle of Angels* and Williams's philosophy of writing.

   Pharos 1/2 (Spring 1945): 110-21. Rpt. Van Antwerp (F
   1): 44-50.

"HOMAGE TO KEY WEST": Tribute to one of his places of residence.

   Harper's Bazaar 106 (Jan. 1973): 50-51. Rpt. Van Antwerp
   (F 1): 286-87.

   Where I Live, 1978: 160-64 (D 2).

"THE HUMAN PSYCHE - ALONE": Review of Paul Bowles's collection of stories *The Delicate Prey*.

   Saturday Review of Literature 33 (23 Dec. 1950): 19-20.
   Rpt. Van Antwerp (F 1): 128-29.

   Where I Live, 1978: 35-39 (D 2).

"'I AM WIDELY REGARDED AS THE GHOST OF A WRITER'": Reflec-
tion on his temperamental nature, written for New York
opening of *Vieux Carré* but largely concerned with a Key
West production of *The Eccentricities of a Nightingale*.

   New York Times 8 May 1977, sec. 2: 3, 20.

"'I HAVE REWRITTEN A PLAY FOR ARTISTIC PURITY'": Essay
written for New York opening of *Eccentricities of a
Nightingale* concerning its origins.

   New York Times 21 Nov. 1976, sec. 2: 1, 5.

"IF THE WRITING IS HONEST": see Introductions (Inge, below)

**INTRODUCTION TO CARSON McCULLERS'S *REFLECTIONS IN A GOLDEN
   EYE***: see Introductions (McCullers, below)

INTRODUCTIONS AND NOTES: Paragraphs to full-length essays written for the following ten works.

Bowles, Jane. *Feminine Wiles*. Santa Barbara, CA: Black Sparrow, 1976. 7-8. "Foreword."

Carr, Virginia Spencer. *The Lonely Hunter: A Biography of Carson McCullers*. Garden City: Doubleday, 1975. xvii-xix. "Some Words Before."

Choukri, Mohamed. *Tennessee Williams in Tangier* (F 1): 89. "Note."

Evans, Oliver. *Young Man with a Screwdriver*. Lincoln: Univ. of Nebraska Pr., 1950. 1-3. "Foreword." Review (mentioning Williams):
    Crane, Milton. *New York Times Book Review* 4 June 1950: 28.

Gallaway, Marian. *Constructing a Play*. New York: Prentice-Hall, 1950. vii-xi. "Foreword" [to work by fellow student at Univ. of Iowa, stressing need for technique in writing].

Inge, William. *The Dark at the Top of the Stairs*. New York: Random House, 1958. vii-vix. New York: Bantam, 1960. "Introduction." Rpt. "The Writing Is Honest," *New York Times* 16 Mar. 1958, sec. 2: 1, 3; *The Passionate Playgoer...*, ed. George Oppenheimer (New York: Viking, 1958): 246-49; "If the Writing Is Honest," *Where I Live*, 1978: 100-04 (D 2).

Leavitt, R. F., ed. *The World of Tennessee Williams* (F 1): 9-10. "Introduction."

McCullers, Carson. *Reflections in a Golden Eye*. New Classics. New York: New Directions, 1950. ix-xxi. New York: Bantam Books, 1960. vii-xvi. "Introduction: This Book" [including reflections on the Southern Gothic]. Rpt. *Where I LIve*, 1978: 40-48 (D 2).

Maxwell, Gilbert. *Go Looking: Poems 1933-1953*. Boston: Bruce Humphries, 1954. 5-6. "Some Words Before" [containing a note on Hart Crane].

Williams, Dakin. *The Bar Bizarre*. Ed. Lucy Freeman. New York: Sunrise, 1980. 5. "Foreword."

"LET ME HANG IT ALL OUT": Essay written for New York opening of *Out Cry* but largely concerned with *A Streetcar
Named Desire* and *Cat on a Hot Tin Roof.*

New York Times 4 Mar. 1973, sec. 2: 1, 3.

"THE MAN IN THE OVERSTUFFED CHAIR": Memoir of Williams's
father, written about 1960. Ms., Columbia (G).

Antaeus 45-46 (Spring-Summer 1982): 281-91.

Collected Stories, 1985: vii-xvi; 1986: ix-xx (B 2).

Trans. (H): French.

"THE MEANING OF *THE ROSE TATTOO*": Essay written for New
York opening.

Untitled. *Vogue* 117 (15 Mar. 1951): 96.

Where I Live, 1978: 55-57 (D 2).

MEMOIRS/"SURVIVAL NOTES: A JOURNAL": Autobiography.
   "Survival Notes" was incorporated into Chaps. 1, 4, 5 of
Memoirs with only two cuts (one of which explains the
reference to "leaves" in the opening of Chap. 5) and much
added. Williams added four pages (229-33) to the British
edition.

Publication: "Survival Notes: A Journal"

Esquire 78 (Sept. 1972): 130-34, 166-68.

Times Saturday Review (London) 20 Jan. 1973: 8-9.

Publication: American Edition

Memoirs. Garden City: Doubleday, 1975. xxii, 264 pp.
   Ils. Limited and trade editions; Book-of-the-Month
   Club selection. Rpt. "Born Forty Years Too Soon,"
   Vogue 1965 (Nov. 1975): 193-95, 232-38 (excerpts).
   Reviews:
      Choice 12 (Feb. 1976): 1578.
      Times (London) 22 Nov. 1975: 10.
      Virgina Quarterly Review 52 (Spring 1976): 42.
      Barnes, Clive. *Times* (London) 22 Nov. 1975: 10.

Bodeen, Dewitt. *Films in Review* 27 (Apr. 1976):
238-39.
Carey, Gary. *Library Journal* 100 (1 Nov. 1975):
2045.
Cooke, M. G. *Yale Review* 65 (Summer 1976): 587-93.
Dvosin, Andrew. *Gay Sunshine* 29-30 (Summer-Fall
1976): 11. Response: see D 3.
Ganz, Arthur. *Tennessee Williams Newsletter* 1.1
(Spring 1979): 16-17.
Hughes, Catherine. *America* 134 (10 Jan. 1976): 10-
11. Rpt. Stanton (A 3): 171-73.
Kalem, T. E. *Time* 1 Dec. 1975: 83-84.
Kauffmann, Stanley. *Saturday Review/World* 1 Nov.
1975: 29-31.
Keith, Don Lee. *New Orleans Courier* 27 Nov.-3 Dec.
1975: 3-4.
Lassell, Michael. *Yale Theatre* 8 (Fall 1976): 78-
82.
Lehmann-Haupt, Christopher. *New York Times* 7 Nov.
1975: 35.
Mano, D. Keith. *National Review* 28 (16 Apr. 1976):
405-06.
Mewshaw, Michael. *Texas Monthly* Mar. 1976: 52.
Richardson, Jack. *New York Times Book Review* 2 Nov.
1975: 42-44.
Rosenthal, Raymond. *New Leader* 29 Mar. 1976: 18.
Tyler, Ralph. *Village Voice* 10 Nov. 1975: 55.
Vidal, Gore. *New York Review of Books* 5 Feb. 1976:
13-18. Rpt. *Matters of Fact and Fiction* (New
York: Random House, 1977): 129-47.
Von Bargen, Cathleen. *Cresset* Sept. 1976: 26.
Weales, Gerald. *New Republic* 27 Dec. 1975: 31-32.
Wilson, Frank. *Best Sellers* 35 (Mar. 1976): 378.

Memoirs. New York: Bantam Books, 1976. xiv, 334 pp.
Ils.

Publication: British Edition

Memoirs. London: W. H. Allen, 1976. London: W. H.
Allen, 1977. Star Book. xvi, 268 pp. Ils. Reviews:
Sunday Times (London) 12 Dec. 1976: 40.
Times (London) 18 Nov. 1976: 11.
Bailey, Paul. *Times Literary Supplement* 17 Dec.
1976: 1576.
Brien, Alan. *Spectator* 237 (20 Nov. 1976): 19.
Davies, Russell. *New Statesman* 92 (12 Nov. 1976):
683.

Trans. (H): Chinese, French, German, Spanish (version
uncertain).

"THE MISUNDERSTANDINGS AND FEARS OF AN ARTIST'S REVOLT":
Set of notes about his vision of the world at the moment.

Where I Live, 1978: 168-71.

"A MOVIE NAMED *LA TERRA TREMA*": Review of film by Luchino
Visconti. Ms., Texas (G).

'48: the Magazine of the Year 2.6 (June 1948).

NOTE ON EVE ADAMSON: Comments on artistic director of Jean
Cocteau Repertory Theatre.

Other Stages, 30 July 1981. Rpt. *Tennessee Williams
Review* 3.2 (1982): 38-39.

NOTE ON HART CRANE: see E 1

"NOTES FOR *THE TWO-CHARACTER PLAY*": Notes dated Mar. 1970;
given to Thomas P. Adler, Purdue Univ., 27 Apr. 1972.

Tennessee Williams Review 3.2 (1982): 3-5. Rpt. Van
Antwerp (F 1): 246-47.

"ON A STREETCAR NAMED SUCCESS"/"THE CATASTROPHE OF SUCCESS":
Essay written for opening of *Streetcar Named Desire*.
Ms., Texas (G).
  Story added a paragraph cut by *New York Times* and
changed the first sentence. Titles in subsequent collec-
tions do not indicate the source of text.

"On a Streetcar Named Success." *New York Times* 30 Nov.
1947, sec. 2: 1,3.

"The Catastrophe of Success." *Story* 32 (Spring 1948):
67-72.

Same. *Glass Menagerie*, 1948 and subsequent editions (A
1).

"On a Streetcar Named Success." *A Streetcar Named
Desire*, 1951 and subsequent editions (A 1)

Same. *American Playwrights on Drama*. Ed. Horst Frenz.
New York: Hill & Wang, 1965). 63-67.

Same. *Where I Live*, 1978: 15-22 (D 2).

"The Catastrophe of Success." *Harper's Bazaar* Jan. 1984: 132, 176.

"ON MEETING A YOUNG WRITER": Essay concerning Françoise Sagan.

Harper's Bazaar 90 (Aug. 1956): 124.

"ON THE ART OF BEING A TRUE NON-CONFORMIST": see "Something Wild"

"ON THE *CAMINO REAL*"/"FOREWORD TO *CAMINO REAL*": Essay written for New York opening.

New York Times 15 Mar. 1953, sec. 2: 1-3.

"Foreword": *Camino Real*, 1953 and subsequent editions (A 1)

Same. *Where I Live*, 1978: 63-67 (D 2).

"THE PAST, THE PRESENT, AND THE PERHAPS": Essay written for New York opening of *Orpheus Descending*, giving much information about his life in the 1930s and about *Battle of Angels* Ms., Texas (G).

"Tennessee Williams on the Past, the Present, and the Perhaps." *New York Times* 17 Mar. 1957, sec. 2: 1, 3.

Orpheus Descending, 1958 and subsequent editions (A 1).

Where I Live, 1978: 81-87 (D 2).

"PERSON-TO-PERSON": Essay written for New York opening of *Cat on a Hot Tin Roof*.

New York Times 20 Mar. 1955, sec. 2: 1, 3.

Cat on a Hot Tin Roof, 1955 and subsequent editions of first version (A 1).

Where I Live, 1978: 75-80 (D 2).

"THE PLEASURES OF THE TABLE":   Travel essay.

Where I Live, 1978: 165-67 (D 2).

"PRAISE TO ASSENTING ANGELS":   Essay about Carson McCullers.
Mss., Delaware, Texas (G).

Excerpts qtd. by Margarita G. Smith in intro. to Carson
McCullers's *The Mortgaged Heart*. Boston: Houghton
Mifflin, 1971. xii-xiii, xvii-xix.

"PRELUDE TO A COMEDY":   Essay written for New York opening
of *Period of Adjustment*.

New York Times 6 Nov. 1960, sec. 2: 1, 3.

Where I Live, 1978: 121-26 (D 2).

PROGRAM NOTES: Brief comments about plays in production.

Camino Real. Los Angeles: Mark Taper Forum Theatre,
1968.

The Milk Train Doesn't Stop Here Anymore. Spoleto:
Quinto Festival dei due Mondi, July 1962.

The Notebook of Trigorin. Press releases, 1981.

Stairs to the Roof. *Pasadena Playhouse News* 26 Feb.
1947: 3.

The Starless Sky by Donald Windham. Houston: Playhouse
Theatre, 13 May 1953.

Sweet Bird of Youth. Coral Gables, FL: Studio M Playhouse, 16 Apr. 1956. Rpt. Leavitt (F 1): 114.

"QUESTIONS WITHOUT ANSWERS":   Essay written for New York
opening of *Summer and Smoke*.

New York Times 3 Oct. 1948, sec. 2: 1, 3. Rpt. Van
Antwerp (F 1): 114-16.

Where I Live, 1978: 23-27 (D 2).

"REFLECTIONS ON A REVIVAL OF A CONTROVERSIAL FANTASY":
Essay written for New York revival of *Camino Real*.

New York Times 15 May 1960, sec. 2: 1, 3.

"SOME MEMOIRS OF A CON MAN": Autobiographical notes, 1971,
pub. St. Just (D 3): 233-43.

"SOMETHING WILD...": Autobiographical essay about nature of
the artist, a tribute to the Little Theatre of his youth.

"On the Art of Being a True Non-Conformist." *New York
Star* 7 Nov. 1948, leisure sec.: 5, 14.

"Something Wild...." *27 Wagons Full of Cotton*, 1953,
1966: vii-xii (A 1).

Same. *Where I Live*, 1978: 7-14 (D 2).

"A SUMMER OF DISCOVERY": Essay written for New York opening
of *Night of the Iguana*, giving the play's background.

New York Herald Tribune 24 Dec. 1961.

Where I Live, 1978: 137-47 (D 2).

"SURVIVAL NOTES: A JOURNAL": see *Memoirs* (above)

"T. WILLIAMS'S VIEW OF T. BANKHEAD": Tribute to Tallulah
Bankhead, written for second New York opening of *Milk
Train Doesn't Stop Here Anymore*.

New York Times 29 Dec. 1963, sec. 2: 1, 3.

Where I Live, 1978: 148-54 (D 2).

"A TALK WITH TENNESSEE WILLIAMS": see "The World I Live In"

"TENNESSEE, NEVER TALK TO AN ACTRESS": Essay concening
rehearsals, written for New York opening of *In the Bar of
a Tokyo Hotel*; tribute to six actresses: Laurette Taylor, Tallulah Bankhead, Diana Barrymore, Estelle Parsons,
Anne Meacham, Maureen Stapleton.

New York Times, 4 May 1969, sec. 2: 1, 16.

"TENNESSEE WILLIAMS PRESENTS HIS POV":   Response to essay
written by Marya Mannes (A 3).   Ms., California-Los
Angeles (G).

New York Times Magazine 12 June 1960: 19, 78.   Rpt. Van
Antwerp (F 1): 207-10.   Response:
New York Times Magazine 26 June 1960: 16; 7 Aug.
1960: 2.

*Background and Foregrounds: An Anthology of Articles from
the New York Times Magazine.*   Ed. Lester Markel.   Great
Neck, NY: Channel, 1960.   301-05.

Where I Live, 1978: 114-20 (D 2).

"THE TIMELESS WORLD OF A PLAY":   Essay written for New York
opening of *Rose Tattoo*.   Ms., Texas (G).

"Concerning the Timeless World of a Play."   *New York
Times* 14 Jan. 1951, sec. 2: 1, 3.

Rose Tattoo, 1951 and subsequent editions (A 1).

Hurrel, John D., ed., 1961:   see A 1 (*Streetcar*, Criticism): 49-52.

American Playwrights on Drama.   Ed. Horst Frenz.   New
York: Hill & Wang, 1965.   84-88.

Where I Live, 1978: 49-54 (D 2).

Inclusion in Textbooks

Corrigan, Robert W., ed.   *The Making of Theatre: From
Drama to Performance.*   New York: Scott, 1980.   24-26.

---, ed.   *The Modern Theatre.*   New York: Macmillan, 1964.
1216-18.

Weiss, Samuel A., ed.   *Drama in the Modern World: Plays
and Essays.*   Boston: Heath, 1964.

"TO WILLIAM INGE: AN HOMAGE":   Eulogy for fellow playwright,
written in Italy, June 1973.

New York Times 1 July 1973, sec. 2: 1, 8.

"TOO PERSONAL?":   Essay written for *New York Times* for opening of *Small Craft Warnings* (the newspaper chose to publish an interview instead).

Small Craft Warnings, 1972 and subsequent editions (A 1).

Where I Live, 1978: 155-59 (D 2).

"W. H. AUDEN: A FEW REMINISCENCES":   Tribute to poet.

Harvard Advocate 108.2-3 (Sept. 1975): 59.

"WE ARE DISSENTERS NOW":   Series of notes about the political situation in America.

Harper's Bazaar 105 (Jan. 1972): 40-41.

"WHAT COLLEGE HAS NOT DONE FOR ME":   Anonymous essay probably by Williams.

Eliot (Washington Univ.) 5 (June 1937): 11, 22, 24.

"WHAT'S NEXT ON THE AGENDA, MR. WILLIAMS?":   Autobiographical piece about 1969 confinement in a St. Louis mental
hospital. Ms., California-Los Angles (G).
  Williams read the piece at the 1970 London Poetry Festival.

Mediterranean Review 1 (Winter 1971): 15-19. Rpt. Maria
St. Just (D 3).

"WHERE MY HEAD IS NOW AND OTHER QUESTIONS":   Autobiographical notes.

Performing Arts 7 (Apr. 1973): 26-27.

**"WILLIAMS' WELLS OF VIOLENCE"/"FOREWORD TO *SWEET BIRD OF
YOUTH*"**:   Essay written for New York opening, reviewing
several of his plays.

New York Times 8 Mar. 1959, sec. 2: 1, 3.

  "Foreword": *Sweet Bird of Youth*, 1959 and subsequent
  editionss (A 1).

Same. *Where I Live*, 1978: 105-10 (D 2).

"THE WOLF AND I": Autobiographical piece about problems with a dog, written for New York opening of *Slapstick Tragedy*.

> *New York Times* 20 Feb. 1966, sec. 2: 1, 5. Rpt. Van Antwerp (F 1): 240-42.

"THE WORLD I LIVE IN": Self-interview. Ms., California-Los Angeles (G)?

> "A Talk with Tennessee Williams." *New York Post Magazine* 17 Mar. 1957: 4.

> "The World I Live In." *London Observer* 7 Apr. 1957: 14.

> Same. *Where I Live*, 1978: 88-92 (D 2).

> Trans. (H): German.

"A WRITER'S QUEST FOR A PARNASSUS": Travel essay.

New York Times Magazine 13 Aug. 1950: 16, 35.

Where I Live, 1978: 28-34 (D 2).

2. COLLECTION

Where I Live: Selected Essays. Ed. Christine R. Day and Bob Woods. New York: New Directions, 1978; Toronto: McClelland & Stewart, 1978. vi, 171 pp. Also New Directions Paperbook. Contents: Christine R. Day: Introduction: "Personal Lyricism," vii-xiv; "Preface to My Poems" (C 2), 1-6; "Something Wild...," 7-14; "On a Streetcar Named Success," 15-22; "Questions without Answer," 23-27; "A Writer's Quest for a Parnassus," 28-34; "The Human Psyche - Alone," 35-39; "Introduction to Carson McCullers's *Reflections in a Golden Eye*," 40-48; "The Timeless World of a Play," 49-54; "The Meaning of *The Rose Tattoo*," 55-57; "Facts about Me," 58-62; "Foreword to *Camino Real*," 63-67; "Afterword to *Camino Real*" (A 1), 68-69; "Critic Says 'Evasion,' Writer Says 'Mystery,'" 70-74; "Person-to-Person," 75-80; "The Past, the Present, and the Perhaps," 81-87; "The World I Live In," 88-92; "Author and Director: A Delicate Situation," 93-99; "If the Writing

Is Honest," 100-104; "Foreword to *Sweet Bird of Youth*,"
105-10; "Reflections on a Revival of a Controversal Fan-
tasy," 111-13; "Tennessee Williams Presents His POV,"
114-20; "Prelude to a Comedy," 121-26; "Five Fiery
Ladies," 127-32; "Biography of Carson McCullers," 133-36;
"A Summer of Discovery," 137-47; "T. Williams's View of
T. Bankhead," 148-54; "Too Personal?" 155-59; "Homage to
Key West," 160-64; "The Pleasures of the Table," 165-67;
"The Misunderstandings and Fears of an Artist's Revolt,"
168-71. Reviews:
   Antioch Review 37 (Summer 1979): 379.
   Booklist 75 (1 Nov. 1978): 451
   Choice 16 (Mar. 1979): 83.
   Kirkus 46 (15 Oct. 1978): 1180.
   Publishers Weekly 214 (16 Oct. 1978): 112.
   Adler, Jacob H. *Southern Literary Journal* 12 (Fall
      1979): 96-99.
   Bone, Larry Earl. *Library Journal* 104 (1 Feb. 1979):
      404.
   Chesler, S. Alan. *Tennessee Williams Newsletter* 2.2
      (Fall 1979): 17-18.
   Holditch, W. Kenneth. *Southern Review* 15 (July 1979):
      753-62.
   Langer, Ingeborg. *Best Sellers* 39 (Apr. 1979): 33.
   Sullivan, Jack. *Saturday Review* Dec. 1978: 54.

                    3. PUBLISHED LETTERS

LETTERS TO THE EDITOR:

   Atlantic Jan. 1971: 34-35. ["An Open Response to Tom
      Buckley"; reply to interview (F 1)]

   Esquire May 1948: 46. [Reply to Sidney Carroll's note (F
      1)]

   Gay Sunshine 31 (Winter 1977): 26. [Reply to Andrew
      Dvosin's review of *Memoirs* (D 1)]

   Link (Alpha Tau Omega, Gamma Rho Chapter) Aug. 1932: 4.
      ["Dictator of Fashion Comments on Style"]

   New York Post 4 May 1958, sec. 2: 5. Rpt. Van Antwerp (F
      1): 187. [Correction to Robert Rice's article (F 1)]

   New York Times 4 Mar. 1956, sec. 2: 3. Rpt. Van Antwerp
      (F 1): 160-61. [Tribute to Tallulah Bankhead] Com-
      ment: *Theatre Arts* June 1956: 11.

294 Occasional Pieces, Autobiography, Letters

New York Times 12 Dec. 1972: 46. Rpt. Leavitt (F 1):
151. [On Dr. Max Jacobson]

New York Times 3 Aug. 1980, sec. 2: 4, 14. [Response to
Harold Clurman's letter on *Clothes for a Summer Hotel*
(A 1)]

New York Times Book Review 15 Jan. 1978: 14, 18. [Reply
to Robert Brustein's review of Donald Windham's collection of letters (below)]

Newsweek 18 Feb. 1963: 6. [Response to quotation, *Newsweek* 4 Feb. 1963: 5]

St. Louis Dispatch 2 Jan. 1948. Rpt. Van Antwerp (F 1):
102. [Apology for comments in Irwin interview (F 1)]

Saturday Review of Literature 19 Aug. 1950: 24. [On Oliver Evans and Jose Garcia Villa]

Syracuse Review 2 (Jan. 1957): 19. [Reply to Charles
Thomas Samuels (A 3)]

Theatre Arts Oct. 1955: 3. [Reply to Arthur B. Waters's
article (F 1)]

Time 8 Sept. 1980. [Praise of Harold Clurman]

LETTER TO GENERAL PUBLIC:

Appeal for contributions, Privacy Rights '82, summer
1982. Note:
Hammond, John. "Without a Single Apology: Sean
O'Brien Runs for Congress." *New York Native* 17
Sept. 1990: 18-19. [Background identifying Alan
Baron as actual author]

LETTERS TO FAMILY, FRIENDS, AND PEERS:

Foley, Martha. *The Story of Story Magazine: A Memoir.*
Ed. Jay Neugeboren. New York: Norton, 1980. 265.

Garfield, David, 1980 (F 1): 194-95.

Goodrum, Charles A. *Treasures of the Library of Congress.* New York: Abrams, 1980, 1991. 297. [To Joseph
Wood Krutch]

Leavitt, Richard F., ed., 1978 (F 1): 38, 40-41, 47, 49,
    52-53, 67, 82, 85, 118. [To family, Maria Vaccaro,
    Audrey Wood]

Nelson, Benjamin, 1961 (A 1): 43-44, 50, 76-77, 89, 155,
    288. [To Paul Bigelow, Jordan Massee, Audrey Wood]

St. Just, Maria Britneva, ed. *Five O'Clock Angel: Let-
    ters of Tennessee Williams to Maria St. Just 1948-1982.*
    New York: Knopf, 1990. London: Deutsch, 1991. xix,
    407 pp. Contents: Elia Kazan, Preface, ix; Introduc-
    tion, xiii-xix; letters with commentary, 3-393.
    Reviews:
        New York Times 15 July 1990: 16. [Advertisement
            with blurbs]
        New Yorker 18 June 1990: 951.
        Athas, Daphne. *Greensboro News & Record* 22 July
            1990, sec. E: 5.
        Holditch, W. Kenneth. *Tennessee Williams Literary
            Journal* 2.1 (Winter 1990-91): 51-54.
        Kakutani, Michiko. *New York Times*
        Nash, Charles C. *Library Journal* 15 Apr. 1990: 95.
        Stuttaford, Genevieve. *Publishers Weekly* 30 Mar.
            1990: 44.
        White, Edmund. *New York Times Book Review* 27 May
            1990: 1, 24-25.
        Windham, Donald. *New York Review of Books* 19 July
            1990: 12-14.

Steen, Mike, ed., 1969 (F 1): 179, 181. Rpt. Leavitt (F
    1): 77. [To Jessica Tandy]

"Tennessee Williams Talks about His Play *In the Bar of a
    Tokyo Hotel*." *New York Times* 14 May 1969: 36. Rpt.
    Leavitt (F 1): 146. [To cast; used in advertisement]

Williams, Edwina Dakin, and Lucy Freeman, 1963 (F 1): 45,
    52-53 (rpt. Van Antwerp [F 1]: 19-20), 64, 71 (rpt. Van
    Antwerp [F 1]: 22), 79-83, 89-96, 101-03, 109-12, 114-
    17, 119, 125-29, 141, 152-53, 158, 187, 195-96, 219,
    224-30, 233-34, 242-47. [To family]

Windham, Donald, ed. *Tennessee Williams' Letters to
    Donald Windham 1940-65.* Verona, Italy: Sandy M. Camp-
    bell, 1976. Limited edition. *Tennessee Williams' Let-
    ters to Donald Windham 1940-1965.* New York: Holt,
    Rinehart & Winston, 1977. xi, 333 pp. Ils. Ham-
    mondsworth/New York: Penguin, 1980. Contents: Intro-
    duction, v-xi; letters, 1-317; Appendix, 319-323. Rpt.
    Christopher Street Oct. 1977: 4-17; Van Antwerp (F 1):

50-53, 102-03, 142-44 (excerpts). Reviews, Controvery
over Publication:
  Choice 15 (Mar. 1978): 75.
  Bailey, Paul. *Times Literary Supplement* 17 Dec.
    1976: 1576.
  Bone, Larry Earl. *Library Journal* 102 (15 Oct.
    1977): 2164.
  Brustein, Robert. *New York Times Book Review* 20
    Nov. 1977: 9. Rpt. *Critical Moments: Reflections
    on Theatre and Society 1973-1979* (New York: Random
    House, 1980): 30-34. Response: *New York Times
    Book Review* 15 Jan. 1978: 14, 18; *New York Times
    Book Review* 5 Feb. 1978: 44-45.
  Clarke, Gerald. *Time* 7 Feb. 1977: 94.
  Demott, Benjamin. *Atlantic* Sept. 1977: 90.
  Dlugos, Tim. *Christopher Street* Aug. 1977: 53-56.
  Holditch, W. Kenneth. *Southern Review* 15 (July
    1979): 753-62.
  Kinnucan, William A. H. *New Republic* 4 Feb. 1978:
    38.
  Leigh, D. J. *Best Sellers* 37 (Mar. 1978): 394.
  Lester, Elenore. *Soho Weekly News* 20 Oct. 1977: 57.
  Rader, Dotson. "The Private Letters of Tennessee
    Williams." *London Magazine* July 1978: 18-28.
    Court case, letter from Windham, apology: *London
    Magazine* Feb.-Mar. 1981: 80-88. Resume: *Tennes-
    see Williams Review* 3.1 (1981): 29-31. [Result of
    libel suit against Rader settled in Windham's
    favor]
  Rodman, Selden. *National Review* 30 (1 Sept. 1978):
    1094.
  Sullivan, Jack. *Saturday Review* 15 Oct. 1977: 35.
  Weales, Gerald. *Tennessee Williams Newsletter* 1.1
    (Spring 1979): 11-13.
  Whitmore, George. *Washington Post Book World* 8 Jan.
    1978: 4.

4. LAST WILL AND TESTAMENT

LAST WILL AND TESTAMENT: Document dated 11 Sept. 1980, with
codicil dated Dec. 1982.

  Tennessee Williams Review 4.1 (1983): 82-90. Rpt. Van
  Antwerp (F 1): 389 (page of codicil).

Filing and Probation

"Author's Papers Donated." *USA Today* 23 Mar. 1988.

Desruisseaux, Paul. "2 Universities Named Playwright's Beneficiaries." *Chronicle of Higher Education* 23 Mar. 1983: 3.

Gruson, Lindsay. "Harvard to Direct Williams Bequest." *New York Times* 22 Mar. 1983: 13.

McGrath, Ellie, and John E. Yang. "Sewanee, How I Love You...." *Time* 4 Apr. 1983: 67.

"Sewanee, How I Love You." *Tennessee Williams Literary Journal* 2.1 (Winter 1990-91): 67-70.

"Tennessee Williams Leaves Most of Estate for Writers." *New York Times* 12 Mar. 1983: 10.

"University Elated by $10 Million Williams Bequest." *New York Times* 13 Mar. 1983: 34.

E. MISCELLANEOUS MATERIALS

Here are included various items that did not fit well anywhere else. E 1 lists readings recorded by Williams. Others exist in studios and universities. (Recorded interviews are listed in F 1.)

E 2 is concerned with Williams's artistic career. He was interested in painting and sketching from the 1940s. There have been showings in Charleston, SC (1979) and at Key West Community College (1990). Larry Berk, the college reference librarian, says that most of the paintings are in private collections and that so far as he knows no catalogue has ever been published.

E 3 lists productions, with reviews, based on Williams's own writings or on his ideas. See also C 4.

1. RECORDED READINGS

The Donsinger Woman and Their Handy Man Jack. Videotape. Washington, DC: Devillier-Donegan, 1982. [short story]

Tennessee Williams Reading from The Glass Menagerie, The Yellow Bird, and Five Poems. Caedmon Records, 1952. On record: *Tennessee Williams Reading from His Works*. Contents: *The Glass Menagerie* (A 1 excerpts); "Cried the Fox" (C 1); "The Eyes" (C 1); "The Summer Belvedere" (C 1); Some Poems Meant for Music: "Which Is My Little Boy?" (C 1), "Little Horse," "Gold Tooth Blues," "Kitchen Door Blues" (C 1), "Heavenly Grass" (C 1); "My Little One"; "The Yellow Bird" (B 1). On record jacket: "Facts about Me" (D 1). Review:
   Publishers Weekly 6 Nov. 1987: 43.

Tennessee Williams Reads Hart Crane. Caedmon Records, 1965. On record jacket: Note on Hart Crane.

2. PAINTINGS AND SKETCHES

Britton, Burt, ed. *Book People Picture Themselves*. New York: Random House, 1976. 75. [Reproduction]

Hjerter, Kathleen G., ed. *Doubly Gifted: The Author as
  Visual Artist*. New York: Abrams, 1986. 140-41. [Repro-
  ductions]

Lambert, Arthur. "Vassilis Voglis: A Painter from Two
  Worlds." *Advocate* 6 June 1989: 81-83. [Williams at work
  in his company]

Leavitt, Richard (F 1): facing 64. [Reproduction]

Phillips, Jane. "Art Beat." *Island Life* (Key West) 4 Jan.
  1990: 19.

Rader, Dotson (F 1): following 231. [Photograph of Williams painting]

St. Just, Maria (D 3): 132, 186, 322. [Reproductions]   See
  also 385. [Photograph of Williams painting]

Staton, Robert W. "Tennessee Williams: The Playwright as
  Painter." *Advocate* 1 Nov. 1978. [Modeling for Williams]

Van Antwerp, Margaret A. (F 1): 159, 355, 376. [Reproduc-
  tions]

"Williams' Paintings." *Key West Citizen* 11 Jan. 1990, sec.
  A: 7. [Photograph]

Williams, Tennessee. *Androgyne, Mon Amour*, 1977 (C 2):
  dustjacket. [Reproduction]

3.   PRODUCTIONS BASED ON WORDS OR IDEAS

An Evening with Tennessee Williams. Westhampton, NY, Writers Festival: 14 May 1988. With Dakin Williams. Report:
  Ketcham Diane. *New York Times* (Long Island Weekly) 22
    May 1988, sec. 21: 3. [Budd Schulberg's objections]

Tennessee's Belles. Script by Cynthia Wood and John G. Moy-
nihan. Galveston, TX: Strand Street Theatre, fall 1983; 25
May-17 June 1984. John G. Moynihan, dir. Music by Henry
Aronson. With Cynthia Wood.

Tennessee Williams: A Celebration. Williamstown Theatre
Festival. Williamstown, MA: 1-10 July 1982. Nikos Psacha-
ropoulos, dir. With Karen Allen, Joyce Ebert, Carrie Nye.
Notes:
  New York Times 23 June 1982, sec. 3: 21.
  Graham, Jennifer W. *Horizon* Oct.-Nov. 1982: 63.

Tennessee Williams's South.   Television script by Harry
Rasky.   CBC–TV (Canada), 26 Mar. 1973.   PBS–TV, 8 Dec. 1976.
Harry Rasky, dir.   With Tennessee Williams, Burl Ives,
Maureen Stapleton, Colleen Dewhurst, Jessica Tandy.
Reviews, Prod. Notes:

  Harris, Radie.   *Hollywood Reporter* 18 Apr. 1972: 4.

  Miller, Jack.   *Toronto Star* 27 Mar. 1973.   Rpt. Rasky (F
    1): 93.

  O'Connor, John J.   *New York Times* 8 Dec. 1976, sec. C:
    24.

  Rasky, Harry.   *Tennessee Williams*, 1986 (F 1).

Tennessee Williams' "The Migrants."   Television play by Lan-
ford Wilson.   Playhouse 90.   CBS–TV, 3 Feb. 1974.   Tom
Gries, dir.   With Cloris Leachman (Mother), Ron Howard
(Son), Sissy Spacek (Daughter).   Reviews:

  New York Times 3 Feb. 1974, sec. 2: 19.

  O'Connor, John J.   *New York Times* 1 Feb. 1974: 61.

F. BIOGRAPHICAL SOURCES

F 1 lists, in alphabetical order, biographies and the great number of interviews which are more or less readily available. (Since early interviews blurred into biography, it seemed best to group all this material. Note: Newspapers and some magazines use quotation marks to indicate titles within titles; for clarity I have italicized them.) Alan M. Cohn (I), John S. McCann (I), and Donald Spoto (F 1) list still other interviews; and the files assembled by Ken Craven at the University of Texas Humanities Research Center contain others from local newspapers across the country. Williams was generous with reporters.

F 2 lists eulogies and F 3 other tributes paid to Williams, both alphabetically. F 4 includes romans and drames à clef. Finally F 5 lists productions based on his life. The scholar should also look to Section D and to entries in E 2, as well as the chronology provided at the beginning of the bibliography. A picture of Williams's life is beginning to emerge as various friends publish their memoirs and as biographers start putting information together, but we are too close to the subject to see him clearly.

1. INTERVIEWS AND BIOGRAPHIES

Acton, Harold. *More Memoirs of an Aesthete*. London: Methuen, 1970. *Memoirs of an Aesthete 1939-1969*. New York: Viking, 1970. Vol. 2: 212-15. [Meeting in Rome]

Adler, Jacob H. *Southern Writers: A Biographical Dictionary*. Ed. Robert Bain et al. Baton Rouge: Louisiana State Univ. Pr., 1979. 497-99.

Alfieri, Richard. "Tennessee Williams: A Remembrance." *Mandate* Sept. 1983: 38.

Alsop, Kenneth. "Tennessee Williams - and the Albatross." *The Curtain Rises....* Ed. Dick Richards. London: Frewin, 1966. 88-92.

Amory, Cleveland. *Celebrity Register: An Irreverent Compendium of American Quotable Notables*. New York: Harper, 1963. Rpt. *McCall's* Jan. 1964: 4.

Atkins, Thomas R. "The Astonishing Mystery of Life: The
    Playwright Talks about His Work." *Tennessee Williams
    Literary Journal* 1.2 (Winter 1989-90): 35-40. [Inter-
    view, Orlando, Mar. 1981]

Baker, Joe. "Key West Thugs Mug Tennessee Williams." *Advo-
    cate* 5 Apr. 1979: 10.

Baker, John. Interview with Kate Medina. Van Antwerp (be-
    low): 313-15. [Doubleday editor of *Memoirs*]

Balch, Jack S. "A Profile of Tennessee Williams." *Theatre*
    Apr. 1958: 15, 36, 40.

Banker, Stephen. *Tennessee Williams.* Washington, DC: Tapes
    for Readers, 1978. [Interview]

Barnes, Clive. "Tennessee Williams." *American Way* May
    1975: 21-24.

---. "Tennessee Williams: A Toast at Turning 70." *New York
    Post* 26 Mar. 1981: 39.

Barnett, Lincoln. "Tennessee Williams." *Life* 16 Feb. 1948:
    113-27. Rpt. *Writings on Life...* (New York: Sloane,
    1951): 243-61. Response: *Life* 8 Mar. 1948: 16 (Carson
    McCullers).

Barron, Mark. "Newest Find on Broadway Is a Mississippi
    Playwright Named Tennessee Williams." *Memphis Commercial
    Appeal* 24 Nov. 1940, sec. 1: 14. Rpt. Devlin (below), 3-
    5.

Becker, Samuel L. *Department of Communication and Theatre
    Arts Newsletter* (Univ. of Iowa) Dec. 1980: [5-6]. [Peri-
    od at Univ.]

Bell, Arthur. "'I've Never Faked It.'" *Village Voice* 24
    Feb. 1972: 58-62. Rpt. Leavitt (below): 154.
    [Interview]

Bellavance-Johnson, Marsha. *Tennessee Williams in Key West
    & Miami: A Guide.* Ils. Allison Gosney. Ketchum, ID:
    Computer Lab, 1989.

Berkvist, Robert. "The Big Daddy of Playwrights." *After
    Dark* Oct. 1981: 52-53.

---. "Broadway Discovers Tennessee Williams." *New York
    Times* 21 Dec. 1975, sec. 2: 1, 4-5. [Interview]

Bilowit, Ira J.   "Roundtable: Tennessee Williams, Craig
    Anderson, and T. E. Kalem Talk about *Creve Coeur*." *New
    York Theatre Review* Mar. 1979: 14-18. Rpt. Devlin (be-
    low): 308-17.

"A Birthday for Williams." *New York Times* 25 Mar. 1980,
    sec. B: 18.

Blais, Madeleine.   "Three Scenes from the Life of a Tor-
    mented Playwright: At Wit's End at Land's End." *Miami
    Herald Tropic Magazine* 1 Apr. 1979: 12-16. Rpt. Van
    Antwerp (below): 350-57. [Interview]

Blum, David J.   "The Art and Anger of Tennessee Williams."
    Wall Street Journal 21 Nov. 1980: 29.

Bolton, Whitney.   Interview. *New York Morning Telegraph* 26
    Jan. 1959: 1-2.

---.   "Of Tennessee and the Sheriff." *New York Morning
    Telegraph* 1 July 1958: 3.

---.   "Tennessee Williams' First Comedy Has 'Humor,' Not
    Jokes and Gags." *New York Morning Telegraph* 3 Oct. 1960:
    2. [Interview, *Period of Adjustment*]

Book of the Year.   Chicago: Encyclopedia Britannica, 1984.
    [Obituary]

Bowles, Jane.   *Out in the World: Selected Letters...1935-
    1970*. Ed. Millicent Dillon. Santa Barbara: Black Spar-
    row, 1985. Passim.

Bowles, Paul.   *Without Stopping: An Autobiography*. New
    York: Putnam's, 1972. Passim.

Bragg, Melvin.   "The Imaginary World of Tennessee Williams."
    Listener 7 Oct. 1976: 445-46.

Braggiotti, Mary.   "Away from It All." *New York Post Maga-
    zine* 12 Dec. 1947: 65. [Interview]

"Brandeis Presents Awards in the Arts." *New York Times* 29
    Mar. 1965: 43. [Creative Arts Award]

Breit, Harvey.   "In and Out of Books." *New York Times Book
    Review* 3 July 1955: 8.

Brinnin, John Malcolm.   *Truman Capote: Dear Heart, Old
    Buddy*. New York: Delacourte, 1986. Passim.

Brooks, Peter.   "Portrait Galley: A Provocative Playwright."
   Sunday Times (London) 7 Apr. 1957: 3.

Brown, Cecil.   "Interview with Tennessee Williams."   *Partisan Review* 45 (1978): 276-305.   Rpt. Van Antwerp
   (below): 331-42 (excerpts); Devlin (below): 251-83.

Brown, Dennis.   "Tennessee Williams' Mom: She Still Has Her
   Memories."   *Calendar* (*Los Angeles Times*) 11 Feb. 1979:
   58.

Buchwald, Art.   "*Baby Doll* Wasn't Good for Him."   *Paris
   Herald Tribune* 19 Apr. 1957.   [Interview]

Buckley, Peter.   "Tennessee Williams' New Lady."   *Horizon*
   Apr. 1980: 66-71.   Resume: *Tennessee Williams Newsletter*
   2.1 (Spring 1980): 43-45.   [*Clothes for a Summer Hotel*]

Buckley, Tom.   "Tennessee Williams Survives."   *Atlantic* Nov.
   1970: 98-108.   Rpt. Van Antwerp (below): 269-79; Devlin
   (below): 161-83.   [Interview]   Response to Williams (D
   3): *Atlantic* Jan. 1971: 35.

Burgess, Charles E.   "An American Experience: William Inge
   in St. Louis, 1943-1949."   *Papers in Language and Literature* 12 (1976): 438-68.

Calendo, John.   "Tennessee Talks to John Calendo."   *Interview* Apr. 1973: 26-28, 43.

Calmer, Charles.   "Tennessee's Years at Iowa: 1937-38."
   Playbill (Univ. of Iowa) 63 (June 1984): 16-19.

Canby, Vincent.   "I Never Depended on the Kindness of Strangers."   *New York Times* 8 May 1966, sec. 2: 1, 3.   [Inter-
   view with Audrey Wood]

Capote, Truman.   "Remembering Tennessee."   *Playboy* Jan.
   1984.   Rpt. *A Capote Reader* (New York: Random House,
   1987): 590-94.

Carr, Virginia Spencer.   *The Lonely Hunter: A Biography of
   Carson McCullers*.   Garden City: Doubleday, 1975.   271-77
   and passim.

---.   "Williams, An Aside."   *On Broadway: Performance Photographs by Fred Fehl*.   Ed. William Stott and Jane Stott.
   Austin: Univ. of Texas Pr., 1978.   334-35.   [Photograph]

Carragher, Bernard. "Born-Again Playwright: Tennessee."
New York Daily News 8 May 1977, leisure sec.: 3, 14.
[Interview]

Carroll, Sidney. "A Streetcar Named Tennessee." *Esquire*
May 1948: 46. [Interview] Response: see D 3.

Cassidy, Claudia. "Tennessee Williams - A Theater Orpheus
Who Looked Back." *Chicago Tribune* 4 July 1971. Rpt. Van
Antwerp (below): 279-82.

"Celluloid Brassiere." *New Yorker* 14 Apr. 1945: 18-19.
[Biography]

Chamberlain, John. "Meeting on an Island." *New Leader* 3
June 1950: 16-17. [Berlin Convention on Western culture]

Chambers, Andrea. "In Winter, U.S. Writing Talent Pools on
the Sensual, Timeless Port of Key West." *People Weekly*
23 Feb. 1981: 24-28.

Chandler, Charlotte. *The Ultimate Seduction*. Garden City:
Doubleday, 1984. 317-55. [Interview]

Chesler, S. Alan. "An Interview with Eve Adamson: Artistic
Director of Jean Cocteau Repertory Theatre." *Tennessee
Williams Review* 3.2 (1982): 39-45.

Choukri, Mohamed. *Tennessee Williams in Tangier*. Trans.
Paul Bowles. Santa Barbara: Cadmus, 1979. 91 pp. Il.
Limited edition. Contents: Gavin Lambert, Foreword, 9-
12; memoir, 15-85; Tennessee Williams, Note, 89.

Christiansen, Richard. "At 70, Even Tennessee Williams Is
Impressed." *New York Daily News* 23 Apr. 1981: 65. [In-
terview]

Ciment, Michael. *Kazan on Kazan*. London: Secker, 1973.
66-82. Rpt. Van Antwerp (below): 167-76.

Clarity, James F. "Williams Finds Cannes Festival a Crass
Menagerie." *New York Times* 24 May 1976: 36.

Clurman, Harold. "The Neon Sickness." *London Observer* 17
May 1959: 19.

Coe, Richard L. "Quiet Words from a Prolific Playwright."
Washington Post 2 Mar. 1975, sec. E: 1, 3. [Interview]

Cowan, Thomas. *Gay Men & Women Who Enriched the World*. New
Canaan, CT: Mulvey, 1989. 210-15.

Crawford, Cheryl. *One Naked Individual: My Fifty Years in the Theatre*. Indianapolis: Bobbs-Merrill, 1977. 183-201.

Creelman, Eileen. "Screen *Streetcar* Gets Author's Nod." *New York World-Telegram* 9 Sept. 1950. Rpt. Van Antwerp (below): 125-27.

Cummingham, Miles. "Tennessee Williams Talks to Press." *Rochester Times-Union* 4 Nov. 1961, sec. A: 14.

Cummings, Judith, and Laurie Johnston. "14 Win Medal of Freedom." *New York Times* 22 Apr. 1980, sec. B: 8.

Daley, Suzanne. "Williams Choked on a Bottle Cap." *New York Times* 27 Feb. 1983: 1, 39.

Da Ponte, Durant. "Tennessee's Tennessee Williams." *University of Tennessee Studies in the Humanities* 1 (1956): 11-17. [Ancestory]

Davis, Louise. "That Baby Doll Man." *Nashville Tennesssean Magazine* 3 Mar. 1957: 12-13, 30-31. Rpt. Devlin (below): 43-49. [Interview]

"Death of Playwright Questioned." *St. Louis Globe-Democrat* 9 Mar. 1983. Rpt. Van Antwerp (below): 400. [Dakin Williams]

Demaret, Kent. "In His Beloved Key West, Tennessee Williams Is Center Stage in a Furor over Gays." *People Weekly* 7 May 1979: 32-35. [Alleged mugging]

DeNoux, O'Neil. "'Mayor' Elected for Tennessee Tours." *New Orleans Times Picayune* 17 Mar. 1991, sec. F: 1, 7. [Dan Mosley, guide]

Devlin, Albert J., ed. *Conversations with Tennessee Williams*. Jackson/London: Univ. Pr. of Mississippi, 1986. xx, 369 pp. Review:
    Griffin, Joseph. *Canadian Review of American Studies* 18.4 (Winter 1987): 522-23.

Dillon, Millicent. *A Little Original Sin: The Life and Work of Jane Bowles*. New York: Holt, 1981. Passim.

Donahue, Francis. *The Dramatic World of Tennessee Williams*. New York: Frederick Ungar, 1964. 243 pp.

"Donates Pulitzer Cash." *New York Times* 9 June 1955: 33. [To Columbia School of Journalism]

Drew, Michael H. "Tennesse Williams' Life of Success and
    Sorrow." *Milwaukee Journal* 29 Jan. 1976. Rpt. *Authors
    in the News*, ed. Barbara Nykoruk (Detroit: Gale, 1976),
    vol. 2: 288. [Interview]

"Drugs Linked to Death of Tennessee Williams." *New York
    Times* 22 Aug. 1983: 37.

Drutman, Irving. "No New Play by Williams for a Year." *New
    York Herald Tribune* 31 Oct. 1948. Rpt. Van Antwerp (be-
    low): 120-22.

"Edwina Williams Is Dead at 95; Mother of Tennessee Wil-
    liams." *New York Times* 4 June 1980: 26. [Obituary]

[Evans, Jean.] "The Life and Ideas of Tennessee Williams."
    New York PM Magazine 6 May 1945: 6-7. Rpt. Van Antwerp
    (below): 70-72, 74; Devlin (above): 12-19. [Interview]

Evans, Oliver. *The Ballad of Carson McCullers*. London:
    Owens, 1965; New York: Coward-McCann, 1966. 144-46 and
    passim.

---. "A Pleasant Evening with Yukio Mishima." *Esquire* May
    1972: 126-30, 174-80.

Evans, Peter. "Tennessee Wants to Unsweeten Ava." *New York
    World-Telegram* 24 Oct. 1963: 12. [Film *Night of the
    Iguana*]

"An Evening Celebrates James Laughlin and Mourns Tennessee
    Williams." *Publishers Weekly* 11 Mar. 1983: 15.

Fawkes, Sandy. "Still Laughing - Though Love Has Passed Him
    By." *London Daily Express* 15 Aug. 1973: 8. [Interview]

Feineman, Neil. "Talking with Tennessee: A Playwright in
    Reticence." *Advocate* 28 June 1979: 31.

"15 Creative Artists to Get $1,000 Each." *New York Times* 27
    Apr. 1940: 18. [Rockefeller Fellowship]

"The Final Horror." *London Observer* 28 Mar. 1965: 23. [In-
    terview]

"5 in Arts to Be Honored." *New York Times* 13 Sept. 1979,
    sec. C: 11. [Kennedy Center Awards]

Flanner, Janet. *Darlinghissima: Letters to a Friend*. Ed.
    Natalie Danes. Murray, NY: Random House, 1985. Passim.

308   Biographical Sources

Fleming, Shirley. "Lee Hoiby - Tennessee Williams." *High Fidelity & Musical America* July 1971: MA 16, 32. [Interview]

"14 Win Admission to Arts Institute." *New York Times* 8 Feb. 1952: 18. [National Institute of Arts and Letters]

Fosburgh, Lacey. "Art and Literary People Urged to Look Inward." *New York Times* 22 May 1969: 52. [Academy Gold Medal for Drama]

Fraser, C. Gerald. "Miss Woodward, Newman Feted." *New York Times* 6 May 1975: 48.

Frazer, Winifred L. "A Day in the Life of Tennessee Williams." *Tennessee Williams Review* 3.2 (1982): 30-37. [Interview, Atlanta, Oct. 1979]

Freedley, George. "The Role of Poetry in the Modern Theatre," 1945. Rpt. Devlin (above): 20-24. [Interview] Resume: Wilella Waldorf, "Tennessee Williams Talks on Poetry in the Theatre," *New York Post* 4 Oct. 1945: 33.

Freedman, Samuel G. "The Life and Death of an Agent." *New York Times* 31 Dec. 1985, sec. C: 9. [Audrey Wood]

Frost, David. "Will God Talk Back to a Playwright?" *The Americans*. New York: Stein, 1970. 33-40. New York: Avon, 1970. London: Heinemann, 1971. Rpt. Van Antwerp (below): 157-69; Devlin (above): 140-46. [Interview] Analysis: Henry Raynor, "Intimate Conversation," *Times* (London) 16 July 1970: 9.

Funke, Lewis. "News and Gossip Gathered on the Rialto." *New York Times* 6 Dec. 1959, sec. 2: 5. [Four new plays]

---. "News of the Rialto: Renunciation." *New York Times* 5 Nov. 1961, sec. 2: 1.

---. "Rialto Gossip." *New York Times* 8 Mar. 1959, sec. 2: 1.

---. "Tennessee's 'Cry.'" *New York Times* 3 Dec. 1972, sec. 2: 1, 27.

---. "Williams Revival? Ask the Playwright." *New York Times* 8 Jan. 1970: 45. [Interview]

---, and John E. Booth. "Williams on Williams. *Theatre Arts* Jan. 1962: 16-19, 72-73. Rpt. Van Antwerp (below): 218-24; Devlin (above): 97-106. [Interview]

Gaines, Jim. "A Talk about Life and Style with Tennessee
Williams." *Saturday Review* 29 Apr. 1972: 25-29. Rpt.
Devlin (above): 213-23. [Interview]

Galligan, David. "Director José Quintero: Recollections of
a Friendship." *Advocate* 15 Sept. 1983: 42-43, 45.

Gamarekian, Barbara. "Kennedy Center Honors Five for Life
Achievements in Arts." *New York Times* 3 Dec. 1979, sec.
C: 14.

Garfield, David. A *Player's Place: The Story of the Actors
Studio.* New York: Macmillan, 1980. Passim.

Gassner, John, and Edward Quinn. *The Reader's Encyclopedia
of Drama.* New York: Crowell, 1969.

Gauen, Patrick, and Bill Smith. "Playwright's Bitter Days
Here Recalled." *St Louis Globe-Democrat* 26-27 Feb. 1983:
1, 12. Rpt. Van Antwerp (below): 394, 396-97.

Gehman, Richard. "Guardian Agent." *Theatre Arts* July 1950:
18. [Audrey Wood]

Gelb, Arthur. "Williams and Kazan and the Big Walkout."
New York Times 1 May 1960, sec. 2: 1, 3. Rpt. Van
Antwerp (below): 205-07; Devlin (above): 64-68.

Gill, Brendan. *Tallulah.* New York: Holt, 1972. 55, 79-80,
83-84.

Gilroy, Harry. "Mr. Williams Turns to Comedy." *New York
Times* 28 Jan. 1951, sec. 2: 1, 3. [*Rose Tattoo*]

Glover, William. "Backstage with Tennessee Williams."
Christian Science Monitor 7 Jan. 1963: 11. [Interview]

---. "Outraged Puritan." *International Herald Tribune* 10
May 1972: 16. [Interview]

Goldman, William. *The Season: A Candid Look at Broadway.*
New York: Harcourt, 1969. 94-96.

"Gossip of the Rialto." *New York Times* 24 Dec. 1939, sec.
9: 1. [Rockefeller Fellowship]

"Gossip of the Rialto." *New York Times* 7 Sept. 1941, sec.
9: 2. [Cronyn's option on one-acts]

Gould, Jean R.   "Tennessee Williams."   *Modern American Playwrights*.   New York: Dodd, Mead, 1966.   225-46.   [Bio-
graphy]

Grauerholz, James.   "Orpheus Holds His Own: William Bur-
roughs Talks with Tennessee Williams."   *Village Voice* 16
May 1977: 44-45.   Rpt. Devlin (above): 199-307.

"The Great Survivor."   *Sunday Times* (London) 28 Jan. 1973:
32.

Green, Blake.   "Tennessee Williams Takes a Long Look Back."
San Francisco Chronicle 25 Mar. 1976: 26.

Green, Michelle.   *The Dream at the End of the World: Paul
Bowles and the Literary Renegades in Tangier*.   New York:
Harper Collins, 1991.   368 pp.

Grobel, Lawrence.   *Conversations with Capote*.   New York: New
American Library, 1985.   Passim.

Gross, Jesse.   "Williams' Rap for Film Version."   *Variety* 30
Mar. 1960: 69, 75.   [Interview, *Sweet Bird*]

Gruen, John.   "The Inward Journey of Tennessee Williams."
New York Herald Tribune Magazine 2 May 1965: 29.   Rpt.
Close-Up (New York: Viking, 1968): 86-98; Devlin (above):
112-23 (exp. ver.).   [Interview]

Grunwald, Beverly.   "A Haunted Williams Is Writing about
Ghosts."   *Women's Wear Daily* 9 Apr. 1979: 17.   [Inter-
view]

---.   "Williams Longs for Togetherness."   *Houston Post* 22
July 1979.   [Interview]

Gunn, Drewey Wayne.   *American and British Writers in Mexico
1556-1973*.   Austin/London: Univ. of Texas Pr., 1974.
208-15.

Gussow, Mel.   "Tennessee Williams Is Dead Here at 71."   *New
York Times* 26 Feb. 1983: 1, 10.   Rpt. *Playbill* (Univ. of
Iowa) 63 (June 1984): 10-13; Van Antwerp (below): 388-92.
[Obituary]

---.   "Tennessee Williams on Art and Sex."   *New York Times* 3
Nov. 1975: 49.   [Interview]

---.   "Williams Is Mourned by Friends and Others."   *New York
Times* 28 Feb. 1983, sec. B: 3.

---. "Williams Looking to Play's Opening." *New York Times*
   31 Mar. 1972: 10. [Interview, *Small Craft Warnings*]

---. "Williams Still Hopes to Bring *The Red Devil* to Broadway Despite Boston Closing." *New York Times* 15 July
   1975: 39. [Interview]

Guthmann, Edward. "Franco Zeffirelli." *Advocate* 9 June
   1983: 46. [Comment on origins of *Streetcar*]

Hale, Allean. "Tennessee Williams at Missouri." *Missouri
   Alumnus* Jan.-Feb. 1986: 18-19.

---. "Two on a Streetcar." *Tennessee Williams Journal* 1.1
   (Spring 1989): 31-43. [New Orleans]

---: see A 1 (*Cat*: Criticism)

Haller, Scot. "The Twilight of Tennessee Williams: A Portrait of the Playwright in the Last Stages of a Great
   Career." *People Weekly* 14 Mar. 1983: 60-66. [Interview]

Harte, Barbara, and Carolyn Riley, eds. *200 Contemporary
   Authors: Bio-Bibliographies of Selected Leading Writers
   of Today with Critical and Personal Sidelights*. Detroit:
   Gale, 1969. 296-301.

Hayes, Robert, and Christopher Makos. "Tennessee Sings for
   Madame Sophia." *Interview* June 1976: 20.

Herbert, Hugh. "The Solid Gold Streetcar." *Guardian* 16
   Mar. 1974: 8. [Interview]

Herridge, Frances. "Tennessee Williams Adds to *Bar of a
   Tokyo Hotel*." *New York Post* 25 Apr. 1969: 40.
   [Interview]

Hewes, Henry. "Tennessee Williams - Last of Our Solid Gold
   Bohemians." *Saturday Review* 28 Mar. 1953: 25-27. Rpt.
   Devlin (above): 30-33.

Hicks, John. "Bard of Duncan Street: Scene Four." *Florida
   Magazine (Orlando Sentinel)* 29 July 1979: 18-19. Rpt.
   Devlin (above): 318-24. [Interview]

Highwater, Jamake. "Lifestyles: Tennessee Williams Is Alive
   and Well at the Plaza Hotel." *Playgirl* July 1974: 35-36.
   [Interview]

Hirshhorn, Clive. "When I'm Alone I'm Just Hell." *London
   Sunday Express* 28 Mar. 1965. [Interview]

Hoffman, Peter, with Anita Shreve, Fred Waitzkin. "The Last
    Days of Tennessee Williams." *New York* 25 July 1983: 41-
    49.

Hofmann, Paul. "Williams Tells Brother He's Fine." *New
    York Times* 30 June 1968: 54. Rpt. Leavitt (below): 149.

Holditch, W. Kenneth. "The Last Frontier of Bohemia: Ten-
    nessee Williams in New Orleans 1938-1983." *Southern
    Quarterly* 23.2 (1985): 1-37.

Holmes, Ann. "Baby, I've Come Back to Life." *Houston
    Chronicle* 17 Oct. 1971: 15. [Interview]

Hopkins, Thomas. "Rewrites of a Gothic Past." *Maclean's* 3
    Nov. 1980: 66-67. [Writer in Residence, Vancouver]

Hornak, Richard Wray. Interview. *Soho Weekly News* (New
    York) 25 Jan. 1979.

Houghton, Norris. "Tomorrow Arrives Today: Young Talent on
    Broadway." *Theatre Arts* Feb. 1946: 85-86.

House, Charles. *The Outrageous Life of Henry Faulkner: Por-
    trait of an Appalachian Artist.* Knoxville: Univ. of Ten-
    nessee Pr., 1988. 151-291 passim.

Hubbard, Kim, and Laura Sanderson Healy. "The Original Mag-
    gie the Cat, Maria St. Just, Remembers Her Loving Friend
    Tennessee Williams." *People Weekly* 2 Apr. 1990: 93-95.

Hughes, Catherine. "Tennessee Williams at 65." *America* 134
    (1 May 1976): 382-83.

Hyams, Joe. "Tennessee Williams Turns Critic." *New York
    Herald Tribune* 23 Dec. 1959: 13. [Interview]

Iachetta, Michael. "Tennessee Williams: A Playwright Reju-
    venated." *New York Sunday News* 1 Oct. 1972, sec. 3: 1,
    28.

Inge, M. Thomas, ed. *Truman Capote: Conversations.* Jack-
    son: Univ. Pr. of Mississippi, 1987. Passim.

Inge, William. "'Tennessee' Williams, Playwright, Author."
    St. Louis Star-Times 11 Nov. 1944: 11. Rpt. Van Antwerp
    (below): 58-59; Devlin (above): 6-8.

"Inside Stuff - Legit." *Variety* 4 Apr. 1945: 52. [Early
    sketch]

"Inside Stuff - Legit." *Variety* 24 June 1953: 62. [In
  Paris]

Interview. *London Daily Express* 5 May 1959: 10.

Interview. *Sunday Times* (London) 13 Aug. 1978: 35.

"Interview with Author." *New Orleans Times-Picayune* 30 Apr.
  1972, sec. 2: 8.

Irwin, Virginia. "'St. Louisans Cold, Smug, Complacent.'"
  St. Louis Post-Dispatch 22 Dec. 1947. Rpt. Van Antwerp
  (below): 101. [Interview] Response: see D 3.

Isaac, Dan. "Talking with Tennessee Williams." *After Dark*
  Oct. 1969: 46-50. Rpt. Devlin (above): 134-39.

Israel, Lee. *Miss Tallulah Bankhead*. New York: Puntman's,
  1972. 300-04, 340-44.

Jampel, Dave. "Tennessee Williams Touring Orient, Working
  in Mornings on Four Scripts." *Variety* 30 Sept. 1959: 1.

Jennings, C. Robert. "*Playboy* Interview: Tennessee Williams." *Playboy* Apr. 1973: 69-84. Rpt. *The Playboy
  Interviews*, ed. G. Barry Golson (New York: Playboy,
  1981): 352-69; Van Antwerp (below): 289-92 (excerpts);
  Devlin (above): 224-50.

Johnson, Harriett. "Tennessee Does His Own Thing in S.C."
  New York Post 10 June 1978: 31.

Johnston, Laurie. "Tennessee Williams Receives Centennial
  Medal of Cathedral Church of St. John the Divine." *New
  York Times* 10 Dec. 1973: 13.

Kakutani, Michiko. "Tennessee Williams: 'I Keep Writing,
  Sometimes I Am Pleased.'" *New York Times* 13 Aug. 1981,
  sec. C: 17. [Interview]

Kalem, T. E. "Angel of the Odd." *Time* 9 Mar. 1962: 53-60.
  Report: "A Desire Named Tennessee," *Palm* (Alpha Tau
  Omega) May 1962: 35; rpt. Van Antwerp (below): 229.

Karsh, Yousuf. *Portraits of Greatness*. New York: Nelson,
  1959; Toronto: Univ. of Toronto Pr., 1959. Rpt. "Tennessee Williams," *Coronet* May 1960: 62-63. [Photograph]

Kazan, Elia. *A Life*. New York: Knopf, 1988.

Keith, Don Lee. "The Bead Lady & Others." *New Orleans Magazine* Feb. 1991: 137.

---. "New Tennessee Williams Rises from 'Stoned Age.'" *New
Orleans Times-Picayune* 18 Oct. 1970, sec. 3: 6. Rpt.
"Phoenix Rising from a Stoned Age," *After Dark* Aug. 1971:
28-35; Devlin (above): 147-60.   [Interview]

---. "The State of Tennessee." *New Orleans Courier* 26
Jan.-1 Feb. 1978: 3-5.

---. "The Williams/Capote Clash: Fear and Loathing 'neath
the Old Magnolias." *New Orleans Courier* 28 Apr.-4 May
1977: 4-7. Rpt. Van Antwerp (below): 321-29.

Kernan, Michael. "Tennessee Williams: The Laughter of a Shy
Man." *Washington Post* 4 Feb. 1973, sec. G: 1, 3. [In-
terview]

Klebs, Albin. "Notes on People." *New York Times* 4 Dec.
1976: 30.

Klemesrud, Judy. "Tennessee Williams Is a Reluctant Per-
former for an Audience of High School Students." *New
York Times* 13 Mar. 1977: 51.

Kobal, John. *People Will Talk.* New York: Knopf, 1985.
241, 673-74, 701. [Comments by Arletty, Tallulah Bankhead, Kim Stanley]

Krementz, Jill. *The Writer's Image: Literary Portraits.*
Boston: Godine, 1980. 10-11. [Photograph]

Kriebel, Charles. "An Afternoon in Gray with Tennessee Williams." *After Dark* Apr. 1980: 39, 76-77. [Interview]

Kunitz, Stanley J., ed. *Twentieth Century Authors: First
Supplement: A Biographical Dictionary of Modern Literature.* New York: Wilson, 1955. 1087-89.

Laing, Margaret. "Day after the *Night of the Iguana*." *London Sunday Times* 28 Mar. 1965: 12. Rpt. "Tennessee Williams - A Loner," *New York Journal-American* 11 Apr. 1965,
sec. L: 38. [Interview]

Lambert, Arthur: see E 2

Langley, Stephen. "The Night of Hurricane Williams." *Tennessee Williams Review* 4.1 (1983): 31-43. [Meeting, Cape
Cod, Aug. 1976]

Lannone, Carol.   Report.   *Villager* 17 May 1979.   Resume:
   Tennessee Williams Newsletter 1.2 (Fall 1979): 41-42.
   [Reading of three works, New York Univ.]

Lardner, James.   "Williams on Williams."   *Washington Post* 3
   Dec. 1979, sec. B: 1, 8.   [Interview]

Laudwehr, Shelly.   "Manhattan Tips."   *Theatre* Dec. 1959: 10.

Leavitt, Richard F, ed.   *The World of Tennessee Williams.*
   New York: Putnam's, 1978; London: Allen, 1978.   169 pp.
   Ils.   Reviews:
      Best Seller 38 (Jan. 1979): 317.
      Choice 15 (Dec. 1978): 1369.
      Christian Century 95 (4 Oct. 1978): 932.
      Critic 15 Oct. 1978: 8.
      West Coast Review of Books 4 Nov. 1978: 52.
      Bone, Larry Earl.   *Library Journal* 103 (15 Nov. 1978):
         2330.
      Fisher, James.   *Tennessee Williams Newsletter* 2.2 (Fall
         1979): 19.
      Maves, Karl.   *Advocate* 22 Feb. 1979.

Leverich, Lyle.   "The Shattered Mirror."   *Tennessee Williams
   Literary Journal* 2.1 (Winter 1990-91): 7-15.

---.   "Tennessee Williams' Vieux Carré."   *Tennessee Williams
   Review* 4.1 (1983): 26-30.   [New Orleans]

Lewis, R. C.   "A Playwright Named Tennessee."   *New York
   Times Magazine* 7 Dec. 1947: 19, 67-70.   Rpt. Van Antwerp
   (below): 97-99 (excerpt); Devlin (above): 25-29.

Londré, Felicia: see A 3

"Lowell Gets Medal."   *New York Times* 19 May 1977, sec. C:
   14.   [Induction into American Academy of Arts and Let-
   ters]

Ludwig, Richard M.   *McGraw-Hill Encyclopedia of World Biography.*   New York: McGraw-Hill, 1973.   Vol. 2: 392-93.

Lyons, Leonard.   "The Lyons Den."   *New York Post* 20 Sept.
   1961: 19.

---.   "The Lyons Den."   *New York Post* 19 Oct. 1961: 37.

---.   "The Lyons Den."   *New York Post* 5 Oct. 1962: 43.

---.   "The Lyons Den."   *New York Post* 29 Apr. 1972: 27.

Mann, William John.   "The Fey Musketeers." *Advocate* 21 Nov.
    1989: 27-28.

Marks, J.   "Remembered Brilliance from a Suspiciously Gra-
    cious Artist." *Los Angeles Free Press* 18 June 1971: 3,
    18.   [Interview]

Marriott, R. B.   "Tennessee Williams Loves Tenderness - But
    Brutality Makes Better Copy." *Stage* 21 May 1959: 8.

Matlaw, Myron. *Modern World Drama: An Encyclopedia*.   New
    York: Dutton, 1972. 820-32.

Maxwell, Gilbert. *Tennessee Williams and Friends*.   Cleve-
    land: World, 1965. 333 pp. Reviews:
        Baru, Gene. *New York Times Book Review* 7 Nov. 1965:
            83.
        Freedley, George. *Library Journal* 90 (July 1965):
            3024.

McCann, John.   "Tennessee without Taboos." *Washington Post*
    11 June 1978, sec. K: 1, 10-11.   [Interview]

McCullers, Carson.   "The Flowering Dream: Notes on Writing."
    Esquire Dec. 1959: 164. Rpt. *The Mortgaged Heart*, ed.
    Margarita G. Smith (Boston: Houghton Mifflin, 1971): 280-
    81.

McCullough, David W. *People, Books, and Book People*.   New
    York: Harmony, 1981. 175-77.

McGraw-Hill Encyclopedia of World Drama.   New York: Mc-Graw-
    Hill, 1972. Vol. 4: 410-20.

McKenna, John J.   "Interviews with Williams." *Tennessee
    Williams Newsletter* 2.2 (Fall 1980): 26-28.   [Summary]

Mead, Shepherd.   "The Secret Year of Tennessee Williams."
    Washington University Magazine 97 (Spring 1977): 8-11.
    [Period at Washington Univ.] Response: see Williams,
    Dakin (below).

Medved, Harry, and Michael Medved. *Son of Golden Turkey
    Awards*.   New York: Villard, 1986. 163-64. [On *Wild
    Women of Wongo* set, 1958]

"Menagerie of Managers on Williams Plays." *Variety* 21 Nov.
    1951: 57-60.

"*Menagerie*'s Author Calls Taxes Unfair." *New York Herald
    Tribune* 4 Apr. 1945: 19.

Mewborn, Brant.   "Tennessee and His Ghost - Present: An Interview."   *ScriptWriter* Apr. 1980: 20-21, 61-64.

"Miss Woodward, Newman Feted."   *New York Times* 6 May 1975:
48.

"Mississippi Writer Profiled."   *New Orleans Times-Picayune*
22 Oct. 1972: 32.

Mississippi Writers: A Portfolio of Portraits.   Jackson:
Univ. Pr. of Mississippi, 1981.   [Photograph]

"Mr. Tennessee Williams at the Crossroads."   *Times* (London)
19 June 1957: 3.   [Interview]

Mitgang, Herbert.   "Annals of Government: Policing America's
Writers."   *New Yorker* 5 Oct. 1987: 82.   Rpt. *Dangerous
Dossiers: Exposing the Secret War against America's
Greatest Authors* (New York: Fine, 1988): 161-62.   [FBI
surveillance]

Mok, Michel.   "Tennessee Williams Writes Off Boredom."   *New
York World Telegram* 17 Nov. 1960: 17.   Rpt. Van Antwerp
(below): 214-15.   [Interview]

Monteiro, G.   "Tennessee Williams Misremembers Hemingway."
Hemingway Review 10 (Fall 1990): 71.

Moor, Paul.   "A Mississippian Named Tennessee."   *Harper's*
July 1948: 63-71.

Moore, Dick.   "Tennessee Williams."   *Equity* Dec. 1959: 8-14.
Rpt. Van Antwerp (below): 198-203.

Moore, Sally.   "Lonely Loser...Who Has Found the Way Back."
London Daily Mirror 26 Mar. 1974.   [Interview]

Moritz, Charles, ed.   *Current Biography Yearbook 1972.*   New
York: Wilson, 1973.   448-51.

Morrow, Mark.   *Images of the Southern Writer.*   Athens: Univ.
of Georgia, 1985.   96-97.   [Photograph]

Mosher, Greg.   "Working with Tennessee."   *Tennessee Williams
Review* 4.1 (1983): 59.

Moss, Kirby.   "Playwright's Friend Using UT Resources."
Austin American-Statesman 15 July 1990, sec. B: 3.   [In-
terview with Maria St. Just]

Murphy, Brenda. "Tennessee Williams Was Alive and Well and Living in St. Louis." *Riverfront Times* (St. Louis) 22-28 July 1987: 46.

Murrow, Edward R. Interview with Tennessee Williams, Yukio Mishima, and Dilys Powell, 1960. Rpt. Devlin (above): 69-77. [1960]

"Naya Wins Play Prize." *New York Times* 21 Mar. 1939: 26. [Prize for *American Blues*; see Molly Day Thacher's letter, Van Antwerp (below): 30]

Nelson, Benjamin. *Tennessee Williams*, 1961: see A 3.

"A New Bag for Tennessee Williams." *New York* 28 June 1982: 11. [*Bag People* project]

"New Playwright." *New York Herald Tribune* 4 Aug. 1940, sec. 6: 1-2. [Early sketch]

Newlove, Donald. "A Dream of Tennessee Williams." *Esquire* Nov. 1969: 172-78, 64-80. [Interview]

---. *Those Drinking Days: Myself and Other Writers*. New York: Horizon, 1981. 80-95.

Newman, David. "The Agent as Catalyst, Part II." *Esquire* Dec. 1962: 217-18, 261-64. [Audrey Wood (see D 1)]

"Newsmakers." *Newsweek* 29 Jan. 1979: 37. [Imogene Coca celebration]

Nin, Anaïs. *The Diary of Anaïs Nin 1947-1955*. Ed. Gunther Stuhlmann. New York: Harcourt, 1974. 64-65, 77, 81, 88, 194.

"No More Southern Belles." *Times* (London) 1 Aug. 1962: 12. Report: *New York Times* 2 Aug. 1962: 16; *Time* 10 Aug. 1962: 26. [British press conference]

Norse, Harold. *Memoirs of a Bastard Angel*. New York: Morrow, 1989. Inc. "Adventures of a Bastard Angel," *City Magazine of San Francisco* Fall 1975; "Of Time and Tennessee Williams: The Summer of '44," *Advocate* 2 Oct. 1984: 38-41.

Norton, Elliot. *Focus on Tennessee Williams: A Giant of Stage Realism Discusses His Foremost Plays*. Videotape. Motivational Programming, 1969. [Interview]

---. "Williams' Career Nearly Ended at Its Start Here."
Boston Daily Record 13 Jan. 1958: 40.

Oakes, Philip. "Return Ticket." *Sunday Times* (London) 17
Mar. 1974: 35. [Interview]

---. "Strictly in Character." *Sunday Times* (London) 24
July 1977: 35. [Interview with Williams and Maria Brit-
neva]

O'Connor, John. "The Great God Gadg." *Audience* Winter
1960: 25-31. [Elia Kazan]

O'Haire, Patrick. "Tennessee's Dream." *New York Daily News*
3 June 1975: 42.

O'Shea, Michael. Interview. *Santa Barbara Magazine* Spring
1976.

Paller, Michael. "Meade Roberts, Playwright." *Advocate* 23
Oct. 1990: 62.

Palmer, Susan Snowden. "An Interview with Tennessee in
Georgia." *New Orleans Review* 6 (1979): 28-30.

Parker, Jerry. "Tennessee." *Newsday* 15 Oct. 1972, sec. 2:
4-5, 26-27. [Interview]

Parrott, Jim. "Tennessee Travels to Taos." *Tennessee Williams Literary Journal* 1.1 (Spring 1989): 9-13.

Pawley, Thomas D. "Experimental Theatre Seminar; or, The
Basic Training of Tennessee Williams." *Iowa Review* 19
(Winter 1989): 65-76.

Peck, Seymour. "Williams and *The Iguana*." *New York Times*
24 Dec. 1961, sec. 2: 5.

"People." *Time* 19 June 1950: 45.

"People at Top of Entertainment World." *Life* 22 Dec. 1958:
165.

Petschek, Willa. "Named Desire." *Guardian* 27 Oct. 1976:
12.

Phillips, Gene D. "Tennessee Williams and the Jesuits."
America 136 (25 June 1977): 564-65.

Pickering, John M. "Remembering Tennessee." *Washington
University Magazine* 53 (Summer 1983): 24.

"Playwright Dead." *Key West Citizen* 25 Feb. 1983. Rpt. Van
Antwerp (below): 387-88. [Obituary]

"The Playwright: Man Named Tennessee." *Newsweek* 1 Apr.
1957: 81. [Interview]

"Playwrights Spotlighted." *New York Times* 20 Nov. 1981,
sec. B: 4 [Common Wealth Award]

"Playwrights Will Get Award." *New York Times* 8 Nov. 1981:
71. [Common Wealth Award]

Pope, John. "Freedom He Found in N.O. Made City Home to
Tennessee." *New Orleans Times-Picayune* 26 Feb. 1983: 1.
Rpt. Van Antwerp (below): 392-94.

Portrait. *Vogue* 15 Apr. 1951: 85.

Probst, Leonard. "The Shirley Temple of Modern Letters."
Village Voice 13 Apr. 1972: 64, 84. [Interview]

"Profile - Tennessee Williams." *London Observer* 26 Jan.
1958: 5.

Rader, Dotson. "The Art of Theatre V: Tennessee Williams."
Paris Review 81 (Fall 1981): 144-85. Rpt. *Writers at
Work: The Paris Review Interviews*, 6th ser., ed. George
Plimpton (New York: Viking: 1984): 75-121; Van Antwerp
(below): 361-81; Devlin (above): 325-60; *Paris Review* 29
(Winter 1987): 214 (excerpt on Isherwood). Resume: *Ten-
nessee Williams Review* 3.2 (1982): 59-60. [Interview]

---. "The Last Years of Tennessee Williams." *Esquire* Dec.
1983: 316-18. Rpt. *Fifty Who Made the Difference* (New
York: Villard, 1984): 245-52.

---. *Tennessee: Cry of the Heart.* Garden City: Doubleday,
1985. x, 348 pp. Ils. *Tennessee Williams: An Intimate
Memoir.* London: Grafton, 1986. 360 pp. Reviews:
    Bennett, Elizabeth. *Houston Post* 26 May 1985, sec. F:
    10.
    Carr, Virginia Spencer. *America* 153 (7 Sept. 1985):
    108-09.
    Galligan, David. *Advocate* 25 June 1985: 40-41, 52-53.
    [Interview]
    Hackett, George. *Newsweek* 25 Mar. 1985: 60-61.
    Henry, William A. III. *Time* 13 May 1985: 74.
    Jurrist, Charles. *Mandate* Dec. 1985: 55-60.
    Lasky, Michael. *Bay Area Reporter* 9 May 1985: 22, 25.
    [Interview]

Lehmann-Haupt, Christopher. *New York Times* 15 Apr.
   1985, sec. 3: 20.
McDonald, Boyd. *Advocate* 25 June 1985: 40, 53.
O'Toole, Lawrence. *Maclean's* 20 May 1985: 58-59.
Real, Jere. *Advocate* 25 June 1985: 42-43.
Rich, Frank. *New York Times Book Review* 21 Apr. 1985:
   3, 48.
Simon, John. *New Leader* 1985. Rpt. *The Sheep from the
   Goats*... (New York: Weidenfeld, 1989): 52-61.
Stitt, Milan. *Horizon* Nov. 1985: 64.
Vidal, Gore: see "Immortal Bird" (below).
Walker, Craig. *New York Native* 1 Sept. 1985: 31-32.
Weales, Gerald. *Nation* 241 (20 July 1985): 54.

---. "Tennessee Williams." *Parade* 17 May 1981: 19-22.
[Interview] Resume: *Tennessee Williams Review* 3.1
(1981): 28-29.

---. "Tennessee Williams: A Friendship." *Paris Review* 81
(Fall 1981): 186-96.

Radin, Victoria. "Fighting Off the Furies." *London Observer* 22 May 1977: 22. [Interview]

Rasky, Harry. *Nobody Swings on Sunday: The Many Lives and
Films of Harry Rasky*. Don Mills, Ont.: Collier Macmillan, 1980. 194-211.

---. *Tennessee Williams: A Portrait in Laughter and Lamen-
tation*. New York: Dodd, Mead, 1986. xii, 148 pp. Ils.
Review:
   Variety 17 June 1987: 18.

Raynor, Henry. "Intimate Conversation." *Times* (London) 16
July 1970: 9.

Real, Jere. "Down in Virginia on a Visit." *Advocate* 15
Sept. 1983: 42-44. [1979]

---. "An Interview with Tennessee Williams." *Southern
Quarterly* 26.3 (1988): 40-49. [Same]

Reed, Rex. "Tennessee Williams Turns Sixty." *Esquire* Sept.
1971: 105-08, 216-23. Rpt. *People Are Crazy Here* (New
York: Delacorte, 1974): 12-40; (New York: Dell, 1974):
23-50; Devlin (above): 184-207. [Interview]

Reiley, Franklin C. "A Playwright Named Tennessee." *Palm*
(Alpha Tau Omega) Mar. 1948: 6-7. [Interview]

"Rev. Walter E. Dakin." *New York Times* 16 Feb. 1955: 29.
[Obituary]

Rice, Robert. "A Man Named Tennessee." *New York Post* 21
Apr.- 4 May 1958. Rpt. Van Antwerp (below): 187-90
(excerpt). Response: see D 3.

Rice, Vernon. "The Talking Tennessee Williams." *New York
Post* 18 Mar. 1953: 66. Rpt. Van Antwerp (below): 135-37.
[Interview]

Rich, Frank. "A Place for Revivals." *New York Times* 31
Mar. 1983, sec. C: 14. [Jessica Tandy at Memorial Serv-
ice]

---. "A Playwright Whose Greatest Act Was His First." *New
York Times* 26 Feb. 1983: 1, 39. [Obituary]

Roberts, Meade. "Tennessee Rising." *Vogue* Sept. 1989: 706-
09, 798.

---. "Williams and Me." *Films and Filming* 6 (Aug. 1960):
71.

Rorem, Ned. *The Later Diaries of Ned Rorem, 1961-1972.* New
York: Holt, 1974. San Francisco: North Point, 1983.
Passim.

---. *The New York Diary.* New York: Braziller, 1967. *The
Paris and the New York Diaries of Ned Rorem, 1951-1961.*
San Francisco: North Point, 1983. Passim.

Ross, Don. "*Sweet Bird of Youth* Violent in Tennessee Williams' Style." *New York Herald Tribune* 8 Mar. 1959: 1,
9. [Interview]

---. "Williams in Art and Morals: An Anxious Foe of Un-
truth." *New York Herald Tribune* 3 Mar. 1957, sec. 4: 1-
2. Rpt. Van Antwerp (below): 176-79; Devlin (above): 38-
42. [Interview]

---. "Williams on a Hot Tin Roof." *New York Herald Tribune*
5 Jan. 1958, sec. 4: 1, 7. Rpt. Van Antwerp (below):
182-84; Devlin (above): 50-53. [Interview]

---. "A Williams Play Ends Happily." *New York Herald Tribune* 6 Nov. 1960, sec. 4: 1, 3. [Interview, *Period of
Adjustment*]]

Ross, George. "Tennessee Williams Has Yen for Moving." *New
York World-Telegram* 30 Nov. 1940: 6. [Early sketch]

Rothe, Anna, ed. *Current Biography: Who's News and Why
1946*. New York: Wilson, 1947. 644-46.

"Roving Playwright Is from St. Louis." *St. Louis Daily
Globe-Democrat* 24 Nov. 1940. Rpt. Van Antwerp (below):
40-42.

Ruas, Charles. *Conversations with American Writers*. New
York: Knopf, 1985. 75-90. Rpt. Devlin (above): 284-95.
[Interview, 1975]

Sagan, Françoise. *Avec mon meilleur souvenir*. Paris: Gallimard, 1984. 55-81. Trans. Christine Donougher: *With
Fondest Regards* (New York: Dutton, 1985): 39-61.

Sandomir, Richard. "Tennessee Williams: On Age and Arro-
gance." *New York Sunday News* 23 Mar. 1980, leisure sec.:
5, 12. [Interview]

Sarotte, George Michel. "La carrière de Tennessee Williams." Sarotte (A 3): 9-17.

"Saroyan's Heir." *Time* 7 June 1948: 85.

Sawyer-Lauçanno, Christopher. *An Invisible Spectator: A
Biography of Paul Bowles*. Weidenfeld, 1989. Passim.

Schumach, Murray. "Tennessee Williams Expresses Fear for
Life in Note to Brother." *New York Times* 29 June 1969:
19. Rpt. Leavitt (above): 150.

Seidleman, Arthur Allen. "Tennessee Williams: Author and
Director Discuss *Vieux Carré*." *Interview* 7 (Apr. 1977):
14-15. [Interview]

Selznick, Irene Mayer. *A Private View*. New York: Knopf,
1983. 294-328.

Shanley, John P. "Tennessee Williams on Television." *New
York Times* 13 Apr. 1958, sec. 2: 13. [Interview]

Sharbutt, Jay. "The Play's Still His Thing." *Dallas Morning News* 19 Apr. 1980, sec. C: 1, 10. [Syndicated inter-
view]

Sharp, Christopher. "Tennessee Williams: 'Scandal Exists
with Me Always, My Dear.'" *Women's Wear Daily* 16 May
1975: 8. [Interview]

Sheaffer, Louis. "Tennessee Williams: Just Another American
in Italy." *Brooklyn Eagle-Sun* 13 Jan. 1952: 23-24.

Sheehy, Helen. *Margo: The Life and Theatre of Margo Jones.*
    Dallas: Southern Methodist Univ. Pr., 1989. Esp. 50-99,
    123-25, 128-78.

Shewey, Don. "I Hear America Talking." *Rolling Stone* 22
    July 1982: 18-20. [Interview with Lanford Wilson]

Silverman, Stephen M. "Tennessee Takes Aim at Zelda's
    Life." *New York Post* 12 Jan. 1980: 18. [Interview]

"Sketches of the Pulitzer Prize Winners...." *New York Times*
    3 May 1955: 28.

"Sketches of Those Added by Columbia to the Roll of Pulitzer
    Prize Winners." *New York Times* 4 May 1948: 22.

Smith, Bruce. *Costly Performances: Tennessee Williams: The
    Last Stage.* New York: Paragon, 1990. x, 262 pp.
    [Period 1979-82] Reviews:
      Holditch, W. Kenneth. *New Orleans Time-Picayune* 15
        July 1990, sec. E: 7.
      ---. *Tennessee Williams Literary Journal* 2.1 (Winter
        1990-91): 51-54.
      Holleran, Andrew. *Christopher Street* 144 (1990): 4-8.
      Satuloff, Bob. *New York Native* 23 July 1990: 22.
      Stuttaford, Genevieve. *Publishers Weekly* 16 Mar. 1990:
        57.
      Windham, Donald: see D 3 (St. Just).

Smith, Helen. "Tennessee Williams: 'I'm Hanging in There,
    Baby!" *Arts Journal* 5 (Mar. 1980): 2-3. [Interview]

Smith, Liz. "Making It Up as We Go Along." *New York Daily
    News* 16 July 1980: 8.

---. "Tough Talk from Tennessee." *New York Daily News* 18
    May 1979: 8. [Response to Mickey Mantle's antigay re-
    marks]

---. "Truman and Tennessee Try on Some Suits." *New York
    Daily News* 2 Feb. 1977: 10. [Two lawsuits]

Smith, William Jay. *Army Brat: A Memoir.* New York: Persea,
    1980. 189-94. Harmondsworth: Penguin, 1982.

"Sorry I Wrote." *Sunday Times* (London) 31 July 1977: 35.

Spoto, Donald. *The Kindness of Strangers: The Life of Ten-
    nessee Williams.* Boston/Toronto: Little, Brown, 1985.
    xix, 409 pp. Ils. New York: Ballantine, 1986. Reviews:
      Economist 6 July 1985: 84.

Variety 22 May 1985: 108.
Bennett, Elizabeth: see Rader.
Carr, Virginia Spencer: see Rader.
Edmonds, Michael. *Library Journal* 1 May 1985: 57.
Henry, William A. III: see Rader.
Jurrist, Charles: see Rader.
Lehmann-Haupt, Christopher: see Rader.
O'Toole, Lawrence: see Rader.
Real, Jere: see Rader.
Rich, Frank: see Rader.
Simon, John: see Rader.
Stitt, Milan: see Rader.
Vidal, Gore: see "Immortal Bird" (below).
Walker, Craig: see Rader.
Weales, Gerald: see Rader.
White, Edmund. *New Republic* 13 May 1985: 33-36.

Stang, Joanne. "Williams: 20 Years after *Glass Menagerie*."
New York Times 28 Mar. 1965, sec. 2: 1, 3. Rpt. Van
Antwerp (below): 235-38; Devlin (above): 107-11. [Inter-
view]

Stanton, Robert J., ed. *Views from a Window: Conversations
with Gore Vidal*. Secaucus, NJ: Lyle Stuart, 1980. 87,
89, 132-33, 177-78, 186-87, 195, 213, 178-79, 288.

Staton, Robert W.: see E 2

Steen, Mike. *A Look at Tennessee Williams*. New York: Hawthorn, 1969. xviii, 318 pp. Ils. Contents: William S.
Gray, Introduction, xii-xvi; interviews with Karl Malden,
1-15; Irving Rapper, 16-39; George Cuckor, 40-55; Hal
Wallis, 56-62; Margaret Leighton and Michael Wilding, 63-
78; Hermione Baddeley, 79-92; William Inge, 93-123; Alice
Ghostly and Felice Orlandi, 124-40; Paul Bowles, 141-56;
Hume Cronyn, 157-66; Jessica Tandy, 167-78; Deborah Kerr
and Peter Viertel, 182-92; Anais Nin, 193-207; Rip Torn,
208-21; Geraldine Page, 222-45; Shelley Winters, 246-60;
Estelle Parsons, 261-81; Maureen Stapleton, 282-87; Anne
Jackson and Eli Wallach, 288-99; Mildred Dunnock, 300-09.
Reviews:
    Choice 7 (Nov. 1970): 1245.
    Myers, Paul. *Library Journal* 94 (1 Sept. 1969): 2913.

Stein, Harry. "A Day in the Life: Tennessee Williams."
Esquire 5 June 1979: 79-80. [Interview] Resume: *Tennessee Williams Newsletter* 1.2 (Fall 1979): 35-36.

Stuart, Roxana. "The Southernmost *Desire*." *Tennessee Williams Newsletter* 1.2 (Fall 1979): 3-7; 2.1 (Spring 1980):
5-10.

Sturdevant, John. "Tennessee Williams." *American Weekly* 21 June 1959: 12-15. [Interview]

Sullivan, Dan. "Tennessee Williams May Learn Something from Failure." *Austin American-Statesman* 23 Mar. 1980: 42-43. [Syndicated article from *Los Angeles Times*]

---. "Tennessee Williams on a Streetcar Named Restraint." *Calendar (Los Angeles Times)* 11 Mar. 1973: 1, 32-33. Rpt. *Authors in the News*, ed. Barbara Nykorak (Detroit: Gale, 1976), vol. 1: 498 (shorter ver.). [Interview]

Swanson, Gloria. *Swanson on Swanson.* New York: Random House, 1980. 252.

Syse, Glenna. Interview. *Chicago Sun Times* ? Nov. 1975.

Taft, Adon. "Tennessee Williams Converts." *Christianity Today* 13 (31 Jan. 1969): 75.

Tailleur, Roger. *Elia Kazan.* Paris: Seghers, 1966. 2nd ed., 1971.

"Talk with the Playwright." *Newsweek* 23 Mar. 1959: 75-76.

Taylor, Robert. "Williams: A Playwright Named Desire." *Calendar (Los Angeles Times)* 14 Dec. 1975: 1, 3. [Interview]

"Tennessee Plays for New Agent." *New York* 4 Dec. 1978: 9. [Milton Goldman]

"Tennessee Sez he's Finished Scripting Pix; Hates to Re-Create." *Variety* 4 Nov. 1959: 23.

"Tennessee Tells It All." *Cue* 20 Dec. 1947: 14-15.

"Tennessee Williams." *Harper's Bazaar* Nov. 1981: 262-63.

"Tennessee Williams." *Miami Herald* 17 Nov. 1974. Rpt. *Authors in the News*, ed. Barbara Nykoruk (Detroit: Gale, 1976), vol. 1: 499-500. [Interview]

Tennessee Williams. Up Close. WTBS, 11 May 1980. [Videocassette]

"Tennessee Williams Ailing." *New York Times* 22 Feb. 1969: 20.

"Tenneessee Williams Gala to Aid Fellowship." *New York Times* 15 Nov. 1981: 76. [70th birthday]

"Tennessee Williams Gives Brief Autobiography."   *New Orleans
    Times-Picayune* 8 Jan. 1956: 10.

"Tennessee Williams Ill."   *New York Times* 4 Oct. 1969: 24.

"Tennessee Williams in City for Premiere of Play."   *New Or-
    leans Times-Picayune* 15 Jan. 1955: 2.

"Tennessee Williams Is Baptized at St. Mary's."   *Key West
    Citizen* 12 Jan. 1969.   Rpt. Van Antwerp (below): 153-55.

"Tennessee Williams Recharges."   *Newsweek* 1 Oct. 1973: 23.

"Tennessee Williams Reflects on Fragility of Friendship."
    New York Times 15 Mar. 1979, sec. C: 16.   [Murder of Key
    West caretaker]

"Tennessee Williams Speaks at Theater of the Performing
    Arts."   *New Orleans Times-Picayune* 26 Jan. 1978, sec. 5:
    9.

"Tennessee Williams Stalks the Sweet Bird of Youth in New
    Orleans."   *People Weekly* 14 Feb. 1977: 50.

"Tennessee Williams' Take Home Pay Now $7,500 Weekly."
    Variety 6 Oct. 1948: 1, 62.

"Tennessee Williams to Present First Creative Film Awards."
    Village Voice 23 Jan. 1957: 6.

"Tennessee Williams Today."   *WPAT Gaslight Review* Mar. 1966:
    15-18.   [Interview]

"Tennessee Williams Turns to Roman Catholic Faith."   *New
    York Times* 12 Jan. 1969, sec. 1: 86.

"Tennessee Williams Visits City with Grandfather."   *New Or-
    leans Times-Picayune* 27 Dec. 1951: 1, 6.

"Tennessee Williams Visits City with Grandfather."   *New Or-
    leans Times-Picayune* 6 Apr. 1954: 22.

Terkel, Studs.   "Talks with Tennessee Williams."   Devlin
    (above): 78-96.

Thompson, Howard.   "TV: Cavett and Williams."   *New York
    Times* 22 Aug. 1974: 67.   [Review of interview taped in
    New Orleans]

Timnick, Lois. "A Visit with Tennessee Williams." *St. Louis Globe-Democrat* 9 Feb. 1974, sec. F: 1, 3. [Interview]

"To Honor Three Iowa Alumni." *New York Times* 9 May 1945: 27.

"Top Agent Audrey Wood Dies at 80." *Variety* 1 Jan. 1986: 135. [Obituary]

Topor, Tom. "The New Tennessee Williams Retains the Old Mastery." *New York Post* 21 Mar. 1972: 8. [Interview]

Tynan, Kenneth. "Valentine to Tennessee Williams." *Mademoiselle* Feb. 1956: 130-31, 200-03. Rpt. *Curtains...* (New York: Atheneum, 1961): 266-71; Van Antwerp (below): 158-60.

"Unbeastly Williams"; "$3,000 a Week." *Newsweek* 27 June 1960: 96. Rpt. Van Antwerp (below): 210-11 ("Unbeastly Williams").

"Up Front." *People Weekly* 23 Feb. 1981: 24-25. [Key West]

Van Antwerp, Margaret A., and Sally Johns, eds. *Tennessee Williams*. Dictionary of Literary Biography: Documentary Series, Vol. 4. Detroit: Gale, 1984. xviii, 436 pp. Ils. Contents: Jerrold A. Phillips, Foreword, xiii-xiv; collection of materials, 3-412, inc. interviews with William Jay Smith, 25-31; Hume Cronyn, 79-81; Dakin Williams, 399-405.

Van Gelder, Robert. "Playwright with 'A Good Conceit.'" *New York Times* 22 Apr. 1945, sec. 2: 1. Rpt. Devlin (above): 9-11.

Vidal, Gore. "Immortal Bird." *New York Review of Books* 13 June 1985: 5-10. Rpt. "Tennessee Williams: Someone to Laugh at the Squares With," *At Home: Essays 1982-1988* (New York: Random House, 1988): 43-56.

---. "Selected Memories of the Glorious Bird and the Golden Age." *New York Review of Books* 5 Feb. 1976: 13-18. Rpt. *Matters of Fact and Fiction: Essays 1973-1976* (New York: Random House, 1977): 129-47; Van Antwerp (above): 303-12.

---. "Tennessee Williams." *Double Exposure*. Ed. Roddy McDowell. New York: Delacorte, 1966. Rpt. *McCalls* Oct. 1966: 107.

---. *Two Sisters: A Memoir in the Form of a Novel*. Boston: Little, Brown, 1970; London: Heinemann, 1970.

Vils, Ursula. "A Lunch with Tennessee Williams." *Los Angeles Times* 21 Mar. 1979, sec. D: 16.

Volland, Victor. "Tennessee Williams' Body Arrives Here." *St. Louis Post-Dispatch* 3 Mar. 1983, sec. A: 5.

Voss, Ralph F. *A Life of William Inge: The Strains of Triumph*. Lawrence: Univ. Pr. of Kansas, 1989. 315 pp.

Wagner, Walter. "Playwright as Individual: A Conversation with Tennessee Williams." *Playbill* Mar. 1966: 13-15, 42-45. Rpt. *The Playwrights Speak* (New York: Delacorte, 1967): 213-37; Devlin (above): 124-33 [expanded ver.].

Wahls, Robert. "Of Time and Money." *New York Sunday News* 18 Jan. 1977, leisure sec.: 4. [Interview]

Wallace, Mike. *Mike Wallace Asks: Highlights from 46 Controversial Interviews*. New York: Simon, 1958. 20-23. Rpt. Van Antwerp (above): 192-95; Devlin (above): 54-58. Report: *New York Post* 30 Dec. 1957: 28.

Wallis, Claudia. "People." *Time* 18 Aug. 1980. [Chicago Goodman Theatre]

Washburn, Beatrice. "Tennessee Williams: Mankind Is Doomed." *Miami Herald* 28 June 1958, sec. G: 1, 6. [Interview]

"The Watched and the Watchers." *Look* 26 Mar. 1963: 54. [Photograph]

Waters, Arthur B. "Tennessee Williams: Ten Years Later." *Theatre Arts* July 1955: 72-73, 96. Rpt. Devlin (above): 34-37. [Interview] Response: see D 3.

Watt, Douglas. "Tennessee Williams: Is His Future behind Him?" *New York Sunday News* 19 Oct. 1975: 3. Rpt. Van Antwerp (above): 298-300.

Watts, Richard Jr. "Word from Tennessee Williams." *New York Post* 13 Apr. 1969: 23. [Interview]

"Way Down Yonder in Tenn." *Time* 3 Mar. 1958: 72-74. [Interview]

Weatherby, W. J. "Lonely in Uptown New York." *Manchester
Guardian Weekly* 23 July 1959: 14. Rpt. Devlin (above):
59-63. [Interview]

Webster, Margaret. *Don't Put Your Daughter on the Stage.*
New York: Knopf, 1972. 68-74.

Weiner, Bernard. "Tennessee Williams Talks about His New
Play, Life, and People." *Datebook (San Francisco Sunday
Examiner & Chronicle)* 9 Nov. 1975: 14. [Interview]

---. "Why Tennessee Williams Is Running Scared." *San Francisco Chronicle* 21 May 1979: 12.

Weisman, John. "Tennessee Williams 'Turns On' with Youth."
Philadelphia Inquirer 30 Jan. 1972, sec. G: 1, 5. [In-
terview]

"What They Are Saying." *Look* July 1957. [Quotation]

Whitmore, George. "Interview: Tennessee Williams." *Gay
Sunshine* 33/34 (Summer-Fall 1977): 1-4. Rpt. *Gay Sunshine Interviews*, Vol. 1, ed. Winston Leyland (San Francisco: Gay Sunshine, 1978): 309-25. [Interview, 1976]

Wilkins, B. J. "Tennessee and His Ghosts – Past: A Candid
History." *ScriptWriter* Apr. 1980: 18, 22-24, 63.

Williams, Dakin. *The Bar Bizarre*. Ed. Lucy Freeman. New
York: Sunrise, 1980. 270 pp. Passim.

---. "Is Tennessee Williams a Catholic Playwright?"
Information Apr. 1960: 2-7. Resume: "Brother's Eye-View
of Tennessee Williams," *Variety* 30 Mar. 1960: 1, 79;
"That Sweet Bird," *Time* 11 Apr. 1960: 76-78.

---. "A Peak Too Soon." *Washington University Magazine* 47
(Summer 1977): 38-39. [Period at Washington Univ.]

---, and Shepherd Mead. *Tennessee Williams: An Intimate
Biography*. New York: Arbor House, 1983. 352 pp. Ils.
Inc. *My Brother's Keeper* (New York: Sunrise, 1983).

Williams, Edwina Dakin, as told to Lucy Freeman. *Remember
Me to Tom*. New York: Putnam's, 1963; London: Cassell,
1964. 255 pp. Rpt. "Remember Me to Tom," *Show* Feb.
1963: 60-63, 103-05; "My Son's Heroines," *Cosmopolitan*
June 1963: 46-53 (excerpts). Reviews:
    Hartley, Lois. *America* 108 (23 Mar. 1963): 416.
    Jackson, K. G. *Harper's* Feb. 1963: 107.

Morgenstern, Joseph.   *New York Herald Tribune Books* 5
   May 1963: 7.
Quinn, J. J.   *Best Sellers* 22 (15 Mar. 1963): 463.
Yivisaker, Mariam.   *Library Journal* 88 (1 Feb. 1963):
   558.
Zolotow, Maurice.   *New York Times Book Reviews* 7 Apr.
   1963: 6.

"Williams Gets Theater Award."   *New York Times* 8 Dec. 1972:
   33.   [National Theatre Conference]

"Williams in Sicily Never Saw *Condemned*."   *Variety* 1 June
   1966: 15.

"Williams Play Opens Florida Arts Center."   *New York Times*
   26 Jan. 1980: 12.

"Williams: Playwright to Try Hard as Actor."   *New York Times*
   19 Mar. 1970: 60.   [Key West prods.]

"Williams to Get Literature Medal."   *New York Times* 15 Feb.
   1975: 35.   [National Arts Club]

"Williams to Get Medal at St. John's."   *New York Times* 8
   Dec. 1973: 42.

"Williams Writing Play during Pacific Cruise."   *Variety* 30
   Sept. 1970: 57.

Windham, Donald.   *Lost Friendships: A Memoir of Truman
   Capote, Tennessee Williams, and Others*.   New York: Morrow, 1987; New York: Paragon, 1989.   270 pp.   Inc. *Footnote to a Friendship: A Memoir of Truman Capote and
   Others* (Verona, Italy: Sandy Campbell, 1983); rpt. "Early
   Friends," *Tennessee Williams Review* 4.1 (1983): 44-45
   (excerpt); and *As If...: A Personal View of Tennessee
   Williams* (Verona, Italy: Sandy Campbell, 1985), both
   limited editions.   Reviews:
      Collins, Geneva.   AP release.   *Houston Post* 12 Apr.
         1987, sec. F: 13.
      Drabelle, Dennis.   *USA Today* 17 Mar. 1987.
      Esposito, Michael J.   *Library Journal* 1 Mar. 1987: 78.
      Real, Jere.   *Advocate* 26 May 1987: 52
      Stuttaford, Genevieve.   *Publishers Weekly* 231 (16 Jan.
         1987): 65.

---.   Letter to the Editor.   *New York Times Book Review* 15
   Jan. 1978: 14, 18.

Wood, Audrey, with Max Wilk.   *Represented by Audrey Wood*.
   Garden City: Doubleday, 1981.   89-93, 120-203.   Rpt. *Show*

(*Washington Post*) 25 Oct. 1981, sec. L: 1, 5-6 (excerpts).

"Writing and the Theatre." *Folio* (Univ. of Miami) 3 (Spring
1958): 6-9. [Interview]

Wulf, W. "Tennessee Williams: Leben und Legende." *Kunst
und Literatur* 31 (1983): 673-82.

Zadan, Craig. "Big Daddy's Back in Full Swing...." *Plays
and Players* Dec. 1972: 20-22.

Zolotow, Sam. "Tennessee Williams Gives Play to Actors
Studio." *New York Times* 12 Apr. 1962: 43. ["The Mutilated"]

Zunser, Jesse. "The 'Off-Broadway' Phenomenon." *Cue* 11
Jan. 1958: 10, 15.

2. EULOGIES

Barnes, Bill. My Last *Gig* with Tennessee." *Tennessee Williams Review* 4.1 (1983): 21.

Baumgartner, Jill. "Glimpses Only...." *Christianity Today*
20 May 1983: 69, 71.

Colt, Jay Leo. "In Memoriam: 'What Tenacity to Existence
Some Creatures Do Have.'" *Christopher Street* 71 (1983):
16-21.

Czarnecki, Mark. "The Man Who Named Desire." *Maclean's* 7
Mar. 1983: 63.

Dworkin, Andrea. "Tennessee Williams' Legacy." *Ms.* June
1983: 106.

Evanier, David. "Tennessee Williams, RIP." *National Review*
35 (18 Mar. 1983): 301.

Faber, Charles. "Theatre." *Advocate* 14 Apr. 1983: 50-51.

Gielgud, John. "Reminiscing about Tennessee." *Tennessee
Williams Review* 4.1 (1983): 7.

Gilmore, Richard. "Tennessee Williams." *Nation* 231 (11
Mar. 1983): 347-48.

Griesman, Eugene B.   "Williams: A Rebellious Puritan."   *Chicago Sun-Times* 27 May 1983: 4.

Hannah, Barry.   "Tennessee Williams... 1."   *Rolling Stone* 14 Apr. 1983: 124.   [See Mamet below]

Hughes, Catherine.   "Tennessee Williams, Remembered."   *America* 148 (26 Mar. 1983): 231-33.

Kakutani, Michiko.   "The Legacy of Tennessee Williams."   *New York Times* 6 Mar. 1983, sec. B: 1, 14.

Kalem, T. E.   "The Laureate of Greatness."   *Time* 7 Mar. 1983: 88.

Kempton, Murray.   "Tennessee Williams (1911-1983)."   *New York Review of Books* 31 Mar. 1983: 37.

Kroll, Jack.   "The Laureate of Loss."   *Newsweek* 7 Mar. 1983: 53.

Leavitt, Richard F., ed.   *Ave atque vale! Memorial Pages Preserving the Final Notices and Other Memorabilia Connected with the Death and Burial of America's Great Playwright/Poet, Tennessee Williams*.   Miami, FL: 1983.   Limited edition.

Mamet, David.   "Tennessee Williams... 2."   *Rolling Stone* 14 Apr. 1983: 124.   [See Hannah above]

Marowitz, Charles.   Obituary.   *Plays and Players* July 1983: 48.

"Orpheus Ascendant."   *Nation* 236 (12 Mar. 1983): 292.

Phillips, Gene D.   "A Giant's Passing - Press Coverage of Williams' Death."   *Tennessee Williams Review* 4.1 (1983): 60-72.   [Resume of 39 articles]

Prosser, William.   "A Memorial to Tennessee."   *Tennessee Williams Review* 4.1 (1983): 18-20.

Quintero, José.   "The Imprint He Left."   *Performing Arts* Aug. 1983.

Rader, Dotson.   "'He Walks with Me....'"   *Tennessee Williams Review* 4.1 (1983): 22-25.

Real, Jere.   "Tennessee Williams' Brilliant Legacy."   *Advocate* 22 Dec. 1983: 52.

Rogoff, Gordon. "Tennessee Williams: Transfer at Elysian
Fields." *Village Voice* 8 Mar. 1983: 75.

Sibley, William. "Remembering Tennessee." *New York Native*
14-27 Mar. 1983: 36.

Simon, John. "Poet of the Theater." *New York* 14 Mar. 1983:
76-77. Rpt. Van Antwerp (F 1): 405-08.

Sullivan, Dan. "Tennessee Williams - The Jokes and Hoo-
doos." *Los Angeles Times* 26 Feb. 1983, sec. V: 1.

Turner, Dan. "A Tennessee Waltz." *Advocate* 15 Sept. 1983:
47.

Vidal, Gore. "The 'Bird' Has Flown." *Los Angeles Times* 27
Feb. 1983, sec. 4: 3. Rpt. Van Antwerp (F 1): 397, 398.

Watt, Douglas. "Tennessee Remembered." *New York Daily News*
26 Feb. 1983.

Weales, Gerald. "'What's left/is keeping hold of breath.'"
Tennessee Williams Review 4.1 (1983): 4-6.

Wilkerson, Jerome F. "Homily at the Funeral of Thomas Lanier (Tennessee) Williams, St. Louis Cathedral, March 5,
1983." *Tennessee Williams Review* 4.1 (1983): 73-81.

3. OTHER TRIBUTES

Auchincloss, Louis. "Tennessee Williams: The Last Puritan."
Van Antwerp (F 1): 409-10.

Cassin, Maxine. "Curtain Call for Tennessee." *Tennessee
Williams Literary Journal* 1.1 (Spring 1989): 44. [Poem]

Hellman, Lillian. "Presentation to Tennessee Williams of
the Gold Medal for Drama." *Proceedings of the National
Institute of Arts and Letters and the American Academy of
Arts and Letters* 20, 2nd ser. (1970): 17-28. Rpt. Van
Antwerp (F 1): 255.

Hiette, James. "A Bus Named Desire." *Tennessee Williams
Literary Journal* 1.2 (Winter 1989-90): 41. [Poem]

Howe, Tina. "'Like a God in Our Midst.'" *Tennessee Williams Literary Journal* 2.1 (Winter 1990-91): 17-18.

Laughlin, James. "Tennessee." Van Antwerp (F 1): 393.
   [Poem]

Lewald, Ann Jared. "For Tennessee." *Tennessee Williams
   Literary Journal* 2.1 (Winter 1990-91): 32. [Poem]

Listfield, Emily. "New Orleans, Tennessee." *American Way* 1
   June 1990: 64-72, 114-18.

Miller, Arthur. "Tennessee Williams' Legacy: 'An Eloquence
   and Amplitude of Feeling.'" *TV Guide* 3-9 Mar. 1984: 30.

Neill, Michael, and Maria Wilhelm. "At This Unique Oregon
   Hotel, There's a Novel Idea in Each Room." *People Weekly*
   5 Sept. 1988: 105-06. [Sylvia Beach Hotel, Newport, OR,
   with Tennessee Williams room]

Nicklaus, Frederick. "Tangier: Three Poems for T.W." *The
   Man Who Bit the Sun: Poems*. New York: New Directions,
   1964. 29-32.

"The Poet of Obsession." *Harper's Bazaar* Apr. 1985: 213.

Rader, Dotson. "Tennessee Fever." *Harper's Bazaar* Sept.
   1989: 364, 412-14.

Sweet, James M. "Goodbye, Angel"; "The Man behind the
   Curtain." *Tennessee Williams Review* 3.1 (1981): 40-42.
   [Poetic tributes]

"Tennessee Williams." *Life* Fall 1990: 78-79.

Turner, Allan. "Tennessee's New Orleans." *Houston Chronicle* 10 May 1987, travel sec.: 6. [Cynthia Radcliffe's
   Tennessee Williams's walk]

Wallis, Hal. Letter to Jean W. Ross. Van Antwerp (F 1):
   398.

"Williams Festival." *USA Today* 4 Apr. 1987. [Plaque on New
   Orleans house dedicated]

                4.   ROMANS AND DRAMES À CLEF

Barton, Lee. *Nightride*. Unpublished play, 1971. [Jon
   Bristow, a closeted playwright who supposedly resembles
   Williams] Notes:
       Harris, Radie. *Hollywood Reporter* 4 Jan. 1972: 4.
       Parker, Jerry. "Tennessee" (F 1).

Capote, Truman. "Unspoiled Monsters." *Esquire* May 1976:
  122-24. Rpt. *Answered Prayers: The Unfinished Novel* (New
  York: Random House, 1987): 57-64. [Mr. Wallace as Wil-
  liams]

Lawrence, Jerome. *Live Spelled Backwards: A Moral
  Immorality Play.* New York: Dramatists Play Service,
  1970. [The Most Famous Playwright of Our Time, loosely
  based on Williams and Inge]

Windham, Donald. *The Hero Continues.* New York: Crowell,
  1960. 191 pp. [Dennis Freeman as Williams]

5. PRODUCTIONS BASED ON WILLIAMS'S LIFE

a/k/a Tennessee. Script by Maxim Mazumdar. New York: South
Side Theater, 26 Sept. 1982. Albert Takazauckas, dir.
Peter Harvey, Mal Sturchis, design. With Maxim Mazumdar,
Carrie Nye, J. T. Walsh. Review:
  Simon, John. *New York* 11 Oct. 1982: 83-85.

Confessions of a Nightingale. Script by Charlotte Chandler
and Ray Stricklyn. Los Angeles: Beverly Hills Playhouse,
Jan. 1985-24 Feb. 1986. Houston: Alley Theater, spring
1986. New York: Audrey Wood Playhouse, 23 Sept.-2 Nov.
1986. John Tillinger, dir. Natasha Katz, design. New Or-
leans: Petit Theatre, 26-27 Mar. 1988. With Ray Stricklyn
(Williams). Reviews:
  Variety 1 Oct. 1986: 116.
  Garfield, Kim. *Advocate* 23 Dec. 1986: 54-55.
  Henry, William A. III. *Time* 6 Oct. 1986: 97.
  Ison, John M. *Advocate* 5 Mar. 1985: 42.
  Shea, Al. *New Orleans* Apr. 1987: 66.
  Simon, John. *New York* 6 Oct. 1986: 86.
  Tree, Noah. *Advocate* 10 Dec. 1985: 64-65.

Mr. Williams and Miss Wood. Play by Max Wilk. Waterford,
CT: Eugene O'Neill Theatre Conference, summer 1989. New
York: Lucille Lortel Theatre, Nov. 1989. New Orleans: Ten-
nessee Williams Festival, 1 Apr. 1990. Note:
  Dodds, Richard. *New Orleans Picayune* (Lagniappe) 30 Mar.
    1990: 18, 20.

Seven Portraits. Film by Edvard Lieber, 1983. Note:
  International Herald Tribune 12 Jan. 1983: 16.

Tennessee in the Summer. Play by Joe Besecker. San Francisco: Valencia Rose, winter 1985. John Peterson, dir.
With Bob Fairfield (Williams the writer), Christine M. Sul-

livan (Williams the sensualist) Betsey Burke, Joe Peer.
Review, Background:
   Bean, Joseph. *Advocate* 5 July 1988: 52-53.
   Spunberg, Bernard. *Advocate* 21 Jan. 1986.

The Tennessee Williams Show. Play by Meade Roberts. New
York: Actors Studio, 1990? (reading only).

G. MANUSCRIPTS

This section is arranged alphabetically by institution. Under each heading are listed manuscript holdings alphabetically by title. There is no attempt to indicate length or state of the manuscript or number of copies.

In 1963 Williams gave the University of Texas at Austin his manuscripts and continued to add to the collection until 1969. Andreas Brown catalogued the enormous holdings as well as an extensive collection of published editions. Through his final will and testament (D 4) the playwright bequeathed all manuscripts which remained with him to Harvard University. They were turned over to the Harvard Theatre Collection in 1988 and are being catalogued by Catherine Johnson, a process scheduled for completion in 1992.

I appreciate the help that the following persons provided: Anne Caiger, University of California-Los Angeles; Bernard R. Crystal, Columbia University; Ellen S. Dunlap, University of Texas; Elizabeth A. Falsey, Catherine Johnson, Martha R. Mahard, Frank J. Connors (Office of the General Counsel), and Jessica S. Owaroff, Harvard University; Lynda Fuller-Clendenning, University of Viriginia; Timothy D. Murray, University of Delaware; Barbara Nytes-Baron, University of Houston; Bob Taylor, New York Public Library; and Elizabeth Stege Teleky, University of Chicago.

AMERICAN ACADEMY OF ARTS AND LETTERS

Letters

UNIVERSITY OF BUFFALO: LOCKWOOD LIBRARY

The Eyes (C 1)

UNIVERSITY OF CALIFORNIA-LOS ANGELES: LIBRARY

Ain't It a Pity (poem)
And Tell Sad Stories of the Death of Queens (play)
Baby Doll (A 1)
Candles to the Sun (A 1)

338

The Day on Which a Man Dies (An Occidental Noh Play) (A 1:
   In the Bar) [See Hale (A 3)]
The Demolition Downtown (A 1)
Do It Yourself Interview (D 1?)
The Drunken Fiddler (poem)
Golden Rules for Playwrights
Happy August the Tenth (B 1)
Letter
Mama's Old Stucco House (B 1)
Man Bring This Up Road (B 1)
The man grows long (poem)
The Milk Train Doesn't Stop Here Anymore (A 1)
The Moment in a Room (poem)
The Night of the Iguana (A 1)
No Sight Would Be Worth Seeing (play)
Now and at the Hour of Our Death (play)
One Arm (A 1)
A Recluse and His Guest (B 1)
She That Comes Late to the Dance (C 1)
Slapstick Tragedy (A 1)
Stairs to the Roof (A 1)
Sweet Bird of Youth (A 1)
Tennnessee Williams Presents His POV (D 1)
The Treadmill (story)
The Twister (screenplay)
We are coming home to die (poem)
What's Next on the Agenda, Mr. Williams (D 1)
A witch and her daughter (poem)

UNIVERSITY OF CHICAGO: REGENSTEIN LIBRARY

Letters
My Love Was Light (C 1)
This Hour (C 1)

COLUMBIA UNIVERSITY: BUTLER LIBRARY

"The Fugitive Kind." *Tennessee Williams Literary Journal*
   1.2 (Winter 1989-90): 63.

*The Fugitive Kind: The Theater of Tennessee Williams: An
   Exhibition.* New York: Columbia Univ., 1989. Text by
   Kenneth A. Lohf and Marvin J. Taylor.

Mitgang, Herbert. "Pages from the Life of Tennessee Williams." *New York Times* 29 Apr. 1989, sec. Y: 13.

"Tennessee Williams Exhibit." *Cite AB* 20 Mar. 1989: 1282-
   83.

A Balcony in Ferrara (play)
Battle of Angels (A 1)
Blanket Roll Blues (C 1)
Broken Glass in the Morning (play)
Camino Real (A 1)
Cat on a Hot Tin Roof (A 1)
A Cavalier for Milady (play)
The Christus of Guadalajara (C 1)
Dark Arm (C 1)
Desire and the Black Masseur (B 1)
Dragon Country (A 1?)
The Eyes (C 1)
Faint as Leaf Shadow (C 1)
The Fugitive Kind (A 1)
The fulsome summer opened both her hands (sonnet)
The Glass Menagerie (A 1)
The Gnädiges Fräulein (A 1)
Grand (D 1)
Hard Candy (B 1)
A House Not Meant to Stand (A 1)
I Never Get Dressed till after Dark on Sundays (A 1: *Vieux
    Carré*)
The Ice Blue Wind (C 1)
In the Bar of a Tokyo Hotel (A 1)
Interviews (F 1)
A Kind of Love (play)
The Kingdom of Earth (B 1)
Kingdom of Earth (A 1)
The Last of My Solid Gold Watches (A 1)
Letters
A Lovely Sunday for Creve Coeur (A 1)
The Man in the Overstuffed Chair (D 1)
Masks Outrageous and Austere (play)
Mes Cahiers Noirs (autobiography)
The Milk Train Doesn't Stop Here Anymore (A 1)
Moony's Kid Don't Cry (A 1)
Morgenlied (C 1)
The Night of the Iguana (A 1)
Now and at the Hour of Our Death (play)
Now the Cats with Jewelled Claws (A 1)
O thou who art all joy (sonnet)
Orpheus Descending (A 1)
Plenty of Zip (play)
Poem for Paul
Portrait of a Girl in Glass (B 1)
The Red Devil Battery Sign (A 1)
The Roman Spring of Mrs. Stone (B 1)
The Rose Tattoo (A 1)
Sonnets
A Streetcar Named Desire (A 1)
Suddenly Last Summer (A 1)

Summer and Smoke (A 1)
Sweet Bird of Youth (A 1)
Tennessee Williams' "Grand" (script by Trace Johnston)
Tenor Sax Taking the Breaks (C 1)
This Is (An Entertainment) (A 1)
This Property Is Condemned (A 1)
Tiger Tail (A 1)
The Two-Character Play (A 1)
Valediction (note)
Vieux Carré (A 1)
The Youthfully Departed (play)
You Touched Me (A 1)

LIBRARY OF CONGRESS

Baby Doll (A 1)
Confessional (A 1)
The Fugitive Kind (screenplay)
In the Bar of a Tokyo Hotel (A 1)
Kingdom of Earth (A 1)
The Milk Train Doesn't Stop Here Anymore (A 1)
The Night of the Iguana (A 1; inc. screenplay by A. Veiller)
The Parade (play)
Old Folks at Home, or The Frosted Glass Coffin (A 1)
Orpheus Descending (A 1)
Sweet Bird of Youth (A 1)

UNIVERSITY OF DELAWARE: UNIVERSITY LIBRARY

"Evolving Texts." *Tennessee Williams Literary Journal* 1.2
   (Winter 1989-90): 63.

Murray, Timothy D. *Evolving Texts: The Writings of Tennes-
   see William*. Catalog of an Exhibtion at the Hugh M.
   Morris Library, University of Delaware. Newark: Univ. of
   Delaware Pr., 1988. 51 pp. Ils.

Baby Doll (Hide and Seek) (A 1)
Brush Hangs Burning (play)
Camino Real (A 1)
Cat on a Hot Tin Roof (A 1; inc. screenplay by James Poe)
Chronicle of a Demise (B 1)
The Coming of Something to the Widow Holly (B 1)
The Eccentricities of a Nightingale (A 1)
The Enemy: Time (A 1)
Fragments
Fugitive Kind (A 1)
The Fugitive Kind (A 1)

The Glass Menagerie (A 1)
Hard Candy (B 1)
The Important Thing (B 1)
Kirche, Kutchen und Kinder (A 1)
Letters
The Loss of a Tear-Drop Diamond (A 1)
The Milk Train Doesn't Stop Here Anymore (A 1)
The Mysteries of the Joy Rio (B 1)
The Night of the Iguana (A 1; inc. screenplay by A. Veiller
   and J. Huston)
The Night of the Iguana (B 1)
One Arm (B 1)
Orpheus Descending (A 1)
Orpheus Descending (C 1)
Period of Adjustment (A 1)
The Poet (B 1)
Praise to Assenting Angels (D 1)
The Red Devil Battery Sign (A 1)
The Resemblance between a Violin-Case and a Coffin (B 1)
The Roman Spring of Mrs. Stone (B 1)
The Rose Tattoo (A 1)
Rubio y Moreno (B 1)
Slapstick Tragedy (A 1)
Snowfall (broadside poem)
A Streetcar Named Desire (screenplay, A 1)
Suitable Entrances to Springfield (play)
Summer and Smoke (A 1)
Sweet Bird of Youth (A 1)
The Tender Ones (poem)
This Is (An Entertainment) (A 1)
The Travelling Companion (A 1)
Three Players of a Summer Game (B 1)
Two on a Party (B 1)
The Vine (B 1)
Das Wasser ist kalt (B 1)
The Yellow Bird (B 1)

HARVARD UNIVERSITY: HARVARD THEATER COLLECTION

Cat on a Hot Tin Roof (A 1)
Letters
The Night of the Iguana (A 1)
Period of Adjustment (A 1)
The Purification (Dos Ranchos) (A 1)
Slapstick Tragedy (A 1)
A Streetcar Named Desire (A 1)

UNIVERSITY OF HOUSTON

Letters
Sweet Bird of Youth (A 1)

UNIVERSITY OF ILLINOIS AT URBANA

The Glass Menagerie (A 1)
A Streetcar Named Desire (A 1)

UNIVERSITY OF MISSOURI: ELLIS LIBRARY

Beauty Is the Word (A 1)
Hot Milk at Three in the Morning (A 1)

UNIVERSITY OF MISSOURI: UNIVERSITY ARCHIVES

Big Black: A Mississippi Idyll (B 1)
Something by Tolstoi (B 1)

NEW YORK PUBLIC LIBRARY: BERG COLLECTION

(16 Blocks on the) Camino Real (A 1)

NEW YORK PUBLIC LIBRARY: THEATER COLLECTION

The Glass Menagerie (A 1)
A House Not Meant to Stand (A 1)
In the Bar of a Tokyo Hotel (A 1)
The Night of the Iguana (A 1)
Orpheus Descending (A 1)
The Rose Tattoo (A 1)
A Streetcar Named Desire (A 1)
Sweet Bird of Youth (A 1)

PRINCETON UNIVERSITY: WILLIAM SEYMOUR THEATER COLLECTION

Baby Doll (Hide and Seek) (A 1)
The Glass Menagerie, or The Gentleman Caller (A 1)
Kingdom of Earth (B 1)
Period of Adjustment (A 1)
The Roman Spring of Mrs. Stone (Moon of Pause) (B 1)
Suddenly Last Summer (Cabeza de Lobo, or Composition in the
    Twelve-Tone Scale) (A 1)

Summer and Smoke (A 1)

PRIVATE COLLECTION

"Homage to Tennessee." *Tennessee Williams Literary Journal*
   1.2 (Winter 1989-90): 62. [Exhibit at Provincetown, MA,
   Fine Arts Work Center]

UNIVERSITY OF ROCHESTER

Letters

UNIVERSITY OF TEXAS: HUMANITIES RESEARCH CENTER

"Williams Gives Scripts to Texas University Library.' *Variety* 20 Feb. 1963: 63.

"Williams to Give Papers to Texas U." *New York Times* 23
   Jan. 1963: 5.

The Accent of a Coming Foot (B 1)
Accidents (poem)
Acknowledgement (poem)   /
Act of Love (play and story)
Adam and Eve on a Ferry (play about D. H. Lawrence)
After a Visit (C 1)
An Afternoon Off for Death (poem)
Age of Retirement (story)
Alice at the Country Club (play)
The Alien Heart: A Group of Sonnets (poems)
All Kinds of Salvation (story)
All the words have been spoken (poem)
All through the night (poem)
Alladin in the Orchard of Jewels (poem)
An Allegory in Pink (play)
An American Chorus (dialogue)
American Gothic: A One-Act Play
Amor Perdido, or How It Feels to Become a Professional Play-
   wright (essay)
And all the while Armand kept smiling
And I would have in my hands (poem)
The Angel in the Alcove (B 1)
The Angels of Fructification (C 1)
Apt. F 3rd Flo. So. (play and story)
Apocalypse (poem)
Apostrophe to Peace (poem)
Apricots Too Sweet (poem)
An April Rendezvous (story)

An April Sermon (poem)
April Song (poem)
An Appreciation [Laurette Taylor] (D 1)
The armed have always their weapons (poem)
The Art of Acting and Anna (essay)
The Artist (poem)
As a Man Thinketh (essay)
Ask the man who died in the electric chair (poem)
At break of dawn (poem)
At Daybreak (poem)
At seven o'clock or eleven
Ate Toadstools But Didn't Quite Die (story)
August Evening: Lindell Blvd. (poem)
Auto-da-Fé: A Tragedy in One Act (A 1)
An Autobiographical Note (poem)
An Autumn Song (poem)
Autumn Sunlight (story)
Baby Doll (A 1) [see Johnson (A 1)]
The Ballad of Billy the Kid (screenplay for ballet)
Ballad of an Old War (poem)
Battle of Angels (A 1)
The Beaded Bag (B 1)
The Beanstalk Country (C 1)
Beauty Is No Cheap Thing (poem)
Beauty the Cross (poem)
The Beetle of the Sun: A Lyric Play
Beginning and End of a Story, or Souvenir for Bennie and Eva
    (story)
Being in a foreign nation (poem)
Being Man (poem)
The Big Flashy Tiffany Diamond Blues (poem)
The Big Game: A One-Act Play
The Big Time Operators (play)
Biography: Sonnet
The Black Cygnet (story)
Black Faced Comedians Blown Out of Smoking Room
The Black Nurse (poem)
Blanket Roll Blues (C 1)
Blood of the Wolf (poems)
Blood on the Snow (poem)
Blossoms' Treat
Blue Mountain Blues: A Collection of Folk-Verse (twelve
    poems)
The Blue Ornament: A Christmas Play
Blue Roses (story)
The 'Boss' Complex (essay)
The Bottle of Brass (story)
A Branch for Birds (C 1)
Bride of the Night (poem)
The Bridegroom's Song (poem)
Burn me! Burn me (poem)

But play it sweetly (poem)
But that iron master heard no bells (poem)
But the lady in the little milk house (poem)
But thou as the moon (poem)
By your hand's miracle (poem)
Byron (story)
Cabin (C 1)
Cacti (C 1)
Cairo, Shanghai, Bombay! A One-Act Melodrama (A 1)
Camino Real (A 1)
Camino Real (TV screenplay, ed. Hugh Leonard)
Camino Real, or The Rich and Eventful Death of Oliver
  Winemiller (compare *One Arm* [A 1])
The campfire flickers (poem)
Can it be again (poem)
Candles to the Sun (A 1)
The Carnival (poem)
Carnival Night (story)
Carol's Song (poem)
Cat on a Hot Tin Roof (A 1)
The Cataract (poem)
The Caterpillar Dogs (story)
Cathedral (poem)
Celebration of Mass (poem)
Cellophane Boxes (story)
Change and Resistance and Change (poem)
Changling (C 1)
Chant (poem)
A Chant for My Former Companions (poem)
Chaplinesque, or The Funniest Pair of Lovers (play)
The Chart (poem)
Cheap silks and perfumes (poem)
A Chicken Farm in Idaho (story)
The Christmas Blocks
The Christus of Guadalajara (C 1)
The Chronicle of a Demise (B 1)
Cinder Hill: A Narrative Poem (C 1)
Cinquaine (poem)
Clothed in seventy years of love and sorrow (poem)
La Coeur a ses raisons: Sonnet (C 1)
Cold Stream (story)
College essays [see D 1]
Combination Forgotten (TV play)
The Comforter and the Betrayer (C 1)
The Coming of Something to the Widow Holly (B 1)
Commencing at Meridian (poem)
Compass (poem)
Compromise
Confessional (A 1)
Convenience (poem)
Conversation (story)

Corduroy Pants (story)
Cortege (C 1)
Counsel (C 1)
Crazy Night (story)
Cried the Fox (C 1)
Crooked (poem)
Crooked Blues (poem)
The Crowded Street (poem)
Cruel the torture (poem)
Cupid on a Corner
Curtains for the Gentleman: A One-Act Play
Cut Out (story)
Dago Hill (story)
Daisy Lanier was eight minutes (poem)
The Dangerous Painters (C 1)
Danse Macabre (poem)
Dark Arm, Hanging over the Edge of Infinity (C 1)
The Dark Pine Wood (poem)
The Dark Room (B 1)
The Darkling Plain (essay)
Daughter of Revolution
The Day Is Not Enough (poem)
De Preacher's Boy (story)
A Dead Hero and the Living (story)
Dead Planet, the Moon (play)
Dear Diary (story)
Dear Silent Ghost (poem)
Death: Celebration (poem)
Death Is a Word
Death Is High (C 1)
Death of a God (play)
The Death of Venus (poem)
Decision (poem)
Deep in distant waters (poem)
Deepest Instinct, or Fate (essay)
Definition of Verbs (poem)
Delle (story)
Departure (poem)
Desertion
Desire and the Black Masseur (B 1)
Destroy me (poem)
Dialogue between Dances (play)
Diver (C 1)
A Do-It-Yourself Interview (D 1?)
The Doctor's Waiting Room (play)
The Dog Can Speak (poem)
Dolores Sleeps under the Roses (story)
Dos Ranchos (poem)
Down Shropshire Lane (poem)
The Drab of Jericho (poem)
Dragon Country (play)

The Dream of Permanence (poem)
Driftwood: For Hart Crane (poem)
The Drunken Faun of Herculaneum (poem)
The Drunken Fiddler (poem)
The Dual Angel (poem)
Dynamics of Play (essay)
Early Frost (poem)
The earth will seduce me (poem)
Earth's Brief Passion (poem)
E'en before noonday, neighbor (poem)
Élégie matinale (poem)
Elegy for an Artist (poem)
Elegy for Rose (poem)
End of Summer
The Enemy: Time (A 1)
Envoi
Episode (poem)
Episode: Cafeteria (poem)
Episode in Connecticut (poem)
Epitome (poem)
Epode (poem)
Eros: Metropolis (poem)
Escape (play)
Every Friday Nite Is Kiddies Nite (story)
Every Twenty Minutes: A Satire (play)
Everyman (C 1)
Exaltations (poem)
An Extraordinary Disaster (poem)
The Eye That Saw Death (story)
The Eyes (C 1)
Facts about Me (D 1)
Faint as Leaf Shadow (C 1)
Fallen Leaves (story)
Family Pew (play)
The Fat Man's Wife (play)
Fatal Moment (poem)
Fate and the Fishpole: A One-Act Play
Fear (poem)
The Field of Blue Children (B 1)
Field of Gold (poem)
A Film in Sicily (D 1)
Fin du Monde: A Postscript to the Casualty List (story)
First Syllable (poem)
Fish have colors that are pale (poem)
Flight (poem)
Floor Show Every Saturday Nite (story)
The Flower-Girl of Carthage (story)
Flowers (story)
Fontana Vecchia: A Masque
For My Grandmother Rosina Maria Francesca von Albertzart-
    Otte Larkin (or Rose) (play)

For Spain (poem)
For the Punishment of Rage
For those impossible things (poem)
For you are not stars (poem)
For You, Pygmalion (poem)
The Foreign Country (poem)
The Four-Leaf Clover (story)
Français Deux
Frieze: Les Bos
The Front Porch Girl (play)
Frost
The Frosted Glass Coffin (A 1)
Fugitive Kind (A 1)
The Fugitive Kind (A 1)
A Gallantry of Maidens (play)
Gambler's Song (poem)
The Garden of Emile Kroger (story)
Garden Scene: Recitation after a Painting by Pierre Bonnard
   (poem)
Gatto Romano
The Gay Cat (poem)
A Gentleman behind the Bars (story)
Gethsemane (poem)
Gift of an Apple (B 1)
A gilded cock upon a steeple (poem)
La Gioconda
Girl (poem)
Girl from Joe's (play)
The Glass Menagerie (A 1)
The Glass Menagerie (TV adapt. by Hugh Leonard)
Go Down, Moses (play)
Goat Song (play)
God in the Free Ward (story)
Gods Passed This Way (poem)
Gold Tooth Blues (C 1)
The Good Time House (play)
Goofer Song (poem)
The Goths (C 1)
The Gravedigger's Speech (poem)
Green Shade
The Green Situation (poem)
Grenada to West Plains (story)
A Guest at the Gables
Gunner Jack (poem)
A hand that makes medieval stones (poem)
Hans Hofmann: An Appreciation (D 1)
Hard Candy (B 1)
The Harlequin of the Dance (poem)
The Harp of Wales (C 1)
The hawk that high in heaven wheels (poem)
The hawthorn is withered (poem)

He fingered his vest (poem)
Heart Continues
The Heaven Tree
Heavenly (story)
Heavenly Grass (C 1)
Heavenly Grass, or The Miracle at Granny's [see Debusscher
   (A 3)]
Hefts, hifts and whatnots (poem)
Helen before Troy (poem)
Hell: An Expressionistic Drama Based on the Prison Atrocity
   in Philadelphia County
Hello from Bertha (A 1)
Her Admired Exaltation (story)
Her body swims in passion (poem)
Her Head on the Pillow (C 1)
Here It Is Winter (poem)
Here was love's pain (poem)
The Hill (poem)
His Father's Home (story)
His Mark on You (poem)
Histoire du Cirque (poem)
The History of a Play (with Parentheses) (D 1)
Homage to Ophelia: A Pretentious Foreword (essay)
Honor the Living (play)
The House of Stone (poem)
House of the Heart's Early Wonder (play)
House of Vines: A Period Play (play)
Housing Problem (poem)
How like a caravan (poem)
How shall I speak to you (poem)
How Sleeps My Lord (poem)
How straight my love lies on her bed (poem)
Hyacinths in the Window Bloom (poem)
Hymns to Eros (poem)
I am in debt to you (poem)
I came upon a fragment of a speech
I cannot deny I have lost in crossing (poem)
I Cannot Tell (poem)
I did not elect this problem (poem)
I don't know how a woman gets an idea (poem)
I envy you, Thomas (poem)
I Fly My Colors (poem)
I give my love (poem)
I Got Fired (poem)
I Got Pneumonia in the Heart (poem)
I had a warnin' (poem)
I have a vast traumatic eye (C 1)
I Have Concluded Lately (poem)
I have kept this love (poem)
I have put my passion (poem)
I Have Not Long to Love (poem)

I Haven't an Open Car (poem)
I must depend on you (poem)
I once observed the mechanical antics (poem)
I remained there (poem)
I Rise in Flame, Cried the Phoenix: A Play about D. H.
   Lawrence (A 1)
I said to myself, said I (poem)
I saw how the green sea's denial (poem)
I think I have heard you (poem)
I think it is time (poem)
I think I am beginning to remember death more kindly (poem)
I think the strange, the crazed, the queer (C 1)
I, Vaslev (play)
I Walk through the City (poem)
I walked down five steps to hell (poem)
I walked this morning along the esplanade (poem)
I Want to Go Away (play)
I want to go down to the sea (poem)
I wanted music (poem)
I Would Dance (poem)
I would like to infect you with the excitement of living
   (poem)
I wounded a man I know (poem)
Ice and Roses (poem)
The Iceberg (poem)
The Ice Blue Wind (C 1)
Ice-Edge (poem)
Idiot and Spinner (poem)
If ever the bell (poem)
If I could march (poem)
If I Wore (poem)
If you be wanton in my arms (poem)
If You Breathe It Breaks, or Portrait of a Girl in Glass: A
   One-Act Play (basis for *The Glass Menagerie*)
If you should return (poem)
Il Canne Incantato delle Divina Costiera: 1-Act Sketch
   (basis for *The Rose Tattoo*)
The Image of the Bell and Dove (poem)
Imaginary Interview, *re* Orpheus Descending (essay)
Imagism Old and New (essay)
The Important Thing (B 1)
In a Mood of Wistful Tenderness (story)
In Memory of a Rose (poem)
In Memory of an Aristocrat (play)
In Memory of an Aristocrat, or Disturbance at the Spring
   Display (B 1)
In Our Profession (play)
In Praise of Zinnias, and Similar Flora (poem)
In Spain There Was Revolution (story)
In terraces the buried city lies (poem)
In the beginning there was the word (poem)

In the middle of the crazed painter's hair (poem)
In this precinct the holy light is held (poem)
The indifference to life or death
Inheritors (C 1)
Interior: Panic (play)
The Interior of the Pocket (C 1)
Interval (poem)
The Interval (B 1)
Intimations (C 1)
The Inventory (story)
Iron Is the Winter (C 1)
Ironweed (story)
Is Fives
Ishtar: A Babylonia Fantasy (play)
The Island Is Memorable to Us (C 1)
It Can Turn (poem)
Its Light Is Longer (poem)
Jean qui pleur ou Jean qui rit?
The Jockeys at Hialeah (C 1)
Joe Clay's Fiddle (poem)
John's Bird (poem)
Joy Rio (play)
Joyous was I (poem)
Jungle (play)
The juniper is dead (poem)
Katharsis (story)
The Kewpie Doll (play)
The Kingdom of Earth (B 1)
The Kitchen Door Blues (C 1)
Knowledge (poem)
Lady, Anemone (C 1)
The Lady from the Village of Falling Flowers: A Japanese
   Fantasy in One Act
Lady Misunderstood (poem)
The Lady of Larkspur Lotion (A 1)
Lament for the Moths (C 1)
Last March (poem)
Last Night When I Was Young (poem)
The Last of My Solid Gold Watches (A 1)
Last Star (poem)
The Last Verse: A Fantasy in One Act (play)
The Last Wine (C 1)
Laugh Not So Proudly (poem)
Laughter (poem)
Laurel (poem)
Law, law! She never had no 'ligion! (poem)
The Legend (C 1)
The Lemon Tree (poem)
Let me review once more (poem)
Let the gloomy bards deny it (poem)
Let us go tight-lipped (poem)

A Letter from the See (poem)
A Letter of Explanation and Apology (poem)
A Letter to Irene (essay)
Letter to an Old Friend (poem)
Letter to an Old Love (C 1)
Letters
Life Is for the Living
The Life of a Sitting Target
Life Story (C 1)
Light (poem)
Lily and *la vie*, or One of Picasso's Blues (play)
A Literary Clique (story)
Little Eva's Dilemma
Little Horse (C 1)
The Little Town (C 1)
The Little White Lady of Tsarko-Toye: A One-Act Tragedy of
   the Russian Revolution
A Liturgy of Roses (C 1)
The Log Book
Lonesome Man (C 1)
The Long Goodbye (A 1)
A Long Road with Pines (story)
The Long Stay Cut Short (poem)
The Long Stay Cut Short, or The Unsatisfactory Supper (A 1)
Look Both Ways before Crossing Streets (C 1)
Lord Buddha Speaks to the Novice (poem)
Lord Byron's Love Letter (A 1)
The Lost Girl (poem)
Loudspeaker
Love Having Owned You (poem)
The Love Is Never (poem)
Love, O Literary Love! (story)
Love Only (story)
Love Song (poem)
The Love Trip (story)
The Lovers (story)
Lyric (C 1 and several other poems with same title)
Madrigal (poem)
The Magic Tower: One-Act Play (A 1)
The Malediction (B 1)
The Man in the Dining Car (C 1)
Marine (poem)
The Mark of the Mahki (story)
Marriage Is a Private Affair (screenplay)
Mars (poem)
The Marvelous Children (C 1)
The Mattress by the Tomato Patch (A 1)
Me, Vashya (A 1)
The Mebby's Cabin (story)
The Meeting of People (play and story)
Memories of War

The Mercury
Meridian
Mesalliance (poem)
Message (poem)
A Military Funeral (poem)
The Milk Train Doesn't Stop Here Anymore (A 1)
The Mind Does Not Forget (C 1)
The Minstrel Jack (poem)
Mirrors and Metals (poem)
Miss Jelkes' Recital (poem)
Miss Wilkins and Archie
A Moment in a Room (poem)
Monotony (poem)
Moon (poem)
Moon of My Delight: A One-Act Play
Moon Song: Key West (poem)
Moony's Kid Don't Cry (A 1)
More Poetry than Truth (poem)
Morgenlied (C 1)
Morning (poem)
Morning at Midnight
Mornings with Martial Music (story)
Mornings on Bourbon Street (C 1)
Mr. Paradise (play)
Mrs. Young (play)
Much green water (poem)
Much shall they suffer (poem)
Las Muchachas (story)
The Mutilated (poem)
My Escape
My feasting is among the damned (poem)
My Grandmother's Favorite Color (story)
My grandmother's name was Rosina Maria Francesca (poem)
My Joy Killing Roomie (story)
My Little One (C 1)
My Love Was Light (C 1)
My sister is discretion's self (poem)
My wife is a white lady (poem)
Myra My Brother's Wife
The Mystery of Your Smile (poem)
The Mystery Play at Chat Noire (story)
Neighing warning of early disaster
Never Completely (poem)
Never Spit against the Wind
The New Boarder
The New Home
The New Poet (poem)
Night before Sailing: A One-Act Play
A Night in Madrid (story)
The Night of the Iguana (A 1)
The Night of the Iguana (C 1)

The Night of the Zeppelin (play)
Night Passage (poem)
Nirvana (story)
No compliments or apologies are called for (poem)
No Warmer Garment (poem)
None but the Lonely Heart
Not about Nightingales (play) [see Ishida (A 3)]
Not long of leave, this residence (poem)
Not that I should or that it matters much (poem)
Not with the curved remembrance of the hand (poem)
Notes for a Coffin Maker (poem)
November Grief (poem)
Now I am a logical sailor (poem)
Now I divide again the already split particles (poem)
Now a memory that's painful (poem)
O I am burning (poem)
O shallow, glittering, unarrested, profound (poem)
Oak Leaves (story)
Observe His Heart: A Choral Elegy (play)
October Song (C 1)
Oh, the long marvelous letters (poem)
Oh, they complain, they complain (poem)
Old Ladies Skulls (poem)
An Old Lady Falls with Two Books (essay)
Old Men Are Fond (C 1)
Old Men with Stocks (C 1)
Old Shoe (poem)
Old Wife's Warning (poem)
Ole 'Serphus: Monologue to a Coon Dog (C 1)
Omer (poem)
On the Beat (story)
On a Streetcar Named Success (D 1)
On Summer Evenings (poem)
Once in a Life Time (play)
One and Two (C 1)
One Arm (B 1)
One Hand in Space (C 1)
One Morning in May
One that thunders (poem)
The opaque casinos were raided (poem)
The Orchard
The Orchards of Night (poem)
Orpheus among the Shades (screenplay)
Orpheus Descending (A 1)
Orpheus Descending (C 1)
Our daughter was Evelyn (poem)
Our death was yesterday (poem)
Our Faith (play)
Our hearts are damaged (poem)
Our new and very tender guest (poem)
Out Cry (A 1)

Ozark (poem)
The Painted Masque (poem)
Las Palomas (story)
The Palooka (play)
A Panic Renaissance in the Lobos Mountains (play)
The Paper Lantern: A Dance Play for Martha Graham
Parentheses (poem)
Part of a Hero (C 1)
The Partner of the Acrobat (play)
The Past, the Present, and the Perhaps (D 1)
Peace bought at fifteen cents a glass (poem)
The Pearl of Greater Price (story)
The pediment of our land (poem)
Penates (C 1)
Pensee Cynique (poem)
A Perfect Analysis Given by a Parrot (A 1)
Perhaps I should tell you (poem)
Period of Adjustment (A 1)
Period of Adjustment (story)
The Pet of Princess Angh (poem)
Pierrot and Pierrette (play)
Pieta
The Pink Bedroom (play and story)
Plato's Address to the United Artists of America
The Play of Character (essay)
Poem (several poems with this title)
Poor Katie with Her Crystal Gone (poem)
The Poppy Paradise (story)
Portrait (poem)
Portrait of a Girl in Glass (B 1)
Pragmatic Compendium: 1936 (poem)
Praise to Assenting Angels (D 1)
Prayer (poem)
The Preacher's Boy (story)
Preface to Action (play)
A Preface to Browning's "My Last Duchess" (play)
The Private Hedge (poem)
The Problems of a Long Run (essay)
The Prodigal Race (poem)
The Puppets of the Levantine (play)
Psyche: Letter to an Old Friend (poem)
Pulse (C 1)
The Purification (story)
Quest
The Radiant Guest (C 1)
The Rebellion (poem)
The Recital (poem)
Recollection (C 1)
Recuerdo (C 1)
The Red Part of a Flag (B 1)
Remember Me as One of Your Lovers (poem)

"Silver Dollar" West (poem)
A simple ring can hold together (poem)
The Simplification (poem)
Sissy (story)
Situation Wanted
Slapstick Tragedy (A 1)
Slide Area (play)
The Smooth Black Lake and the Swan (play)
So Glad! (play)
So, let the sweet singers laugh
So Long, Moon (play)
So we'll go no more a roving (poem)
A Social Problem (poem)
The Soft City (C 1)
Sold for a Penny (poem)
Soldier's Memoranda (poem)
Some folks are niggardly of love (poem)
Some look for destiny within a cup (poem)
Some Notes on "Camino Real" (D 1)
Something about Him (B 1)
Something by Tolstoi (B 1)
Something Unspoken (A 1)
Sometimes the space between
Son of --- (story)
Song (two poems with this title)
Song among Leaves (poem)
Song for the Damned (poem)
Sonnet (poem)
Sonnet for a Prodigal (poem)
Sonnet to a Fool in Love (poem)
Sonnet to Pygmalion (C 1)
Sonnets for the Spring: A Sequence (C 1)
Sonnets in My Sixteenth Year (poem)
Soon after the event is past (poem)
Speech (poem)
Speech from the Stairs (C 1)
The Spinning Song (play and story)
Spreading havoc among them while on the subject (poem)
Spring from the west (poem)
Spring Night: Adventure (poem)
Spring Storm (play) [see Ishida (A 3)]
Springfield, Illinois (play outline, based on Vachel Lind-
    say's life)
Square Pegs
Stains of a Tender Outrage
Stairs to the Roof (A 1)
Stairs to the Roof (story)
Stars are Candles for the Dead (poem)
Stella for Star (see B 1)
Still Waters (poem)
Stone and Plaster (poem)

The Stonecutter's Angels (C 1)
Storm Clouds over the Wheat
The Stage Play
The Stranger (story)
Stranger in Yellow Gloves
The Strangers (radio play)
The strangers pass me on the street (C 1)
The Strangest Kind of Romance (A 1)
The Street (poem)
Street Music
A Streetcar Named Desire (A 1) [See Dickinson; Johns (A 1)]
Sub Terra (poem)
Suburbs (poem)
Such a Reverence for Tea-Cups: A Dramatic Monologue
Suddenly Last Summer (A 1)
Sugar in the Cane (C 1)
Summer and Smoke (A 1)
Summer and Somke (screenplay by James Poe)
Summer and Smoke (story)
Summer at the Lake/Escape: Play in One Act
The Summer Belvedere (C 1)
A Summer Husbandry (poem)
Summer: Manhattan (poem)
Summer: Meridan (poem)
Summer Night (poem)
Summer Notes and Some Ain't
Sun Flower (poem)
The Swan (story)
Swan Song (poem)
Sweet Bird of Youth (A 1) [See Debusscher; Gunn (A 1)]
A System of Wheels (story)
A Tale of Two Writers, or The Ivory Tower (story)
Talisman of Roses (poem)
Talisman Roses (play)
Talk to Me like the Rain and Let Me Listen (A 1)
The Talk Went On (poem)
Te Moraturi Salutamus (essay)
The tears that pass (poem)
The Temple of Yama and Yu (story)
Temples to the Red Earth Shook (poem)
Ten Minute Stop (B 1)
The Tender Ones (poem)
Tennessee Williams: The Author (D 1)
Tenor Sax Taking the Breaks (C 1)
Testa dell' Effebo (C 1)
Testament (poem)
Thank You, Kind Spirit (play)
That Horse (play)
That Red-Headed Woman of Mine (story)
Their distance asserts your dereliction (poem)
Then I must twist and turn (poem)

Then I must weave my thread (poem)
There is a wistful shepherd-girl (poem)
There Was Light (play)
These in the Sun's Temple (poem)
A Thing Called "Personal Lyricism" (essay)
Thinking Our Thoughts (essay)
This Book (D 1)
This Can't Last Forever (story)
This Cryptic Bone (C 1)
This Hour (C 1)
This is at once his pride and his disgrace (poem)
This Property Is Condemned (A 1)
This Spring (story)
This Year's Debutante: A Three-Act Farce
Those Who Ignore the Appropriate Time of Their Going (C 1)
Three (C 1)
Three against Grenada
Three Myths and a Malediction
Three Players of a Summer Game (A 1)
Three Players of a Summer Game (B 1)
Three Songs for the Damned (poem)
The tide runs full (poem)
Till One or the Other Gits Back
Time and Life and Dance (essay)
Time in Motion
Time of the Locust (poem)
The Timeless World of a Play (D 1)
Timothy the Tinker: A Puppet Farce (play)
The tinkling of glasses (poem)
To a Lost Friend (poem)
To Me Who Loved You Once (poem)
To Mr. Ustinov: A Gentle Objection (essay)
Tomorrow Is Another Day (play)
The Tongue (poem)
The too limpid streets have grown narrow (poem)
Tourists
Towns Become Jewels (C 1)
The Threadmill (story)
A Tree of Gold Apples (play)
Tuesday's Child (C 1)
27 Wagons Full of Cotton (A 1)
Twenty-Seven Wagons Full of Cotton (B 1)
Twenty-Three (story)
Two Friends (play)
Two Metaphysical Sonnets (C 1)
Two on a Party (B 1)
Two Out of Three
The Uglie Queen
Unarmed (poem)
Under the April Rain (C 1)
Unemployment (poem)

The unexpressed and ever wonderful (poem)
Unidentified works and fragments
The Union With (poem)
Unresigned (poem)
Until the Man Jumped (poem)
Unwilling Hero (poem)
An Urban Fantasy (poem)
Useless (story)
The Valediction (C 1)
Valentine's Story of Vivien
The Valkyr's Ride (poem)
Venite Adoremus (story)
Victim of a Hunter
Vieux Carré (poem)
The Vine (play)
The Vine (B 1)
La Violletta Romance
The Virgin (poem)
Virgin's Dream
Virgo (poem)
A Vision of Tyre (poem)
Visions (poem)
The Vocal Dead: An Act in Verse
Waiting in line for bread (poem)
Waiting Room (play)
A Walk through Snow (poem)
Warning (poem)
The wayward flash has made me wise (poem)
We are coming here to die (poem)
We Have Not Long to Love (C 1)
The Weight of a Stone: A Verse Play for Dancers
We were the pioneers (poem)
Wedding Day
What did he think of as he died? (poem)
What does the bird in his eyrie sing? (poem)
What Harp Unmangled (poem)
What have you done (poem)
What ornament will be upon your breast? (poem)
What would you like for lunch? they ask (poem)
When (poem)
When Love Went Out (poem)
When will the sleeping tiger stir (poem)
Which Is My Little Boy? (C 1)
The Whisper of the Marsh (story)
The White Cafe (poem)
Who goes between their awful world and ours (poem)
Who is able to breathe? (poem)
Who Possibly Will (poem)
Why Did Desdemona Love the Moor? (story)
Why Do You Smile So Much, Lilly? (play and story)
Why should I seek the lofty things (poem)

Wild Girl (poem)
Will You Believe (story)
Wind of the Night (poem)
The Windows of the Blue Hotel (play)
The Wine-Drinkers (C 1)
Wings in the Night (poem)
Winter Is Death's Season (poem)
A Winter Song
With a necklace of amber and agate (poem)
With the first crocus (poem)
The Woman from Alice Regan's (play)
Woman Key: A Melodrama for Tallulah Bankhead (play)
Woman of the Hills (story)
Woman of the Winter Wood (poem)
The Wooden Cross
Words to the Wise (poem)
World of Light and Shadow (story)
The Wounds of Vanity (essay)
A Writer's Quest for a Parnassus (D 1)
The Years of Vision (poem)
The Yellow Bird (B 1)
Yes, I suppose that art was a form of misogyny (poem)
You and I (C 1)
You Could Not Understand (poem)
You never saw him (poem)
You Touched Me (A 1)

UNIVERSITY OF VIRGINIA: BARRETT LIBRARY

"Tennessee Williams Manuscript Comes to Auction Block." *New York Herald Tribune* 10 Dec. 1961: 50. [*Glass Menagerie*]

"Virginia Players Plan to Use Original Williams Manuscript." *Charlottesville Daily Progress* 18 Dec. 1961.

"Williams Draft of Play Brings $6,000 at Auction." *New York Herald Tribune* 13 Dec. 1961: 18.

The Blanket Roll Blues (C 1)
A Call (poem)
Come to me like a deep breath (poem)
Elegy for an Artist (poem)
Fragments
The Glass Menagerie (A 1)   [See Beaurline (A 1)]
I dream and in my dreams (poem)
Letters
My eyes sometimes swim past enormous crowds (poem)
The Painted Masque (poem)
The Roman Spring of Mrs. Stone (Moon of Pause) (B 1)
Rose (poem)

Suddenly Last Summer (A 1)
The Vanished Nymph (poem)
Virginia H. Jones: An Appreciation (poem)

WASHINGTON UNIVERSITY: OLIN LIBRARY

Letters
Me, Vashya (A 1)

STATE HISTORICAL SOCIETY OF WISCONSIN

Letters

YALE UNIVERSITY: LIBRARY

Letters

H. TRANSLATIONS AND FOREIGN-LANGUAGE PRODUCTIONS

This section is arranged alphabetically by language. For each of the 36 languges, first any bibliographies and general surveys are listed. Then follows a short-title list of published translations. Last comes a record of productions in that language. Williams's plays have been successful on European, Asian, and Latin American stages, but the production record below is sketchy. Reviews are limited to English-language notices, but many of the general surveys list local reviews. Many such local reviews as well as programs are available in the horizontal files at the University of Texas Humanities Research Center.

The list of published translations depends heavily on information provided by the *Index Translationum* published by UNESCO, 1948-83. However, the *Index* is not exhaustive. In the Humanities Research Center are copies of translations not found in it, and I have encountered others elsewhere. Nor do the *Index*'s descriptions always correspond to books I have actually held in my hand. The University of Mississippi and the University of Texas have particularly rich collections of translations.

I am grateful to Val Almendarez, Academy of Motion Pictures Arts and Sciences Library; Ruslana Antonowicz of Vienna; Karen Kirk-Sorensen, librarian for the United States Embassy in Copenhagen; Mitsunobu Osada of Tokyo; Hon Ying Tang of Hong Kong; and Odette Tavolara of Robert Laffont's for bringing works to my attention.

General Problems in Translating Williams

Zuber[-Skerritt], Ortrun. "Problems of Propriety and Authenticity in Translating Modern Drama." *Pacific Quarterly* (Moana) 3 (1978): 383-94. Rpt. *The Language of Theatre: Problems in the Translation and Transposition of Drama* (Oxford: Pergamon, 1980): 92-103.

———. "Towards a Typology of Literary Translation: Drama Translation Science." *Meta* 33.4 (1988): 485-90.

———. "The Translation of Non-Verbal Signs in Drama." *Pacific Quarterly* (Moana) 5 (1980): 61-74.

ARABIC

Arabah Ismuhä Al-Raghbah.   Trans. Azîz Mitrî 'Abd-Al-Malik.
Cairo: 1961.   245 pp.   [*Streetcar Named Desire*]

Fatrat al-tawäfug.   Trans. Färüq 'Abd Al-Qädir.   Cairo:
1964.   271 pp.   [*Period of Adjustment*]

Fatrat al-täwafug; Laylat al-sîhliyah.   Trans. Färûq 'Abd
Al-Qädir.   Cairo: 1980.   216 pp.   [*Period of Adjustment;
Night of the Iguana*]

Hewayat al hayawanat al zogagiah.   Trans. Hussein Al-Hote.
Cairo: 1957.   154 pp.   [*Glass Menagerie*]

Hubät ûrfyûs.   Trans. Muhammad Samîr 'Abd Al-Rahmân.   Cairo:
1966.   208 pp.   [*Orpheus Descending*]

Qittah 'alä när.   Trans. Muhammad Samîr 'Abd Al-Hamîd.
Cairo, 1965.   268 pp.   [*Cat on a Hot Tin Roof*]

Qittah 'alä sath min al-safih al-säkhin.   Trans. Abdel Halîm
Al-Bishlawi.   Cairo: 1980.   159 pp.   [*Cat on a Hot Tin
Roof*]

Sayf wa-dukhân.   Trans. 'Abd Al-Khaliq 'Amir Al-Qitt.   Cairo:
1962.   120 pp.   Cairo: 1980.   159 pp.   [*Summer and Smoke*]

Al-wadä al-tawil.   Trans. 'Abdal-Mun'im Subhi Samihah
Hasanin.   Cairo: 1967.   123 pp.   ["Long Goodbye"]

Washam al-wardah....   Cairo: 1959.   101 pp.   [*Rose Tattoo*]

Al-zawjah al-'adhrä'.   Trans. Zaynab Mûsä.   Cairo: 1967.   81
pp.   [*Baby Doll*]

BENGALI

Garir nam bashanapur.   Trans. Munier and Lily Chowdhury.
Dacca: 1981.   158 pp.   [*Streetcar Named Desire*]

Hindayer ritu.   Trans. Shamsur Rahman.   Chittagong: Shahin,
1967.   149 pp.   [*Summer and Smoke*]

Rupar kheya.   Trans. Prasun Mitra.   Calcutta: 1965.   108 pp.
[*Streetcar Named Desire*]

BULGARIAN

Orfej sliza v ada. Trans. B. Vinarova. Sofia: 1961. 78 pp. [*Orpheus Descending*]

Rimskata prolet na misis Stoun. Trans. Krasimira Abadzieva and Julija Toseva. Sofia: 1983. 173 pp. [*Roman Spring of Mrs. Stone*]

Tramvaj "želanie." Trans. Grigor Pavlov. Sofia: Nar Kultura, 1973. 204 pp. [*Streetcar Named Desire*]

Production

Tramvaj "želanie" [*Streetcar Named Desire*]. Gabrovo, 25 Mar. 1978. Review:
   Weeks, Robert P. *Tennessee Williams Newsletter* 1.1 (Spring 1979): 18-20.

CATALAN

Figuretes de vidre. Trans. B. Vallespinosa. Barcelona: Agrupación Dramática, 1959. 32 pp. [*Glass Menagerie*]

CHINESE

Ch'ang Ch'un Chih Niao. Trans. Chang Shih. Taipei: Buffalo Book, 1969. 122 pp. [*Sweet Bird of Youth*]

Mei Kuei Mêng. Trans. Mai Chia. Taipei: 1956. [*Rose Tattoo*: excerpt]

Mei Kuei Wên Shên. Trans. Tien Yao et al. Kao Hsiung: 1956. [*Rose Tattoo*]

T'ien na hsi wei lien ssu ch'an hui lu. Trans. Yang Yueh-sun. Taipei: 1986. [*Memoirs*]

Wei Lien Shih Hsi Chu Hsüan Chi. Trans. Lin Ke Tuan and Liao Hwei-mei. Taipei: Chin Shein, 1970. [*Streetcar Named Desire; Orpheus Descending*]

Productions

Kolin, Philip C., and Sherry Shao. "The First Production of *A Streetcar Named Desire* on Mainland China." *Tennessee Williams Literary Journal* 2.1 (Winter 1990-91): 19-31. [Also *Cat on a Hot Tin Roof*]

CZECH

Kralóvská cesta. Trans. Stanislav Mares. Prague: Delia,
1966. 190 pp. [*Camino Real*]

Království boží na zemi. Trans. Ota Ornest. Prague: Delia,
1969. 99 pp. [*Kingdom of Earth*]

Léto a dým. Trans. Hana Budínová. Prague: Orbis, 1964.
106 pp. [*Summer and Smoke*]

Manzelstvi v záběhu. Trans. Luba Pellarová and Rudolf Pellar. Prague: Delia, 1967. 115 pp. [*Period of Adjustment*]

Noc s Leguánen. Trans. Luba Pellarová and Rudolf Pellar.
Prague: Delia, 1967. 135 pp. [*Night of the Iguana*]

Rímska jaro paní Stoneové. Trans. J. Z. Novak. *Revue
Svetovej Literatury* 2 (Aug. 1965): 68-104. Prague:
Spisovatel, 1966. 133 pp. [*Roman Spring of Mrs. Stone*]

Rodim se v plamendi, vzkrikl ptak Ohnivak. Trans. Jiri
Konupek. Prague: Delia, 1965. 34 pp. ["I Rise in
Flame"]

7 x Tennessee Williams: "Podivuhodny příběh jedné lásky";
"Dům na zbouráni"; "Autodafé"; "27 vagonú bavlny";
"Milostný dopis lorda Byrona"; "Mluv ke mně jako déšt
..."; "Cosi nevysloveného." Trans. Hana Budínová.
Prague: Orbis, 1966. 133 pp. [One-act plays]

Sestup Orfeův. Trans. Jan Grossman and Jiri Kolar. Prague:
Orbis, 1962. 138 pp. Trans. Věra Šedá. Prague: Dilia,
1973. 120 pp. [*Orpheus Descending*]

Skleněný zvěřinec. Trans. Ota Ornest. Prague: Delia, 1960.
Trans. Milan Lukeš. Prague: Delia, 1982. 88 pp. [*Glass
Menagerie*]

Sladké ptáce mládí. Trans. Luba Pellarova and Redolf Pellar. Prague: Delia, 1960. 70 pp. [*Sweet Bird of Youth*]

Tri Hráči jedné letní hry. *Svetova* 6 (1964): 106-18. [*Cat
on a Hot Tin Roof*]

Vytetetovaná ruže. Trans. Hana Budínová. Prague: Orbis,
1964. 108 pp. [*Rose Tattoo*]

DANISH

Englen i alkoven. Trans. Aage Dons. Copenhagen: Fremad,
   1956. 177 pp. [*One Arm*]

Glassmenageriet. Trans. Knud Sonderby. Copenhagen: Byl-
   dendal, 1966. 97 pp. [*Glass Menagerie*]

Mrs. Stones Romerske Forår. Trans. Aage Dons. Copenhagen:
   Fremad, 1951. 158 pp. Copenhagen: Vintens, 1965. 149
   pp. [*Roman Spring of Mrs. Stone*]

Den tatoverende rose. Trans. Holger Bech. Copenhagen: Fremad, 1951. 96 pp. [*Rose Tattoo*]

"Tre kroketspillere." Trans. Ole Storm. *Modern Amerikanske
   noveller.* Copenhagen: Thaming & Appels, 1954. ["Three
   Players of a Summer Game"]

DUTCH

"Drie Spelers van een Zomerspel." *Amerikaans Cultureel Per-
   spectief.* Utrecht: W. DeHaan, 1954. 45-72. ["Three
   Players of a Summer Game"]

Een Kwestie van Aanpassen of Voorstadje Boren. Trans.
   Alfred Pleiter. Baarn: Hollandia, 1969. 90 pp. [*Period
   of Adjustment*]

De Romeinse Lente von Mrs. Stone. Trans. Max Schuchart.
   Amsterdam: Querido, 1951. 195 pp. [*Roman Spring of Mrs.
   Stone*]

"Het Veld de Blauw Kinderen." *Zo Begonnen Ze.* Amsterdam:
   Meulenhoft, 1964. 178-88. ["Field of Blue Children"]

ESTONIAN

Klaasist loomaaedja teisi naidendeid. Trans. Jaak Rähesoo.
   Tallin: Eésti raamat, 1976. 339 pp. [*Glass Menagerie
   and other plays*]

FINNISH

Mrs. Stonen Rooman Kevät. Trans. Jorma Partanen. Jyvas-
   kyla: Gummerus Osakeyhtio, 1952. 195 pp. [*Roman Spring
   of Mrs. Stone*]

FRENCH

Falb, Lewis W. *American Drama in Paris 1945-1970: A Study of Its Critical Reception.* Chapel Hill: Univ. of North Carolina Pr., 1973. 24-36. [Includes record of French reviews]

Translations

Baby Doll (Scénario). Paris: Livre de Poche, 1972. 189 pp.

Le boxer manchot. Trans. Maurice Pons. Paris: Union Generale, 1981. 270 pp. Ils. [*One Arm*]

La chatte sur un toit brûlant. Trans. André Obey. *Paris Théâtre* 11 (1958): 19-50. [*Cat on a Hot Tin Roof*]

Le cri du phoenix. Trans. F. J. Temple. Montpellier: Licorne, 1960. 38 pp. Ils., Arthur Secunda. Limited edition. ["I Rise in Flame, Cried the Phoenix"]

Dans l'hiver des villes. Trans. Renaud de Jouvenel. Paris: Pierre Seghers, 1964. 87 pp. Bilingual. ["Eyes," "Faint as Leaf Shadow," "Orpheus Descending," "Pulse," "Angels of Fructification," "Those Who Ignore the Appropriate Time of Their Going," "Summer Belvedere," "Cortege," "Part of a Hero," "Intimations," Life Story," "Man in the Dining Car," "Death Embrace"]

La descente d'Orphée. Trans. Raymond Rouleau. *Les Oeuvres Libres* 158 (1959): 155-244. *L'Avant Scène* 200 (1 July 1959): 8-33. Paris: Avant-Scène, 1959. 46 pp. Ils. Paris: Librairie Théâtrale, 1979. 124 pp. [*Orpheus Descending*]

Été et fumées. Trans. Paule de Beaumont. *Paris Théâtre* 8 (Jan. 1954): 15-49. Paris: Mauclaire, 1954. 66 pp. [*Summer and Smoke*]

Une femme nommée Moïse. Trans. Francis Ledoux. Paris: Robert Laffont, 1976. 197 pp. [*Moise and the World of Reason*]

"Homme monte ça par chemin." Trans. Henri Robillot. *Revue de Poche* 5 (Sept. 1965): 3-21. ["Man Bring This Up Road"]

Interview avec Beatrix Andrade: "Les charmes discrets d'un sudiste." *Nouvelles Littéraires* 20 May 1976: 4.

Interview avec Jeanne Fayard: "Rencontre avec Tennessee Williams." *Tennessee Williams* (A 3): 130-35. Trans. Marlene J. Devlin: Devlin (F 1): 108-12.

Interview avec Stéphane Groueff: "Un 'comdamné' nommé Tennessee." *Paris Match* 9 Feb. 1957: 10-15.

Interview avec Kurt Singer. *Tribune de Genève* 15 July 1959.

"Un long séjour interrompu, ou les suites d'un mauvais dîner." *Profils* 8 (Summer 1954): 92-104. Paris: Librairie Théâtrale, 1977. ["Unsatisfactory Supper"]

"Je renais dans les flammes, cria le phénix." Trans. Benoît Braun. *Les Oeuvres Libres* 122 (1956): 3-20. ["I Rise in Flame, Cried the Phoenix"]

"Les joueurs de l'été." *Profils* 11 (Spring 1955): 58-82. ["Three Players of a Summer Game"]

Mémoires. Trans. Maurice Pons and Michèle Witta. Paris: Robert Laffont, 1977 (c 1978). 310 pp. [*Memoirs*]

La ménagerie de verre. Trans. Marcel Duhamel. Paris: Librairie Théâtrale, 1977. 104 pp. [*Glass Menagerie*]

Poèmes. *L'Album Masques: Tennessee Williams.* Ed. Georges-Michel Sarotte. Paris: Association Masques, 1986. 120-23. Bilingual. ["You and I"; "Winter Smoke Is Blue and Bitter"]

Poèmes. *Trente-cinq jeunes poètes américains.* Ed. Alain Bosquet. Paris: Gallimard, 1960. 250-51, 448. ["Man in the Dining Car"; "Life Story"; Autobiographical Note]

Le printemps romain de Mrs. Stone. Trans. Jean Tournier and Jacques Tournier. *La Table Ronde* 44 (Aug. 1951); 45 (Sept. 1951). Paris: Plon, 1951. 199 pp. Limited and trade editions. Paris: Club Français du Livre, 1955. 185 pp. Lausanne: Guilde du Livre, 1963. 191 pp. Paris: Livre de Poche, 1964. 190 pp. Paris: Union Générale d'Éditions, 1981. 175 pp. [*Roman Spring of Mrs. Stone*]

Propriété condamnée. Trans. Jacques Guicharnaud. Paris: Librairie Théâtrale, 1977. 23 pp. ["This Property Is Condemned"]

La quête du chevalier. Trans. Henriette de Sarbois. Paris: Robert Laffont, 1968. 232 pp. [*Knightly Quest*]

La rose tatouée. Trans. Paule de Beaumont. *Les Oeuvres Libres* 87 (1953): 225-312. *France Illustration* Supplément 87 (1953): 1-32. Paris: Librairie Théâtrale, 1977. 124 pp. [*Rose Tattoo*]

Soudain l'été dernier. Trans. Jacques Guicharnaud. Paris: Librairie Théâtrale, 1977. 79 pp. [*Suddenly Last Summer*]

La statue mutilée. Trans. Maurice Pons. Paris: Robert Laffont, 1960. 271 pp. Paris: Livre de Poche, 1970. [*One Arm*]

Sucre d'orge. Trans. Bernard Willerval. Paris: Robert Laffont, 1964. 236 pp. [*Hard Candy*]

Théâtre. Various translators. Paris: Robert Laffont, 1958. 656 pp. [*Rose Tattoo; Glass Menagerie; Streetcar Named De-sire; Cat on a Hot Tin Roof; Summer and Smoke*]

Théâtre II. Various translators. Paris: Robert Laffont, 1962. 468 pp. [*Orpheus Descending; Suddenly Last Summer;* "Portrait of a Madonna"; "This Property Is Condemned"; "Talk to Me like the Rain"; *Baby Doll;* "Unsatisfactory Supper"; "27 Wagons Full of Cotton"]

Théâtre III. Trans. Maurice Pons; Marcel Ayme. Paris: Robert Laffont, 1972. 293 pp. [*Sweet Bird of Youth; Night of the Iguana*]

Théâtre IV. Trans. Michel Arnaud; Matthieu Galey. Paris: Robert Laffont, 1972. 293 pp. [*Milk Train Doesn't Stop Here Anymore; Kingdom of Earth*]

Toutes ses nouvelles...(1928-1977). Various translators. Éditions Pavillons. Paris: Robert Lafont, 1989. 583 pp. [*Collected Stories*]

Un tramway nommé Désir. Trans. Paule de Beaumont; adpt. Jean Cocteau. Paris: Bordas, 1949. 218 pp. Paris: Librairie Theatrale, 1977. 166 pp. [*Streetcar Named Desire*]

Un tramway nommé Désir, suivi de la Chatte sur un toit brûlant. Trans. Paule de Beaumont, André Obey. Paris: Livre de Poche, 1963. 431 pp. [*Streetcar Nmed Desire; Cat on a Hot Tin Roof*]

"Un Williams nommé Tennessee." *Arts Spectacle* 13-19 Mar. 1953: 1. ["Facts about Me"]

Productions

La chatte sur un toit brûlant [*Cat on a Hot Tin Roof*], adpt.
André Obey. Paris: Théâtre Antoine, 18 Dec. 1956. Peter
Brook, dir. With Paul Guers (Brick), Jeanne Moreau (Mag-
gie), Antoine Balpêtre (Big Daddy), Jane Marken (Big Mama).
Reviews:
   New York Times 20 Dec. 1956: 37.
   Curtiss, Thomas Quinn. *Paris Herald Tribune* 27 Dec.
     1956.

La descente d'Orphée [*Orpheus Descending*], adpt. Ramond
Rouleau. Paris: Théâtre de l'Athenee, 16 Mar. 1959. Ray-
mond Rouleau, dir. Lila de Nobili, design. With Jean
Babilée (Val), Arletty (Lady), Claude Génia (Carol), Andrée
Tainsy (Vee). Reviews:
   New York Times 18 Mar. 1959: 44. Rpt. *New York Times*
     Theatre Reviews.
   Bishop, Thomas W. *French Review* 33 (May 1960): 551-57.
   Curtiss, Thomas Quinn. *Paris Herald Tribune* 19 Mar.
     1959.

Le doux oiseau de la jeunesse [*Sweet Bird of Youth*], adpt.
Françoise Sagan. Paris: Théâtre de l'Atelier, 1 Oct. 1971.
André Barsacq, dir. Jacques Dupont, design. Music by
Frédéric Botton. With Bernard Fresson (Chance), Edwige
Feuillère (Princess), Jacques Monod (Boss Finley).

Été et fumées [*Summer and Smoke*], adpt. Paule de Beaumont.
Paris: Théâtre de l'Oeuvre, 16 Dec. 1953. Michel le Pulain,
dir. Léonor Fini, design. With Silvia Monfort (Alma), Gilbert Edard (John). Review:
   Curtiss, Thomas Quinn. *Paris Herald Tribune* 25 Dec.
     1953.

"Je n'imagine pas ma vie demain" ["I Can't Imagine Tomorrow"]. Paris: Le Coupe Chou, spring 1976. Andreas Voput-
sines, dir. With Reine Bartere (One), François Nocher
(Two). Review:
   Curtiss, Thomas Quinn. *International Herald Tribune* 30
     Apr. 1976.

La ménagerie de verre [*Glass Menagerie*], adpt. Marcel Duha-
mel. Compagnie de Geneve. Paris: Théâtre du Vieux-
Colombier, 18 Apr. 1947. Claude Maritz, dir. With Claude
Maritz (Tom), Jane Marken (Amanda), Hélène Vita (Laura),
Daniel Ivernel (Jim). Review:
   Theatre Arts Aug. 1947: 39.

La ménagerie de verre, adpt. Robert Antelme. Communauté
Theatrale Mouffetard. Paris: Théâtre de la Bruyère, 19 Mar.
1963.

La ménagerie de verre, adpt. Marcel Duhamel. Paris: The-
atre 347, winter 1977. M. Lupovici, dir. With Daniel Colas
(Tom), Odile Versois or Hélène Vallier (Amanda), Anne Saint-
Mor (Laura), Bernard Crommbey (Jim).

Noir et Blanc ["Desire and the Black Masseur"]. Screenplay
by Claire Devers. Film, 1986. Claire Devers, dir. Daniel
Desbois et al., camera. With Francis Farppat, Jacques Mar-
tial, Claire Rigolleir, Josephine Fresson, Marc Berman,
Benoît Regent, Christophe Galland. Reviews:
 Variety 20 Aug. 1986.
 Bronski, Michael. *Gay Community News* 28 July-3 Aug.
  1991: 10; 4-10 Aug. 119: 4.
 Satuloff, Bob. *New York Native* 27 May 1991: 32.

La nuit de l'iguane [*Night of the Iguana*], adpt. Sophie Bec-
ker. Paris: Bouffes du Nord, winter 1977. Andreas Vout-
sinas, dir. Hubert Monloup, Luc Perini, design. With
Pierre Vaneck (Shannon), Catherine Savage (Maxine), Natasha
Parry (Hannah), Donald Eccles (Nonno). Review:
 Curtiss, Thomas Quinn. *International Herald Tribune* 18
  Feb. 1977.

Le paradis sur terre [*Kingdom of Earth*]. Le Théâtre de la
Balance. Paris: Théâtre Aquarium, Cartoucherie, 1-23 June
1985. E. Chailloux, dir. With Jean-François Vlerik,
Christiane Cohendy, Adel Hakim.

"Une parfaite analyse donnée par un perroquet" ["Perfect
Analysis Given by a Parrot"]. Paris: L'Ecume, June 1984.
M. Giunta, dir. With Marie-Brigitte Andrei, Peggy Marlow.

"Parle-moi comme la pluie et laisse-moi écouter"; "Propriété
condamnée" ["Talk to Me like the Rain," "This Property Is
Condemned"], adpt. Jacques Guicharnaud. Paris: Café Théâtre
"Le Tripot," 1969, 1970. With Valery Quincy, Stephen
Meldegg.

"La plus étrange des idylles" ["Strangest Kind of Romance"],
adpt. Jacques Guicharnaud. Paris: Café-Théâtre de l'Ile
Saint-Louis, Feb. 1968. With Jean Menaud (Little Man),
Yvette Petit (Landlady).

Quatre pièces en un acte ["Talk to Me like the Rain,"
"Strangest Kind of Romance," "Portrait of a Madonna," "This
Property Is Condemned"], adpt. Jacques Guicharnaud. La Com-
pagnie Robert Postec. Paris: Théâtre des Champs-Elysées,

20 Apr. 1962. Robert Postec, dir. André Acquart, design.
With Robert Postec, Reine Courtois, Paul Chevalier, Madeleine Parion, Rosette Zuchelli, François Perez.

La rose tatouée [Rose Tattoo], adpt. Raymond Gerome. Brus-
sels: Rideau de Bruxelles, 7-20 Jan. 1952. Maurice Vaneau,
dir. Bill: Leavitt (F), color section.

La rose tatouée, adpt. Paule de Beaumont. Paris: Théâtre
Gramont, 21 Mar. 1953. Pierre Valde, dir. Annenkof, de-
sign. With Lila Kedrova (Serafina), René Havard (Alvaro),
Jane Lysa (Rosa), Gilbert Eduard (Jack).

Soudain l'été dernier [Suddenly Last Summer], adpt. Jacques
Guicharnaud. Paris: Théâtre des Maturins, 12 Nov. 1965.
Jean Danet, dir. With Silvia Monfort (Catherine), Jeanine
Crispin (Mrs. Venable), Jean Danet (Dr. Cukrowicz).

Soudain l'été dernier, adpt. Jacques Guicharnaud. Les Tré-
teaux de France. French tour, 1967.

Un spectacle Tennessee Williams ["Moony's Kid Don't Cry"],
adpt. Robert Postec; ["Talk to Me like the Rain"] adpt. Jacques Guicharnaud. La Compagnie Robert Postec. Paris: Théâtre de l'Alliance Française, 1962.

Tokyo Bar Hotel [In the Bar of a Tokyo Hotel]. Compagnie du
Théâtre à 2 Têtes. Paris: Roseau Théâtre, 10 Aug. 1988.
With Patrick Olivier (Mark), Odile Michel (Miriam), Roger
Ilann-Waich (Leonard), Michel Tchang (Barman).

*Le train de l'aube ne s'arrete plus ici [Milk Train Doesn't
Stop Here Anymore]*, adpt. Michel Arnaud. Paris: Théâtre
Edouard VII, 3 Feb. 1971. Jean-Pierre Laruy, dir. Pace,
design. With Claude Génia (Mrs. Goforth), Claude Titre
(Chris), Denis Grey (Witch of Capri), Dominique Arden
(Blackie).

Un tramway nommé Désir [Streetcar Named Desire], trans.
Paule de Beaumont, adpt. Jean Cocteau. Paris: Théâtre
Edouard VII, 15 Oct. 1949. Raymond Rouleau, dir. Lila de
Nobili, design. With Arletty (Blanche), Yves Vincent
(Stan), Helena Bossis (Stella), Daniel Ivernel (Mitch).
Reviews:
   Life 19 Dec. 1949: 66.
   New York Times 19 Oct. 1949: 36. Rpt. *New York Times
      Theatre Reviews.*
   Theatre Arts Jan. 1950: 35.
   Time 31 Oct. 1949: 54.
   Dorsey, Frank. *Paris Herald Tribune* 19 Oct. 1949.

MacColl, Rene. *Atlantic* July 1950: 94-95. Rpt. Miller
(A 1: *Streetcar*): 49-52.

Un tramway nommé Désir. adpt. Paule de Beaumont. Paris:
Théâtre de l'Atelier, Feb. 1975. Michel Fagadau, dir. With
Andrée Lachapelle (Blanche), Jean-Claude Drouot (Stan),
Colette Castel (Stella), Claude Brosset (Mitch). Review:
   Curtiss, Thomas Quinn. *International Herald Tribune* 14
   Feb. 1975.

"27 remorques pleines de coton" ["27 Wagons Full of Cot-
ton"], adpt. Jean-Marc Bajulaz and B. Tatem. Paris: Le
Funambule, spring 1991. With Marie Borowski, Bruno Lochet,
Jean-Marc Bajulaz.

GERMAN

Dobson, Eugene Jr. "The Reception of the Plays of Tennessee
   Williams in Germany." Diss., Univ. of Arkansas, 1967.
   Dissertation Abstracts 28 (1967): 226-27.

Frenz, Horst. "American Playwrights and the German Psyche."
   Neueren Sprachen 10 (Apr. 1961): 170-78.

---, and Ulrich Weisstein. "Tennessee Williams and His German Critics." *Symposium* 14 (Winter 1960): 258-75.

Groene, Horst. "Tennessee Williams im Zwiespalt der Mei-
   nungen: Ein Forschungsbericht über die englische und
   deutschspachige Literatur zu Williams' dramatischem
   Werk." *Literatur in Wissenschaft und Unterricht* (Kiel) 5
   (1971): 66-87.

Kratch, Fritz Andre. "Rise and Decline of U.S. Theater on
   German Stages." *American-German Review* 22 (June-July
   1968): 13-15.

Lange, Wigand. *Theater in Deutschland nach 1945: Zur The-
   aterpolitik der amerikanischen Besatzungbehorden.* Frankfurt: Lang, 1980.

Scheller, Bernhard. "Die Gestalt der Farbigen bei Williams,
   Albee und Baldwin und ihre szenische Realisierung in DDR-
   Auffuhrungen." *Zeitschrift für Anglistik und Amerikanis-
   tik* 20 (1972): 137-57.

Translations

"Der abgebrochene Aufenthalt, oder Das unbefriedigende
   Abendessen." Trans. Elisabeth Viertel. *Perspektiven* 8

(Summer 1954): 119-28. Ms. Ausg. Frankfurt: Fischer, 1976. ["Unsatisfactory Supper"]

Acht Damen, besessen und sterblich. Trans. Erich Wolfgang Skwara. Frankfurt: Fischer, 1977. 133 pp. [*Eight Mortal Ladies Possessed*]

"Begierde und der schwarze Masseur." *Das Lot* 5 (May 1951): 11-17. ["Desire and the Black Masseur"]

"Bildnis eines Mädchens in Glas." *Der Baum mit den bitteren Feigen.* Ed. Elisabeth Schnack. Zurich: Diogenes, 1959. 377-92. ["Portrait of a Girl in Glass"]

Camino Real. Trans. Berthold Viertel. Frankfurt: Fischer, 1954. 113 pp.

Endstation Sehnsucht. 2nd ed. Frankfurt: Fisher, 1989.

Endstation Sehnsucht; Die Glasmenagerie. Trans. Berthold Viertel. Frankfurt: Fischer, 1954. 203 pp. Frankfurt: Fischer-Taschensuch, 1973. 168 pp. [*Streetcar Named Desire; Glass Menagerie*]

Endstation Sehnsucht und andere Dramen. Trans. Berthold Viertel, Hans Sahl. Stuttgart/Berlin/Vienna: various publishers, 1978. 446 pp. [Plays]

Etwas Unausgesprochenes. Trans. Martin Beheim-Schwarzbach. Ms. Ausg. Frankfurt: Fischer, 1970. 116 pp. ["Something Unspoken" and three other one-act plays]

Die exzentrische Nachtigall. Trans. Jan Lustig. Ms. Ausg. Frankfurt: Fischer, 1977. 107 pp. [*Eccentricities of a Nightingale*]

Der fahrende Ritter und andere Erzählungen. Trans. Hellmut Jaesrich. Frankfurt: Fischer, 1970. 119 pp. [*Knightly Quest*]

Ein Fall zertretener Petunien. Trans. Alf Leegaard. Ms. Ausg. Frankfurt: Fischer, 1970. 30 pp. ["Case of the Crushed Petunias"]

"Frage und Antwort: Ein Selbst-Interview." *Monat* 104 (May 1957): 63-64. ["World I Live In"]

Die Glasmenagerie. Trans. Berthold Viertel. Berlin: U.S. Military Gov. Inf., n.d. 98 pp. Ms. Ausg. Frankfurt: Fischer, 1970. 167 pp. New trans. Frankfurt: Fisher, 1987. [*Glass Menagerie*]

*Die Glasmenagerie; Endstation Sehnsucht; Die tätowierte
Rose; Die Katze auf dem heissen Blechdach.* Zurich: Buch-
club Ex Libris, 196-. 464 pp. [*Glass Menagerie; Streetcar Named Desire; Rose Tattoo; Cat on a Hot Tin Roof*]

Glasporträt eines Mädchens. Trans. Elga Abramowitz, Hellmut
Jaesrich, Paridam von dem Knesebeck. Berlin/Weimar: Aufbau, 1976. 236 pp. [Twelve short stories]

In einer Hotelbar in Tokio. Trans. Alf Leegaard. Frankfurt: Fischer, 1970. 106 pp. [*In the Bar of a Tokyo
Hotel*]

Interview. *Theater und Zeit* Nov. 1955: 41-44.

Interview mit Ludwig Heinrich. *Frankfurt Abendpost-Nach-
tausgabe* 27 Dec. 1975.

Interview mit Lothar Schmidt-Mulisch. *Welt* (West Berlin) 29
Dec. 1975. Trans. Kathryn Wright Brady: Devlin (F 1):
196-98.

Die Katze auf dem heissen Blechdach. Trans. S. Melchinger.
Frankfurt/Vienna/Zurich: Gulenberg, 1963. Trans. Hans
Sahl. Frankfurt: Fischer-Taschenbuch, 1982. 117 pp.
[*Cat on a Hot Tin Roof*]

Die Katze auf dem heissen Blechdach; Die tätowierte Rose.
Trans. Hans Sahl; Berthold Viertel. Frankfurt: Fischer,
1956. 196 pp. [*Cat on a Hot Tin Roof; The Rose Tattoo*]

Königreich auf Erden. Trans. Jan Lustig. Ms. Ausg. Frankfurt: Fischer, 1970. 195 pp. [*Kingdom of Earth*]

Der lange Abschied; Das dunkle Zimmer. Trans. Hans Sahl.
Ms. Ausg. Frankfurt: Fischer, 1975. 61 pp. ["Long
Goodbye"; "Dark Room"]

"Die letzte meiner echtgoldenen Uhren." Trans. Hans Sahl.
Almanach 1962: 72-84. ["Last of My Solid Gold Watches"]

*Die letzte meiner echtgoldenen Uhren; Moonys Kindchen weint
nicht.* Trans. Hans Sahl. Ms. Ausg. Frankfurt: Fischer,
1970. 55 pp. ["Last of My Sold Gold Watches"; "Moony's
Kid Don't Cry"]

*Meisterdramen: Die Glasmenagerie; Endstation Sehnsucht; Die
tätowierte Rose,* etc. Trans. Berthold Viertel; Hans
Sahl. Frankfurt: Fischer, 1978. 446 pp. [*Glass Menagerie; Streetcar Named Desire; Rose Tattoo*]

Memoiren. Trans. Kai Molvig. Frankfurt: Fischer, 1977.
Frankfurt: Fischer-Taschenbuch, 1979. Zurich: Ex Libris,
1979. 327 pp. Ils. [*Memoirs*]

Der Milchzug hält hier nicht mehr. Trans. Hans Sahl. Ms.
Ausg. Frankfurt: Fischer, 1970. 204 pp. [*Milk Train
Doesn't Stop Here Anymore*]

Der Milchzug hält hier nicht mehr...; Königreich auf Erden.
Trans. Hans Sahl; Jan Lustig. Frankfurt: Fischer, 1969.
160 pp. [*Milk Train Doesn't Stop Here Anymore; Kingdom
of Earth*]

Mississippi-Melodie. Trans. Hans Sahl. Ms. Ausg. Frankfurt: Fischer, 1970. 167 pp. [Five one-act plays]

Mrs. Stone und ihr römischer Frühling. Trans. Kurt Heinrich
Hansen. Frankfurt: Fischer, 1953. 163 pp. Ed. Horst
Kruger. Frankfurt: Fischer, 1978. 157 pp. Berlin/
Weimar: Aufbau, 1980. 128 pp. [*Roman Spring of Mrs.
Stone*]

Moise und die Welt der Vernunft. Frankfurt: Fischer, 1987.
[*Moise and the World of Reason*]

Die Nacht des Leguan. Trans. Franz Hoellering. Frankfurt:
Fischer, 1962. 189 pp. *Theater Heute* 3 (1963): iii-xx.
[*Night of the Iguana*]

*Die Nacht des Leguan; Porträt einer Madonna, und vier
weitere Einakter.* Trans. Franz Hollering; Hans Sahl.
Frankfurt: Fischer, 1963. 177 pp. [*Night of the Iguana*;
"Portrait of a Madonna"; four other one-act plays]

Orpheus steigt herab. Trans. Hans Sahl. Ms. Ausg. Frankfurt: Fischer, 1973. 202 pp. [*Orpheus Descending*]

Plötzlich letzten Sommer. Trans. Hans Sahl. *Almanach* 1958:
69-72. Ms. Ausg. Frankfurt: Fischer, 1975. 102 pp.
[*Suddenly Last Summer*]

Plötzlich letzten Sommer; Orpheus steigt herab. Trans. Hans
Sahl. Frankfurt: Fischer, 1962. 160 pp. [*Suddenly Last
Summer; Orpheus Descending*]

Die sizilianische Rose. Trans. Berthold Viertel. Ms. Ausg.
Frankfurt: Fischer, 1970. xii, 180 pp. [*Rose Tattoo*]

Sommer und Rauch. Trans. Berthold Viertel. *Theatrum mundi
Amerikanische Dramen der Gegenwart.* Frankfurt: Fischer,

1962. 217-95. Ms. Ausg. Frankfurt: Fischer, 1970. 213 pp. [*Summer and Smoke*]

"Sommerspiel zu dritt." *Perspektiven* 11 (Spring 1955): 15-38. ["Three Players of a Summer Game"]

Sommerspiel zu dritt. Trans. Paridam von dem Knesebeck. Frankfurt: Fischer, 1962. 262 pp. [*Three Players of a Summer Game and Other Stories*]

"Sprich zu mir wie der Regen." Trans. Hans Sahl. *Die neue Rundschau* 1 (1956). ["Talk to Me like the Rain..."]

Der steinerne Engel. Frankfurt: Fischer, n.d. 209 pp. [*Summer and Smoke*]

Sturmwarnung. Trans. Alf Leegaard. Ms. Ausg. Frankfurt: Fischer, 1973. 121 pp. [*Small Craft Warnings*]

Süsser Vogel Jugend. Trans. Hans Sahl and Franz Hollering. Frankfurt: Fischer, 1962. Ms. Ausg. Frankfurt: Fischer, 1974. 191 pp. [*Sweet Bird of Youth*]

Süsser Vogel Jugend; Zeit der Anpassung, oder Hochpunkt uber einer Höhle. Trans. Hans Sahl and Franz Hollering. Frankfurt: Fischer, 1962. 168 pp. [*Sweet Bird of Youth; Period of Adjustment*]

Die tätowierte Rose. Trans. Berthold Vierte. Frankfurt: Fischer, 1983. 121 pp. [*Rose Tattoo*]

"Tatsachen über mich selbst." Frankfurt: Fischer, n.d. ["Facts about Me"]

Die Verstümmelte. Trans. Hans Sahl. Ms. Ausg. Frankfurt: Fischer, 1970. 93 pp. ["Mutilated"]

Vieux Carré. Frankfurt: Fischer, 1986.

Zeit der Anpassung, oder Hochpunkt über einer Höhle. Trans. Franz Hollering. Ms. Ausg. Frankfurt: Fischer, 1970. 148 pp. [*Period of Adjustment*]

Productions

Bourbon Street Blues ["Lady of Larkspur Lotion"]. Film, 1978. Detlef Sierck (Douglas Sirk), dir. Michael Ballhaus, camera. With Annemarie Dueringer, Doris Schade, Rainer Werner Fassbinder. Review:
Allan, Tom. *Village Voice* 21 Jan. 1980.

Camino Real, adpt. Berthold Viertel. Darmstadt: Hessisches Landestheater, 6 Nov. 1954. Gustav Rudolf Sellner, dir. Franz Mertz, design. With Claus Hofer (Kilroy), Brigitte Konig (Marguerite), Alwin Michael Rueffer (Casanova), Julia Costa (Esmeralda), Max Noack (Gutman).

Endstation Sehnsucht [*Streetcar Named Desire*], adpt. Berthold Viertel. Pforzheim: Theater der Stadt, 17 Mar. 1950. Hanskarl Zeiser, dir. With Giesela Hagenua (Blanche), Heinz Kiefer (Stan), Giesela Leininger (Stella).

Endstation Sehnsucht, adpt. Berthold Viertel. Berlin: Komödie, 1950. Berthold Viertel, dir. With Marianne Hoppe (Blanche), Peter Mosbacher (Stan).

Die Glasmenagerie [*Glass Menagerie*], adpt. Berthold Viertel. Basel: Theater der Stadt, Nov. 1946. Kurt Horwitz, dir. With Leopold Biberti (Tom), Therese Giehse (Amanda), Margrit Winter (Laura), James Meyer (Jim). Program: Leavitt (F 1): 58.

Die Katze auf dem heissen Blechdach [*Cat on a Hot Tin Roof*], adpt. Hans Sahl. Dusseldorf: Schauspielhaus, 16 Nov. 1955. Leo Mittler, dir. With Peter Mosbacher (Brick), Ida Kroftendorf (Maggie), Alfred Schieske (Big Daddy), Gerda Marus (Big Mama).

Königreich auf Erden [*Kingdom of Earth*], adpt. Jan Lustig. Hamburg: Thaliatheater, 1969. Detlef Sierck (Douglas Sirk), dir. Gunther Walback, design. With Gisela Peltzer (Myrtle), Siefried Wischnewski (Chicken), Joachim Ansorge (Lot).

Nacht des Leguan [*Night of the Iguana*], adpt. Franz Hollering. Berlin: Renaissancetheater, 1963. Willi Maertens, dir. Erich Crandeit, design. With Peter Mosbacher (Shannon), Tilly Lauenstein (Maxine), Grete Mosheim (Hannah), Walter Janssen (Nonno).

Der steinerne Engel [*Summer and Smoke*]. Stuttgart: Jungentheater, 22 Nov. 1951. Franz Essel, dir. With Rosemarie Kilian (Alma), Horst Otto Reiner (John).

Süsser Vogel Jugend [*Sweet Bird of Youth*], adpt. Hans Sahl. Berlin: Schillertheater, 1959. Hans Lietzau, dir. A. M. Vargas, design. With Klaus Kammer (Chance), Marianne Hoppe (Princess).

Die tätowierte Rose [*Rose Tattoo*], adpt. Berthold Viertel. Hamburg: Thaliatheater, 30 Sept. 1952. Leo Mittler, dir. With Inge Meysel (Serafina), Wolfgang Wahl (Alvaro), Ingrid Andree (Rosa), Klaus Kammer (Jack).

Zeit der Anpassung [Period of Adjustment], adpt. Frank Hol-
lering. Hamburg: 2 Jan. 1962. Review:
New York Times 3 Jan. 1962: 25. Rpt. *New York Times
Theatre Reviews*.

Other Productions:
New York Times 21 Mar. 1955: 21. [*Camino Real*]
Halloway, Ronald. *Variety* 17 July 1974: 103. [*Endsta-
tion Sehnsucht*]

GREEK

Georgoudaki, Catherine (Katia). "Elliniki Bibliographia tou
Tennessee Williams." *Ta Mimika* 314 (Dec. 1984): 180-94.

---. "The Plays of Tennessee Williams in Greece 1946-1983."
Notes on Mississippi Writers 16.1-2 (1984): 59-93. [In-
cludes reviews and other productions not listed below]

---. "E theatriki parousia tou Tennessee Williams stin
Ellada, 1946-1985"; "Ellinikes metaphrases ergon tou Tennessee Williams." *Diavazo* 139 (12 Mar. 1986): 31-35; 43.

Translations

O akrotiriasmenos Apollonas. Trans. Annika Fertaki.
Athens: Papadimitriou, 1971. Athens: Angyra, 1972.
[*One Arm*]

Kalokairia ke katachnia. Trans. Marios Pioritis. *Theatro*
58: 121-38. [*Summer and Smoke*]

Leoforio o pothos. Trans. Gerasimos Stavrou. *Theatro 65*
(1965): 169-90. [*Streetcar Named Desire*]

Leoforio o pothos ke exi monoprakta. Trans. Kostoula Mitro-
poulou. Athens: Govostis, 1969. [*Streetcar Named Desire; six one-act plays*]

O Orfeas ston Adi. Trans. Mersina Ioakim. *Sira Pangosmio
Theatro 68*. Athens: Dodoxi, 1979. [*Orpheus Descending*]

*E romaiki anixi tis Kyrias Stoun; Treis s'ena kalokerino
pegnidi; Ti sou na be stin Isabela Holy; Dyo poulia s'ena
petagma*. Trans. Kosmos Polites, Fondas Kondylis.
Athens: Zaharoupoulos, 1969. 248 pp. [*Roman Spring of
Mrs. Stone*; "Three Players of a Summer Game"; "Coming of
Something to the Widow Holly"; "Two on a Party"]

Theatrika erga: Kalokeria ke katachnia; Triantaphyllo sto stethos; E lyssasmene gata. Trans. Marios Plorites. Athens: Gones, 1962. 346 pp. [*Summer and Smoke; Rose Tattoo; Cat on a Hot Tin Roof*]

Theatro, Theatro, Theatro. Trans. Stefanos Katsabis. Athens: 1968. 1-10, 100-06. ["Portrait of a Madonna"; "Lord Byron's Love Letter"]

Interview. *Vema* 3 Jan. 1963.

Title unknown. Trans. Marios Ploritis. *Theatro 59* (1959): 191-202. [*Suddenly Last Summer*]

Title unknown. Trans. Marios Ploritis. *Theatro 60* (1960): 185-204. [*Sweet Bird of Youth*]

Productions

Kalokeria ke katachnia [*Summer and Smoke*], trans. Marios Poloritis. Athens: Apr. 1958. Karolos Koun, dir.

E lyssasmene gata [*Cat on a Hot Tin Roof*], trans. Marios Ploritis. Athens: winter 1955. Dimitris Myrat, dir.

Leoforis o pothos [*Streetcar Named Desire*], trans. N. Gatsos, M. Volanakis, N. Economopoulos. Theatro Technis. Athens: Mar. 1949. Karolos Koun, dir. With Melina Mercouri (Blanche).

Mila mou san ti vrohi [five one-act plays], trans. Nikos Gatsos. Teatro Technis. Athens: fall 1955. Karolos Koun, dir.

O Orfeas ston Adi [*Orpheus Descending*], trans. Mersina Ioakim. Athens: 1963. Elsa Vergi, dir.

Triantaphyllo sto stethos [*Rose Tattoo*], trans. Marios Ploritis. Athens: Oct. 1956. Karolos Koun, dir. With Nelli Angelidou (Serafina), Georgos Lazanis (Alvaro).

Title unknown [*Camino Real*], trans. Alexis Solomos. Piraeus: National Theatre, Jan. 1974. Alexis Solomos, dir.

Title unknown [*Glass Menagerie*], trans. Nikos Spanias. Theatro Technis. Athens: Aliki, 8 Nov. 1946. Karolos Koun, dir. Manos Hadzidakis, music. With Karolos Koun (Tom), Maria Yannakopoulou (Amanda), Elli Lambeti (Laura), Lykourgos Kallergis (Jim).

Title unknown [*Glass Menagerie*], trans. Michalis Kakoyannis.
Athens: National Theatre, spring 1978. With Vaso Manolidou
(Amanda).

Title unknown [*Night of the Iguana*]. Athens: 1964. Karolos
Koun, dir.

Title unknown [*Period of Adjustment*], trans. Kety Kasimati-
Myrivili. Cyclico Theatro. Athens?: Oct. 1963. Leonidas
Trivizas, dir.

Title unknown [*Suddenly Last Summer*], trans. Marios Ploritis; "The Long Goodbye," trans. Nikos Gatsos. Athens:
1959. Karolos Koun, dir.

Title unknown [*Sweet Bird of Youth*], trans. Marios Ploritis.
Athens: 1960. Karolos Koun, dir. With Yannis Fertis
(Chance), Melina Mercouri (Princess).

Title unknown [*You Touched Me*], trans. Platon Mousaios.
Athens: 1961. Minas Christides, dir. With Alekos Alexan-
drakis, Vera Zavitsianou.

HEBREW

Ashuvato she Paolo. Trans. Aryeh Hashavya. Tel Aviv:
Deshe, 1959. 152 pp. [*Roman Spring of Mrs. Stone*]

HINDI

Title unknown. In collection of classics of American literature: drama. Delhi: Rajpal, 1965. 1-108. [*Glass
Menagerie*]

HUNGARIAN

Autóbusz es Iguána. Trans. Ottliki Géza. Budapest: Európa
Könyvkiadó, 1968. 409 pp. [Collection]

Drámák. Budapest: Európa Könyvkiadó, 1964. 615 pp.
[*Streetcar Named Desire; Summer and Smoke*; "This Property
Is Condemned"; "Talk to Me like the Rain..."; *Cat on a
Hot Tin Roof; Orphesus Descending; Suddenly Last Summer;
Period of Adjustment*]

"Két elbeszélés üvegkisasszony arcképe." *Nagyvilág* 8 (June
1963): 824-34. ["Portrait of a Girl in Glass"]

"Az eltiport petúniák esete." *Nagyvilág* 10 (July 1965): 1016-23. ["Case of the Crushed Petunias"]

Az ifjusag szep madara. Nagyvilág 9 (Aug. 1964): 1162-1210. [*Sweet Bird of Youth*]

Az iguna ékazaláka. Nem félünk a farkastól. Budapest: Európa Könyvkiadó, 1966. 5-129. [*Night of the Iguana*]

Maeska a forró bádogteton. Nagvilág 7 (Aug. 1962): 1146-1207. [*Cat on a Hot Tin Roof*]

"Az uvegguyüjtu lány portréja." *Legjobb elbeszélések angolból.* Ed. Mirka Janos Forditasai. Winnipeg: Canadian Hungarian News, 1966. 19-30. ["Portrait of a Girl in Glass"]

A *vágy villamosa.* Trans. Czimer József. *Nagyvilág* 6 (Feb. 1961): 204-67. Bucarest: Irodalmikonyvkiado, 1968. 128 pp. [*Streetcar Named Desire*]

ITALIAN

"Auto-da-Fe: Tragedia in un atto." Trans. Mino Roli. *Il Dramma* 63 (15 July 1948): 61-66.

I "blues." Trans. Gerardo Guerrieri. Torino: Einaudi, 1952. 84 pp. [*American Blues*] Intro. rpt. *Lo spottatore critico* (Rome: Levi, 1987): 13-18.

La calata di Orfeo. Trans. Gerardo Guerrieri. *Sipario* June 1961: 39-62. [*Orpheus Descending*]

"Il Cristo di Guadalajara"; "Gli angeli dello sculpellino." *Bottighe Oscure* 4 (1949): 37-40. ["Christus of Guadalajara"; "Stonecutter's Angels"]

"La dama dell' insetticida Larkspur." Trans. Mino Roli. *Il Dramma* 65 (15 July 1948): 55-57. ["Lady of Larkspur Lotion"]

Una donna chiamata Moise. Trans. Maria Teresa Marenco. Milan: Garzanti, 1976. 166 pp. [*Moise and the World of Reason*]

La gatta sul tetto che scotta. Trans. Gerardo Guerrieri. *Sipario* 144 (Apr. 1958): 40-58. [*Cat on a Hot Tin Roof*]

"Gioco estivo." *Prospetti* 11 (Spring 1955): 15-36. ["Three Players of a Summer Game"]

Intervista: "E' proprio vero quello che dice Williams."
Ultima 25 Mar. 1948.

Intervista con Giuseppe di Bernardo: "Desiderio a Taormina."
Sicilia 9 July 1980.

Intervista con Trudy Goth: "Tutto va bene per Williams."
Fiera Litteraria 22 Mar. 1953: 2.

Intervista con E. G. Mattia. *Fiera Litteraria* Feb. 1948.

"Una lettera d'amore di Lord Byron." Trans. Gigi Cane. *Il
Dramma* 85 (15 May 1949): 53-54. ["Lord Byron's Love Letter"]

Una lettera d'amore di Lord Byron: Opera. Milan: Ricordi,
1955. 39 pp. [*Lord Byron's Love Letter: Opera*]

La notte dell' iguana. Trans. Bruno Fonzi. Torino:
Einaudi, 1965. 130 pp. [*Night of the Iguana*]

Un ospite indiscreto. Trans. Luciano Bianciardi. Milan:
Rizzoli, 1970. 217 pp. [*Knightly Quest*]

La primavera romana della Signora Stone. Trans. Bruno
Tasso. Milan: Garzanti, 1954. 138 pp. [*Roman Spring of
Mrs. Stone*]

"Properieta espropriata." Trans. Sergio Cenalino. *Il
Dramma* 161 (15 July 1952): 22-26. ["This Property Is
Codemned"]

"Rinasco nelle fiamme gridava la fenice." Trans. Luigi
Candoni. *Sipario* 138 (Oct. 1957): 53-56. ["I Rise in
Flames"]

Teatro. Trans. Gerardo Guerrieri. Torino: Einaudi, 1963.
529 pp. ["Dark Room"; "Portrait of a Madonna"; "Unsatisfactory Supper"; "This Property Is Condemned; *Glass
Menagerie; Streetcar Named Desire; Summer and Smoke; Cat
on a Hot Tin Roof; Baby Doll; Orpheus Descending*]

"La terra dei fagioli gigante." *Il Tarocco* 7/8 (1968): 39.
["Beanstalk Country"]

Un tram che se chiama Desiderio. Trans. Gerardo Guerrieri.
Sipario 68 (Dec. 1951): 49-72. Torino: Einaudi, 1973.
106 pp. [*Streetcar Named Desire*]

Tutti i racconti. Trans. Giuliana Beltrami Gadola and Nora
Finzi. Torino: Einaudi, 1966. 260 pp. [Short stories]

"27 vagoni di cotone." Trans. Gigi Cane. *Il Dramma* 67/69
(1 Aug.-1 Sept. 1948): 79-88. ["27 Wagons Full of Cotton"]

Lo zoo di vetro. Trans. Alfredo Segre. Milan: Garzanti,
1948. 142 pp. [*Glass Menagerie*]

Title unknown. Trans. Gigi Cane. *Il Dramma* 15 Jan. 1949:
37-41. ["Hello from Bertha"]

Productions

Un tram che se chiama Desiderio [*Streetcar Named Desire*].
Rome: Teatre Eliseo, 21 Jan. 1949. Luchino Visconti, dir.
Franco Zeffirelli, design. With Rina Morelli (Blanche),
Vittorio Gassman (Stan), Vivi Gioi (Stella), Marcello Mas-
troianni (Mitch).

Zoo di vetro [*Glass Menagerie*], adpt. Alfredo Segre. Rome:
Theatro Eliseo, 12 Dec. 1946. Luchino Visconti, dir. Mario
Chiari, Uberto Petrassi, Renato Morozzo, Amleto Neoccia,
design. Music by Paul Bowles. With Paolo Stoppa (Tom),
Tatiana Pavlova (Amanda), Nina Morelli (Laura), Girgio de
Lullo (Jim). Review:
   Theatre Arts Aug. 1947: 38-39.

JAPANESE

Ishida, Akira. [A bibliography of Tennessee Williams in
   Japan. *Annual Report of Studies*] (Doshisha Woman's College) 22 (1971): 355-86.

---. [Tennessee Williams and Japan. *Annual Report of
   Studies*] 23 (1973): 217-38.

Translations

Aru madonna no shôzo. Trans. Takashi Sugawara. *Gendai
   sekai gikyoku senshu* 6. Tokyo: Hakusuisha, 195-. ["Portrait of a Madonna"]

Bara no irezumi. Trans. Takashi Sugawara. Tokyo: Hakusuisha, 1956. 167 pp. Trans. Hiroshi Tajima. Tokyo: Shinchosha, 1973. 186 pp. [*Rose Tattoo*]

Garasu no dobutsuen. Trans. Hiroshi Tajima. Tokyo: Shinchosha, 1957. 177 pp. [*Glass Menagerie*]

Hâdo kyandi. Trans. Yasuhiko Terakado. Tokyo: Hakusuisha,
   1981. 277 pp. [*Hard Candy*]

Ichimaku geki shû. Trans. Shirô Narumi et al. Tokyo: Hayakawa shobo, 1966. 512 pp. ["Moony's Kid Don't Cry."
etc.]

Kaisôroku. Trans. Shirô Narumi. Tokyo: Hakusuisha, 1978.
453 pp. [*Memoirs*]

Moise. Trans. Shirô Narumi. Tokyo: Hakusuisha, 1981. 290
pp. [*Moise and the World of Reason*]

Natsu to kemuri. Trans. Shirô Narumi. *Gendai America Bun-
gaku Zenshu* 13. Tokyo: Kochi Shuppanshu, 1959. [*Summer
and Smoke*]

Natsu to kemura. Trans. Hiroshi Tajima. Tokyo: Shinchôsha,
1972. 279 pp. [*Eccentricities of a Nightingale; Summer
and Smoke*]

Noroi. Trans. Shimura Masao and Kono Ichirô. Tokyo: Hakusuisha, 1972. 288 pp. [*One Arm*]

Shi ni tsukareta hachinin no onna. Trans. Shizuo Suyama.
Tokyo: Hakusuisha, 1981. 214 pp. [*Eight Mortal Ladies
Possessed*]

Stone fujin no Rôma no haru. Trans. Tomoko Saitô. Tokyo:
Hakusuisha, 1981. 219 pp. [*Roman Spring of Mrs. Stone*]

Yaketa totan-yane no ue no neko. Trans. Tajima Hiroshi.
Tokyo: Shinchosha, 1959. 304 pp. [*Cat on a Hot Tin
Roof*]

Yokubô to yû na no densha. Trans. Hiroshi Tajima and Yama-
shita Osamu. Tokyo: Sogensha, 1952. 204 pp. Ils.
Trans. Shirô Narumi. Tokyo: Hayakawa shobo, 1977. 387
pp. [*A Streetcar Named Desire*]

Also translated: *Period of Adjustment;* "The Vengeance of
Nitocris."

KANNADA

Gajina gombe. Trans. H. K. Ramachandramurti. Mysore:
Suruchi, 1979. 95 pp. [*Glass Menagerie*]

KOREAN

Yogmaniraneun ireumeui jeoncha. Trans. Mun Il-yeong.
Seoul: Juyeongsa, 1975. [*Streetcar Named Desire*]

Also translated: *Cat on a Hot Tin Roof; Glass Menagerie.*

LITHUANIAN

Interview: "Kuo toliau nuo Kranto."   *Literatura in Menas* 33
   (1979): 5.

MARATHI

Kacheci khelne.   Trans. Vasant Vaikuntha Kamat.   Bombay:
   Popular Prakashan, 1965.   76 pp.   [*Glass Menagerie*]

Vasanachakra.   Trans. Vijay Dhondopant Tandulkar.   Bombay:
   Popular Praks-ashan, 1966.   122 pp.   [*Streetcar Named
   Desire*]

NORWEGIAN

Skei, Hans H.   "The Reception and Reputation of Tennessee
   Williams in Norway."   *Notes on Mississippi Writers* 17.2
   (1985): 63-81.   [Includes mention of other productions
   and many reviews; some of the information below is at
   odds with this article]

Translations

"En arm."   Trans. Olav Andre Manum.   In unidentified collection.   Oslo: Pax, 1983.   ["One Arm"]

Flyvende sommer.   Trans. Elvind Hauge?   Oslo: Gyldendal
   Norsk, 1956.   [*Summer and Smoke*]

Glassmenasjeriet.   Trans. Helge Hagerup.   Oslo: Gyldendal
   Norsk, 1956.   [*Glass Menagerie*]

Katt paa varmt blikktak.   Trans. Peter Magnus.   Oslo: Gyldendal Norsk, 1955.   104 pp.   [*Cat on a Hot Tin Roof*]

"Sommerspill."   Trans. Daisy Schelderup.   *Amerika forteller.*
   Oslo: Norske Borklubben, 1973.

En Sporvogn til Begjaer.   Trans. Peter Magnus.   Oslo: Gyldendal Norsk, 1950.   116 pp.   [*Streetcar Named Desire*]

Den tatoverte rosen.   Trans. Peter Magnus.   Oslo: Gyldendal
   Norsk, 1951.   106 pp.   [*Rose Tattoo*]

Productions

Note: The scripts used for the Nationaltheatret productions have been catalogued and are apparently available.

Camino Real (musical version), trans. Svein Selvig. Oslo: Nationaltheatret, 21 Aug. 1982 (35). 119 pp.

Du deilige ungdom [*Sweet Bird of Youth*], trans. Arne Skouen. Oslo: Nye Teater, 4 Dec. 1969.

Flyvende sommer [*Summer and Smoke*], trans. Elvind Hauge. Oslo: National Scene, 6 Mar. 1952 (15).

"Forbudt omraade" ["Long Goodbye"?]. Oslo: Nye Theater, 1953.

Glassmenasjeriet [*Glass Menagerie*], trans. Lizzie Juvkam. Bergon: Nationale Scene, 4 Jan. 1947; Oslo: National-theatret, 3 Mar. 1947 (24). With Ada Kramm (Amanda).

Glassmenasjeriet, trans. Inger Hagerup (?). Oslo: National-theatret, 6 Oct. 1966 (47). With Ada Kramm (Amanda), Liv Thorsen (Laura).

"Hilsin fra Bertha" ["Hello from Bertha"]. Bergen: Nation-ale Scene, 1953 (19).

Iguananatten [*Night of the Iguana*], trans. Peter Magnus. Oslo: Nationaltheatret, 9 Nov. 1962 (17).

Katt paa hett blikktak [*Cat on a Hot Tin Roof*], trans. Peter Magnus. Oslo: Nationaltheatret, 23 Feb. 1956 (15). Gerda Ring, dir. With Liv Stromsted (Maggie).

"Madame de Politur," "Portrett av en Madonna," "Mitt aller siste quillar, eller skumringstimen," "Huset skal Rives" ["Lady of Larkspur Lotion," "Portrait of a Madonna," "Last of My Solid Gold Watches," "This Property Is Condemned"], trans. Peter Magnus. Oslo: Nationaltheatret, 5 Oct. 1963 (47).

"Mot hvit horison." "This Property Is Condemned." Bergen: Nationale Scene, 1953 (25).

En sporvogn til begjaer [*Streetcar Named Desire*], trans. Peter Magnus. Oslo: Nationaltheatret, 26 Apr. 1949 (24). With Aase Bye (Blanche).

Den tatoverterte rosen [*Rose Tattoo*], trans. Peter Magnus.
Oslo: Nationaltheatret, 16 Sept. 1951 (46). With Aase Bye
(Serafina).

Varsel for smaa forty [*Small Craft Warnings*], trans. Bjorn
Endreson. Oslo: Norske Teatret, 27 Oct. 1973 (21). With
Rut Tellefsen (Leona).

PERSIAN

Gorbe ruye shirvāni-ye dāqb. Trans. Parviz Arshad.   Tehran:
Morvarid, 1963. 130 pp. [*Cat on a Hot Tin Roof*]

Havas-e bahāri. Trans. Abdollah Gallédāri.   Tehran: Pocket
Books, 1963. 119 pp. [*Roman Spring of Mrs. Stone*]

POLISH

Natanson, Wojciech. "American Plays on Polish Stages."
Polish Review 5 (Winter 1960): 86-87. [Productions in
eight cities, with reviews, of *Streetcar Named Desire*]

Translations

"Laka niebieskich dzieci." *Tematy* 3 (1964): 102-11.
["Field of Blue Children"]

PORTUGUESE

O anjo de pedra. Trans. Sérgio Viotti. Rio de Janeiro:
Letras e Artes, 1964. 150 pp. Rio de Janeiro: Bloch,
1968. 190 pp. [*Summer and Smoke*]

Bruscamente no verão passado. Lisbon: Presença, 1964.   158
pp. [*Suddenly Last Summer*]

Entrevistado por George Whitmore. *Sexualidade e Criação
literaria.* Ed. Winston Leyland. Trans. Raul de Sa Bar-
bosa. Rio de Janeiro: Civilização Brasileira, 1980.
231-51. [*Gay Sunshine* interview]

Fumo de verão. Trans. Luís de Stau Monteiro. Lisbon:
Europa-America, 1962. 131 pp. [*Summer and Smoke*]

A margem da vida. Trans. Léo Gilson Ribeiro. Rio de
Janeiro: Bloch, 1954. 191 pp. Rio de Janeiro: Letras e
Artes, 1964. 150 pp. [*Glass Menagerie*]

Moisés e o mundo da razão. Trans. Leonel Vallandro. Rio de
Janeiro: Nova Fronteira, 1976. 210 pp. [*Moise and the
World of Reason*]

A *noite da iguana.* Trans. Idalina S. N. Piña Amaro. Rio de
Janeiro: Europa-America, 1965. 129 pp. [*Night of the
Iguana*]

A *rosa tatuada.* Trans. Eurico da Costa and Manuel Pina.
Lisbon: Europa-America, 1956. 199 pp. Trans. R. Magal-
haes, Jr. Rio de Janeiro: Civilização Brasileira, 1956.
187 pp. Rio de Janeiro: Biblioteca Universal Popular,
1964. 214 pp. [*Rose Tattoo*]

A *ultima primavera.* Trans. José Estêvão Sasportes. Lisbon:
Livros do Brasil, 1960. 146 pp. [*Roman Spring of Mrs.
Stone*]

Production

Uma gata sobre um telhado quente [*Cat on a Hot Tin Roof*].
Lisbon: 21 Oct. 1959. With Laura Alves (Maggie). Review:
New York Times 23 Oct. 1959: 23.

ROMANIAN

Teatru: Orfeu în infern; Menajeria de sticlă; Camino real.
Trans. Mihnea Gheorghiu; Anda Boldur; Dana Crivăy.
Bucharest: Univers, 1978. 264 pp. [*Orpheus Descending;
Glass Menagerie; Camino Real*]

Un tramvia numit Dorinta. Trans. Dorin Dron. *Teatra
American Contemporan.* Bucharest: Pentru Literatura
Universala, 1967. Vol. 2: 109-216. [*Streetcar Named
Desire*]

RUSSIAN

Schmemann, Serge. "The Russian Theatergoers Take Tennessee
Williams to Their Hearts." *New York Times* 21 June 1982,
sec. C: 13.

Shaland, Irene. *Tennessee Williams on the Soviet Stage.*
Lanhan, MD: Univ. Pr. of America, 1987. 90 pp. [In-
cludes mention of Soviet reviews]

Translations

"Chem bolshe chernovikov, tem piesa Luchshe." *Literaturraia*
12 July 1972: 15. [Interview]

Rimskaja vesna missis stoun. Moscow: Hudoz lit., 1978.   143
pp. [*Roman Spring of Mrs. Stone*]

Sladkogolosaja ptica junosti. Trans. V. Vulf and A.
Dorosevic. Moscow: VAAP, 1975.   85 pp. [*Sweet Bird of
Youth*]

Stekljanny zverinets i ešče devjat p'es. Trans. Yakov
Bereznitsky. Moscow: Iskusstvo, 1967.   721 pp. Ils.
[Intro., V Nedelin; *Glass Menagerie* and nine other plays]

Productions

Koshka na raskalyonnoy kryshe [*Cat on a Hot Tin Roof*],
trans. Vitaly Y. Vulf. Moscow: Mayakovsky Theatre, 28 Dec.
1981.

Sladkogolosaja ptitsa junosti [*Sweet Bird of Youth*], trans.
Vitaly Y. Vulf and Doroshevich. Moscow: Khudozhestvenny
Akademichesky Teatr, 1975. V. Shilovsky, dir. Boris Mes-
serer, design. With I. Vasiliev (Chance), Angelina Stepa-
nova (Princess).

Steklyanny zverinets [*Glass Menagerie*]. Moscow: Ermolova,
1969. Kaarin Rayad, dir. Lalevich, Sosunov, design. With
V. Larirev (Tom), E. Kirillova (Amanda), H. Vasilieva
(Laura).

Tatuirovannaya roza [*Rose Tattoo*], trans. Vitaly Y. Vulf.
Moscow Art Theatre, Jan. 1982.

Tsarstvie zemnoe [*Kingdom of Earth*], trans. Vitaly Y. Vulf.
Moscow: Teatr imeni Mossoveta, 1977. Pavel Khomsky, dir.
Mark Kitaev, design. With Valentina Talyzina (Myrtle),
Georgy Zhzhenov (Chicken), Gennady Bortnikov (Lot).

Title unknown [*Night of the Iguana*], trans. Vitaly Y. Vulf.
Moscow: Maly Theatre, 2 June, Nov. 1989; tour, summer 1989.
Theodore Mann, dir. With Vitaly Solomin (Shannon), Lyudmila
Titova (Hannah), Y. V. Samoilov (Nonno). Prod. Notes:
    Tennesee Williams Literary Journal 1.2 (Winter 1989-90):
        67, 69.
    Bohlen, Celestine. *New York Times* 6 Aug. 1989, sec. 2:
        12-13. [Rehearsals; excerpts from Theodore Mann's
        diary]

Clines, Francis X. *New York Times* 23 May 1989, sec. C: 15. [Rehearsals]

Title unknown [*Orpheus Descending*]. Moscow: 17 Aug. 1961. Irina Anisimova-Wolf, dir. Music by Kirill Molchanov. With Vera Maretskaya (Lady).

Title unknown [*Orpheus Descending*]. Moscow: Tsentralny Teatr Sovetskoy Armii, 1977. A. Burdonsky, dir. S. Barkhin, design. With A. Vasiliev (Val), Ludmila Kasatkina (Lady).

Title unknown [*Streetcar Named Desire*]. Moscow: Mayakovsky, 1971. A. Goncharov, dir. Yuri Bogoyavlensky, design. With Svetlana Nemolyaeva (Blanche), Armen Dzhigarkhanyan (Stanley), Okhlupin (Mitch).

SERBO-CROATIAN

Rimsko proleće gospodje Ston. Trans. Miloš Marinovič. Sarajero: Džepna kngiga, 1957. 110 pp. [*Roman Spring of Mrs. Stone*]

Tramvaj nazvan želja (Scenario filma). Belgrade: Sportska Knjiga, 1953. 48 pp. [Screenplay?, *Streetcar Named Desire*]

SLOVAK

Električka zvaná túžha. Trans. Jan Trachta. *Moderna svetova drama*. Bratislava: Slovenské Vydavatelstvo, 1964. 7-102. [*Streetcar Named Desire*]

Král'ovstvo na zemi. Trans. Eduard Castiglione. Bratislava: Diliza, 1969. 74 pp. [*Kingdom of Earth*]

Nedel'a pre bolest' ako stvorenná. Trans. Eduard Castiglione. Bratislava: Lita, 1981. 55 pp. [*Lovely Sunday for Creve Coeur*]

Noc s leguánon. Trans. Eduard Castiglione. Bratislava: Diliza, 1968. 100 pp. [*Night of the Iguana*]

Sklenený zverinec. Trans. Karel Dlouhy. Bratislava: Diliza, 1961. 78 pp. [*Glass Menagerie*]

Sladky vták mladosti. Trans. Eduard Castiglione. Bratislava: Dilzia, 1969. 57 pp. [*Sweet Bird of Youth*]

Vytetovaná Ruža. Trans. Eduard V. Tvarožek. Bratislavia:
Dilzia, 1964. 101 pp. [*Rose Tattoo*]

SLOVENE

Rimska pomlad gospe slonove. Trans. Maila Golob. Ljubl-
jana: Mladinska Knjiga, 1965. 125 pp. [*Roman Spring of
Mrs. Stone*]

Tja in nazal: Osem ameriskih zgodb. Ed. Herbert Grun.
Maribor: Obzorja, 195-. ["I Rise in Flame," in collec-
tion]

SPANISH

Advertencias para barcos pequeños; Batalla de ángeles.
Buenos Aires: Losada, 198-. [*Small Craft Warnings;
Battle of Angels*]

La caída de Orfeo. Trans. Antonio de Cabo. Madrid: Alfil,
1962. 112 pp. [*Orpheus Descending*]

Camino Real. Trans. Diego Hurtado. Madrid: Alfil, 1963.
91 pp.

Caramelo fundido. Trans. Roberto Bixio. Buenos Aires: Sur,
1966. 217 pp. [*Hard Candy*]

Dulce pájaro de juventud. Buenos Aires: Sur, 1962. 166 pp.
[*Sweet Bird of Youth*]

Un empeño caballeresco. Trans. Juan Ribalta. Barcelona:
Lumen, 1972. 151 pp. [*Knightly Quest*]

En el invierno de las ciudades. Buenos Aires: Flor, 198-.
[*In the Winter of Cities*]

La gata sobre el tejado de zinc caliente. Trans. Antonio de
Cabo and Luis Sáenz. Madrid: Alfil, 1962. 80 pp. [*Cat
on a Hot Tin Roof*]

Hasta llegar a entenderse. Trans. Alfonso Paso and Julio
Mathias. Madrid: Alfil, 1964. 83 pp. [*Period of Adjustment*]

El manco y otros cuentos. Trans. Carlos María Tejedor.
Buenos Aires: Sur, 1968. 160 pp. [*One Arm*]

Memorias. Trans. Antonio Samous. Barcelona: Bruguera,
   1983. 352 pp. [*Memoirs*]

Moisa y el mundo de la razón. Trans. Pilar Giralt Gorina.
   Barcelona: Caralt, 1978. 197 pp. [*Moise and the World
   of Reason*]

La noche de la iguana. Trans. Manuel Barbera. Buenos
   Aires: Losada, 1964. 105 pp. Trans. José Méndez Herrera. Madrid: Alfil, 1965. [*Night of the Iguana*]

*La noche de la iguana; Lo que no se dice; Súbitamente el
   último verano; Período de ajuste.* Trans. Manuel Barbera.
   Buenos Aires: Losada, 1967. 254 pp. [*Night of the
   Iguana*; "Something Unspoken"; *Suddenly Last Summer;
   Period of Adjustment*]

Ocho mujeres poseídas. Trans. Pilar Giralt Gorina. Barcelona: Caralt, 1977. 139 pp. [*Eight Mortal Ladies Possessed*]

Orfeo desciende. Trans. Roberto Bixio. Buenos Aires: Sur,
   1960. 163 pp. [*Orpheus Descending*]

El país del dragón. Trans. Ángela Pérez and José Manuel
   Álvarez Florez. Madrid: Jucar, 1975. 282 pp. Buenos
   Aires: Losada, 198-. 2 vols. [*Dragon Country*]

Piezas cortas. Trans. María Dolores López de Cervera.
   Madrid: Alianza, 1968. 201 pp. [One-act plays]

La primavera romana de la Señora Stone. Trans. Martín de
   Ezcurdia. Barcelona/Buenos Aires: Plaza Janes, 1964.
   175 pp. [*Roman Spring of Mrs. Stone*]

Teatro. Trans. León Mirlas. Buenos Aires: Losada, 1951.
   305 pp. [*Streetcar Named Desire; Glass Menagerie; Summer
   and Smoke*]

Un tranvía llamado Deseo. Trans. José Méndez Herrera.
   Madrid: Alfil, 1962. 122 pp. Trans. Juan García-Puerte.
   Teatro norteamericano contemporáneo. Madrid: Aguilar,
   1963. 179-284. [*Streetcar Named Desire*]

*Un tranvía llamado Deseo; Lo que no se dice; Súbitamente el
   último verano.* Trans. León Mirlas and Manuel Barbera.
   Buenos Aires: Losada, 1979. 181 pp. [*Streetcar Named
   Desire*; "Something Unspoken"; *Suddenly Last Summer*]

Tres dramas. Trans. Floreal Mazía. Buenos Aires: Sudameri-
cana, 1958. 378 pp. [*Rose Tattoo; Cat on a Hot Tin
Roof; Camino Real*]

Verano y humo; La noche de la iguana. Trans. León Mirlas
and Manuel Barbera. Buenos Aires: Losada, 1979. 178 pp.
[*Summer and Smoke; Night of the Iguana*]

El zoo de cristal. Trans. José Gordon and José María de
Quinto. Madrid: Alfil, 1965. 96 pp. [*Glass Menagerie*]

El zoológico de cristal; Período de ajuste. Trans. León
Mirlas and Manuel Barbera. Buenos Aires: Losada, 1979.
159 pp. [*Glass Menagerie; Period of Adjustment*]

Productions

Mundo de cristal [*Glass Menagerie*]. Repertorio Español.
New York: Gramercy Arts Theatre, 3-28 Sept. 1980; tour of
Spanish America, beginning 30 Sept. 1980. René Buch, dir.
With Yolanda Arenas, Ofelia González, Mateo Gómez,
Christofer de Oni.

La rosa tatuada [*Rose Tattoo*], adpt. Antonio de Cabo and
Luis Sáenz. Madrid: Teatro Infanta Beatriz, spring 1958.
Miguel Narros, dir. With Maria Arias (Serafina), Ramón Cor-
rot (Alvaro).

Un tranvía llamado Deseo [*Streetcar Named Desire*]. Teatro
de la Reforma. México: Palacio de Bellas Artes, 4 Dec.
1948; México: Teatro Esperanza Iris, 4 May 1949. Seki Sano,
dir. With María Douglas (Blanche), Wolf Ruvinskis (Stanley), Lillian Oppenheim (Stella), Reynaldo Rivera (Mitch).
Reviews:
   Mexico Life Dec. 1948: 41.
   Theatre Arts June 1949: 44.

Un tranvía llamado Deseo. Havana: El Sotano, 17 Feb. 1965.
Review:
   Hofmann, Paul. *New York Times* 19 Feb. 1965: 27. Rpt.
   New York Times Theatre Reviews.

El zoológico de cristal [*Glass Menagerie*]. México: Casa de
la Paz, 5 July 1965. Juan López Moctezuma, Sergio Guzik,
dir. Roberto Donis, Roberto Cirou, Raúl Díaz González,
design. Music by Juan José Calatayud. With María Socorro
Cano de Delgado (Amanda), Virginia O. de Gutierrez (Laura),
Juan López Moctezuma (Tom), Constantino Gutiérrez (Jim).

Other Productions:
New York Times 12 Dec. 1949: 28. Response: *New York Times* 23 Dec. 1949, sec. 3: 16. [Williams's refusal to permit Spanish prod.]

SWEDISH

"Det kan man kalla kariek." *Radiotjansts Teaterbibliotek* 97. ["Strangest Kind of Romance"]

Linje Lusta. Stockholm: Bonniers, 1949. 130 pp. [*Streetcar Named Desire*]

Mrs. Stones Romerska Vaar. Trans. Th. Warburton. Stockholm: Bonniers, 1951. 120 pp. [*Roman Spring of Mrs. Stone*]

"Portratt av en glasflicken." *All Varlders Beratare* 11 (Nov. 1955): 8-15. ["Portrait of a Girl in Glass"]

Productions

Linje Lusta [*Streetcar Named Desire*]. Goteborg: 1949. With Kairn Koali (Blanche).

Rosen [*Rose Tattoo*], trans. Sven Berthel. Goteborg: Stads Teatern, 31 Aug. 1951. Stig Torsslov, dir. With Berta Hall (Serafina).

Title unknown [*Glass Menagerie*]. Stockholm: Royal Dramatic Theatre, 1947. With Nancy Dalunde (Laura), Olof Bergstrom (Jim). Review:
Theatre Arts Aug. 1947: 38-39.

TAMIL

Title unknown. Trans. T. N. Suki Subramaniyam. Madras: Jothi Nilayam, 1966. 339 pp. [*Glass Menagerie*]

TURKISH

Arzu tramvayi. Trans. Halit Cakir. Istanbul: Milli Eğitim Basimevi, 1965. 148 pp. [*Streetcar Named Desire*]

Iguana gecesi. Trans. Canset Unan. Istanbul: Altin Kitaplar, 1966. 288 pp. [*Night of the Iguana*]

Soğuk gúnes. Istanbul: Samim-Sadik Yayinevi, 1960. [*Roman Spring of Mrs. Stone*]

Sirça kümes. Trans. Can Yucel. Istanbul: Milli Egitim Bokanligt, 1964. 103 pp. [*Glass Menagerie*]

WELSH

Pethe brau. Trans. Emyr Edwards. Llandysul: Gwasg & Gler, 1963. 74 pp. [*Glass Menagerie*]

I. PRIOR BIBLIOGRAPHIES

Here are listed those bibliographies which look specif-
ically at Williams. The user should also consult the works
listed in the preliminary notes to the bibliography and to
works listed under some languages of Section G.

Adler, Thomas P., et al. "Tennessee Williams in the Seventies: A Checklist." *Tennessee Williams Newsletter* 2.1
(Spring 1980): 24-29.

Arnott, Catherine M. *Tennessee Williams on File.* London/
New York: Methuen, 1985. 80 pp.

Balachandran, K. "Tennessee Williams in India: Stagings and
Scholarship." *Notes on Mississippi Writers* 20.1 (1988):
17-27.

Brown, Andreas. "Tennessee Williams by Another Name."
Papers of the Bibliographical Society of America 57
(1963): 377-78.

Carpenter, Charles A. Jr. "Studies of Tennessee Williams'
Drama: A Selective International Bibliography 1966-1978."
Tennessee Williams Newsletter 2.1 (Spring 1980): 11-23.

---, and Elizabeth Cook. "Addenda to Tennessee Williams: A
Selected Bibliography." *Modern Drama* 2 (Dec. 1959): 220-
23. [See Dony below]

Cohn, Alan M. "More Tennessee Williams in the Seventies:
Additions to the Checklist and the Gunn Bibliography."
Tennessee Williams Newsletter 3.2 (1982): 46-50. [See
Adler above and Gunn below]

Dony, Nandine. "Tennessee Williams: A Selected Bibliography." *Modern Drama* 1 (Dec. 1958): 181-91.

Gunn, Drewey Wayne. *Tennessee Williams: A Bibliography.*
Metuchen, NJ/London: Scarecrow, 1980. xiv, 255 pp.
Reviews:
    Booklist July 15-Aug. 1981: 1468-69.
    Choice Jan. 1981.
    Wilson Library Journal Oct. 1981: 141-42.

Adler, Thomas P. *Library Research Newsletter* Spring-
    Summer 1982: 127-28.
Cherry, Grady. *South Central Bulletin* (SCMLA) Spring-
    Summer 1981: 23-24.
Eddleman, Floyd Eugene. *Modern Drama* 25 (Dec. 1982):
    585-87.
Gleaves, Edwin S. *ARBA* 81: 586-87.
Miller, George. *Tennessee Williams Review* 3.2 (1982):
    51-54.

---. "The Various Texts of Tennessee Williams's Plays."
    Educational Theatre Journal 30 (Oct. 1978): 368-75.

Harris, Richard H. *Modern Drama in America and England
    1950-1970*. Detroit: Gale, 1982. 519-29.

Hayashi, Tetsumaro. *Arthur Miller and Tennessee Williams:
    Research Opportunities and Dissertation Abstracts*. Jef-
    ferson, NC/London: McFarland, 1983. 59-124, 129-33.

Londré, Felicia Hardison. "Tennessee Williams." *American
    Playwrights since 1945: A Guide to Scholarship, Criti-
    cism, and Performance*. Ed. Philip C. Kolin. Westport,
    CT: Greenwood, 1989. 488-517.

McCann, John S. *The Critical Reputation of Tennessee Wil-
    liams: A Reference Guide*. Boston: Hall, 1983. xxxix,
    430 pp. Review:
        Gunn, Drewey Wayne. *Analytical and Enumerative Bib-
            liography* 8.1 (1984): 57-59.

McHaney, Pearl Amelia. "A Checklist of Tennessee Williams
    Scholarship, 1980-87." *Tennessee Williams Literary Jour-
    nal* 1.1 (Spring 1989): 65-76.

---. "A Checklist of Tennessee Williams Scholarship, 1988-
    90." *Tennessee Williams Literary Journal* 2.1 (Winter
    1990-91): 57-63.

---. "Tennessee Williams." *Contemporary Authors Biblio-
    graphical Series: American Dramatists*. Ed. Matthew C.
    Rondoné. Detroit: Gale, 1989. 3: 385-429.

Presley, Delma E. "Tennessee Williams: Twenty-Five Years of
    Criticism." *Bulletin of Bibliography* 30 (Jan.-Mar.
    1973): 21-29.

Drewey Wayne Gunn is Professor of English at Texas A&I University. He received his Ph.D. from the University of North Carolina at Chapel Hill in 1968. He has also taught at Presbyterian College, SC; Upward Bound, Texas Southern University; Institut Reine, Versailles; and the Université de Metz. He was a Fulbright teacher in four normal schools and two lycées in Denmark, 1972-73.

He is the author of another Scarecrow bibliography, *Mexico in American and British Letters*, and a study, *American and British Writers in Mexico, 1556-1973*, which was translated into Spanish. In addition to his work on Williams, he has published on Carlos Fuentes, Preston Jones, John Steinbeck, and Mark Twain.